The Broadview Introduction

to Philosophy

VOLUME II | VALUES AND SOCIETY

The Broadview Introduction to

PHILOSOPHY

VOLUME II | VALUES AND SOCIETY

edited by **ANDREW BAILEY**

broadview press

BROADVIEW PRESS – www.broadviewpress.com
Peterborough, Ontario, Canada

Founded in 1985, Broadview Press remains a wholly independent publishing house. Broadview's focus is on academic publishing; our titles are accessible to university and college students as well as scholars and general readers. With over 600 titles in print, Broadview has become a leading international publisher in the humanities, with world-wide distribution. Broadview is committed to environmentally responsible publishing and fair business practices.

Library and Archives Canada Cataloguing in Publication

Title: The Broadview introduction to philosophy / edited by Andrew Bailey.
Other titles: Introduction to philosophy
Names: Bailey, Andrew, 1969– editor.
Description: Includes bibliographical references. | Contents:
   Volume II. Values and society.
Identifiers: Canadiana 20190105038 | ISBN 9781554814022 (v. 2 ;
   softcover)
Subjects: LCSH: Philosophy—Introductions.
Classification: LCC BD21 .B76 2019 | DDC 100—dc23

Broadview Press handles its own distribution in North America:
PO Box 1243, Peterborough, Ontario K9J 7H5, Canada
555 Riverwalk Parkway, Tonawanda, NY 14150, USA
Tel: (705) 743-8990; Fax: (705) 743-8353
email: customerservice@broadviewpress.com

Distribution is handled by Eurospan Group in the UK, Europe, Central Asia, Middle East, Africa, India, Southeast Asia, Central America, South America, and the Caribbean. Distribution is handled by Footprint Books in Australia and New Zealand.

Canada

Broadview Press acknowledges the financial support of the Government of Canada for our publishing activities.

Book design by Michel Vrana
Cover image: borojoint, istockphoto.com

PRINTED IN CANADA

CONTRIBUTING EDITORS AND WRITERS

Editor
Andrew Bailey

Editorial Coordinator
Stephen Latta

Assistant Editor
Tara Bodie

Copyeditor
Robert M. Martin

Proofreaders
Stacey Aspinall
Joe Davies
Michel Pharand
Paige Pinto
Michael Roberts
Helena Snopek

Production Editors
Tara Lowes
Tara Trueman

Permissions Coordinator
Merilee Atos

Contributing Writers
Andrew Bailey
Laura Buzzard
Leslie Dema
Stephen Latta
Melissa MacAulay
Robert M. Martin
Andrew Reszitnyk
Nora Ruddock

CONTENTS

ACKNOWLEDGMENTS

A number of academics provided valuable comments and input that helped to shape this book, including (but not limited to):

Ardis Anderson, University of Lethbridge
Shannon Dea, University of Waterloo
William J. Devlin, Bridgewater State University
Leigh Duffy, Buffalo State College
Mark Ereshefsky, University of Calgary
Erin Frykholm, University of Kansas
Hans V. Hansen, University of Windsor
W. Jim Jordan, University of Waterloo
Karl Laderoute, University of Lethbridge
Christinia Landry, Wilfrid Laurier University
Alison K. McConwell, University of Calgary
Joshua Mugg, Park University
Csaba Nyiri, Lourdes University
Brian Orend, University of Waterloo
Tina Strasbourg, Grande Prairie Regional College
Brynn Welch, University of Alabama at Birmingham
Byron Williston, Wilfrid Laurier University

This book is a successor to *First Philosophy: Fundamental Problems and Readings in Philosophy* (2nd ed.; Broadview Press, 2011). Thanks to Alan Belk, Lance Hickey, Peter Loptson, and Mark Migotti for pointing out errors and omissions in the first edition of that book. The editor would warmly welcome further corrections or suggestions for improvement.

Andrew Bailey
Department of Philosophy
The University of Guelph
abailey@uoguelph.ca

This book is an introduction to philosophy. It is intended to be a reasonably representative—though very far from exhaustive—sampling of important philosophical questions, major philosophers and their most important works, periods of philosophical history, and styles of philosophical thought.* More than half of the included readings, however, were published since 1950, and another important aim of the book is to provide some background for *current* philosophical debates, to give the interested reader a springboard for the plunge into the exciting world of contemporary philosophy (debates about the nature of consciousness, say, or quantum theories of free will, or feminist ethics, or the status of scientific knowledge, or welfarist vs. libertarian accounts of social justice, or ...).

The aim of this book is to introduce philosophy through philosophy itself: it is not a book *about* philosophy but a book *of* philosophy, in which more than sixty great philosophers speak for themselves. Each of the readings is prefaced by a set of notes, but these notes are not intended to explain or summarize the reading. Instead, the goal of the notes is to provide *background information* helpful for understanding the reading—to remove as many of the unnecessary barriers to comprehension as possible, and to encourage a deeper and more sophisticated encounter with great works of philosophy. The notes to selections, therefore, do not stand alone and *certainly* are not a substitute for the reading itself: they are meant to be consulted in combination with the reading.

Readers can of course take or leave these notes as they choose, and read them (or not) in any order. One good way of proceeding, however, would be the following. First, read the selection (so that nothing said in the notes inadvertently taints your first impression of the piece). Then, go back and read some of the notes—the biographical sketch, information on the author's philo-

sophical project, structural and background information—and with these things in mind read the selection again. Spend some time *thinking* about the reading: ask yourself if you really feel you have a good grasp of what the author is trying to say, and then—no less importantly—ask yourself whether the author gives good reasons to believe that what is said is *true*. (The general Introduction tries to give some helpful suggestions for this process of critical reflection.) After this, it should be worthwhile going back to the notes, checking your impressions against any 'common misconceptions,' and then running through at least some of the suggestions for critical reflection. Finally, you might want to go on and read more material by the philosopher in question, or examine what other philosophers have said about those ideas: the suggestions for further reading, available at the companion website, will point you in the right direction.

The philosophical selections are also quite heavily annotated throughout by the editors, again in an effort to get merely contingent difficulties for comprehension out of the way and allow the reader to devote all her or his effort to understanding the philosophy itself. Many of the original texts also include their own notes, all of which have been presented here as endnotes following the reading, so as to keep those notes separate from the editors' annotations. The original endnotes are marked with numbers, while the added annotations are marked with symbols (*, †, ‡, etc.) and placed at the bottom of each page.

A word of explanation about the 'Suggestions for Critical Reflection' section: although the notes to the readings contain no philosophical critique of the selection, the questions in this section are largely intended to help the reader generate his or her own critique. As such, they are supposed to be thought-provoking, rather than straightforwardly easy to answer. They try to sug-

---

* There are two major exceptions to this. First, this book focuses exclusively on 'Western' philosophy—that is, roughly, on the philosophical traditions of Europe and of the descendants of European settlers in North America and Australasia. In particular, it does not attempt to encompass the rich philosophical heritage of Asia or Africa. Second, this collection under-represents an important strain of twentieth-century philosophy, 'Continental' philosophy, which includes thinkers such as Husserl, Heidegger, Sartre, Foucault, Derrida, and Habermas, and is characterized by such movements as existentialism, hermeneutics, structuralism, and deconstructionism.

gest fruitful avenues for critical thought (though they do not cover every possible angle of questioning, or even all the important ones), and only very rarely is there some particular 'right answer' to the question. Thus, these questions should not be considered a kind of 'self-test' to see if you understand the material: even people with a very good grasp of the material will typically be puzzled by the questions—because they are *supposed* to be puzzling questions.

The readings and their accompanying notes are designed to be 'modular'; that is, in general, one reading can be understood without the benefit of having read any of the other selections. This means that the selections can be read in any order. The current arrangement of the readings groups them by topic, and then orders them so that they follow a reasonably natural progression through a particular philosophical problem. However, quite different courses of study could be plotted through this book, emphasizing, say, philosophers grouped by nationality, by historical period, by philosophical approach, and so on. Furthermore, often readings from one section can quite naturally be brought into another (e.g., Plato's *Republic* into the section on justice).

The readings in this anthology are, so far as is practicable, 'complete': that is, they are entire articles, chapters, or sections of books. The editors feel it is important for students to be able to see an argument in the context in which it was originally presented; also, the fact that the readings are not edited to include only what is relevant to one particular philosophical concern means that they can be used in a variety of different ways following a variety of different lines of thought across the ages. Some instructors will wish to assign for their students shorter excerpts of some of these readings, rather than having them read all of the work included: the fact that complete, or almost complete, works of philosophy are included in this anthology gives instructors the freedom to select the excerpts that best fit their pedagogical aims.

The notes to the readings in this anthology are almost entirely a work of synthesis, and many books and articles were consulted in their preparation; it is impossible—without adding an immense apparatus of notes and references—to acknowledge them in detail. This is, I believe, appropriate for a textbook, but it is not intended to model good referencing practices for student essays. All the material and annotations accompanying the readings was written by the editors, and none of it (unless otherwise noted) was copied from other sources. Typically, the notes for each reading amalgamate information from up to a dozen or so sources; in a few instances, especially for biographical information on still-living philosophers, the notes rely heavily on a smaller number of sources (and I tried to indicate this in the text when it occurred).

INTRODUCTION

What Is Philosophy?

Philosophy, at least according to the origin of the word in classical Greek, is the "love of wisdom"—philosophers are lovers of wisdom. The first philosophers of the Western tradition lived on the shores of the Mediterranean in the sixth century BCE (that is, more than 2,500 years ago);* thinkers such as Thales, Xenophanes, Pythagoras, Heraclitus, and Protagoras tried systematically to answer questions about the ultimate nature of the universe, the standards of knowledge, the objectivity of moral claims, and the existence and nature of God. Questions like these are still at the core of the discipline today.

So what is philosophy? It can be characterized either as a particular sort of *method*, or in terms of its *subject matter*, or as a kind of intellectual *attitude*.

busily mapping out correlations between brain states and mental states—finding which parts of the visual cortex play a role in dreaming, for example—and building computer models of intelligent information processing (such as software for self-driving vehicles). Philosophers are also involved in cognitive science, trying to discover just what would *count* as discovering that dreaming is really nothing more than certain electro-chemical events in the brain, or would count as building a computer which feels pain or genuinely has beliefs. These second kinds of questions are crucial to the whole project of cognitive science, but they are not empirical, scientific questions: there simply is no fact about the brain that a scientist could observe to answer them. And so these questions—which are part of cognitive science—are dealt with by philosophers.

PHILOSOPHY AS A METHOD

One view is that philosophers study the same things—the same world—as, for example, scientists do, but that they do so in a different, and complementary, way. In particular, it is often claimed that while scientists draw conclusions from empirical *observations* of the world, philosophers use *rational arguments* to justify claims about the world. For instance, both scientists and philosophers are involved in contemporary studies of the human mind. Neuroscientists and psychologists are

Here are two more examples. Economists study the distribution of wealth in society, and develop theories about how wealth and other goods can come to be distributed one way rather than another (e.g., concentrated in a small proportion of the population, as in Brazil, or spread more evenly across society, as in Sweden). However, questions about which kind of distribution is more *just*, which kind of society is best to live in, are not answered within economic theory—these are philosophical questions. Medical professionals are concerned with facts about sickness and death, and often have to

---

* In the East, Lao-Tzu, the founder of Taoism, probably lived at about the same time in China. Buddha and Confucius were born a few decades later. In India, an oral literature called the Veda had been asking philosophical questions since at least 1500 BCE.

make decisions about the severity of an illness or weigh the risk of death from a certain procedure. Philosophers also examine the phenomenon of death, but ask different questions: for example, they ask whether people can survive their own deaths (i.e., if there is a soul), whether death is really a harm for the person who dies, under what conditions—if any—we should assist people in committing suicide, and so on.

One reason why philosophers deal differently with phenomena than scientists do is that philosophers are using different techniques of investigation. The core of the philosophical method is the application of *rational thought* to problems. There are (arguably) two main aspects to this: the use of conceptual or linguistic *analysis* to clarify ideas and questions, and the use of formal or informal *logic* to argue for certain answers to those questions.

For example, questions about the morality of abortion often pivot on the following question: is a fetus a *person* or not? A person is, roughly, someone who has a similar moral status to a normal adult human being. Being a person is not simply *the same thing* as being a member of the human species, however, since it is at least possible that some human beings are not persons (brain-dead individuals in permanent comas, for example?) and some persons might not be human beings (intelligent life from other planets, or gorillas, perhaps?). If it turns out that a fetus *is* a person, abortion will be morally problematic—it may even be a kind of murder. On the other hand, if a fetus is no more a person than, say, one of my kidneys, abortion may be as morally permissible as a transplant. So *is* a fetus a person? How would one even go about discovering the answer to this question? Philosophers proceed by using *conceptual analysis*. What we need to find out, first of all, is what makes something a person—what the essential difference is between persons and non-persons—and then we can apply this general account to human fetuses to see if they satisfy the definition. Put another way, we need to discover precisely what the word "person" means.

Since different conceptual analyses will provide importantly different answers to questions about the morality of abortion, we need to *justify* our definition: we need to give reasons to believe that one particular analysis of personhood is correct. This is where logic comes in: logic is the study of arguments, and its techniques are designed to distinguish between good arguments—by which we should be persuaded—and bad arguments, which we should not find persuasive. (The

next main section of this introduction will tell you a little more about logic.)

PHILOSOPHY AS A SUBJECT MATTER

Another way of understanding philosophy is to say that philosophers study a special set of issues, and that it is this subject matter which defines the subject. Philosophical questions fit three major characteristics:

1. They are of deep and lasting interest to human beings;
2. They have answers, but the answers have not yet been settled on;
3. The answers cannot be decided by science, faith, or common sense.

Philosophers try to give the best possible answers to such questions. That is, they seek the one answer which is more justified than any other possible answer. There are lots of questions which count as philosophical, according to these criteria. All can be classified as versions of one of three basic philosophical questions.

The first foundational philosophical question is *What exists?* For example: Does God exist? Are quarks really real, or are they just fictional postulates of a particular scientific theory? Are numbers real? Do persons exist, and what is the difference between a person and her physical body, or between a person and a 'mere animal'? The various questions of existence are studied by the branch of philosophy called Metaphysics, and by its various sub-fields such as Philosophy of Mind and the study of Personal Identity.

The second fundamental philosophical question is *What do we know?* For example, can we be sure that a scientific theory is actually true, or is it merely the currently dominant simplification of reality? The world appears to us to be full of colors and smells, but can we ever find out whether it really is colored or smelly (i.e., even if no one is perceiving it)? Everyone believes that 5+6=11, but what makes us so sure of this—could we be wrong, and if not, why not? The branch of philosophy which deals with these kinds of questions is called Epistemology. Philosophy of Science examines the special claims to knowledge made by the natural sciences, and Logic is the study of the nature of rational justification.

The third major philosophical question is *What should we do?* If I make a million dollars selling widgets or playing basketball, is it okay for me to keep all of that money and do what I want with it, or do I have some kind of moral obligation to give a portion of my income to the less well off? If I could get out of trouble by telling a lie, and no one else will really be harmed by my lie, is it alright to do so? Is Mozart's *Requiem* more or less artistically valuable than The Beatles' *Sgt. Pepper's Lonely Hearts Club Band*? Questions like these are addressed by Value Theory, which includes such philosophical areas as Ethics, Aesthetics, Political Philosophy, and Philosophy of Law.

PHILOSOPHY AS AN ATTITUDE

A third view is that philosophy is a state of being—a kind of intellectual independence. Philosophy is a reflective activity, an attitude of critical and systematic thoughtfulness. To be philosophical is to continue to question the assumptions behind every claim until we come to our most basic beliefs about reality, and then to critically examine those beliefs. For example, most of us assume that criminals are responsible for their actions, and that this is at least partly why we punish them. But *are* they responsible for what they do? We know that social pressures are very powerful in affecting our behavior. Is it unfair to make individuals entirely responsible for society's effects on them when those effects are negative? How much of our personal identity is bound up with the kind of community we belong to, and how far are we free to choose our own personalities and values? Furthermore, it is common to believe that the brain is the physical cause of all our behavior, that the brain is an entirely physical organ, and that all physical objects are subject to deterministic causal laws. If all of this is right, then presumably all human behavior is just the result of complex causal laws affecting our brain and body, and we could no more choose our actions than a falling rock could choose to take a different route down the mountainside. If this is true, then can we even make sense of the notion of moral responsibility? If it is not true, then where does free will come from and how (if at all) does it allow us to escape the laws of physics? Here, a questioning attitude towards our assumptions about criminals has shown that we might not have

properly considered the bases of our assumptions. This ultimately leads us to fundamental questions about the place of human beings in the world.

Here are three quotations from famous philosophers which give the flavor of this view of philosophy as a critical attitude:

Socrates, one of the earliest Western philosophers, who lived in Greece around 400 BCE, is said to have declared that it "is the greatest good for a man, to talk every day about virtue and the other things you hear me converse about when I examine both myself and others, and that the unexamined life is not worth living for a man."*

Immanuel Kant—the most important thinker of the late eighteenth century—called this philosophical state of being "Enlightenment."

> Enlightenment is the emergence of man from the immaturity for which he is himself responsible. Immaturity is the inability to use one's understanding without the guidance of another. Man is responsible for his own immaturity, when it is caused, by lack not of understanding, but of the resolution and the courage to use it without the guidance of another. *Sapere aude!* Have the courage to use your own reason! is the slogan of Enlightenment.†

Finally, in the twentieth century, Bertrand Russell wrote the following assessment of the value of philosophy:

> Philosophy is to be studied, not for the sake of any definite answers to its questions, since no definite answers can, as a rule, be known to be true, but rather for the sake of the questions themselves; because these questions enlarge our conception of what is possible, enrich our intellectual imagination and diminish the dogmatic assurance which closes the mind against speculation; but above all because, through the greatness of the universe which philosophy contemplates, the mind also is rendered great, and becomes capable of that union with the universe which constitutes its highest good.‡

---

* Plato, *Apology* 38a, in *The Apology and Related Dialogues*, ed. Andrew Bailey, trans. Cathal Woods and Ryan Pack (Broadview, 2016), 75–76.

† Immanuel Kant, "An Answer to the Question: What Is Enlightenment?" in *Practical Philosophy*, ed. Mary J. Gregor (Cambridge University Press, 1996), 17.

‡ Bertrand Russell, *The Problems of Philosophy* (Oxford University Press, 1912), 93–94.

SUGGESTIONS FOR CRITICAL REFLECTION

1. Here are some more examples of phenomena which are studied by both scientists and philosophers: color, sense perception, medical practices like abortion and euthanasia, human languages, mathematics, quantum mechanics, the evolution of species, democracy, taxation. What contribution (if any) might philosophers make to the study of these topics?

2. How well does *mathematics* fit into the division between science and philosophy described above? How does *religion* fit into this classification?

3. Here are a few simple candidate definitions of "person": a person is anything which is capable of making rational decisions; a person is any creature who can feel pain; a person is any creature with a soul; a person is any creature which has the appropriate place in a human community. Which of these, if any, do you think are plausible? What are the consequences of these definitions for moral issues like abortion or vegetarianism? Try to come up with a more sophisticated conceptual analysis of personhood.

4. Do you think criminals are responsible for their actions?

5. Should society support philosophy, and to what degree (e.g., should tax dollars be spent paying philosophers to teach at public universities? Why (not)?)?

A Brief Introduction to Arguments

EVALUATING ARGUMENTS

The main tool of philosophy is the *argument*. An argument is any sequence of statements intended to establish—or at least to make plausible—some particular claim. For example, if I say that Vancouver is a better place to live in than Toronto because it has a beautiful setting between the mountains and the ocean, is more relaxed, and has a lower cost of living, then I am making an argument. The claim which is being defended is called the *conclusion*, and the statements which together are supposed to show that the conclusion is (likely to be) true are called the *premises*. Often arguments will be strung together in a sequence, with the conclusions of earlier arguments featuring as premises of the later ones. For example, I might go on to argue that since Vancouver is a better place to live in than Toronto, and since one's living conditions are a big part of what determines one's happiness, then the people who live in Vancouver must, in general, be happier than those living in Toronto. Usually, a work of philosophy is primarily made up of chains of argumentation: good philosophy consists of good arguments; bad philosophy contains bad arguments.

What makes the difference between a good and a bad argument? It's important to notice, first of all, that the difference is *not* that good arguments have true conclusions and bad arguments have false ones. A perfectly good argument might, unluckily, happen to have a conclusion that is false. For example, you might argue that you know this rope will bear my weight because you know that the rope's rating is greater than my weight, you know that the rope's manufacturer is a reliable one, you have a good understanding of the safety standards which are imposed on rope makers and vendors, and you have carefully inspected this rope for flaws. Nevertheless, it still might be the case that this rope is the one in 50 million which has a hidden defect causing it to snap. If so, that makes me unlucky, but it doesn't suddenly make your argument a bad one—we were still being quite reasonable when we trusted the rope. On the other hand, it is very easy to give appallingly bad arguments for true conclusions: Every sentence beginning with the letter "c" is true; "Chickens lay eggs" begins with the letter "c"; therefore, chickens lay eggs.

But there is a deeper reason why the evaluation of arguments doesn't begin by assessing the truth of the conclusion. The whole point of making arguments is to establish *whether or not* some particular claim is true or false. An argument works by starting from some claims which, ideally, everyone is willing to accept as true—the premises—and then showing that something interesting—something *new*—follows from them: i.e., an argument tells you that *if* you believe these premises, *then* you should also believe this conclusion. In general, it would be unfair, therefore, to simply reject the conclusion and suppose that the argument must be a bad one—in fact, it would often be intellectually dishonest. If the argument *were* a good one, then it would show you that you might be *wrong* in supposing its conclusion to be false; and to refuse to accept this is not to respond to the argument but simply to ignore it.*

It follows that there are exactly two reasonable ways to criticize an argument. The first is to question the truth of the *premises*. The second is to question the claim that if the premises are true then the conclusion is true as well—that is, one can critique the *strength* of the argument. Querying the truth of the premises (i.e., asking whether it's really true that Vancouver is cheaper than Toronto) is fairly straightforward. The thing to bear in mind is that you will usually be working backwards down a chain of argumentation: that is, each premise of a philosopher's main argument will often be supported by sub-arguments, and the controversial premises in these sub-arguments might be defended by further arguments, and so on. Normally it is not enough to merely demand to know whether some particular premise is true: one must look for *why* the arguer thinks it is true, and then engage with *that* argument.

Understanding and critiquing the strength of an argument (either your own or someone else's) is somewhat more complex. In fact, this is the main subject of most books and courses in introductory logic. When dealing with the strength of an argument, it is usual to divide arguments into two classes: *deductive* arguments and *inductive* arguments. Good deductive arguments are the strongest possible kind of argument: if their premises are true, then their conclusion *must necessarily* be true. For example, if all bandicoots are rat-like marsupials, and if Billy is a bandicoot, then it cannot possibly be false that Billy is a rat-like marsupial. On the other hand, good inductive arguments establish that, if the premises are true, then the conclusion is *highly likely* (but not absolutely certain) to be true as well. For example, I may notice that the first bandicoot I see is rat-like, and the second one is, and the third, and so on; eventually, I might reasonably conclude that all bandicoots are rat-like. This is a good argument for a probable conclusion, but nevertheless the conclusion can never be shown to be *necessarily* true. Perhaps a non-rat-like bandicoot once existed before I was born, or perhaps there is one living now in an obscure corner of New Guinea, or perhaps no bandicoot

so far has ever been non-rat-like but at some point, in the future, a bandicoot will be born that in no way resembles a rat, and so on.

DEDUCTIVE ARGUMENTS AND VALIDITY

The strength of deductive arguments is an on/off affair, rather than a matter of degree. Either these arguments are such that if the premises are true then the conclusion necessarily must be, or they are not. Strong deductive arguments are called *valid*; otherwise, they are called *invalid*. The main thing to notice about validity is that its definition is an *if ... then ...* statement: *if* the premises *were* true, then the conclusion *would* be. For example, an argument can be valid even if its premises and its conclusion are not true: all that matters is that if the premises *had* been true, the conclusion necessarily would have been as well. This is an example of a valid argument:

1. Either bees are rodents or they are birds.
2. Bees are not birds.
3. Therefore bees are rodents.

If the first premise were true, then (since the second premise is already true) the conclusion would *have* to be true—that's what makes this argument valid. This example makes it clear that validity, though a highly desirable property in an argument, is not enough all by itself to make a good argument: good deductive arguments are both valid *and* have true premises. When arguments are good in this way they are called *sound*: sound arguments have the attractive feature that they necessarily have true conclusions. To show that an argument is unsound, it is enough to show that it is either invalid or has a false premise.

It bears emphasizing that even arguments which have true premises and a true conclusion can be unsound. For example:

1. Only US citizens can become the President of America.

---

* Of course, occasionally, you might legitimately know for sure that the conclusion is false, and then you could safely ignore arguments which try to show it is true: for example, after the rope breaks, I could dismiss your argument that it is safe (again, though, this would not show that your argument was bad, just that I need not be persuaded that the conclusion is true). However, this will not do for philosophical arguments: all interesting philosophy deals with issues where, though we may have firm opinions, we cannot just insist that we know all the answers and can therefore afford to ignore relevant arguments.

2. George W. Bush is a US citizen.
3. Therefore, George W. Bush was elected President of America.

This argument is not valid, and therefore it should not convince anyone who does not already believe the conclusion to start believing it. It is not valid because the conclusion could have been false even though the premises were true: Bush could have lost to Gore in 2000, for example. The question to ask, in thinking about the validity of arguments, is this: Is there a coherent possible world, which I can even *imagine*, in which the premises are true and the conclusion false? If there is, then the argument is invalid.

When assessing the deductive arguments that you encounter in philosophical work, it is often useful to try to lay out, as clearly as possible, their *structure*. A standard and fairly simple way to do this is simply to pull out the logical connecting phrases and to replace, with letters, the sentences they connect. Five of the most common and important 'logical operators' are *and, or, it is not the case that, if ... then ...*, and *if and only if*.... For example, consider the following argument: "If God is perfectly powerful (omnipotent) and perfectly good, then no evil would exist. But evil does exist. Therefore, God cannot be both omnipotent and perfectly good; so either God is not all-powerful or he is not perfectly good." The structure of this argument could be laid bare as follows:

1. If (O and G) then not-E.
2. E.
3. Therefore, not-(O and G).
4. Therefore, either not-O or not-G.

Revealing the structure in this way can make it easier to see whether or not the argument is valid. And in this case, it is valid. In fact, no matter what O, G, and E stand for—no matter how we fill in the blanks—*any* argument of this form must be valid. You could try it yourself—invent random sentences to fill in for O, G, and E, and no matter how hard you try, you will never produce an argument with all true premises and a false conclusion.* What this shows is that validity is often a property of the *form* or structure

of an argument. (This is why deductive logic is known as "formal logic." It is not formal in the sense that it is stiff and ceremonious, but because it has to do with argument forms.)

Using this kind of shorthand, therefore, it is possible to describe certain general argument forms which are *invariably* valid and which—since they are often used in philosophical writing—it can be handy to look out for. For example, a very common and valuable form of argument looks like this: if P then Q; P; therefore Q. This form is often called *modus ponens*. Another—which appears in the previous argument about God and evil—is *modus tollens*: if P then Q; not-Q; therefore not-P. A *disjunctive syllogism* works as follows: either P or Q; not-P; therefore Q. A *hypothetical syllogism* has the structure: if P then Q; if Q then R; therefore if P then R. Finally, a slightly more complicated but still common argument structure is sometimes called a *constructive dilemma*: either P or Q; if P then R; if Q then R; therefore R.

INDUCTIVE ARGUMENTS AND
INDUCTIVE STRENGTH

I noted above that the validity of deductive arguments is a yes/no affair—that a deductive argument is either extremely strong or it is hopelessly weak. This is not true for inductive arguments. The strength of an inductive argument—the amount of support the premises give to the conclusion—is a matter of degree, and there is no clear dividing line between the 'strong' inductive arguments and the 'weak' ones. Nevertheless, some inductive arguments are obviously much stronger than others, and it is useful to think a little bit about what factors make a difference.

There are lots of different types and structures of inductive arguments; here I will briefly describe four which are fairly representative and commonly encountered in philosophy. The first is *inductive generalization*. This type of argument is the prototypical inductive argument—indeed, it is often what people mean when they use the term "induction"—and it has the following form:

1. *x* per cent of observed Fs are G.
2. Therefore *x* per cent of all Fs are G.

---

* Since the argument about God and evil is valid, then we are left with only two possibilities. Either all its premises are true, and then it is sound and its conclusion must inescapably be true. Or one of its premises is false, in which case the conclusion might be false (though we would still not have shown that it is false). The only way to effectively critique this argument, therefore, is to argue against one of the claims 1 and 2.

That is, inductive generalizations work by inferring a claim about an entire *population* of objects from data about a *sample* of those objects. For example:

(a) Every swan I have ever seen is white, so all swans (in the past and future, and on every part of the planet) are white.

(b) Every swan I have ever seen is white, so probably all the swans around here are white.

(c) 800 of the 1,000 rocks we have taken from the Moon contain silicon, so probably around 80% of the Moon's surface contains silicon.

(d) We have tested two very pure samples of copper in the lab and found that each sample has a boiling point of 2,567°C; we conclude that 2,567°C is the boiling point for copper.

(e) Every intricate system I have seen created (such as houses and watches) has been the product of intelligent design, so therefore all intricate systems (including, for example, frogs and volcanoes) must be the product of intelligent design.

The two main considerations when assessing the strength of inductive generalizations are the following. First, ask how *representative* is the sample? How likely is it that whatever is true of the sample will also be true of the population as a whole? For instance, although the sample size in argument (c) is much larger than that in argument (d), it is much more likely to be biased: we know that pure copper is very uniform, so a small sample will do; but the surface of the Moon might well be highly variable, and so data about the areas around moon landings may not be representative of the surface as a whole. Second, it is important to gauge how cautious and *accurate* the conclusion is, given the data—how far beyond the evidence does it go? The conclusion to argument (a) is a much more radical inference from the data than that in argument (b); consequently, though less exciting, the conclusion of argument (b) is much better supported by the premise.

A second type of inductive argument is an *argument from analogy*. It most commonly has the following form:

1. Object (or objects) *A* and object (or objects) *B* are alike in having features F, G, H, ...
2. *B* has feature X.
3. Therefore *A* has feature X as well.

These examples illustrate arguments from analogy:

(a) Human brains and dolphin brains are large, compared to body size. Humans are capable of planning for the future. So, dolphins must also be capable of planning for the future.

(b) Humans and dolphins are both mammals and often grow to more than five feet long. Humans are capable of planning for the future. So, dolphins must also be capable of planning for the future.

(c) Eagles and robins are alike in having wings, feathers, claws, and beaks. Eagles kill and eat sheep. Therefore, robins kill and eat sheep.

(d) Anselm's ontological argument has the same argumentative form as Gaunilo's "Lost Island" argument. But Gaunilo's argument is a patently bad argument. So there must be something wrong with the ontological argument.

(e) An eye and a watch are both complex systems in which all of the parts are inter-dependent and where any small misadjustment could lead to a complete failure of the whole. A watch is the product of intelligent design. Therefore, the eye must also be the product of intelligent design (i.e., God exists).

The strength of an argument from analogy depends mostly on two things: first, the degree of *positive relevance* that the noted similarities (F, G, H ...) have to the target property X; and second, the absence of *relevant dissimilarities*—properties which *A* has but *B* does not, which make it *less* likely that *A* is X. For example, the similarity (brain size) between humans and dolphins cited in argument (a) is much more relevant to the target property (planning) than are the similarities cited in argument (b). This, of course, makes (a) a much stronger argument than (b). The primary problem with argument (c), on the other hand, is that we know that robins are much smaller and weaker than eagles and this dissimilarity makes it far less likely that they kill sheep.

A third form of inductive argument is often called *inference to the best explanation* or sometimes *abduction*. This kind of argument works in the following way. Suppose we have a certain quantity of data to explain (such as the behavior of light in various media, or facts about the complexity of biological organisms, or a set of ethical claims). Suppose also that we have a number of theories which account for this data in different ways (e.g., the theory that light is a particle, or the theory that light is a wave, or the theory that it is somehow both). One way of arguing for the truth of one of these theories, over the others, is to show that one theory provides a much *better explanation* of the data than the others. What counts as making a theory a better explanation can be a bit tricky, but some basic criteria would be:

1. The theory predicts all the data we know to be true.
2. The theory explains all this data in the most economical and theoretically satisfying way (scientists and mathematicians often call this the most *beautiful* theory).
3. The theory predicts some *new* phenomena which turn out to exist and which would be a big surprise if one of the competing theories were true. (For example, one of the clinchers for Einstein's theory of relativity was the observation that starlight is bent by the sun's gravity. This would have been a big surprise under the older Newtonian theory, but was predicted by Einstein's theory.)

Here are some examples of inferences to the best explanation:

(a) When I inter-breed my pea plants, I observe certain patterns in the properties of the plants produced (e.g., in the proportion of tall plants, or of plants which produce wrinkled peas). If the properties of pea plants were generated randomly, these patterns would be highly surprising. However, if plants pass on packets of information (genes) to their offspring, the patterns I have observed would be neatly explained. Therefore, genes exist.

(b) The biological world is a highly complex and inter-dependent system. It is highly unlikely that such a system would have come about (and would continue to hang together) from the purely random motions of particles. It would be much less surprising if it were the result of conscious design from a super-intelligent creator. Therefore, the biological world was deliberately created (and therefore, God exists).

(c) The biological world is a highly complex and inter-dependent system. It is highly unlikely that such a system would have come about (and would continue to hang together) from the purely random motions of particles. It would be much less surprising if it were the result of an evolutionary process of natural selection which mechanically preserves order and eliminates randomness, and which (if it existed) would produce a world much like the one we see around us. Therefore, the theory of evolution is true.

The final type of inductive argument that I want to mention here is usually called *reductio ad absurdum*, which means "reduction to absurdity." It is always a negative argument, and has this structure:

1. Suppose (for the sake of argument) that position *p* were true.
2. If *p* were true then something else, *q*, would also have to be true.
3. However *q* is absurd—it can't possibly be true.
4. Therefore *p* can't be true either.

In fact, this argument style can be either inductive or deductive, depending on how rigorous premises 2 and 3 are. If *p* logically implies *q*, and if *q* is a logical contradiction, then it is deductively certain that *p* can't be true (at least, assuming the classical laws of logic). On the other hand, if *q* is merely absurd but not literally *impossible*, then the argument is inductive: it makes it highly likely that *p* is false, but does not prove it beyond all doubt.

Here are a few examples of *reductio* arguments:

(a) Suppose that gun control were a good idea. That would mean it's a good idea for the government to gather information on anything we own which, in the wrong hands, could be a lethal weapon, such as kitchen knives and baseball bats. But that would be ridiculous. This shows gun control cannot be a good idea.

(b) If you think that fetuses have a right to life because they have hearts and fingers and toes, then you must believe that anything with a heart, fingers, and toes has a right to life. But that would be absurd. Therefore, a claim like this about fetuses cannot be a good argument against abortion.

(c) Suppose, for the sake of argument, that this is not the best possible world. But that would mean God had either deliberately chosen to create a sub-standard world or had failed to notice that this was not the best of all possible worlds, and either of these options is absurd. Therefore, it must be true that this is the best of all possible worlds.

(d) "The anti-vitalist says that there is no such thing as vital spirit. But this claim is self-refuting. The speaker can be taken seriously only if his claim cannot. For if the claim is true, then the speaker does not have vital spirit and must be dead. But if he is dead, then his statement is a meaningless string of noises, devoid of reason and truth."*

The critical questions to ask about *reductio* arguments are simply: *Does* the supposedly absurd consequence follow from the position being attacked? and Is it *really* absurd?

A FEW COMMON FALLACIES

Just as it can be useful to look for common patterns of reasoning in philosophical writing, it can also be helpful to be on guard for a few recurring fallacies—and, equally importantly, to take care not to commit them in your own philosophical writing. Here are four common ones:

Begging the question does not mean, as the media would have us believe, stimulating one to ask a further question; instead, it means to assume as true (as one of your premises) the very same thing which you are supposedly attempting to prove. This fallacy is sometimes called *circular reasoning* or even (the old Latin name) *petitio principii*. To argue, for example, that God exists because (a) the Bible says that God exists, (b) God wrote the Bible, and (c) God would not lie, is to commit a blatant case of begging the question. In this case, of course, one would have no reason to accept the premises as true unless one *already* believed the conclusion. Usually, however, arguments that beg the question are a little more disguised. For example, "Adultery is immoral, since sexual relations outside marriage violate ethical principles," or "Terrorism is bad, because it encourages further acts of terrorism," are both instances of circular reasoning.

Arguing *ad hominem* means attacking or rejecting a position not because the arguments for it are poor, but because the person presenting those arguments is unattractive in some way: i.e., an attack is directed at the person (which is what *ad hominem* means) rather than at their argument. The following are implicit *ad hominem* arguments: "You say churches have too much influence on society? Well, Hitler and Stalin would agree with you!" and "We shouldn't trust the claim, by philosophers such as Anselm, Aquinas, and Leibniz, that God exists, since they were all Christian philosophers and so of course they were biased." Such attacks are fallacious because they have nothing at all to do with how reasonable a claim is: even if the claim is false, *ad hominem* attacks do nothing to show this.

Straw person arguments are particularly devious, and this fallacy can be hard to spot (or to avoid committing) unless great care is taken. The *straw person* fallacy consists in misrepresenting someone else's position so that it can be more easily criticized. It is like attacking a dummy stuffed with straw instead of a real opponent. For example, it's not uncommon to see attacks on "pro-choice" activists for thinking that abortion is a good thing. However, whatever the merits of either position, this objection is clearly unfair—no serious abortion advocates think it is a positively *good thing* to have an abortion; at most they claim that (at least in some circumstances) it is a lesser evil than the alternative. Here's an even more familiar example, containing two straw persons, one after the other: "We should clean out the closets. They're getting a bit messy." "Why, we just went through those closets last year. Do we have to clean them out every day?" "I never said anything about cleaning them out every day. You just want to keep all your junk forever, which is simply ridiculous."

Arguments from ignorance, finally, are based on the assumption that lack of evidence *for* something is evidence that it is false, or that lack of evidence *against* something is evidence for its truth. Generally, neither of these assumptions is reliable. For example, even if we could find no good proof to show that God exists, this would not, all by itself, suffice to show that God does *not* exist: it would still be possible, for example, that God exists but transcends our limited human reason. Consider the following 'argument' by Senator Joseph McCarthy, about some poor official in the State Department: "I do not have much information on this except the general statement of the agency that there is nothing in the files to disprove his Communist connections."†

---

* This example is from Paul Churchland's "Eliminative Materialism and the Propositional Attitudes," *Journal of Philosophy* 78 (1981). (Note, however, that it is not Churchland's argument.)

† McCarthy on the Senate floor, quoted by Richard H. Rovere in *Senator Joe McCarthy* (University of California Press, 1996), 132.

SUGGESTIONS FOR CRITICAL REFLECTION

1. Suppose some deductive argument has a premise which is necessarily false. Is it a valid argument?
2. Suppose some deductive argument has a conclusion which is necessarily true. Is it a valid argument? From this information alone, can you tell whether it is sound?
3. Is the following argument form valid: if P then Q; Q; therefore P? How about: if P then Q; not-P; so not-Q?
4. No inductive argument is strong enough to *prove* that its conclusion is true: the best it can do is to show that the conclusion is highly probable. Does this make inductive arguments bad or less useful? Why don't we restrict ourselves to using only deductive arguments?
5. Formal logic provides mechanical and reliable methods for assessing the validity of deductive arguments. Do you think there might be some similar system for evaluating the strength of inductive arguments?
6. I have listed four important fallacies; can you identify any other common patterns of poor reasoning?

Introductory Tips on Reading and Writing Philosophy

READING PHILOSOPHY

As you will soon find out, if you haven't already, it is not easy to read philosophy. It can be exhilarating, stimulating, life-changing, or even annoying, but it isn't easy. There are no real shortcuts for engaging with philosophy (though the notes accompanying the readings in this book are intended to remove a few of the more unnecessary barriers); however, there are two things to remember which will help you get the most out of reading philosophy—*read it several times*, and *read it actively*.

Philosophical writing is not like a novel, a historical narrative, or even a textbook: it is typically dense, compressed, and written to contribute to an on-going debate with which you may not yet be fully familiar. This means, no matter how smart you are, it is highly unlikely that you will get an adequate understanding of any halfway interesting piece of philosophy the first time through, and it may even take two or three more readings before it really becomes clear. Furthermore, even after that point, repeated readings of good philosophy will usually reveal new and interesting nuances to the writer's position, and occasionally you will notice some small point that seems to open a mental door and show you what the author is trying to say in a whole new way. As they say, if a piece of philosophy isn't worth reading at least twice, it isn't worth reading once. Every selection in this book, I guarantee, is well worth reading once.

As you go through a piece of philosophy, it is very important to engage with it: instead of just letting the words wash over you, you should make a positive effort, first, to understand, and then, to critically assess the ideas you encounter. On your first read-through it is a good idea to try to formulate a high-level understanding of what the philosopher is attempting: What are the main claims? What is the overall structure of the arguments behind them? At this stage, it can be useful to pay explicit attention to section headings and introductory paragraphs.

Ideally during a second reading, you should try to reconstruct the author's arguments and sub-arguments in more detail. To help yourself understand them, consider jotting down their outlines on a sheet of paper. At this point, it can be extremely fruitful to pay attention to special definitions or distinctions used by the author in the arguments. It is also helpful to consider the historical context in which the philosopher wrote, and to look for connections to ideas found in other philosophical works.

Finally, on third and subsequent readings, it is valuable to expressly look for *objections* to the writer's argument (Are the premises true? Is the argument strong?), *unclarities* in position statements, or *assumptions* they depend upon, but do not argue for. I make these suggestions partly because the process of critical assessment is helpful in coming to understand a philosopher's work; but more importantly for the reason that—perhaps contrary to popular opinion—philosophers are typically playing for very high stakes. When philosophers write about whether God exists, whether science is a rational enterprise, or whether unfettered capitalism creates a just society, they are seriously interested in discovering the *answers* to these questions. The arguments they make, if they are good enough, will be strong reasons to believe one thing rather than another. If you are reading philosophy properly, you must sincerely join the debate and be honestly prepared to be persuaded—but it is also important not to let yourself be persuaded too easily.

WRITING PHILOSOPHY

Writing philosophy consists, in roughly equal measures, of *thinking* about philosophy and then of trying to express your ideas *clearly and precisely*. This makes it somewhat unlike other writing: the point of writing philosophy is not, alas, to entertain, nor to explain some chunk of knowledge, nor to trick or cajole the reader into accepting a certain thesis. The point of philosophical writing is, really, to *do* philosophy. This means that, since philosophy is based on arguments, most philosophical essays will have the underlying structure of an argument. They will seek to defend some particular philosophical claim by developing one or more good arguments for that claim.*

There is no particular template to follow for philosophical writing (there are lots of different kinds of good philosophical writing—lots of different ways of arguing well), but here are seven suggestions you might find useful:

1. Take your time. Spend time thinking, and then leave yourself enough time to get the writing right.
2. After you've thought for a while, begin by making an outline of the points you want to make (rather than immediately launching into prose). Then write several drafts, preferably allowing some cooling-off time between drafts so you can come back refreshed and with a more objective eye. Be prepared for the fact that writing a second draft doesn't mean merely tinkering with what you've already got, but starting at the beginning and writing it again.
3. Strive to be clear. Avoid unnecessary jargon, and use plain, simple words whenever possible; concrete examples can be extremely useful in explaining what you mean. It's also worth remembering that the clarity of a piece of writing has a lot to do with

its structure. Ideally, the argumentative structure of your essay should be obvious to the reader, and it is a good idea to use your introduction to give the reader a 'road map' of the argument to follow.

4. Aim for precision. Make sure the *thesis* of your essay is spelled out in sufficient detail that the reader is left in no doubt about what you are arguing for (and therefore what the implications will be, if your arguments are strong ones). Also, take care to define important terms so the reader knows exactly what you mean by them. Terms should normally be defined under any of the following three conditions: (a) the word is a technical term whose meaning a layperson probably won't know (e.g., "intrinsic value"); (b) it is an ordinary word whose meaning is not sufficiently clear or precise for philosophical purposes (e.g., "abortion"); or (c) it is an ordinary word that you are going to use to mean something other than what it normally means (e.g., "person").
5. Focus. Everything you write should directly contribute to establishing your thesis. Anything which is unnecessary for your arguments should be eliminated. Make every word count. Also, don't be over-ambitious; properly done, philosophy moves at a fairly slow pace—it is unlikely that anyone could show adequately that, for example, there is no such thing as matter in three pages or less.
6. Argue as well and as carefully as you can. Defend your position using reason and not rhetoric; critically assess the strength of your arguments, and consider the plausibility of your premises. It's important to consider alternatives to your own position and possible counter-arguments; don't be afraid to raise and attempt to reply to objections to your position. (If you make a serious objection, one which you cannot answer, perhaps you should change your position.)
7. When you think you are finished, read the essay out loud and/or give it to someone else to read—at a minimum, this is a good way of checking for ease of reading, and it may reveal problems with your essay or argument that hadn't previously occurred to you.

---

* The conclusion of a philosophical essay, however, need not always be something like: "God exists," or "Physical objects are not colored." It could just as legitimately be something like: "Philosopher A's third argument is flawed," or "When the arguments of philosopher A and those of philosopher B are compared, B wins," or "No one has yet given a good argument to show either P or not-P," or even "Philosopher A's argument is not, as is widely thought, X, but instead it is Y." Though these kinds of claims are, perhaps, less immediately exciting than the first two examples, they are still philosophical claims, they still need to be argued for, and they can be extremely important in an overall debate about, say, the existence of God.

PART I: ETHICS

Ethical Theory

HOW OUGHT WE TO LIVE OUR LIVES?

Ethics, of course, is the philosophical sub-discipline which examines morality;* along with metaphysics and epistemology, it is one of the largest and most important areas of philosophy. It can usefully be thought of as divided into three main parts: *normative ethics*, *applied ethics,* and *metaethics*.

i) Normative ethics is the philosophical study of the standards of right and wrong, or of good and bad. Normative ethical theories do not attempt to merely *describe* how people actually do behave, or report what people *think* is right: they lay out prescriptions (rooted in rationally supported philosophical theory) for how people *really ought* to think and behave. It is common—though by no means universal—to assume that the proper aim of normative ethics should be to develop a systematic and comprehensive moral theory which has as many of the virtues of a scientific theory as possible: it should capture all the phenomena of moral life, place them within a simple and unified theoretical structure, and provide the resources for answering any ethical question whatsoever—i.e.,

an adequate moral theory should always be able to tell you what to do, and it should always give you the correct answer.

One way of classifying different normative moral theories is in terms of their emphasis on 'the Right' or 'the Good.' Some moral theories—such as that of Kant—are primarily theories of *right action*: they are moral codes (usually derived from, and justified by, some fundamental principle or set of principles, such as Kant's Categorical Imperative) that define the duties human beings have to themselves and others. A (morally) good life is then defined simply as a life of duty—a life spent doing the right thing. By contrast, other moral theories—such as Mill's utilitarianism—*begin* by developing a theory of the good: they are accounts of those things that are *good in themselves* (or at least which are essential components of human flourishing). For example, for Mill, what is good is the happiness of sentient creatures. Right actions are then defined derivatively as those (whichever they are) that best contribute to the good.

---

* There are various important philosophical usages which treat 'ethical' and 'moral' as meaning slightly different things. For example, some philosophers (such as Bernard Williams) use the word 'ethics' to denote systems of *rules* for conduct, while 'morality' has a more open-ended, less institutionalized content ... while others (such as Jürgen Habermas), interestingly, use the terms in almost exactly the opposite way! I am ignoring such niceties here, however, and simply treat the two words as being interchangeable.

ii) Applied ethics is the study of how ethical norms or rules ought to be applied in particular cases of unusual difficulty, such as abortion, mercy-killing, the treatment of animals, genetic research, corporate responsibility to the community, "just" wars, and so on. It encompasses several sub-fields, such as bioethics, business ethics, environmental ethics, legal ethics, and so forth.

iii) Metaethics deals with the philosophical underpinnings of normative ethics: that is, it applies philosophical scrutiny to a part of philosophy itself. The main kinds of metaethical inquiry are the study of the ethical *concepts* used in normative ethics (such as 'duty,' 'right,' 'good,' 'responsibility'), moral *epistemology* (questions about whether and how moral truths can be known), and moral *ontology* (which is concerned with the nature of 'moral reality'—e.g., whether it is objective or subjective, relative or absolute).

The sequence of readings in this section begins in the realm of metaethics, then moves into normative ethics; some applied ethical issues are dealt with in the next section. The question which is being pursued throughout this section is simple, but profound: "How should I live my life?" That is, what kind of *person* should I be? What *values* should guide my plans and choices? Which kinds of *behavior* are morally acceptable, and which unacceptable?

The first selection, from Plato, is a metaethical consideration of the notion of moral value itself: what exactly is the connection between moral virtue and 'the good life'? Are moral goodness and well-being *simply the same thing* (perhaps because only the virtuous are really happy, as Plato goes on to argue, or because what is morally good just is happiness, which is Mill's view)? Or do happiness and virtue come apart (as Kant believes): could one be moral but miserable, vicious yet fulfilled? Along similar lines, another excerpt from Plato asks: what is the connection between moral virtue and religion? Are certain behaviors morally good because the gods (or God) approve of them, or do the gods approve of them because they are good?

The next readings introduce three of the historically most important and influential theories of normative ethics. Aristotle lays the foundations for a theory called 'virtue ethics,' which holds that morality cannot be captured by any set of moral rules or principles—instead, what is right or wrong will vary from situation to situation and the trick is to educate people to be wise in their ethical judgments. Kant defends the view that moral actions have to be understood independently of their merely contingent motivations, and thus that certain actions are simply right or wrong *in themselves*. Mill lays out a moral theory, called utilitarianism, which is based on the principle that the moral value of actions must be understood in terms of their effect on human happiness or well-being.

The next two readings can be thought of as challenges to traditional approaches to ethics. Nietzsche, who called himself an "immoralist," argues that our modern moral views are merely historically contingent opinion (rather than any kind of insight into 'the truth'), and furthermore that they are heavily infected with what he labels "slave morality." He urges a "revaluation" of our moral values which will take us "beyond good and evil." Virginia Held presents a feminist critique of traditional moral theory, arguing that the history of ethical thought has been dominated by sexist attitudes towards women and that only a *radical transformation* of moral philosophy will allow us to escape from these distorting preconceptions. One of the things this article does is to introduce a recent approach called "care ethics."

Finally, an influential article by Judith Jarvis Thomson introduces the famous "trolley problem," which illustrates the use of imaginary scenarios to tease out our ethical intuitions and to assess how adequately different moral theories can deal with them.

Several good introductory books on moral philosophy are available, including Piers Benn, *Ethics* (McGill-Queen's University Press, 1998); Simon Blackburn, *Being Good: A Short Introduction to Ethics* (Oxford University Press, 2003); Julia Driver, *Ethics: The Fundamentals* (Blackwell, 2013); Gilbert Harman, *The Nature of Morality* (Oxford University Press, 1977); Colin McGinn, *Moral Literacy, or How to Do The Right Thing* (Hackett, 1992); Pojman and Fieser, *Ethics: Discovering Right and Wrong* (Cengage, 2016); Rachels, *The Elements of Moral Philosophy* (McGraw Hill, 2018); Russ Shafer-Landau, *The Fundamentals of Ethics* (Oxford University Press, 2017); Peter Singer, *Practical Ethics* (Cambridge University Press, 2011); Bernard Williams, *Morality: An Introduction to Ethics* (Cambridge University Press, 1993); and Lewis Vaughn, *Beginning Ethics: An Introduction to Moral Philosophy* (W.W. Norton, 2014). Good reference works are David Copp, ed., *The Oxford Handbook of Ethical Theory* (Oxford University Press, 2007), LaFollette and Persson, eds., *The Blackwell Guide to Ethical Theory* (Blackwell, 2013), and Peter Singer, ed., *A Companion to Ethics* (Blackwell, 1993).

PLATO

FROM *Republic* AND *Euthyphro*

Who Was Plato?

The historical details of Plato's life are shrouded in uncertainty. He is traditionally thought to have been born in about 427 BCE and to have died in 347 BCE. His family, who lived in the Greek city-state of Athens, was aristocratic and wealthy. Legend has it that Plato's father, Ariston, was descended from Codrus, the last king of Athens, and his mother, Perictione, was related to the great Solon, who wrote the first Athenian constitution. While Plato was still a boy, his father died and his mother married Pyrilampes, a friend of the revered Athenian statesman Pericles, who in the 450s had transformed Athens into one of the greatest cities in the Greek world.

As a young man, Plato probably fought with the Athenian army against Sparta during the Peloponnesian war (431–404 BCE)—which Athens lost—and he may have served again when Athens was involved in the Corinthian war (395–386 BCE).

Given his family connections, Plato looked set for a prominent role in Athenian political life and, as it happens, when he was about 23, a political revolution occurred in Athens which could have catapulted Plato into public affairs. The coup swept the previous democratic rulers—who had just lost the war against Sparta—out of power and into exile, and replaced them with the so-called Thirty Tyrants, several of whom were Plato's friends and relatives. Plato, an idealistic young man, expected this would usher in a new era of justice and good government, but he was soon disillusioned when the new regime was even more violent and corrupt than the old. He withdrew from public life in disgust. The rule of the Thirty lasted only about 90 days before the exiled democrats were restored to power, and Plato—impressed by their relative lenience towards the coup leaders—apparently thought again about entering politics. But then, in 399 BCE, the city rulers arrested Plato's old friend and mentor, Socrates, and accused him of the trumped-up charge of impiety towards the city's gods and of corrupting the youth of Athens. Socrates was convicted by a jury of the townspeople and—since he declared that he would rather die than give up philosophy, even though he was given a chance to escape—he was executed by being forced to drink poison.

> The result was that I, who had at first been full of eagerness for public affairs, when I considered all this and saw how things were shifting about every which way, at last became dizzy. I didn't cease to consider ways of improving this particular situation, however, and, indeed, of reforming the whole constitution. But as far as action was concerned, I kept waiting for favorable moments and finally saw clearly that the constitutions of all actual cities are bad and that their laws are almost beyond redemption without extraordinary resources and luck as well. Hence I was compelled to say in praise of the true philosophy that it enables us to discern what is just for a city or an individual in every case and that the human race will have no respite from evils until those who are really and truly philosophers acquire political power or until, through some divine dispensation, those who rule and have political authority in cities become real philosophers.*

After the death of Socrates, it appears that Plato, along with some other philosophical followers of Socrates, fled Athens and went to the city of Megara in east-

---

* This is a quotation from the so-called *Seventh Letter*, supposed to have been written by Plato when he was 70 years old. It is not certain that Plato actually wrote this document, but if it was not his, it was probably written by one of his disciples shortly after his death. See Plato, *Seventh Letter*, translated by C.D.C. Reeve in his Introduction to Plato's *Republic*, trans. G.M.A. Grube, revised by C.D.C. Reeve (Indianapolis: Hackett, 1992), ix–x. The later fragmentary quote is from the translation of the *Seventh Letter* by Glen R. Morrow, in *Plato: Complete Works*, ed. John M. Cooper and D.S. Hutchinson (Indianapolis: Hackett, 1997), 1648.

central Greece to stay with the philosopher Eucleides (a follower of the great Greek philosopher Parmenides of Elea). He may also have visited Egypt, though his travels at this time are shrouded in myth. It appears that Plato started doing philosophy in earnest at about this time, and his earliest writings date from this point. Almost all of Plato's writings are in the form of dialogues between two or more characters and, in most of them, the character leading the discussion is Socrates. Since Plato never wrote himself into any of his dialogues, it is usually—though not uncontroversially—assumed that the views expressed by the character of Socrates more or less correspond with those that Plato is trying to put forward in his dialogues.

Later, when Plato was about 40, he made another trip away from Athens, visiting Italy to talk with the Pythagorean philosophers. Plato was deeply impressed by Pythagorean philosophy—especially their emphasis on mathematics—but he was horrified by the luxury and sensuality of life in Italy, "with men gorging themselves twice a day and never sleeping alone at night."

After Italy, Plato visited Syracuse on the island of Sicily where, during a long stay, he became close friends with Dion, the brother-in-law of the ruling tyrant Dionysius I.* Dion became Plato's pupil, and (according to legend) came to prefer the philosophical life of moral goodness to the pleasure, luxury, and power of his surroundings. Exactly what happened next is historically unclear, but there is some reason to believe Plato was captured by a displeased Dionysius, sold into slavery, and subsequently rescued from the slave market when his freedom was purchased by an unidentified benevolent stranger.

On Plato's return to Athens, he bought land in a precinct named for an Athenian hero called Academus, and there, in about 385, he founded the first European university (or at least, the first of which there is any real historical knowledge). Because of its location, this school was called the Academy, and it was to remain in existence for over 900 years, until 529 CE. For most of the rest of his life, Plato stayed at the Academy, directing its stud-

ies, and he probably wrote the *Republic* there (in about 380 BCE). Very quickly, the school became a vital center for research in all kinds of subjects, both theoretical and practical. It was probably one of the first cradles for the subjects of metaphysics, epistemology, psychology, ethics, politics, aesthetics, and mathematical science, and members were invited, by various Greek city-states, to help draft new political constitutions.

In 368 Dionysius I of Sicily died and Dion persuaded his successor, Dionysius II, to send for Plato to advise him on how the state should be run. Plato, by now about 60, agreed with some misgivings, possibly hoping to make the younger Dionysius an example of a philosopher-king and to put the doctrines of the *Republic* into practice. However, the experiment was a disastrous failure. Dionysius II—though he gave himself airs as a philosopher—had no inclination to learn philosophy and mathematics in order to become a better ruler. Within four months Dion was banished, and Plato returned to Greece shortly afterwards. However, four years later Dionysius II convinced Plato to return, pressuring him with testimonials from eminent philosophers describing Dionysius's love for philosophy, and bribing him by offering to reinstate Dion at Syracuse within a year. Once again, the king proved false: he not only kept Dion in exile but confiscated and sold his lands and property. Plato was imprisoned on Sicily for nearly two years until, in 360, he finally escaped and returned to Athens for good. He died 13 years later, at the ripe old age of 80.†

What Was Plato's Overall Philosophical Project?

Plato is probably the single person with the best claim to being the inventor of western philosophy. His thought encompassed nearly all the areas central to philosophy today—metaphysics, epistemology, ethics, political theory, aesthetics, and the philosophy of science and mathematics—and, for the first time in European history, dealt with them in a unified way.‡ Plato thought of

---

* Indeed, Plato later wrote a poem about Dion and spoke of being driven out of his mind with love for him.

† Dion, meanwhile, attempted to recover his position at Syracuse by force—an endeavor Plato, wisely, refused to support—and was later assassinated by a supposed friend, and fellow member of the Academy, called Callippus.

‡ In fact the mathematician and philosopher Alfred North Whitehead (1861–1947) famously was moved to say that "The safest general characterization of the European philosophical tradition is that it consists of a series of footnotes

philosophy as a special discipline with its own intellectual method, and he was convinced it had foundational importance in human life. Only philosophy, Plato thought, could provide genuine understanding, since only philosophy scrutinized the assumptions that other disciplines left unquestioned. Furthermore, according to Plato, philosophy reveals a realm of comprehensive and unitary hidden truths—indeed, a whole level of reality that the senses cannot detect—which goes far beyond everyday common sense and which, when properly understood, has the power to revolutionize the way we live our lives and organize our societies. Philosophy, and only philosophy, holds the key to genuine human happiness and well-being.

This realm of objects which Plato claimed to have discovered is generally known as that of the Platonic Forms. The Forms—according to Plato—are changeless, eternal objects, which lie outside of both the physical world and the minds of individuals, and which can only be encountered through pure thought rather than through sensation. One of Plato's favorite examples of a Form is the mathematical property of Equality. In a dialogue called the *Phaedo* he argues that Equality itself cannot be identical with two equal sticks, or with any other group of physical objects of equal length, since we could always be mistaken about whether any two observed objects are really equal with one another, but we could not possibly be mistaken about Equality itself and somehow take *it* to be unequal. When two sticks are equal in length, therefore, they "participate in" Equality—it is their relation to Equality which makes them equal rather than unequal—but Equality itself is an abstract object which exists over and above all the instances of equal things. The form of Equality is what one succeeds in understanding when one has a proper conception of what Equality really is in itself: real knowledge, therefore, comes not from observation but from acquaintance with the Forms. Other central examples of Platonic Forms, are Sameness, Number, Motion, Beauty, Justice, Piety, and (the most important Form of all) Goodness.

Plato describes the relation of the ordinary world of perceivable, concrete objects to the realm of the Forms in Book VII of the *Republic*, using the allegory of a cave. Ordinary people, lacking the benefit of a philosophical education, are like prisoners trapped underground in a cave since birth and forced to look only at shadows cast on the wall in front of them by puppets behind their backs, dancing in front of a fire. With the proper philosophical encouragement, they can—if they have the courage to do so—break their bonds and turn around to see that what they believed was reality was really only an illusory puppet show. The philosophers among them can even leave the cave to encounter the true reality—of which even the puppets are only copies—illuminated by the light of the sun which, for Plato, represents the form of the Good. The perceptible world is thus merely an imperfect image of—and sustained by—the quasi-divine, eternal realm of the unchanging and unobservable Forms.

What Is the Structure of This Reading?

The *Republic* is written in the form of a dramatic dialogue. The narrator, Socrates, speaking directly to the reader, describes a conversation in which he took part and which is supposed to have happened the previous day at the Athenian port city of Piraeus. The dialogue is traditionally divided into ten parts or "Books," and the first half of Book II is reprinted here. In the first book, Thrasymachus, a boorish character, has asserted that justice, or morality, is simply the rule of the strong over the weak, and that it is, in fact, not in everybody's self-interest to be just—it is only in the best interests of the ruling powers for everyone else to follow the social rules they lay down. Socrates has, characteristically, attempted to show that Thrasymachus's reasons for this claim are muddled and confused, but although Thrasymachus is unable to defend himself against Socrates' attacks he remains convinced of the truth of his position. As Book II opens, two brothers, Glaucon and Adeimantus, take up Thrasymachus's cause not because they think he is right, but because they want to challenge Socrates to defeat it properly and to conclusively show that being a just and moral person is valuable *in itself*.

Glaucon begins by introducing a classification of "goods" into three types and asks Socrates to which class justice belongs. Socrates replies it belongs to the

---

to Plato." (Alfred North Whitehead, *Process and Reality*, corrected edition, ed. D.R. Griffin and D.W. Sherburne [Free Press, 1978], 39.)

highest type of good, but Glaucon points out that this conflicts with the popularly held assumption that justice belongs in the lowest class of good. Glaucon then presents three arguments in favor of this common view. First, he describes an account of the "origin and essence of justice" which treats it as only a 'second best' solution to a social problem. Second, he uses the myth of the Ring of Gyges to argue that people are unwillingly just and that, given the chance, anyone would behave immorally. Finally, he describes 'ideal cases' of just and unjust people to show that, if one had the option of living a perfectly just or a totally unjust life, the only rational choice would be the latter. When Glaucon has finished, Adeimantus argues at length that even those who defend justice—parents, poets, and politicians—defend it on the basis of its beneficial *effects* only, and never go so far as to claim it is intrinsically worthwhile to be a morally just person. Glaucon and Adeimantus challenge Socrates to refute all of these arguments.

The reading breaks off just as Socrates is about to respond to this challenge (a response not completed until at least the end of Book IX of the *Republic*). Socrates argues, in effect, that the virtue of justice is such a good thing that it is better to be a just person, even if severe misfortune and loss of reputation occur, than it is to be unjust and to enjoy all possible social rewards; that being a just person always makes you *happier* than being an unjust one, no matter what other circumstances may hold.

In crude outline, Plato's response goes like this. There are three fundamentally different kinds of psychological impulses in human beings: *appetitive desires* (e.g., food, sex, money), *spirited desires* (e.g., fame, power, honor), and *rational desires* (knowledge and truth). Because of this three-fold division of desire, the human soul must also be divided into three parts, and people can be classified according to the dominant part of their soul: that is, people are either money-lovers, honor-lovers, or wisdom-lovers (philosophers). Since these three types of people have very different sorts of desires, they must also have quite different views of what it is to lead a good and morally virtuous life. For one, it is a life of hedonistic pleasure, for the second, a life of political power and influence, and for the philosopher, a life spent in the pursuit of knowledge.

However, according to Plato, only one of these views of the good life is *correct*. Only the philosopher, he argues, has access to the genuinely good life. This is so because the true nature of reality—including moral reality—is the realm of the Forms, and only the philosopher has knowledge of this fundamental reality. Since philosophers are the only ones to understand the true nature of virtue, it seems to Plato to follow that they are the only ones with the specialized knowledge necessary to live a truly good life.* Since capacity for the good life is thus connected with the *kind of person* one is (i.e., a money-lover, an honor-lover, or a philosopher), the Platonic conception of virtue can thus be understood as a particular kind of hierarchy in the soul. According to Plato, to be virtuous is to have a soul ruled by its rational part. Morality, properly understood, fulfils one's highest nature—it is a kind of psychic harmony or mental health—and so leads to the deepest and most genuine form of happiness.†

After the selection from the *Republic* we have included an excerpt from another Socratic dialogue by Plato called the *Euthyphro*. This dialogue was written about fifteen years before the *Republic*, and is set a few weeks before Socrates' trial and conviction for impiety. Socrates is waiting to attend a preliminary hearing before the city's magistrates when he strikes up a conversation with another legal petitioner, Euthyphro, who—to Socrates' amazement—is suing his own father for the crime of murder.

---

* There is also a quasi-religious interpretation of Plato which sees him holding that the Forms—rather than anything in the shifting, illusory spatio-temporal world—are the supreme objects of value. Instead of wealth, power, or pleasure, the most perfect object of devotion is the realm of the Forms, and in particular the Form of the Good (which Plato seems to think of as almost a kind of divinity).

† Plato introduces and explains this account of justice in the human soul by drawing an analogy with the structure of an ideal city-state (which is why the dialogue is called the *Republic*). Briefly, a properly run state would contain three specialized types of citizens: craftspeople, warrior-guardians, and rulers. The rulers would have to have a proper philosophical education, in order to truly know what is best for the state and its citizens, and for this reason they are often called "philosopher kings." The state only functions properly and justly, according to Plato, when these three classes work together in harmony—for example, the craftspeople must be appropriately skilled and must also be properly subservient to the other two classes.

The main subject of the *Euthyphro* is a particular moral virtue: that of piety or holiness, which is to say showing proper respect for religion and the gods (literally, knowledge of how to properly perform ritual prayers and sacrifices). However, the notion is somewhat broader than it might initially seem: insofar as the gods approve on the whole of morally good behavior, to show proper respect for the gods will involve behaving well more generally. Socrates fairly quickly turns the discussion to an attempt to find the essence or definition of piety—the fundamental thing that all pious actions have in common—and this is the point at which this selection begins. Euthyphro's first attempt to answer this question is to say that "what is beloved by the gods is pious, and what is not beloved by them is impious," but Socrates shows him that this is inadequate as a definition. He argues against it in two ways, but it is the second that really counts; this more fundamental objection to the definition emerges when Socrates asks, "Is the pious loved by the gods because it's pious, or it is pious because it is loved?"

Some Useful Background Information

1. All the characters who take part in discussions in the *Republic* were historical figures. Of those mentioned here, Glaucon and Adeimantus were actually Plato's brothers and Thrasymachus was a well-known contemporary teacher of rhetoric, oratory, and "sophist" philosophy (roughly, what we might think of today as a "self-help" guru).* The main character of the *Republic*, however, is its narrator Socrates, Plato's primary intellectual influence. Though he left no writings, Socrates' personality and ideas were so powerful that he appears to have had a tremendous impact upon everyone he encountered, inspiring either fervent devotion or intense irritation. Socrates' main philosophical concern was the ethical question of how one's life should best be lived, and his method was to engage in systematic cross-examination (*elenchus*) of those he encountered, challenging them to state and then justify their beliefs about justice and virtue. The effect of this was to demonstrate to them that their uncritically held beliefs about moral virtue are self-contradictory and hence *have* no justification. The state of bewildered awareness of their own ignorance in which Socrates left his unfortunate victims is called *aporia*, and Socrates' technique of remorseless questioning is sometimes known as the "aporetic method."

2. Though famous for insisting he was wiser than his fellow Athenians only because he alone realized that he knew nothing, Socrates did subscribe to a handful of substantive philosophical positions, at least two of which he passed on to Plato. First, for Socrates, virtue (*aretē*) is a kind of knowledge. To be a virtuous person is, fundamentally, to *understand* what virtue is, in much the same way as being an expert shoemaker consists in knowing everything there is to know about shoes. Socrates (and Plato after him) held that it was vitally important to find correct definitions—to understand the essence (*eidos*)—of ethical concepts, otherwise we will not know how to live.

   The second crucial Socratic doctrine is that the real essence of a person is not their body but their soul, and that this soul is immortal. The health of one's own soul is thus of paramount importance, far more significant than the mere slings and arrows of physical life. Indeed, Socrates was convinced that, even while we are living in the physical world, the quality of our souls is a far more important determinant of our happiness than external circumstances like health, wealth, popularity, or power.

3. The topic of the *Republic* is *dikaiosúnē*, a Greek word usually translated into English as "justice." Strangely enough, it is a matter of some controversy just what Plato means by *dikaiosúnē* (and thus just what, exactly, the *Republic* is about); clearly, though, the notion covers more than we might normally understand by the word "justice," though probably somewhat less than we would, today, understand by "morality." Plato is not merely interested in the virtue of treating other people fairly and impartially (and, in the *Republic*, he is hardly interested at all in the formulation and

---

* Similarly, Euthyphro was a real person and one of Socrates' contemporaries: he was a seer or prophet—that is, someone who was a professional interpreter of the wishes of the gods.

administration of civil and criminal law). Rather, Plato is discussing something like *the right way to live*, where it is understood (as was generally assumed by the ancient Greeks) that human beings are *social* animals, for whom the good life can only exist in a particular sort of political context and all the virtues—such as courage, moderation, generosity, and even piety—have to do, in one way or another, with our relationships with other people. Therefore, by "justice," Plato probably means all the areas of morality that regulate our relationships with other people.

On the other hand, it is important to notice that Plato does *not* think of justice as primarily a way of behaving, as a set of rules for correct action, or as a kind of relationship between people. Justice, for Plato, is an *internal property of individual souls*, and only secondarily of their actions. You have the virtue of justice if your soul has a certain configuration, and then it is this virtue of yours which regulates your treatment of other people; but your treatment of other people is not *itself* justice, it is just the manifestation of your justice. To put it another way, you are not a just person because your actions are just—on the contrary, your actions are just because you are.

4. The description of the "popular view" of justice by Glaucon and Adeimantus is philosophically more complicated than it might at first seem, and the following distinction is a useful one to bear in mind when you are trying to get it straight. This distinction is one between what are often called the "artificial" and the "natural" consequences of justice. The artificial consequences of justice are those "rewards and reputations" which society provides for those who give the appearance of being just. They are artificial rewards because they would not exist if it were not for human social conventions and practices and, more importantly, because they are connected only to the *appearance* of justice rather than justice itself. Thus, someone who appeared just, but was not, would still get all of the artificial rewards of justice. On the other hand, the natural rewards of being just are supposed to follow simply from justice itself, in the same way that health, sight, and knowledge have, in themselves, beneficial consequences for their possessors.

Some Common Misconceptions

1. All the protagonists in this selection from the *Republic*—Glaucon, Adeimantus, and Socrates—*agree* that justice is good in itself. Glaucon and Adeimantus present certain arguments as strongly as they can in order to force Socrates to properly respond to them, but they do not, themselves, endorse the conclusion of those arguments (and they hope Socrates will give them a way to legitimately evade that conclusion).

2. The discussion is about the benefits of justice *for just people themselves*, not for those with whom they interact or for society generally. The topic asks whether *acting justly* is intrinsically worthwhile (rather than whether it is nice to be *treated* justly).

How Important and Influential Is This Passage?

The *Republic* is generally acknowledged to be Plato's greatest work (indeed, one of the very greatest works in all philosophy), and is often thought of as the centerpiece of Plato's philosophy. Though it presents only a partial picture of his developing philosophical views, it is the dialogue where most of Plato's central ideas about ethics, metaphysics, epistemology, politics, psychology, aesthetics, and so on, come together into a single unified theory. This excerpt from the *Republic* is by no means the best-known part of the work, but it is where Plato sets up the philosophical question his book is intended to answer. As with much of Plato's writing, it is the questions he asked which have proved to be of enduring philosophical importance as much as the answers he gave to them. The questions developed here about the relationship between morality and self-interest lie at the very foundation of ethical study, and the myth of the Ring of Gyges, in particular, has been a particularly evocative image through the centuries for exploring these issues.

The *Euthyphro*, also, is a very influential Socratic dialogue and the key argument that Socrates makes there—known as the Euthyphro dilemma—has been an important problem for theists who argue that god is the source of morality (a stance sometimes called Divine Command Theory) for hundreds of years.

FROM *Republic*

BOOK II (357A–367E)[*]

When I said this, I thought I had done with the discussion, but it turned out to have been only a prelude. Glaucon showed his characteristic courage on this occasion too and refused to accept Thrasymachus' abandonment of the argument. Socrates, he said, do you want to seem to have persuaded us that it is better in every way to be just than unjust, or do you want truly to convince us of this?

I want truly to convince you, I said, if I can.

Well, then, you certainly aren't doing what you want. Tell me, do you think there is a kind of good we welcome, not because we desire what comes from it, but because we welcome it for its own sake—joy, for example, and all the harmless pleasures that have no results beyond the joy of having them?

Certainly, I think there are such things.

And is there a kind of good we like for its own sake and also for the sake of what comes from it—knowing, for example, and seeing and being healthy? We welcome such things, I suppose, on both counts.

Yes.

And do you also see a third kind of good, such as physical training, medical treatment when sick, medicine itself, and the other ways of making money? We'd say that these are onerous[†] but beneficial to us, and we wouldn't choose them for their own sakes, but for the sake of the rewards and other things that come from them.

There is also this third kind. But what of it?

Where do you put justice?

I myself put it among the finest goods, as something to be valued by anyone who is going to be blessed with happiness, both because of itself and because of what comes from it.

That isn't most people's opinion. They'd say that justice belongs to the onerous kind, and is to be practiced for the sake of the rewards and popularity that come from a reputation for justice, but is to be avoided because of itself as something burdensome.

I know that's the general opinion. Thrasymachus faulted justice on these grounds a moment ago and praised injustice, but it seems that I'm a slow learner.

Come, then, and listen to me as well, and see whether you still have that problem, for I think that Thrasymachus gave up before he had to, charmed by you as if he were a snake.[‡] But I'm not yet satisfied by the argument on either side. I want to know what justice and injustice are and what power each itself has when it's by itself in the soul. I want to leave out of account their rewards and what comes from each of them. So, if you agree, I'll renew the argument of Thrasymachus. First, I'll state what kind of thing people consider justice to be and what its origins are. Second, I'll argue that all who practice it do so unwillingly, as something necessary, not as something good. Third, I'll argue that they have good reason to act as they do, for the life of an unjust person is, they say, much better than that of a just one.

It isn't, Socrates, that I believe any of that myself. I'm perplexed, indeed, and my ears are deafened listening to Thrasymachus and countless others. But I've yet to hear anyone defend justice in the way I want, proving that it is better than injustice. I want to hear it praised *by itself*, and I think that I'm most likely to hear this from you. Therefore, I'm going to speak at length in praise of the unjust life, and in doing so I'll show you the way I want to hear you praising justice and denouncing injustice. But see whether you want me to do that or not.

I want that most of all. Indeed, what subject could someone with any understanding enjoy discussing more often?

---

* The *Republic* was probably written in about 380 BCE. This translation is by G.M.A. Grube, revised by C.D.C. Reeve, and was published in 1992 by the Hackett Publishing Company. Reprinted by permission of Hackett Publishing Company, Inc. All rights reserved.

† Burdensome, troublesome.

‡ As if he were calmed by the music of a snake-charmer.

Excellent. Then let's discuss the first subject I mentioned—what justice is and what its origins are.

They say that to do injustice is naturally good and to suffer injustice bad, but that the badness of suffering it so far exceeds the goodness of doing it that those who have done and suffered injustice and tasted both, but who lack the power to do it and avoid suffering it, decide that it is profitable to come to an agreement with each other neither to do injustice nor to suffer it. As a result, they begin to make laws and covenants, and what the law commands they call lawful and just. This, they say, is the origin and essence of justice. It is intermediate between the best and the worst. The best is to do injustice without paying the penalty; the worst is to suffer it without being able to take revenge. Justice is a mean between these two extremes. People value it not as a good but because they are too weak to do injustice with impunity. Someone who has the power to do this, however, and is a true man wouldn't make an agreement with anyone not to do injustice in order not to suffer it. For him that would be madness. This is the nature of justice, according to the argument, Socrates, and these are its natural origins.

We can see most clearly that those who practice justice do it unwillingly and because they lack the power to do injustice, if in our thoughts we grant to a just and an unjust person the freedom to do whatever they like. We can then follow both of them and see where their desires would lead. And we'll catch the just person red-handed travelling the same road as the unjust. The reason for this is the desire to outdo others and get more and more.* This is what anyone's nature naturally pursues as good, but nature is forced by law into the perversion of treating fairness with respect.

The freedom I mentioned would be most easily realized if both people had the power they say the ancestor of Gyges of Lydia† possessed. The story goes that he was a shepherd in the service of the ruler of Lydia. There was a violent thunderstorm, and an earthquake broke open the ground and created a chasm at the place where he was tending his sheep. Seeing this, he was filled with amazement and went down into it. And there, in addition to many other wonders of which we're told, he saw a hollow bronze horse. There were windowlike openings in it, and, peeping in, he saw a corpse, which seemed to be of more than human size, wearing nothing but a gold ring on its finger. He took the ring and came out of the chasm. He wore the ring at the usual monthly meeting that reported to the king on the state of the flocks. And as he was sitting among the others, he happened to turn the setting‡ of the ring towards himself to the inside of his hand. When he did this, he became invisible to those sitting near him, and they went on talking as if he had gone. He wondered at this, and, fingering the ring, he turned the setting outwards again and became visible. So he experimented with the ring to test whether it indeed had this power—and it did. If he turned the setting inward, he became invisible; if he turned it outward, he became visible again. When he realized this, he at once arranged to become one of the messengers sent to report to the king. And when he arrived there, he seduced the king's wife, attacked the king with her help, killed him, and took over the kingdom.

Let's suppose, then, that there were two such rings, one worn by a just and the other by an unjust person. Now, no one, it seems, would be so incorruptible that he would stay on the path of justice or stay away from other people's property, when he could take whatever he wanted from the marketplace with impunity, go into people's houses and have sex with anyone he wished, kill or release from prison anyone he wished, and do all the other things that would make him like a god among humans. Rather his actions would be in no way different from those of an unjust person and both would follow the same path. This, some would say, is a great proof that one

---

* This is the vice of *pleonexia*, the desire to out-compete everybody else and get more than you are entitled to. According to Plato, *pleonexia* is the root cause of injustice, and proper virtue consists in keeping *pleonexia* in check; Thrasymachus, however, has argued that *pleonexia* is not a vice at all, but a reasonable impulse which is only stifled by artificial social conventions.

† Lydia was an ancient kingdom located in western Asia Minor, where northwestern Turkey lies today. Gyges was king of Lydia from 670 to 652 BCE. Probably the first realm to use coins as money, Lydia was renowned for its immense wealth and reached the height of its power in the seventh century BCE. In 546 BCE its final king, Croesus, was defeated by the Persians, and Lydia was absorbed into the Persian Empire.

‡ The setting for a jewel.

is never just willingly but only when compelled to be. No one believes justice to be a good when it is kept private, since, wherever either person thinks he can do injustice with impunity, he does it. Indeed, every man believes that injustice is far more profitable to himself than justice. And any exponent of this argument will say he's right, for someone who didn't want to do injustice, given this sort of opportunity, and who didn't touch other people's property would be thought wretched and stupid by everyone aware of the situation, though, of course, they'd praise him in public, deceiving each other for fear of suffering injustice. So much for my second topic.

As for the choice between the lives we're discussing, we'll be able to make a correct judgment about that only if we separate the most just and the most unjust. Otherwise we won't be able to do it. Here's the separation I have in mind. We'll subtract nothing from the injustice of an unjust person and nothing from the justice of a just one, but we'll take each to be complete in his own way of life. First, therefore, we must suppose that an unjust person will act as clever craftsmen do: A first-rate captain or doctor, for example, knows the difference between what his craft can and can't do. He attempts the first but lets the second go by, and if he happens to slip, he can put things right. In the same way, an unjust person's successful attempts at injustice must remain undetected, if he is to be fully unjust. Anyone who is caught should be thought inept, for the extreme of injustice is to be believed to be just without being just. And our completely unjust person must be given complete injustice; nothing may be subtracted from it. We must allow that, while doing the greatest injustice, he has nonetheless provided himself with the greatest reputation for justice. If he happens to make a slip, he must be able to put it right. If any of his unjust activities should be discovered, he must be able to speak persuasively or to use force. And if force is needed, he must have the help of courage and strength and of the substantial wealth and friends with which he has provided himself.

Having hypothesized such a person, let's now in our argument put beside him a just man, who is simple and noble and who, as Aeschylus* says, doesn't want to be believed to be good but to be so.† We must take away his reputation, for a reputation for justice would bring him honour and rewards, so that it wouldn't be clear whether he is just for the sake of justice itself or for the sake of those honours and rewards. We must strip him of everything except justice and make his situation the opposite of an unjust person's. Though he does no injustice, he must have the greatest reputation for it, so that his justice may be tested full-strength and not diluted by wrong-doing and what comes from it. Let him stay like that unchanged until he dies—just, but all his life believed to be unjust. In this way, both will reach the extremes, the one of justice and the other of injustice, and we'll be able to judge which of them is happier.

Whew! Glaucon, I said, how vigorously you've scoured each of the men for our competition, just as you would a pair of statues for an art competition.

I do the best I can, he replied. Since the two are as I've described, in any case, it shouldn't be difficult to complete the account of the kind of life that awaits each of them, but it must be done. And if what I say sounds crude, Socrates, remember that it isn't I who speak but those who praise injustice at the expense of justice. They'll say that a just person in such circumstances will be whipped, stretched on a rack, chained, blinded with fire, and, at the end, when he has suffered every kind of evil, he'll be impaled, and will realize then that one shouldn't want to be just but to be believed to be just. Indeed, Aeschylus' words are far more correctly applied to unjust people than to just ones, for the supporters of injustice will say that a really unjust person, having a way of life based on the truth about things and not living in accordance with opinion, doesn't want simply to be believed to be unjust but actually to be so—

Harvesting a deep furrow in his mind,
Where wise counsels propagate.

---

*   Aeschylus (525–456 BCE) was a great and influential Greek tragic dramatist. He is sometimes said to have created drama itself, through his innovative introduction of multiple actors speaking different parts. His most famous plays are the *Oresteia* trilogy—*Agamemnon*, *The Libation Bearers*, and *The Eumenides*.
†   This refers to Aeschylus's play *Seven Against Thebes*. It is said of a character that "he did not wish to be believed to be the best but to be it." The next two lines of the passage are quoted by Glaucon below.

He rules his city because of his reputation for justice; he marries into any family he wishes; he gives his children in marriage to anyone he wishes; he has contracts and partnerships with anyone he wants; and besides benefiting himself in all these ways, he profits because he has no scruples about doing injustice. In any contest, public or private, he's the winner and outdoes his enemies. And by outdoing them, he becomes wealthy, benefiting his friends and harming his enemies. He makes adequate sacrifices to the gods and sets up magnificent offerings to them. He takes better care of the gods, therefore, (and, indeed, of the human beings he's fond of) than a just person does. Hence it's likely that the gods, in turn, will take better care of him than of a just person. That's what they say, Socrates, that gods and humans provide a better life for unjust people than for just ones.

When Glaucon had said this, I had it in mind to respond, but his brother Adeimantus intervened: You surely don't think that the position has been adequately stated?

Why not? I said.

The most important thing to say hasn't been said yet.

Well, then, I replied, a man's brother must stand by him, as the saying goes.* If Glaucon has omitted something, you must help him. Yet what he has said is enough to throw me to the canvas† and make me unable to come to the aid of justice.

Nonsense, he said. Hear what more I have to say, for we should also fully explore the arguments that are opposed to the ones Glaucon gave, the ones that praise justice and find fault with injustice, so that what I take to be his intention may be clearer.

When fathers speak to their sons, they say that one must be just, as do all the others who have charge of anyone. But they don't praise justice itself, only the high reputations it leads to and the consequences of being thought to be just, such as the public offices, marriages, and other things Glaucon listed. But they elaborate even further on the consequences of reputation. By bringing in the esteem of the gods, they are able to talk about the abundant good things that they themselves and the noble Hesiod and Homer say that the gods give to the pious, for Hesiod says that the gods make the oak trees

Bear acorns at the top and bees in the middle
And make fleecy sheep heavy laden with wool‡

for the just, and tells of many other good things akin to these. And Homer is similar:

When a good king, in his piety,
Upholds justice, the black earth bears
Wheat and barley for him, and his trees are heavy
  with fruit.
His sheep bear lambs unfailingly, and the sea yields up
  its fish.§

Musaeus¶ and his son make the gods give the just more headstrong goods than these. In their stories, they lead the just to Hades,** seat them on couches, provide them with a symposium†† of pious people, crown them with wreaths, and make them spend all their time drinking—as if they thought drunkenness was the finest wage of virtue. Others stretch even further the wages that virtue receives from the gods, for they

---

* In Homer's *Odyssey* (part 16, lines 97–98).
† To throw me to the floor of a wrestling ring.
‡ Hesiod, *Works and Days*, lines 232–34. Hesiod was an early Greek poet—widely considered the second greatest Greek epic poet after Homer—who lived around 700 BCE. His poem *Works and Days* reflects his experiences as a farmer, giving practical advice on how to live, and also shows Hesiod lamenting the loss of a historic Golden Age which has been replaced, he complains, with a modern era of immorality and suffering.
§ Homer, *Odyssey*, part 19, lines 109 and 111–13.
¶ This Musaeus (as opposed to a Greek poet of the same name, who lived some 1,000 years later) was a mythical poet and singer connected with the cult of Orphism, a Greek mystery religion of the sixth century BCE. His son, Eumolpus, is said to have founded the Eleusinian mysteries, an annual celebration to honor Demeter, goddess of agriculture and fertility.
** The site of the Greek afterlife, where the good were rewarded and the wicked punished.
†† A gathering for drinking, music, and intellectual conversation. (Greek: *sumposion*, literally, 'drinking party.')

say that someone who is pious and keeps his promises leaves his children's children and a whole race behind him. In these and other similar ways, they praise justice. They bury the impious and unjust in mud in Hades; force them to carry water in a sieve; bring them into bad repute while they're still alive, and all those penalties that Glaucon gave to the just person they give to the unjust. But they have nothing else to say. This, then, is the way people praise justice and find fault with injustice.

Besides this, Socrates, consider another form of argument about justice and injustice employed both by private individuals and by poets. All go on repeating with one voice that justice and moderation are fine things, but hard and onerous, while licentiousness and injustice are sweet and easy to acquire and are shameful only in opinion and law. They add that unjust deeds are for the most part more profitable than just ones, and, whether in public or private, they willingly honour vicious people* who have wealth and other types of power and declare them to be happy. But they dishonour and disregard the weak and the poor, even though they agree that they are better than the others.

But the most wonderful of all these arguments concerns what they have to say about the gods and virtue. They say that the gods, too, assign misfortune and a bad life to many good people, and the opposite fate to their opposites. Begging priests and prophets frequent the doors of the rich and persuade them that they possess a god-given power founded on sacrifices and incantations. If the rich person or any of his ancestors has committed an injustice, they can fix it with pleasant rituals. Moreover, if he wishes to injure some enemy, then, at little expense, he'll be able to harm just and unjust alike, for by means of spells and enchantments they can persuade the gods to serve

them. And the poets are brought forward as witnesses to all these accounts. Some harp on the ease of vice, as follows:

> Vice in abundance is easy to get;
> The road is smooth and begins beside you,
> But the gods have put sweat between us and virtue,†

and a road that is long, rough, and steep. Others quote Homer to witness that the gods can be influenced by humans, since he said:

> The gods themselves can be swayed by prayer,
> And with sacrifices and soothing promises,
> Incense and libations, human beings turn them from
>   their purpose
> When someone has transgressed and sinned.‡

And they present a noisy throng of books by Musaeus and Orpheus,§ offspring as they say of Selene and the Muses,¶ in accordance with which they perform their rituals. And they persuade not only individuals but whole cities that the unjust deeds of the living or the dead can be absolved or purified through sacrifices and pleasant games, whether those who have committed them are still alive, or have died. These initiations, as they call them, free people from punishment hereafter, while a terrible fate awaits those who have not performed rituals.

When all such sayings about the attitudes of gods and humans to virtue and vice are so often repeated, Socrates, what effect do you suppose they have on the souls of young people? I mean those who are clever and are able to flit from one of these sayings to another, so to speak, and gather from them an impression of what sort of person he should be and of how best to

---

*   Those having many vices, wicked people.

†   Hesiod, *Works and Days*, lines 287–89.

‡   *Iliad*, part 9, lines 497 and 499–501.

§   Orpheus was a legendary poet who lived (if he is a real figure at all) in the sixth or seventh century BCE. According to Greek myth, he was the first living mortal to travel to the underworld, on a quest to retrieve his dead wife Eurydice. Hades, ruler of the underworld, was so moved by the poet's music that he gave back Eurydice, on the condition that Orpheus not look back at her until they reached the world of the living. Orpheus glanced back a moment too soon, and Eurydice vanished. Heart-broken, he wandered alone in the wilds until a band of Thracian women killed him and threw his severed head in the river, where it continued to call for his lost love, Eurydice.

¶   Selene is the Greek goddess of the Moon. The Muses were nine goddesses, daughters of Zeus, who presided over the arts and sciences.

travel the road of life. He would surely ask himself Pindar's* question, "Should I by justice or by crooked deceit scale this high wall and live my life guarded and secure?" And he'll answer: "The various sayings suggest that there is no advantage in my being just if I'm not also thought just, while the troubles and penalties of being just are apparent. But they tell me that an unjust person, who has secured for himself a reputation for justice, lives the life of a god. Since, then, 'opinion forcibly overcomes truth' and 'controls happiness,' as the wise men† say, I must surely turn entirely to it. I should create a façade of illusory virtue around me to deceive those who come near, but keep behind it the greedy and crafty fox of the wise Archilochus."‡

"But surely," someone will object, "it isn't easy for vice to remain always hidden." We'll reply that nothing great is easy. And, in any case, if we're to be happy, we must follow the path indicated in these accounts. To remain undiscovered we'll form secret societies and political clubs. And there are teachers of persuasion to make us clever in dealing with assemblies and law courts. Therefore, using persuasion in one place and force in another, we'll outdo others without paying a penalty.

"What about the gods? Surely, we can't hide from them or use violent force against them!" Well, if the gods don't exist or don't concern themselves with human affairs, why should we worry at all about hiding from them? If they do exist and do concern themselves with us, we've learned all we know about them from the laws and the poets who give their genealogies—nowhere else. But these are the very people who tell us that the gods can be persuaded and influenced by sacrifices, gentle prayers, and offerings. Hence, we should believe them on both matters or neither. If we believe them, we should be unjust and offer sacrifices from the fruits of our injustice. If we are just, our only gain is not to be punished by the gods, since we lose the profits of injustice. But if we are unjust, we get the profits of our crimes and transgressions and

afterwards persuade the gods by prayer and escape without punishment.

"But in Hades won't we pay the penalty for crimes committed here, either ourselves or our children's children?" "My friend," the young man will say as he does his calculation, "mystery rites have great power and the gods have great power of absolution. The greatest cities tell us this, as do those children of the gods who have become poets and prophets."

Why, then, should we still choose justice over the greatest injustice? Many eminent authorities agree that, if we practice such injustice with a false façade, we'll do well at the hands of gods and humans, living and dying as we've a mind to. So, given all that has been said, Socrates, how is it possible for anyone of any power—whether of mind, wealth, body, or birth—to be willing to honor justice and not laugh aloud when he hears it praised? Indeed, if anyone can show that what we've said is false and has adequate knowledge that justice is best, he'll surely be full not of anger but of forgiveness for the unjust. He knows that, apart from someone of godlike character who is disgusted by injustice or one who has gained knowledge and avoids injustice for that reason, no one is just willingly. Through cowardice or old age or some other weakness, people do indeed object to injustice. But it's obvious that they do so only because they lack the power to do injustice, for the first of them to acquire it is the first to do as much injustice as he can.

And all of this has no other cause than the one that led Glaucon and me to say to you: "Socrates, of all of you who claim to praise justice, from the original heroes of old whose words survive, to the men of the present day, not one has ever blamed injustice or praised justice except by mentioning the reputations, honours, and rewards that are their consequences. No one has ever adequately described what each itself does of its own power by its presence in the soul of the person who possesses it, even if it remains hidden from gods and humans. No one, whether in poetry or in private

---

*   Pindar (520–440 BCE) was a Greek lyric poet.

†   Simonides of Ceos (c. 556–468 BCE), a Greek poet.

‡   Archilochus of Paros (who lived around 650 BCE), yet another Greek poet, and author of the famous fable about a fox and a hedgehog. All that remains of his writing now is this quotation: "a fox knows many things, but a hedgehog one important thing." In the fable, apparently, the clever fox tries many strategies to eat the hedgehog, who simply repels each attempt by rolling up into a spiny ball. It's not clear how the moral of this story—the success of the hedgehog—applies here, other than by its reference to a greedy and crafty animal.

conversations, has adequately argued that injustice is the worst thing a soul can have in it and that justice is the greatest good. If you had treated the subject in this way and persuaded us from youth, we wouldn't now be guarding against one another's injustices, but each would be his own best guardian, afraid that by doing injustice he'd be living with the worst thing possible."

Thrasymachus or anyone else might say what we've said, Socrates, or maybe even more, in discussing justice and injustice—crudely inverting their powers, in my opinion. And, frankly, it's because I want to hear the opposite from you that I speak with all the force I can muster. So don't merely give us a theoretical argument that justice is stronger than injustice, but tell us what each itself does, because of its own powers, to someone who possesses it, that makes injustice bad and justice good. Follow Glaucon's advice, and don't take reputations into account, for if you don't deprive justice and injustice of their true reputations and attach false ones to them, we'll say that you are not praising them but their reputations and that you're encouraging us to be unjust in secret. In that case, we'll say that you agree with Thrasymachus that justice is the good

of another, the advantage of the stronger, while injustice is one's own advantage and profit, though not the advantage of the weaker.

You agree that justice is one of the greatest goods, the ones that are worth getting for the sake of what comes from them, but much more so for their own sake, such as seeing, hearing, knowing, being healthy, and all other goods that are fruitful by their own nature and not simply because of reputation. Therefore, praise justice as a good of that kind, explaining how—because of its very self—it benefits its possessors and how injustice harms them. Leave wages and reputations for others to praise.

Others would satisfy me if they praised justice and blamed injustice in that way, extolling the wages of one and denigrating those of the other. But you, unless you order me to be satisfied, wouldn't, for you've spent your whole life investigating this and nothing else. Don't, then, give us only a theoretical argument that justice is stronger than injustice, but show what effect each has because of itself on the person who has it—the one for good and the other for bad—whether it remains hidden from gods and human beings or not....

FROM *Euthyphro**

SOCRATES: ... So now, by Zeus, explain to me what you were just now claiming to know clearly: what sort of thing do you say holiness is, and unholiness, with respect to murder and everything else as well? Or isn't the pious the same as itself in every action,[†] and the impious in turn is the complete opposite of the pious but the same as itself, and everything that in fact turns out to be impious has a single form with respect to its impiousness?

EUTHYPHRO: It certainly is, Socrates.

SOCRATES: So tell me, what do you say the pious is, and what is the impious?

EUTHYPHRO: Well then, I claim that the pious is what I am doing now, prosecuting someone who is guilty of wrongdoing—either of murder or temple robbery or anything else of the sort, whether it happens to be one's father or mother or whoever else—and the impious is failing to prosecute. For observe, Socrates, how great a proof I will give you that this is how the law stands, one I have already given to others as well, which shows such actions to be correct—not yielding to impious people, that is, no matter who they happen to be. Because these very people also happen to worship Zeus as the best and most just of the gods, and agree that he put his own father in bonds because he unjustly swallowed his sons, and the father too castrated his own father for other similar reasons.[‡] Yet

---

* The *Euthyphro* was probably written in about 395 BCE. This translation is by Cathal Woods and Ryan Pack and was published in 2016 by Broadview Press.
† That is, there is just one kind of piety—all pious actions have something in common.
‡ For the stories of Zeus, Cronos, and Ouranos, see Hesiod, *Theogony*, 154–82 and 453–506.

they are sore at me because I am prosecuting my father for his injustice. And so they say contradictory things about the gods and about me.

SOCRATES: Maybe this, Euthyphro, is why I am being prosecuted for this crime, that whenever someone says such things about the gods, for some reason I find them hard to accept? For this reason, I suppose, someone will claim I misbehave. But now if you, with your expertise in such matters, also hold these beliefs, it's surely necessary, I suppose, that we too must accept them—for indeed what *can* we say, we who admit openly that we know nothing about these matters? But before the god of friendship* tell me, do you truly believe these things happened like this?

EUTHYPHRO: These and still more amazing things, Socrates, that most people are unaware of.

SOCRATES: And do you believe there is really a war amongst the gods, with terrible feuds, even, and battles and many other such things, such as are recounted by the poets and the holy artists, and that have been elaborately adorned for us on sacred objects, too, and especially the robe covered with such designs which is brought up to the acropolis at the great Panathenaea?† Are we to say that these things are true, Euthyphro?

EUTHYPHRO: Not only these, Socrates, but as I said just now, I could also describe many other things about the gods to you, if you want, which I am sure you will be astounded to hear.

SOCRATES: I wouldn't be surprised. But you can describe these to me at leisure some other time. For the time being, however, try to state more clearly what I asked you just now, since previously, my friend, you did not teach me well enough when I asked what the pious was but you told me that what you're doing is something pious, prosecuting your father for murder.

EUTHYPHRO: And I spoke the truth, too, Socrates.

SOCRATES: Perhaps. But in fact, Euthyphro, you say there are many other pious things.

EUTHYPHRO: Indeed there are.

SOCRATES: So do you remember that I did not request this from you, to teach me one or two of the many pious things, but to teach me the form itself by which everything pious is pious? For you said that it's by one form that impious things are somehow impious and pious things pious. Or don't you remember?

EUTHYPHRO: I certainly do.

SOCRATES: So then tell me whatever this form itself is, so that, by looking at it and using it as a paradigm, if you or anyone else do anything of that kind I can say that it is pious, and if it is not of that kind, that it is not.

EUTHYPHRO: Well if that's what you want, Socrates, that's what I'll tell you.

SOCRATES: That's exactly what I want.

EUTHYPHRO: Well, what is beloved by the gods is pious, and what is not beloved by them is impious.

SOCRATES: Excellent, Euthyphro! And you have answered in the way I was looking for you to answer. Whether you have done so truly or not, that I don't quite know—but you will obviously spell out how what you say is true.

EUTHYPHRO: Absolutely.

SOCRATES: Come then, let's look at what we said. An action or a person that is beloved by the gods is pious, while an action or person that is despised by the gods is impious. It is not the same, but the complete opposite, the pious to the impious. Isn't that so?

EUTHYPHRO: Indeed it is.

---

* Zeus Philios, or Zeus in his aspect of the champion of friendship.

† The Panathenaea was an annual celebration of Athena's birthday, with a larger ("great") celebration every four years. A new robe would be presented to the statue of the goddess Athena.

SOCRATES: And this seems right?

EUTHYPHRO: I think so, Socrates.

SOCRATES: But wasn't it also said that the gods are at odds with each other and disagree with one another and that there are feuds among them?

EUTHYPHRO: Yes, it was.

SOCRATES: What is the disagreement about, my good man, that causes hatred and anger? Let's look at it this way. If we disagree, you and I, about quantity, over which of two groups is greater, would our disagreement over this make us enemies and angry with each other, or wouldn't we quickly resolve the issue by resorting to counting?

EUTHYPHRO: Of course.

SOCRATES: And again, if we disagreed about bigger and smaller, we would quickly put an end to the disagreement by resorting to measurement?

EUTHYPHRO: That's right.

SOCRATES: And we would weigh with scales, I presume, to reach a decision about heavier and lighter?

EUTHYPHRO: How else?

SOCRATES: Then what topic, exactly, would divide us and what difference would we be unable to settle such that we would be enemies and angry with one another? Perhaps you don't have an answer at hand, so as I'm talking, see if it's the just and the unjust, the noble and the shameful, and the good and the bad. Isn't it these things that make us enemies of one another, any time that happens, whether to me and you or to any other men, when we quarrel about them and are unable to come to a satisfactory judgment about them?

EUTHYPHRO: It is indeed this disagreement, Socrates, and over these things.

SOCRATES: And what about the gods, Euthyphro? If they indeed disagree over something, don't they disagree over these very things?

EUTHYPHRO: It's undoubtedly necessary.

SOCRATES: Then some of the gods think different things are just—according to you, worthy Euthyphro—and noble and shameful, and good and bad, since they surely wouldn't be at odds with one another unless they were disagreeing about these things. Right?

EUTHYPHRO: You're right.

SOCRATES: And so whatever each group thinks is noble and good and just, they also love these things, and they hate the things that are the opposites of these?

EUTHYPHRO: Certainly.

SOCRATES: Then according to you the things some of them think are just, others think are unjust, and by disagreeing about these things they are at odds and at war with each other. Isn't this so?

EUTHYPHRO: It is.

SOCRATES: The same things, it seems, are both hated by the gods and loved, and so would be both despised and beloved by them?

EUTHYPHRO: It seems so.

SOCRATES: And the same things would be both pious and impious, Euthyphro, according to this argument?

EUTHYPHRO: I'm afraid so.

SOCRATES: So you haven't answered what I was asking, you remarkable man! I didn't ask you for what is both pious and impious at once: what is beloved by the gods is also hated by the gods, as it appears. As a result, Euthyphro, it wouldn't be surprising if in doing what you're doing now—punishing your father—you were doing something beloved by Zeus but despised by Cronos and Uranus, and while it is dear to Hephaestus, it is despised by Hera, and if any other god disagrees with another on the subject, your action will also appear to them similarly.

EUTHYPHRO: But I believe, Socrates, that none of the gods will disagree with any other on this matter at least: that any man who has killed another person unjustly need not pay the penalty.

SOCRATES: What's that? Have you never heard any *man* arguing that someone who killed unjustly or did something else unjustly should not pay the penalty?

EUTHYPHRO: There's no end to these arguments, both outside and inside the courts, since people commit so many injustices and do and say anything to escape the punishment.

SOCRATES: Do they actually agree that they are guilty, Euthyphro, and despite agreeing they nonetheless say that they shouldn't pay the penalty?

EUTHYPHRO: They don't agree on that at all.

SOCRATES: So they don't do or say *everything*, since, I think, they don't dare to claim or argue for this: that if they are in fact guilty they should *not* pay the penalty. Rather, I think they claim that they're not guilty. Right?

EUTHYPHRO: That's true.

SOCRATES: So they don't argue, at least, that the guilty person shouldn't pay the penalty, but perhaps they argue about who the guilty party is and what he did and when.

EUTHYPHRO: That's true.

SOCRATES: Doesn't the very same thing happen to the gods, too, if indeed, as you said, they are at odds about just and unjust things, some saying that a god commits an injustice against another one, while others deny it? But absolutely no one at all, you remarkable man, either god or human, dares to say that the guilty person need not pay the penalty.

EUTHYPHRO: Yes. What you say is true, Socrates, for the most part.

SOCRATES: But I think that those who quarrel, Euthyphro, both men and gods, if the gods actually quarrel, argue over the particulars of what was done. Differing over a certain action, some say that it was done justly, others that it was done unjustly. Isn't that so?

EUTHYPHRO: Certainly.

SOCRATES: Come now, my dear Euthyphro. So that I can become wiser, teach me too what evidence you have that all gods think the man was killed unjustly—the one who committed murder while he was working for you, and was bound by the master of the man he killed, and died from his bonds before the servant could learn from the interpreters what ought to be done in his case, and is the sort of person on whose behalf it is proper for a son to prosecute his father and make an allegation of murder. Come, try to give me a clear indication of how in this case all the gods believe beyond doubt that this action is proper. If you could show me this satisfactorily I would never stop praising you for your wisdom.

EUTHYPHRO: But this is probably quite a task, Socrates, though I could explain it to you very clearly, even so.

SOCRATES: I understand. It's because you think I'm a slower learner than the judges, since you could make it clear to *them* in what way these actions are unjust and how the gods all hate such things.

EUTHYPHRO: Very clear indeed, Socrates, if only they would listen to me when I talk.

SOCRATES: Of course they'll listen, so long as they think you speak well. But while you were speaking the following occurred to me: I'm thinking to myself, "Even if Euthyphro convincingly shows me that every god thinks this kind of death is unjust, what more will I have learned from Euthyphro about what the pious and the impious are? Because while this particular deed might be despised by the gods, as is likely, it was already apparent, just a moment ago, that the pious and impious aren't defined this way, since we saw that what is despised by the gods is also beloved by them." So I acquit you of this, Euthyphro. If you want, let us allow that all gods think this is unjust and that all of them despise it. But this current correction to the definition—that what all the gods despise is impious while what they love is pious, and what some love and some hate is neither or both—do you want us to now define the pious and the impious in this way?

EUTHYPHRO: Well, what is stopping us, Socrates?

SOCRATES: For my part nothing, Euthyphro, but think about whether adopting this definition will make it easiest for you to teach me what you promised.

EUTHYPHRO: I do indeed say that the pious is what all the gods love, and the opposite, what all gods hate, is impious.

SOCRATES: Then let's look again, Euthyphro, to see whether it's well stated. Or will we be content to simply accept our own definition or someone else's, agreeing that it is right just because somebody says it is? Or must we examine what the speaker is saying?

EUTHYPHRO: We must examine it. But I'm quite confident that what we have now is well put.

SOCRATES: We'll soon know better, my good man. Think about this: Is the pious loved by the gods because it's pious, or it is pious because it is loved?

EUTHYPHRO: I don't know what you mean, Socrates.

SOCRATES: I'll try to express myself more clearly. We speak of something being carried and of carrying, and being led and leading, and being seen and seeing, and so you understand that all of these are different from one another and how they are different?

EUTHYPHRO: I think I understand.

SOCRATES: So there's a thing loved and different from this there's the thing that loves?

EUTHYPHRO: How could there not be?

SOCRATES: Then tell me whether what is carried is a carried thing because it is carried, or because of something else?

EUTHYPHRO: No, it's because of this.

SOCRATES: And also what is led because it is led, and what is seen because it is seen?

EUTHYPHRO: Absolutely.

SOCRATES: So it is not that because it is something seen, it is seen, but the opposite, that because it is seen it is something seen. And it is not because it is something led that it is led, but because it is led it is something led. And it is not because it is something carried that it is carried, but because it is carried, it is something carried. Is it becoming clear what I'm trying to say, Euthyphro? I mean this: that if something becomes or is affected by something, it's not because it is a thing coming to be that it comes to be; but because it comes to be it is a thing coming into being. Nor is it affected by something because it is a thing that is affected; but because it is affected, it is a thing that is being affected. Or don't you agree?

EUTHYPHRO: I do.

SOCRATES: And is a loved thing either a thing coming to be or a thing affected by something?

EUTHYPHRO: Certainly.

SOCRATES: And does the same apply to this as to the previous cases: it is not because it is a loved thing that it is loved by those who love it, but it is a loved thing because it is loved?

EUTHYPHRO: Necessarily.

SOCRATES: So what do we say about the pious, Euthyphro? Precisely that is it loved by all the gods, according to your statement?

EUTHYPHRO: Yes.

SOCRATES: Is it because of this: that it is pious? Or because of something else?

EUTHYPHRO: No, it's because of that.

SOCRATES: Because it is pious, then, it is loved, rather than being pious because it is loved?

EUTHYPHRO: It seems so.

SOCRATES: Then because it loved by the gods it is a loved thing and beloved by the gods?

EUTHYPHRO: How could it not?

SOCRATES: So the beloved is not pious, Euthyphro, nor is the pious beloved by the gods, as you claim, but the one is different from the other.

EUTHYPHRO: How so, Socrates?

SOCRATES: Because we agree that the pious is loved because of this—that is, because it's pious—and not that it is pious because it is loved. Right?

EUTHYPHRO: Yes.

SOCRATES: The beloved, on the other hand, because it is loved by gods, is beloved due to this very act of being loved, rather than being loved because it is beloved?

EUTHYPHRO: That's true.

SOCRATES: But if the beloved and the pious were in fact the same, my dear Euthyphro, then, if the pious were loved because of being the pious, the beloved would be loved because of being the beloved; and again, if the beloved was beloved because of being loved by gods, the pious would also be pious by being loved. But as it is, you see that the two are opposites and are completely different from one another, since the one, because it is loved, is the kind of thing that is loved, while the other is loved because it is the kind of thing that is loved.

So I'm afraid, Euthyphro, that when you were asked what in the world the pious is, you did not want to reveal its nature to me, but wanted to tell me some one of its qualities—that the pious has the quality of being loved by all the gods—but as for what it *is*, you did not say at all. So if I am dear to you, don't keep me in the dark but tell me again from the beginning what in the world the pious is. And we won't differ over whether it is loved by the gods or whatever else happens to it, but tell me without delay, what is the pious, and the impious?

... ■

Suggestions for Critical Reflection

1. How does Glaucon distinguish between the three different kinds of good? Do his examples make sense, and can you think of any examples of goods that do not fit easily into his classification? Into which of the three classes would *you* place justice?

2. Many modern debates about justice or morality tend to assume that there are only two fundamental, mutually exclusive positions one might take. Either something is morally right in itself, *regardless* of its consequences—often called a "deontological" view—or things are morally right or wrong *because* of their consequences (a view called "consequentialism"). For example, one might hold that taking human life is intrinsically morally wrong, no matter what the justification (e.g., because human life is 'sacred'); alternately, one might believe killing is wrong because of its harmful consequences (suffering, death, etc.), or perhaps even that sometimes it can be morally justified to kill human beings if the net consequences of doing so are sufficiently desirable (e.g., if a killing prevents more deaths than it brings about). How does the view of justice Socrates is being asked to defend fit here? Is his position *either* deontological or consequentialist? If not, what is it? How tenable a view is it?

3. How plausible is Glaucon's story of the origin of justice? If he were historically right about it, what would this show us (if anything) about the *moral* value of behaving justly?

4. If you had the Ring of Gyges, how would you behave? Do you agree with the claim that nearly everybody who possessed such a ring would behave immorally? What, if anything, would the answer to this question show about how people *ought* to behave?

5. Do unjust people generally lead more pleasant lives than just people? If so, what, if anything, would this show about the nature of morality?

6. Some commentators have claimed that the speeches of Glaucon and Adeimantus are not, as they purport to be, making the same point, but, in fact, are arguing for two quite *different* conclusions. Glaucon, it is said, emphasizes the need to defend justice *in itself*, without concern for the consequences, while Adeimantus urges that the virtue of justice must be shown to have beneficial *consequences* for those who have it. What do you think about this? Is this characterization of the speeches correct and, if so, does it mean they must be arguing for different conclusions?

7. Socrates agrees with Glaucon and Adeimantus that if justice is to be properly defended, it must be defended in isolation from its artificial or conventional consequences (such as reputation, wealth, and political influence). He also agrees that a good theory of justice must be capable of accommodating such extreme and unrealistic examples as the Ring of Gyges. But is this the right methodology to adopt? Couldn't we say that an essential part of what makes justice valuable is its pragmatic role in regulating social interactions in the kind of political societies in which we find ourselves? For example, perhaps part of the *point* of being just *is* that it entitles us to certain social rewards, or allows us to escape social penalties, and so justice does lose at least some of its value if this connection to social reality breaks down. What do you think?

8. If being just would make a person unhappy, would it then be irrational to be moral? Does Plato think so? Why does Socrates accept the challenge of showing that being just is in one's self-interest? Why not agree that justice is onerous, but is, nevertheless, our moral duty?

9. In the *Euthyphro*, Socrates famously asks whether right action (piety) is loved by the gods because it is right, or if an action is right simply because it is approved of by the gods. What is the difference between the two options? Socrates does not seem to take the second option seriously, instead focusing on the first; why do you think this might be?

10. Socrates claims that "the beloved is not pious, Euthyphro, nor is the pious beloved by the gods, as you claim, but the one is different from the other." How does he reach this conclusion?

ARISTOTLE

FROM *Nicomachean Ethics*

Who Was Aristotle?

Aristotle was born in 384 BCE in Stageira, a small town in the northeast corner of the Chalcidicé peninsula in the kingdom of Macedon, many days journey north of the intellectual centers of Greece. His father—Nicomachus, a physician at the Macedonian court—died when Aristotle was young, and he was brought up by his mother's wealthy family. At 17 Aristotle traveled to Athens to study at Europe's most important center of learning, the Academy, set up and presided over by Plato. As a young philosopher, Aristotle showed exceptional promise and made a name for himself as being industrious and clever, a good speaker, argumentative (if rather sarcastic), original, and an independent thinker. He was apparently a bit of a dandy—cutting his hair in a fashionably short style, and wearing jeweled rings—and is said to have suffered from poor digestion, to have lisped, and to have had spindly legs.

After Plato's death in about 347 BCE, Aristotle left Athens (possibly pushed out by a surge of anti-Macedonian feeling in the city—though one story suggests he left in a fit of pique after failing to be granted leadership of the Academy, and yet another account has it that Aristotle was unhappy with the Academy's turn towards pure mathematics under Plato's successor Speusippus). He traveled to Atarneus on the coast of Asia Minor (present-day Turkey) where his mother's family had connections and where the pro-Macedonian tyrant, Hermias, was a patron of philosophical studies. There, with three colleagues from the Academy, Aristotle started his own school at the town of Assos. Aristotle married Hermias's niece and adopted daughter, Pythias, and they had a daughter, also called Pythias.

This happy familial situation did not last long, however. In about 345 BCE Hermias was betrayed and executed (in a particularly grisly fashion) by the Persians.

Aristotle and his family fled to the nearby island of Lesbos, in the eastern Aegean Sea, where Aristotle founded another school at a town called Mytilene. There, with his student Theophrastus, he engaged in a hugely impressive series of studies in botany, zoology, and marine biology, collecting observations which were still of unrivaled scientific interest 2,000 years later. (Indeed, as late as the nineteenth century, Charles Darwin was able to praise Aristotle's biological researches as a work of genius which every professional biologist should read.)

Aristotle's stay on Lesbos was of short duration. In 343 BCE, invited by Philip II, the ruler of Macedonia, he returned home to tutor the 13-year-old prince Alexander. Little is reliably known about Aristotle's life during this period, though many fanciful stories have been written, clouding it in myth. Three years later, on Philip's death, Alexander became king and launched the military career which, in fairly short order, made him conqueror of much of the known world and earned him the epithet Alexander the Great. (One history claims that when Alexander embarked on his conquest of the East—his armies advanced as far as the Indian sub-continent—he took along scientists whose sole job it was to report their discoveries back to Aristotle.)

In 335 BCE, after Alexander's troops had completed their conquest of the Greek city-states, Aristotle moved back to Athens where, once again, he started his own research institute. This university became known as the Lyceum (after the grove, dedicated to the god Apollo Lyceus, where it was located), and it continued to flourish for 500 years after Aristotle's death.* There he spent the next twelve years teaching, writing, and building up the first great library of the ancient world. Most of his known philosophical writings probably date from this time. After his wife Pythias died, Aristotle became the lover of a woman called Herpyllis. Their son Nicomachus was named, following the Greek custom, after his grandfather.

---

* Because philosophical discussions at the Lyceum were often conducted while strolling around a colonnaded walk called a *peripatos*, Aristotle's group became known as "the Peripatetics" (the walkers).

This peaceful existence was shattered in 323 BCE by news of Alexander's death in Babylon at the age of 33. Almost instantly, open revolt against the Macedonian conquerors broke out, and Aristotle—because of his connection with Alexander—was suddenly no longer welcome in Athens. One of the citizens brought an indictment of impiety towards him—the same "crime" for which the Athenians had executed Socrates three-quarters of a century earlier. It is said that in order to prevent the Athenians from sinning against philosophy a second time, Aristotle and his family beat a hasty retreat to Chalcis, on the island of Euboea, where his mother's family had estates. There Aristotle soon died, in November 322 BCE, at age 62. In his humane and sensible will, which has been preserved for posterity, Aristotle directed that Pythias's bones should be placed in his grave, in accordance with her wishes. He also freed several of his slaves and made generous and flexible financial provisions for Herpyllis and Nicomachus.

What Was Aristotle's Overall Philosophical Project?

Aristotle's life-work was nothing less than the attempt to collect together and systematically arrange all human knowledge. His consuming ambition was to get as close as possible to *knowing everything*—about the natural world, the human social world, and even the unchanging and eternal world of the heavens and the gods. However, unlike many other philosophers with similar ambitions before and since, Aristotle probably did not believe that there is some single, unified set of truths—some single *theory*—which provides the key to unlocking all of reality. He was not looking for a deeper, more authentic realm lying behind and explaining the world we live in, but instead was simply trying to find out as much as he could about *our* world, as we experience it. Thus, it is sometimes said, Aristotle's basic theoretical commitment was to *common sense*: he wanted to develop a system that provided a place for both scientific and moral-political truths, but did not depend on mysteriously invisible and inaccessible objects such as Plato's Forms (see the notes to the previous reading).* For Aristotle, the ultimate reality is the concrete world with which we are already acquainted—people, animals, plants, minerals—which Aristotle thought of as *substances* and their properties.

Often, Aristotle worked in the following way: after choosing a domain of study (such as rhetoric or metaphysics), he would begin by summarizing and laying out all the serious claims made about it—"what seems to be the case," including all the "reputable opinions." He would also pay attention to the way in which the matters in question were ordinarily spoken of—the assumptions about them built into everyday language. Then, Aristotle would survey the puzzles or problems generated by this material, and would set out to solve those puzzles, preferably without disturbing too many of the received opinions. Typically he would not stop there: new puzzles or objections would be raised by the solutions, and he would try to clear up those matters, and then new puzzles would be generated, and so on, each time, he hoped, getting closer to the final truth.

Since Aristotle did not believe in a single "theory of everything," he divided the branches of knowledge, or "sciences," into three main groups: theoretical sciences (whose aim is to discover truths), practical sciences (governing the performance of actions), and productive sciences (whose goal is the making of objects). The major theoretical sciences, according to Aristotle, are theology (which he thought of as the study of "changeless items"), mathematics, and the natural sciences. The chief practical sciences are ethics and politics. Examples of productive sciences are poetics, rhetoric, medicine, and agriculture. According to Aristotle, these various sciences are quite different: although they add up to a composite picture of reality, they share no single set of theoretical concepts or assumptions, no single methodology, and no single set of standards for scientific rigor. The proper methods of mathematics differ from those of zoology, which differ again from those of ethics.

---

* Another, then contemporary, theory which Aristotle opposed, also on the grounds of mystery-mongering, was a theory called "atomism," put forward by philosophers like Leucippus (who flourished between 450 and 420 BCE) and Democritus (c. 460–371 BCE). This theory postulated the existence of huge numbers of invisibly tiny, eternal, unchangeable particles—*atoma*, Greek for "uncuttables"—whose hidden behaviors and interactions were supposed to explain all the observable properties of the visible spatio-temporal world.

On the other hand, Aristotle hoped each science, or at least all theoretical sciences, would share the same *structure*: Aristotle was the first philosopher to conceive of science as a body of knowledge arranged according to a particular logical structure, which he modeled on that of geometry. As in geometry, there are two kinds of scientific truth, according to Aristotle: truths which are simply "evident" and need no explanation, and a much larger body of further truths which are justified or explained by being logically derived from the self-evident truths. (Aristotle, more or less single-handedly, invented the study of logic—which he called the science of "syllogisms"—partly to be able to describe the proper structure of scientific knowledge.) Unlike the case with geometry, however, Aristotle insisted that the "axioms" of any theoretical science—the self-evident truths upon which it is based—should ideally capture the *essences* of the things being described by that science. In this way, according to Aristotle, the logical structure of science would exactly reflect the structure of the world itself. Just as the properties of things (say, plants) are caused by their essential natures, so will the claims of the relevant science (e.g., botany) be logically derived from its basic assumptions about the essences of the things in its domain.

So where, according to Aristotle, do we get these first principles of the different sciences? The answer, Aristotle believed, was not from the exercise of pure reason but from careful *observation* of the world around us. By looking very hard and carefully at a particular domain (such as botany or ethics) we discern some fundamental truths about the things in that domain, from which everything else about it will follow. Because of this practical emphasis on observation rather than mere thought, Aristotle is described as "the father of modern empiricism." On the other hand, Aristotle never developed anything like an experimental method: his method for testing theories—verifying and falsifying them—consisted more in reasoned analysis than in empirical testing.

What Is the Structure of This Reading?

Judging by Alexandrian-age library catalogues, Aristotle wrote some 150 works in his lifetime—ranging in length from essays to books—covering a huge variety of topics: logic, physics, biology, meteorology, philosophy of science, history of science, metaphysics, psychology (including works on love, friendship, and the emotions), ethics and political theory, political science, rhetoric, poetics (and some original poetry), and political and legal history. Only a fraction of these writings—perhaps less than a fifth—survive: many of Aristotle's works, including all the dialogues he wrote for popular consumption, are now lost.* Most of what remains are summaries of lectures delivered at various times during his career, which were deposited in Aristotle's own library at the Lyceum to be consulted by teachers and students. Most of these notes were probably edited and re-edited, both by Aristotle and his successors; the *Nicomachean Ethics*, for example, is so-called because it is thought to have been edited by Aristotle's son Nicomachus after his father's death.†

The *Nicomachean Ethics* is traditionally divided into 10 books (though the divisions were probably not Aristotle's own). Book I examines the nature of the good for human beings—happiness—and divides it into two categories: intellectual excellence and moral excellence. Books II to IV deal with moral excellence, beginning with a general account of it and going on to discuss several of the moral virtues in detail. Book V looks at the virtue of justice, while Book VI describes some of the forms of intellectual excellence. Book VII deals with moral self-control and the nature of pleasure, and Books VIII and IX are about friendship. Finally, Book X concludes with a discussion of *eudaimonia* or well-being, and of the role that education and society play in bringing about individual happiness.

Excerpted here are the first few pages of Book I, which introduce Aristotle's view of the study of ethics, and then section 7 of Book I, where Aristotle lays out his so-called function argument for the view that human

---

* This lost *oeuvre* is a particular tragedy because Aristotle's prose style was greatly admired by the ancients—more so than Plato's, for example—and yet (not unnaturally, considering their purpose) the lecture notes, which are the only things of Aristotle's we have left to us, are generally agreed to be rather dryly written: terse and elliptical, full of abrupt transitions, inadequate explanations, and technical jargon.

† Aristotle's other main ethical work—an earlier set of lecture notes, generally thought to be superseded by the more mature *Nicomachean Ethics*—is similarly called the *Eudemian Ethics*, possibly after its ancient editor Eudemus of Rhodes.

happiness consists in a life of excellent activity in accordance with reason. There follows the second half of Book II, where Aristotle defines moral virtue as a disposition to choose the mean—illustrating this with examples of particular moral virtues—and then discusses the practical corollaries of this account of virtue. Finally, part of Book X is included: here, Aristotle discusses further the nature of happiness and argues that the highest form of happiness is to be found in a life of philosophical "contemplation."

Much of Book V of the *Nicomachean Ethics* is also reprinted in the Justice section of this book.

Some Useful Background Information

1. Aristotle categorized ethics as a practical, rather than a theoretical, science. The *Nicomachean Ethics* is written "not in order to know what virtue is, but in order to become good." In other words, for Aristotle, the point of ethics is not merely to know what good people are like, but to learn to act as good people do: the *Nicomachean Ethics* is intended to foster what he calls "practical wisdom" (*phronesis*) in those who study it. The science of ethics is continuous, for Aristotle, with two others—biology and politics. It is continuous with biology because ethics is the study of the good life for humankind *as a biological species*. A good life for the member of *any* species (whether a horse or a daffodil) is a life of continuous flourishing, but what *counts* as flourishing will depend upon the biological nature of that species. Ethics is continuous with politics—the study of human society— because the arena in which human beings live their lives, in which they develop as moral agents and exercise their moral capacities, is necessarily a social one.

2. According to Aristotle, the goal of human life is to achieve *eudaimonia*. *Eudaimonia* is usually—as it is in our selection—translated as "happiness," but this can be misleading. The Greek word does not refer to a psychological state or feeling, such as pleasure, but instead means a certain kind of desirable *activity* or *way of life*—it is the activity of living well. The happy person is, for Aristotle, someone who has lived a genuinely *successful* or fulfilling life.

3. Aristotle's understanding of nature, and in particular of biology, is what is called *teleological*: a thing's *telos* is its goal or purpose and, for Aristotle, all of nature is goal-directed. For example, the nature of some processes (such as digestion) or biological organs (such as the eye) is plausibly determined by their *function*—their goal or *telos*— and not by their physical composition at some particular time. Eyes are things, any things, that have the function of seeing. Aristotle extended this model to the entire natural world, so that, in his view, the essence of fire consists in its goal (of, roughly, rising upwards), the essence of an acorn is its purpose to grow into an oak tree, and the essence of the species *horse* is to flourish and procreate as horses are supposed to do. Since human beings are as much a part of the biological world as anything else, it follows that a proper understanding of human nature—and thus of the good life for human beings—must involve an investigation into the function of the human species.

Some Common Misconceptions

1. When Aristotle refers to the *telos*—the function or goal—of living creatures like plants, animals, and human beings, he is not thinking of these creatures as having a purpose for *something else*. He is not, for example, assuming that there is some great universal plan (perhaps God's plan) and that living creatures have a role to play in fulfilling this plan. Instead, the *telos* of living creatures is *internal* to them: it is, so to speak, built into their biological natures. So, for another example, the fact that apples serve our purposes as food does not mean that this is their *telos*.

2. It is sometimes easy to forget that Aristotle's Doctrine of the Mean urges us to avoid *both* excess and deficiency. Aristotle's account not only instructs us to moderate our anger or curb our drinking, it also warns us against feeling too *little* anger or not drinking *enough* wine.

3. When Aristotle refers to "the mean" of a spectrum of behavior, he does not intend to speak of something like an arithmetical average, and thus does not suggest we should, literally, choose the *mid-point* of that range of behavior. The mean or mid-point of two

numbers (as 6 is the mean of 2 and 10) is an example of what Aristotle calls a mean "in the object." Aristotle contrasts this mathematical use with his own usage of "mean," which is a mean "relative to us." For example, we should eat neither too many, nor too few, cookies; but exactly how many cookies we should eat depends on our personal circumstances (our weight, our lifestyle, how many other people also want cookies, whether we are allergic to ingredients in the cookies, and so on). Certainly, Aristotle does not want to say that we should eat *exactly half* of all the available cookies.

4. Aristotle does not think of his ethical theory as a sort of moral rulebook. Unlike most modern moral philosophers, such as Immanuel Kant and J.S. Mill, Aristotle is not trying to find a theory that will, by itself, generate moral principles to tell us how to act. Instead, he is trying to develop an account of moral *character*—a theory of the good person. It is salutary to recall that, although the topic of Aristotle's book is indeed *ēthika*, which is usually translated as "ethics," the Greek word means "matters to do with character." Similarly, when Aristotle writes of *ēthikē aretē*—which is almost invariably translated as "moral virtue"—the literal meaning is "excellence of character," and by "excellence" is meant simply what we would mean if we spoke of an excellent horse or an excellent phone. The modern sense of ethics, as involving *obedience to some sort of moral law*, is substantially more recent than Aristotle, and arose (more or less) with the monotheistic religions of Judaism, Christianity, and Islam.

5. The Doctrine of the Mean does not apply to particular *actions*, but to *virtues*—to states of character. Thus, the idea is not that one always *acts* in a way which is intermediate between two extremes, but that one's actions are guided by a *character trait* which is neither excessive nor insufficient. For example, in certain situations, someone possessing the virtue of generosity might nevertheless refuse to give anything at all to a particular person in a particular circumstance (or, conversely, might give away everything they own); or a person with the virtue of being even-tempered might nevertheless find it appropriate, sometimes, to become very angry (or, in another situation, to meekly suppress any angry feelings whatsoever).

How Important and Influential Is This Passage?

Many professional philosophers consider Aristotle to be the greatest philosopher who ever lived (for example, Oxford philosopher J.L. Ackrill called him "a philosophical super-genius"[*]); throughout the Middle Ages he was simply "the Philosopher." The system of ethics developed in the *Nicomachean Ethics* has had a profound effect on all subsequent moral philosophy. In every age of philosophy it has been either fervently embraced or fiercely rejected, but never ignored. Several of its central tenets—that morality consists in finding a "golden mean," or that the rational aim of human life is happiness (though not necessarily pleasure)—have become part of our everyday moral consciousness. On the other hand, for much of the post-medieval period, Aristotle's emphasis on the *virtues*, rather than on *types of action*, as the basis of morality was paid relatively little attention. More recently, there has been a surge of interest in so-called virtue ethics, and Aristotle is generally considered the original source for this 'new' theory. (Modern virtue theories, however, diverge from Aristotle's ethical philosophy in important ways. In particular, they tend to reject or ignore his emphasis on *eudaimonia* as the ultimate moral good.)

---

* J.L. Ackrill, *Aristotle the Philosopher* (Oxford University Press, 1981), 8.

FROM *Nicomachean Ethics**

BOOK I

1 [Ends and Goods]

Every craft and every line of inquiry, and likewise every action and decision, seems to seek some good; that is why some people were right to describe the good as what everything seeks.[†] But the ends[‡] [that are sought] appear to differ; some are activities, and others are products apart from the activities. Wherever there are ends apart from the actions, the products are by nature better than the activities.

Since there are many actions, crafts, and sciences, the ends turn out to be many as well; for health is the end of medicine, a boat of boat building, victory of generalship, and wealth of household management. But some of these pursuits are subordinate to some one capacity; for instance, bridle making and every other science producing equipment for horses are subordinate to horsemanship, while this and every action in warfare are, in turn, subordinate to generalship, and in the same way other pursuits are subordinate to further ones. In all such cases, then, the ends of the ruling sciences are more choiceworthy[§] than all the ends subordinate to them, since the lower ends are also pursued for the sake of the higher. Here it does not matter whether the ends of the actions are the activities themselves, or something apart from them, as in the sciences we have mentioned.

2 [The Highest Good and Political Science]

Suppose, then, that the things achievable by action have some end that we wish for because of itself, and because of which we wish for the other things, and that we do not choose everything because of something else—for if we do, it will go on without limit, so that desire will prove to be empty and futile. Clearly, this end will be the good, that is to say, the best good.

Then does knowledge of this good carry great weight for [our] way of life, and would it make us better able, like archers who have a target to aim at, to hit the right mark? If so, we should try to grasp, in outline at any rate, what the good is, and which is its proper science or capacity.

It seems proper to the most controlling science—the highest ruling science. And this appears characteristic of political science.[¶] For it is the one that prescribes which of the sciences ought to be studied in cities, and which ones each class in the city should learn, and how far; indeed we see that even the most honored capacities—generalship, household management, and rhetoric, for instance—are subordinate to it. And since it uses the other sciences concerned with action, and moreover legislates what must be done and what avoided, its end will include the ends of the other sciences, and so this will be the human good. For even

---

[*] The *Nicomachean Ethics* was probably written, as a series of lecture notes which would have undergone frequent revision, sometime between 334 and 322 BCE. This selection is reprinted from *Aristotle, Nicomachean Ethics*, 2nd edition, translated, with introduction, notes, and glossary by Terence Irwin (Hackett, 1999). The section headings are not Aristotle's own, but are supplied by the translator.

[†] This definition is consistent with the views of Plato, but Aristotle is probably thinking mostly of the work of a philosopher, mathematician, and astronomer called Eudoxus of Cnidus. Eudoxus taught at Plato's Academy in Athens from 368 until his death in 355 BCE, and was in charge of the school (during one of Plato's absences in Sicily) when Aristotle arrived there to study at the age of 17.

[‡] Here, and throughout this reading, "end" means "goal" or "purpose," rather than merely "stopping place."

[§] More worthy of pursuit, to be preferred.

[¶] For Aristotle the study of politics (*politikē*) would be broader than our modern political science, and would include all aspects of the study of society. The goal of political science, according to Aristotle, ought to be to achieve happiness (*eudaimonia*) for all the citizens of the state, and this is why he thinks that the investigation into human happiness (ethics) is continuous with politics.

if the good is the same for a city as for an individual, still the good of the city is apparently a greater and more complete good to acquire and preserve. For while it is satisfactory to acquire and preserve the good even for an individual, it is finer and more divine to acquire and preserve it for a people and for cities. And so, since our line of inquiry seeks these [goods, for an individual and for a community], it is a sort of political science.

3 [The Method of Political Science]

Our discussion will be adequate if we make things perspicuous enough to accord with the subject matter; for we would not seek the same degree of exactness in all sorts of arguments alike, any more than in the products of different crafts. Now, fine and just things, which political science examines, differ and vary so much as to seem to rest on convention only, not on nature. But [this is not a good reason, since] goods also vary in the same way, because they result in harm to many people—for some have been destroyed because of their wealth, others because of their bravery. And so, since this is our subject and these are our premises, we shall be satisfied to indicate the truth roughly and in outline; since our subject and our premises are things that hold good usually [but not universally], we shall be satisfied to draw conclusions of the same sort.

Each of our claims, then, ought to be accepted in the same way [as claiming to hold good usually]. For the educated person seeks exactness in each area to the extent that the nature of the subject allows; for apparently it is just as mistaken to demand demonstrations from a rhetorician as to accept [merely] persuasive arguments from a mathematician....

7 [An Account of the Human Good]

But let us return once again to the good we are looking for, and consider just what it could be. For it is apparently one thing in one action or craft, and another thing in another; for it is one thing in medicine, another in generalship, and so on for the rest. What, then, is the good of each action or craft? Surely it is that for the sake of which the other things are done; in medicine this is health, in generalship victory, in house-building a house, in another case something else, but in every action and decision it is the end, since it is for the sake of the end that everyone does the other actions. And so, if there is some end of everything achievable in action, the good achievable in action will be this end; if there are more ends than one, [the good achievable in action] will be these ends.

Our argument, then, has followed a different route to reach the same conclusion. But we must try to make this still more perspicuous. Since there are apparently many ends, and we choose some of them (for instance, wealth, flutes,* and, in general, instruments) because of something else, it is clear that not all ends are complete. But the best good is apparently something complete. And so, if only one end is complete, the good we are looking for will be this end; if more ends than one are complete, it will be the most complete end of these.

We say that an end pursued in its own right is more complete than an end pursued because of something else, and that an end that is never choiceworthy because of something else is more complete than ends that are choiceworthy both in their own right and because of this end. Hence an end that is always choiceworthy in its own right, never because of something else, is complete without qualification.

Now happiness,† more than anything else, seems complete without qualification. For we always choose it because of itself, never because of something else. Honor, pleasure, understanding, and every virtue we certainly choose because of themselves, since we would choose each of them even if it had no further result; but we also choose them for the sake of happiness, supposing that through them we shall be happy. Happiness, by contrast, no one ever chooses for their sake, or for the sake of anything else at all.

The same conclusion [that happiness is complete] also appears to follow from self-sufficiency. For the complete good seems to be self-sufficient. What we count as self-sufficient is not what suffices for a solitary person by himself, living an isolated life, but what suffices also for parents, children, wife, and, in general,

---

*   Strictly speaking, Aristotle means an *aulos*, an ancient Greek double-reed instrument.
†   *Eudaimonia* (see the "Some Useful Background Information" section of the introduction to this reading).

for friends and fellow citizens, since a human being is a naturally political [animal]. Here, however, we must impose some limit; for if we extend the good to parents' parents and children's children and to friends of friends, we shall go on without limit; but we must examine this another time.

Anyhow, we regard something as self-sufficient when all by itself it makes a life choiceworthy and lacking nothing; and that is what we think happiness does. Moreover, we think happiness is most choiceworthy of all goods, [since] it is not counted as one good among many. [If it were] counted as one among many, then, clearly, we think it would be more choiceworthy if the smallest of goods were added; for the good that is added becomes an extra quantity of goods, and the larger of two goods is always more choiceworthy.

Happiness, then, is apparently something complete and self-sufficient, since it is the end of the things achievable in action.

But presumably the remark that the best good is happiness is apparently something [generally] agreed, and we still need a clearer statement of what the best good is. Perhaps, then, we shall find this if we first grasp the function of a human being. For just as the good, i.e., [doing] well, for a flautist, a sculptor, and every craftsman, and, in general, for whatever has a function and [characteristic] action, seems to depend on its function, the same seems to be true for a human being, if a human being has some function.

Then do the carpenter and the leather worker have their functions and actions, but has a human being no function? Is he by nature idle, without any function?* Or, just as eye, hand, foot, and, in general, every [bodily] part apparently has its function, may we likewise ascribe to a human being some function apart from all of these?

What, then, could this be? For living is apparently shared with plants, but what we are looking for is the special function of a human being; hence we should set aside the life of nutrition and growth. The life next in order is some sort of life of sense perception; but this too is apparently shared with horse, ox, and every animal.

The remaining possibility, then, is some sort of life of action of the [part of the soul] that has reason. One [part] of it has reason as obeying reason; the other has it as itself having reason and thinking. Moreover, life is also spoken of in two ways [as capacity and as activity], and we must take [a human being's special function to be] life as activity, since this seems to be called life more fully. We have found, then, that the human function is activity of the soul† in accord with reason or requiring reason.

Now we say that the function of a [kind of thing]—of a harpist, for instance—is the same in kind as the function of an excellent individual of the kind—of an excellent harpist, for instance. And the same is true without qualification in every case, if we add to the function the superior achievement in accord with the virtue; for the function of a harpist is to play the harp, and the function of a good harpist is to play it well. Moreover, we take the human function to be a certain kind of life, and take this life to be activity and actions of the soul that involve reason; hence the function of the excellent man is to do this well and finely.

Now each function is completed well by being completed in accord with the virtue proper [to that kind of thing]. And so the human good proves to be activity of the soul in accord with virtue, and indeed with the best and most complete virtue, if there are more virtues than one. Moreover, in a complete life. For one swallow does not make a spring,‡ nor does one

---

* In the original Greek, this would have been a pun: the word for being "without function" (*argon*) was also colloquially used to mean a "good for nothing" or a "dropout."

† By "soul"—*psuchē*—Aristotle means, very roughly, that which makes us alive or animates us. The religious or Cartesian connotations of the word—the notion of the soul as a sort of substantial spiritual self, housed in a temporary material vessel (the body)—only came about much later in history.

‡ An allusion to the return of migrating swallows at the start of the summer, this remark has become a well-known cliché—the idea is that seeing the first swallow of the year does not mean that spring has fully arrived yet. (Aristotle himself, as it happens, believed that swallows hibernated over winter in holes in the ground—and claimed that this was something he had personally observed—and his authority was so great that this 'scientific fact' was believed for centuries.)

day; nor, similarly, does one day or a short time make us blessed and happy.

This, then, is a sketch of the good; for, presumably, we must draw the outline first, and fill it in later. If the sketch is good, anyone, it seems, can advance and articulate it, and in such cases time discovers more, or is a good partner in discovery. That is also how the crafts have improved, since anyone can add what is lacking [in the outline].

We must also remember our previous remarks, so that we do not look for the same degree of exactness in all areas, but the degree that accords with a given subject matter and is proper to a given line of inquiry. For the carpenter's and the geometer's inquiries about the right angle are different also; the carpenter restricts himself to what helps his work, but the geometer inquires into what, or what sort of thing, the right angle is, since he studies the truth. We must do the same, then, in other areas too, [seeking the proper degree of exactness], so that digressions do not overwhelm our main task.

Nor should we make the same demand for an explanation in all cases. On the contrary, in some cases it is enough to prove rightly that [something is true, without also explaining why it is true]. This is so, for instance, with principles, where the fact that [something is true] is the first thing, that is to say, the principle.

Some principles are studied by means of induction,* some by means of perception,† some by means of some sort of habituation,‡ and others by other means. In each case we should try to find them out by means suited to their nature, and work hard to define them rightly. For they carry great weight for what follows; for the principle seems to be more than half the whole,§ and makes evident the answer to many of our questions.

...

BOOK II

5 [Virtue of Character: Its Genus¶]

Next we must examine what virtue is. Since there are three conditions arising in the soul—feelings, capacities, and states—virtue must be one of these.

By feelings I mean appetite, anger, fear, confidence, envy, joy, love, hate, longing, jealousy, pity, and in general whatever implies pleasure or pain. By capacities I mean what we have when we are said to be capable of these feelings—capable of being angry, for instance, or of being afraid or of feeling pity. By states I mean what we have when we are well or badly off in relation to feelings. If, for instance, our feeling is too intense or slack, we are badly off in relation to anger, but if it is intermediate, we are well off; the same is true in the other cases.

First, then, neither virtues nor vices are feelings. For we are called excellent or base insofar as we have virtues or vices, not insofar as we have feelings. Further, we are neither praised nor blamed insofar as we have feelings; for we do not praise the angry or the frightened person, and do not blame the person who is simply angry, but only the person who is angry in a particular way. We are praised or blamed, however,

---

* This, for Aristotle, is the process of moving from particular facts, observations, or examples to a general or universal claim (for example, from particular examples of courage and cowardice to a general understanding of the relation between them). The Greek word is *epagōgē*, which literally means "leading on."

† The word Aristotle uses, *aisthēsis*, can be used to mean sense-perception, but Aristotle probably means something more like "direct intuition" of (moral) facts—just *seeing* that something is right or wrong.

‡ This, in Aristotle's view, is how the moral virtues are inculcated: by repeatedly and self-consciously acting in a particular way (e.g., bravely) until that manner of behaving (e.g., bravery) becomes a habit or a character trait.

§ This was apparently a Greek proverb.

¶ Aristotle defined a category by stating the family—what genus—it belonged to, then by explaining what differentiated it from other categories in the same family—the differentia: that is, what species it was among others in the genus. For example, humans are defined as belonging to the genus animals, and were, in particular, the species of animals that are rational.

insofar as we have virtues or vices. Further, we are angry and afraid without decision; but the virtues are decisions of some kind, or [rather] require decision. Besides, insofar as we have feelings, we are said to be moved; but insofar as we have virtues or vices, we are said to be in some condition rather than moved.

For these reasons the virtues are not capacities either; for we are neither called good nor called bad, nor are we praised or blamed, insofar as we are simply capable of feelings. Further, while we have capacities by nature, we do not become good or bad by nature; we have discussed this before.

If, then, the virtues are neither feelings nor capacities, the remaining possibility is that they are states. And so we have said what the genus of virtue is.

6 [Virtue of Character: Its Differentia]

But we must say not only, as we already have, that it is a state, but also what sort of state it is.

It should be said, then, that every virtue causes its possessors to be in a good state and to perform their functions well. The virtue of eyes, for instance, makes the eyes and their functioning excellent, because it makes us see well; and similarly, the virtue of a horse makes the horse excellent, and thereby good at galloping, at carrying its rider, and at standing steady in the face of the enemy. If this is true in every case, the virtue of a human being will likewise be the state that makes a human being good and makes him perform his function well.

We have already said how this will be true, and it will also be evident from our next remarks, if we consider the sort of nature that virtue has.

In everything continuous and divisible we can take more, less, and equal, and each of them either in the object itself or relative to us; and the equal is some intermediate between excess and deficiency. By the intermediate in the object I mean what is equidistant from each extremity; this is one and the same for all. But relative to us the intermediate is what is neither superfluous nor deficient; this is not one, and is not the same for all.

If, for instance, ten are many and two are few, we take six as intermediate in the object, since it exceeds [two] and is exceeded [by ten] by an equal amount, [four]. This is what is intermediate by numerical proportion. But that is not how we must take the intermediate that is relative to us. For if ten pounds [of food], for instance, are a lot for someone to eat, and two pounds a little, it does not follow that the trainer will prescribe six, since this might also be either a little or a lot for the person who is to take it—for Milo* [the athlete] a little, but for the beginner in gymnastics a lot; and the same is true for running and wrestling. In this way every scientific expert avoids excess and deficiency and seeks and chooses what is intermediate—but intermediate relative to us, not in the object.

This, then, is how each science produces its product well, by focusing on what is intermediate and making the product conform to that. This, indeed, is why people regularly comment on well-made products that nothing could be added or subtracted; they assume that excess or deficiency ruins a good [result], whereas the mean preserves it. Good craftsmen also, we say, focus on what is intermediate when they produce their product. And since virtue, like nature, is better and more exact than any craft, it will also aim at what is intermediate.

By virtue I mean virtue of character; for this is about feelings and actions, and these admit of excess, deficiency, and an intermediate condition. We can be afraid, for instance, or be confident, or have appetites, or get angry, or feel pity, and in general have pleasure or pain, both too much and too little, and in both ways not well. But having these feelings at the right times, about the right things, toward the right people, for the right end, and in the right way, is the intermediate and best condition, and this is proper to virtue. Similarly, actions also admit of excess, deficiency, and an intermediate condition.

Now virtue is about feelings and actions, in which excess and deficiency are in error and incur blame, whereas the intermediate condition is correct and wins praise, which are both proper to virtue. Virtue, then, is a mean, insofar as it aims at what is intermediate.

---

* Milo of Croton, supposed to have lived in the second half of the sixth century BCE in southern Italy, was a legendary wrestler and athlete, famous for his immense strength.

Moreover, there are many ways to be in error—for badness is proper to the indeterminate, as the Pythagoreans* pictured it, and good to the determinate. But there is only one way to be correct. That is why error is easy and correctness is difficult, since it is easy to miss the target and difficult to hit it. And so for this reason also excess and deficiency are proper to vice, the mean to virtue; "for we are noble in only one way, but bad in all sorts of ways."†

Virtue, then, is a state that decides, consisting in a mean, the mean relative to us, which is defined by reference to reason, that is to say, to the reason by reference to which the prudent person would define it. It is a mean between two vices, one of excess and one of deficiency.

It is a mean for this reason also: Some vices miss what is right because they are deficient, others because they are excessive, in feelings or in actions, whereas virtue finds and chooses what is intermediate.

That is why virtue, as far as its essence and the account stating what it is are concerned, is a mean, but, as far as the best [condition] and the good [result] are concerned, it is an extremity.

Now not every action or feeling admits of the mean. For the names of some automatically include baseness—for instance, spite, shamelessness, envy [among feelings], and adultery, theft, murder, among actions. For all of these and similar things are called by these names because they themselves, not their excesses or deficiencies, are base. Hence in doing these things we can never be correct, but must invariably be in error. We cannot do them well or not well—by committing adultery, for instance, with the right woman at the right time in the right way. On the contrary, it is true without qualification that to do any of them is to be in error.

[To think these admit of a mean], therefore, is like thinking that unjust or cowardly or intemperate action also admits of a mean, an excess and a deficiency. If it did, there would be a mean of excess, a mean of deficiency, an excess of excess and a deficiency of deficiency. On the contrary, just as there is no excess or deficiency of temperance or of bravery (since the intermediate is a sort of extreme), so also there is no mean of these vicious actions either, but whatever way anyone does them, he is in error. For in general there is no mean of excess or of deficiency, and no excess or deficiency of a mean.

7 [The Particular Virtues of Character]

However, we must not only state this general account but also apply it to the particular cases. For among accounts concerning actions, though the general ones are common to more cases, the specific ones are truer, since actions are about particular cases, and our account must accord with these. Let us, then, find these from the chart.‡

First, then, in feelings of fear and confidence the mean is bravery. The excessively fearless person is nameless (indeed many cases are nameless), and the one who is excessively confident is rash. The one who is excessive in fear and deficient in confidence is cowardly.

In pleasures and pains—though not in all types, and in pains less than in pleasures—the mean is temperance and the excess intemperance. People deficient in pleasure are not often found, which is why they also lack even a name; let us call them insensible.

In giving and taking money the mean is generosity, the excess wastefulness and the deficiency ungenerosity. Here the vicious people have contrary excesses and defects; for the wasteful person is excessive in spending and deficient in taking, whereas the ungenerous person is excessive in taking and deficient in spending. At the moment we are speaking in outline and summary, and that is enough; later we shall define these things more exactly.

In questions of money there are also other conditions. Another mean is magnificence; for the magnificent person differs from the generous by being concerned with large matters, while the generous person is concerned with small. The excess is ostentation and vulgarity, and the deficiency is stinginess. These differ

---

* The followers of philosopher and mystic Pythagoras of Samos (c. 570–495 BCE). One of their most influential beliefs was that everything in the universe can be understood in terms of *harmonia* or number, and the notion of a "limit" which Aristotle refers to here is a quasi-mathematical notion.

† The source of this quotation is unknown.

‡ Aristotle must have used a diagram at this point during his lectures, to illustrate graphically the various virtues and their extremes.

from the vices related to generosity in ways we shall describe later.

In honor and dishonor the mean is magnanimity, the excess something called a sort of vanity, and the deficiency pusillanimity. And just as we said that generosity differs from magnificence in its concern with small matters, similarly there is a virtue concerned with small honors, differing in the same way from magnanimity, which is concerned with great honors. For honor can be desired either in the right way or more or less than is right. If someone desires it to excess, he is called an honor-lover, and if his desire is deficient he is called indifferent to honor, but if he is intermediate he has no name. The corresponding conditions have no name either, except the condition of the honor-lover, which is called honor-loving.

This is why people at the extremes lay claim to the intermediate area. Moreover, we also sometimes call the intermediate person an honor-lover, and sometimes call him indifferent to honor; and sometimes we praise the honor-lover, sometimes the person indifferent to honor. We will mention later the reason we do this; for the moment, let us speak of the other cases in the way we have laid down.

Anger also admits of an excess, deficiency, and mean. These are all practically nameless; but since we call the intermediate person mild, let us call the mean mildness. Among the extreme people, let the excessive person be irascible, and his vice irascibility, and let the deficient person be a sort of inirascible person, and his deficiency inirascibility.

There are also three other means, somewhat similar to one another, but different. For they are all concerned with common dealings in conversations and actions, but differ insofar as one is concerned with truth telling in these areas, the other two with sources of pleasure, some of which are found in amusement, and the others in daily life in general. Hence we should also discuss these states, so that we can better observe that in every case the mean is praiseworthy, whereas the extremes are neither praiseworthy nor correct, but blameworthy. Most of these cases are also nameless, and we must try, as in the other cases also, to supply names ourselves, to make things clear and easy to follow.

In truth-telling, then, let us call the intermediate person truthful, and the mean truthfulness; pretense that overstates will be boastfulness, and the person who has it boastful; pretense that understates

will be self-deprecation, and the person who has it self-deprecating.

In sources of pleasure in amusements let us call the intermediate person witty, and the condition wit; the excess buffoonery and the person who has it a buffoon; and the deficient person a sort of boor and the state boorishness.

In the other sources of pleasure, those in daily life, let us call the person who is pleasant in the right way friendly, and the mean state friendliness. If someone goes to excess with no [ulterior] aim, he will be ingratiating; if he does it for his own advantage, a flatterer. The deficient person, unpleasant in everything, will be a sort of quarrelsome and ill-tempered person.

There are also means in feelings and about feelings. Shame, for instance, is not a virtue, but the person prone to shame as well as [the virtuous people we have described] receives praise. For here also one person is called intermediate, and another—the person excessively prone to shame, who is ashamed about everything—is called excessive; the person who is deficient in shame or never feels shame at all is said to have no sense of disgrace; and the intermediate one is called prone to shame.

Proper indignation is the mean between envy and spite; these conditions are concerned with pleasure and pain at what happens to our neighbors. For the properly indignant person feels pain when someone does well undeservedly; the envious person exceeds him by feeling pain when anyone does well, while the spiteful person is so deficient in feeling pain that he actually enjoys [other people's misfortunes].

There will also be an opportunity elsewhere to speak of these. We must consider justice after these. Since it is spoken of in more than one way, we shall distinguish its two types and say how each of them is a mean. Similarly, we must also consider the virtues that belong to reason.

8 [Relations between Mean and Extreme States]

Among these three conditions, then, two are vices— one of excess, one of deficiency—and one, the mean, is virtue. In a way, each of them is opposed to each of the others, since each extreme is contrary both to the intermediate condition and to the other extreme, while the intermediate is contrary to the extremes.

For, just as the equal is greater in comparison to the smaller, and smaller in comparison to the greater, so also the intermediate states are excessive in comparison to the deficiencies and deficient in comparison to the excesses—both in feelings and in actions. For the brave person, for instance, appears rash in comparison to the coward, and cowardly in comparison to the rash person; the temperate person appears intemperate in comparison to the insensible person, and insensible in comparison with the intemperate person; and the generous person appears wasteful in comparison to the ungenerous, and ungenerous in comparison to the wasteful person. That is why each of the extreme people tries to push the intermediate person to the other extreme, so that the coward, for instance, calls the brave person rash, and the rash person calls him a coward, and similarly in the other cases.

Since these conditions of soul are opposed to each other in these ways, the extremes are more contrary to each other than to the intermediate. For they are further from each other than from the intermediate, just as the large is further from the small, and the small from the large, than either is from the equal.

Further, sometimes one extreme—rashness or wastefulness, for instance—appears somewhat like the intermediate state, bravery or generosity. But the extremes are most unlike one another; and the things that are furthest apart from each other are defined as contraries. And so the things that are further apart are more contrary.

In some cases the deficiency, in others the excess, is more opposed to the intermediate condition. For instance, cowardice, the deficiency, not rashness, the excess, is more opposed to bravery, whereas intemperance, the excess, not insensibility, the deficiency, is more opposed to temperance.

This happens for two reasons: One reason is derived from the object itself. Since sometimes one extreme is closer and more similar to the intermediate condition, we oppose the contrary extreme, more than this closer one, to the intermediate condition. Since rashness, for instance, seems to be closer and more similar to bravery, and cowardice less similar, we oppose cowardice, more than rashness, to bravery; for what is further from the intermediate condition seems to be more contrary to it. This, then, is one reason, derived from the object itself.

The other reason is derived from ourselves. For when we ourselves have some natural tendency to one extreme more than to the other, this extreme appears more opposed to the intermediate condition. Since, for instance, we have more of a natural tendency to pleasure, we drift more easily toward intemperance than toward orderliness. Hence we say that an extreme is more contrary if we naturally develop more in that direction; and this is why intemperance is more contrary to temperance, since it is the excess [of pleasure].

9 [How Can We Reach the Mean?]

We have said enough, then, to show that virtue of character is a mean and what sort of mean it is; that it is a mean between two vices, one of excess and one of deficiency; and that it is a mean because it aims at the intermediate condition in feelings and actions.

That is why it is also hard work to be excellent. For in each case it is hard work to find the intermediate; for instance, not everyone, but only one who knows, finds the midpoint in a circle. So also getting angry, or giving and spending money, is easy and everyone can do it; but doing it to the right person, in the right amount, at the right time, for the right end, and in the right way is no longer easy, nor can everyone do it. Hence doing these things well is rare, praiseworthy, and fine.

That is why anyone who aims at the intermediate condition must first of all steer clear of the more contrary extreme, following the advice that Calypso* also gives: "Hold the ship outside the spray and surge."† For one extreme is more in error, the other less. Since, therefore, it is hard to hit the intermediate extremely accurately, the second-best tack, as they say, is to take the lesser of the evils. We shall succeed best in this by the method we describe.

---

*   In Homer's *Odyssey*, Calypso is a sea nymph who is in love with Odysseus and keeps him on her island for seven years.
†   A line from Homer's *Odyssey* (part 12, lines 219–20). However, it is actually Circe (an enchantress), not Calypso (the nymph who detained Odysseus and his crew on her island), who gave the advice. The actual quotation is from Odysseus's orders to his steersman when he acts on Circe's suggestion that he take the ship closer to Scylla (a sea

We must also examine what we ourselves drift into easily. For different people have different natural tendencies toward different goals, and we shall come to know our own tendencies from the pleasure or pain that arises in us. We must drag ourselves off in the contrary direction; for if we pull far away from error, as they do in straightening bent wood, we shall reach the intermediate condition.

And in everything we must beware above all of pleasure and its sources; for we are already biased in its favor when we come to judge it. Hence we must react to it as the elders reacted to Helen, and on each occasion repeat what they said;* for if we do this, and send it off, we shall be less in error.

In summary, then, if we do these things we shall best be able to reach the intermediate condition. But presumably this is difficult, especially in particular cases, since it is not easy to define the way we should

be angry, with whom, about what, for how long. For sometimes, indeed, we ourselves praise deficient people and call them mild, and sometimes praise quarrelsome people and call them manly.

Still, we are not blamed if we deviate a little in excess or deficiency from doing well, but only if we deviate a long way, since then we are easily noticed. But how great and how serious a deviation receives blame is not easy to define in an account; for nothing else perceptible is easily defined either. Such things are among particulars, and the judgment depends on perception.

This is enough, then, to make it clear that in every case the intermediate state is praised, but we must sometimes incline toward the excess, sometimes toward the deficiency; for that is the easiest way to hit the intermediate and good condition.

...

BOOK X

6 [Conditions for Happiness]

We have now finished our discussion of the types of virtue; of friendship; and of pleasure. It remains for us to discuss happiness in outline, since we take this to be the end of human [aims]. Our discussion will be shorter if we first take up again what we said before.

We said, then, that happiness is not a state. For if it were, someone might have it and yet be asleep for his whole life, living the life of a plant, or suffer the greatest misfortunes. If we do not approve of this, we count happiness as an activity rather than a state, as we said before.

Some activities are necessary, i.e., choiceworthy for some other end, while others are choiceworthy in their own right. Clearly, then, we should count happiness as one of those activities that are choiceworthy

in their own right, not as one of those choiceworthy for some other end. For happiness lacks nothing, but is self-sufficient.

An activity is choiceworthy in its own right if nothing further apart from it is sought from it. This seems to be the character of actions in accord with virtue; for doing fine and excellent actions is choiceworthy for itself. But pleasant amusements also [seem to be choiceworthy in their own right]; for they are not chosen for other ends, since they actually cause more harm than benefit, by causing neglect of our bodies and possessions. Moreover, most of those people congratulated for their happiness resort to these sorts of pastimes. That is why people who are witty participants in them have a good reputation with tyrants, since they offer themselves as pleasant [partners] in the tyrant's aims, and these are the sort of people

---

monster) than to Charybdis (a great whirlpool). Aristotle's quotations from Homer were apparently made from memory, and are rarely exact.

* See Homer's *Iliad*, part 3, lines 156–60 (here translated by Richmond Lattimore):
   Surely there is no blame on Trojans and strong-greaved Achaians
   if for long time they suffer hardship for a woman like this one.
   Terrible is the likeness of her face to immortal goddesses.
   Still, though she be such, let her go away in the ships, lest
   she be left behind, a grief for us and our children.

the tyrant requires. And so these amusements seem to have the character of happiness because people in supreme power spend their leisure in them.

These sorts of people, however, are presumably no evidence. For virtue and understanding, the sources of excellent activities, do not depend on holding supreme power. Further, these powerful people have had no taste of pure and civilized pleasure, and so they resort to bodily pleasures. But that is no reason to think these pleasures are most choiceworthy, since boys also think that the things they honor are best. Hence, just as different things appear honorable to boys and to men, it is reasonable that in the same way different things appear honorable to base and to decent people.

As we have often said, then, what is honorable and pleasant is what is so to the excellent person. To each type of person the activity that accords with his own proper state is most choiceworthy; hence the activity in accord with virtue is most choiceworthy to the excellent person [and hence is most honorable and pleasant].

Happiness, then, is not found in amusement; for it would be absurd if the end were amusement, and our lifelong efforts and sufferings aimed at amusing ourselves. For we choose practically everything for some other end—except for happiness, since it is [the] end; but serious work and toil aimed [only] at amusement appears stupid and excessively childish. Rather, it seems correct to amuse ourselves so that we can do something serious, as Anacharsis* says; for amusement would seem to be relaxation, and it is because we cannot toil continuously that we require relaxation. Relaxation, then, is not [the] end; for we pursue it [to prepare] for activity. But the happy life seems to be a life in accord with virtue, which is a life involving serious actions, and not consisting in amusement.

Besides, we say that things to be taken seriously are better than funny things that provide amusement, and that in each case the activity of the better part and

the better person is more serious and excellent; and the activity of what is better is superior, and thereby has more the character of happiness.

Besides, anyone at all, even a slave, no less than the best person, might enjoy bodily pleasures; but no one would allow that a slave shares in happiness, if one does not [also allow that the slave shares in the sort of] life [needed for happiness]. Happiness, then, is found not in these pastimes, but in the activities in accord with virtue, as we also said previously.

7 [Happiness and Theoretical Study]

If happiness is activity in accord with virtue, it is reasonable for it to accord with the supreme virtue, which will be the virtue of the best thing. The best is understanding, or whatever else seems to be the natural ruler and leader, and to understand what is fine and divine, by being itself either divine or the most divine element in us. Hence complete happiness will be its activity in accord with its proper virtue; and we have said that this activity is the activity of study.†

This seems to agree with what has been said before, and also with the truth. For this activity is supreme, since understanding is the supreme element in us, and the objects of understanding are the supreme objects of knowledge.

Further, it is the most continuous activity, since we are more capable of continuous study than any continuous action.

Besides, we think pleasure must be mixed into happiness; and it is agreed that the activity in accord with wisdom is the most pleasant of the activities in accord with virtue. Certainly, philosophy seems to have remarkably pure and firm pleasures, and it is reasonable for those who have knowledge to spend their lives more pleasantly than those who seek it.

Moreover, the self-sufficiency we spoke of will be found in study more than in anything else. For

---

* Anacharsis was a prince of Scythia (today the southern Ukraine), said to have lived early in the sixth century BCE, whose travels throughout the Greek world gave him a reputation for wisdom. He was known for his aphorisms, which were believed to be particularly profound.

† The Greek word *theōria*, translated here as "study," denotes something like the theoretical study of reality for the sake of knowledge alone, and would include, for example, astronomy, biology, mathematics, and anthropology as well as what we call philosophy. Furthermore, it is not so much the *search* for this knowledge that Aristotle is thinking of, but the quasi-aesthetic *appreciation* of it—a tranquil surveying of it in one's mind—once it has been acquired. (*Theōrein* is a Greek verb which originally meant to look at something, to gaze at it steadily.)

admittedly the wise person, the just person, and the other virtuous people all need the good things necessary for life. Still, when these are adequately supplied, the just person needs other people as partners and recipients of his just actions; and the same is true of the temperate person, the brave person, and each of the others. But the wise person is able, and more able the wiser he is, to study even by himself; and though he presumably does it better with colleagues, even so he is more self-sufficient than any other [virtuous person].

Besides, study seems to be liked because of itself alone, since it has no result beyond having studied. But from the virtues concerned with action we try to a greater or lesser extent to gain something beyond the action itself.

Besides, happiness seems to be found in leisure; for we deny ourselves leisure so that we can be at leisure, and fight wars so that we can be at peace. Now the virtues concerned with action have their activities in politics or war, and actions here seem to require trouble. This seems completely true for actions in war, since no one chooses to fight a war, and no one continues it, for the sake of fighting a war; for someone would have to be a complete murderer if he made his friends his enemies so that there could be battles and killings. But the actions of the politician also deny us leisure; apart from political activities themselves, those actions seek positions of power and honors, or at least they seek happiness for the politician himself and for his fellow citizens, which is something different from political science itself, and clearly is sought on the assumption that it is different.

Hence among actions in accord with the virtues those in politics and war are preeminently fine and great; but they require trouble, aim at some [further] end, and are choiceworthy for something other than themselves. But the activity of understanding, it seems, is superior in excellence because it is the activity of study, aims at no end apart from itself, and has its own proper pleasure, which increases the activity. Further, self-sufficiency, leisure, unwearied activity (as far as is possible for a human being), and any other features ascribed to the blessed person, are evidently features of this activity. Hence a human being's complete happiness will be this activity, if it receives a complete span of life, since nothing incomplete is proper to happiness.

Such a life would be superior to the human level. For someone will live it not insofar as he is a human being, but insofar as he has some divine element in him. And the activity of this divine element is as much superior to the activity in accord with the rest of virtue as this element is superior to the compound.* Hence if understanding is something divine in comparison with a human being, so also will the life in accord with understanding be divine in comparison with human life. We ought not to follow the makers of proverbs and 'Think human, since you are human', or 'Think mortal, since you are mortal'. Rather, as far as we can, we ought to be pro-immortal, and go to all lengths to live a life in accord with our supreme element; for however much this element may lack in bulk, by much more it surpasses everything in power and value.

Moreover, each person seems to be his understanding, if he is his controlling and better element. It would be absurd, then, if he were to choose not his own life, but something else's. And what we have said previously will also apply now. For what is proper to each thing's nature is supremely best and most pleasant for it; and hence for a human being the life in accord with understanding will be supremely best and most pleasant, if understanding, more than anything else, is the human being. This life, then, will also be happiest.

8 [Theoretical Study and the Other Virtues]

The life in accord with the other kind of virtue [i.e., the kind concerned with action] is [happiest] in a secondary way, because the activities in accord with this virtue are human. For we do just and brave actions, and the other actions in accord with the virtues, in relation to other people, by abiding by what fits each person in contracts, services, all types of actions, and also in feelings; and all these appear to be human conditions. Indeed, some feelings actually seem to arise from the body; and in many ways virtue of character seems to be proper to feelings.

Besides, prudence is inseparable from virtue of character, and virtue of character from prudence. For the principles of prudence accord with the virtues

---

* The view that human beings are made up of both soul and body, while the divine is pure intellect.

of character; and correctness in virtues of character accords with prudence. And since these virtues are also connected to feelings, they are concerned with the compound. Since the virtues of the compound are human virtues, the life and the happiness in accord with these virtues is also human. The virtue of understanding, however, is separated [from the compound]. Let us say no more about it, since an exact account would be too large a task for our present project.

Moreover, it seems to need external supplies very little, or [at any rate] less than virtue of character needs them. For let us grant that they both need necessary goods, and to the same extent; for there will be only a very small difference, even though the politician labors more about the body and suchlike. Still, there will be a large difference in [what is needed] for the [proper] activities [of each type of virtue]. For the generous person will need money for generous actions; and the just person will need it for paying debts, since wishes are not clear, and people who are not just pretend to wish to do justice. Similarly, the brave person will need enough power, and the temperate person will need freedom [to do intemperate actions], if they are to achieve anything that the virtue requires. For how else will they, or any other virtuous people, make their virtue clear?

Moreover, it is disputed whether decision or action is more in control of virtue, on the assumption that virtue depends on both. Well, certainly it is clear that the complete [good] depends on both; but for actions many external goods are needed, and the greater and finer the actions the more numerous are the external goods needed.

But someone who is studying needs none of these goods, for that activity at least; indeed, for study at least, we might say they are even hindrances. Insofar as he is a human being, however, and [hence] lives together with a number of other human beings, he chooses to do the actions that accord with virtue. Hence he will need the sorts of external goods [that are needed for the virtues], for living a human life.

In another way also it appears that complete happiness is some activity of study. For we traditionally suppose that the gods more than anyone are blessed and happy; but what sorts of actions ought we to ascribe to them? Just actions? Surely they will appear ridiculous making contracts, returning deposits, and so on. Brave actions? Do they endure what [they find] frightening and endure dangers because it is fine? Generous actions? Whom will they give to? And surely it would be absurd for them to have currency or anything like that. What would their temperate actions be? Surely it is vulgar praise to say that they do not have base appetites. When we go through them all, anything that concerns actions appears trivial and unworthy of the gods. Nonetheless, we all traditionally suppose that they are alive and active, since surely they are not asleep like Endymion.* Then if someone is alive, and action is excluded, and production even more, what is left but study? Hence the gods' activity that is superior in blessedness will be an activity of study. And so the human activity that is most akin to the gods' activity will, more than any others, have the character of happiness.

A sign of this is the fact that other animals have no share in happiness, being completely deprived of this activity of study. For the whole life of the gods is blessed, and human life is blessed to the extent that it has something resembling this sort of activity; but none of the other animals is happy, because none of them shares in study at all. Hence happiness extends just as far as study extends, and the more someone studies, the happier he is, not coincidentally but insofar as he studies, since study is valuable in itself. And so [on this argument] happiness will be some kind of study.

But happiness will need external prosperity also, since we are human beings; for our nature is not self-sufficient for study, but we need a healthy body, and need to have food and the other services provided. Still, even though no one can be blessedly happy without external goods, we must not think that to be happy we will need many large goods. For self-sufficiency and action do not depend on excess.

Moreover, we can do fine actions even if we do not rule earth and sea; for even from moderate resources we can do the actions that accord with virtue. This is evident to see, since many private citizens seem to do decent actions no less than people in power do—even

---

*   According to Greek myth, Endymion was such a beautiful man that the Moon fell in love with him. She made him immortal, but cast him into an eternal sleep so that she could descend and embrace him every night.

more, in fact. It is enough if moderate resources are provided; for the life of someone whose activity accords with virtue will be happy.

Solon* surely described happy people well, when he said† they had been moderately supplied with external goods, had done what he regarded as the finest actions, and had lived their lives temperately. For it is possible to have moderate possessions and still to do the right actions. And Anaxagoras‡ would seem to have supposed that the happy person was neither rich nor powerful, since he said he would not be surprised if the happy person appeared an absurd sort of person to the many. For the many judge by externals, since these are all they perceive. Hence the beliefs of the wise would seem to accord with our arguments.

These considerations, then, produce: some confidence. But the truth in questions about action is judged from what we do and how we live, since these are what control [the answers to such questions]. Hence we ought to examine what has been said by applying it to what we do and how we live; and if it harmonizes with what we do, we should accept it, but if it conflicts we should count it [mere] words.

The person whose activity accords with understanding and who takes care of understanding would seem to be in the best condition, and most loved by the gods. For if the gods pay some attention to human beings, as they seem to, it would be reasonable for them to take pleasure in what is best and most akin to them, namely understanding; and reasonable for them to benefit in return those who most of all like and honor understanding, on the assumption that these people attend to what is beloved by the gods, and act correctly and finely. Clearly, all this is true of the wise person more than anyone else; hence he is most loved by the gods. And it is likely that this same person will be happiest; hence, by this argument also, the wise person, more than anyone else, will be happy. ■

Suggestions for Critical Reflection

1. When Aristotle talks of the "precision" of a subject matter, what exactly does he mean? What kind of precision can mathematics have which ethics must always lack? Does this mean there can be no universally true moral principles (but, perhaps, just 'rules of thumb')?

2. Does Aristotle assume there is just one thing which is the goal of every human life? Is he right?

3. Aristotle seems to define the (biological) function of human beings as the thing "which is peculiar to man"—i.e., as something only human beings can do. Is this a plausible way of identifying the human function? Is reason the *only* capacity which human beings have uniquely? Does Aristotle believe that only human beings are rational, or does he say things elsewhere which are inconsistent with this?

4. What if human beings do not *have* a function? How much damage would this do to Aristotle's moral theory?

5. Aristotle concedes that not every *vice* is a matter of degree, but he does seem to hold that every *virtue is* in the middle between two vices. Does this claim seem plausible? What about, for example, the virtue of kindness?

6. Does Aristotle's Doctrine of the Mean actually help us at all in making moral decisions? If not, how much of a problem is this for Aristotle's ethics? Do you think Aristotle *expects* his Doctrine of the Mean to guide our moral behavior? If the Doctrine of the Mean *cannot* tell us what to do, then what (if anything) is its point?

7. Many commentators on Aristotle's ethics have worried about what is sometimes called the

---

* Solon (c. 640–558 BCE) was an Athenian lawmaker and poet, considered the founder of Athenian democracy, whose name was a byword for wisdom.

† As quoted in Book I of Herodotus's *History*.

‡ Anaxagoras of Clazomenae (c. 500–428 BCE) was the first philosopher to teach in Athens—though he, like Socrates and Plato, was prosecuted for impiety by the Athenians (in part for believing that the sun is a fiery body larger than Greece and that the light of the moon is reflected light from the sun).

"Aristotelian circle." Aristotle can be seen as making the following claims: virtuous action is what the practically wise person would choose; the practically wise are those who can successfully act in such a way as to achieve *eudaimonia*; but *eudaimonia*, for Aristotle, simply consists in wise action (it is "activity of soul exhibiting excellence"). If this is an accurate description of Aristotle's claims, how are we to *recognize* wise or virtuous action without an independent standard by which to judge it, and when Aristotle's inter-connected definitions go around in an endless circle? Do you agree that Aristotle's theory is circular? If so, do you think that makes it simply vacuous?

8. How plausible do you find Aristotle's arguments that the life of a philosopher is the best and happiest possible kind of life for human beings? How consistent is the emphasis in Book X on the activity of *theoria*—on *theoretical* reason—with Aristotle's earlier focus on *practical* wisdom?

9. Is Aristotle too egoistic? Does he pay too much attention to the question of how we as *individuals* can lead a good life, and not enough on moral issues to do with helping other people? For example, is generosity a virtue just because of its good effects on others, or simply because being generous makes one happy?

IMMANUEL KANT

FROM *Foundations of the Metaphysics of Morals*

Who Was Immanuel Kant?

Immanuel Kant—by common consent the most important philosopher of the past 300 years, and arguably the most important of the past 2,300—was born in 1724 on the coast of the Baltic Sea, in Königsberg, a regionally important harbor city in East Prussia.* Kant spent his whole life living in this town, and never ventured outside its region. His family were devout members of an evangelical Protestant sect (rather like the Quakers or early Methodists) called the Pietists, and Pietism's strong emphasis on moral responsibility, hard work, and distrust of religious dogma had a deep effect on Kant's character. Kant's father was a craftsman (making harnesses and saddles for horses) and his family was fairly poor; Kant's mother, whom he loved deeply, died when he was 13.

Kant's life is notorious for its outward uneventfulness. He was educated at a strict Lutheran school in Königsberg, and after graduating from the University of Königsberg in 1746 (where he supported himself by some tutoring but also by his skill at billiards and card games) he served as a private tutor to various local families until he became a lecturer at the university in 1755. However his position—that of *Privatdozent*—carried no salary, and Kant was expected to support himself by the income from his lecturing; financial need caused Kant to lecture for 30 or more hours a week on a huge range of subjects (including mathematics, physics, geography, anthropology, ethics, and law). During this period Kant published several scientific works and his reputation as a scholar grew; he turned down opportunities for professorships in other towns (Erlangen and Jena), having his heart set on a professorship in Königsberg. Finally, at the age of 46, Kant became professor of logic and metaphysics at the University of Königsberg, a position he held until his retirement 26 years later in 1796. After a tragic period of senility he died in 1804, and was buried with pomp and circumstance in the "professors' vault" at the Königsberg cathedral.[†]

Kant's days were structured by a rigorous and unvarying routine—indeed, it is often said that the housewives of Königsberg were able to set their clocks by the regularity of his afternoon walk. He never married (though twice he nearly did), had very few close friends, and lived by all accounts an austere and outwardly unemotional life. He was something of a hypochondriac, hated noise, and disliked all music except for military marches. Nevertheless, anecdotes by those who knew him give the impression of a warm, impressive, rather noble human being, capable of great kindness and dignity and sparkling conversation. He did not shun society, and in fact his regular daily routine included an extended lunchtime gathering at which he and his guests—drawn from the cosmopolitan stratum of Königsberg society—would discuss politics, science, philosophy, and poetry.

Kant's philosophical life is often divided into three phases: his "pre-Critical" period, his "silent" period, and his "Critical" period. His pre-Critical period began in 1747 when he published his first work (*Thoughts on the True Estimation of Living Forces*) and ended in 1770 when he wrote his Inaugural Dissertation—*Concerning the Form and Principles of the Sensible and Intelligible World*—and became a professor. Between 1770 and 1780, Kant published almost nothing. In 1781, however, at the age of 57, Kant made his first major contribution to philosophy with his monumental *Critique of Pure Rea-*

---

* Prussia is a historical region which included what is today northern Germany, Poland, and the western fringes of Russia. It became a kingdom in 1701, and then a dominant part of the newly unified Germany in 1871. Greatly reduced after World War I, the state of Prussia was formally abolished after World War II, and Königsberg—renamed Kaliningrad during the Soviet era, after one of Stalin's henchmen—now sits on the western rump of Russia (between Poland and Lithuania).

† His body no longer remains there: in 1950 his sarcophagus was broken open by unknown vandals and his corpse was stolen and never recovered.

son (written, Kant said, over the course of a few months "as if in flight"). He spent the next 20 years in unrelenting intellectual labor, trying to develop and answer the new problems laid out in this masterwork. First, in order to clarify and simplify the system of the *Critique* for the educated public, Kant published the much shorter *Prolegomena to Any Future Metaphysics* in 1783. In 1785 came Kant's *Foundations of the Metaphysics of Morals*, and in 1788 he published what is now known as his "second Critique": the *Critique of Practical Reason*. His third and final Critique, the *Critique of Judgement*, was published in 1790—an amazing body of work produced in less than 10 years.

By the time he died, Kant had already become known as a great philosopher, with a permanent place in history. Over his grave was inscribed a quote from the *Critique of Practical Reason*, which sums up the impulse for his philosophy: "Two things fill the mind with ever new and increasing admiration and reverence, the more often and more steadily one reflects on them: the starry heavens above me and the moral law within me."*

What Was Kant's Overall Philosophical Project?

Kant's core ethical idea is that the guiding principle for morality is delivered by pure reason—it is an objectively rational way to behave, and any other way of behaving is irrational—and that all particular moral injunctions are either justified or shown to be unjustified by this principle of reason. This supreme principle of morality is called the Categorical Imperative, and it is introduced and explained in this reading.

Kant argues that the Categorical Imperative is rational in a particular, and somewhat unfamiliar, way. Often, when we speak of something being rational, we really mean that it is *instrumentally* rational: that is, *if* you wish to achieve a certain outcome, *then* the rational thing to do is such-and-such. For example, if you want to make a sandwich then it is rational to collect bread and sandwich fillings, and to put them together with the bread on the outside and the fillings inside; if you want to win a battle under certain circumstances then it might be rational to send your cavalry around to the left to outflank the enemy's artillery; and so on. But is it rational to *want* to make a sandwich or win a battle? That depends: it might be instrumentally rational to seek these outcomes, depending on what else you want (to give yourself energy for a busy afternoon of study, or to win the war), but if you had different overall goals (to avoid procrastination, to preserve your forces to fight in a later more important battle) it might not. Instrumental rationality can tell you how to achieve your goals effectively, but it cannot by itself tell you what those goals should be.

Another way in which we often think about being rational has to do with consistency. For example, in logic, *if* you begin from particular premises, *then* you are required to conclude that some other claim is true as well. To believe in the truth of the premises while asserting the falsity of the conclusion would be logically inconsistent and hence irrational. For example, suppose you believe that ice is cold, and that if you put something cold in contact with something warm then the warm thing will lose its heat to the cold thing; then it would be irrational, because inconsistent, to believe that you can heat up your coffee by adding ice cubes to it. But, just as with instrumental rationality what it is rational to do depends on some ultimately non-rational fact about what you want to achieve, this kind of appeal to consistency is relative to what else you already happen to believe. If you thought that ice was hot then it would be quite rational to try and use it to heat up a drink.

The way in which the Categorical Imperative is rational is neither of these. It is, according to Kant, *unconditionally* rational (otherwise, he thinks, it wouldn't really be moral). The Categorical Imperative specifies a principle of action that is rational all by itself, under any circumstances, no matter what else we want or believe, or what else is true. Any rational agent whatever can recognize that the Categorical Imperative is true and, because they are rational agents, they will *want* to act in accordance with it. People don't need to be (in fact can't be) externally compelled to behave morally, according to Kant; once they think reflectively about the principles that are guiding their behavior, they will freely bind their will to the moral law because choosing anything else is irrational. It is impossible to want to violate the Categorical Imperative (though of course we might unreflectively do so by mistake), similar to the way it is impossible to

---

* Immanuel Kant, *Critique of Practical Reason*, ed. Mary Gregor (Cambridge University Press, 1997), 133.

consciously believe that P is true and that it is false at the same time.

Where does the Categorical Imperative come from? How do we discover it and come to know that it is true? This is a complex issue for Kant, and he considers it a branch of metaphysics—the metaphysics of practical reason. Prior to Kant, seventeenth- and eighteenth-century philosophers divided knowledge into exactly two camps: "truths of reason" (or "relations of ideas") on the one hand, and "truths of fact" (or "matters of fact") on the other. A major school of thought called rationalism was characterized by the doctrine that all final, complete knowledge was a truth of reason: that is, it was made up entirely of claims that could be proven *a priori* (without the need for sensory observations) as being necessarily true, as a matter of logic, since it would be self-contradictory for them to be false. The opposing school, empiricists, on the other hand, believed that all genuinely *informative* claims were truths of fact: if we wanted to find out about the world itself, rather than merely the logical relations between our own concepts, we had to rely upon the (*a posteriori*) data of sensory experience. At the center of Kant's contribution to the history of thought was the way he reshaped this distinction in a new framework. Instead of merely drawing a distinction between truths of reason and truths of fact, Kant replaced this with *two* separate distinctions: that between "*a priori*" and "*a posteriori*" propositions, and that between "analytic" and "synthetic" judgments.* On this more complex scheme, the rationalists' truths of reason turn out to be "analytic *a priori*" knowledge, while empirical truths of fact are "synthetic *a posteriori*" propositions. But, Kant pointed out, this leaves open the possibility that there is at least a *third* type of knowledge: *synthetic a priori* judgments. These are judgments which we know *a priori* and thus do not need to learn from experience, but which nevertheless go beyond merely "analytic" claims about our own concepts.

Kant's question therefore becomes: *How* is synthetic *a priori* knowledge possible? After all, the source of this knowledge can be neither experience (since it is *a priori*) nor the logical relations of ideas (since it is synthetic), so where could this kind of knowledge possibly come from? In bald (and massively simplified) summary, Kant's answer to these questions in the *Critique of Pure Reason* is the following. Synthetic *a priori* knowledge is possible insofar as it is knowledge of the *conditions of our experience of the world* (or indeed, of any *possible* experience). For example, for Kant, our judgments about the fundamental nature of space and time are not claims about our experiences themselves, nor are they the results of logic: instead, the forms of space and time are the conditions under which we are capable of having experience *at all*—we *can* only undergo sensations (either perceived or imaginary) that are arranged in space, and spread out in time; anything else is just impossible for us. So we can know *a priori*, but not analytically, that space and time must have a certain nature, since they are the forms of (the very possibility of) our experience.

Kant sets out to address the question of the Categorical Imperative in a similar way. The Categorical Imperative, he argues is *a priori* and necessary, but it is not analytic—it is not to be discovered merely by analysis of certain concepts (such as our concept of "good" or "right"; it isn't merely true by definition). As such it is a synthetic *a priori* claim. If we are to establish it, it must be required by some sort of built-in condition or limit of an appropriate domain of human experience. In the case of morality, the domain is not perception but what Kant called *practical reason*, because we are dealing here with a law that should govern our behavior, rather than laws that describe how the world is. The Categorical Imperative, according to Kant, is made necessary by the structure or limits of our freedom to act—the common features of our practical life. For Kant, genuine freedom does not consist in lawlessness but in being bound by laws that are of one's own making: freedom is autonomy. A rational will is one that operates on the basis of reasons, and this means that a free will is one that is not influenced by non-rational factors—such as psychological impulses or the laws of neuroscience—but only by its grasp of rational principles. For this to be true—for us to be genuinely free, as we believe we are—there therefore must *be* a rational law to which we can conform our behavior: there must be a Categorical Imperative.

---

* "Analytic" judgments are true due to the meanings of their words alone (e.g., "All bachelors are unmarried"), while synthetic truths are true at least in part due to the way the world is (e.g., "The sky is blue").

What Is the Structure of This Reading?

Kant's *Foundations of the Metaphysics of Morals* was written not just for professional philosophers, but for the general educated reader. Nevertheless, it can be pretty hard going, especially for those coming to Kant for the first time; the effort, however, is richly rewarded.

The *Foundations* forms a single, continuous argument running the whole length of the book, and each step of that overall argument is supported by sub-arguments. Kant's goals for the work are first, to establish that there is such a thing as morality—that there really are laws that should govern our conduct—and, second, to discover and justify the "supreme principle of morality." This "supreme principle," which Kant announces he has uncovered, is now famous as the Categorical Imperative.

Each section of the *Foundations* plays a role in Kant's overall argument. He begins, in the First Section, by simply trying to discover *what we already think morality is*. He is not, at this stage, trying to *justify* these beliefs: he merely wants to analyze our moral "common sense" to bring to light the principle behind it. He argues that the only thing which is "unconditionally" morally good is a good will, and that this insight is embedded in our ordinary moral judgments. (He then backs this argument with another, longer but less plausible—not included here—which appeals to "the purpose of nature.") The key to understanding morality, therefore, must be a proper understanding of the good will; if we can understand the principles that people of good will try to act on, Kant thinks, then we can see what the moral law tells us to do. In order to carry out this investigation, Kant announces he will focus on examples that make the moral will especially clear: i.e., on cases where the person performing an action has other motives that would normally lead to *not* doing that thing, but where she does it anyway because she recognizes it as her moral duty. He illustrates this contrast between people doing things "from duty" and doing them for some other reason by giving examples (each of which can be done for the sake of duty or not): a merchant who does not overcharge customers, a person who refrains from committing suicide, a man who performs kind actions to help others, and someone taking care to preserve their own happiness.

Consideration of examples like these shows us, Kant argues, that what gives a particular action moral worth is not the kind of action it is, nor the consequences of that action, nor even the purpose for which the action is performed, but the psychological rule, or *maxim*, motivating that action. This in turn, Kant claims, shows moral worth is a kind of *respect for moral law* and that, in order to have the form of a law, moral principles must be *universalizable*.* This important result is then illustrated and further explained using the example of truth-telling.

Kant concludes the First Section by explaining the need for philosophy to bolster these insights of common sense. The Second Section, therefore, is devoted to developing the fundamental elements of a proper "metaphysics of morals," which, in turn, Kant argues, must ultimately be embedded within a general theory of *practical reason*. Since the theory of practical reason is a theory of what reason tells us we ought to do (whether or not we actually do it), it must be a theory of what Kant calls *imperatives*. Kant therefore embarks on a discussion of the different types of imperative, distinguishing between *hypothetical* imperatives and *categorical* imperatives. Moral imperatives, he argues, must be categorical and not hypothetical.

He then asks: What makes these imperatives "possible," that is, what makes them legitimate requirements of rationality? Why are they *laws* that are binding on rational beings? The answer for hypothetical imperatives, Kant argues, is easy: that hypothetical imperatives are laws of reason is an *analytic* truth. However, in the case of categorical imperatives, the issue is more difficult. That these imperatives are rationally binding can only be, in Kant's terms, a *synthetic a priori* practical principle— something which we can know, independently of experience, to be true, but which is not merely true 'logically' or by virtue of the meanings of the words involved. Thus, showing there really *are* moral laws that are binding on all rational creatures is a difficult problem for Kant—and he postpones it until the Third Section of his book.

---

* That is, a rule that can rationally be applied to everyone. Kant does not mean that we should act only in ways we'd want others to act. He means that in some sense it's impossible to conceive of the universalization of some maxims (such as 'tell lies when it's beneficial to you'); as these maxims are not universalizable, they cannot be moral principles. See the "Misconceptions" section below for further explanation.

First, he turns to a more detailed analysis of the concept of a categorical imperative and, by emphasizing the *unconditional* character of categorical imperatives, arrives at his first major formulation of the moral law: the so-called Formula of Universal Law. Kant then illustrates how this law constrains our duties by ruling out certain maxims as being immoral. He gives four (carefully chosen) examples: someone contemplating suicide, someone considering borrowing money by making a false promise to repay it, someone wasting their talents in a life of self-indulgence and idleness, and someone refusing to help others.

If this helps us see *what* the categorical imperative requires us, morally, to do, the next issue is to discover *why* our wills should be consistent with the categorical imperative: what could motivate us to adopt universalizable maxims? The imperative is categorical and not hypothetical, so we cannot appeal to any contingent or variable motivations: the goal of morality—the *value* of being moral—must be something shared by every possible rational creature, no matter how they are situated. This, Kant argues, means all rational creatures must be ends-in-themselves and the ultimate source of all objective value. The categorical imperative can thus be expressed according to the Formula of Humanity as End in Itself. The reason non-universalizable maxims are immoral is, according to Kant, because they fail to properly respect rational creatures as ends in themselves; Kant illustrates this by reconsidering his four examples in light of this latest formulation.

This notion of rational beings as having (and indeed being the source of) objective, intrinsic worth leads Kant to the idea of the *kingdom of ends*: an ideal human community in which people treat each other as ends in themselves. Acting morally, Kant claims, can be thought of as *legislating* moral laws for this ideal community: we guide our own behavior by principles which we realize should be followed by all the free and equal members of the kingdom of ends. This formulation of the categorical imperative is often called the Formula of Autonomy (autonomy comes from the Greek words for self—*autos*—and law—*nomos*—and hence means something like

"following one's own laws"). Again, this shows us something new about the categorical imperative: the reason we ought to follow the moral law is not because we are forced to conform to it by something outside ourselves (such as society or God), but because these are laws that rational people lay down *for themselves*.* Morality, thus, does not infringe on freedom—on the contrary, it is the fullest expression of freedom, and also of respect for the freedom of others. Furthermore, it is the capacity of rational creatures to be legislators in the kingdom of ends which is the source of what Kant calls their *dignity*.

This brings us to the final stage of Kant's argument: the last problem he faces is that of showing moral law really does exist—that we really are rationally bound by it. He has shown that we *would* be bound by it if we were autonomous, rational beings capable of being legislative citizens in the kingdom of ends; now Kant has to show that human beings really do have an autonomous will, and this is the project of the Third Section (which is not reprinted here). To do this, Kant needs to show that the human will is not subject to the laws of nature, for otherwise we would not be free to legislate the moral law for ourselves. On the other hand, if we are free, then—since our wills must be governed by *some* law or other or they would not be causal—we must be governed by the moral law. Morality and freedom are thus intimately connected, for Kant, and we cannot have one without the other. He then argues that if we are to think of ourselves as *rational*, we must necessarily think of ourselves as free. Thus, to be rational just is to be governed by the moral law.

But how is this freedom possible—how *can* human beings be rational, given that we are surely part of the natural world and hence entangled in the web of the laws of nature? Here Kant appeals to and summarizes parts of his *Critique of Pure Reason*, where he argued that the empirical world of appearance—the world of nature—is not the way things are in themselves, but merely how they appear to us: 'behind' this world of appearance is the deeper reality of things as they are in themselves. Human beings, too, are subject to this duality: as members of the natural world, we are subject to

---

* Moreover, we do not need to be told, by some external authority, what the moral law is. We can each reliably discover *for ourselves* what we ought to do. In fact, for Kant, acting in accordance with a moral law merely because some moral authority has told you to does not make you a good person. That would be to obey a merely hypothetical, and not a categorical, imperative.

the laws of causality, but our real selves—our *egos*—are "above nature" and so, at least potentially, are autonomous. Kant's overall conclusion in the *Foundations of the Metaphysics of Morals*, then, is not that we can actually know there *is* a moral law, but that a) if there were a moral law it would have to be the way he has described, b) it is at least possible the moral law really does exist, and c) in any case we are forced to *believe* the moral law exists, simply in virtue of thinking of ourselves as rational beings.

Some Useful Background Information

1. The goal of Kant's *Foundations* is not to tell people how to act or to introduce a new theory of morality. Kant thought that, on the whole, people know perfectly well what they are and are not supposed to do and, indeed, that any moral theory having prescriptions that substantially diverged from "common sense" beliefs about morality was likely to be erroneous. When criticized by his contemporaries for merely providing a new formula for old beliefs, Kant replied, "... who would even want to introduce a new principle of all morality and, as it were, first invent it? Just as if, before him, the world had been ignorant of what duty is, or in thoroughgoing error about it."* Instead, Kant aimed to provide a new philosophical *underpinning* for morality: he thought people had misunderstood *why* the prescriptions of morality are the way they are, and that they lacked a reliable *method* for making sure they always did the right thing.

2. In the Preface to the *Foundations of the Metaphysics of Morals* Kant divides philosophy into three parts: logic (the study of thought), physics (the study of the way the world is), and ethics (the study of what we ought to do). Kant thinks of each of these as a domain of *laws*: logic deals with the laws of thought, physics deals with the laws of nature, and ethics deals with what Kant calls the *laws of freedom*—that is, with laws governing the conduct of those beings not subject to the laws of nature. In this way, Kant sets up the study of morality as the study of a particular kind of law (as opposed to, say, of character traits, states of affairs, or types of actions), and he thinks of these laws as being analogous to, but different from, laws of nature.

3. According to Kant, there are in general two routes to knowledge: experience and reason. The study of logic is within the domain of pure reason, but for Kant physics and ethics each have both a "pure" and an empirical part. Particular physical laws—for example that infection is transmitted by micro-organisms—are empirical, but the general *framework* for these laws—the idea that all events must have a lawlike cause—is not itself empirical (after all, we have not *seen* every event and its cause). That ethics must be built upon a non-empirical foundation is even more obvious, according to Kant. Ethics is the study, not of how things actually are, but of how things *ought* to be. Scrutinizing the way human beings actually behave, and describing the things they actually believe, will never be sufficient to tell you what we *ought* to do and think. Moral laws and concepts, therefore, must be established by pure reason alone (though experience will certainly play a role in determining the *concrete content* of moral principles in actual circumstances). This body of non-empirical knowledge, which sets out what Kant calls the "synthetic *a priori*" framework for physics and ethics, is called *metaphysics*; that is why Kant labels the subject of this work the "metaphysics of morals."

4. While all things in nature are bound by laws, rational beings instead govern their behavior by their *conception* of laws. For example, while objects fall because of the law of gravity, rational entities refrain from stepping off high places, not because of this law itself, but because of their *understanding* or conception of the law. A *maxim*, for Kant, is the subjective psychological principle that lies behind volition. It is, roughly, a stable motive that makes people do things in one way rather than another, a tacit 'rule' that guides their behavior. Examples of maxims might be "never kill innocent people," "don't tell lies unless it is clearly to your advantage to do so," "don't eat meat (except on special occasions)," "always give people the

---

*   Immanuel Kant, *Critique of Practical Reason*, Preface, footnote to p. 7. This translation is by Mary Gregor.

correct change," "never sleep with someone before the third date," and "never shop-lift, but it's okay to take office supplies from your workplace."

Some Common Misconceptions

1. Kant is not an ethical grinch or an unfeeling puritan. He does not claim that we cannot be glad to perform a moral action, that we only act morally when we do something we don't want to do, or that happiness is incompatible with goodness. Kant's examples in the *Foundations* are only supposed to be thought experiments which pull apart, as clearly as possible, actions we *want* to do from actions we *ought* to do, in order to show what makes actions distinctively moral. He does not claim that the mere presence of an inclination to do something detracts from its moral worth: the key idea is just that one's *motive* must be duty and not inclination. (In fact, Kant argues that we have a kind of indirect moral duty to seek our own happiness, and that since generous inclinations are helpful in doing good actions, we should cultivate these feelings in ourselves.)

2. Similarly, Kant does not—as is sometimes claimed—assert that the good will is the *only thing* which is good, that everything else which is good is merely a *means* to the achievement of a good will, or even that a good will is *all* we require for a completely good life. It is perfectly consistent with Kant's views to point out that, say, health or pleasure are valuable for their own sake. Kant's claim is that the good will is the *highest* good, and that it is the *precondition* of all the other goods (i.e., nothing else is good unless it is combined with a good will). When Kant says health is not "unconditionally" good, what he means is that it is not good at all unless it is combined with a good will—though when it *is* so combined, it really does have value in itself. By contrast, a good will is unconditionally good: it has its goodness in

all possible circumstances, independently of its relation to anything else, and this is what makes it the "highest" good.

3. The categorical imperative is (arguably) not intended by Kant to be *itself* a recipe for moral action. It does not, and is not supposed to, tell you what you ought to do. Instead, the categorical imperative acts as a *test* for particular maxims— permitting some and prohibiting others. To put it another way, Kant does not expect us to *deduce* particular moral maxims from the categorical imperative alone; rather, we take the maxims upon which we are *already* disposed to act and scrutinize them to see if they are formally consistent with the moral law.

4. The categorical imperative—say, the Formula of Universal Law—applies to maxims, not to actions or even intentions. Thus, for example, there is no requirement that our *actions* be universalizable: it need not be immoral for me to use my toothbrush or live in my house, even though not *everyone* could do those things. Instead, the *maxims* which guide my actions must be universalizable, and one and the same maxim (e.g., the principle of taking care of one's teeth) can give rise to different actions by different people in different circumstances. Conversely, two actions of exactly the same type (e.g., refusing to give someone a loan) could be of vastly different moral significance since the maxims that lie behind them might be of vastly different moral worth. It is also important to notice that maxims are not the same thing as *intentions*: one can intend to do something (such as make someone happy) for any of several quite different maxims (e.g., because you realize that being nice to people is part of moral duty, or because you want to be remembered in their will), and thus sometimes this intention is moral and sometimes it is not.*

5. When Kant claims certain maxims cannot be universalized, he cannot mean by this merely that it would be *immoral* or *bad* if these maxims were universal laws. (This would make his reasoning

---

* One significant consequence of this is that Kant is not coldly saying that all of our actions should be done *because* it is our duty, in the sense that the purpose of our acting is to be dutiful. On the contrary, good people will typically do the things they do because they want to help others, or to cultivate their own talents, or to be good parents, and so on: it is just that the maxims they are following in acting on these intentions are maxims which are consistent with the moral law.

circular; if he is trying to define immorality in terms of non-universalizable maxims, he can't turn around and define universalizability in terms of immorality. Also, Kant has disavowed the relevance of the *consequences* of an action as part of what makes it moral or immoral, so he cannot now appeal to the consequences of making a maxim universal.) Instead, Kant means it is *literally impossible* to will that certain maxims be universal laws—that it would go against rationality itself to do so, rather like willing that 2+2=5 or wanting my desires to be always and everywhere frustrated.

6. Kant did not hold that *all* universalizable maxims are moral; it would be a problem for his account if he had done so, since some obviously trivial and non-moral maxims appear to be consistent with the categorical imperative (e.g., a policy of always wearing socks on Tuesdays). Kant is able to exclude such examples from the sphere of the moral by distinguishing between actions that merely *conform* to a law, and actions performed *because* of a law. It is these latter kind of actions that are genuinely moral, since in these cases I decide what to do *by* working out what I would will that every rational being should do (rather than doing something for *other* reasons—e.g., to keep my feet warm—that also happens to be something that every rational being could do).

7. Kant's philosophy is not, as is often assumed, authoritarian or dictatorial. Although he places great emphasis on a rigid adherence to duty, it is important to realize that, for Kant, this duty is not imposed from the outside: it is not a matter of the laying down of moral laws by the state, society, or even by God. Quite the opposite: for Kant, constraining one's own behavior by the moral law actually *constitutes* genuine freedom or autonomy, which is being guided by rationality and not by mere inclination. Moral duty, for Kant, is *self*-legislated.

How Important and Influential Is This Passage?

Kant's *Foundations of the Metaphysics of Morals* is one of the most important ethical works ever written. Philosopher H.J. Paton called it "one of the small books which are truly great: it has exercised on human thought an influence almost ludicrously disproportionate to its size.... Its main topic—the supreme principle of morality—is of the utmost importance to all who are not indifferent to the struggle of good against evil."* Since their introduction in this work, some of Kant's themes—the idea that human beings are ends-in-themselves and so not to be treated as mere means by others; that our own humanity finds its greatest expression through the respect we have for others; that morality is freedom and vice a form of enslavement—have become central parts of contemporary moral culture. Many modern moral philosophers have been heavily influenced by his work, and descendants of his moral theory form one of the main strands in contemporary ethical theory. Kant's ethical theory is very much a 'live' philosophical position today.

---

* H.J. Paton, "Preface" to his translation of *The Moral Law, or Kant's Groundwork of the Metaphysics of Morals* (Hutchinson University Library, 1949), 7.

FROM *Foundations of the Metaphysics of Morals**

FIRST SECTION

Transition from the Common Rational Moral Cognition to the Philosophical Moral Cognition

Nothing can possibly be conceived in the world, or even out of it, which can be called good without qualification, except a *good will*. Intelligence, wit, judgment, and the other *talents* of the mind, however they may be named, or courage, resolution, perseverance, as qualities of *temperament*, are undoubtedly good and desirable in many respects; but these gifts of nature may also become extremely bad and mischievous if the will which is to make use of them, and which, therefore, constitutes what is called *character*, is not good. It is the same with the *gifts of fortune*. Power, riches, honor, even health, and the general well-being and contentment with one's condition which is called *happiness*, inspire pride, and often presumption, if there is not a good will to correct the influence of these on the mind, and with this also to rectify the whole principle of acting, and adapt it to its end. The sight of a being who is not adorned with a single feature of a pure and good will, enjoying unbroken prosperity, can never give pleasure to an impartial spectator. Thus a good will appears to constitute the indispensable condition even of being worthy of happiness.

There are even some qualities which are of service to this good will itself, and may facilitate its action, yet which have no inner unconditional value, but always presuppose a good will, and this qualifies the esteem that we justly have for them, and does not permit us to regard them as absolutely good. Moderation in the affections and passions, self-control, and calm deliberation are not only good in many respects, but even seem to constitute part of the *inner* worth of the person; but they are far from deserving to be called good without qualification, although they have been so unconditionally praised by the ancients. For without the principles of a good will, they may become extremely evil; and the coldness of a villain not only makes him far more dangerous, but also directly makes him more abominable in our eyes than he would have been without it.

A good will is good not because of what it accomplishes or effects, not by its aptness for the attainment of some proposed end, but simply by virtue of the volition—that is, it is good in itself, and considered by itself is to be esteemed much higher than all that can be brought about by it in favor of any inclination, or even the sum total of all inclinations.[†] Even if it should happen that, owing to a step-motherly nature,[‡] this will should wholly lack power to accomplish its purpose, if with its greatest efforts it should yet achieve nothing, and there should remain only the good will (not, to be sure, a mere wish, but the summoning of all means in our power), then, like a jewel, it would still shine by its own light, as a thing which has its whole value in itself. Its usefulness or fruitlessness can neither add to nor take away anything from this value. It would be, as it were, only the setting to enable us to handle it more conveniently in common commerce, or to attract to it the attention of those who are not yet connoisseurs, but not to recommend it to true connoisseurs, or to determine its value....

We have then to develop the concept of a will which deserves to be highly esteemed for itself, and is good without a view to anything further, a concept which exists already in the sound natural understanding, requiring rather to be clarified than to be taught, and which in estimating the value of our actions always takes the first place and constitutes the condition of all the rest. In order to do this, we will take concept of duty, which includes that of a

---

* Kant's *Grundlegung zur Metaphysik der Sitten* was first published in Riga in 1785. This translation is by Thomas K. Abbott with revisions by Lara Denis, from *Groundwork for the Metaphysics of Morals* (Broadview Press, 2005).

† One's inclinations are things one wants or likes to do.

‡ Owing to a step-motherly nature: because the world is ungenerous or uncooperative.

good will, although implying certain subjective limitations and hindrances. These, however, far from concealing it or rendering it unrecognizable, rather bring it out by contrast and make it shine forth so much the brighter.

I omit here all actions which are already recognized as contrary to duty, although they may be useful for this or that purpose, for with these the question whether they are done *from duty* cannot arise at all, since they even conflict with it. I also set aside those actions which really conform to duty, but to which men have *no* immediate *inclination*, performing them because they are impelled thereto by some other inclination. For in this case we can readily distinguish whether the action which agrees with duty is done *from duty* or from a selfish purpose. It is much harder to make this distinction when the action accords with duty, and the subject has besides an *immediate* inclination to it. For example, it is always a matter of duty that a dealer should not overcharge an inexperienced purchaser; and wherever there is much commerce the prudent tradesman does not overcharge, but keeps a fixed price for everyone, so that a child buys from him as well as any other. People are thus *honestly* served; but this is not enough to make us believe that the tradesman has so acted from duty and from principles of honesty; his own advantage required it; it is unwarranted in this case to suppose that he might besides have an immediate inclination in favor of the buyers, so that, as it were, from love he should give no advantage to one over another. Accordingly the action was done neither from duty nor from immediate inclination, but merely with a selfish purpose.

On the other hand, it is a duty to preserve one's life; and, in addition, everyone has also an immediate inclination to do so. But on this account the often anxious care which most people take for it has no intrinsic worth, and their maxim* has no moral content. They preserve their life *in conformity with duty*, no doubt, but not *from duty*. On the other hand, if adversity and hopeless sorrow have completely taken away the relish for life, if the unfortunate one, strong in mind, indignant to his fate rather than desponding or dejected, wishes for death, and yet preserves his life without loving it—not from inclination or fear, but from duty—then his maxim has moral content.

To be beneficent† when one can is a duty; and besides this, there are many minds so sympathetically constituted that, without any other motive of vanity or self-interest, they find a pleasure in spreading joy around them, and can take delight in the satisfaction of others so far as it is their own work. But I maintain that in such a case an action of this kind, however proper, however amiable it may be, has nevertheless no true moral worth, but is on a level with other inclinations, for example, the inclination to honor, which if it is happily directed to that which is in fact of public utility and accordant with duty, and consequently honorable, deserves praise and encouragement, but not esteem. For the maxim lacks the moral content, namely, that such actions be done *from duty*, not from inclination. Put the case that the mind of that philanthropist was clouded by sorrow of his own, extinguishing all sympathy with the lot of others, and that while he still has the power to benefit others in distress, he is not touched by their trouble because he is absorbed with his own; and now suppose that he tears himself out of this dead insensibility and performs the action without any inclination to it, but simply from duty, then for the first time his action has its genuine moral worth. Further still, if nature has put little sympathy in the heart of this or that man, if he, supposed to be an upright man, is by temperament cold and indifferent to the sufferings of others, perhaps because in respect of his own he is provided with the special gifts of patience and fortitude, and supposes, or even requires, that others should have the same—and such a man would certainly not be the meanest product of nature—but if nature had not specially framed him for a philanthropist, would he not still find in himself a source from which to give himself a far higher worth than that of a good-natured temperament could be? Unquestionably. It is just in this that the moral worth of the character is brought out which is incomparably the highest of all, namely, that he is beneficent, not from inclination, but from duty....

---

*　A general rule of conduct.
†　Generous, kind.

The second proposition* is: That an action done from duty derives its moral worth, *not from the purpose* which is to be attained by it, but from the maxim by which it is determined, and therefore does not depend on the realization of the object of the action, but merely on the *principle of volition* by which the action has taken place, without regard to any object of desire. It is clear from what precedes that the purposes which we may have in view in our action, or their effects regarded as ends and incentives of the will, cannot give to actions any unconditional or moral worth. In what, then, can their worth lie if it is not to consist in the will in reference to its expected effect? It cannot lie anywhere but in the *principle of the will* without regard to the ends which can be attained by the action. For the will stands between its *a priori* principle, which is formal, and its *a posteriori* incentive, which is material, as between two roads, and as it must be determined by something, it follows that it must be determined by the formal principle of volition when an action is done from duty, in which case every material principle has been withdrawn from it.

The third proposition, which is a consequence of the two preceding, I would express thus: *Duty is the necessity of acting from respect for the law.* I may have *inclination* for an object as the effect of my proposed action, but *never respect* for it, just because it is an effect and not an activity of will. Similarly, I cannot have respect for inclination, whether my own or another's; I can at most, if my own, approve it; if another's, sometimes even love it, that is, look on it as favorable to my own interest. It is only what is connected with my will as a principle, by no means as an effect—what does not serve my inclination, but outweighs it, or at least in case of choice excludes it from its calculation—in other words, simply the law of itself, which can be an object of respect, and hence a command. Now an action done from duty must wholly exclude the influence of inclination, and with it every object of the will, so that nothing remains which can determine the will except objectively the *law*, and subjectively *pure respect* for this practical law, and consequently the maxim[1] that I should follow this law even to the thwarting of all my inclinations.

Thus the moral worth of an action does not lie in the effect expected from it, nor in any principle of action which needs to borrow its motive from this expected effect. For all these effects—agreeableness of one's condition, and even the promotion of the happiness of others—could have been also brought about by other causes, so that for this there would have been no need of the will of a rational being; whereas it is in this alone that the supreme and unconditional good can be found. The pre-eminent good which we call moral can therefore consist in nothing else than *the representation of the law* in itself, *which certainly is only possible in a rational being*, insofar as this representation, and not the expected effect, determines the will. This is a good which is already present in the person who acts accordingly, and we need not wait for it to appear first in the result....

But what sort of law can that be, the conception of which must determine the will, even without paying any regard to the effect experienced from it, in order that this will may be called good absolutely and without qualification? As I have deprived the will of every impulse which could arise for it from obedience to any particular law, there remains nothing but the universal conformity of its actions to law in general, which alone is to serve the will as a principle, that is, I am never to act otherwise than so *that I could also will that my maxim should become a universal law.* Here, now, it is the simple lawfulness in general, without assuming any particular law applicable to certain actions, that serves the will as its principle, and must so serve it if duty is not to be a vain† delusion and a chimerical‡ notion. The common reason of human beings in its practical judgments perfectly coincides with this, and always has in view the principle here suggested.

Let the question be, for example: May I when in distress make a promise with the intention not to keep it? I readily distinguish here between the two significations which the question may have: whether it is prudent or whether it is right to make such a false promise. The former may undoubtedly often be the case. I see clearly indeed that it is not enough to extricate myself from a present difficulty by means

---

* Kant does not say explicitly what the first proposition was—it is that only an action done from duty has moral worth.
† Pointless, useless.
‡ A product of fantasy.

of this subterfuge, but it must be well considered whether there may not hereafter spring from this lie much greater inconvenience than that from which I now seek to free myself, and as, with all my supposed *cunning*, the consequences cannot be so easily foreseen but that credit once lost may be much more injurious to me than any mischief which I seek to avoid at present, it should be considered whether it would not be *more prudent* to act herein according to a universal maxim, and to make it a habit to promise nothing except with the intention of keeping it. But it is soon clear to me that such a maxim will still only be based on the fear of consequences. Now it is a wholly different thing to be truthful from duty than to be so from apprehension of injurious consequences. In the first case, the very notion of the action already implies a law for me; in the second case, I must first look about elsewhere to see what results may be combined with it which would affect myself. For to deviate from the principle of duty is beyond all doubt evil; but to be unfaithful to my maxim of prudence may often be very advantageous to me, although to abide by it is certainly safer. The shortest way, however, and an unerring one, to discover the answer to this question whether a lying promise is consistent with duty, is to ask myself: Would I be content that my maxim (to extricate myself from difficulty by a false promise) should hold as a universal law, for myself as well as for others? And would I be able to say to myself, "Everyone may make a deceitful promise when he finds himself in a difficulty from which he cannot otherwise extricate himself"? Then I presently become aware that, while I can will the lie, I can by no means will that lying become a universal law. For with such a law there would be no promises at all, since it would be in vain to profess my intention in regard to my future actions to those who would not believe this profession, or if they over-hastily did

so, would pay me back in my own coin. Hence my maxim, as soon as it should be made a universal law, would necessarily destroy itself.

I do not, therefore, need any far-reaching penetration* to discern what I have to do in order that my volition may be morally good. Inexperienced in the course of the world, incapable of being prepared for all its contingencies, I only ask myself: Can you also will that your maxim should be a universal law? If not, then it must be rejected, and that not because of a disadvantage accruing from it to myself or even to others, but because it cannot enter as a principle into a possible universal legislation, and reason extorts from me immediate respect for such legislation. I do not indeed as yet *discern* on what this respect is based (this the philosopher may inquire), but at least I understand this—that it is an estimation of the worth which far outweighs all worth of what is recommended by inclination, and that the necessity of acting from *pure* respect for the practical law is what constitutes duty, to which every other motive must give place because it is the condition of a will that is good *in itself*, and the worth of such a will is above everything.

Thus, then, without quitting the moral cognition of common human reason, we have arrived at its principle. And although, no doubt, common human reason does not conceive it in such an abstract and universal form, yet it really always has it before its eyes and uses it as the standard of judgment. Here it would be easy to show how, with this compass in hand, common human reason is well able to distinguish, in every case that occurs, what is good, what evil, conformably to duty or inconsistent with it, if, without in the least teaching it anything new, we only, like Socrates,† direct its attention to the principle it itself employs; and that, therefore, we do not need science and philosophy to know what we should do to be honest and good, yes, even to be wise and virtuous....

---

*   Extreme cleverness or deep insight.
†   This ancient Athenian is famous for (among other things) a technique of teaching—today called the "Socratic method"—in which the master, instead of imparting knowledge, asks a sequence of questions to prompt the pupil to reflect on their own ideas and to uncover knowledge they already have within themselves. Because of this technique, Socrates compared himself to a midwife helping people give birth to philosophical ideas. See the Plato readings from earlier in this section for examples of this method.

SECOND SECTION

Transition from Popular Moral Philosophy to the Metaphysics of Morals

If we have so far drawn our notion of duty from the common use of our practical reason, it is by no means to be inferred that we have treated it as an empirical concept. On the contrary, if we attend to the experience of human conduct, we meet frequent and, as we ourselves allow, just complaints that one cannot find a single, certain example of the disposition to act from pure duty. Although many things are done *in conformity with* what *duty* prescribes, it is nevertheless always doubtful whether they are done strictly *from duty*, and so have moral worth. Hence there have at all times been philosophers who have altogether denied that this disposition actually exists at all in human actions, and have ascribed everything to a more or less refined self-love. Not that they have on that account questioned the soundness of the conception of morality; on the contrary, they spoke with sincere regret of the frailty and impurity of human nature, which, though noble enough to take as its rule an idea so worthy of respect, is yet too weak to follow it; and employs reason, which ought to give it the law, only for the purpose of providing for the interest of the inclinations, whether singly or at the best in the greatest possible harmony with one another.

In fact, it is absolutely impossible to make out by experience with complete certainty a single case in which the maxim of an action, however right in itself, rested simply on moral grounds and on the representation of duty. Sometimes it happens that with the sharpest self-examination we can find nothing beside the moral principle of duty which could have been powerful enough to move us to this or that action and to so great a sacrifice; yet we cannot from this infer with certainty that it was not really some secret impulse of self-love, under the false appearance of duty, that was the actual determining cause of the will. We like then to flatter ourselves by falsely taking credit for a more noble motive; whereas in fact we can never, even by the strictest examination, get completely behind the secret incentives, since, when the question is of moral worth, it is not with the actions which we see that we are concerned, but with those inward principles of them which we do not see.

Moreover, we cannot better serve the wishes of those who ridicule all morality as mere chimera of human imagination overstepping itself from vanity, than by conceding to them that concepts of duty must be drawn only from experience (as, from indolence, people are ready to think is the case with all other concepts also); for this is to prepare for them a certain triumph. I am willing to admit out of love for humanity that even most of our actions are in conformity with duty; but if we look closer at them we everywhere come upon the dear self which is always prominent; and it is this they have in view, and not the strict command of duty, which would often require self-denial. Without being an enemy of virtue, a cool observer, one that does not mistake the wish for good, however lively, for its reality, may sometimes doubt whether true virtue is actually found anywhere in the world, and this especially as years increase and the judgment is partly made wiser by experience, and partly also more acute in observation. This being so, nothing can secure us from falling away altogether from our ideas of duty, or maintain in the soul a well-grounded respect for its law, but* the clear conviction that although there should never have been actions which really sprang from such pure sources, yet whether this or that takes place is not at all the question; but that reason itself, independent of all experience, ordains what ought to take place, that accordingly actions of which perhaps the world has so far never given an example, the feasibility even of which might be very much doubted by one who founds everything on experience, are nevertheless inflexibly commanded by reason; that, for example, even though there might never have been a sincere friend, yet not a whit less is pure sincerity in friendship required of everyone, because, prior to all experience, this duty is involved (as duty in general) in the idea of a reason determining the will by *a priori* principles.

---

* Except.

When we add further that, unless we deny that the notion of morality has any truth or reference to any possible object, we must admit that its law must be valid, not merely for human beings, but for all *rational beings as such*, not merely under certain contingent conditions or with exceptions, but with *absolute necessity*, then it is clear that no experience could enable us to infer even the possibility of such apodictic* laws. For with what right could we bring into unbounded respect as a universal precept for all rational nature that which perhaps holds only under the contingent conditions of humanity? Or how could laws of the determination of *our* will be regarded as laws of the determination of the will of rational beings as such, and for us only as such, if they were merely empirical and did not take their origin wholly *a priori* from pure but practical reason?

Nor could anything be more fatal to morality than that we should wish to derive it from examples. For every example of it that is set before me must first itself be judged by principles of morality, as to whether it is worthy to serve as an original example, that is, as a model; but by no means can it authoritatively furnish the conception of morality. Even the Holy One of the Gospels† must first be compared with our ideal of moral perfection before we can recognize Him as such; and so He says of Himself, "Why do you call Me (whom you see) good; none is good (the model of good) but God only (whom you do not see)?"‡ But whence have we the conception of God as the supreme good? Simply from the *idea* of moral perfection, which reason frames *a priori* and connects inseparably with the notion of a free will. Imitation finds no place at all in morality, and examples serve only for encouragement, that is, they put beyond all doubt the feasibility of what the law commands, they make visible that which the practical rule expresses more generally, but they can never authorize us to set aside the true original which lies in reason, and to guide ourselves by examples....

Such a metaphysics of morals, completely isolated, not mixed with any anthropology, theology, physics, or hyperphysics, and still less with occult qualities (which we might call hypophysical),§ is not only an indispensable substratum of all sound theoretical knowledge of duties, but is at the same time a desideratum¶ of the highest importance to the actual fulfilment of their precepts. For the pure thought of duty, unmixed with any foreign addition of empirical attractions, and, in a word, the thought of the moral law, exercises on the human heart, by way of reason alone (which first becomes aware with this that it can of itself be practical), an influence so much more powerful than all other incentives ... which may be derived from the field of experience that in the consciousness of its dignity** it despises the latter, and can by degrees become their master; whereas a mixed doctrine of morals, compounded partly of incentives drawn from feelings and inclinations, and partly also of conceptions of reason, must make the mind waver between motives which cannot be brought under any principle, which lead to good only by mere accident, and very often also to evil.

From what has been said, it is clear that all moral concepts have their seat and origin completely *a priori* in reason, and that, moreover, in the commonest reason just as truly as in that which is in the highest degree speculative; that they cannot be obtained by abstraction from any empirical, and therefore merely contingent, cognitions; that it is just this purity of their origin that makes them worthy to serve as our supreme practical principle, and that just in proportion as we add anything empirical, we detract from their genuine influence and from the absolute value of actions; that it is not only of the greatest necessity, in a purely speculative point of view, but is also of the greatest practical importance, to derive these concepts and laws from pure reason, to present them pure and unmixed, and even to determine the compass of this practical or pure rational cognition, that is,

---

* Necessarily true, clearly demonstrated or established.

† Jesus Christ.

‡ Matthew 19:17.

§ Hyperphysics is that which goes beyond physics. The term is usually used in a similar way as "paranormal" or "supernatural." "Hypophysics" is a coinage meaning that which lies *below* physics.

¶ Something very much needed or desired.

** For Kant, "dignity" is a technical term meaning something like *intrinsic worth*.

to determine the whole faculty of pure practical reason; and, in doing so, we must not make its principles dependent on the particular nature of human reason, though in speculative philosophy this may be permitted, or may even at times be necessary; but since moral laws ought to hold good for every rational being, we must derive them from the universal concept of a rational being. In this way, although for its *application* to human beings morality has need of anthropology, yet, in the first instance, we must treat it in itself (a thing which in such distinct branches of science is easily done); knowing well that, unless we are in possession of this, it would not only be vain to determine the moral element of duty in right actions for purposes of speculative criticism, but it would be impossible to base morals on their genuine principles, even for common practical purposes, especially for moral instruction, so as to produce pure moral dispositions, and to engraft them on people's minds to the promotion of the greatest possible good in the world.

But in order that in this study we may not merely advance by the natural steps from the common moral judgment (in this case very worthy of respect) to the philosophical, as has been already done, but also from a popular philosophy, which goes no further than it can reach by groping with the help of examples, to metaphysics (which does not allow itself to be checked by anything empirical and, as it must measure the whole extent of this kind of rational knowledge, goes as far as ideal conceptions, where even examples fail us), we must follow and clearly describe the practical faculty of reason, from the general rules of its determination to the point where the concept of duty springs from it.

Everything in nature works according to laws. Rational beings alone have the capacity to act *in accordance with the representation* of laws—that is, according to principles, that is, have a *will*. Since the deduction of actions from principles requires *reason*, the will is nothing but practical reason. If reason infallibly determines the will, then the actions of such a being which are recognized as objectively necessary* are subjectively necessary also, that is, the will is a capacity to choose *that only* which reason independent of inclination recognizes as practically necessary, that is, as good. But if reason of itself does not sufficiently determine the will, if the latter is subject also to subjective conditions (particular incentives) which do not always coincide with the objective conditions, in a word, if the will does not *in itself* completely accord with reason (which is actually the case with human beings), then the actions which objectively are recognized as necessary are subjectively contingent, and the determination of such a will according to objective laws is *necessitation*, that is to say, the relation of the objective laws to a will that is not thoroughly good is conceived as the determination of the will of a rational being by principles of reason, but which the will from its nature does not necessarily follow.

The conception of an objective principle, in so far as it is obligatory for a will, is called a command (of reason), and the formula of the command is called an *imperative.*

All imperatives are expressed through an *ought*, and thereby indicate the relation of an objective law of reason to a will which from its subjective constitution is not necessarily determined by it (a necessitation). They say that something would be good to do or to forbear, but they say it to a will which does not always do a thing because it is represented to be good to do it. That is *practically good*, however, which determines the will by means of the representations of reason, and consequently not from subjective causes, but objectively, that is, on principles which are valid for every rational being as such. It is distinguished from the agreeable as that which influences the will only by means of feeling from merely subjective causes, valid only for the senses of this or that one, and not as a principle of reason which holds for everyone....

A perfectly good will would therefore be equally subject to objective laws (viz. laws of good), but could not be conceived as *necessitated* thereby to act lawfully, because of itself from its subjective constitution it can only be determined by the conception of good. Therefore no imperatives hold for the Divine will, or in general for a *holy* will; *ought* is here out of place because the volition is already of itself necessarily in unison with the law. Therefore imperatives are only formulae to express the relation of objective laws of all volition to the subjective imperfection of the will of this or that rational being, for example, a human will.

---

* As determined by the objective principles of rationality.

Now all imperatives command either *hypothetically* or *categorically*. The former represent the practical necessity of a possible action as means to something else that is willed (or at least which one might possibly will). The categorical imperative would be that which represented an action as necessary of itself without reference to another end, that is, as objectively necessary.

Since every practical law represents a possible action as good, and on this account, for a subject who is practically determinable by reason, as necessary, all imperatives are formulae determining an action which is necessary according to the principle of a will good in some respects. If now the action is good only as a means *to something else*, then the imperative is *hypothetical*; if it is conceived as good *in itself* and consequently as being necessarily the principle of a will which of itself conforms to reason, then it is *categorical*.

Thus the imperative declares what action possible by me would be good, and presents the practical rule in relation to a will which does not forthwith perform an action simply because it is good, whether because the subject does not always know that it is good, or because, even if it know this, yet its maxims might be opposed to the objective principles of practical reason.

Accordingly the hypothetical imperative only says that the action is good for some purpose, *possible* or *actual*. In the first case, it is a *problematic*, in the second an *assertoric*, practical principle. The categorical imperative which declares an action to be objectively necessary in itself without reference to any purpose, without any other end, is valid as an *apodictic* (practical) principle.

Whatever is possible only by the power of some rational being may also be conceived as a possible purpose of some will; and therefore the principles of action as regards the means necessary to attain some possible purpose are in fact infinitely numerous. All sciences have a practical part consisting of problems expressing that some end is possible for us, and of imperatives directing how it may be attained. These may, therefore, be called in general imperatives of *skill*. Here there is no question whether the end is rational and good, but only what one must do in order to attain it. The precepts for the physician to make his patient thoroughly healthy, and for a poisoner to ensure certain death, are of equal value in this respect, that each serves to effect its purpose perfectly. Since in early youth it cannot be known what ends are likely to occur to us in the course of life, parents seek to have their children taught a *great many things*, and provide for their *skill* in the use of means for all sorts of *discretionary* ends, of none of which can they determine whether it may not perhaps hereafter be an object to their pupil, but which it is at all events *possible* that he might aim at; and this anxiety is so great that they commonly neglect to form and correct their children's judgment of the value of the things which may be chosen as ends.

There is *one* end, however, which may be assumed to be actually such to all rational beings (so far as imperatives apply to them, viz. as dependent beings), and therefore, one purpose which they not merely *may* have, but which we may with certainty assume that they all actually *do have* by a natural necessity, and this is *happiness*. The hypothetical imperative which expresses the practical necessity of an action as means to the advancement of happiness is *assertoric*. We are not to present it as necessary for an uncertain and merely possible purpose, but for a purpose which we may presuppose with certainty and *a priori* in every human being, because it belongs to his being. Now skill in the choice of means to his own greatest well-being may be called *prudence*, ... in the narrowest sense. And thus the imperative which refers to the choice of means to one's own happiness, that is, the precept of prudence, is still always *hypothetical*; the action is not commanded absolutely, but only as means to another purpose.

Finally, there is an imperative which commands a certain conduct immediately, without having as its condition any other purpose to be attained by it. This imperative is *categorical*. It concerns not the matter of the action, or its intended result, but its form and the principle of which it is itself a result; and what is essentially good in it consists in the mental disposition, let the consequence be what it may. This imperative may be called that of *morality*.

There is a marked distinction also between the volitions on these three sorts of principles in the *dissimilarity* of the necessitation of the will. In order to mark this difference more clearly, I think they would be most suitably named in their order if we said they are either *rules* of skill, or *counsels* of prudence, or *commands* (*laws*) of morality. For it is law only that involves the concept of an *unconditional* and objective necessity, which is consequently universally valid; and commands are laws which must be obeyed, that is, must be followed, even in opposition to inclination. *Counsels*, indeed, involve necessity, but one which can only hold under a contingent subjective condition, viz., they depend on whether this or that human being counts this or that as part of his happiness; the categorical imperative, on the contrary, is not limited by any condition, and as being absolutely, although practically, necessary may be quite properly called a command. We might also call the first kind of imperatives *technical* (belonging to art), the second *pragmatic* ... (belonging to welfare), and the third *moral* (belonging to free conduct as such, that is, to morals).

Now arises the question, how are all these imperatives possible? This question does not seek to know how we can conceive the performance of the action which the imperative ordains, but merely how we can conceive the necessitation of the will which the imperative expresses. No special explanation is needed to show how an imperative of skill is possible. Whoever wills the end wills also (so far as reason has decisive influence on his action) the means in his power which are indispensably necessary to it. This proposition is, as regards the volition, analytic;* for in willing an object as my effect there is already thought the causality of myself as an acting cause, that is to say, the use of the means; and the imperative educes† from the concept of a volition of an end the concept of actions necessary to this end. Synthetic propositions must no doubt be employed in defining the means to a proposed end; but they do not concern the principle, the act of the will, but the object and its realization. For example, that in order to bisect a line on an unerring principle I must draw from its extremities two intersecting arcs; this no doubt is taught by mathematics only in synthetic propositions; but if I know that it is only by this process that the intended operation can be performed, then to say that if I fully will the operation, I also will the action required for it, is an analytic proposition; for it is one and the same thing to represent something as an effect which I can produce in a certain way, and to represent myself as acting in this way.

If it were only equally easy to give a definite conception of happiness, the imperatives of prudence would correspond exactly with those of skill, and would likewise be analytic. For in this case as in that, it could be said whoever wills the end wills also (necessarily in accordance with reason) the indispensable means thereto which are in his power. But, unfortunately, the notion of happiness is so indeterminate that although every human being wishes to attain it, yet he never can say definitely and consistently what it is that he really wishes and wills. The reason for this is that all the elements which belong to the concept of happiness are altogether empirical, that is, they must be borrowed from experience, and nevertheless the idea of happiness requires an absolute whole, a maximum of welfare in my present and all future circumstances. Now it is impossible that the most clear-sighted and at the same time most powerful being (supposed finite) should frame for himself a definite conception of what he really wills in this. If he wills riches, how much anxiety, envy, and snares might he not thereby draw upon his shoulders? If he wills knowledge and discernment, perhaps it might prove to be only an eye so much sharper to show him so much the more fearfully the evils that are now concealed from him and that cannot be avoided, or to impose more wants on his desires, which already give him concern enough. Would he have long life? Who guarantees to him that it would not be a long misery? Would he at least have health? How often has uneasiness of the body restrained from excesses into which perfect health would have allowed one to fall, and so on? In short, he is unable, on any principle, to determine with certainty what would make him truly happy; because to do so he would need to be omniscient. We cannot therefore act on any definite principles to secure happiness, but only on empirical counsels, for example, of regimen, frugality, courtesy, reserve, etc., which experience teaches do, on the average, most promote well-being. Hence it follows that the imperatives of prudence do not, strictly speaking,

---

* Something is analytically true if it is true in virtue of the meanings involved, particularly in cases where, as Kant put it, the concept of the predicate is "contained in" the concept of the subject (e.g., "All aunts are female" or "This poodle is a dog"). Synthetic propositions, according to Kant, are simply propositions that are not analytic: thus, in synthetic propositions, the predicate provides *new* information about the subject (e.g., "My aunt is called Dora" or "Poodles come in many colors").

† Brings out, makes explicit.

command at all, that is, they cannot present actions objectively as practically *necessary*; that they are rather to be regarded as counsels (*consilia*) than precepts (*praecepta*) of reason, that the problem to determine certainly and universally what action would promote the happiness of a rational being is completely insoluble, and consequently no imperative respecting it is possible which would, in the strict sense, command him to do what makes him happy; because happiness is not an ideal of reason but of imagination, resting solely on empirical grounds, and it is vain to expect that these should determine an action by which one could attain the totality of a series of consequences which is really endless. This imperative of prudence would, however, be an analytic proposition if we assume that the means to happiness could be certainly assigned; for it is distinguished from the imperative of skill only by this, that in the latter the end is merely *possible*, in the former it is *given*; as, however, both only ordain the means to that which we suppose to be willed as an end, it follows that the imperative which ordains the willing of the means to him who wills the end is in both cases analytic. Thus there is no difficulty in regard to the possibility of an imperative of this kind either.

On the other hand, the question, how the imperative of *morality* is possible, is undoubtedly one, the only one, demanding a solution, as this is not at all hypothetical, and the objective necessity which it presents cannot rest on any hypothesis, as is the case with the hypothetical imperatives. Only here we must never leave out of consideration that we *cannot* make out *by means of any example*, in other words, empirically, whether there is such an imperative at all; but it is rather to be feared that all those which seem to be categorical may yet be at bottom hypothetical. For instance, when the precept is: "You ought not to promise deceitfully," and it is assumed that the necessity of this is not a mere counsel to avoid some other ill, so that it should mean: "You shall not make a lying promise, lest if it become known you should destroy your credit," but that an action of this kind must be regarded as evil in itself, so that the imperative of the prohibition is categorical; then we cannot show with certainty in any example that the will was determined merely by the law, without any other incentives, although it may appear to be so. For it is always possible that fear of disgrace, perhaps also obscure dread

of other dangers, may have a secret influence on the will. Who can prove by experience the non-existence of a cause when all that experience tells us is that we do not perceive it? But in such a case the so-called moral imperative, which as such appears to be categorical and unconditional, would in reality be only a pragmatic precept, drawing our attention to our own interests, and merely teaching us to take these into consideration.

We will therefore have to investigate *a priori* the possibility of a *categorical* imperative, as we have not in this case the advantage of its reality being given in experience, so that [the elucidation of] its possibility should be requisite only for its explanation, not for its establishment. In the meantime it may be discerned beforehand that the categorical imperative alone has the purport of a practical law; and the rest may indeed be called *principles* of the will but not laws, since whatever is only necessary for the attainment of some discretionary purpose may be considered as in itself contingent, and we can at any time be free from the precept if we give up the purpose; on the contrary, the unconditional command leaves the will no liberty to choose the opposite, consequently it alone carries with it that necessity which we require of a law.

Secondly, in the case of this categorical imperative or law of morality, the difficulty (of describing its possibility) is a very profound one. It is an *a priori* synthetic practical proposition; ... and as there is so much difficulty in discerning the possibility of speculative propositions of this kind, it may readily be supposed that the difficulty will be no less with the practical.

In this problem we will first inquire whether the mere concept of a categorical imperative may not perhaps supply us also with the formula of it, containing the proposition which alone can be a categorical imperative; for even if we know the tenor of such an absolute command, yet how it is possible will require further special and laborious study, which we postpone to the last section.

When I conceive a hypothetical imperative, in general I do not know beforehand what it will contain until I am given the condition. But when I conceive a categorical imperative, I know at once what it contains. For as the imperative contains besides the law only the necessity that the maxims[2] shall conform to this law, while the law contains no conditions restricting it, there remains nothing but the general statement that the maxim of the action should conform to universal law, and it is this conformity alone that the imperative properly represents as necessary.

There is therefore but one categorical imperative, namely, this: *Act only on that maxim whereby you can at the same time will that it become a universal law.**

Now if all imperatives of duty can be deduced from this one imperative as their principle, then, although it should remain undecided whether what is called duty is not merely a vain notion, yet at least we shall be able to show what we understand by it and what this notion means.

Since the universality of the law according to which effects are produced constitutes what is properly called *nature* in the most general sense (as to form)—that is, the existence of things so far as it is determined by general laws—the imperative of duty may be expressed thus: *Act as if the maxim of your action were to become by your will a universal law of nature.*†

We will now enumerate a few duties, adopting the usual division of them into duties to ourselves and duties to others, and into perfect and imperfect duties.[3]

1. Someone reduced to despair by a series of misfortunes feels wearied of life, but is still so far in possession of his reason that he can ask himself whether it would not be contrary to his duty to himself take his own life. Now he inquires whether the maxim of his action could become a universal law of nature. His maxim is: From self love I adopt it as my principle to shorten my life when its longer duration is likely to bring more ill than satisfaction. It is asked then simply whether this principle founded on self-love can become a universal law of nature. Now we can see at once that a system of nature of which it should be a law to destroy life by means of the very feeling whose vocation it is to impel to the improvement of life would contradict itself, and therefore could not exist as a system of nature; hence that maxim cannot possibly exist as a universal law of nature, and consequently would be wholly inconsistent with the supreme principle of all duty.

2. Another finds himself forced by necessity to borrow money. He knows that he will not be able to repay it, but sees also that nothing will be lent to him unless he promises firmly to repay it within in a determinate time. He wants to make this promise, but he has still so much conscience as to ask himself: Is it not unlawful and inconsistent with duty to get out of a difficulty this way? Suppose, however, that he resolves to do so, then the maxim of his action would be expressed thus: When I think myself in want of money, I will borrow money and promise to repay it, although I know that I never can do so. Now this principle of self-love or of one's own advantage may perhaps be consistent with my whole future welfare; but the question now is, Is it right? I change then the suggestion of self-love into a universal law, and state the question thus: How would it be if my maxim were a universal law? Then I see at once that it could never hold as a universal law of nature, but would necessarily contradict itself. For supposing it to be a universal law that everyone when he thinks himself in a difficulty should be able to promise whatever he pleases, with the purpose of not keeping his promise, the promise itself would become impossible, as well as the end that he might have in view in it, since no one would consider that anything was promised to him, but would ridicule all such statements as vain pretenses.

3. A third finds in himself a talent which with the help of some culture might make him a useful human being in many respects. But he finds himself in comfortable circumstances and prefers to indulge in pleasure rather than to take pain in enlarging and improving his fortunate natural predispositions. He asks, however, whether his maxim of neglect of his natural gifts, besides agreeing with his inclination to indulgence, agrees also with what is called duty. He sees then that a system of nature could indeed subsist with such a universal law, although human beings (like the South Sea islanders‡) should let their talents rust and resolve to devote their lives merely to idleness, amusement, and propagation of their species—in a word, to enjoyment; but he cannot possibly *will* that this should be a universal law of nature, or be implanted in us as such by a natural instinct. For as a rational being, he necessarily wills that his faculties be

---

*   This formulation of the categorical imperative is often called the Formula of Universal Law.

†   This is often called the Formula of the Law of Nature.

‡   The inhabitants of the islands of the southern Pacific, such as Polynesia and Micronesia.

developed, since they serve him, and have been given him, for all sorts of purposes.

4. Yet a fourth, who is in prosperity, while he sees that others have to contend with great wretchedness and that he could help them, thinks: What concern is it of mine? Let everyone be as happy as heaven pleases, or as he can make himself; I will take nothing from him nor even envy him, only I do not wish to contribute anything to his welfare or to his assistance in need! Now no doubt, if such a mode of thinking were a universal law, the human race might very well subsist, and doubtless even better than in a state in which everyone talks of sympathy and good-will, or even takes care occasionally to put it into practice, but, on the other side, also cheats when he can, betrays the rights of human beings, or otherwise violates them. But although it is possible that a universal law of nature might exist in accordance with that maxim, it is impossible to *will* that such a principle should have the universal validity of a law of nature. For a will which resolved this would contradict itself, inasmuch as many cases might occur in which one would have need of the love and sympathy of others, and in which, by such a law of nature, sprung from his own will, he would deprive himself of all hope of the aid he desires.

These are a few of the many actual duties, or at least what we regard as such, which obviously fall into two classes on the one principle that we have laid down. We must *be able to will* that a maxim of our action should be a universal law. This is the canon of the moral judgment of the action generally. Some actions are of such a character that their maxim cannot without contradiction be even *conceived* as a universal law of nature, far from it being possible that we should *will* that it *should* be so. In others, this intrinsic impossibility is not found, but still it is impossible to *will* that their maxim should be raised to the universality of a law of nature, since such a will would contradict itself. It is easily seen that the former violate strict or rigorous (inflexible) duty; the latter only wide (meritorious) duty. Thus it has been completely shown by these examples how all duties depend as regards the nature of the obligation (not the object of the action) on the same principle.

If now we attend to ourselves on occasion of any transgression of duty, we will find that we in fact do not will that our maxim should be a universal law, for that is impossible for us; on the contrary, we will that

the opposite should remain a universal law, only we assume the liberty of making an *exception* in our own favor or (just for this time only) in favor of our inclination. Consequently, if we considered all cases from one and the same point of view, namely, that of reason, we should find a contradiction in our own will, namely, that a certain principle should be objectively necessary as a universal law, and yet subjectively should not be universal, but admit of exceptions. As, however, we at one moment regard our action from the point of view of a will wholly conformed to reason, and then again look at the same action from the point of view of a will affected by inclination, there is not really any contradiction, but an opposition (*antagonismus*) of inclination to the precept of reason, whereby the universality (*universalitas*) of the principle is changed into a mere generality (*generalitas*), so that the practical principle of reason shall meet the maxim half way. Now, although this cannot be justified in our own impartial judgment, yet it proves that we do really recognize the validity of the categorical imperative and (with all respect for it) only allow ourselves a few exceptions which we think unimportant and forced upon us.

We have thus established at least this much—that if duty is a conception which is to have any import and real legislative authority for our actions, it can only be expressed in categorical, and not at all in hypothetical, imperatives. We have also, which is of great importance, exhibited clearly and definitely for every practical application the content of the categorical imperative, which must contain the principle of all duty if there is such a thing at all. We have not yet, however, advanced so far as to prove *a priori* that there actually is such an imperative, that there is a practical law which commands absolutely of itself and without any other incentive, and that the following of this law is duty.

With the view of attaining to this it is of extreme importance to remember that we must not allow ourselves to think of deducing the reality of this principle from the *particular attributes of human nature*. For duty is to be a practical, unconditional necessity of action; it must therefore hold for all rational beings (to whom an imperative can apply at all), and *for this reason only* be also a law for all human wills. On the contrary, whatever is deduced from the particular natural characteristics of humanity, from certain feelings and propensities, or even, if possible, from any particular tendency proper to human reason, and which need not necessarily hold for the will of every rational being—this may indeed supply us with a maxim but not with a law; with a subjective principle on which we may have a propensity and inclination to act, but not with an objective principle on which we should be *enjoined* to act, even though all our propensities, inclinations, and natural dispositions were opposed to it. In fact, the sublimity and intrinsic dignity of the command in duty are so much the more evident, the less the subjective impulses favor it and the more they oppose it, without being able in the slightest degree to weaken the obligation of the law or to diminish its validity....

The question then is this: Is it a necessary law *for all rational beings* that they should always judge their actions by maxims of which they can themselves will that they should serve as universal laws? If there is such a law, then it must be connected (altogether *a priori*) with the very concept of the will of a rational being as such. But in order to discover this connection we must, however reluctantly, take a step into metaphysics, although into a domain of it which is distinct from speculative philosophy—namely, the metaphysics of morals....

The will is conceived as a capacity of determining itself to action in accordance with the *representation of certain laws*. And such a capacity can be found only in rational beings. Now that which serves the will as the objective ground of its self-determination is the *end*, and if this is assigned by reason alone, it must hold for all rational beings. On the other hand, that which merely contains the ground of possibility of the action of which the effect is the end, this is called the *means*. The subjective ground of the desire is the *incentive*, the objective ground of the volition is the *motive*; hence the distinction between subjective ends which rest on incentives, and objective ends which depend on motives valid for every rational being. Practical principles are *formal* when they abstract from all subjective ends; they are *material* when they assume these, and therefore particular incentives. The ends which a rational being proposes to himself at pleasure as *effects* of his actions (material ends) are all only relative, for it is only their relation to the particular desires of the subject that gives them their worth, which therefore cannot furnish principles universal and necessary for all rational beings and for every volition, that is to say, practical laws. Hence all these relative ends can give rise only to hypothetical imperatives.

Supposing, however, that there were something *whose existence* has *in itself* an absolute worth, something which, being *an end in itself*, could be a source of definite laws, then in this and this alone would lie the source of a possible categorical imperative, that is, a practical law.

Now I say: the human being and in general every rational being exists as an end* in itself, *not merely as a means* to be arbitrarily used by this or that will, but in all his actions, whether they concern himself or other rational beings, must be always regarded at the same time as an end. All objects of the inclinations have only a conditional worth; for if the inclinations and the needs founded on them did not exist, then their object would be without any value. But the inclinations themselves, being sources of needs, are so far from having an absolute worth for which they should be desired that, on the contrary, it must be the universal wish of every rational being to be wholly free from them. Thus the worth of any object which is *to be acquired* by our action is always conditional. Beings whose existence depends not on our will but on nature's, have nevertheless, if they are nonrational beings, only a relative value as means, and are therefore called *things*; rational beings, on the contrary, are called *persons*, because their very nature restricts all choice (and is an object of respect). These, therefore, are not merely subjective ends whose existence has a worth *for us* as an effect of our action, but *objective ends*, that is, things whose existence is an end in itself—an end, moreover, for which no other can be substituted, to which they should serve *merely* as means, for otherwise nothing whatever would possess *absolute worth*; but if all worth were conditioned and therefore contingent, then there would be no supreme practical principle of reason whatever.

If then there is a supreme practical principle or, with respect to the human will, a categorical imperative, it must be one which, being drawn from the conception of that which is necessarily an end for everyone because it is *an end in itself*, constitutes an *objective*

---

*   A source of value and meaning, a goal or purpose.

principle of will, and can therefore serve as a universal practical law. The foundation of this principle is: *rational nature exists as an end in itself*. The human being necessarily conceives of his own existence as being so; so far then this is a *subjective* principle of human actions. But every other rational being regards its existence similarly, just on the same rational principle that holds for me; ... so that it is at the same time an objective principle from which as a supreme practical law all laws of the will must be capable of being deduced. Accordingly the practical imperative will be as follows: *So act as to treat humanity, whether in your own person or in that of any other, in every case at the same time as an end, never as a means only.** We will now inquire whether this can be practically carried out.

To abide by the previous examples:

First, under the head of necessary duty to oneself: Someone who contemplates suicide should ask himself whether his action can be consistent with the idea of humanity *as an end in itself*. If he destroys himself in order to escape from painful circumstances, he uses a person merely as a *means* to maintain a tolerable condition up to the end of life. But a human being is not a thing, that is to say, something which can be used merely as a means, but must in all his actions be always considered as an end in itself. I cannot, therefore, dispose in any way of a human being in my own person by mutilating, damaging, or killing him. (It belongs to morals proper to define this principle more precisely, so as to avoid all misunderstanding, for example, as to the amputation of the limbs in order to preserve myself; as to exposing my life to danger with a view to preserve it, etc. This question is therefore omitted here.)

Second, as regards necessary duties, or those of strict obligation, towards others: He who is thinking of making a lying promise to others will see at once that he would be using another human being *merely as a means*, without the latter at the same time containing in himself the end. For he whom I propose by such a promise to use for my own purposes cannot possibly assent to my mode of acting toward him, and therefore cannot himself contain the end of this action. This violation of the principle of humanity in other human beings is more obvious if we take in examples of attacks on the freedom and property of others. For then it is clear that he who transgresses the rights of human beings intends to use the person of others merely as means, without considering that as rational beings they ought always to be esteemed also as ends, that is, as beings who must be capable of containing in themselves the end of the very same action.[4]

Third, as regards contingent (meritorious) duties to oneself: It is not enough that the action does not violate humanity in our own person as an end in itself, it must also *harmonize with* it. Now there are in humanity capacities of greater perfection which belong to the end that nature has in view with regard to humanity in ourselves as the subject; to neglect these might perhaps be consistent with the *maintenance* of humanity as an end in itself, but not with the *advancement* of this end.

Fourth, as regards meritorious duties toward others: The natural end which all human beings have is their own happiness. Now humanity might indeed subsist although no one should contribute anything to the happiness of others, provided he did not intentionally withdraw anything from it; but after all, this would only harmonize negatively, not positively, with *humanity as an end in itself*, if everyone does not also endeavor, as far as he can, to forward the ends of others. For the ends of any subject which is an end in itself ought as far as possible to be *my* ends also, if that conception is to have its *full* effect in me.

This principle that humanity and generally every rational nature is *an end in itself* (which is the supreme limiting condition of every human being's freedom of action), is not borrowed from experience, *first*, because it is universal, applying as it does to all rational beings whatever, and experience is not capable of determining anything about them; *second*, because it does not present humanity as an end to human beings (subjectively), that is, as an object which human beings do of themselves actually adopt as an end; but as an objective end which must as a law constitute the supreme limiting condition of all our subjective ends, let them be what they will; it must therefore spring from pure reason. In fact the ground of all practical legislation lies (according to the first principle) *objectively in the rule* and its form of universality which makes it capable of being a law (say, for example, a law of nature);

---

*   This is often called the Formula of Humanity as End in Itself.

but *subjectively* in the *end*; now by the second principle, the subject of all ends is each rational being inasmuch as it is an end in itself. From this follows the third practical principle of the will, which is the ultimate condition of its harmony with the universal practical reason, viz., the idea of *the will of every rational being as a will giving universal law.**

On this principle all maxims are rejected which are inconsistent with the will being itself universal legislator. Thus the will is not merely subject to the law, but subject to it so that it must be regarded *as itself giving the law*, and on this ground only subject to the law (of which it can regard itself as the author).

In the previous imperatives, namely, that based on the conception of the conformity of actions to general laws, as in a *system of nature*, and that based on the universal *prerogative* of rational beings as *ends* in themselves—these imperatives just because they were conceived as categorical excluded from any share in their authority all admixture of any interest as an incentive; they were, however, only *assumed* to be categorical, because such an assumption was necessary to explain the conception of duty. But we could not prove independently that there are practical propositions which command categorically, nor can it be proved in this section; one thing, however, could be done, namely, to indicate in the imperative itself, by some determinate expression, that in the case of volition from duty all interest is renounced, which is the specific criterion of categorical as distinguished from hypothetical imperatives. This is done in the present third formula of the principle, namely, in the idea of the will of every rational being as a *will giving universal law.*

For although a will *which is subject to laws* may be attached to this law by means of an interest, yet a will which is itself a supreme lawgiver, so far as it is such, cannot possibly depend on any interest, since a will so dependent would itself still need another law restricting the interest of its self-love by the condition that it should be valid as universal law.

Thus the *principle* of every human will as *a will which in all its maxims ... gives universal laws*, provided it be otherwise correct, would be very *well suited* to be the categorical imperative in this respect,

namely, that just because of the idea of universal legislation it is *not based on any interest*, and therefore it alone among all possible imperatives can be *unconditional*. Or still better, converting the proposition, if there is a categorical imperative (that is, a law for the will of every rational being), it can only command that everything be done from maxims of one's will regarded as a will which could at the same time will that it should itself give universal laws, for in that case only the practical principle and the imperative which it obeys are unconditional, since they cannot be based on any interest.

Looking back now on all previous attempts to discover the principle of morality, we need not wonder why they all failed. It was seen that the human being is bound to laws by duty, but it was not observed that the laws to which he is subject are *only those of his own giving*, though at the same time they are *universal*, and that he is only bound to act in conformity with his own will—a will, however, which is designed by nature to give universal laws. For when one has conceived the human being only as subject to a law (no matter what), then this law required some interest, either by way of attraction or constraint, since it did not originate as a law from *his own* will, but this will was according to a law obliged by *something else* to act in a certain manner. Now by this necessary consequence all the labor spent in finding a supreme principle of *duty* was irrevocably lost. For one never elicited duty, but only a necessity of acting from a certain interest. Whether this interest was private or otherwise, in any case the imperative had to be conditional, and could not by any means be capable of being a moral command. I will therefore call this the principle of *autonomy* of the will, in contrast with every other which I accordingly count under *heteronomy*.†

The concept of every rational being as one which must consider itself as giving in all the maxims of its will universal laws, so as to judge itself and its actions from this point of view—this concept leads to another which depends on it and is very fruitful, namely, that of a *kingdom of ends*.

By a *kingdom* I understand the systematic union of different rational beings through common laws.

---

* This is sometimes called the Formula of Autonomy.
† Autonomy = self-rule. Heteronomy = rule by another.

Now since it is by laws that the universal validity of ends are determined, hence, if we abstract from the personal differences of rational beings, and likewise from all the content of their private ends, we shall be able to conceive all ends combined in a systematic whole (including both rational beings as ends in themselves, and also the special ends which each may propose to himself), that is to say, we can conceive a kingdom of ends, which on the preceding principles is possible.

For all rational beings come under the *law* that each of them must treat itself and all others *never merely as means*, but in every case *at the same time as ends in themselves*. From this results a systematic union of rational beings through common objective laws, that is, a kingdom which may be called a kingdom of ends, since what these laws have in view is just the relation of these beings to one another as ends and means. It is certainly only an ideal.

A rational being belongs as a *member* to the kingdom of ends when, although giving universal laws in it, he is also himself subject to these laws. He belongs to it *as sovereign* when, while giving laws, he is not subject to the will of any other.

A rational being must always regard himself as giving laws either as member or as sovereign in a kingdom of ends which is rendered possible by the freedom of will. He cannot, however, maintain the latter position merely by maxims of his will, but only in case he is a completely independent being without needs and with unrestricted power adequate to his will.

Morality consists then in the reference of all action to the legislation which alone can render a kingdom of ends possible.* This legislation must be capable of existing in every rational being, and of emanating from his will, so that the principle of this will is never to act on any maxim which could not without contradiction be also a universal law, and accordingly always so to act that *the will could at the same time regard itself as giving through its maxims universal laws*. If now the maxims of rational beings are not by their own nature coincident with this objective principle, then the necessity of acting on it is called practical necessitation, that is, *duty*. Duty does not apply to the sovereign in the kingdom of ends, but it does apply to every member of it and to all in the same degree.

The practical necessity of acting on this principle, that is, duty, does not rest at all on feelings, impulses, or inclinations, but solely on the relation of rational beings to one another, a relation in which the will of a rational being must always be regarded as *legislative*, since otherwise it could not be regarded as *an end in itself*. Reason then refers every maxim of the will, regarding it as legislative universally, to every other will and also to every action towards oneself; and this not on account of any other practical motive or any future advantage, but from the idea of the *dignity* of a rational being, obeying no law but that which he himself also gives.

In the kingdom of ends everything has either *price* or *dignity*. Whatever has price can be replaced by something else which is *equivalent*; whatever, on the other hand, is above all price, and therefore admits of no equivalent, has a dignity.

Whatever has reference to the general inclinations and wants of humankind has a *market price*; whatever, without presupposing a need, corresponds to a certain taste, that is, to a delight in the mere purposeless play of our faculties, has a *fancy price*;† but that which constitutes the condition under which alone anything can be an end in itself, this has not merely relative worth, that is, price, but an inner worth, that is, *dignity*.

Now morality is the condition under which alone a rational being can be an end in himself, since by this alone it is possible that he should be a legislating member in the kingdom of ends. Thus morality, and humanity, insofar as it is capable of morality, is that which alone has dignity. Skill and diligence in labor have a market price; wit, lively imagination, and humor have a fancy price; on the other hand, fidelity to promises, benevolence from principle (not from instinct), have an inner worth. Neither nature nor art contains anything which in default of these it could put in their place, for their worth consists not in the effects which spring from them, not in the use and advantage which they secure, but in the disposition, that is, the maxims of the will which are ready to manifest themselves in such actions, even if they do

---

* This is sometimes called the Formula of the Kingdom of Ends.
† A capricious or arbitrary preference; individual taste; an inclination, a liking.

not have the desired effect. These actions also need no recommendation from any subjective taste or sentiment, that they may be looked upon with immediate favor and delight; they need no immediate propensity or feeling for them; they exhibit the will that performs them as an object of an immediate respect, and nothing but reason is required to *impose* them on the will; not to *flatter* it into them, which, in the case of duties, would be a contradiction. This estimation therefore shows that the worth of such a disposition is dignity, and places it infinitely above all price, with which it cannot for a moment be brought into comparison or competition without as it were violating its sanctity.

What then is it which justifies virtue or the morally good disposition, in making such lofty claims? It is nothing less than the *privilege* it secures to the rational being of participating *in the giving of universal laws*, by which it qualifies him to be a member of a possible kingdom of ends, a privilege to which he was already destined by his own nature as being an end in itself, and on that account legislating in the kingdom of ends; free as regards all laws of nature, and obeying only those laws which he himself gives, and by which his maxims can belong to a system of universal law to which at the same time he submits himself. For nothing has any worth except what the law assigns it. Now the legislation itself which assigns the worth of everything must for that very reason possess dignity, that is, an unconditional incomparable worth; and the word *respect*** alone supplies a becoming expression for the esteem which a rational being must have for it. *Autonomy* then is the basis of the dignity of human nature and of every rational nature.

The three modes of presenting the principle of morality that have been adduced are at bottom only so many formulae of the very same law, and each unites in itself the other two. There is, however, a difference among them, but it is subjectively rather than objectively practical, intended, namely, to bring an idea of reason nearer to intuition (by means of a certain analogy), and thereby nearer to feeling. All maxims, in fact, have—

1. A *form*, consisting in universality; and in this view the formula of the moral imperative is expressed thus, that the maxims must be so chosen as if they were to serve as universal laws of nature.

2. A *matter*, namely, an end, and here the formula says that the rational being, as it is an end by its own nature and therefore an end in itself, must in every maxim serve as the condition limiting all merely relative and arbitrary ends.

3. A *complete determination* of all maxims by means of that formula, namely, that all maxims ought, by their own legislation, to harmonize with a possible kingdom of ends as with a kingdom of nature.[5] ... ■

Suggestions for Critical Reflection

1. Kant gives four examples in which it is supposed to be impossible to will that your maxim become universal law. Just exactly *how* does Kant think this is impossible? Is there more than one kind of 'impossibility' here? Is Kant *correct* that it is, in some way, impossible to universalize these four maxims? (If you don't think he is, what does this show about his moral theory?)

2. Could Kant's moral theory lead to a potential conflict of duties? For example, the duty to tell the truth seems to conflict, potentially, with the duty to save the lives of innocent people: what, for example, if you are faced with a mad axman demanding to know where his victim—whom you happen to know is cowering under your kitchen table—is hiding? (Here the key idea is that, in some situations, two universalizable *maxims* must tend toward different and incompatible actions. Mere conflicts of rules for action—e.g., "always return what you have borrowed"—will tend to miss the mark as criticisms of Kant, as the maxims which lie behind them may well allow for exceptions

---

*   Other translators have preferred the English word "reverence." The German word is *Achtung*, which in this context has religious overtones of awe before the sublimity of the moral law.

in particular cases.) If duties mandated by the categorical imperative *can* conflict with each other, how much destruction does this wreak on Kant's moral theory?

3. On the other hand, does Kant's moral theory produce any concrete ethical prescriptions at all? The German philosopher G.W.F. Hegel called Kant's Formula of Universal Law an "empty formalism" and said it reduced "the science of morals to the preaching of duty for duty's sake.... No transition is possible to the specification of particular duties nor, if some such particular content for acting comes under consideration, is there any criterion in that principle for deciding whether it is or is not a duty. On the contrary, by this means any wrong or immoral line of conduct may be justified."* What do you make of this objection?

4. Kant provides several—up to five—different formulations of the categorical imperative. What is the relationship between them? For example, do some of the formulations yield different sets of duties than the others?

5. Kant denies that "the principles of morality are ... to be sought anywhere in knowledge of human nature." Does this seem like a reasonable position to take? What reasons does he have for this striking claim, and how persuasive are they?

6. At one point Kant argues that the function of reason cannot, primarily, be to produce happiness, since then it would not have been well adapted by nature to its purpose, and it must therefore have some other purpose (to produce a will which is good in itself). What do you think of this argument? How much does it rely upon the assumption that nature has purposes?

7. Kant suggests our ordinary, everyday moral beliefs and practices contain within them the "ultimate principle" of morality (the categorical imperative). Is he successful in showing we *already* tacitly believe the categorical imperative? If not, how much of a problem is this for his later arguments?

8. Do all of our actions rest on maxims? Do you think that Kant thinks they do (and if so, how does that affect your understanding of what he means by "maxim")? If they do not, does this cause serious problems for Kant's moral theory?

9. "There are ... many persons so sympathetically constituted that without any motive of vanity or self-ishness they find an inner satisfaction in spreading joy and rejoice in the contentment of others which they have made possible. But I say that, however dutiful and however amiable it may be, that kind of action has no true moral worth." What do you think of this claim of Kant's? When properly understood, do you think it is plausible?

10. Does Kant's moral theory require us to be perfectly rational in order to be perfectly moral? If so, is this a reasonable expectation? What place can the irrational elements of human psychology—such as emotions—have in Kant's moral philosophy?

11. How well can Kant's moral theory handle the following question: Now you've shown me what morality is, *why* should I be moral? Why is morality binding on me? For example, when Kant rules out all hypothetical imperatives as grounds for moral behavior, does he thereby rule out all possible *reasons* to be moral?

12. How accurately can we make moral judgments about *other people*, if Kant's theory is correct? How easily could we tell what maxim is guiding their behavior? For that matter, how accurately can we make moral judgments about our *own* behavior? Do we always know our own motives for action? How much, if at all, is any of this a problem for Kant's theory?

13. Even if you disagree with the details in Kant's moral theory, do you think his fundamental claim is sound? Is there a sharp distinction between moral actions and those performed for the sake of self-interest or emotional inclination? Must genuinely moral actions be motivated by a categorical or universally rational duty?

---

* G.W.F. Hegel, *Philosophy of Right*, trans. T.M. Knox (Oxford University Press, 1967), 90.

Notes

1 A maxim is the subjective principle of volition. The objective principle (i.e., that which would serve all rational beings also subjectively as a practical principle if reason had full power over the faculty of desire) is the practical law.

2 A maxim is the subjective principle of acting and must be distinguished from the objective principle (i.e., the practical law). The former contains the practical rule which reason determines according to the conditions of the subject (often his ignorance or inclinations) and is thus the principle according to which the subject acts. The law, on the other hand, is the objective principle valid for every rational being, and the principle by which it ought to act, i.e., an imperative.

3 ... [B]y a perfect duty I here understand a duty which permits no exception in the interest of inclination; thus I have not merely outer but also inner perfect duties....

4 Let it not be thought that the banal "what you do not wish to be done to you ..." could here serve as guide or principle, for it is only derived from the principle and is restricted by various limitations. It cannot be a universal law, because it contains the ground neither of duties to one's self nor of the benevolent duties to others (for many a man would gladly consent that others should not benefit him, provided only that he might be excused from showing benevolence to them). Nor does it contain the ground of obligatory duties to another, for the criminal would argue on this ground against the judge who sentences him. And so on.

5 Teleology considers nature as a realm of ends; morals regards a possible realm of ends as a realm of nature. In the former the realm of ends is a theoretical Idea for the explanation of what actually is. In the latter it is a practical Idea for bringing about that which does not exist but which can become actual through our conduct and for making it conform with this Idea.

JOHN STUART MILL

FROM *Utilitarianism*

Who Was John Stuart Mill?

John Stuart Mill, the most important British philosopher of the nineteenth century, was born in London in 1806, the eldest son of Scottish utilitarian philosopher and political radical James Mill (1773–1836). His childhood was shaped—some might say, misshaped—by his father's fervent belief in the importance of education. James Mill held that every variation in the talents and capacities of individual human beings could be explained by their education and experiences, and therefore he believed that a proper educational regime, beginning more or less from birth, could train any child to be an almost superhuman intellect. To prove these theories, Mill raised his first son, John Stuart, to be the British radical movement's secret weapon: a prodigious intellect who would be a living demonstration of what could be achieved through properly scientific educational methods, and who would go out into the world to spread the secular gospel of utilitarianism and liberalism.

His father took sole charge of little John Stuart's education from the time he was a toddler, keeping him isolated from other children (who might be harmful influences) and even from other adults who were not Mill's own philosophical compatriots. John was therefore kept out of schools—which his father believed reinforced ignorant and immoral social attitudes—and educated at home, learning Greek and Latin in the same large study where his father was hard at work on a monumental history of India (and, since no English-Greek dictionary had yet been written, frequently interrupting his father to ask questions about vocabulary). In his autobiography, the younger Mill wrote, "I have no remembrance of the time when I began to learn Greek. I have been told that it was when I was three years old."*

By the time he was eight—the age at which he began to learn Latin and arithmetic—he had studied much of Greek literature in the original, including all of Herodotus's *Histories* and six dialogues by Plato. At 12 he started on logic and the serious study of philosophy; political economy began at 13; and at 20 he was sent to France for a year to become fluent in that language and to study chemistry and mathematics.†

Despite these prodigious achievements, Mill's early life seems not to have been a happy one. He had no toys or children's books—not so much, apparently, because his father forbade them as simply because it never occurred to him to provide them—and John Stuart later remarked that he had never learned to play. Until he was 14 he never really mixed with children his own age at all. An early draft of his autobiography contained the following passage, deleted before publication:

> I believe there is less personal affection in England than in any other country of which I know anything, and I give my father's family not as peculiar in this respect but only as a faithful exemplification of the ordinary fact. That rarity in England, a really warm hearted mother, would in the first place have made the children grow up loving and being loved. But my mother with the very best intentions, only knew how to pass her life in drudging for them ... but to make herself loved, looked up to, or even obeyed, required qualities which she unfortunately did not possess. I thus grew up in the absence of love and in the presence of fear: and many and indelible are the effects of this bringing-up, in the stunting of my moral growth.‡

* This and other passages below are from J.S. Mill, *Autobiography* (Penguin Books, 1989), 27, 112, 117, 68.
† At around this time Mill was offered a place at Cambridge University. His father refused it for him, saying he already knew more than Cambridge could ever teach him.
‡ *The Early Draft of John Stuart Mill's "Autobiography,"* ed. Jack Stillinger (University of Illinois Press, 1961), 184.

At the age of 22, Mill suffered a nervous breakdown and was plunged into suicidal despair. The trigger—according to his autobiography—was a sudden realization that living the life for which his father had trained him could not make him happy:

> ... [I]t occurred to me to put the question directly to myself, "Suppose that all your objects in life were realized; that all the changes in institutions and opinions which you are looking forward to, could be completely effected this very instant: would this be a great joy and happiness to you?" And an irrepressible self-consciousness distinctly answered, "No!" At this my heart sank within me: the whole foundation on which my life was constructed fell down. All my happiness was to have been found in the continual pursuit of this end. The end had ceased to charm, and how could there ever again be any interest in the means? I seemed to have nothing left to live for.

Mill's response to this crisis was not to *abandon* utilitarianism and the radical philosophy of his father, but instead to *modify* the theories by which he had been brought up. He came to adopt the view that "those only are happy ... who have their minds fixed on some object other than their own happiness": that is, true happiness—which, as his father had taught him, is the measure of all action—comes not from the pursuit of one's own happiness in itself, but from living a life filled with concern for the happiness of others and with a love of other things, such as poetry and music, for their own sake. Mill, in fact, claimed his sanity was saved by his discovery of Romantic poetry—especially that of William Wordsworth (1770–1850), Samuel Taylor Coleridge (1772–1834), and Johann Wolfgang von Goethe (1749–1832)—and he later placed great emphasis on the proper development of the emotional and sentimental side of one's character, as well as one's intellect.

In 1830, at 24, Mill began a deeply passionate love affair with a beautiful, vivacious, but married woman, Harriet Hardy Taylor (b. 1807), the wife of John Taylor, a merchant. Mill's relationship with Harriet was central to his life, and she had a great influence on his writings.

For 15 years, between 1834 and John Taylor's death in 1849, Harriet and the two Johns lived out a curiously Victorian compromise: Harriet and Mill agreed never to be seen in "society" as a couple—which would cause a scandal—but were allowed by Harriet's husband to go on frequent holidays together. In 1851, two years after her husband's death, Harriet and Mill were finally able to marry, but in 1858, Harriet died of tuberculosis—a disease she probably caught from her new husband, who in turn had probably caught it from his father, who had died of TB in 1836.

Mill never held an academic position, but he spent 35 years working as an administrator for the British East India Company in London. The East India Company, which had also employed Mill's father, was a private trading company formed in 1600 which, by the end of the eighteenth century, had its own army and political service and was effectively administering the sub-continent of India on behalf of the British government. Mill started his career in 1823, at 17, as a clerk in the office of the Examiner of India Correspondence; by 1856 he had become Chief Examiner of India Correspondence, as his father had been before him. In 1858 the East India Company was taken over by the British Crown following the Indian Rebellion of 1857, and Mill retired with a substantial pension.

Mill's work for the company left him plenty of time for his writing, and he was also very active in public life. In 1823 he was arrested for distributing birth-control pamphlets, and in 1825 he helped to found the London Debating Society. In 1824 his father had established the *Westminster Review*, a quarterly magazine advocating a radically liberal political and social agenda, and John Stuart—only 18 years old at the time of its founding—was a frequent and enthusiastic contributor of articles during its early years. In 1835 he started his own radical periodical, the *London Review*, which soon became the influential *London and Westminster Review* and ran, under his editorship, until 1840. Between 1865 and 1868 Mill was the Liberal Member of Parliament for Westminster, and in 1866 he secured a law guaranteeing freedom of speech in London's Hyde Park.* In 1867 he tried, but failed, to amend the second Reform Bill to introduce proportional representation and the vote for women. In

---

*   This is the location, since that date, of London's famous Speakers' Corner—a place where "soapbox orators" can say whatever they like with legal impunity.

1866—by now something of a 'grand old man' of English society—he was made Rector of the University of St. Andrews in Scotland. In 1872 he became godfather to the newborn Bertrand Russell.

Mill died suddenly, from a fever, in 1873, at Aix-en-Provence, France. From about 1860 until 1870 he had been at the peak of his powers and influence. The moral philosopher Henry Sidgwick wrote in 1873, "from about 1860–1865 or thereabouts he ruled England in the region of thought as very few men ever did. I do not expect to see anything like it again."* A few decades later the former prime minister James Arthur Balfour noted that the authority of Mill's thought in English universities had been "comparable to that wielded ... by Hegel in Germany and in the middle ages by Aristotle."† By the First World War, however, Mill's reputation as a philosopher had suffered a precipitous decline, and he remained in ill-favor in the English-speaking philosophical world until the early 1970s, when new scholarship and changing philosophical fashions made possible a gradual increase in the appreciation of Mill as a major philosophical figure—the finest flowering of nineteenth-century British philosophy, and a precursor for the "naturalist" philosophers of the second half of the twentieth century.

What Was Mill's Overall Philosophical Project?

Mill is important less for the *originality* of his philosophic thought than for his brilliant *synthesis* of several major strands in nineteenth-century (and especially British) thought into a single, compelling, well-developed picture. The main ingredients for his worldview were empiricism, associationism, utilitarianism, and elements of German Romanticism. Together, these elements became what John Skorupski has called Mill's "liberal naturalism."‡

The bedrock of Mill's philosophy is empiricism: he believed all human knowledge comes ultimately from sense-experience, and his most substantial intellectual project was the attempt to construct a system of empirical knowledge that could underpin not just science but also moral and social affairs. One of his main interests was in showing that empiricism need not lead to skepticism, such as that espoused by Scottish philosopher David Hume (1711–76). Mill's main discussion of the foundation of knowledge and the principles of inference is the massive *System of Logic*, published in six volumes in 1843. In this work he discusses both deductive inference (including mathematics, which Mill argues is—like all human knowledge—reducible to a set of generalizations of relations among sense-experiences) and inductive inference in the natural sciences. He also tries to show how these methods can be applied in politics and the social sciences. Social phenomena, he argues, are just as much the result of causal laws as are natural events, and thus the social sciences—though they will never make us perfectly able to predict human behavior—are capable of putting social policy on an objective footing that goes beyond the mere "intuitions" of conservative common sense.

His prescriptions for scientific practice—today called "Mill's methods"—were highly influential in the development of the philosophy of science in the twentieth century, and his work is still the foundation of modern methodologies for discovering causal laws. The key engine of science, for Mill, is simply *enumerative induction* or generalization from experience. Crudely put, once we have observed a sequence of events that all obey some regularity—ravens that are black, say, or moving magnetic fields being accompanied by an electrical current—we are justified in inferring that all future events of that type will follow the same law.

Mill's work was also a precursor of what is now called "naturalized epistemology." He proposed that all the phenomena of the human mind, including rationality, be treated as the result of the operation of psychological laws acting upon the data of experience. This psychological theory is called *associationism*—since it holds that ideas arise from the psychological associations between sensations—and is particularly defended by Mill in his *Examination of Sir William Hamilton's Philosophy* (1865).

---

* Henry Sidgwick, in a May 1873 letter to C.H. Pearson; he is quoted in Stefan Collini, *Public Moralists, Political Thought and Intellectual Life in Great Britain 1850–1930* (Oxford University Press, 1991), 178.

† Arthur James Balfour, *Theism and Humanism* (Hodder and Stoughton, 1915), 138.

‡ John Skorupski, "Introduction: The Fortunes of Liberal Naturalism," in *The Cambridge Companion to Mill*, ed. John Skorupski (Cambridge University Press, 1998), 1–34.

In his own time, Mill was for many years most widely known for his *Principles of Political Economy* (1848), which tried to show that the science of economics—criticized by some for its tendency to predict disaster and starvation—could be reformulated as a progressive force for social progress. Mill pointed out the mismatch between what economics measures and what human beings really value, and this led him to argue for limiting economic growth for the sake of the environment, for controlling populations in order to allow an adequate standard of living for everyone, and for what he considered the economically ideal form of society—a system of worker-owned cooperatives.

Mill's main ethical position is utilitarianism, which is set out in this selection. As he wrote in his autobiography, of reading Jeremy Bentham's work on utilitarianism (at the age of 15), "it gave unity to my conceptions of things. I now had opinions; a creed, a doctrine, a philosophy; in one among all the best senses of the word, a religion; the inculcation and diffusion of which could be made the principal outward purpose of a life." Mill was also concerned to apply this moral theory to wider questions of social policy. Of all social institutions—including both formal institutions such as laws and churches, and informal ones like social norms—Mill wants to ask: Does this institution contribute to human welfare, and does it do so better than any of the alternatives? If the answer is "No," Mill argues, then that institution should (gradually and non-violently) be changed for the better.

Mill's *On Liberty* (1859; see elsewhere in this volume)—which, during his lifetime, was probably his most famous writing—is a classic defense of the freedom of thought and discussion, arguing that "the only purpose for which power can be rightfully exercised over any member of a civilized community, against his will, is to prevent harm to others. His own good, either physical or moral, is not a sufficient warrant." This essay was sparked partly by Mill's growing fear of the middle-class conformism (which he saw in America and detected increasing signs of in Britain) that he thought dangerously stifled originality and the critical consideration of ideas. Central to these concerns is Mill's view of human nature as "progressive," as well as the importance of individuality and autonomy. These themes, with their emphasis on the power and importance of the human spirit, were part of what he took from the European Romantic movement.

One of Mill's last works, *The Subjection of Women* (1869), is a classic statement of liberal feminism. Mill argues that women should have just as much freedom as men, and he attacks the conservative view that women and men have different "natures" that suit them for different spheres of life by arguing that no one could possibly know this—since all knowledge comes only from experience—unless women were first allowed to throw off their oppression and, over several generations, try to do all the things that men were allowed to do.

What Is the Structure of This Reading?

Utilitarianism was not written as a scholarly treatise but as a sequence of articles, published in a monthly magazine and intended for the general educated reader: consequently, although *Utilitarianism* is philosophically weighty and—just below the surface—often difficult, its overall structure is quite straightforward. Mill begins by making some general remarks in the first chapter, attacking moral intuitionism and suggesting, among other things, that the principle of utilitarianism has always had a major tacit influence on moral beliefs. In Chapter 2, where our selection begins, he defines utilitarianism, attempts to head off several common misunderstandings of the doctrine, and raises and responds to about ten possible objections to the theory (such as that utilitarianism is a godless morality worthy only of pigs, or alternatively that it sets an impracticably high standard that can never be attained by mere mortal human beings). In the third chapter, Mill considers the question of moral motivation and discusses how people might come to feel themselves morally bound by the principles of utilitarianism, arguing that utilitarianism is grounded in the natural social feelings of humanity. In Chapter 4 Mill sets out to give a positive "proof" (insofar as that is possible) for the claim that utilitarianism is the correct moral theory: he argues, first, that one's own happiness is desirable to oneself; second that it follows that happiness is simply desirable in itself, no matter whose it is; and third that *only* happiness is intrinsically desirable. It is this third stage in the argument that takes up most of the chapter. The final chapter of *Utilitarianism*, not included here, is a long discussion dealing with the relationship between utilitarianism and justice.

Some Useful Background Information

1. Mill frames much of *Utilitarianism* in terms of a debate between two basic positions on the nature of morality: the "intuitive" school and the "inductive" school. The intuitionists, whom Mill attacks, believed that ethical facts—though as real and as objectively true as any others—are *non-empirical*: that is, moral truths cannot be detected or confirmed using the five senses, but instead are known through the special faculty of "moral intuition." This philosophical position was represented in Mill's time by, among others, Sir William Hamilton (1788–1856) and William Whewell (1794–1866), and Mill's frequent criticism of the notion of "transcendental" moral facts is directed at intuitionists such as them. Mill considered intuitionism to be not only false but also a serious obstacle to social and moral progress. He thought the claim that (educated) human beings can "just tell" which moral principles are true, without needing or being able to cite evidence for these beliefs, tended to act as a disguise for prejudice and social conservatism. Mill's own moral methodology, by contrast, was what he called "inductive": he believed that *all* human knowledge, including ethical knowledge, comes ultimately from sense experience and therefore that moral judgments must be explained and defended by showing their connections to actual human experience.

2. The notion of *happiness* is a very important part of Mill's moral philosophy, so it is useful to be clear about exactly what his theory of happiness is. Because of Mill's empiricist and associationist philosophical upbringing, it was most natural for him to adopt a kind of hedonistic view of happiness. In keeping with his emphasis on sense experience as the key to understanding knowledge and the mind, Mill thinks of happiness as a kind of *pleasurable mental state* (*hēdonē* is the classical Greek word for "pleasure"). For Mill, a happy life is, roughly, one filled with as many pleasurable sensations, and as few painful ones, as possible.

Mill followed his philosophical predecessors in thinking that pleasurable experiences can be classified according to their duration and their intensity: thus rational people seeking their own happiness will aim to arrange their lives so that, over time, they will have more longer-lasting pleasures than short-lived ones, and more intense pleasures than dilute ones. For example, the initial painfulness of learning the violin might be more than offset by the intense and long-lasting pleasure of playing it well.* In addition, however, Mill distinguishes between different *qualities* of pleasure. For Mill (unlike, say, Bentham), pleasure is not just one type of mental sensation but comes in "higher" and "lower" varieties. For example, according to Mill, the pleasant feeling that accompanies advanced intellectual or creative activity is a more valuable kind of pleasure—even if it is no more intense or long-lasting—than that which comes from physical satisfactions like eating and sex.

3. One of Mill's philosophical presuppositions that is significant for his moral and social philosophy is *individualism*. Mill assumed that individual persons are the basic unit of political analysis—that social structures are nothing more than constructions out of these individuals and are nothing over and above particular people and the relations between them. It follows that the analysis of social phenomena must be approached through a study of the actions and intentions of individuals (as opposed to the study of larger social groups), and similarly that social change is possible only through a large number of changes to individual people. What matters to Mill is not "the general happiness" in some abstract sense, but the happiness of large numbers of individual human beings. He views social institutions as merely *instruments* for benefiting all these people. Furthermore, for Mill (influenced, as he was, by European Romanticism), there is a special kind of *value* in individuality: the particular uniqueness of each person is a thing to be treasured in itself.

---

* Mill's mentor Jeremy Bentham (1748–1832) even proposed what he called a "felicific calculus": a mathematical system for measuring the total net quantity of pleasure to be expected from a given course of action. Roughly, calculate the balance of pleasure and pain that would accompany a particular outcome of your actions—taking into account their intensity and duration—and then multiply this number by the probability of that outcome actually occurring. This yields what Bentham called the "expected utility" of an action. The rational agent—according to Bentham—acts in a way that has the greatest expected utility.

Some Common Misconceptions

1. For Mill, mere *exemption* from pain is not itself a good. He holds that pleasure is the only good, and pain the only bad, and the overall goodness of states of affairs consists in the *balance* of pleasure over pain. The absence of pain is thus morally neutral, unless it is accompanied by the positive presence of pleasure.

2. Mill is not arguing that people already *do* act in order to produce the greatest happiness of the greatest number: he is arguing that we *should*. He is not merely describing an already prevalent moral psychology, but arguing for a certain set of moral attitudes that he thinks we ought to cultivate in ourselves and in society in general.

3. Utilitarianism is a theory of actions and not motives. It does not require that people *intend* to maximize utility but rather that their behavior, in fact, does so. Mill insists that the criterion for what makes an action right is that it maximize utility; it does not follow from this that all our actions must have the conscious goal of maximizing utility. In fact, there is a good case to be made that a community where everyone is *trying* to maximize utility all the time would actually be self-defeating and a much less happy society than it would be if people acted from other motivations. If this is right, it would follow that, according to utilitarianism itself, it would be immoral to be always consciously trying to maximize utility. This is not a paradox or a problem for the theory, however; it simply shows there is a difference between the criterion of right action and the best advice one can give moral agents for actually meeting that criterion.

   Actions, according to Mill, include within themselves two parts: an *intention* (which is different from a motive—it is not *why* the action is done but *what* the action is intended to achieve), and the action's *effects*. Mill sometimes appeals to differences of intention to distinguish between kinds of actions (as in his Chapter 3 footnote about a tyrant rescuing a drowning man), but, strictly speaking, only the *effects* or consequences of an action can be morally relevant in Mill's view.

4. One common complaint against utilitarianism is that it makes *every* action, no matter how trivial, a moral issue: pretty much everything we do (e.g., getting a haircut) will have *some* effect on someone's pleasure and pain, and so it appears we have a moral duty to ensure we *always* act in such a way as to maximize the general happiness—and this, to say the least, would seem to put a bit of a strain on everyday life. However, even if this is, in fact, an implication of Mill's utilitarian theory, he did not intend to commit us to such an onerous regime. Something that Mill writes elsewhere is illuminating in this regard: "It is not good that persons should be bound, by other people's opinion, to do everything that they would deserve praise for doing. There is a standard of altruism to which all should be required to come up, and a degree beyond which it is not obligatory, but meritorious."*

5. Despite how *Utilitarianism* can strike us today, in the aftermath of the grand and often massively destructive social-engineering projects of the twentieth century, Mill was actually a bitter foe of what might be called "social constructivism." He emphatically did *not* see society as merely a machine built to help human beings to live together, a machine that can be broken into bits and reconstructed if it is not working optimally, and one where the rational, technical vision of collective planners should override individual initiative in the public good. On the contrary, Mill was very much an individualist and a humanist. He saw society as built from the actions of separate individual human beings and held that it is a kind of historical "consensus" that has created traditions and cultural practices that are continually but gradually evolving over time. Mill's vision for the reform of society, then, was not the imposition of central planning, but instead the gradual construction of a set of cultural norms—including, especially, a progressive educational system—to create human beings with the best possible moral character.

---

* From *Auguste Comte and Positivism*, in *Collected Works of J.S. Mill*, vol. 10 (University of Toronto Press, 1979), 337.

How Important and Influential Is This Work?

John Stuart Mill did not *invent* utilitarianism (and never pretended to have done so). Indeed, he was brought up by people who already considered themselves utilitarians. Mill's importance to utilitarianism is that he gave it what is arguably its single greatest and most influential formulation, in the essay *Utilitarianism*. It is this work that, ever since it was written, has been the starting point for both defenders and foes of utilitarianism. Furthermore, utilitarianism is itself a very important and influential moral theory.

Along with Marxism, it was arguably the most prevalent moral theory among philosophers, economists, political scientists, and other social theorists for much of the twentieth century (completely eclipsing—or in some cases, as with G.E. Moore's moral philosophy, absorbing—the moral "intuitionism" that Mill saw as his theory's main competitor in 1861). Utilitarianism's influence has waned since the 1970s and it has been subjected to several damaging philosophical attacks, but it is still, uncontroversially, one of the four or five most discussed and appealed-to moral theories in contemporary philosophical discourse.

FROM *Utilitarianism**

Chapter 2: What Utilitarianism Is

... The creed which accepts as the foundation of morals, Utility, or the Greatest Happiness Principle, holds that actions are right in proportion as they tend to promote happiness, wrong as they tend to produce the reverse of happiness. By happiness is intended pleasure, and the absence of pain; by unhappiness, pain, and the privation of pleasure. To give a clear view of the moral standard set up by the theory, much more requires to be said; in particular, what things it includes in the ideas of pain and pleasure; and to what extent this is left an open question. But these supplementary explanations do not affect the theory of life on which this theory of morality is grounded—namely, that pleasure, and freedom from pain, are the only things desirable as ends; and that all desirable things (which are as numerous in the utilitarian as in any other scheme) are desirable either for the pleasure inherent in themselves, or as means to the promotion of pleasure and the prevention of pain.

Now, such a theory of life excites in many minds, and among them in some of the most estimable in feeling and purpose, inveterate dislike. To suppose that life has (as they express it) no higher end than pleasure—no better and nobler object of desire and pursuit—they designate as utterly mean and grovelling; as a doctrine worthy only of swine, to whom the followers of Epicurus[†] were, at a very early period, contemptuously likened;[‡] and modern holders of the doctrine are occasionally made the subject of equally polite comparisons by its German, French, and English assailants.

When thus attacked, the Epicureans have always answered, that it is not they, but their accusers, who represent human nature in a degrading light; since the accusation supposes human beings to be capable of no pleasures except those of which swine are capable. If

---

*   *Utilitarianism* was first published in 1861 as a series of three essays in volume 64 of *Fraser's Magazine*. It was first published as a book in 1863; this text is from the fourth edition, published in 1871 (by Longmans, Green, Reader, and Dyer), the last to be printed in Mill's lifetime.

†   Epicurus (341–270 BCE) was a Greek philosopher and founder of the loosely knit school of thought called Epicureanism. A central plank of this doctrine is—as the modern connotations of the word "epicurean" suggest—that the good life is one filled with pleasure. Indeed, for Epicurus, the only rational goal in life is one's own pleasure. However, contrary to the popular association of "Epicureanism" with mere sensual self-indulgence, Epicurus placed much greater emphasis on stable, non-sensory pleasures (say, the pleasures of friendship and psychological contentment) and also stressed the importance of dispensing with unnecessary desires, harmful fears (such as the fear of death), and hollow gratifications. For more on Epicurus, see the reading from Kathy Behrendt later in this volume.

‡   For example, in Diogenes Laertius's *Lives of Eminent Philosophers*, written c. 230 CE.

this supposition were true, the charge could not be gainsaid,* but would then be no longer an imputation; for if the sources of pleasure were precisely the same to human beings and to swine, the rule of life which is good enough for the one would be good enough for the other. The comparison of the Epicurean life to that of beasts is felt as degrading, precisely because a beast's pleasures do not satisfy a human being's conceptions of happiness. Human beings have faculties more elevated than the animal appetites, and when once made conscious of them, do not regard anything as happiness which does not include their gratification. I do not, indeed, consider the Epicureans to have been by any means faultless in drawing out their scheme of consequences from the utilitarian principle. To do this in any sufficient manner, many Stoic,† as well as Christian elements require to be included. But there is no known Epicurean theory of life which does not assign to the pleasures of the intellect, of the feelings and imagination, and of the moral sentiments, a much higher value as pleasures than to those of mere sensation. It must be admitted, however, that utilitarian writers in general have placed the superiority of mental over bodily pleasures chiefly in the greater permanency, safety, uncostliness, etc., of the former—that is, in their circumstantial advantages rather than in their intrinsic nature. And on all these points utilitarians have fully proved their case; but they might have taken the other, and, as it may be called, higher ground, with entire consistency. It is quite compatible with the principle of utility to recognise the fact, that some *kinds* of pleasure are more desirable and more valuable than others. It would be absurd that while, in estimating all other things, quality is considered as well as quantity, the estimation of pleasures should be supposed to depend on quantity alone.

If I am asked, what I mean by difference of quality in pleasures, or what makes one pleasure more valuable than another, merely as a pleasure, except its being greater in amount, there is but one possible answer. Of two pleasures, if there be one to which all or almost all who have experience of both give a decided preference, irrespective of any feeling of moral obligation to prefer it, that is the more desirable pleasure. If one of the two is, by those who are competently acquainted with both, placed so far above the other that they prefer it, even though knowing it to be attended with a greater amount of discontent, and would not resign it for any quantity of the other pleasure which their nature is capable of, we are justified in ascribing to the preferred enjoyment a superiority in quality, so far outweighing quantity as to render it, in comparison, of small account.

Now it is an unquestionable fact that those who are equally acquainted with, and equally capable of appreciating and enjoying, both, do give a most marked preference to the manner of existence which employs their higher faculties. Few human creatures would consent to be changed into any of the lower animals, for a promise of the fullest allowance of a beast's pleasures; no intelligent human being would consent to be a fool, no instructed person would be an ignoramus, no person of feeling and conscience would be selfish and base, even though they should be persuaded that the fool, the dunce, or the rascal is better satisfied with his lot than they are with theirs. They would not resign what they possess more than he for the most complete satisfaction of all the desires which they have in common with him. If they ever fancy they would, it is only in cases of unhappiness so extreme, that to escape from it they would exchange their lot for almost any other, however undesirable in their own eyes. A being of higher faculties requires more to make him happy, is capable probably of more acute suffering, and certainly accessible to it at more points, than one of an inferior type; but in spite of these liabilities, he can never really wish to sink into what he feels to be a lower grade of existence. We may give what explanation we please of this unwillingness; we may attribute it to pride, a name which is given indiscriminately to some of the most and to some of the least estimable feelings of which mankind are capable:

---

*   Denied.

†   Stoicism was, with Epicureanism, one of the two main strands of "Hellenistic" philosophy (roughly, that associated with Greek culture during the 300 years after the death of Alexander the Great in 323 BCE). Its main ethical doctrine was that wise and virtuous persons accept, with calm indifference, their place in the impartial, rational, inevitable order of the universe—even if it is their fate to suffer hardship or painful death—but also work dutifully to foster a social order that mirrors the rational order of the cosmos. For more on stoicism, see the reading from Epictetus later in this volume.

we may refer it to the love of liberty and personal independence, an appeal to which was with the Stoics one of the most effective means for the inculcation of it; to the love of power, or to the love of excitement, both of which do really enter into and contribute to it: but its most appropriate appellation* is a sense of dignity, which all human beings possess in one form or other, and in some, though by no means in exact, proportion to their higher faculties, and which is so essential a part of the happiness of those in whom it is strong, that nothing which conflicts with it could be, otherwise than momentarily, an object of desire to them. Whoever supposes that this preference takes place at a sacrifice of happiness—that the superior being, in anything like equal circumstances, is not happier than the inferior—confounds the two very different ideas, of happiness, and content. It is indisputable that the being whose capacities of enjoyment are low, has the greatest chance of having them fully satisfied; and a highly endowed being will always feel that any happiness which he can look for, as the world is constituted, is imperfect. But he can learn to bear its imperfections, if they are at all bearable; and they will not make him envy the being who is indeed unconscious of the imperfections, but only because he feels not at all the good which those imperfections qualify. It is better to be a human being dissatisfied than a pig satisfied; better to be Socrates dissatisfied than a fool satisfied. And if the fool, or the pig, are of a different opinion, it is because they only know their own side of the question. The other party to the comparison knows both sides.

... From this verdict of the only competent judges, I apprehend there can be no appeal. On a question which is the best worth having of two pleasures, or which of two modes of existence is the most grateful† to the feelings, apart from its moral attributes and from its consequences, the judgment of those who are qualified by knowledge of both, or, if they differ, that of the majority among them, must be admitted as final. And there needs be the less hesitation to accept this judgment respecting the quality of pleasures, since there is no other tribunal to be referred to even on the question of quantity. What means are there of determining which is the acutest of two pains, or the intensest of two pleasurable sensations, except the general suffrage‡ of those who are familiar with both? Neither pains nor pleasures are homogeneous, and pain is always heterogeneous with pleasure. What is there to decide whether a particular pleasure is worth purchasing at the cost of a particular pain, except the feelings and judgment of the experienced? When, therefore, those feelings and judgment declare the pleasures derived from the higher faculties to be preferable *in kind*, apart from the question of intensity, to those of which the animal nature, disjoined from the higher faculties, is susceptible, they are entitled on this subject to the same regard.

I have dwelt on this point, as being a necessary part of a perfectly just conception of Utility or Happiness, considered as the directive rule of human conduct. But it is by no means an indispensable condition to the acceptance of the utilitarian standard; for that standard is not the agent's own greatest happiness, but the greatest amount of happiness altogether; and if it may possibly be doubted whether a noble character is always the happier for its nobleness, there can be no doubt that it makes other people happier, and that the world in general is immensely a gainer by it. Utilitarianism, therefore, could only attain its end§ by the general cultivation of nobleness of character, even if each individual were only benefited by the nobleness of others, and his own, so far as happiness is concerned, were a sheer deduction¶ from the benefit. But the bare enunciation of such an absurdity as this last, renders refutation superfluous.

According to the Greatest Happiness Principle, as above explained, the ultimate end, with reference to and for the sake of which all other things are desirable (whether we are considering our own good or that of other people), is an existence exempt as far as possible from pain, and as rich as possible in enjoyments, both in point of quantity and quality; the test

---

* Name, label.
† Pleasing.
‡ A view expressed by voting (or the right to make such a vote).
§ Here, as elsewhere, 'end' means goal or object aimed at.
¶ Subtraction (as opposed to an inference).

of quality, and the rule for measuring it against quantity, being the preference felt by those who in their opportunities of experience, to which must be added their habits of self-consciousness and self-observation, are best furnished with the means of comparison. This, being, according to the utilitarian opinion, the end of human action, is necessarily also the standard of morality; which may accordingly be defined, the rules and precepts for human conduct, by the observance of which an existence such as has been described might be, to the greatest extent possible, secured to all mankind; and not to them only, but, so far as the nature of things admits, to the whole sentient creation.*

Against this doctrine, however, arises another class of objectors, who say that happiness, in any form, cannot be the rational purpose of human life and action; because, in the first place, it is unattainable: and they contemptuously ask, what right hast thou to be happy? a question which Mr. Carlyle† clenches by the addition, What right, a short time ago, hadst thou even *to be*? Next, they say, that men can do without happiness; that all noble human beings have felt this, and could not have become noble but by learning the lesson of Entsagen,‡ or renunciation; which lesson, thoroughly learnt and submitted to, they affirm to be the beginning and necessary condition of all virtue.

The first of these objections would go to the root of the matter were it well founded; for if no happiness is to be had at all by human beings, the attainment of it cannot be the end of morality, or of any rational conduct. Though, even in that case, something might still be said for the utilitarian theory; since utility includes not solely the pursuit of happiness, but the prevention or mitigation of unhappiness; and if the former aim be chimerical,§ there will be all the greater scope and more imperative need for the latter, so long at least as mankind think fit to live, and do not take refuge in the simultaneous act of suicide recommended under certain conditions by Novalis.¶ When, however, it is thus positively asserted to be impossible that human life should be happy, the assertion, if not something like a verbal quibble, is at least an exaggeration. If by happiness be meant a continuity of highly pleasurable excitement, it is evident enough that this is impossible. A state of exalted pleasure lasts only moments, or in some cases, and with some intermissions, hours or days, and is the occasional brilliant flash of enjoyment, not its permanent and steady flame. Of this the philosophers who have taught that happiness is the end of life were as fully aware as those who taunt them. The happiness which they meant was not a life of rapture; but moments of such, in an existence made up of few and transitory pains, many and various pleasures, with a decided predominance of the active over the passive, and having as the foundation of the whole, not to expect more from life than it is capable of bestowing. A life thus composed, to those who have been fortunate enough to obtain it, has always appeared worthy of the name of happiness. And such an existence is even now the lot of many, during some considerable portion of their lives. The present wretched education, and wretched social arrangements, are the only real hindrance to its being attainable by almost all.

The objectors perhaps may doubt whether human beings, if taught to consider happiness as the end of life, would be satisfied with such a moderate share

---

* All creatures capable of sensation (and thus of feeling pleasure and pain).

† Thomas Carlyle (1795–1881) was a popular Scottish writer and (somewhat reactionary) social critic. This quotation is from his 1836 book *Sartor Resartus*. As a young man Mill was heavily influenced by Carlyle's allegiance to German Romanticism, but once Carlyle began to realize that Mill did not see himself as one of his disciples, their relationship took a sharp turn for the worse. (The fact that Mill's maid accidentally used the only manuscript copy of Carlyle's *History of the French Revolution* to light a fire when Carlyle was visiting him—forcing Carlyle to rewrite all of Volume I—cannot have helped.) *Utilitarianism* is largely intended as a response to criticisms of Mill's moral theories leveled by Carlyle and others.

‡ German for "to renounce or abjure." The idea it is supposed to capture is that moral behavior must be painful or difficult to be genuinely virtuous.

§ Unrealistic, fanciful.

¶ Novalis was the pseudonym of an early German poet and philosopher in the Romantic movement, Friedrich von Hardenberg (1772–1801). His most famous poem, "Hymns to the Night," was written after the death of his young fiancée from tuberculosis in 1799. Just months after its publication, von Hardenberg also succumbed to the disease.

of it. But great numbers of mankind have been satisfied with much less. The main constituents of a satisfied life appear to be two, either of which by itself is often found sufficient for the purpose: tranquillity, and excitement. With much tranquillity, many find that they can be content with very little pleasure: with much excitement, many can reconcile themselves to a considerable quantity of pain. There is assuredly no inherent impossibility in enabling even the mass of mankind to unite both; since the two are so far from being incompatible that they are in natural alliance, the prolongation of either being a preparation for, and exciting a wish for, the other. It is only those in whom indolence amounts to a vice, that do not desire excitement after an interval of repose: it is only those in whom the need of excitement is a disease, that feel the tranquillity which follows excitement dull and insipid, instead of pleasurable in direct proportion to the excitement which preceded it. When people who are tolerably fortunate in their outward lot do not find in life sufficient enjoyment to make it valuable to them, the cause generally is, caring for nobody but themselves. To those who have neither public nor private affections, the excitements of life are much curtailed, and in any case dwindle in value as the time approaches when all selfish interests must be terminated by death: while those who leave after them objects of personal affection, and especially those who have also cultivated a fellow-feeling with the collective interests of mankind, retain as lively an interest in life on the eve of death as in the vigour of youth and health. Next to selfishness, the principal cause which makes life unsatisfactory is want* of mental cultivation. A cultivated mind—I do not mean that of a philosopher, but any mind to which the fountains of knowledge have been opened, and which has been taught, in any tolerable degree, to exercise its faculties—finds sources of inexhaustible interest in all that surrounds it; in the objects of nature, the achievements of art, the imaginations of poetry, the incidents of history, the ways of mankind, past and present, and their prospects in the future. It is possible, indeed, to become indifferent to all this, and that too without having exhausted a thousandth part of it; but only when one has had from the beginning no moral or human interest in these things, and has sought in them only the gratification of curiosity.

Now there is absolutely no reason in the nature of things why an amount of mental culture sufficient to give an intelligent interest in these objects of contemplation, should not be the inheritance of every one born in a civilised country. As little is there an inherent necessity that any human being should be a selfish egotist, devoid of every feeling or care but those which centre in his own miserable individuality. Something far superior to this is sufficiently common even now, to give ample earnest of what the human species may be made. Genuine private affections and a sincere interest in the public good, are possible, though in unequal degrees, to every rightly brought up human being. In a world in which there is so much to interest, so much to enjoy, and so much also to correct and improve, every one who has this moderate amount of moral and intellectual requisites is capable of an existence which may be called enviable; and unless such a person, through bad laws, or subjection to the will of others, is denied the liberty to use the sources of happiness within his reach, he will not fail to find this enviable existence, if he escape the positive evils of life, the great sources of physical and mental suffering—such as indigence, disease, and the unkindness, worthlessness, or premature loss of objects of affection. The main stress of the problem lies, therefore, in the contest with these calamities, from which it is a rare good fortune entirely to escape; which, as things now are, cannot be obviated, and often cannot be in any material degree mitigated. Yet no one whose opinion deserves a moment's consideration can doubt that most of the great positive evils of the world are in themselves removable, and will, if human affairs continue to improve, be in the end reduced within narrow limits. Poverty, in any sense implying suffering, may be completely extinguished by the wisdom of society, combined with the good sense and providence of individuals. Even that most intractable of enemies, disease, may be indefinitely reduced in dimensions by good physical and moral education, and proper control of noxious influences; while the progress of science holds out a promise for the future of still more direct conquests over this detestable foe.

---

* Lack, absence.

And every advance in that direction relieves us from some, not only of the chances which cut short our own lives, but, what concerns us still more, which deprive us of those in whom our happiness is wrapt up.* As for vicissitudes of fortune, and other disappointments connected with worldly circumstances, these are principally the effect either of gross imprudence, of ill-regulated desires, or of bad or imperfect social institutions. All the grand sources, in short, of human suffering are in a great degree, many of them almost entirely, conquerable by human care and effort; and though their removal is grievously slow—though a long succession of generations will perish in the breach before the conquest is completed, and this world becomes all that, if will and knowledge were not wanting, it might easily be made—yet every mind sufficiently intelligent and generous to bear a part, however small and unconspicuous, in the endeavour, will draw a noble enjoyment from the contest itself, which he would not for any bribe in the form of selfish indulgence consent to be without.

And this leads to the true estimation of what is said by the objectors concerning the possibility, and the obligation, of learning to do without happiness. Unquestionably it is possible to do without happiness; it is done involuntarily by nineteen-twentieths of mankind, even in those parts of our present world which are least deep in barbarism; and it often has to be done voluntarily by the hero or the martyr, for the sake of something which he prizes more than his individual happiness. But this something, what is it, unless the happiness of others or some of the requisites of happiness? It is noble to be capable of resigning entirely one's own portion of happiness, or chances of it: but, after all, this self-sacrifice must be for some end; it is not its own end; and if we are told that its end is not happiness, but virtue, which is better than happiness, I ask, would the sacrifice be made if the hero or martyr did not believe that it would earn for others immunity from similar sacrifices? Would it be made if he thought that his renunciation of happiness for himself would produce no fruit for any of his

fellow creatures, but to make their lot like his, and place them also in the condition of persons who have renounced happiness? All honour to those who can abnegate for themselves the personal enjoyment of life, when by such renunciation they contribute worthily to increase the amount of happiness in the world; but he who does it, or professes to do it, for any other purpose, is no more deserving of admiration than the ascetic mounted on his pillar.† He may be an inspiriting proof of what men *can* do, but assuredly not an example of what they *should*.

... I must again repeat, what the assailants of utilitarianism seldom have the justice to acknowledge, that the happiness which forms the utilitarian standard of what is right in conduct, is not the agent's own happiness, but that of all concerned. As between his own happiness and that of others, utilitarianism requires him to be as strictly impartial as a disinterested‡ and benevolent spectator. In the golden rule of Jesus of Nazareth, we read the complete spirit of the ethics of utility. To do as you would be done by, and to love your neighbour as yourself, constitute the ideal perfection of utilitarian morality. As the means of making the nearest approach to this ideal, utility would enjoin, first, that laws and social arrangements should place the happiness, or (as speaking practically it may be called) the interest, of every individual, as nearly as possible in harmony with the interest of the whole; and secondly, that education and opinion, which have so vast a power over human character, should so use that power as to establish in the mind of every individual an indissoluble association between his own happiness and the good of the whole; especially between his own happiness and the practice of such modes of conduct, negative and positive, as regard for the universal happiness prescribes; so that not only he may be unable to conceive the possibility of happiness to himself, consistently with conduct opposed to the general good, but also that a direct impulse to promote the general good may be in every individual one of the habitual motives of action, and the sentiments connected therewith may fill a large and prominent

---

* For example, Mill's wife Harriet Taylor, who died of "pulmonary congestion" in 1858.

† Mill is probably thinking of St. Simeon Stylites (c. 390–459), a Syrian ascetic who spent more than 30 years living at the top of various pillars, the highest of which was 20 meters tall.

‡ Free from bias or self-interest (not *un*interested or bored!).

place in every human being's sentient existence. If the impugners of the utilitarian morality represented it to their own minds in this, its true character, I know not what recommendation possessed by any other morality they could possibly affirm to be wanting to it; what more beautiful or more exalted developments of human nature any other ethical system can be supposed to foster, or what springs of action, not accessible to the utilitarian, such systems rely on for giving effect to their mandates.

The objectors to utilitarianism cannot always be charged with representing it in a discreditable light. On the contrary, those among them who entertain anything like a just idea of its disinterested character, sometimes find fault with its standard as being too high for humanity. They say it is exacting too much to require that people shall always act from the inducement of promoting the general interests of society. But this is to mistake the very meaning of a standard of morals, and confound the rule of action with the motive of it. It is the business of ethics to tell us what are our duties, or by what test we may know them; but no system of ethics requires that the sole motive of all we do shall be a feeling of duty; on the contrary, ninety-nine hundredths of all our actions are done from other motives, and rightly so done, if the rule of duty does not condemn them. It is the more unjust to utilitarianism that this particular misapprehension should be made a ground of objection to it, inasmuch as utilitarian moralists have gone beyond almost all others in affirming that the motive has nothing to do with the morality of the action, though much with the worth of the agent. He who saves a fellow creature from drowning does what is morally right, whether his motive be duty, or the hope of being paid for his trouble; he who betrays the friend that trusts him, is guilty of a crime, even if his object be to serve another friend to whom he is under greater obligations.[1]

But to speak only of actions done from the motive of duty, and in direct obedience to principle: it is a misapprehension of the utilitarian mode of thought, to conceive it as implying that people should fix their minds upon so wide a generality as the world, or society at large. The great majority of good actions are intended not for the benefit of the world, but for that of individuals, of which the good of the world is made up; and the thoughts of the most virtuous man need not on these occasions travel beyond the particular persons concerned, except so far as is necessary to assure himself that in benefiting them he is not violating the rights—that is, the legitimate and authorised expectations—of any one else. The multiplication of happiness is, according to the utilitarian ethics, the object of virtue: the occasions on which any person (except one in a thousand) has it in his power to do this on an extended scale, in other words to be a public benefactor, are but exceptional; and on these occasions alone is he called on to consider public utility; in every other case, private utility, the interest or happiness of some few persons, is all he has to attend to. Those alone the influence of whose actions extends to society in general, need concern themselves habitually about so large an object. In the case of abstinences indeed— of things which people forbear to do from moral considerations, though the consequences in the particular case might be beneficial—it would be unworthy of an intelligent agent not to be consciously aware that the action is of a class which, if practised generally, would be generally injurious, and that this is the ground of the obligation to abstain from it. The amount of regard for the public interest implied in this recognition, is no greater than is demanded by every system of morals, for they all enjoin to abstain from whatever is manifestly pernicious to society.

The same considerations dispose of another reproach against the doctrine of utility, founded on a still grosser misconception of the purpose of a standard of morality, and of the very meaning of the words right and wrong. It is often affirmed* that utilitarianism renders men cold and unsympathising; that it chills their moral feelings towards individuals; that it makes them regard only the dry and hard consideration of the consequences of actions, not taking into their moral estimate the qualities from which those actions emanate. If the assertion means that they do not allow their judgment respecting the rightness or wrongness of an action to be influenced by their opinion of the qualities of the person who does it, this is a complaint not against utilitarianism, but against having any standard of morality at all; for certainly no

---

*   For example, in Charles Dickens's novel *Hard Times* (1854), especially through the character of Gradgrind.

known ethical standard decides an action to be good or bad because it is done by a good or a bad man, still less because done by an amiable, a brave, or a benevolent man, or the contrary. These considerations are relevant, not to the estimation of actions, but of persons; and there is nothing in the utilitarian theory inconsistent with the fact that there are other things which interest us in persons besides the rightness and wrongness of their actions. The Stoics, indeed, with the paradoxical misuse of language which was part of their system, and by which they strove to raise themselves above all concern about anything but virtue, were fond of saying that he who has that has everything; that he, and only he, is rich, is beautiful, is a king. But no claim of this description is made for the virtuous man by the utilitarian doctrine. Utilitarians are quite aware that there are other desirable possessions and qualities besides virtue, and are perfectly willing to allow to all of them their full worth. They are also aware that a right action does not necessarily indicate a virtuous character, and that actions which are blameable, often proceed from qualities entitled to praise. When this is apparent in any particular case, it modifies their estimation, not certainly of the act, but of the agent. I grant that they are, notwithstanding, of opinion, that in the long run the best proof of a good character is good actions; and resolutely refuse to consider any mental disposition as good, of which the predominant tendency is to produce bad conduct. This makes them unpopular with many people; but it is an unpopularity which they must share with every one who regards the distinction between right and wrong in a serious light; and the reproach is not one which a conscientious utilitarian need be anxious to repel....

It may not be superfluous to notice a few more of the common misapprehensions of utilitarian ethics, even those which are so obvious and gross that it might appear impossible for any person of candour and intelligence to fall into them....

... Utility is often summarily stigmatised as an immoral doctrine by giving it the name of Expediency, and taking advantage of the popular use of that term to contrast it with Principle. But the Expedient, in the sense in which it is opposed to the Right, generally means that which is expedient for the particular interest of the agent himself; as when a minister sacrifices the interests of his country to keep himself in place. When it means anything better than this, it means that which is expedient for some immediate object, some temporary purpose, but which violates a rule whose observance is expedient in a much higher degree. The Expedient, in this sense, instead of being the same thing with the useful, is a branch of the hurtful. Thus, it would often be expedient, for the purpose of getting over some momentary embarrassment, or attaining some object immediately useful to ourselves or others, to tell a lie. But inasmuch as the cultivation in ourselves of a sensitive feeling on the subject of veracity, is one of the most useful, and the enfeeblement of that feeling one of the most hurtful, things to which our conduct can be instrumental; and inasmuch as any, even unintentional, deviation from truth, does that much towards weakening the trustworthiness of human assertion, which is not only the principal support of all present social well-being, but the insufficiency of which does more than any one thing that can be named to keep back civilisation, virtue, everything on which human happiness on the largest scale depends; we feel that the violation, for a present advantage, of a rule of such transcendent expediency, is not expedient, and that he who, for the sake of a convenience to himself or to some other individual, does what depends on him to deprive mankind of the good, and inflict upon them the evil, involved in the greater or less reliance which they can place in each other's word, acts the part of one of their worst enemies. Yet that even this rule, sacred as it is, admits of possible exceptions, is acknowledged by all moralists; the chief of which is when the withholding of some fact (as of information from a malefactor, or of bad news from a person dangerously ill) would save an individual (especially an individual other than oneself) from great and unmerited evil, and when the withholding can only be effected by denial. But in order that the exception may not extend itself beyond the need, and may have the least possible effect in weakening reliance on veracity, it ought to be recognised, and, if possible, its limits defined; and if the principle of utility is good for anything, it must be good for weighing these conflicting utilities against one another, and marking out the region within which one or the other preponderates.

Again, defenders of utility often find themselves called upon to reply to such objections as this—that there is not time, previous to action, for calculating and weighing the effects of any line of conduct on the general happiness. This is exactly as if any one were to say that it is impossible to guide our conduct by Christianity, because there is not time, on every occasion on which anything has to be done, to read through the Old and New Testaments. The answer to the objection is, that there has been ample time, namely, the whole past duration of the human species. During all that time, mankind have been learning by experience the tendencies of actions; on which experience all the prudence, as well as all the morality of life, are dependent. People talk as if the commencement of this course of experience had hitherto been put off, and as if, at the moment when some man feels tempted to meddle with the property or life of another, he had to begin considering for the first time whether murder and theft are injurious to human happiness. Even then I do not think that he would find the question very puzzling; but, at all events, the matter is now done to his hand. It is truly a whimsical supposition that, if mankind were agreed in considering utility to be the test of morality, they would remain without any agreement as to what *is* useful, and would take no measures for having their notions on the subject taught to the young, and enforced by law and opinion. There is no difficulty in proving any ethical standard whatever to work ill, if we suppose universal idiocy to be conjoined with it; but on any hypothesis short of that, mankind must by this time have acquired positive beliefs as to the effects of some actions on their happiness; and the beliefs which have thus come down are the rules of morality for the multitude, and for the philosopher until he has succeeded in finding better. That philosophers might easily do this, even now, on many subjects; that the received code of ethics is by no means of divine right; and that mankind have still much to learn as to the effects of actions on the general happiness, I admit, or rather, earnestly maintain. The corollaries from the principle of utility, like the precepts of every practical art, admit of indefinite improvement, and, in a progressive state of the human mind, their improvement is perpetually going on. But to consider the rules of morality as improvable, is one thing; to pass over the intermediate generalisations entirely, and endeavour to test

each individual action directly by the first principle, is another. It is a strange notion that the acknowledgment of a first principle is inconsistent with the admission of secondary ones. To inform a traveller respecting the place of his ultimate destination, is not to forbid the use of landmarks and direction-posts on the way. The proposition that happiness is the end and aim of morality, does not mean that no road ought to be laid down to that goal, or that persons going thither should not be advised to take one direction rather than another. Men really ought to leave off talking a kind of nonsense on this subject, which they would neither talk nor listen to on other matters of practical concernment. Nobody argues that the art of navigation is not founded on astronomy, because sailors cannot wait to calculate the Nautical Almanack.* Being rational creatures, they go to sea with it ready calculated; and all rational creatures go out upon the sea of life with their minds made up on the common questions of right and wrong, as well as on many of the far more difficult questions of wise and foolish. And this, as long as foresight is a human quality, it is to be presumed they will continue to do. Whatever we adopt as the fundamental principle of morality, we require subordinate principles to apply it by; the impossibility of doing without them, being common to all systems, can afford no argument against any one in particular; but gravely to argue as if no such secondary principles could be had, and as if mankind had remained till now, and always must remain, without drawing any general conclusions from the experience of human life, is as high a pitch, I think, as absurdity has ever reached in philosophical controversy.

The remainder of the stock arguments against utilitarianism mostly consist in laying to its charge the common infirmities of human nature, and the general difficulties which embarrass conscientious persons in shaping their course through life. We are told that a utilitarian will be apt to make his own particular case an exception to moral rules, and, when under temptation, will see a utility in the breach of a rule, greater than he will see in its observance. But is utility the only creed which is able to furnish us with excuses for

---

* An annual government publication that tabulates the astronomical data required for maritime navigation. (For example, the almanac might give the coordinates of a particular star as it would be seen at a particular time and date from various places on the earth's surface: observation will therefore tell you where you are.)

evil doing, and means of cheating our own conscience? They are afforded in abundance by all doctrines which recognise as a fact in morals the existence of conflicting considerations; which all doctrines do, that have been believed by sane persons. It is not the fault of any creed, but of the complicated nature of human affairs, that rules of conduct cannot be so framed as to require no exceptions, and that hardly any kind of action can safely be laid down as either always obligatory or always condemnable. There is no ethical creed which does not temper the rigidity of its laws, by giving a certain latitude, under the moral responsibility of the agent, for accommodation to peculiarities of circumstances; and under every creed, at the opening thus made, self-deception and dishonest casuistry* get in. There exists no moral system under which there do not arise unequivocal cases of conflicting obligation. These are the real difficulties, the knotty points both in the theory of ethics, and in the conscientious guidance of personal conduct. They are overcome practically, with greater or with less success, according to the intellect and virtue of the individual; but it can hardly be pretended that any one will be the less qualified for dealing with them, from possessing an ultimate standard to which conflicting rights and duties can be referred. If utility is the ultimate source of moral obligations, utility may be invoked to decide between them when their demands are incompatible. Though the application of the standard may be difficult, it is better than none at all: while in other systems, the moral laws all claiming independent authority, there is no common umpire entitled to interfere between them; their claims to precedence one over another rest on little better than sophistry,† and unless determined, as they generally are, by the unacknowledged influence of considerations of utility, afford a free scope for the action of personal desires and partialities. We must remember that only in these cases of conflict between secondary principles is it requisite that first principles should be appealed to. There is no case of moral obligation in which some secondary principle is not involved; and if only one, there can seldom be any real doubt which one it is, in the mind of any person by whom the principle itself is recognised.

Chapter 3: Of the Ultimate Sanction‡ of the Principle of Utility

The question is often asked, and properly so, in regard to any supposed moral standard—What is its sanction? what are the motives to obey it? or more specifically, what is the source of its obligation? whence does it derive its binding force? It is a necessary part of moral philosophy to provide the answer to this question; which, though frequently assuming the shape of an objection to the utilitarian morality, as if it had some special applicability to that above others, really arises in regard to all standards....

The principle of utility either has, or there is no reason why it might not have, all the sanctions which belong to any other system of morals. Those sanctions are either external or internal. Of the external sanctions it is not necessary to speak at any length. They are, the hope of favour and the fear of displeasure, from our fellow creatures or from the Ruler of the Universe, along with whatever we may have of sympathy or affection for them, or of love and awe of Him, inclining us to do his will independently of selfish consequences. There is evidently no reason why all these motives for observance should not attach themselves to the utilitarian morality, as completely and as powerfully as to any other. Indeed, those of them which refer to our fellow creatures are sure to do so, in proportion to the amount of general intelligence; for whether there be any other ground of moral obligation than the general happiness or not, men do desire happiness; and however imperfect may be their own practice, they desire and commend all conduct in others towards themselves, by which they think their happiness is promoted. With regard to the religious motive, if men believe, as most profess to do, in the goodness of God, those who think that conduciveness

---

* Unsound and deceptive reasoning; or, reasoning from particular cases rather than general rules.
† Plausible but misleading argument.
‡ "Sanction" was a technical term in eighteenth- and nineteenth-century philosophy. Sanctions are the considerations that motivate adherence to rules of conduct. For example, Bentham—in his *Introduction to the Principles of Morals and Legislation*—distinguished between four different types of sanction: "physical" (e.g., hunger or sexual desire), "political" (e.g., prison), "religious" (e.g., heaven and hell), and "moral" (e.g., social disapproval).

to the general happiness is the essence, or even only the criterion of good, must necessarily believe that it is also that which God approves. The whole force therefore of external reward and punishment, whether physical or moral, and whether proceeding from God or from our fellow men, together with all that the capacities of human nature admit of disinterested devotion to either, become available to enforce the utilitarian morality, in proportion as that morality is recognised; and the more powerfully, the more the appliances of education and general cultivation are bent to the purpose.

So far as to external sanctions. The internal sanction of duty, whatever our standard of duty may be, is one and the same—a feeling in our own mind; a pain, more or less intense, attendant on violation of duty, which in properly cultivated moral natures rises, in the more serious cases, into shrinking from it as an impossibility. This feeling, when disinterested, and connecting itself with the pure idea of duty, and not with some particular form of it, or with any of the merely accessory circumstances, is the essence of Conscience; though in that complex phenomenon as it actually exists, the simple fact is in general all encrusted over with collateral associations, derived from sympathy, from love, and still more from fear; from all the forms of religious feeling; from the recollections of childhood and of all our past life; from self-esteem, desire of the esteem of others, and occasionally even self-abasement. This extreme complication is, I apprehend, the origin of the sort of mystical character which, by a tendency of the human mind of which there are many other examples, is apt to be attributed to the idea of moral obligation, and which leads people to believe that the idea cannot possibly attach itself to any other objects than those which, by a supposed mysterious law, are found in our present experience to excite it. Its binding force, however, consists in the existence of a mass of feeling which must be broken through in order to do what violates our standard of right, and which, if we do nevertheless violate that standard, will probably have to be encountered afterwards in the form of remorse. Whatever theory we have of the nature or origin of conscience, this is what essentially constitutes it.

The ultimate sanction, therefore, of all morality (external motives apart) being a subjective feeling in our own minds, I see nothing embarrassing to those whose standard is utility, in the question, what is the sanction of that particular standard? We may answer, the same as of all other moral standards—the conscientious feelings of mankind. Undoubtedly this sanction has no binding efficacy on those who do not possess the feelings it appeals to; but neither will these persons be more obedient to any other moral principle than to the utilitarian one. On them morality of any kind has no hold but through the external sanctions. Meanwhile the feelings exist, a fact in human nature, the reality of which, and the great power with which they are capable of acting on those in whom they have been duly cultivated, are proved by experience. No reason has ever been shown why they may not be cultivated to as great intensity in connection with the utilitarian, as with any other rule of morals....

It is not necessary, for the present purpose, to decide whether the feeling of duty is innate* or implanted. Assuming it to be innate, it is an open question to what objects it naturally attaches itself, for the philosophic supporters of that theory are now agreed that the intuitive perception is of principles of morality and not of the details. If there be anything innate in the matter, I see no reason why the feeling which is innate should not be that of regard to the pleasures and pains of others. If there is any principle of morals which is intuitively obligatory, I should say it must be that. If so, the intuitive ethics would coincide with the utilitarian, and there would be no further quarrel between them. Even as it is, the intuitive moralists, though they believe that there are other intuitive moral obligations, do already believe this to be one; for they unanimously hold that a large *portion* of morality turns upon the consideration due to the interests of our fellow-creatures. Therefore, if the belief in the transcendental origin of moral obligation gives any additional efficacy to the internal sanction, it appears to me that the utilitarian principle has already the benefit of it.

On the other hand, if, as is my own belief, the moral feelings are not innate, but acquired, they are not for that reason the less natural. It is natural to

---

* Inborn, possessed at birth.

man to speak, to reason, to build cities, to cultivate the ground, though these are acquired faculties. The moral feelings are not indeed a part of our nature, in the sense of being in any perceptible degree present in all of us; but this, unhappily, is a fact admitted by those who believe the most strenuously in their transcendental origin. Like the other acquired capacities above referred to, the moral faculty, if not a part of our nature, is a natural outgrowth from it; capable, like them, in a certain small degree, of springing up spontaneously; and susceptible of being brought by cultivation to a high degree of development. Unhappily it is also susceptible, by a sufficient use of the external sanctions and of the force of early impressions, of being cultivated in almost any direction: so that there is hardly anything so absurd or so mischievous that it may not, by means of these influences, be made to act on the human mind with all the authority of conscience. To doubt that the same potency might be given by the same means to the principle of utility, even if it had no foundation in human nature, would be flying in the face of all experience.

But moral associations which are wholly of artificial creation, when intellectual culture goes on, yield by degrees to the dissolving force of analysis: and if the feeling of duty, when associated with utility, would appear equally arbitrary; if there were no leading department of our nature, no powerful class of sentiments, with which that association would harmonise, which would make us feel it congenial, and incline us not only to foster it in others (for which we have abundant interested motives), but also to cherish it in ourselves; if there were not, in short, a natural basis of sentiment for utilitarian morality, it might well happen that this association also, even after it had been implanted by education, might be analysed away.

But there is this basis of powerful natural sentiment; and this it is which, when once the general happiness is recognised as the ethical standard, will constitute the strength of the utilitarian morality. This firm foundation is that of the social feelings of mankind; the desire to be in unity with our fellow creatures, which is already a powerful principle in human nature, and happily one of those which tend to become stronger, even without express inculcation,* from the influences of advancing civilisation. The social state is at once so natural, so necessary, and so habitual to man, that, except in some unusual circumstances or by an effort of voluntary abstraction, he never conceives himself otherwise than as a member of a body; and this association is riveted more and more, as mankind are further removed from the state of savage independence. Any condition, therefore, which is essential to a state of society, becomes more and more an inseparable part of every person's conception of the state of things which he is born into, and which is the destiny of a human being. Now, society between human beings, except in the relation of master and slave, is manifestly impossible on any other footing than that the interests of all are to be consulted. Society between equals can only exist on the understanding that the interests of all are to be regarded equally. And since in all states of civilisation, every person, except an absolute monarch, has equals, every one is obliged to live on these terms with somebody; and in every age some advance is made towards a state in which it will be impossible to live permanently on other terms with anybody. In this way people grow up unable to conceive as possible to them a state of total disregard of other people's interests. They are under a necessity of conceiving themselves as at least abstaining from all the grosser injuries, and (if only for their own protection) living in a state of constant protest against them. They are also familiar with the fact of co-operating with others and proposing to themselves a collective, not an individual interest as the aim (at least for the time being) of their actions. So long as they are co-operating, their ends are identified with those of others; there is at least a temporary feeling that the interests of others are their own interests. Not only does all strengthening of social ties, and all healthy growth of society, give to each individual a stronger personal interest in practically consulting the welfare of others; it also leads him to identify his *feelings* more and more with their good, or at least with an even greater degree of practical consideration for it. He comes, as though instinctively, to be conscious of himself as a being who *of course* pays regard to others. The good of others becomes to him a thing naturally and necessarily to be attended to, like any of the physical

---

* Frequent repetition or instruction, intended to firmly impress something in someone's mind.

conditions of our existence. Now, whatever amount of this feeling a person has, he is urged by the strongest motives both of interest and of sympathy to demonstrate it, and to the utmost of his power encourage it in others; and even if he has none of it himself, he is as greatly interested as any one else that others should have it. Consequently the smallest germs of the feeling are laid hold of and nourished by the contagion of sympathy and the influences of education; and a complete web of corroborative association is woven round it, by the powerful agency of the external sanctions. This mode of conceiving ourselves and human life, as civilisation goes on, is felt to be more and more natural. Every step in political improvement renders it more so, by removing the sources of opposition of interest, and levelling those inequalities of legal privilege between individuals or classes, owing to which there are large portions of mankind whose happiness it is still practicable to disregard. In an improving state of the human mind, the influences are constantly on the increase, which tend to generate in each individual a feeling of unity with all the rest; which, if perfect, would make him never think of, or desire, any beneficial condition for himself, in the benefits of which they are not included. If we now suppose this feeling of unity to be taught as a religion, and the whole force of education, of institutions, and of opinion, directed, as it once was in the case of religion, to make every person grow up from infancy surrounded on all sides both by the profession and the practice of it, I think that no one, who can realise this conception, will feel any misgiving about the sufficiency of the ultimate sanction for the Happiness morality....

Chapter 4: Of What Sort of Proof the Principle of Utility Is Susceptible

It has already been remarked, that questions of ultimate ends do not admit of proof, in the ordinary acceptation of the term. To be incapable of proof by reasoning is common to all first principles; to the first premises of our knowledge,* as well as to those of our conduct. But the former, being matters of fact, may be the subject of a direct appeal to the faculties which

judge of fact—namely, our senses, and our internal consciousness.† Can an appeal be made to the same faculties on questions of practical ends? Or by what other faculty is cognisance taken of them?

Questions about ends are, in other words, questions about what things are desirable. The utilitarian doctrine is, that happiness is desirable, and the only thing desirable, as an end; all other things being only desirable as means to that end. What ought to be required of this doctrine—what conditions is it requisite that the doctrine should fulfil—to make good its claim to be believed?

The only proof capable of being given that an object is visible, is that people actually see it. The only proof that a sound is audible, is that people hear it: and so of the other sources of our experience. In like manner, I apprehend, the sole evidence it is possible to produce that anything is desirable, is that people do actually desire it. If the end which the utilitarian doctrine proposes to itself were not, in theory and in practice, acknowledged to be an end, nothing could ever convince any person that it was so. No reason can be given why the general happiness is desirable, except that each person, so far as he believes it to be attainable, desires his own happiness. This, however, being a fact, we have not only all the proof which the case admits of, but all which it is possible to require, that happiness is a good: that each person's happiness is a good to that person, and the general happiness, therefore, a good to the aggregate of all persons. Happiness has made out its title as *one* of the ends of conduct, and consequently one of the criteria of morality.

But it has not, by this alone, proved itself to be the sole criterion. To do that, it would seem, by the same rule, necessary to show, not only that people desire happiness, but that they never desire anything else. Now it is palpable that they do desire things which, in common language, are decidedly distinguished from happiness. They desire, for example, virtue, and the absence of vice, no less really than pleasure and the absence of pain. The desire of virtue is not as universal, but it is as authentic a fact, as the desire of happiness. And hence the opponents of the utilitarian standard deem that they have a right to infer that there are

---

*   The foundations of our beliefs.
†   Mill means the memory of something previously experienced.

other ends of human action besides happiness, and that happiness is not the standard of approbation and disapprobation.

But does the utilitarian doctrine deny that people desire virtue, or maintain that virtue is not a thing to be desired? The very reverse. It maintains not only that virtue is to be desired, but that it is to be desired disinterestedly, for itself. Whatever may be the opinion of utilitarian moralists as to the original conditions by which virtue is made virtue; however they may believe (as they do) that actions and dispositions are only virtuous because they promote another end than virtue; yet this being granted, and it having been decided, from considerations of this description, what is virtuous, they not only place virtue at the very head of the things which are good as means to the ultimate end, but they also recognise as a psychological fact the possibility of its being, to the individual, a good in itself, without looking to any end beyond it; and hold, that the mind is not in a right state, not in a state conformable to Utility, not in the state most conducive to the general happiness, unless it does love virtue in this manner—as a thing desirable in itself, even although, in the individual instance, it should not produce those other desirable consequences which it tends to produce, and on account of which it is held to be virtue. This opinion is not, in the smallest degree, a departure from the Happiness principle. The ingredients of happiness are very various, and each of them is desirable in itself, and not merely when considered as swelling an aggregate. The principle of utility does not mean that any given pleasure, as music, for instance, or any given exemption from pain, as for example health, is to be looked upon as means to a collective something termed happiness, and to be desired on that account. They are desired and desirable in and for themselves; besides being means, they are a part of the end. Virtue, according to the utilitarian doctrine, is not naturally and originally part of the end, but it is capable of becoming so; and in those who love it disinterestedly it has become so, and is desired and cherished, not as a means to happiness, but as a part of their happiness.

To illustrate this farther, we may remember that virtue is not the only thing, originally a means, and which if it were not a means to anything else, would be and remain indifferent, but which by association with what it is a means to, comes to be desired for itself, and that too with the utmost intensity. What,

for example, shall we say of the love of money? There is nothing originally more desirable about money than about any heap of glittering pebbles. Its worth is solely that of the things which it will buy; the desires for other things than itself, which it is a means of gratifying. Yet the love of money is not only one of the strongest moving forces of human life, but money is, in many cases, desired in and for itself, the desire to possess it is often stronger than the desire to use it, and goes on increasing when all the desires which point to ends beyond it, to be compassed by it, are falling off. It may, then, be said truly, that money is desired not for the sake of an end, but as part of the end. From being a means to happiness, it has come to be itself a principal ingredient of the individual's conception of happiness. The same may be said of the majority of the great objects of human life—power, for example, or fame; except that to each of these there is a certain amount of immediate pleasure annexed, which has at least the semblance of being naturally inherent in them; a thing which cannot be said of money. Still, however, the strongest natural attraction, both of power and of fame, is the immense aid they give to the attainment of our other wishes; and it is the strong association thus generated between them and all our objects of desire, which gives to the direct desire of them the intensity it often assumes, so as in some characters to surpass in strength all other desires. In these cases the means have become a part of the end, and a more important part of it than any of the things which they are means to. What was once desired as an instrument for the attainment of happiness, has come to be desired for its own sake. In being desired for its own sake it is, however, desired as *part* of happiness. The person is made, or thinks he would be made, happy by its mere possession; and is made unhappy by failure to obtain it. The desire of it is not a different thing from the desire of happiness, any more than the love of music, or the desire of health. They are included in happiness. They are some of the elements of which the desire of happiness is made up. Happiness is not an abstract idea, but a concrete whole; and these are some of its parts. And the utilitarian standard sanctions and approves their being so. Life would be a poor thing, very ill provided with sources of happiness, if there were not this provision of nature, by which things originally indifferent, but conducive to, or otherwise associated with, the satisfaction of our primitive desires, become in themselves sources of pleasure more valuable than the primitive pleasures, both in permanency, in the space of human existence that they are capable of covering, and even in intensity.

Virtue, according to the utilitarian conception, is a good of this description. There was no original desire of it, or motive to it, save its conduciveness to pleasure, and especially to protection from pain. But through the association thus formed, it may be felt a good in itself, and desired as such with as great intensity as any other good; and with this difference between it and the love of money, of power, or of fame, that all of these may, and often do, render the individual noxious to the other members of the society to which he belongs, whereas there is nothing which makes him so much a blessing to them as the cultivation of the disinterested love of virtue. And consequently, the utilitarian standard, while it tolerates and approves those other acquired desires, up to the point beyond which they would be more injurious to the general happiness than promotive of it, enjoins and requires the cultivation of the love of virtue up to the greatest strength possible, as being above all things important to the general happiness.

It results from the preceding considerations, that there is in reality nothing desired except happiness. Whatever is desired otherwise than as a means to some end beyond itself, and ultimately to happiness, is desired as itself a part of happiness, and is not desired for itself until it has become so. Those who desire virtue for its own sake, desire it either because the consciousness of it is a pleasure, or because the consciousness of being without it is a pain, or for both reasons united; as in truth the pleasure and pain seldom exist separately, but almost always together, the same person feeling pleasure in the degree of virtue attained, and pain in not having attained more. If one of these gave him no pleasure, and the other no pain, he would not love or desire virtue, or would desire it only for the other benefits which it might produce to himself or to persons whom he cared for.

We have now, then, an answer to the question, of what sort of proof the principle of utility is susceptible. If the opinion which I have now stated is psychologically true—if human nature is so constituted as to desire nothing which is not either a part of happiness or a means of happiness, we can have no other proof, and we require no other, that these are the only things desirable. If so, happiness is the sole end of human action, and the promotion of it the test by which to judge of all human conduct; from whence it necessarily follows that it must be the criterion of morality, since a part is included in the whole.

And now to decide whether this is really so; whether mankind do desire nothing for itself but that which is a pleasure to them, or of which the absence is a pain; we have evidently arrived at a question of fact and experience, dependent, like all similar questions, upon evidence. It can only be determined by practised self-consciousness and self-observation, assisted by observation of others. I believe that these sources of evidence, impartially consulted, will declare that desiring a thing and finding it pleasant, aversion to it and thinking of it as painful, are phenomena entirely inseparable, or rather two parts of the same phenomenon; in strictness of language, two different modes of naming the same psychological fact: that to think of an object as desirable (unless for the sake of its consequences), and to think of it as pleasant, are one and the same thing; and that to desire anything, except in proportion as the idea of it is pleasant, is a physical and metaphysical* impossibility....

But if this doctrine be true, the principle of utility is proved. Whether it is so or not, must now be left to the consideration of the thoughtful reader. ∎

---

* Mill probably means "psychological." In his view, not only do human beings actually desire things "in proportion as the idea of it is pleasant," but there is no possible human psychology that would be otherwise.

Suggestions for Critical Reflection

1. One of the attractions of utilitarianism, it is often supposed, is that it is 'scientific' or objective in a way that intuitionism (or other ethical theories such as Kantianism, or virtue theory) is not. The Greatest Happiness Principle apparently provides a quasi-mathematical, bias-free, and theoretically motivated way of working out what we ought to do in literally any moral situation. But is this really so? For example, can the pleasures and pains of sentient creatures really be 'objectively' measured and compared, in order to calculate the net effect of actions on utility? Even if pleasures and pains are measurable, do you think all the consequences of an action can be properly predicted and measured? How serious are these problems for utilitarianism?

2. Does Mill's notion of "higher" or more "noble" pleasure make sense? How could the "nobility" of an experience add to the pleasure of it? Why couldn't an experience be noble but not pleasant? In that case, would Mill be able to say that it is still valuable? In other words, is Mill *really* a hedonist (i.e., someone who thinks that only pleasure has intrinsic value—and only pain intrinsic disvalue)?

3. An influential criticism of the hedonistic component of utilitarianism was invented by philosopher Robert Nozick (1938–2002) and is called the "experience machine." The experience machine is a fictional device that keeps your body alive in a tank of fluids, for a normal human life-span, all the while stimulating your brain so that you continuously feel as if you are having the most pleasant and satisfying experiences imaginable. Since—properly designed—this would be an utterly reliable way of maximizing the quality and number of pleasant sensations during your lifetime, it seems that the utilitarian is forced to conclude that it would be our *moral duty* to plug ourselves into one of these machines (especially if they are such reliable and long-lasting devices that nearly everyone can be plugged in at the same time). But Nozick argues that this result is clearly unsatisfactory: surely there is more to a valuable life than a mere succession of pleasant experiences, and so utilitarianism must be a faulty moral theory. What do you think about Nozick's argument? What exactly does it suggest is wrong with utilitarianism (or at least Mill's version of the theory)? Could this problem—if it is a problem—be fixed?

4. Roger Crisp has called the third paragraph of the fourth chapter of *Utilitarianism* "the most notorious [passage] in Mill's writings."* In it Mill compares desirability with visibility in an effort to argue that desire is a faculty that reveals what we morally ought to do. The most famous and apparently devastating criticism of this argument came from G.E. Moore in 1903: "The fact is that 'desirable' does not mean 'able to be desired' as 'visible' means 'able to be seen.' The desirable means simply what *ought* to be desired or deserves to be desired."† How does Moore's complaint cause problems for Mill's argument? Does Mill really make the mistake Moore is suggesting? If Mill's own arguments fail to show that we *ought* to desire happiness, is there any other way a utilitarian could consistently argue for this claim? Does utilitarianism need to provide arguments for it?

5. How well does Mill refute moral egoism? That is, does his argument show that I ought to care about *everyone*'s happiness, and not just my own? Does he have an *argument* for the "impartiality" component of utilitarianism? Does he need one?

6. Is Mill right that we desire *only* happiness? In other words, is his claim that, "to desire anything, except in proportion as the idea of it is pleasant, is a physical and metaphysical impossibility," a plausible one? If he is wrong, how seriously does this undercut his argument for the truth of utilitarianism? For example, what about Mill's own example of virtue: is he right in arguing that we value our own virtue only as a "part" of our happiness?

7. Mill appears to argue that happiness is the only thing desired, because the satisfaction of any desire is part of happiness. This seems to *define* happiness as desire satisfaction; if so, what do you

---

* Roger Crisp, *The Routledge Philosophy Guidebook to Mill on Utilitarianism* (Routledge, 1997), 73.

† G.E. Moore, *Principia Ethica* (Cambridge University Press, 1903), 67.

think of his further claim that this conclusion is an empirical matter, to be settled by observation?

8. Utilitarianism is a kind of moral theory that is sometimes called "welfarist": for such theories, the only thing of intrinsic value is the welfare of moral agents (according to Mill, sentient beings). One consequence of welfarism is that *nothing else* is of intrinsic value. Thus, for example, the beauty of art and nature, ecological sustainability, scientific knowledge, justice, equality, loyalty, kindness, or self-sacrifice—none of these things have any value in themselves but are valuable *only* insofar as they increase the welfare of sentient creatures (and are actually *immoral* if they reduce this welfare). Is this something Mill would agree with? Does this seem to be an acceptable consequence of a moral theory?

9. Utilitarianism is often accused of being an extremely demanding moral theory. According to utilitarianism, a certain unit of pleasure or pain should matter *equally* to me whether it belongs to me, to a member of my family, to a stranger halfway across the world, or even to an animal. Utilitarianism requires us to maximize overall happiness, and does not allow us to think of the happiness of ourselves and our friends as being especially important. If you or I were to spend all of our free time, and use almost all of our money, working to help victims of famine and other natural disasters around the world, this might well produce more overall utility than the lives we currently lead. If so, then utilitarianism apparently commits us to a moral *duty* to behave in this way, and we are being flat-out *immoral* in spending time with our families or watching movies. Does a careful reading support the claim that this is a consequence of Mill's position? Is this acceptable? If not, what is wrong with it?

10. According to utilitarianism, should we be morally responsible for all the consequences of our actions, including the unforeseen ones? What would Mill say (bear in mind his distinction between the morality of actions and of agents)? Are we just as responsible for *not* doing things that could have

prevented great pain? For example, according to utilitarianism, am I equally morally deficient if I fail to give money to charity as I am if I send poisoned food to famine-stricken areas (supposing the outcomes in terms of human death and suffering would be the same)?

11. Act (or "direct") utilitarianism is the view that one should act in any circumstance so as to produce the greatest overall balance of pleasure over pain. (You would have a moral duty to break an important promise to your best friend if doing so would increase overall utility by even a tiny amount, for example.) Rule (or "indirect") utilitarianism, on the other hand, is the view that one should act in accordance with certain moral rules, rules fixed as those which, over time, can be expected to maximize utility if they are generally followed. (For example, you should never break an important promise, even if you can foresee that keeping it, in a particular case, will cause far more pain than pleasure.) Is Mill an act or rule utilitarian? Which is the better theory? Is *either* version attractive and, if not, can you think of a third option for utilitarianism?

12. According to utilitarianism, *how* should we maximize utility? Should we aim to maximize the *total* utility of the world, the *average* utility, or what? (For example, if we chose to maximize total utility, we might be morally obliged to aim for an extremely large population, even if each member has only a low level of happiness; on the other hand, if we opt for the highest possible average utility we might be committed to keeping the population small and select, perhaps killing, before birth, people who look as though they might drag the average down.) What would Mill say?

13. Mill thought utilitarianism to be the one true fundamental moral theory and to be consistent with (what is right in) the moral theories of Aristotle and Kant. If you are familiar with Aristotle's and Kant's ethical views, consider whether utilitarianism is in fact consistent with them. For example, could Kant accept that consequences are what is morally important about our actions?

Note

1 An opponent, whose intellectual and moral fairness it is a pleasure to acknowledge (the Rev. J. Llewellyn Davies), has objected to this passage, saying, "Surely the rightness or wrongness of saving a man from drowning does depend very much upon the motive with which it is done. Suppose that a tyrant, when his enemy jumped into the sea to escape from him, saved him from drowning simply in order that he might inflict upon him more exquisite tortures, would it tend to clearness to speak of that action as 'a morally right action'? Or suppose again, according to one of the stock illustrations of ethical inquiries, that a man betrayed a trust received from a friend, because the discharge of it would fatally injure that friend himself or some one belonging to him, would utilitarianism compel one to call the betrayal 'a crime' as much as if it had been done from the meanest motive?"

I submit, that he who saves another from drowning in order to kill him by torture afterwards, does not differ only in motive from him who does the same thing from duty or benevolence; the act itself is different.

The rescue of the man is, in the case supposed, only the necessary first step of an act far more atrocious than leaving him to drown would have been. Had Mr. Davies said, "the rightness or wrongness of saving a man from drowning does depend very much"—not upon the motive but—"upon the *intention*," no utilitarian would have differed from him. Mr. Davies, by an oversight too common not to be quite venial, has in this case confounded the very different ideas of Motive and Intention. There is no point at which utilitarian thinkers (and Bentham pre-eminently) have taken more pains to illustrate than this. The morality of the action depends entirely upon the intention—that is, upon what the agent *wills to do*. But the motive, that is, the feeling which makes him will to do so, when it makes no difference to the act, makes none in the morality: though it makes a great difference in our moral estimation of the agent, especially if it indicates a good or a bad habitual *disposition*—a bent of character from which useful, or from which hurtful actions are likely to arise.

FRIEDRICH NIETZSCHE

FROM *Beyond Good and Evil*

In the end, what is there for it? There is no other means to bring philosophy again into honor: one must first hang all moralists—Friedrich Nietzsche*

Who Was Friedrich Nietzsche?

Friedrich Wilhelm Nietzsche was one of the most original, important, and—belatedly—influential voices of the nineteenth century, and is (arguably) among the greatest of the German-speaking philosophers since Kant. He was born in 1844, on the birthday of King Friedrich Wilhelm IV of Prussia (after whom he was named), in the village of Röcken near Leipzig in the region of Saxony. His father and both grandfathers were Lutheran ministers. Nietzsche's father, Carl Ludwig, died of a head injury before he was five and Nietzsche's younger brother died the next year, and so he and his sister Elisabeth were brought up by their mother, Franziska, and two aunts. As a young boy he struggled with his schoolwork, but persevered, rising at 5 a.m. to begin his school day and then studying extra hours in the evening to keep up with his Greek. He spent much of his free time playing the piano—Nietzsche was a skilled pianist—and, beginning before the age of 10 and continuing throughout his life, composed many pieces of music and wrote a great deal of poetry.

In 1858 Nietzsche was admitted to Schulpforta, one of Germany's oldest and most prestigious private boarding schools. The fourteen-year-old Nietzsche found the transition to the school's rigorous, almost monastic, regime hard, but again he persevered and played an energetic role in the school's intellectual, musical, and cultural life. By 1861, however, he was beginning to be plagued by headaches, fevers, eyestrain, and weakness—the first signs of the ill health from which he would suffer for the rest of his life. In 1864 Nietzsche graduated, and

although his grades were patchy he had already shown signs of great intellectual promise, especially in the study of languages.

After a brief stint as a theology student at the University of Bonn, Nietzsche enrolled at the university in Leipzig and began work in classical philology, studying the linguistic, interpretative, and historical aspects of Greek and Roman literature. At this time, he discovered the work of philosopher Arthur Schopenhauer (1788–1860), a pessimistic German philosopher who saw the world as an irrational, godless sequence of ceaseless striving and suffering. He also met and became friends with the composer Richard Wagner (1813–83), a creative genius who revolutionized opera with his concept of "music drama," which fused music, poetry, drama, and legend, culminating with his famous *Ring* cycle. Both these men would greatly influence Nietzsche's philosophical thought.

Even before he had completed his studies, and at the unprecedentedly young age of 24, Nietzsche was invited to take up a post as professor of classical philology at the University of Basel in Switzerland. Leipzig University hastily gave him a doctorate, not even bothering with the formality of an examination. Nietzsche began work at Basel in 1869, after renouncing his Prussian citizenship, and in 1870 was promoted to the rank of full professor. In that same year, the French parliament declared war on Prussia and Nietzsche volunteered for Prussian military service but, because of Switzerland's neutrality, he was allowed only to serve as a medical orderly. He was on the front lines for approximately a week before he fell ill—of diphtheria—and spent most of the rest of the short Franco-Prussian war (Paris surrendered in January 1871) recuperating and continuing his academic work.

His first book, *The Birth of Tragedy Out of the Spirit of Music*, appeared in 1872 and was expected to secure his reputation as a brilliant young scholar. Instead, it caused

---

* Friedrich Nietzsche, *Nachlass* [Nietzsche's previously unpublished notebooks], Division VIII, Volume 3, Nietzsche's *Werke Kritische Gesamtausgabe*, ed. Colli and Montinari (de Gruyter, 1967), 412. This translation is by Tracy Strong.

a small tempest of academic controversy, a battle which Nietzsche was deemed by his professional contemporaries to have lost. Rather than publishing a traditional work of classical scholarship, Nietzsche presented a rhapsodic, free-flowing essay which attempted to apply Schopenhauer's philosophical ideas to an interpretation of the origins of Greek tragedy, and which argued that the spirit of Greek tragedy was reborn in the music-dramas of Richard Wagner. Nietzsche hoped this work would establish him as a philosopher (and allow him to transfer to the philosophy department at Basel), but it did not resemble a traditional work of philosophy either. Nietzsche's reputation as a professional scholar was irreparably damaged.

Nietzsche continued to teach philology at Basel—where, for several years after the publication of *The Birth of Tragedy* he was generally shunned by the students—until 1879. In that year he resigned due to ill health: by this time he could hardly see to read and write, and was beset with headaches and other pains. He was given a pension of two-thirds his salary, not quite enough money for Nietzsche to live comfortably, but this freed him to devote all his time to his real love: the writing of philosophy.

Disliking the increasingly nationalist climate of Bismarck's "Second Reich," Nietzsche spent most of the next decade, from 1880 to 1889, in self-imposed exile from Germany, wandering around Europe (France, Italy, Switzerland) staying with various friends. In 1882, in Rome, Nietzsche met the bewitching Lou von Andreas-Salomé, fell madly in love with her, and within two months asked her to marry him; she refused. A month later, in Lucerne, he proposed again, and was again rejected. Nevertheless, Nietzsche, Salomé, and their mutual friend Paul Rée became, for a time, firm companions, traveling together and calling themselves the *Dreieinigkeit* or "trinity" of free spirits. The capricious Salomé, however, was not warmly received by Nietzsche's possessive mother and sister—eventually his mother refused to have Lou in the house. This caused such family bickering that Nietzsche, upset and depressed, broke off his relations with Rée and Salomé and also ceased his correspondence with his mother and sister for a few months. On his (rather bumpy) reconciliation with his

sister Elisabeth, she began a campaign to turn Nietzsche decisively against Rée and Salomé, and was quickly successful in making the split between Nietzsche and his former friends irrevocable.

Despite this and various other emotional upsets, Nietzsche produced several substantial philosophical books during the first few years of his "wandering" decade: *Human, All Too Human: A Book for Free Spirits* (1878–80), *Daybreak: Thoughts on the Prejudices of Morality* (1881), *The Gay Science* (1882), and *Thus Spake Zarathustra* (1883–85). They sold so few copies, however, that by the time he came to write *Beyond Good and Evil* (1886) he was having great difficulty finding publishers and was rapidly running out of money. The late 1880s were lonely, worried years: his health was very bad, he had little money, he had destroyed his relationships with most of his friends (including Wagner and his circle), and his philosophical work was falling on deaf ears.

In 1887 Nietzsche published *On the Genealogy of Morals* and, at long last, in 1888 began to see the first signs of public recognition—for example, public lectures on his work were held in Copenhagen. However, by this time Nietzsche, never a modest man, was starting to show signs of full-blown megalomania, referring to himself in letters as, for example, "the first spirit of the age" and "a genius of the Truth."* Yet in this final year of his sanity he managed to write no fewer than five new books: *The Case of Wagner, Twilight of the Idols (or How to Philosophize with a Hammer), The Anti-Christ: Curse on Christianity, Ecce Homo,* and *Nietzsche Contra Wagner.* By January of 1889, however, his communications were so bizarre—they are the so-called *Wahnbriefe,* or "mad letters"—that his remaining friends became concerned and called in the director of the Psychiatric Clinic in Basel, Dr. Ludwig Wille.

Nietzsche, by now completely insane, was tracked down in Turin and (with the help of a local dentist named Dr. Bettmann) was brought back to Basel and quickly transferred to a psychiatric clinic in the central German city of Jena. He was only 44. The doctors quickly agreed that the prospects for recovery were slim, even after Nietzsche's condition improved somewhat with confinement and treatment. They reported that he

---

* Quoted from a letter to Peter Gast dated 8 June 1887. Printed in *Friedrich Nietzsche's Briefe an Peter Gast* (Leipzig, 1908), and cited by, for example, Walter Kaufmann in the preface to his translation of *Beyond Good and Evil* (Random House, 1996), xi.

speaks more coherently and ... the episodes with screaming are more seldom. Different delirious notions appear continually, and auditory hallucinations still occur.... He recognizes his environment only partially, e.g., he calls the chief orderly Prince Bismarck etc. He does not know exactly where he is.*

In 1890, Nietzsche was released into the care of his mother and his mental health declined into a kind of permanent apathy and, gradually, paralysis.

Meanwhile, his sister Elisabeth seized control of Nietzsche's literary remains.† She created a Nietzsche Archive in Naumburg, near Leipzig, in 1894 and quickly turned out a biography of her brother in which she presented herself as his major influence and closest friend. She even hired a tutor, Rudolf Steiner, to teach her about her brother's philosophy, but after a few months Steiner resigned in disgust, declaring it was impossible to teach her anything about philosophy. After much legal wrangling, editions of many of Nietzsche's previously unpublished works were released, several of his books were translated into English and other languages, and (partly because of his sister's energetic, if self-serving, proselytizing) Nietzsche's intellectual influence began to increase. However, despite her role in publicizing Nietzsche's philosophy, it is now widely agreed that Elisabeth's appalling editing practices caused great harm to Nietzsche's reputation for many years after his death. She had twisted his thoughts to fit her virulent German nationalism and anti-Semitism, and even her own fervent Christianity.

Nietzsche finally died‡ on August 25, 1900, in the German city of Weimar, where Elisabeth had relocated the Nietzsche Archive and her helpless brother. For some time before his death, his sister—who was still enthusiastically encouraging a "Nietzsche cult"—had taken to dressing the half-paralyzed Nietzsche in ridiculous "holy" outfits and propping him up on the balcony of his home for adoring groups below to witness, an indignity which Nietzsche would have loathed.

What Was Nietzsche's Overall Philosophical Project?

Nietzsche's philosophical project was essentially a critique of all previous philosophical projects. He held that all philosophers before him, although they may have *believed* that they sought the pure and objective truth, were in fact merely laying out and defending *their own prejudices*—their philosophical theories were really nothing more than a personal statement, "a rarefied and abstract version of their heart's desire." They were often tricked into sincerely believing in their own objectivity, through the apparent simplicity and clarity of their statements (such as Descartes' "I think therefore I am") but this, according to Nietzsche, is a form of deception built into the very nature of language. For example, the claim "I think" is not *at all* clear and simple when one considers it carefully: the concept of thinking is not clear, and even if it could be *made* clear it would (in Nietzsche's view) fail to capture the reality of things. The world itself has no sharp edges and is not divided sharply into thinking and non-thinking things, for example, but instead contains subtle gradations and complexities. In fact, for Nietzsche, there is no stable, enduring, fixed reality lying behind the endless flux of experience; there is only experience and the human attempt to impose an individual perspective upon it.

The result of all this, for Nietzsche, is that the proper business of philosophy has been misunderstood. The point is not to scrutinize our most fundamental concepts, in order to come closer to a 'true description of reality'; the point is to ask what *function* our concepts have—to ask why we have adopted them, whether they are life-enhancing or destructive, whether it is necessary for us to have them at all. The goal is to affirm life, to live it free from superstitious illusions.

In urging this change, Nietzsche (probably§) does not simply *give up* on the whole project of acquiring 'knowledge,' but he does radically recast it. His philosophers of the future will realize that there is no such thing as 'ob-

---

* From a report by Otto Binswanger on 23 September 1889.

† She and her racist husband Bernhard Förster (whom Nietzsche detested) had been living in Paraguay, South America, where Förster was attempting to establish the pure Aryan colony of "New Germany." However Förster committed suicide in 1889 and, after unsuccessfully trying for a few months to hold the colony together, Elisabeth returned to Germany.

‡ Although there is still controversy, most commentators agree that he probably suffered from and succumbed to syphilis.

§ It should be pointed out that the interpretation of Nietzsche is a tricky business. His philosophical approach is highly unusual, with no sustained arguments or clear statements of philosophical conclusions, and his writing style is more

jective,' non-perspectival knowledge, since this requires the defunct assumption of a 'real' world underlying our ever-changing experience. Instead they will take a *multi-perspectival* approach to understanding reality; roughly, since *all there is* is a set of different individual perspectives on the world, the best way to achieve as full a comprehension of reality as possible is simply to strive to adopt *as many perspectives as possible* (through art, metaphor, construction of dramatic personas, and so on). Clearly, this is a task which can never be completed; there can never be a 'final understanding' of the world, and we should not look for such a thing, since there will always be a new perspective around the next corner not previously encountered.

Nietzsche's term for his new breed of philosopher was "free spirits" (*freien Geistes*), and he believed that these free spirits would be superior human beings who would assume a place of authority in a future social and intellectual hierarchy. Nietzsche's free spirits disdain democracy, equality, and social convention; and are "*delivered* from the crowd, the multitude, the majority, where he is allowed to forget the rule of 'humanity,' being the exception to it."* Instead of toiling for 'objectivity' and consensus, they will revel in their subjectivity and strive for the *extraordinary*. They will be in touch with their own instinctual life—their "will to power"—and will rise beyond, or "overcome," traditional morality and religion.† Traditional ethical systems are merely historical creations, according to Nietzsche, that serve the self-interested purposes of their creators and artificially constrain the horizons of human possibility.

The kind of future morality Nietzsche envisages for his "free spirits" is rather elusive. All his mature life, Nietzsche planned a great work, to be called *The Revaluation of All Values*, which would fill in all of the details, but he never seems to have felt able to get beyond the first step of this project. Furthermore, Nietzsche had a deep distrust of systematization: in his view, the desire to make everything "fit together" and "make sense" is really a desire for death and the end of creativity. As he writes in *Beyond Good and Evil* (section 32):

The overcoming of morality, or even (in a certain sense) the self-overcoming of morality: let that be the name for the long, clandestine work that was kept in reserve for the most subtle and honest (and also the most malicious) people of conscience today, living touchstones of the human heart.

Nevertheless, there are things that can be said about Nietzsche's positive view of morality (or, as he might have put it, the value system that lies *beyond* morality). First, Nietzsche approaches morality *naturalistically*. He treats it as a natural phenomenon, observable in certain living things such as human beings, and not as something rooted in a supernatural or metaphysical 'other world.' The emergence of value is to be explained in a roughly Darwinian fashion, as the result of human evolution. The "free spirits" or *Übermenschen* (supermen) of our future, with their "revalued" values, will not somehow escape this evolutionary progress, but will be the next stage in the development of the human race.

Second, for Nietzsche, genuine moral worth is not a matter of our conscious intentions or rational choices; it's not a matter of following the right rules. Instead, moral value is somehow built into our unconscious, non-autonomous, non-rational "inner nature"—the *noble spirit*. For Nietzsche, there is a natural hierarchy (*Rangordnung*) among human beings, a natural division between those with "noble" souls and the lesser creatures of the "herd." Only a value-system which recognizes this, he thought, is biologically natural, life-affirming, creative, and vital.

Finally, another famous thesis of Nietzsche's which is morally relevant (though it does not appear in *Beyond Good and Evil*) is the notion of "eternal recurrence": the idea that time is cyclical, repeating itself in an endless loop over and over again. It is not fully clear whether Nietzsche actually *believed* this cosmological claim, but he did use it as a way of expressing what he thought of as a more positive attitude to life than the moral or Christian one. Instead of the value of one's life being judged *at its end*, Nietzsche suggests that we should see our lives as being subject to eternal recurrence, and thus that we

---

often polemical or metaphorical than analytic. As a result, even more so than for other philosophers, it is more or less impossible to present a summary of 'Nietzsche's views' with which some commentators will not disagree strongly (and this attempt will be no exception).

* *Beyond Good and Evil*, §26.

† One of Nietzsche's most famous aphorisms occurs in *The Gay Science*, where he proclaims, "God is dead" (Book 3, Section 125). In *Beyond Good and Evil* he calls Christianity "an ongoing suicide of reason."

should strive to make *each moment* of life one that we would want to repeat over and over again for eternity.

What Is the Structure of This Reading?

Despite its title, *Beyond Good and Evil* is not only—or even primarily—about moral philosophy. It is a general statement of much of Nietzsche's philosophical thought, including reflections on religion, epistemology, art, and politics. Its central theme is that philosophers must strip themselves of their preconceptions and contingently existing values, and become perfectly non-dogmatic; only then can they begin a "philosophy of the future" which will, for the first time in history, approach the truth. One of Nietzsche's central concerns in this work, as in much of his philosophy, is to persuade us to abandon previously accepted 'truths' inherited both from philosophy and religion. He is much less interested in laying out a new moral system with which to replace them.

Beyond Good and Evil is structured as a set of loosely connected aphorisms—tersely phrased statements, each dealing with a single focussed claim. The aphorisms (numbered 1 through 296) are self-standing, and each has its own point to make: but together—like threads in a tapestry or notes in a piece of music—they combine to form an overall picture. Ideally, the book needs to be read as a whole to get its full effect. Nietzsche arranged the aphorisms into nine chapters, eight of which are designed to pursue a particular theme:

1. On the Prejudices of the Philosophers
2. The Free Spirit
3. The Religious Disposition
4. Epigrams and Interludes
5. Towards a Natural History of Morals
6. We Scholars
7. Our Virtues
8. Peoples and Fatherlands
9. What Is Noble?

The book concludes with a poem—in the style of a Greek ode—called "From High Mountains."

The three aphorisms reprinted here are from the final chapter, What Is Noble? Aphorism 259 urges the "exploitative character" of all living things, 260 describes a distinction, very important for Nietzsche's philosophy, between "master moralities" and "slave moralities," and 261, while primarily a rumination on the nature of vanity, also contains important comments on the *source* of value—juxtaposed with 260 it gives further insight into the nature of "slave morality."

Some Useful Background Information

One of the central concepts in Nietzsche's philosophy is the *will to power*. According to Nietzsche, the will to power is the basic disposition of all life, including human life—it is the principle which provides the ultimate motive force for everything that happens in the natural (or at least the biological) world. Thus, every organic phenomenon—such as plant growth, animal predation, or the establishment of a religion—can be understood, according to Nietzsche, as being brought about by an underlying set of power relationships, where each term of the relation is exerting a "force of will" which strives, with varying success, to expand towards and transform the other terms. For example, a hunting lioness is driven by her will to power to kill antelope, while the will to power of her prey impels them to attempt to frustrate her.

Some Common Misconceptions

1. Though Nietzsche makes it amply clear in his text that he admires master morality more than slave morality, there is nevertheless controversy over whether Nietzsche actually *endorsed* master morality. (The textual evidence on this is mixed. For example, in a later book called *The Antichrist* Nietzsche asserts: "When the exceptional human being treats the mediocre more tenderly than himself and his peers, this is not mere courtesy of the heart—it is simply his *duty*."*) The revalued values of free spirits might have more in common with master morality than slave morality, but might nevertheless supersede *both* types and be a third form of 'morality' entirely.

---

* Friedrich Nietzsche, *The Antichrist*, section 57. (This translation is by Walter Kaufmann.)

2. Nietzsche's "master" and "slave" moralities are ideal types, and cannot be identified in the modern world—where types of morality are jumbled—by simply looking at what contemporary people say and do. Instead, clear paradigms can only be found in the distant historical past: perhaps Homer's *Iliad* as an illustration of master morality, and the *New Testament* to exemplify slave morality.

3. Nietzsche called himself an "immoralist" and was (on the surface at least) centrally concerned with *attacking* morality, but this does not mean Nietzsche encourages people to *behave immorally*—he is certainly not saying that people should do the opposite of what traditional moral systems prescribe. In one of his earlier works, *Daybreak* (1881), he firmly asserts:

    > [I]t goes without saying that I do not deny, presupposing I am no fool, that many actions called immoral ought to be avoided and resisted, or that many called moral ought to be done and encouraged—but *for different reasons than formerly.**

4. Although not a philosophical point, it may be worth mentioning that—although Nietzsche certainly did equate the rise of Judeo-Christianity with the ascendance of "slave morality"—his notorious so-called anti-Semitism, and supposed sympathy for what became ideological themes of the Nazi party, are largely a *myth* created by misunderstandings and deliberate distortions of his work during the fifty years after his death. In fact, Nietzsche had difficulty finding a publisher for *Beyond Good and Evil* because he had split from the publisher of his previous books, Ernst Schmeitzner, in part because Nietzsche *objected* to Schmeitzner's close association with the anti-Semitic movement in Germany and did not want it to seem that he had similar racist sympathies.†

(On the other hand, it *does* seem that Nietzsche, at least late in his life, was avowedly—and very unpleasantly—misogynist, and a fierce opponent of the first wave of tentative female emancipation then moving across Germany.‡)

How Important and Influential Is This Passage?

Beyond Good and Evil is widely considered to be the work which best introduces and encapsulates many of the themes of Nietzsche's mature philosophy. Like the rest of his writings, it had little influence during his sane lifetime, and from 1930 to 1960 Nietzsche (tarred by his supposed association with fascism) was hardly considered worthy of study at all. However, since revisionist scholarship on his work began in earnest in the 1960s, Nietzsche's philosophical reputation has been in the ascendant (especially on the European continent), and *Beyond Good and Evil* has now come to be recognized as one of the most important books of the nineteenth century. As Walter Kaufmann, a leading Nietzsche translator and commentator since 1950, puts it:

> It is possible to say briefly what makes this book great: the prophetic independence of its spirit; the hundreds of doors it opens for the mind, revealing new vistas, problems, and relationships; and what it contributes to our understanding of much of recent thought and literature and history.§

The particular sections excerpted here, though merely a small part of the book and not in any way a 'summary' of the whole, are especially interesting for the introduction of Nietzsche's notorious distinction between "master" and "slave" moralities, and for some hints as to the connection of this distinction with his concept of a "will to power."

---

*   Friedrich Nietzsche, *Daybreak*, section 101. (This translation is by Maudemarie Clark.)

†   In the end, Nietzsche had to pay for printing *Beyond Good and Evil* himself. He needed to sell 300 copies to cover his costs, but after a year only 114 had been purchased (and 66 given away to reviewers). As Nietzsche mournfully put it, "I—may no longer afford the luxury of print."

‡   On the other, other hand, Nietzsche was one of the minority of University of Basel faculty members who voted in *favor* of allowing women to be admitted to doctoral programs in 1874. Clearly, Nietzsche was a complex character.

§   Walter Kaufmann, "Translator's Preface," in *Beyond Good and Evil* (Random House, 1996), xvii.

FROM *Beyond Good and Evil**
§§259–261

259

Mutually refraining from wounding each other, from violence, and from exploitation, and setting one's will on the same level as others—these can in a certain crude sense become good habits among individuals, if conditions exist for that (namely, a real similarity in the quality of their power and their estimates of value, as well as their belonging together within a single body). However, as soon as people wanted to take this principle further and, where possible, establish it as the *basic principle of society*, it would immediately show itself for what it is, as the willed *denial* of life, as the principle of disintegration and decay. Here we must think through to the fundamentals and push away all sentimental weakness: living itself is *essentially* appropriation from and wounding and overpowering strangers and weaker people, oppression, hardness, imposing one's own forms, annexing, and at the very least, in its mildest actions, exploitation—but why should we always use these precise words, which have from ancient times carried the stamp of a slanderous purpose? Even that body in which, as previously mentioned, individuals deal with each other as equals—and that happens in every healthy aristocracy—must itself, if it is a living body and not dying out, do to other bodies all those things which the individuals in it refrain from doing to each other: it will have to be the living will to power, it will seek to grow, grab things around it, pull to itself, and acquire predominance—not because of some morality or immorality, but because it is *alive* and because living *is* simply the will to power. But in no point is the common consciousness of the European more reluctant to be instructed than here. Nowadays people everywhere, even those in scientific disguises, are raving about the coming conditions of society from which "the exploitative character" is to have disappeared:—to my ears that sounds as if people had promised to invent a life which abstained from all organic functions. The "exploitation" is not part of a depraved or incomplete and primitive society: it belongs to the *essential nature* of what is living, as a basic organic function; it is a consequence of the real will to power, which is simply the will to life.

Assuming that this is something new as a theory—it is, nonetheless, in reality the *fundamental fact* of all history: we should at least be honest with ourselves to this extent!

260

As the result of a stroll though the many more sophisticated and cruder moral systems which up to this point have ruled or still rule on earth, I found certain characteristics routinely return with each other, bound up together, until finally two basic types revealed themselves to me and a fundamental difference sprang up. There is *master morality*, and there is *slave morality*†—to this I immediately add that in all higher and more mixed cultures attempts at a mediation between both moralities make an appearance as well, even more often, a confusion and mutual misunderstanding between the two, in fact, sometimes their close juxtaposition—even in the same person, within a single soul. Distinctions in moral value have arisen either among a ruling group which was happily conscious of its difference with respect to the ruled—or among the ruled, the slaves and dependent people of every degree. In the first case, when it's the masters

---

* *Jenseits von Gut und Böse: Vorspiel einer Philosophie der Zukunft* [*Beyond Good and Evil: Prelude to a Philosophy of the Future*] was first published in Leipzig in 1886. This excerpt is translated by Ian Johnston of Vancouver Island University.

† This distinction was first introduced—though not given these now-famous names—in Nietzsche's *Human, All Too Human* (1878), and plays an important role in Essay One of his next book, *On the Genealogy of Morals* (1887).

who establish the idea of the "good," the elevated and proud conditions of the soul emotionally register as the distinguishing and defining order of rank. The noble man separates his own nature from that of people in whom the opposite of such exalted and proud states expresses itself. He despises them. We should notice at once that in this first kind of morality the opposites "good" and "bad" mean no more than "noble" and "despicable"—the opposition between "good" and "evil" has another origin. The despised one is the coward, the anxious, the small, the man who thinks about narrow utility, also the suspicious man with his inhibited look, the self-abasing man, the species of human dogs who allow themselves to be mistreated, the begging flatterer, and, above all, the liar:—it is a basic belief of all aristocrats that the common folk are liars. "We tellers of the truth"—that's what the nobility called itself in ancient Greece. It's evident that distinctions of moral worth everywhere were first applied to *men* and then later, by extension, were established for *actions*; hence, it is a serious mistake when historians of morality take as a starting point questions like "Why was the compassionate action praised?" The noble kind of man experiences *himself* as a person who determines value and who does not need other people's approval. He makes the judgment "What is harmful to me is harmful in itself." He understands himself as something which in general first confers honour on things, as something which *creates values*. Whatever he recognizes in himself he honours. Such a morality is self-glorification. In the foreground stands the feeling of fullness, the power which wants to overflow, the happiness of high tension, the consciousness of riches which wants to give presents and provide:—the noble man also helps the unfortunate, however not, or hardly ever, from pity, but more in response to an impulse which the excess of power produces. The noble person honours the powerful man in himself and also the man who has power over himself, who understands how to speak and how to keep silent, who takes delight in dealing with himself severely

and toughly, and who respects, above all, severity and toughness. "Wotan* set a hard heart in my breast," it says in an old Scandinavian saga: that's poetry emerging from the soul of a proud Viking—and justifiably so. A man of this sort is simply proud of the fact that he has *not* been made for pity. That's why the hero of the saga adds a warning, "In a man whose heart is not hard when he is still young it will never become hard." Noble and brave men who think this way are furthest removed from that morality which sees the badge of morality specifically in pity or in actions for others or in *désintéressement*.† The belief in oneself, pride in oneself, a fundamental hostility and irony against "selflessness" belong to noble morality, just as much as an easy contempt and caution before feelings of pity and the "warm heart."

Powerful men are the ones who *understand* how to honour; that is their art, their realm of invention. The profound reverence for age and for ancestral tradition—all justice stands on this double reverence—the belief and the prejudice favouring forefathers and working against newcomers are typical in the morality of the powerful, and when, by contrast, the men of "modern ideas" believe almost instinctively in "progress" and the "future" and increasingly lack any respect for age, then in that attitude the ignoble origin of these "ideas" already reveals itself well enough. However, a morality of the rulers is most alien and embarrassing to present taste because of the severity of its basic principle that man has duties only with respect to those like him, that man should act towards those beings of lower rank, towards everything foreign, at his own discretion, or "as his heart dictates," and, in any case, "beyond good and evil."‡ Here pity and things like that may belong. The capacity for and obligation to a long gratitude and a long revenge—both only within the circle of one's peers—the sophistication in paying back again, the refined idea in friendship, a certain necessity to have enemies (as, so to speak, drainage ditches for the feelings of envy, quarrelsomeness, and high spirits—basically in order to be capable of being

---

*   Also called Odin, Wotan was the supreme god of Scandinavian and German mythology: creator of the world and god of war, wisdom, poetry, magic, and the dead. He was usually depicted as a one-eyed, wise old man, accompanied by two great ravens. Wednesday—"Wotan's day"—is named for him.

†   French: "disinterestedness" (i.e., lack of bias).

‡   This phrase, in German, has religious as well as moral overtones. *Jenseits* not only means "beyond" but also refers to the afterlife.

a good *friend*): all those are typical characteristics of a noble morality, which, as indicated, is not the morality of "modern ideas" and which is thus nowadays difficult to sympathize with, as well as difficult to dig up and expose.

Things are different with the second type of moral system, *slave morality*. Suppose the oppressed, depressed, suffering and unfree people, those ignorant of themselves and tired out, suppose they moralize: what will be the common feature of their moral estimates of value? Probably a pessimistic suspicion directed at the entire human situation will express itself, perhaps a condemnation of man, along with his situation. The gaze of a slave is not well disposed towards the virtues of the powerful; he possesses scepticism and mistrust; he has a *subtlety* of mistrust of everything "good" that is honoured in those virtues—he would like to persuade himself that even happiness is not genuine there. By contrast, those characteristics will be pulled forward and flooded with light which serve to mitigate existence for those who suffer: here respect is given to pity, to the obliging hand ready to help, to the warm heart, to patience, diligence, humility, and friendliness—for these are here the most useful characteristics and almost the only means to endure the pressure of existence. Slave morality is essentially a morality of utility.* Here is the focus for the origin of that famous opposition of "good" and "evil":—people sense power and danger within evil, a certain terror, subtlety, and strength that does not permit contempt to spring up. According to slave morality, the "evil" man thus inspires fear; according to master morality, it is precisely the "good" man who inspires and desires to inspire fear, while the "bad" man is felt as despicable. This opposition reaches its peak when, in accordance with the consequences of slave morality, finally a trace of disregard is also attached to the "good" of this morality—it may be light and benevolent—because within the

way of thinking of the slave the good person must definitely be the *harmless* person: he is good natured, easy to deceive, perhaps a bit stupid, *un bonhomme.*† Wherever slave morality gains predominance the language reveals a tendency to bring the words "good" and "stupid" into closer proximity.

A final basic difference: the longing *for freedom*, the instinct for happiness, and the refinements of the feeling for freedom belong just as necessarily to slave morality and morals as art and enthusiasm in reverence and in devotion are the regular symptoms of an aristocratic way of thinking and valuing.

From this we can without further ado understand why love as *passion*—which is our European specialty—must clearly have a noble origin: as is well known, its invention belongs to the Provencal knightly poets, those splendidly inventive men of the *"gay saber"*‡ to whom Europe owes so much—almost its very self.

261

Vanity is among the things that are perhaps hardest for a noble man to understand: he will be tempted even to deny its existence where another kind of man thinks he has grasped it with both hands. For him the problem is imagining to himself beings who seek to elicit a good opinion of themselves which they themselves do not possess—and which, as a result, they also have not "earned"—people who, nonetheless, themselves later *believe* in this good opinion. Half of this seems to the noble man so tasteless and disrespectful of oneself and the other half so unreasonably baroque,§ that he would be happy to understand vanity as an exception and has doubts about it in most cases when people talk of it. For example, he'll say: "I can make a mistake about my own value and yet on the other hand still demand that my value, precisely as I determine it, is recognized by others—that, however,

---

* Unsurprisingly, Nietzsche referred to John Stuart Mill as "that blockhead" (*The Genealogy of Morals*).
† French: a simple, good man.
‡ "Gay science" or "joyful art" in the dialect of Provence, in south-eastern France. One of Nietzsche's earlier books is called *The Gay Science* (1882). The phrase was coined in the early fourteenth century to refer to the art of the troubadours: lyric poets and musicians—mostly noblemen, and sometimes even kings—who flourished in southern France, northern Italy, and eastern Spain from the end of the eleventh to the close of the thirteenth century. Their songs typically dealt with themes of chivalry and courtly love.
§ Grotesque, misshapen ornamentation.

is not vanity (but arrogance or, in the more frequent cases, something called "humility" and "modesty"). Or again, "For many reasons I can take pleasure in the good opinion of others, perhaps because I honour and love them and enjoy all of their pleasures, perhaps also because their good opinion underscores and strengthens the faith I have in my own good opinion of myself, or perhaps because the good opinion of others, even in cases where I do not share it, is still useful to me or promises to be useful—but all that is not vanity." The noble man must first compel himself, particularly with the help of history, to see that since time immemorial, in all the levels of people dependent in some way or other, the common man *was* only what people *thought of him*:—not being at all accustomed to set values himself, he measured even himself by no value other than by how his masters assessed him (that is the essential *right of masters*, to create values). We should understand that, as the consequence of an immense atavism,* the common man even today still always *waits* first for an opinion about himself and then instinctively submits himself to it: however, that is by no means merely to a "good" opinion, but also to a bad and unreasonable one (think, for example, of the greatest part of the self-assessment and self-devaluing which devout women learn from their father confessors and the devout Christian in general

learns from his church). Now, in accordance with the slow arrival of the democratic order of things (and its cause, the blood mixing between masters and slaves), the originally noble and rare impulse to ascribe to oneself a value on one's own and "to think well" of oneself will really become more and more encouraged and widespread. But in every moment it has working against it an older, more extensive, and more deeply incorporated tendency—and where the phenomenon of "vanity" is concerned, this older tendency becomes master over the more recent one. The vain person takes pleasure in *every* good opinion which he hears about himself (quite apart from all considerations of its utility and equally apart from its truth or falsity), just as he suffers from every bad opinion. For he submits to both; he *feels* himself subjected to them on the basis of that oldest of instincts for submission which breaks out in him.

It is "the slave" in the blood of the vain man, a trace of the slave's roguishness—and how much of the "slave" still remains nowadays in woman, for example!—that tries to *tempt* him into good opinions of himself; in the same way it's the slave who later prostrates himself immediately in front of these opinions, as if he had not summoned them up.

To state the matter once again: vanity is an atavism. ■

Suggestions for Critical Reflection

1. Why could "good manners" never be an adequate basic principle of society? What does Nietzsche mean when he says that this would be to "deny life"? How plausible do you find his reasons for saying so?

2. Nietzsche distinguishes between two possible understandings of the difference between good and bad: "noble" vs. "despicable," and "good" vs. "evil." How important is this difference? Are they both really *moral* distinctions, or is one of them dealing with a different sort of value altogether?

If they are different kinds of value, does this hurt Nietzsche's argument or help it?

3. "It is obvious that moral value distinctions everywhere are first attributed to *people* and only later and in a derivative fashion applied to *actions*." Is it? If this claim *is* true, then what does it show about the nature of morality?

4. How *historically* and *psychologically* plausible do you find Nietzsche's description of the difference between the moral outlooks of the powerful and their 'slaves'? If it is plausible as a *description* of moral attitudes, what implications should this have

---

* A throwback: a trait which resembles those possessed by remote ancestors, and which has returned after being absent for many generations. (The word comes from the Latin *atavus*, one's great-grandfather's grandfather.)

(if any) for the moral views we *ought* to hold? What implications would Nietzsche think it has?

5. "Within a slave mentality a good person must in any event be *harmless*." What do you think of this claim?

6. What do Nietzsche's claims about the nature of vanity reveal about his views on the way we, as individuals, come to *endorse* or *reject* particular values? Are these views plausible?

7. What do you think Nietzsche's view of democracy is? What reasons might he have for his views?

8. What is your judgment of Nietzsche's style: do you think that it is 'philosophical' in the right way? For example, is it a productive way of pursuing the truth (if that is indeed the proper goal of philosophy), or is it in the end (merely?) a sophisticated kind of creative writing?

VIRGINIA HELD

Feminist Transformations of Moral Theory

Who Is Virginia Held?

Virginia P. Held (b. 1929) is an influential ethicist and social-political philosopher, known especially as one of the central figures in the development of the "ethics of care," along with Carol Gilligan, Sara Ruddick, Nel Noddings, and others. Before becoming a professional philosopher she was a reporter, working for *The Reporter* magazine and other publications. She obtained her PhD from Columbia University in 1968, going on to spend much of her career teaching at Hunter College in New York. A past President of the Eastern Division of the American Philosophical Society, she is now a Distinguished Professor Emerita in the philosophy program of the Graduate Center at the City University of New York. She is the author of several books, including *Feminist Morality: Transforming Culture, Society and Politics* (1993), *Rights and Goods: Justifying Social Action* (1984), and *The Ethics of Care: Personal, Political, and Global* (2006)—and many articles on social and political philosophy, ethics, and feminist philosophy.

What Is the Structure of This Reading?

Held begins her article by arguing that, historically, all ethical theories have been built upon assumptions biased in favor of men and against women. She illustrates this by exploring the implications of the historically important dichotomies of reason vs. emotion and public vs. private, and by discussing the history of our concept of the self or personhood. She then goes on, in the next three sections, to discuss feminist approaches to the transformation of each of these three conceptual areas. In particular, she emphasizes a feminist re-valuing of *emotional responses* in ethics, the importance of *mothering* (which breaks through the public-private distinction), and the notion of the self as being importantly constituted by its *relations* to others.

Some Useful Background Information

The ethics of care, or care ethics, is a modern approach to moral theory that competes with traditional deontological/Kantian and consequentialist/utilitarian ethics. Ethicists working in this mode emphasize the basic moral significance of caring personal relationships, such as those between parents and children, between patients and their care-givers, and between humans and animals. A key moral issue, according to care ethics, is the maintenance of these networks of relationships in such a way that the well-being of each party, including the dependent and the vulnerable, is preserved and fostered; and an important critique of other types of ethical theory is that they are blind to these relationships, and, even worse, by placing an exclusive emphasis on justice and impartiality, that they are positively harmful to them. Care ethicists tend to focus on "actual experience, with an emphasis on reason and emotion, literal rather than hypothetical persons, embodiment, actual dialogue, and contextual, lived methodologies."* Similarly, rather than seeking universalizable moral rules, care ethics somewhat resembles virtue theory (and several non-western ethical traditions) in defining care as more of a lived practice. Two foundational texts for the ethics of care are Carol Gilligan's *In A Different Voice* (Harvard University Press, 1982) and Nel Noddings's *Caring* (University of California Press, 1982).

---

* "Care Ethics" by Maureen Sander-Staudt, in the *Internet Encyclopedia of Philosophy*, 24 October 2018.

Feminist Transformations of Moral Theory[*]

The history of philosophy, including the history of ethics, has been constructed from male points of view, and has been built on assumptions and concepts that are by no means gender-neutral.[1] Feminists characteristically begin with different concerns and give different emphases to the issues we consider than do nonfeminist approaches. And, as Lorraine Code expresses it, "starting points and focal points shape the impact of theoretical discussion."[2] Within philosophy, feminists often start with, and focus on, quite different issues than those found in standard philosophy and ethics, however "standard" is understood. Far from providing mere additional insights which can be incorporated into traditional theory, feminist explorations often require radical transformations of existing fields of inquiry and theory.[3] From a feminist point of view, moral theory along with almost all theory will have to be transformed to take adequate account of the experience of women.

I shall in this paper begin with a brief examination of how various fundamental aspects of the history of ethics have not been gender-neutral. And I shall discuss three issues where feminist rethinking is transforming moral concepts and theories.

The History of Ethics

Consider the ideals embodied in the phrase "the man of reason." As Genevieve Lloyd has told the story, what has been taken to characterize the man of reason may have changed from historical period to historical period, but in each, the character ideal of the man of reason has been constructed in conjunction with a rejection of whatever has been taken to be characteristic of the feminine. "Rationality," Lloyd writes, "has been conceived as transcendence of the 'feminine,' and

the 'feminine' itself has been partly constituted by its occurrence within this structure."[4]

This has of course fundamentally affected the history of philosophy and of ethics. The split between reason and emotion is one of the most familiar of philosophical conceptions. And the advocacy of reason "controlling" unruly emotion, of rationality guiding responsible human action against the blindness of passion, has a long and highly influential history, almost as familiar to non-philosophers as to philosophers. We should certainly now be alert to the ways in which reason has been associated with male endeavor, emotion with female weakness, and the ways in which this is of course not an accidental association. As Lloyd writes, "From the beginnings of philosophical thought, femaleness was symbolically associated with what Reason supposedly left behind—the dark powers of the earth goddesses, immersion in unknown forces associated with mysterious female powers. The early Greeks saw women's capacity to conceive as connecting them with the fertility of Nature. As Plato later expressed the thought, women 'imitate the earth.'"[5]

Reason, in asserting its claims and winning its status in human history, was thought to have to conquer the female forces of Unreason. Reason and clarity of thought were early associated with maleness, and as Lloyd notes, "what had to be shed in developing culturally prized rationality was, from the start, symbolically associated with femaleness."[6] In later Greek philosophical thought, the form/matter distinction was articulated,[†] and with a similar hierarchical and gendered association. Maleness was aligned with active, determinate, and defining form; femaleness with mere passive, indeterminate, and inferior matter. Plato, in the *Timaeus*,[‡] compared the defining aspect of form with the father, and indefinite matter with the

[*]   This article was originally published in *Philosophy and Phenomenological Research* 50 (Supplement Autumn 1990): 321–44.

[†]   For Plato and Aristotle, the matter of something (roughly) is the stuff it is made of, while its form is the organization, shape, or pattern which gives that thing its particular nature. A simple example would be a clay bowl, where the matter—a lump of clay—has been given the form of a bowl by the potter.

[‡]   A dialogue by Plato (427–347 BCE), which describes how a divine (though not omnipotent) craftsman transformed the chaotic materials of the universe into an ordered and harmonious cosmos by consulting the unchanging Forms and using them as his template for the construction of (rather shoddily inadequate and fluctuating) earthly images of those

mother; Aristotle also compared the form/matter distinction with the male/female distinction. To quote Lloyd again, "This comparison ... meant that the very nature of knowledge was implicitly associated with the extrusion* of what was symbolically associated with the feminine."[7]

The associations, between Reason, form, knowledge, and maleness, have persisted in various guises, and have permeated what has been thought to be moral knowledge as well as what has been thought to be scientific knowledge, and what has been thought to be the practice of morality. The associations between the philosophical concepts and gender cannot be merely dropped, and the concepts retained regardless of gender, because gender has been built into them in such a way that without it, they will have to be different concepts. As feminists repeatedly show, if the concept of "human" were built on what we think about "woman" rather than what we think about "man," it would be a very different concept. Ethics, thus, has not been a search for universal, or truly human guidance, but a gender-biased enterprise.

Other distinctions and associations have supplemented and reinforced the identification of reason with maleness, and of the irrational with the female; on this and other grounds "man" has been associated with the human, "woman" with the natural. Prominent among distinctions reinforcing the latter view has been that between the public and the private, because of the way they have been interpreted. Again, these provide as familiar and entrenched a framework as do reason and emotion, and they have been as influential for non-philosophers as for philosophers. It has been supposed that in the public realm, man transcends his animal nature and creates human history. As citizen, he creates government and law; as warrior, he protects society by his willingness to risk death; and as artist or philosopher, he overcomes his human mortality. Here, in the public realm, morality should guide human decision. In the household, in contrast, it has been supposed that women merely "reproduce" life as natural, biological matter. Within the household, the "natural" needs of man for food and shelter are served, and new instances of the biological creature that man is are brought into being. But what is distinctively human, and what transcends any given level of development to create human progress, are thought to occur elsewhere.

This contrast was made highly explicit in Aristotle's conceptions of polis[†] and household; it has continued to affect the basic assumptions of a remarkably broad swath of thought ever since. In ancient Athens, women were confined to the household; the public sphere was literally a male domain. In more recent history, though women have been permitted to venture into public space, the associations of the public, historically male sphere with the distinctively human, and of the household, historically a female sphere, with the merely natural and repetitious, have persisted. These associations have deeply affected moral theory, which has often supposed the transcendent, public domain to be relevant to the foundations of morality in ways that the natural behavior of women in the household could not be. To take some recent and representative examples, David Heyd, in his discussion of supererogation,[‡] dismisses a mother's sacrifice for her child as an example of the supererogatory because it belongs, in his view, to "the sphere of natural relationships and instinctive feelings (which lie outside morality)."[8] J.O. Urmson had earlier taken a similar position. In his discussion of supererogation, Urmson said, "Let us be clear that we are not now considering cases of natural affection, such as the sacrifice made by a mother for her child; such cases may be said with some justice not to fall under the concept of morality...."[9] And in a

---

paradigms. See the Plato reading in this chapter for more information on the Forms.

*   Violent or rigorous expulsion.

†   The *polis* is the ancient Greek city-state. See the Aristotle readings in this volume for more on his interwoven views on politics and society.

‡   Acting in a way which is not strictly required by moral duty but which goes beyond it, as in cases of exceptional generosity or heroism (from the Latin, "beyond what is asked"). The key idea is that a supererogatory act is morally good, but to fail to perform it would not be morally bad. Such acts are of interest partly because several major moral theories—such as utilitarianism, Kantianism, and some versions of Protestantism—appear to be unable to recognize the existence of supererogation.

recent article called "Distrusting Economics," Alan Ryan argues persuasively about the questionableness of economics and other branches of the social sciences built on the assumption that human beings are rational, self-interested calculators; he discusses various examples of non-self-interested behavior, such as of men in wartime, which show the assumption to be false, but nowhere in the article is there any mention of the activity of mothering, which would seem to be a fertile locus for doubts about the usual picture of rational man.[10] Although Ryan does not provide the kind of explicit reason offered by Heyd and Urmson for omitting the context of mothering from consideration as relevant to his discussion, it is difficult to understand the omission without a comparable assumption being implicit here, as it so often is elsewhere. Without feminist insistence on the relevance for morality of the experience in mothering, this context is largely ignored by moral theorists. And yet, from a gender-neutral point of view, how can this vast and fundamental domain of human experience possibly be imagined to lie "outside morality"?

The result of the public/private distinction, as usually formulated, has been to privilege the points of view of men in the public domains of state and law, and later in the marketplace, and to discount the experience of women. Mothering has been conceptualized as a primarily biological activity, even when performed by humans, and virtually no moral theory in the history of ethics has taken mothering, as experienced by women, seriously as a source of moral insight, until feminists in recent years have begun to.[11] Women have been seen as emotional rather than as rational beings, and thus as incapable of full moral personhood. Women's behavior has been interpreted as either "natural" and driven by instinct, and thus as irrelevant to morality and to the construction of moral principles, or it has been interpreted as, at best, in need of instruction and supervision by males better able to know what morality requires and better able to live up to its demands.

The Hobbesian* conception of reason is very different from the Platonic or Aristotelian conceptions before it, and from the conceptions of Rousseau or Kant or Hegel later; all have in common that they ignore and disparage the experience and reality of women. Consider Hobbes' account of man in the state of nature contracting with other men to establish society. These men hypothetically come into existence fully formed and independent of one another, and decide on entering or staying outside of civil society. As Christine Di Stefano writes, "What we find in Hobbes's account of human nature and political order is a vital concern with the survival of a self conceived in masculine terms.... This masculine dimension of Hobbes's atomistic egoism is powerfully underscored in his state of nature, which is effectively built on the foundation of denied maternity."[12] In *The Citizen*, where Hobbes gave his first systematic exposition of the state of nature, he asks us to "consider men as if but even now sprung out of the earth, and suddenly, like mushrooms, come to full maturity, without all kind of engagement with each other."[13] As Di Stefano says, it is a most incredible and problematic feature of Hobbes's state of nature that the men in it "are not born of, much less nurtured by, women, or anyone else."[14] To abstract from the complex web of human reality an abstract man for rational perusal, Hobbes has, Di Stefano continues, "expunged human reproduction and early nurturance, two of the most basic and typically female-identified features of distinctively human life, from his account of basic human nature. Such a strategy ensures that he can present a thoroughly atomistic subject...."[15] From the point of view of women's experience, such a subject or self is unbelievable and misleading, even as a theoretical construct. The Leviathan,† Di Stefano writes, "is effectively comprised of a body politic of orphans who have reared themselves, whose desires are situated within and reflect nothing but independently generated movement.... These essential elements are natural human beings conceived along masculine lines."[16]

---

* That found in the philosophy of Thomas Hobbes (1588–1679). See the notes to the selection from Hobbes in the Justice section of this volume.

† Hobbes's term for the state, in his book *Leviathan* (1651). A leviathan is something monstrously large and powerful—from the name of a sea monster in the Old Testament—and the term was in part supposed to reflect the state's absolute power over its citizens.

Rousseau, and Kant, and Hegel, paid homage to the emotional power, the aesthetic sensibility, and the familial concerns, respectively, of women. But since in their views morality must be based on rational principle, and women were incapable of full rationality, or a degree or kind of rationality comparable to that of men, women were deemed, in the view of these moralists, to be inherently wanting in morality. For Rousseau,* women must be trained from childhood to submit to the will of men lest their sexual power lead both men and women to disaster. For Kant,† women were thought incapable of achieving full moral personhood, and women lose all charm if they try to behave like men by engaging in rational pursuits. For Hegel,‡ women's moral concern for their families could be admirable in its proper place, but is a threat to the more universal aims to which men, as members of the state, should aspire.[17]

These images, of the feminine as what must be overcome if knowledge and morality are to be achieved, of female experience as naturally irrelevant to morality, and of women as inherently deficient moral creatures, are built into the history of ethics. Feminists examine these images, and see that they are not the incidental or merely idiosyncratic suppositions of a few philosophers whose views on many topics depart far from the ordinary anyway. Such views are the nearly uniform reflection in philosophical and ethical theory of patriarchal attitudes pervasive throughout human history. Or they are exaggerations even of ordinary male experience, which exaggerations then reinforce rather than temper other patriarchal conceptions and institutions. They distort the actual experience and aspirations of many men as well as of women. Annette Baier recently speculated about why it is that moral philosophy has so seriously overlooked the trust between human beings that in her view is an utterly central aspect of moral life. She noted that "the great moral theorists in our tradition not only are all men, they are mostly men who had minimal adult dealings with (and so were then minimally influenced by) women."[18] They were

for the most part "clerics, misogynists, and puritan bachelors," and thus it is not surprising that they focus their philosophical attention "so single-mindedly on cool, distanced relations between more or less free and equal adult strangers...."[19]

As feminists, we deplore the patriarchal attitudes that so much of philosophy and moral theory reflect. But we recognize that the problem is more serious even than changing those attitudes. For moral theory as so far developed is incapable of correcting itself without an almost total transformation. It cannot simply absorb the gender that has been "left behind," even if both genders would want it to. To continue to build morality on rational principles opposed to the emotions and to include women among the rational will leave no one to reflect the promptings of the heart, which promptings can be moral rather than merely instinctive. To simply bring women into the public and male domain of the polis will leave no one to speak for the household. Its values have been hitherto unrecognized, but they are often moral values. Or to continue to seek contractual restraints on the pursuits of self-interest by atomistic individuals, and to have women join men in devotion to these pursuits, will leave no one involved in the nurturance of children and cultivation of social relations, which nurturance and cultivation can be of greatest moral import.

There are very good reasons for women not to want simply to be accorded entry as equals into the enterprise of morality as so far developed. In a recent survey of types of feminist moral theory, Kathryn Morgan notes that "many women who engage in philosophical reflection are acutely aware of the masculine nature of the profession and tradition, and feel their own moral concerns as women silenced or trivialized in virtually all the official settings that define the practice."[20] Women should clearly not agree, as the price of admission to the masculine realm of traditional morality, to abandon our own moral concerns as women.

And so we are groping to shape new moral theory. Understandably, we do not yet have fully worked out

---

feminist moral theories to offer. But we can suggest some directions our project of developing such theories is taking. As Kathryn Morgan points out, there is not likely to be a "star" feminist moral theorist on the order of a Rawls or Nozick:* "There will be no individual singled out for two reasons. One reason is that vital moral and theoretical conversations are taking place on a large dialectical scale as the feminist community struggles to develop a feminist ethic. The second reason is that this community of feminist theoreticians is calling into question the very model of the individualized autonomous self presupposed by a star-centered male-dominated tradition.... We experience it as a common labour, a common task."[21]

The dialogues that are enabling feminist approaches to moral theory to develop are proceeding. As Alison Jaggar makes clear in her useful overview of them, there is no unitary view of ethics that can be identified as "feminist ethics." Feminist approaches to ethics share a commitment to "rethinking ethics with a view to correcting whatever forms of male bias it may contain."[22] While those who develop these approaches are "united by a shared project, they diverge widely in their views as to how this project is to be accomplished."[23]

Not all feminists, by any means, agree that there are distinctive feminist virtues or values. Some are especially skeptical of the attempt to give positive value to such traditional "feminine virtues" as a willingness to nurture, or an affinity with caring, or reluctance to seek independence. They see this approach as playing into the hands of those who would confine women to traditional roles.[24] Other feminists are skeptical of all claims about women as such, emphasizing that women are divided by class and race and sexual orientation in ways that make any conclusions drawn from "women's experience" dubious.[25]

Still, it is possible, I think, to discern various important focal points evident in current feminist attempts to transform ethics into a theoretical and practical activity that could be acceptable from a feminist point of view. In the glimpse I have presented of

bias in the history of ethics, I focused on what, from a feminist point of view, are three of its most questionable aspects: 1) the split between reason and emotion and the devaluation of emotion; 2) the public/private distinction and the relegation of the private to the natural; and 3) the concept of the self as constructed from a male point of view. In the remainder of this article, I shall consider further how some feminists are exploring these topics. We are showing how their previous treatment has been distorted, and we are trying to reenvision the realities and recommendations with which these aspects of moral theorizing do and should try to deal.

I. Reason and Emotion

In the area of moral theory in the modern era, the priority accorded to reason has taken two major forms. A) On the one hand has been the Kantian, or Kantian-inspired search for very general, abstract, deontological,† universal moral principles by which rational beings should be guided. Kant's Categorical Imperative is a foremost example: it suggests that all moral problems can be handled by applying an impartial, pure, rational principle to particular cases. It requires that we try to see what the general features of the problem before us are, and that we apply an abstract principle, or rules derivable from it, to this problem. On this view, this procedure should be adequate for all moral decisions. We should thus be able to act as reason recommends, and resist yielding to emotional inclinations and desires in conflict with our rational wills.

B) On the other hand, the priority accorded to reason in the modern era has taken a Utilitarian form. The Utilitarian approach, reflected in rational choice theory, recognizes that persons have desires and interests, and suggests rules of rational choice for maximizing the satisfaction of these. While some philosophers in this tradition espouse egoism,‡ especially of an intelligent and long-term kind, many do not. They begin, however, with assumptions that what are

---

* John Rawls, Robert Nozick: see the Justice section of this volume for information on these contemporary philosophers.

† Based on the notion of a duty or a right (rather than on the value of some kind of state of affairs or type of character).

‡ That one either is, or ought to be, exclusively motivated by self-interest.

morally relevant are gains and losses of utility to the-oretically isolatable individuals, and that the outcome at which morality should aim is the maximization of the utility of individuals. Rational calculation about such an outcome will, in this view, provide moral rec-ommendations to guide all our choices. As with the Kantian approach, the Utilitarian approach relies on abstract general principles or rules to be applied to particular cases. And it holds that although emotion is, in fact, the source of our desires for certain objectives, the task of morality should be to instruct us on how to pursue those objectives most rationally. Emotional attitudes toward moral issues themselves interfere with rationality and should be disregarded. Among the questions Utilitarians can ask can be questions about which emotions to cultivate, and which desires to try to change, but these questions are to be handled in the terms of rational calculation, not of what our feelings suggest.

Although the conceptions of what the judgments of morality should be based on, and of how reason should guide moral decision, are different in Kantian and in Utilitarian approaches, both share a reliance on a highly abstract, universal principle as the appropri-ate source of moral guidance, and both share the view that moral problems are to be solved by the applica-tion of such an abstract principle to particular cases. Both share an admiration for the rules of reason to be appealed to in moral contexts, and both denigrate emotional responses to moral issues.

Many feminist philosophers have questioned whether the reliance on abstract rules, rather than the adoption of more context-respectful approaches, can possibly be adequate for dealing with moral prob-lems, especially as women experience them.[26] Though Kantians may hold that complex rules can be elabo-rated for specific contexts, there is nevertheless an assumption in this approach that the more abstract the reasoning applied to a moral problem, the more satisfactory. And Utilitarians suppose that one highly abstract principle, The Principle of Utility, can be applied to every moral problem no matter what the context.

A genuinely universal or gender-neutral moral theory would be one which would take account of the experience and concerns of women as fully as it would take account of the experience and concerns of men. When we focus on the experience of women,

however, we seem to be able to see a set of moral con-cerns becoming salient that differs from those of tradi-tional or standard moral theory. Women's experience of moral problems seems to lead us to be especially concerned with actual relationships between embod-ied persons, and with what these relationships seem to require. Women are often inclined to attend to rather than to dismiss the particularities of the context in which a moral problem arises. And we often pay attention to feelings of empathy and caring to suggest what we ought to do rather than relying as fully as possible on abstract rules of reason.

Margaret Walker, for instance, contrasts fem-inist moral "understanding" with traditional moral "knowledge." She sees the components of the former as involving "attention, contextual and narrative appre-ciation, and communication in the event of moral deliberation."[27] This alternative moral epistemology holds that "the adequacy of moral understanding decreases as its form approaches generality through abstraction."[28]

The work of psychologists such as Carol Gilligan and others has led to a clarification of what may be thought of as tendencies among women to approach moral issues differently. Rather than interpreting moral problems in terms of what could be handled by applying abstract rules of justice to particular cases, many of the women studied by Gilligan tended to be more concerned with preserving actual human rela-tionships, and with expressing care for those for whom they felt responsible. Their moral reasoning was typ-ically more embedded in a context of particular oth-ers than was the reasoning of a comparable group of men.[29] One should not equate tendencies women in fact display with feminist views, since the former may well be the result of the sexist, oppressive conditions in which women's lives have been lived. But many femi-nists see our own consciously considered experience as lending confirmation to the view that what has come to be called "an ethic of care" needs to be developed. Some think it should supercede "the ethic of justice" of traditional or standard moral theory. Others think it should be integrated with the ethic of justice and rules.

In any case, feminist philosophers are in the pro-cess of reevaluating the place of emotion in morality in at least two respects. First, many think morality requires the development of the moral emotions, in contrast to moral theories emphasizing the primacy of reason. As Annette Baier notes, the rationalism typical of traditional moral theory will be challenged when we pay attention to the role of parent. "It might be important," she writes, "for father figures to have rational control over their violent urges to beat to death the children whose screams enrage them, but more than control of such nasty passions seems needed in the mother or primary parent, or parent-substitute, by most psychological theories. They need to love their children, not just to control their irritation."[30] So the emphasis in many traditional theories on rational control over the emotions, "rather than on cultivating desirable forms of emotion,"[31] is challenged by feminist approaches to ethics.

Secondly, emotion will be respected rather than dismissed by many feminist moral philosophers in the process of gaining moral understanding. The experience and practice out of which feminist moral theory can be expected to be developed will include embodied feeling as well as thought. In a recent overview of a vast amount of writing, Kathryn Morgan states that "feminist theorists begin ethical theorizing with embodied, gendered subjects who have particular histories, particular communities, particular allegiances, and particular visions of human flourishing. The starting point involves valorizing what has frequently been most mistrusted and despised in the western philosophical tradition...."[32] Among the elements being reevaluated are feminine emotions. The "care" of the alternative feminist approach to morality appreciates rather than rejects emotion. The caring relationships important to feminist morality cannot be understood in terms of abstract rules or moral reasoning. And the "weighing" so often needed between the conflicting claims of some relationships and others cannot be settled by deduction or rational calculation. A feminist ethic will not just acknowledge emotion, as do Utilitarians, as giving us the objectives toward which moral rationality can direct us. It will embrace emotion as providing at least a partial basis for morality itself, and for moral understanding.

Annette Baier stresses the centrality of trust for an adequate morality.[33] Achieving and maintaining trusting, caring relationships is quite different from acting in accord with rational principles, or satisfying the individual desires of either self or other.

Caring, empathy, feeling with others, being sensitive to each other's feelings, all may be better guides to what morality requires in actual contexts than may abstract rules of reason, or rational calculation, or at least they may be necessary components of an adequate morality.

The fear that a feminist ethic will be a relativistic "situation ethic" is misplaced. Some feelings can be as widely shared as are rational beliefs, and feminists do not see their views as reducible to "just another attitude."[34] In her discussion of the differences between feminist medical ethics and nonfeminist medical ethics, Susan Sherwin gives an example of how feminists reject the mere case by case approach that has come to predominate in nonfeminist medical ethics. The latter also rejects the excessive reliance on abstract rules characteristic of standard ethics, and in this way resembles feminist ethics. But the very focus on cases in isolation from one another deprives this approach from attending to general features in the institutions and practices of medicine that, among other faults, systematically contribute to the oppression of women.[35] The difference of approach can be seen in the treatment of issues in the new reproductive technologies, where feminists consider how the new technologies may further decrease the control of women over reproduction.

This difference might be thought to be one of substance rather than of method, but Sherwin shows the implications for method also. With respect to reproductive technologies one can see especially clearly the deficiencies of the case by case approach: what needs to be considered is not only choice in the purely individualistic interpretation of the case by case approach, but control at a more general level and how it affects the structure of gender in society. Thus, a feminist perspective does not always counsel attention to specific case vs. appeal to general considerations, as some sort of methodological rule. But the general considerations are often not the purely abstract ones of traditional and standard moral theory, they are the general features and judgments to be made about cases in actual (which means, so far, patriarchal) societies. A feminist evaluation of a moral problem should never omit the political elements involved; and it is likely to recognize that political issues cannot be dealt with adequately in purely abstract terms any more than can moral issues.

The liberal tradition in social and moral philosophy argues that in pluralistic society* and even more clearly in a pluralistic world, we cannot agree on our visions of the good life, on what is the best kind of life for humans, but we can hope to agree on the minimal conditions for justice, for coexistence within a framework allowing us to pursue our visions of the good life.[36] Many feminists contend that the commitment to justice needed for agreement *in actual conditions* on even minimal requirements of justice is as likely to demand relational feelings as a rational recognition of abstract principles. Human beings can and do care, and are capable of caring far more than at present, about the sufferings of children quite distant from them, about the prospects for future generations, and about the well-being of the globe. The liberal tradition's mutually disinterested rational individualists would seem unlikely to care enough to take the actions needed to achieve moral decency at a global level, or environmental sanity for decades hence, as they would seem unable to represent caring relationships within the family and among friends. As Annette Baier puts it, "A moral theory, it can plausibly be claimed, cannot regard concern for new and future persons as an optional charity left for those with a taste for it. If the morality the theory endorses is to sustain itself, it must provide for its own continuers, not just take out a loan on a carefully encouraged maternal instinct or on the enthusiasm of a self-selected group of environmentalists, who make it their business or hobby to be concerned with what we are doing to mother earth."[37]

The possibilities as well as the problems (and we are well aware of some of them) in a feminist reenvisioning of emotion and reason need to be further developed, but we can already see that the views of nonfeminist moral theory are unsatisfactory.

II. *The Public and the Private*

The second questionable aspect of the history of ethics on which I focused was its conception of the distinction between the public and the private. As with the split between reason and emotion, feminists are showing how gender-bias has distorted previous conceptions of these spheres, and we are trying to offer more appropriate understandings of "private" morality and "public" life.

Part of what feminists have criticized has been the way the distinction has been accompanied by a supposition that what occurs in the household occurs as if on an island beyond politics, whereas the personal is highly affected by the political power beyond, from legislation about abortion to the greater earning power of men, to the interconnected division of labor by gender both within and beyond the household, to the lack of adequate social protection for women against domestic violence.[38] Of course we recognize that the family is not identical to the state, and we need concepts for thinking about the private or personal, and the public or political. But they will have to be very different from the traditional concepts.

Feminists have also criticized deeper assumptions about what is distinctively human and what is "natural" in the public and private aspects of human life, and what is meant by "natural" in connection with women.[39] Consider the associations that have traditionally been built up: the public realm is seen as the distinctively human realm in which man transcends his animal nature, while the private realm of the household is seen as the natural region in which women merely reproduce the species.[40] These associations are extraordinarily pervasive in standard concepts and theories, in art and thought and cultural ideals, and especially in politics.

Dominant patterns of thought have seen women as primarily mothers, and mothering as the performance of a primarily biological function. Then it has been supposed that while engaging in political life is a specifically human activity, women are engaged in an activity which is not specifically human. Women accordingly have been thought to be closer to nature than men,[41] to be enmeshed in a biological function involving processes more like those in which other animals are involved than like the rational discussion of the citizen in the polis, or the glorious battles of noble soldiers, or the trading and rational contracting

---

* A society that values (or at least tolerates) a range of different, and even mutually incompatible, views among its members of what constitutes a "good life." For example, toleration of different religions and sexual orientations is a form of pluralism.

of "economic man." The total or relative exclusion of women from the domain of public life has then been seen as either inevitable or appropriate.

The view that women are more determined by biology than are men is still extraordinarily prevalent. It is as questionable from a feminist perspective as many other traditional misinterpretations of women's experience. Human mothering is an extremely different activity from the mothering engaged in by other animals. The work and speech of men is recognized as very different from what might be thought of as the "work" and "speech" of other animals. Human mothering is fully as different from animal mothering. Of course all human beings are animal as well as human. But to whatever extent it is appropriate to recognize a difference between "man" and other animals, so would it be appropriate to recognize a comparable difference between "woman" and other animals, and between the activities—including mothering—engaged in by women and the behavior of other animals.

Human mothering shapes language and culture, it forms human social personhood, it develops morality. Animal behavior can be highly impressive and complex, but it does not have built into it any of the consciously chosen aims of morality. In creating human social persons, human mothering is different in kind from merely propagating a species. And human mothering can be fully as creative an activity as those activities traditionally thought of as distinctively human, because to create *new* persons, and new types of *persons*, can surely be as creative as to make new objects, products, or institutions. *Human* mothering is no more "natural" or "primarily biological" than is any other human activity.

Consider nursing an infant, often thought of as the epitome of a biological process with which mothering is associated and women are identified. There is no reason to think of human nursing as any more simply biological than there is to think of, say, a businessmen's lunch this way. Eating is a biological process, but what and how and with whom we eat are thoroughly cultural. Whether and how long and with whom a woman nurses an infant, are also human, cultural matters. If men transcend the natural by conquering new territory and trading with their neighbors and making deals over lunch to do so, women can transcend the natural by choosing not to nurse their children when they could, or choosing to nurse them when their culture tells them not to, or singing songs to their infants as they nurse, or nursing in restaurants to overcome the prejudices against doing so, or thinking human thoughts as they nurse, and so forth. Human culture surrounds and characterizes the activity of nursing as it does the activities of eating, or governing, or writing, or thinking.

We are continually being presented with images of the humanly new and creative as occurring in the public realm of the polis, or the realms of marketplace or of art and science outside the household. The very term 'reproduction' suggests mere repetition, the "natural" bringing into existence of repeated instances of the same human animal. But human reproduction is not repetition.[42] This is not to suggest that bringing up children in the interstices* of patriarchal society, in society structured by institutions supporting male dominance, can achieve the potential of transformation latent in the activity of human mothering. But the activity of creating new social persons and new kinds of persons is potentially the most transformative human activity of all. And it suggests that morality should concern itself first of all with this activity, with what its norms and practices ought to be, and with how the institutions and arrangements throughout society and the world ought to be structured to facilitate the right kinds of development of the best kinds of new persons. The flourishing of children ought to be at the very center of moral and social and political and economic and legal thought, rather than, as at present, at the periphery, if attended to at all.

Revised conceptions of public and private have significant implications for our conceptions of human beings and relationships between them. Some feminists suggest that instead of seeing human relationships in terms of the impersonal ones of the "public" sphere, as standard political and moral theory has so often done, we might consider seeing human relationships in terms of those experienced in the sphere of the "private," or of what these relationships could be imagined to be like in post-patriarchal society.[43] The traditional approach is illustrated by those who generalize,

---

* Intervening spaces, cracks.

to other regions of human life than the economic, assumptions about "economic man" in contractual relations with other men. It sees such impersonal, contractual relations as paradigmatic, even, on some views, for moral theory. Many feminists, in contrast, consider the realm of what has been misconstrued as the "private" as offering guidance to what human beings and their relationships should be like even in regions beyond those of family and friendship. Sara Ruddick looks at the implications of the practice of mothering for the conduct of peace politics.[44] Marilyn Friedman and Lorraine Code consider friendship, especially as women understand it, as a possible model for human relationships.[45] Others see society as non-contractual rather than as contractual.

Clearly, a reconceptualization is needed of the ways in which every human life is entwined with personal and with social components. Feminist theorists are contributing imaginative work to this project.

III. *The Concept of Self*

Let me turn now to the third aspect of the history of ethics which I discussed and which feminists are re-envisioning: the concept of self. One of the most important emphases in a feminist approach to morality is the recognition that more attention must be paid to the domain between, on the one hand, the self as ego, as self-interested individual, and, on the other hand, the universal, everyone, others in general.[46] Traditionally, ethics has dealt with these poles of individual self and universal all. Usually, it has called for impartiality against the partiality of the egoistic self; sometimes it has defended egoism against claims for a universal perspective. But most standard moral theory has hardly noticed as morally significant the intermediate realm of family relations and relations of friendship, of group ties and neighborhood concerns, especially from the point of view of women. When it has noticed this intermediate realm it has often seen its attachments as threatening to the aspirations of the Man of Reason, or as subversive of "true" morality. In seeing the problems of ethics as problems of reconciling the interests of the self with what would be right or best for "everyone," standard ethics has neglected the moral aspects of the concern and sympathy which people actually feel for particular others, and what

moral experience in this intermediate realm suggests for an adequate morality.

The region of "particular others" is a distinct domain, where what can be seen to be artificial and problematic are the very egoistic "self" and the universal "all others" of standard moral theory. In the domain of particular others, the self is already constituted to an important degree by relations with others, and these relations may be much more salient and significant than the interests of any individual self in isolation.[47] The "others" in the picture, however, are not the "all others," or "everyone," of traditional moral theory; they are not what a universal point of view or a view from nowhere could provide.[48] They are, characteristically, actual flesh and blood other human beings for whom we have actual feelings and with whom we have real ties.

From the point of view of much feminist theory, the individualistic assumptions of liberal theory and of most standard moral theory are suspect. Even if we would be freed from the debilitating aspects of dominating male power to "be ourselves" and to pursue our own interests, we would, as persons, still have ties to other persons, and we would at least in part be constituted by such ties. Such ties would be part of what we inherently are. We are, for instance, the daughter or son of given parents, or the mother or father of given children, and we carry with us at least some ties to the racial or ethnic or national group within which we developed into the persons we are.

If we look, for instance, at the realities of the relation between mothering person (who can be female or male) and child, we can see that what we value in the relation cannot be broken down into individual gains and losses for the individual members in the relation. Nor can it be understood in universalistic terms. Self-development apart from the relation may be much less important than the satisfactory development of the relation. What matters may often be the health and growth of and the development of the relation-and-its-members in ways that cannot be understood in the individualistic terms of standard moral theories designed to maximize the satisfaction of self-interest. The universalistic terms of moral theories grounded in what would be right for "all rational beings" or "everyone" cannot handle, either, what has moral value in the relation between mothering person and child.

Feminism is of course not the only locus of criticism of the individualistic and abstractly universalistic features of liberalism and of standard moral theory. Marxists* and communitarians† also see the self as constituted by its social relations. But in their usual form, Marxist and communitarian criticisms pay no more attention than liberalism and standard moral theory to the experience of women, to the context of mothering, or to friendship as women experience it.[49] Some recent nonfeminist criticisms, such as offered by Bernard Williams, of the impartiality required by standard moral theory, stress how a person's identity may be formed by personal projects in ways that do not satisfy universal norms, yet ought to be admired. Such views still interpret morality from the point of view of an individual and his project, not a social relationship such as that between mothering person and child. And recent nonfeminist criticisms in terms of traditional communities and their moral practices, as seen for instance in the work of Stuart Hampshire and Alasdair MacIntyre, often take traditional gender roles as given, or provide no basis for a radical critique of them.[50] There is no substitute, then, for feminist exploration of the area between ego and universal, as women experience this area, or for the development of a refocused concept of relational self that could be acceptable from a feminist point of view.

Relationships can be evaluated as trusting or mistrustful, mutually considerate or selfish, harmonious or stressful, and so forth. Where trust and consideration are appropriate, which is not always, we can find ways to foster them. But understanding and evaluating relationships, and encouraging them to be what they can be at their best, require us to look at relationships between actual persons, and to see what both standard moral theories and their nonfeminist critics often miss. To be adequate, moral theories must pay attention to the neglected realm of particular others in the actual relationships and actual contexts of women's experience. In doing so, problems of individual self-interest vs. universal rules may recede to a region more

like background, out-of-focus insolubility or relative unimportance. The salient problems may then be seen to be how we ought best to guide or to maintain or to reshape the relationships, both close and more distant, that we have, or might have, with actual other human beings. Particular others can be actual children in need in distant continents, or the anticipated children of generations not yet even close to being born. But they are not "all rational beings" or "the greatest number," and the self that is in relationships with particular others and is composed to a significant degree by such relations is not a self whose ego must be pitted against abstract, universal claims. Developing the needed guidance for maintaining and reshaping relationships presents enormous problems, but a first step is to recognize how traditional and nonfeminist moral theory of both an individualistic and communitarian kind falls short in providing it.

The concept of the relational self which is evolving within feminist thought is leading to interesting inquiry in many fields. An example is the work being done at the Stone Center at Wellesley College.[51] Psychologists there have posited a self-in-relation theory and are conducting empirical inquiries to try to establish how the female self develops. They are working with a theory that a female relational self develops through a mutually empathetic mother-daughter bond.

The work has been influenced by Jean Baker Miller's re-evaluation of women's psychological qualities as strengths rather than weaknesses. In her book *Toward a New Psychology of Women*, published in 1976, Miller identified women's "great desire for affiliation" as one such strength.[52] Nancy Chodorow's *The Reproduction of Mothering*, published in 1978, has also had a significant influence on the work done at the Stone Center, as it has on much feminist inquiry.[53] Chodorow argued that a female affiliative self is reproduced by a structure of parenting in which mothers are the primary caretakers, and sons and daughters develop differently in relation to a parent of the same sex, or a parent of different sex, as primary caretaker.

---

* See the section on Justice from this volume for more on Marx.

† Communitarian political theories tend to stress the social role of a shared sense of common purpose and tradition and mutual ties of kinship and affection, as opposed to the typically "liberal" conception of society as constructed out of a set of contractual relations between otherwise unattached individuals. In North America, communitarianism is especially associated with a wave of criticism of liberalism in the 1980s, spearheaded by such philosophers as Alasdair MacIntyre, Michael Sandel, Charles Taylor, and Michael Walzer.

Daughters develop a sense of self by identifying themselves with the mother; they come to define themselves as connected to or in relation with others. Sons, in contrast, develop a sense of self by differentiating themselves from the mother; they come to define themselves as separate from or unconnected to others. An implication often drawn from Chodorow's work is that parenting should be shared equally by fathers and mothers so that children of either sex can develop with caretakers of both same and different sex.

In 1982, Carol Gilligan, building on both Miller and Chodorow, offered her view of the "different voice" with which girls and women express their understanding of moral problems.[54] Like Miller and Chodorow, Gilligan valued tendencies found especially in women to affiliate with others and to interpret their moral responsibilities in terms of their relationships with others. In all, the valuing of autonomy and individual independence over care and concern for relationships, was seen as an expression of male bias. The Stone Center has tried to elaborate and to study a feminist conception of the relational self. In a series of Working Papers, researchers and clinicians have explored the implications of this conception for various issues in women's psychology (e.g., power, anger, work inhibitions, violence, eating patterns) and for therapy.

The self as conceptualized in these studies is seen as having both a need for recognition and a need to understand the other, and these needs are seen as compatible. They are created in the context of mother-child interaction, and are satisfied in a mutually empathetic relationship. This does not require a loss of self, but a relationship of mutuality in which self and other both express intersubjectivity. Both give and take in a way that not only contributes to the satisfaction of their needs as individuals, but also affirms the "larger relational unit" they compose.[55] Maintaining this larger relational unit then becomes a goal, and maturity is seen not in terms of individual autonomy but in terms of competence in creating and sustaining relations of empathy and mutual inter-subjectivity.

The Stone Center psychologists contend that the goal of mutuality is rarely achieved in adult male-female relationships because of the traditional gender system. The gender system leads men to seek autonomy and power over others, and to undervalue the caring and relational connectedness that is expected of women. Women rarely receive the nurturing and

empathetic support they provide. Accordingly, these psychologists look to the interaction that occurs in mother-daughter relationships as the best source of insight into the promotion of the healthy, relational self. This research provides an example of exploration into a refocused, feminist conception of the self, and into empirical questions about its development and implications.

In a quite different field, that of legal theory, a refocused concept of self is leading to reexaminations of such concepts as property and autonomy and the role these have played in political theory and in constitutional law. For instance, the legal theorist Jennifer Nedelsky questions the imagery that is dominant in constitutional law and in our conceptions of property: the imagery of a bounded self, a self contained within boundaries and having rights to property within a wall allowing it to exclude others and to exclude government. The boundary metaphor, she argues, obscures and distorts our thinking about human relationships and what is valuable in them. "The boundedness of selves," Nedelsky writes, "may seem to be a self-evident truth, but I think it is a wrong-headed and destructive way of conceiving of the human creatures law and government are created for."[56] In the domain of the self's relation to the state, the central problem, she argues, is not "maintaining a sphere into which the state cannot penetrate, but fostering autonomy when people are already within the sphere of state control or responsibility."[57] What we can from a feminist perspective think of as the male "separative self" seems on an endless quest for security behind such walls of protection as those of property. Property focuses the quest for security "in ways that are paradigmatic of the efforts of separative selves to protect themselves through boundaries...."[58] But of course property is a social construction, not a thing; it requires the involvement of the state to define what it is and to defend it. What will provide what it seeks to offer will not be boundaries and exclusions, but constructive relationships.

In an article on autonomy, Nedelsky examines the deficiencies in the concept of self with which so much of our political and legal thinking about autonomy has been developed. She well recognizes that of course feminists are centrally concerned with freedom and autonomy, with enabling women to live our own lives. But we need a language with which to express these concerns which will also reflect "the equally important feminist precept that any good theorizing will start with people in their social contexts. And the notion of social context must take seriously its constitutive quality; social context cannot simply mean that individuals will, of course, encounter one another."[59] The problem, then, is how to combine the claim of the constitutiveness of social relations with the value of self-determination. Liberalism has been the source of our language of freedom and self-determination, but it lacks the ability to express comprehension of "the reality we know: the centrality of relationships in constituting the self."[60]

In developing a new conception of autonomy that avoids positing self-sufficient and thus highly artificial individuals, Nedelsky points out first that "the capacity to find one's own law can develop only in the context of relations with others (both intimate and more broadly social) that nurture this capacity, and second, that the 'content' of one's own law is comprehensible only with reference to shared social norms, values, and concepts."[61] She sees the traditional liberal view of the self as implying that the most perfectly autonomous man is the most perfectly isolated, and finds this pathological.

Instead of developing autonomy through images of walls around one's property, as does the Western liberal tradition and as does U.S. constitutional law, Nedelsky suggests that "the most promising model, symbol, or metaphor for autonomy is not property, but childrearing. There we have encapsulated the emergence of autonomy through relationship with others.... Interdependence [is] a constant component of autonomy."[62] And she goes on to examine how law and bureaucracies can foster autonomy within relationships between citizen and government. This does not entail extrapolating from intimate relations to largescale ones; rather, the insights gained from experience with the context of childrearing allow us to recognize the relational aspects of autonomy. In work such as Nedelsky's we can see how feminist reconceptualizations of the self can lead to the rethinking of fundamental concepts even in terrains such as law, thought by many to be quite distant from such disturbances.

To argue for a view of the self as relational does not mean that women need to remain enmeshed in the ties by which they are constituted. In recent decades, especially, women have been breaking free of relationships with parents, with the communities in which they grew up, and with men, relationships in which they defined themselves through the traditional and often stifling expectations of others.[63] These quests for self have often involved wrenching instability and painful insecurity. But the quest has been for a new and more satisfactory relational self, not for the self-sufficient individual of liberal theory. Many might share the concerns expressed by Alison Jaggar that disconnecting ourselves from particular others, as ideals of individual autonomy seem to presuppose we should, might make us incapable of morality, rather than capable of it, if, as so many feminists think, "an ineliminable part of morality consists in responding emotionally to particular others."[64]

I have examined three topics on which feminist philosophers and feminists in other fields are thinking anew about where we should start and how we should focus our attention in ethics. Feminist reconceptualizations and recommendations concerning the relation between reason and emotion, the distinction between public and private, and the concept of the self, are providing insights deeply challenging to standard moral theory. The implications of this work are that we need an almost total reconstruction of social and political and economic and legal theory in all their traditional forms as well as a reconstruction of moral theory and practice at more comprehensive, or fundamental, levels.[65] ∎

Suggestions for Critical Reflection

1. Do you agree with Held that there has historically been a characteristically "male point of view"? Do you think there is today? If so, what does this show about ethics? (Similarly, do you think there is a characteristically *female* point of view, and what would that show?)

2. Many have argued that the stereotyping of certain characteristics as "female" (e.g., emotional, less concerned with principles, more concerned with relationships than with issues) is harmful for women (not to mention inaccurate). Does an ethics of care risk encouraging these stereotypes?

3. Held argues that the male bias in the history of ethics requires, for its correction, a *wholesale transformation* of ethical theory: she does not think women should want "simply to be accorded entry as equals into the enterprise of morality as so far developed." How persuasively does Held make this case? If—unlike Held—you think traditional ethical theory might be repaired rather than transformed, how might one go about removing the gender bias that Held detects in, for example, utilitarianism or Kantian ethics?

4. Held writes, "The associations between ... philosophical concepts and gender cannot be merely dropped, and the concepts retained regardless of gender, because gender has been built into them in such a way that without it, they will have to be different concepts." What do you make of this argument? What implications does it have for philosophy today?

5. Held suggests that our very concept of *human* has historically been infected with male-biased assumptions. Does this seem plausible? If so, how important a philosophical discovery is this? In what ways should the existing concept be changed (or with what sort of concept should it be replaced)?

6. Should "a mother's sacrifice for her child" be considered an act of moral supererogation (something it is good to do but not a moral duty)? Why, or why not? What implications, if any, does this have for ethical theory?

7. Held draws a contrast between an "ethic of care" and an "ethic of justice," and suggests the former is more appropriate to women's experience than the latter. Does this claim seem right to you? If so, in what ways—if any—does that make an ethic of care a *better moral theory* than an ethic of justice? What potential benefits and pitfalls can you see in the notion of an ethic of care?

8. Held argues that women are no more biologically determined than men, and, in particular, that the activity of mothering is no less "human" than, say, politics or trade. What implications does this have for our view of human relationships, and for morality?

9. Feminist ethicists often pay particular attention to a domain of people intermediate between the self and "everyone": i.e., they focus on our moral relationships to "particular others," our friends, family, and other individuals with whom we have personal relationships. How important, and how defensible, is this shift in focus? *Do* we have special moral responsibilities to particular people—which we do not have to others—just because, for example, they are our friends? If so, is feminist ethics the only theory able to accommodate this insight?

10. Held describes a model of the self which treats it as at least partly constituted by its *relationships* with other people. Does Held mean to suggest that only *women* have a "relational self" or that men do as well? If this model is correct, what are its implications for ethics? For example, how does it affect the problem of moral motivation? What would it do to our conception of justice, rights, and duties? How does it change the nature and value of human autonomy?

Notes

1   See e.g., Cheshire Calhoun, "Justice, Care, Gender Bias," *The Journal of Philosophy* 85 (September, 1988): 451–63.

2   Lorraine Code, "Second Persons," in *Science, Morality and Feminist Theory*, ed. Marsha Hanen and Kai Nielsen (Calgary: University of Calgary Press, 1987), p. 360.

3   See e.g., *Revolutions in Knowledge: Feminism in the Social Sciences*, ed. Sue Rosenberg Zalk and Janice Gordon-Kelter (Boulder: Westview Press, forthcoming).

4   Genevieve Lloyd, *The Man of Reason: 'Male' and 'Female' in Western Philosophy* (Minneapolis: University of Minnesota Press, 1984), p. 104.

5   Ibid., p. 2.

6   Ibid., p. 3.

7   Ibid., p. 4. For a feminist view of how reason and emotion in the search for knowledge might be reevaluated, see Alison M. Jaggar, "Love and Knowledge: Emotion in Feminist Epistemology," *Inquiry* 32 (June, 1989): 151–76.

8   David Heyd, *Supererogation: Its Status in Ethical Theory* (New York: Cambridge University Press, 1982), p. 134.

9   J.O. Urmson, "Saints and Heroes," in *Essays in Moral Philosophy*, ed. A.I. Melden (Seattle: University of Washington Press, 1958), p. 202. I am indebted to Marcia Baron for pointing out this and the previous example in her "Kantian Ethics and Supererogation," *The Journal of Philosophy* 84 (May, 1987): 137–62.

10 Alan Ryan, "Distrusting Economics," *New York Review of Books* (May 18, 1989): 25–27. For a different treatment, see *Beyond Self-Interest*, ed. Jane Mansbridge (Chicago: University of Chicago Press, 1990).

11 See especially *Mothering: Essays in Feminist Theory*, ed. Joyce Trebilcot (Totowa, New Jersey: Rowman and Allanheld, 1984); and Sara Ruddick, *Maternal Thinking: Toward a Politics of Peace* (Boston: Beacon Press, 1989).

12 Christine Di Stefano, "Masculinity as Ideology in Political Theory: Hobbesian Man Considered," *Women's Studies International Forum* (Special Issue: *Hypatia*), Vol. 6, No. 6 (1983): 633–44, p. 637.

13 Thomas Hobbes, *The Citizen: Philosophical Rudiments Concerning Government and Society*, ed. B. Gert (Garden City, New York: Doubleday, 1972 (1651)), p. 205.

14 Di Stefano, op. cit., p. 638.

15 Ibid.

16 Ibid., p. 639.

17 For examples of relevant passages, see *Philosophy of Woman: Classical to Current Concepts*, ed. Mary Mahowald (Indianapolis: Hackett, 1978); and *Visions of Women*, ed. Linda Bell (Clifton, New Jersey: Humana, 1985). For discussion, see Susan Moller Okin, *Women in Western Political Thought* (Princeton, New Jersey: Princeton University Press, 1979); and Lorenne Clark and Lynda Lange, eds., *The Sexism of Social and Political Theory* (Toronto: University of Toronto Press, 1979).

18 Annette Baier, "Trust and Anti-Trust," *Ethics* 96 (1986): 231–60, pp. 247–48.

19 Ibid.

20 Kathryn Pauly Morgan, "Strangers in a Strange Land: Feminists Visit Relativists" in *Perspectives on Relativism*, ed. D. Odegaard and Carole Stewart (Toronto: Agathon Press, 1990).

21 Kathryn Morgan, "Women and Moral Madness," in *Science, Morality and Feminist Theory*, ed. Hanen and Nielsen, p. 223.

22 Alison M. Jaggar, "Feminist Ethics: Some Issues for the Nineties," *Journal of Social Philosophy* 20 (Spring/Fall 1989), p. 91.

23 Ibid.

24 One well-argued statement of this position is Barbara Houston, "Rescuing Womanly Virtues: Some Dangers of Moral Reclamation," in *Science, Morality and Feminist Theory*, ed. Hanen and Nielsen.

25 See e.g., Elizabeth V. Spelman, *Inessential Woman: Problems of Exclusion in Feminist Thought* (Boston: Beacon Press, 1988). See also Sarah Lucia Hoagland, *Lesbian Ethics: Toward New Value* (Palo Alto, California: Institute of Lesbian Studies, 1989); and Katie Geneva Cannon, *Black Womanist Ethics* (Atlanta, Georgia: Scholars Press, 1988).

26 For an approach to social and political as well as moral issues that attempts to be context-respectful, see Virginia Held, *Rights and Goods. Justifying Social Action* (Chicago: University of Chicago Press, 1989).

27 Margaret Urban Walker, "Moral Understandings: Alternative 'Epistemology' for a Feminist Ethics," *Hypatia* 4 (Summer, 1989): 15–28, p. 19.

28 Ibid., p. 20. See also Iris Marion Young, "Impartiality and the Civic Public. Some Implications of Feminist Critiques of Moral and Political Theory," in Seyla Benhabib and Drucilla Cornell, *Feminism as Critique* (Minneapolis: University of Minnesota Press, 1987).

29 See especially Carol Gilligan, *In a Different Voice. Psychological Theory and Women's Development* (Cambridge, Massachusetts: Harvard University Press, 1988); and Eva Feder Kittay and Diana T. Meyers eds., *Women and Moral Theory* (Totowa, New Jersey: Rowman and Allanheld, 1987).

30 Annette Baier, "The Need for More Than Justice," in *Science, Morality and Feminist Theory*, ed. Hanen and Nielsen, p. 55.

31 Ibid.

32 Kathryn Pauly Morgan, "Strangers in a Strange Land...," p. 2.

33 Annette Baier, "Trust and Anti-Trust."

34 See especially Kathryn Pauly Morgan, "Strangers in a Strange Land...."

35 Susan Sherwin, "Feminist and Medical Ethics: Two Different Approaches to Contextual Ethics," *Hypatia* 4 (Summer, 1989): 57–72.

36 See especially the work of John Rawls and Ronald Dworkin; see also Charles Larmore, *Patterns of Moral Complexity* (Cambridge: Cambridge University Press, 1987).

37 Annette Baier, "The Need for More Than Justice," pp. 53–54.

38 See e.g., Linda Nicholson, *Gender and History. The Limits of Social Theory in the Age of the Family* (New York: Columbia University Press, 1986); and Jean Bethke Elshtain, *Public Man, Private Woman* (Princeton, New Jersey: Princeton University Press, 1981). See also Carole Pateman, *The Sexual Contract* (Stanford, California: Stanford University Press, 1988).

39 See e.g., Susan Moller Okin, *Women in Western Political Thought*. See also Alison M. Jaggar, *Feminist Politics and Human Nature* (Totowa, New Jersey: Rowman and Allanheld, 1983).

40 So entrenched is this way of thinking that it was even reflected in Simone de Beauvoir's pathbreaking feminist text *The Second Sex*, published in 1949. Here, as elsewhere, feminists have had to transcend our own early searches for our own perspectives.

41 See e.g., Sherry B. Ortner, "Is Female to Male as Nature Is to Culture?" in *Woman, Culture, and Society*, ed. Michelle Z. Rosaldo and Louise Lamphere (Stanford: Stanford University Press, 1974).

42 For further discussion and an examination of surrounding associations, see Virginia Held, "Birth and Death," in *Ethics* 99 (January 1989): 362–88.

43 See e.g., Virginia Held, "Non-contractual Society: A Feminist View," in *Science, Morality and Feminist Theory*, ed. Hanen and Nielsen.

44 Sara Ruddick, *Maternal Thinking*.

45 See Marilyn Friedman, "Feminism and Modern Friendship: Dislocating the Community," *Ethics* 99 (January 1989): 275–90; and Lorraine Code, "Second Persons."

46 See Virginia Held, "Feminism and Moral Theory," in *Women and Moral Theory*, ed. Kittay and Meyers.

47 See Seyla Benhabib, "The Generalized and the Concrete Other. The Kohlberg-Gilligan Controversy and Moral Theory," in *Women and Moral Theory*, ed. Kittay and Meyers. See also Caroline Whitbeck, "Feminist Ontology: A Different Reality," in *Beyond Domination*, ed. Carol Gould (Totowa, New Jersey: Rowman and Allanheld, 1983).

48 See Thomas Nagel, *The View from Nowhere* (New York: Oxford University Press, 1986). For a feminist critique, see Susan Bordo, "Feminism, Postmodernism, and Gender-Skepticism," in *Feminism/Postmodernism*, ed. Linda Nicholson (New York: Routledge, 1989).

49 On Marxist theory, see e.g., *Women and Revolution*, ed. Lydia Sargent (Boston: South End Press, 1981); Alison Jaggar, *Feminist Politics and Human Nature*; and Ann Ferguson, *Blood at the Root. Motherhood, Sexuality and Male Dominance* (London: Pandora, 1989). On communitarian theory, see Marilyn Friedman, "Feminism and Modern Friendship...," and also her paper "The Social Self and the Partiality Debates," presented at the Society for Women in Philosophy meeting in New Orleans, April 1990.

50 Bernard Williams, *Moral Luck* (Cambridge: Cambridge University Press, 1981); *Public and Private Morality*, ed. Stuart Hampshire (Cambridge: Cambridge University Press, 1978); Alasdair MacIntyre, *After Virtue. A Study in Moral Theory* (Notre Dame, Indiana: University of Notre Dame Press, 1981). For discussion see Susan Moller Okin, *Justice, Gender, and the Family* (New York: Basic Books, 1989).

51 On the Stone Center concept of the self see especially Jean Baker Miller, "The Development of Women's Sense of Self," Wellesley, Massachusetts: Stone Center Working Paper No. 12; Janet Surrey, "The 'Self-in-Relation': A Theory of Women's Development" (Wellesley, Massachusetts: Stone Center Working Paper No. 13); and Judith Jordan, "The Meaning of Mutuality" (Wellesley, Massachusetts: Stone Center Working Paper No. 23). For a feminist but critical view of this work, see Marcia Westkott, "Female Relationality and the Idealized Self," *American Journal of Psychoanalysis* 49 (September, 1989): 239–50.

52 Jean Baker Miller, *Toward a New Psychology of Women* (Boston: Beacon Press, 1976).

53 Nancy Chodorow, *The Reproduction of Mothering: Psychoanalysis and the Sociology of Gender* (Berkeley: University of California Press, 1978).

54 Carol Gilligan, *In a Different Voice*.

55 J.V. Jordan, "The Meaning of Mutuality," p. 2.

56 Jennifer Nedelsky, "Law, Boundaries, and the Bounded Self," *Representations* 30 (Spring, 1990): 162–89, at 167.

57 Ibid., p. 169.

58 Ibid., p. 181.

59 Jennifer Nedelsky, "Reconceiving Autonomy: Sources, Thoughts and Possibilities," *Yale Journal of Law and Feminism* 1 (Spring, 1989): 7–36, p. 9. See also Diana T. Meyers, *Self, Society, and Personal Choice* (New York: Columbia University Press, 1989).

60 Ibid.

61 Ibid, p. 11.

62 Ibid., p. 12. See also Mari J. Matsuda, "Liberal Jurisprudence and Abstracted Visions of Human Nature," *New Mexico Law Review* 16 (Fall, 1986): 613–30.

63 See e.g., *Women's Ways of Knowing. The Development of Self, Voice, and Mind*, by Mary Field Belenky, Blyth McVicker Clinchy, Nancy Rule Goldberger, and Jill Mattuck Tarule (New York: Basic Books, 1986).

64 Alison Jaggar, "Feminist Ethics: Some Issues for the Nineties," p. 11.

65 This paper is based in part on my Truax Lectures on "The Prospect of Feminist Morality" at Hamilton College on November 2 and 9, 1989. Early versions were also presented at Colgate University; at Queen's University in Kingston, Ontario; at the University of Kentucky; and at the New School for Social Research. I am grateful to all who made possible these occasions and commented on the paper at these times, and to Alison Jaggar, Laura Purdy, and Sara Ruddick for additional discussion.

JUDITH JARVIS THOMSON

The Trolley Problem

Who Is Judith Jarvis Thomson?

A distinguished philosopher of ethics and metaphysics, Judith Jarvis Thomson was born in New York City in 1929. The descendent of a long line of Eastern European rabbis, Thomson officially converted to Judaism when she was 14 years old. After obtaining two BA degrees, one from Barnard College and one from Cambridge University, Thomson completed her PhD in philosophy at Columbia in 1959. She taught at Barnard College from 1956 to 1962 and briefly served as a professor at Boston University before securing a permanent professorship at MIT in 1964. Thomson has published numerous influential papers and several books, including *Acts and Other Events* (1977), *The Realm of Rights* (1990), and *Normativity* (2008). She received a prestigious Guggenheim Fellowship in 1986, and was awarded an honorary Doctor of Letters degree from Cambridge in 2015 and from Harvard in 2016.

What Is the Structure of This Reading?

Thomson's argument employs a large number of thought experiments—imaginary scenarios with simplified conditions that are meant to draw out the reader's intuitions. Among the thought experiments Thomson discusses are:

1. *Trolley Driver*: An unstoppable trolley is headed toward a group of five workers repairing a section of track and will run down and kill the workers unless the driver diverts the trolley to a different track. The other track contains only one worker, who will inevitably be killed should the driver choose to divert the trolley. Should the driver divert the trolley?
2. *Bystander at the Switch*: A bystander next to the trolley track is observing the above scenario, and sees that the driver of the trolley has fainted without changing the path of the trolley. The bystander is next to a switch which could be used to divert the trolley to the segment of track containing only one worker. Should the bystander flip the switch?
3. *Fat Man*: While standing on a footbridge overlooking a track, a person sees an out-of-control trolley headed toward a group of five workers. The person is standing next to a rather large man, and knows that they could shove the large man off the bridge and onto the trolley tracks below, and that the man's body would then stop the trolley before it kills the five workers. Should this person shove the man onto the tracks?
4. *Transplant*: A surgeon requires five different organs in order to save the lives of five patients, who will otherwise die within a day. A healthy young person shows up at the transplant clinic, requesting only a routine check-up. The young person happens to be a compatible donor for all five of the other patients; however, the potential donor would have to be killed in order to have all five of their organs transplanted, and is unwilling to consent to such an operation. Should the surgeon operate anyway, killing the potential donor in order to save five other people?
5. *Hospital*: Five hospital patients will die unless a certain gas is manufactured to save their lives. However, in order to manufacture this gas, we would have to flood a nearby room with lethal fumes, killing the patient who inhabits that room. Should we manufacture the gas?

Thomson also discusses a number of variations of these scenarios, teasing out the ways in which slight differences can cause us to have very different intuitions about which actions are permissible and which are not.

Each scenario presents a choice that will lead to more-or-less the same two possible outcomes: one in which five people die, and another in which only one person dies. And yet, for many of us (including Thomson), it seems intuitively as though the act leading to only one person's death is permissible in some of these scenarios but not in others. If our intuitions are a reliable guide to right and wrong, then this would seem to show that the morality of an action depends on more than just its outcome. The bulk of Thomson's article is spent considering possible explanations as to why we're permitted to act in some of these situations but not in others. She examines and rejects a number of potential responses before providing her own solution.

Some Useful Background Information

Many of the thought experiments described in this article are of Thomson's own creation. The first variation of the Trolley Driver scenario, however, is borrowed from another important philosopher, Philippa Foot. Foot presented the example as a way of illustrating the "Doctrine of Double Effect," a principle especially influential in Christian philosophy. According to this Doctrine, it is sometimes morally permissible to cause harm when that harm is a side effect of an action intended to bring about something good.

Some Common Misconceptions

1. It's not uncommon for readers of this paper to reject the set of options on offer—to claim, for example, that the trolley driver should instead look for an emergency brake, or derail the trolley, or find some other mechanical solution that would prevent any loss of life. Though it may be commendable to seek out such alternative solutions in real life, to respond to Thomson's thought experiments in this way is to misunderstand their purpose. Thomson deliberately simplifies the mechanics of each scenario and limits the available options so as to focus attention on the comparative merits of only two possible actions. By limiting the options in this way, we may come to better understand the grounds of our moral reasoning.

2. Thomson's claims about which actions are morally permissible are not meant as predictions of how she would behave or of how the majority of people would behave. Rather, they are meant as assessments of the morality of each possible action, regardless of whether we would act accordingly in a situation of high tension and limited time.

How Important and Influential Is This Passage?

Though Thomson's conclusion is itself important, this paper's greater influence is perhaps not so much found in the conclusion itself but rather in the collection of thought experiments it provides. These scenarios, and their use in drawing out intuitions about morality, are well-known not only within academic philosophy but also in other areas of inquiry such as computing science. And over the years they've entered into some areas of popular culture, with variations presented in television, film, and video games.

The Trolley Problem*

I.

Some years ago, Philippa Foot† drew attention to an extraordinarily interesting problem.[1] Suppose you are the driver of a trolley.‡ The trolley rounds a bend, and there come into view ahead five track workmen, who have been repairing the track. The track goes through a bit of a valley at that point, and the sides are steep, so you must stop the trolley if you are to avoid running the five men down. You step on the brakes, but alas

---

* Judith Jarvis Thomson, "The Trolley Problem," *The Yale Law Journal* 94, 6 (May 1985): 1395–1415.
† Philippa Ruth Foot (1920–2010) was an influential British philosopher who wrote primarily on the rationality of morality and helped to re-popularize and modernize virtue ethics.
‡ That is, a tram or streetcar.

they don't work. Now you suddenly see a spur of track leading off to the right. You can turn the trolley onto it, and thus save the five men on the straight track ahead. Unfortunately, Mrs. Foot has arranged that there is one track workman on that spur of track. He can no more get off the track in time than the five can, so you will kill him if you turn the trolley onto him. Is it morally permissible for you to turn the trolley?

Everybody to whom I have put this hypothetical case says, Yes, it is.[2] Some people say something stronger than that it is morally *permissible* for you to turn the trolley: They say that morally speaking, you *must* turn it—that morality requires you to do so. Others do not agree that morality requires you to turn the trolley, and even feel a certain discomfort at the idea of turning it. But everybody says that it is true, at a minimum, that you *may* turn it—that it would not be morally wrong in you to do so.

Now consider a second hypothetical case. This time you are to imagine yourself to be a surgeon, a truly great surgeon. Among other things you do, you transplant organs, and you are such a great surgeon that the organs you transplant always take. At the moment you have five patients who need organs. Two need one lung each, two need a kidney each, and the fifth needs a heart. If they do not get those organs today, they will all die; if you find organs for them today, you can transplant the organs and they will all live. But where to find the lungs, the kidneys, and the heart? The time is almost up when a report is brought to you that a young man who has just come into your clinic for his yearly check-up has exactly the right blood-type, and is in excellent health. Lo, you have a possible donor. All you need do is cut him up and distribute *his* parts among the five who need them. You ask, but he says, "Sorry. I deeply sympathize, but no." Would it be morally permissible for you to operate anyway? Everybody to whom I have put this second hypothetical case says, No, it would not be morally permissible for you to proceed.

Here then is Mrs. Foot's problem: *Why* is it that the trolley driver may turn his trolley, though the surgeon may not remove the young man's lungs, kidneys, and heart?[3] In both cases, one will die if the agent acts, but five will live who would otherwise die—a net saving of

four lives. What difference in the other facts of these cases explains the moral difference between them? I fancy that the theorists of tort and criminal law* will find this problem as interesting as the moral theorist does.

II.

Mrs. Foot's own solution to the problem she drew attention to is simple, straightforward, and very attractive. She would say: Look, the surgeon's choice is between operating, in which case he kills one, and not operating, in which case he lets five die; and killing is surely worse than letting die[4]—indeed, so much worse that we can even say

(I) Killing one is worse than letting five die.

So the surgeon must refrain from operating. By contrast, the trolley driver's choice is between turning the trolley, in which case he kills one, and not turning the trolley, in which case he does not *let five die*, he positively *kills* them. Now surely we can say

(II) Killing five is worse than killing one.

But then that is why the trolley driver may turn his trolley: He would be doing what is worse if he fails to turn it, since if he fails to turn it he kills five.

I do think that that is an attractive account of the matter. It seems to me that if the surgeon fails to operate, he does not kill his five patients who need parts; he merely lets them die. By contrast, if the driver fails to turn his trolley, he does not merely let the five track workmen die; he drives his trolley into them, and thereby kills them.

But there is good reason to think that this problem is not so easily solved as that.

Let us begin by looking at a case that is in some ways like Mrs. Foot's story of the trolley driver. I will call her case *Trolley Driver*; let us now consider a case I will call *Bystander at the Switch*. In that case you have been strolling by the trolley track, and you can see the situation at a glance: The driver saw the five on the track ahead, he stamped on the brakes, the brakes failed, so

---

* Tort law deals with legal actions seeking a private civil remedy, such as damages, while criminal law addresses criminal wrongs that are punishable by the state.

he fainted. What to do? Well, here is the switch, which you can throw, thereby turning the trolley yourself. Of course you will kill one if you do. But I should think you may turn it all the same.[5]

Some people may feel a difference between these two cases. In the first place, the trolley driver is, after all, captain of the trolley. He is charged by the trolley company with responsibility for the safety of his passengers and anyone else who might be harmed by the trolley he drives. The bystander at the switch, on the other hand, is a private person who just happens to be there.

Second, the driver would be driving a trolley into the five if he does not turn it, and the bystander would not—the bystander will do the five no harm at all if he does not throw the switch.

I think it right to feel these differences between the cases.

Nevertheless, my own feeling is that an ordinary person, a mere bystander, may intervene in such a case. If you see something, a trolley, a boulder, an avalanche, heading towards five, and you can deflect it onto one, it really does seem that—other things being equal—it would be permissible for you to *take* charge, *take* responsibility, and deflect the thing, whoever you may be. Of course you run a moral risk if you do, for it might be that, unbeknownst to you, other things are not equal. It might be, that is, that there is some relevant difference between the five on the one hand, and the one on the other, which would make it morally preferable that the five be hit by the trolley than that the one be hit by it. That would be so if, for example, the five are not track workmen at all, but Mafia members in workmen's clothing, and they have tied the one workman to the right-hand track in the hope that you would turn the trolley onto him. I won't canvass all the many kinds of possibilities, for in fact the moral risk is the same whether you are the trolley driver, or a bystander at the switch.

Moreover, second, we might well wish to ask ourselves what exactly is the difference between what the driver would be doing if he failed to turn the trolley and what the bystander would be doing if he failed to throw the switch. As I said, the driver would be driving a trolley into the five; but what exactly would his driving the trolley into the five consist in? Why,

just sitting there, doing nothing! If the driver does just sit there, doing nothing, then that will have been how come he drove his trolley into the five.

I do not mean to make much of that fact about what the driver's driving his trolley into the five would consist in, for it seems to me to be right to say that if he does not turn the trolley, he does drive his trolley into them, and does thereby kill them. (Though this does seem to me to be right, it is not easy to say exactly what makes it so.) By contrast, if the bystander does not throw the switch, he drives no trolley into anybody, and he kills nobody.

But as I said, my own feeling is that the bystander *may* intervene. Perhaps it will seem to some even less clear that morality requires him to turn the trolley than that morality requires the driver to turn the trolley; perhaps some will feel even more discomfort at the idea of the bystander's turning the trolley than at the idea of the driver's turning the trolley. All the same, I shall take it that he *may*.

If he may, there is serious trouble for Mrs. Foot's thesis (I). It is plain that if the bystander throws the switch, he causes the trolley to hit the one, and thus he kills the one. It is equally plain that if the bystander does not throw the switch, he does not cause the trolley to hit the five, he does not kill the five, he merely fails to save them—he lets them die. His choice therefore is between throwing the switch, in which case he kills one, and not throwing the switch, in which case he lets five die. If thesis (I) were true, it would follow that the bystander may not throw the switch, and that I am taking to be false.

III.

I have been arguing that

(I) Killing one is worse than letting five die

is false, and a fortiori* that it cannot be appealed to to explain why the surgeon may not operate in the case I shall call *Transplant.*

I think it pays to take note of something interesting which comes out when we pay close attention to

---

* Latin: "from the stronger." An *a fortiori* inference is one that draws a weaker conclusion on the basis of a stronger conclusion that has already been reached.

(II) Killing five is worse than killing one.

For let us ask ourselves how we would feel about *Transplant* if we made a certain addition to it. In telling you that story, I did not tell you why the surgeon's patients are in need of parts. Let us imagine that the history of their ailments is as follows. The surgeon was badly overworked last fall—some of his assistants in the clinic were out sick, and the surgeon had to take over their duties dispensing drugs. While feeling particularly tired one day, he became careless, and made the terrible mistake of dispensing chemical X to five of the day's patients. Now chemical X works differently in different people. In some it causes lung failure, in others kidney failure, in others heart failure. So these five patients who now need parts need them because of the surgeon's carelessness. Indeed, if he does not get them the parts they need, so that they die, he will have killed them. Does that make a moral difference? That is, does the fact that he will have killed the five if he does nothing make it permissible for him to cut the young man up and distribute his parts to the five who need them?

We could imagine it to have been worse. Suppose what had happened was this: The surgeon was badly overextended last fall, he had known he was named a beneficiary in his five patients' wills, and it swept over him one day to give them chemical X to kill them. Now he repents, and would save them if he could. If he does not save them, he will positively have murdered them. Does *that* fact make it permissible for him to cut the young man up and distribute his parts to the five who need them?

I should think plainly not. The surgeon must not operate on the young man. If he can find no other way of saving his five patients, he will *now* have to let them die—despite the fact that if he now lets them die, he will have killed them.

We tend to forget that some killings themselves include lettings die, and do include them where the act by which the agent kills takes time to cause death—time in which the agent can intervene but does not.

In face of these possibilities, the question arises what we should think of thesis (II), since it *looks* as if it tells us that the surgeon ought to operate, and thus that he may permissibly do so, since if he operates he kills only one instead of five.

There are two ways in which we can go here. First, we can say: (II) does tell us that the surgeon ought to operate, and that shows it is false. Second, we can say: (II) does not tell us that the surgeon ought to operate, and it is true.

For my own part, I prefer the second. If Alfred kills five and Bert kills only one, then questions of motive apart, and other things being equal, what Alfred did *is* worse than what Bert did. If the surgeon does not operate, so that he kills five, then it will later be true that he did something worse than he would have done if he had operated, killing only one—especially if his killing of the five was murder, committed out of a desire for money, and his killing of the one would have been, though misguided and wrongful, nevertheless a well-intentioned effort to save five lives. Taking this line would, of course, require saying that assessments of which acts are worse than which other acts do not by themselves settle the question what it is permissible for an agent to do.

But it might be said that we ought to by-pass (II), for perhaps what Mrs. Foot would have offered us as an explanation of why the driver may turn the trolley in *Trolley Driver* is not (II) itself, but something more complex, such as

(II′) If a person is faced with a choice between doing something *here and now* to five, by the doing of which he will kill them, and doing something else *here and now* to one, by the doing of which he will kill only the one, then (other things being equal) he ought to choose the second alternative rather than the first.

We may presumably take (II′) to tell us that the driver ought to, and hence permissibly may, turn the trolley in *Trolley Driver*, for we may presumably view the driver as confronted with a choice between here and now driving his trolley into five, and here and now driving his trolley into one. And at the same time, (II′) tells us nothing at all about what the surgeon ought to do in *Transplant*, for he is not confronted with such a choice. If the surgeon operates, he does do something by the doing of which he will kill only one; but if the surgeon does not operate, he does not do something by the doing of which he kills five; he merely fails to do something by the doing of which he would make it be the case that he has not killed five.

I have no objection to this shift in attention from (II) to (II′). But we should not overlook an interesting question that lurks here. As it might be put: *Why* should the present tense matter so much? Why should a person prefer killing one to killing five if the alternatives are wholly in front of him, but not (or anyway, not in every case) where one of them is partly behind him? I shall come back to this question briefly later.

Meanwhile, however, even if (II′) can be appealed to in order to explain why the trolley driver may turn his trolley, that would leave it entirely open why the bystander at the switch may turn *his* trolley. For he does not drive a trolley into each of five if he refrains from turning the trolley; he merely lets the trolley drive into each of them.

So I suggest we set *Trolley Driver* aside for the time being. What I shall be concerned with is a first cousin of Mrs. Foot's problem, viz.: Why is it that the bystander may turn his trolley, though the surgeon may not remove the young man's lungs, kidneys, and heart? Since *I* find it particularly puzzling that the bystander may turn his trolley, I am inclined to call this The Trolley Problem. Those who find it particularly puzzling that the surgeon may not operate are cordially invited to call it The Transplant Problem instead.

IV.

It should be clear, I think, that "kill" and "let die" are too blunt to be useful tools for the solving of this problem. We ought to be looking within killings and savings for the ways in which the agents would be carrying them out.

It would be no surprise, I think, if a Kantian* idea occurred to us at this point. Kant said: "Act so that you treat humanity, whether in your own person or in that of another, always as an end and never as a means only." It is striking, after all, that the surgeon who proceeds in *Transplant* treats the young man he cuts up "as a means only": He literally uses the young man's body to save his five, and does so without the young man's consent. And perhaps we may say that the agent in *Bystander at the Switch* does not use his victim to save his five, or (more generally) treat his victim as a means only, and that that is why he (unlike the surgeon) may proceed.

But what exactly is it to treat a person as a means only, or to use a person? And why exactly is it wrong to do this? These questions do not have obvious answers.[6]

Suppose an agent is confronted with a choice between doing nothing, in which case five die, or engaging in a certain course of action, in which case the five live, but one dies. Then perhaps we can say: If the agent chooses to engage in the course of action, then he uses the one to save the five only if, had the one gone out of existence just before the agent started, the agent would have been unable to save the five. That is true of the surgeon in *Transplant*. He needs the young man if he is to save his five; if the young man goes wholly out of existence just before the surgeon starts to operate, then the surgeon cannot save his five. By contrast, the agent in *Bystander at the Switch* does not need the one track workman on the right-hand track if he is to save his five; if the one track workman goes wholly out of existence before the bystander starts to turn the trolley, then the bystander *can* all the same save his five. So here anyway is a striking difference between the cases.

It does seem to me right to think that solving this problem requires attending to the means by which the agent would be saving his five if he proceeded. But I am inclined to think that this is an overly simple way of taking account of the agent's means.

One reason for thinking so[7] comes out as follows. You have been thinking of the tracks in *Bystander at the Switch* as not merely diverging, but continuing to diverge, as in the following picture:

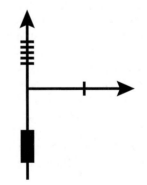

---

* Immanuel Kant (1724–1804) was an influential German philosopher. The adjective "Kantian" refers here to Kant's moral philosophy, which emphasized duties, in particular the "Categorical Imperative," a variation of which is quoted by Thomson. See the readings by Kant elsewhere in this volume.

Consider now what I shall call "the loop variant" on this case, in which the tracks do not continue to diverge—they circle back, as in the following picture:

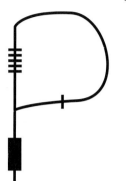

Let us now imagine that the five on the straight track are thin, but thick enough so that although all five will be killed if the trolley goes straight, the bodies of the five will stop it, and it will therefore not reach the one. On the other hand, the one on the right-hand track is fat, so fat that his body will by itself stop the trolley, and the trolley will therefore not reach the five. May the agent turn the trolley? Some people feel more discomfort at the idea of turning the trolley in the loop variant than in the original *Bystander at the Switch*. But we cannot really suppose that the presence or absence of that extra bit of track makes a major moral difference as to what an agent may do in these cases, and it really does seem right to think (despite the discomfort) that the agent may proceed.

On the other hand, we should notice that the agent here needs the one (fat) track workman on the right-hand track if he is to save his five. If the one goes wholly out of existence just before the agent starts to turn the trolley, then the agent cannot save his five[8]— just as the surgeon in *Transplant* cannot save his five if the young man goes wholly out of existence just before the surgeon starts to operate.

Indeed, I should think that there is no plausible account of what is involved in, or what is necessary for, the application of the notions "treating a person as a means only," or "using one to save five," under which the surgeon would be doing this whereas the agent in this variant of *Bystander at the Switch* would

not be. If that is right, then appeals to these notions cannot do the work being required of them here.

V.

Suppose the bystander at the switch proceeds: He throws the switch, thereby turning the trolley onto the right-hand track, thereby causing the one to be hit by the trolley, thereby killing him—but saving the five on the straight track. There are two facts about what he does which seem to me to explain the moral difference between what he does and what the agent in *Transplant* would be doing if *he* proceeded. In the first place, the bystander saves his five by making something that threatens them instead threaten one. Second, the bystander does not do that by means which themselves constitute an infringement of any right of the one's.

As is plain, then, my hypothesis as to the source of the moral difference between the cases makes appeal to the concept of a right. My own feeling is that solving this problem requires making appeal to that concept—or to some other concept that does the same kind of work.[9] Indeed, I think it is one of the many reasons why this problem is of such interest to moral theory that it does force us to appeal to that concept; and by the same token, that we learn something from it about that concept.

Let us begin with an idea, held by many friends of rights, which Ronald Dworkin* expressed crisply in a metaphor from bridge: Rights "trump" utilities.[10] That is, if one would infringe a right in or by acting, then it is not sufficient justification for acting that one would thereby maximize utility. It seems to me that something like this must be correct.

Consideration of this idea suggests the possibility of a very simple solution to the problem. That is, it might be said (i) The reason why the surgeon may not proceed in *Transplant* is that if he proceeds, he maximizes utility, for he brings about a net saving of four lives, but in so doing he would infringe a right of the young man's.

Which right? Well, we might say: The right the young man has against the surgeon that the surgeon

---

* Ronald Dworkin (1931–2013) was an American philosopher and jurist.

not kill him—thus a right in the cluster of rights that the young man has in having a right to life.

Solving this problem requires being able to explain also why the bystander may proceed in *Bystander at the Switch*. So it might be said (ii) The reason why the bystander may proceed is that if he proceeds, he maximizes utility, for he brings about a net saving of four lives, and in so doing he does *not* infringe any right of the one track workman's.

But I see no way—certainly there is no easy way—of establishing that these ideas are true.

Is it clear that the bystander would infringe no right of the one track workman's if he turned the trolley? Suppose there weren't anybody on the straight track, and the bystander turned the trolley onto the right-hand track, thereby killing the one, but not saving anybody, since nobody was at risk, and thus nobody needed saving. Wouldn't that infringe a right of the one workman's, a right in the cluster of rights that he has in having a right to life?

So should we suppose that the fact that there are five track workmen on the straight track who are in need of saving makes the one lack that right—which he would have had if that had not been a fact?

But then why doesn't the fact that the surgeon has five patients who are in need of saving make the young man also lack that right?

I think some people would say there is good (excellent, conclusive) reason for thinking that the one track workman lacks the right (given there are five on the straight track) lying in the fact that (given there are five on the straight track) it is morally permissible to turn the trolley onto him. But if your reason for thinking the one lacks the right is that it is permissible to turn the trolley onto him, then you can hardly go on to explain its being permissible to turn the trolley onto him by appeal to the fact that he lacks the right. It pays to stress this point: If you want to say, as (ii) does, that the bystander may proceed because he maximizes utility and infringes no right, then you need an independent account of what makes it be the case that he infringes no right—independent, that is, of its being the case that he may proceed.

There is *some* room for maneuver here. Any plausible theory of rights must make room for the possibility of waiving a right, and within that category, for the possibility of failing to have a right by virtue of assumption of risk; and it might be argued that that is what is involved here, i.e., that track workmen know of the risks of the job, and consent to run them when signing on for it.

But that is not really an attractive way of dealing with this difficulty. Track workmen certainly do not explicitly consent to being run down with trolleys when doing so will save five who are on some other track—certainly they are not asked to consent to this at the time of signing on for the job. And I doubt that they consciously assume the risk of it at that or any other time. And in any case, what if the six people involved had not been track workmen? What if they had been young children? What if they had been people who had been shoved out of helicopters? Wouldn't it all the same be permissible to turn the trolley?

So it is not clear what (independent) reason could be given for thinking that the bystander will infringe no right of the one's if he throws the switch.

I think, moreover, that there is *some* reason to think that the bystander will infringe a right of the one if he throws the switch, even though it is permissible for him to do so. What I have in mind issues simply from the fact that if the bystander throws the switch, then he does what will kill the one. Suppose the bystander proceeds, and that the one is now dead. The bystander's motives were, of course, excellent—he acted with a view to saving five. But the one did not volunteer his life so that the five might live; the bystander volunteered it for him. The bystander made him pay with his life for the bystander's saving of the five. This consideration seems to me to lend some weight to the idea that the bystander did do him a wrong—a wrong it was morally permissible to do him, since five were saved, but a wrong *to him* all the same.

Consider again that lingering feeling of discomfort (which, as I said, some people do feel) about what the bystander does if he turns the trolley. No doubt it is permissible to turn the trolley, but still ... but still .... People who feel this discomfort also think that, although it is permissible to turn the trolley, it is not morally required to do so. My own view is that they are right to feel and think these things. We would be able to explain why this is so if we supposed that if the bystander turns the trolley, then he does do the one track workman a wrong—if we supposed, in particular, that he infringes a right of the one track workman's which is in that cluster of rights which the workman has in having a right to life.[11]

I do not for a moment take myself to have established that (ii) is false. I have wished only to draw attention to the difficulty that lies ahead of a person who thinks (ii) true, and also to suggest that there is some reason to think that the bystander would infringe a right of the one's if he proceeded, and thus some reason to think that (ii) is false. It can easily be seen that if there is some reason to think the bystander would infringe a right of the one's, then there is also some reason to think that (i) is false—since if the bystander does infringe a right of the one's if he proceeds, and may nevertheless proceed, then it cannot be the fact that the surgeon infringes a right of the young man's if *he* proceeds which makes it impermissible for *him* to do so.

Perhaps a friend of (i) and (ii) can establish that they are true. I propose that, just in case he can't, we do well to see if there isn't some other way of solving this problem than by appeal to them. In particular, I propose we grant that both the bystander and the surgeon would infringe a right of their ones, a right in the cluster of rights that the ones' have in having a right to life, and that we look for some *other* difference between the cases which could be appealed to to explain the moral difference between them.

Notice that accepting this proposal does not commit us to rejecting the idea expressed in that crisp metaphor of Dworkin's. We can still say that rights trump utilities—if we can find a further feature of what the bystander does if he turns the trolley (beyond the fact that he maximizes utility) which itself trumps the right, and thus makes it permissible to proceed.

VI.

As I said, my own feeling is that the trolley problem can be solved only by appeal to the concept of a right—but not by appeal to it in as simple a way as that discussed in the preceding section. What we were attending to in the preceding section was only the fact that the agents would be killing and saving if they proceeded; what we should be attending to is the means by which they would kill and save.[12] (It is very tempting, because so much simpler, to regard a human act as a solid nugget, without internal structure, and to try to trace its moral value to the shape of its surface, as it were. The trolley problem seems to me to bring home that that will not do.)

I said earlier that there seem to me to be two crucial facts about what the bystander does if he proceeds in *Bystander at the Switch*. In the first place, he saves his five by making something that threatens them instead threaten the one. And second, he does not do that by means which themselves constitute infringements of any right of the one's.

Let us begin with the first.

If the surgeon proceeds in *Transplant*, he plainly does not save his five by making something that threatens them instead threaten one. It is organ-failure that threatens his five, and it is not *that* which he makes threaten the young man if he proceeds.

Consider another of Mrs. Foot's cases, which I shall call *Hospital*.

> Suppose [Mrs. Foot says] that there are five patients in a hospital whose lives could be saved by the manufacture of a certain gas, but that this will inevitably release lethal fumes into the room of another patient whom for some reason we are unable to move.[13]

Surely it would not be permissible for us to manufacture the gas.

In *Transplant* and *Hospital*, the five at risk are at risk from their ailments, and this might be thought to make a difference. Let us by-pass it. In a variant on *Hospital*—which I shall call *Hospital'*—all six patients are convalescing. The five at risk are at risk, not from their ailments, but from the ceiling of their room, which is about to fall on them. We can prevent this by pumping on a ceiling-support-mechanism; but doing so will inevitably release lethal fumes into the room of the sixth. Here too it is plain we may not proceed.

Contrast a case in which lethal fumes are being released by the heating system in the basement of a building next door to the hospital. They are headed towards the room of five. We can deflect them towards the room of one. Would that be permissible? I should think it would be—the case seems to be in all relevant respects like *Bystander at the Switch*.

In *Bystander at the Switch*, something threatens five, and if the agent proceeds, he saves the five by making that very thing threaten the one instead of the five. That is not true of the agents in *Hospital'* or *Hospital* or *Transplant*. In *Hospital'*, for example, what threatens the five is the ceiling, and the agent does not save them by making *it* threaten the one, he saves them by doing what will make something wholly different (some lethal fumes) threaten the one.

Why is this difference morally important? Other things being equal, to kill a man is to infringe his right to life, and we are therefore morally barred from killing. It is not enough to justify killing a person that if we do so, five others will be saved: To say that if we do so, five others will be saved is merely to say that utility will be maximized if we proceed, and that is not by itself sufficient to justify proceeding. Rights trump utilities. So if that is all that can be said in defense of killing a person, then killing that person is not permissible.

But that five others will be saved is not all that can be said in defense of killing in *Bystander at the Switch*. The bystander who proceeds does not merely minimize the number of deaths which get caused: He minimizes the number of deaths which get caused by something that already threatens people, and that will cause deaths whatever the bystander does.

The bystander who proceeds does not make something be a threat to people which would otherwise not be a threat to anyone; he makes be a threat to fewer what is already a threat to more. We might speak here of a "distributive exemption," which permits arranging that something that will do harm anyway shall be better distributed than it otherwise would be—shall (in *Bystander at the Switch*) do harm to fewer rather than more. Not just any distributive intervention is permissible: It is not in general morally open to us to make one die to save five. But other things being equal, it is not morally required of us that we let a burden descend out of the blue onto five when we can make it instead descend onto one.

I do not find it clear why there should be an exemption for, and only for, making a burden which is descending onto five descend, instead, onto one. That there is seems to me very plausible, however. On the one hand, the agent who acts under this exemption makes be a threat to one something that is *already* a threat to more, and thus something that will do harm *whatever* he does; on the other hand, the exemption seems to allow those acts which intuition tells us are clearly permissible, and to rule out those acts which intuition tells us are clearly impermissible.

VII.

More precisely, it is not morally required of us that we let a burden descend out of the blue onto five when we can make it instead descend onto one *if* we can make it descend onto the one by means which do not themselves constitute infringements of rights of the one.

Consider a case—which I shall call *Fat Man*—in which you are standing on a footbridge over the trolley track. You can see a trolley hurtling down the track, out of control. You turn around to see where the trolley is headed, and there are five workmen on the track where it exits from under the footbridge. What to do? Being an expert on trolleys, you know of one certain way to stop an out-of-control trolley: Drop a really heavy weight in its path. But where to find one? It just so happens that standing next to you on the footbridge is a fat man, a really fat man. He is leaning over the railing, watching the trolley; all you have to do is to give him a little shove, and over the railing he will go, onto the track in the path of the trolley. Would it be permissible for you to do this? Everybody to whom I have put this case says it would not be. But why?

Suppose the agent proceeds. He shoves the fat man, thereby toppling him off the footbridge into the path of the trolley, thereby causing him to be hit by the trolley, thereby killing him—but saving the five on the straight track. Then it is true of this agent, as it is true of the agent in *Bystander at the Switch*, that he saves his five by making something which threatens them instead threaten one.

But *this* agent does so by means which themselves constitute an infringement of a right of the one's. For shoving a person is infringing a right of his. So also is toppling a person off a footbridge.

I should stress that doing these things is infringing a person's rights even if doing them does not cause his death—even if doing them causes him no harm at all. As I shall put it, shoving a person, toppling a person off a footbridge, are *themselves* infringements of rights of his. A theory of rights ought to give an account of what makes it be the case that doing either of these things is itself an infringement of a right of his. But I think we may take it to be a datum* that it

---

* Singular of "data"—in this case, meaning something we are entitled to assume as true.

is, the job which confronts the theorist of rights being, not to establish that it is, but rather to explain why it is.

Consider by contrast the agent in *Bystander at the Switch*. He too, if he proceeds, saves five by making something that threatens them instead threaten one. But the means he takes to make that be the case are these: Turn the trolley onto the right-hand track. And turning the trolley onto the right-hand track is not *itself* an infringement of a right of anybody's. The agent would do the one no wrong at all if he turned the trolley onto the right-hand track, and by some miracle the trolley did not hit him.

We might of course have imagined it not necessary to shove the fat man. We might have imagined that all you need do to get the trolley to threaten him instead of the five is to wobble the handrail, for the handrail is low, and he is leaning on it, and wobbling it will cause him to fall over and off. Wobbling the handrail would be impermissible, I should think—no less so than shoving. But then there is room for an objection to the idea that the contrast I point to will help explain the moral differences among these cases. For it might be said that if you wobble the handrail, thereby getting the trolley to threaten the one instead of the five, then the means you take to get this to be the case are just these: Wobble the handrail. But doing that is not *itself* an infringement of a right of anybody's. You would do the fat man no wrong at all if you wobbled the handrail and no harm came to him in consequence of your doing so. In this respect, then, your situation seems to be exactly like that of the agent in *Bystander at the Switch*. Just as the means he would be taking to make the trolley threaten one instead of five would not constitute an infringement of a right, so also would the means you would be taking to make the trolley threaten one instead of five not constitute an infringement of a right.

What I had in mind, however, is a rather tighter notion of "means" than shows itself in this objection. By hypothesis, wobbling the handrail will cause the fat man to topple onto the track in the path of the trolley, and thus will cause the trolley to threaten him instead of the five. But the trolley will not threaten him instead of the five unless wobbling the handrail does cause him to topple. Getting the trolley to threaten the fat man instead of the five *requires* getting him into its path. You get the trolley to threaten him instead of them by wobbling the handrail only if,

and only because, by wobbling the handrail you topple him into the path of the trolley.

What I had in mind, then, is a notion of "means" which comes out as follows. Suppose you get a trolley to threaten one instead of five by wobbling a handrail. The means you take to get the trolley to threaten the one instead of the five include wobbling the handrail, *and* all those further things that you have to succeed in doing by wobbling the handrail if the trolley is to threaten the one instead of the five.

So the means by which the agent in *Fat Man* gets the trolley to threaten one instead of five include toppling the fat man off the footbridge; and doing that is itself an infringement of a right of the fat man's. By contrast, the means by which the agent in *Bystander at the Switch* gets the trolley to threaten one instead of five include no more than getting the trolley off the straight track onto the right-hand track; and doing that is not itself an infringement of a right of anybody's.

VIII.

It is arguable, however, that what is relevant is not that toppling the fat man off the footbridge is itself an infringement of *a* right of the fat man's but rather that toppling him off the footbridge is itself an infringement of a particularly stringent right of his.

What I have in mind comes out in yet another variant on *Bystander at the Switch*. Here the bystander must cross (without permission) a patch of land that belongs to the one in order to get to the switch; thus in order to get the trolley to threaten the one instead of five, the bystander must infringe a right of the one's. May he proceed?

Or again, in order to get the switch thrown, the bystander must use a sharply pointed tool, and the only available sharply pointed tool is a nailfile that belongs to the one; here too the bystander must infringe a right of the one's in order to get the trolley to threaten the one instead of five. May he proceed?

For my own part, I do not find it obvious that he may. (Remember what the bystander will be doing to the one by throwing that switch.) But others tell me they think it clear the bystander may proceed in such a case. If they are right—and I guess we should agree that they are—then that must surely be because the rights which the bystander would have to infringe here are minor, trivial, non-stringent—property rights of no great importance. By contrast, the right to not be toppled off a footbridge onto a trolley track is on any view a stringent right. We shall therefore have to recognize that what is at work in these cases is a matter of degree: If the agent must infringe a stringent right of the one's in order to get something that threatens five to threaten the one (as in *Fat Man*), then he may not proceed, whereas if the agent need infringe no right of the one's (as in *Bystander at the Switch*), or only a more or less trivial right of the one's (as in these variants on *Bystander at the Switch*), in order to get something that threatens five to threaten the one, then he may proceed.

Where what is at work is a matter of degree, it should be no surprise that there are borderline cases, on which people disagree. I confess to having been greatly surprised, however, at the fact of disagreement on the following variant on *Bystander at the Switch*:

> The five on the straight track are regular track workmen. The right-hand track is a dead end, unused in ten years. The Mayor, representing the City, has set out picnic tables on it, and invited the convalescents at the nearby City Hospital to have their meals there, guaranteeing them that no trolleys will ever, for any reason, be turned onto that track. The one on the right-hand track is a convalescent having his lunch there; it would never have occurred to him to do so if the Mayor had not issued his invitation and guarantee. The Mayor was out for a walk; he now stands by the switch.[14]

For the Mayor to get the trolley to threaten the one instead of the five, he must turn the trolley onto the right-hand track; but the one has a right against the Mayor that he not turn the trolley onto the right-hand track—a right generated by an official promise, which was then relied on by the one. (Contrast the original *Bystander at the Switch*, in which the one had no such right.) My own feeling is that it is plain the Mayor may not proceed. To my great surprise, I find that some people think he may. I conclude they think the right less stringent than I do.

In any case, that distributive exemption that I spoke of earlier is very conservative. It permits intervention into the world to get an object that already threatens death to those many to instead threaten death to these few, but only by acts that are not themselves gross impingements on the few. That is, the intervenor must not use means that infringe stringent rights of the few in order to get his distributive intention carried out.

It could of course be argued that the fact that the bystander of the original *Bystander at the Switch* makes threaten the one what already threatens the five, and does so by means that do not themselves constitute infringements of any right of the one's (not even a trivial right of the one's), shows that the bystander in that case infringes no right of the one's at all. That is, it could be argued that we have here that independent ground for saying that the bystander does not infringe the one's right to life which I said would be needed by a friend of (ii).[15] But I see nothing to be gained by taking this line, for I see nothing to be gained by supposing it never permissible to infringe a right; and something is lost by taking this line, namely the possibility of viewing the bystander as doing the one a wrong if he proceeds—albeit a wrong it is permissible to do him.

IX.

What counts as "*an* object which threatens death"? What marks one threat off from another? I have no doubt that ingenious people can construct cases in which we shall be unclear whether to say that if the agent proceeds, he makes threaten the one the very same thing as already threatens the five.

Moreover, which are the interventions in which the agent gets a thing that threatens five to instead threaten one by means that themselves constitute infringements of stringent rights of the one's? I have no doubt that ingenious people can construct cases in which we shall all be unclear whether to say that the agent's means do constitute infringements of stringent rights—and cases also in which we shall be unclear whether to say the agent's means constitute infringements of any rights at all.

But it is surely a mistake to look for precision in the concepts brought to bear to solve this problem: There isn't any to be had. It would be enough if cases in which it seems to us unclear whether to say "same threat," or unclear whether to say "non-right-infringing-means," also seemed to us to be cases in which it is unclear whether the agent may or may not proceed; and if also coming to see a case as one to which these expressions do (or do not) apply involves coming to see the case as one in which the agent may (or may not) proceed.

X.

If these ideas are correct, then we have a handle on anyway some of the troublesome cases in which people make threats. Suppose a villain says to us "I will cause a ceiling to fall on five unless you send lethal fumes into the room of one." Most of us think it would not be permissible for us to accede to this threat. Why? We may think of the villain as part of the world around the people involved, a part which is going to drop a burden on the five if we do not act. On this way of thinking of him, nothing *yet* threatens the five (certainly no ceiling as yet threatens them) and a fortiori we cannot save the five by making what (already) threatens them instead threaten the one. Alternatively, we may think of the villain as himself a threat to the five. But sending the fumes in is not making *him* be a threat to the one instead of to the five. The hypothesis I proposed, then, yields what it should: We may not accede.

That is because the hypothesis I proposed says nothing at all about the source of the threat to the five. Whether the threat to the five is, or is caused by, a human being or anything else, it is not permissible to do what will kill one to save the five except by making what threatens the five itself threaten the one.

By contrast, it seems to me very plausible to think that if a villain has started a trolley towards five, we may deflect the trolley towards one—other things being equal, of course. If a trolley is headed towards five, and we can deflect it towards one, we *may*, no matter who or what caused it to head towards the five.

I think that these considerations help us in dealing with a question I drew attention to earlier. Suppose a villain says to us "I will cause a ceiling to fall on five unless you send lethal fumes into the room of one." If we refuse, so that he does what he threatens to do, then he surely does something very much worse than we would be doing if we acceded to his threat and sent the fumes in. If we accede, we do something misguided and wrongful, but not nearly as bad as what he does if we refuse.

It should be stressed: The fact that he will do something worse if we do not send the fumes in does not entail that we ought to send them in, or even that it is permissible for us to do so.

How after all could that entail that we may send the fumes in? The fact that we would be saving five lives by sending the fumes in does not itself make it permissible for us to do so. (Rights trump utilities.) How could adding that the taker of those five lives would be doing what is worse than we would tip the balance? If we may not infringe a right of the one in order to save the five lives, it cannot possibly be thought that we may infringe the right of that one in order, not merely to save the five lives, but to make the villain's moral record better than it otherwise would be.

For my own part, I think that considerations of motives apart, and other things being equal, it does no harm to say that

(II) Killing five is worse than killing one

is, after all, true. *Of course* we shall then have to say that assessments of which acts are worse than which do not by themselves settle the question of what is permissible for a person to do. For we shall have to say that, despite the truth of (II), it is not the case that we are required to kill one in order that another person shall not kill five, or even that it is everywhere permissible for us to do this.

What is of interest is that what holds interpersonally also holds intra-personally. I said earlier that we might imagine the surgeon of *Transplant* to have caused the ailments of his five patients. Let us imagine the worst: He gave them chemical X precisely in order to cause their deaths, in order to inherit from them. Now he repents. But the fact that he would be saving five lives by operating on the one does not itself make it permissible for him to operate on the one. (Rights trump utilities.) And if he may not infringe a right of the one in order to save the five lives, it cannot possibly be thought that he may infringe the right of that one in order, not merely to save the five lives, but to make his own moral record better than it otherwise would be.

Another way to put the point is this: Assessments of which acts are worse than which have to be directly relevant to the agent's circumstances if they are to have a bearing on what he may do. If A threatens to kill five unless B kills one, then although killing five is worse than killing one, these are not the alternatives open to B. The alternatives open to B are: Kill one, thereby forestalling the deaths of five (and making A's moral record better than it otherwise would be), or let it be the case that A kills five. And the supposition that it would be worse for B to choose to kill the one is entirely compatible with the supposition that killing five is worse than killing one. Again, the alternatives open to the surgeon are: Operate on the one, thereby saving five (and making the surgeon's own moral record better than it otherwise would be), or let it be the case that he himself will have killed the five. And the supposition that it would be worse for the surgeon to choose to operate is entirely compatible with the supposition that killing five is worse than killing one.

On the other hand, suppose a second surgeon is faced with a choice between here and now giving chemical X to five, thereby killing them, and operating on, and thereby killing, only one. (It taxes the imagination to invent such a second surgeon, but let that pass. And compare *Trolley Driver*.) Then, other things being equal, it does seem he may choose to operate on the one. Some people would say something stronger, namely that he is required to make this choice. Perhaps they would say that

(II′) If a person is faced with a choice between doing something *here and now* to five, by the doing of which he will kill them, and doing something else *here and now* to one, by the doing of which he will kill only the one, then (other things being equal) he ought to choose the second alternative rather than the first

is a quite general moral truth. Whether or not the second surgeon is morally required to make this choice (and thus whether or not (II′) is a general moral truth), it does seem to be the case that he may. But this did seem puzzling. As I put it: Why should the present tense matter so much?

It is plausible to think that the present tense matters because the question for the agent at the time of acting is about the present, viz., "What may I here and now do?," and because that question is the same as the question "Which of the alternatives here and now open to me may I choose?" The alternatives now open to the second surgeon are: kill five or kill one. If killing five is worse than killing one, then perhaps he ought to, but at any rate he may, kill the one. ■

Suggestions for Critical Reflection

1. Thomson frequently appeals to her own intuitions about which actions are morally permissible. In responding to the various scenarios, she uses phrases such as "my own feeling is," "it really does seem right to think," and "surely it would not." For the most part, these claims are presented without further argument. Do your own intuitions about these scenarios align with Thomson's, or do they differ? Is there a general moral principle you can think of that would justify your intuitive beliefs about which of the actions are permissible and which are not?

2. If you are familiar with some standard moral theories—represented in this chapter by Aristotle (virtue theory), Kant (deontology), Mill (consequentialism), and Held (care ethics)—consider how these theories would approach the various scenarios Thomson describes. When Thomson endorses Dworkin's dictum "rights trump utilities," is she opting for one type of moral theory over others? Is she right to do so?

3. Most of us will not, in the course of our lives, encounter life-or-death moral choices closely resembling Thomson's thought experiments. Are there other contexts of ethical and political decision-making in which our intuitions regarding these thought experiments may provide insight? Think especially of contexts in which we are forced to weigh good consequences against other principles or rights.

4. Some have suggested the trolley problem may have practical relevance in connection with self-driving vehicles. Suppose, for example, that a driver realizes the inevitability of a high-speed collision and is able to either swerve left to kill or injure one person or continue in a straight path to kill or injure five. In most contexts, a human driver simply wouldn't have time to compare and decide between these options. However, this decision

might be possible for a vehicle navigated by artificial intelligence, equipped with sensors and programming capable of assessing the physical variables at play and predicting probable outcomes. In programming such an AI, should we design it to maximize the number of lives saved, always sacrificing one life if doing so is likely to spare multiple lives, even if this means veering off course? Should the AI take into account other factors, such as whether the five people at risk are adhering to the rules of the road, or whether they are young or old? Should the AI favor the life of any human passengers it is transporting, over the lives of people outside of the vehicle?

5. In recent decades, some philosophers have used surveys and experimentation to determine our common intuitions regarding thought experiments of the kind Thomson discusses. One such survey found that 81 per cent of American respondents

agreed that one should change the path of the trolley in the "Bystander at the Switch" scenario, while only 63 per cent of Russian respondents and 52 per cent of Chinese respondents agreed.* Does this apparent cultural variation undermine Thomson's argument in any way? Does this kind of experimental data have bearing on the philosophical issues at hand?

6. Also in recent years, some psychologists and philosophers have raised criticisms of trolley-problem type thought experiments, arguing that they are too extreme and unrealistic to elicit genuine moral intuitions (or teach genuine moral lessons), or that forcing people to think about ethics in this kind of calculating way is a distortion of how we really reason, or should reason, in ethical situations.† What do you make of these kinds of worries?

Notes

1   *See* P. FOOT, *The Problem of Abortion and the Doctrine of the Double Effect*, in VIRTUES AND VICES AND OTHER ESSAYS IN MORAL PHILOSOPHY 19 (1978).

2   I think it possible (though by no means certain) that John Taurek would say No, it is not permissible to (all simply) turn the trolley; what you ought to do is flip a coin. *See* Taurek, *Should the Numbers Count?*, 6 PHIL. & PUB. AFF. 293 (1977). (But he is there concerned with a different kind of case, namely that in which what is in question is not whether we may do what harms one to avoid harming five, but whether we may or ought to choose to save five in preference to saving one.) For criticism of Taurek's article, see Parfit, *Innumerate Ethics*, 7 PHIL. & PUB. AFF. 285 (1978).

3   I doubt that anyone would say, with any hope of getting agreement from others, that the surgeon ought to flip a coin. So even if you think that the trolley driver ought to flip a coin, there would remain, for you, an analogue of Mrs. Foot's problem, namely: Why ought the trolley driver flip a coin, whereas the surgeon may not?

4   Mrs. Foot speaks more generally of causing injury and failing to provide aid; and her reason for thinking that the former is worse than the latter is that the negative duty to refrain from causing injury is stricter than the positive duty to provide aid. *See* P. FOOT, *supra* note 1, at 27–29.

5   A similar case (intended to make a point similar to the one that I shall be making) is discussed in Davis, *The Priority of Avoiding Harm*, in KILLING AND LETTING DIE 172, 194–95 (B. Steinbock ed. 1980).

6   For a sensitive discussion of some of the difficulties, see Davis, *Using Persons and Common Sense*, 94 *Ethics* 387 (1984). Among other things, she argues (I think rightly) that the Kantian idea is not to be identified with the common sense concept of "using a person." *Id.* at 402.

7   For a second reason to think so, see *infra* note 13.

8   It is also true that if the five go wholly out of existence just before the agent starts to turn the trolley, then the one will die whatever the agent does. Should we say, then, that the agent uses one to save five if he acts, *and* uses five to save one if he does not act? No: What

---

*   Henrik Ahlenius and Torbjörn Tännsjö, "Chinese and Westerners Respond Differently to the Trolley Dilemmas," *Journal of Cognition and Culture* 12, 3–4 (2012): 195–201.

†   See, for example, Christopher Bauman et al., "Revisiting External Validity: Concerns about Trolley Problems and Other Sacrificial Dilemmas in Moral Psychology," *Social and Personality Psychology Compass* 8/9 (2014): 536–54.

follows *and* is false. If the agent does not act, he uses nobody. (I doubt that it can even be said that if he does not act, he lets them *be used*. For what is the active for which this is passive? Who or what would be using them if he does not act?)

9   I strongly suspect that giving an account of what makes it wrong to *use* a person, *see supra* text accompanying notes 6–8, would also require appeal to the concept of a right.

10 R. Dworkin, *Taking Rights Seriously* ix (1977).

11 Many of the examples discussed by Bernard Williams and Ruth Marcus plainly call out for this kind of treatment. *See* B. Williams, *Ethical Consistency*, in Problems of the Self 166 (1973); Marcus, *Moral Dilemmas and Consistency*, 77 J. Phil. 121 (1980).

12 It may be worth stressing that what I suggest calls for attention is not (as some construals of "double effect" would have it) whether the agent's killing of the one is his means to something, and not (as other construals of "double effect" would have it) whether the death of the one is the agent's means to something, but rather what are the means by which the agent both kills and saves.

For a discussion of "the doctrine of double effect," see P. Foot, *supra* note 1.

13 *Id*. at 29. As Mrs. Foot says, we do not *use* the one if we proceed in *Hospital*. Yet the impermissibility of proceeding in *Hospital* seems to have a common source with the impermissibility of operating in *Transplant*, in which the surgeon *would* be using the one whose parts he takes for the five who need them. This is my second reason for thinking that an appeal to the fact that the surgeon would be using his victim is an over-simple way of taking account of the means he would be employing for the saving of his five. *See supra* note 7.

14 Notice that in this case too the agent does not *use* the one if he proceeds. (This case, along with a number of other cases I have been discussing, comes from Thomson, *Killing, Letting Die, and the Trolley Problem*, 59 The Monist 204 (1976). Mrs. Thomson seems to me to have been blundering around in the dark in that paper, but the student of this problem may possibly find some of the cases she discusses useful.)

15 *See supra* text accompanying notes 9–11.

Ethical Issues

ABORTION • IMMIGRATION • TERRORISM •
NON-HUMAN ANIMALS

The previous section introduced some main moral theories: Aristotle's view emphasizing moral character and the virtues; Kant's position that certain moral maxims, characterizing types of action, are right or wrong in themselves; Mill's argument for placing moral priority on maximizing the good consequences of our actions; Nietzsche's plea for moving "beyond good and evil"; Held's critique of previous moral theories in favor of an "ethics of care"; and Thomson's rights-based counter to utilitarianism. This section turns to the application of these theories to particular moral issues, an area of philosophy sometimes called "applied ethics."

Four particular topics in applied ethics are introduced here, each with a pair of readings. The first topic is the morality of abortion. Don Marquis argues that the fundamental harm of abortion is that it deprives the fetus of the future it would otherwise have had, and concludes from this that "the overwhelming majority of deliberate abortions are seriously immoral." A contrasting view is developed by Judith Jarvis Thomson, who reasons that the rights of the fetus have to be balanced against the pregnant woman's own rights and uses vivid thought experiments to argue that, in general (though not in every case), the net result is that abortion is permissible.

The selections for the second topic, immigration, also pairs two opposing views, though in this case the opposition is a little more oblique. Kit Wellman presents a nuanced defense of a state's right to control immigration, concluding that "legitimate states are entitled to reject all potential immigrants, even those desperately seeking asylum from corrupt governments." José

Jorge Mendoza's paper, on the other hand, focuses not so much on border control as on immigration enforcement within the borders of a state, and makes the case that it may be immoral for legitimate, liberal-democratic states to use certain methods to identify and deport immigrants, even when they are in the country illegally.

The next two readings grapple with the difficult question of defining terrorism and finding a consistent, appropriately nuanced moral response to it. Here, a lot of the value of the discussions is in their details as much as in their overall (tentative) conclusions, but Virginia Held sets out in general strokes "to compare war and terrorism, and to show how war can be morally worse," while Claudia Card suggests we broaden the definition of terrorism to include things which are not always labeled as such, and notes that "an enormous amount of preventable suffering and death, globally, is caused by terrorism against targets who have lacked a public voice."

Just as, in the case of terrorism, much of the interesting philosophical debate involves calling into question a widely held background assumption—that terrorism is clearly identifiable and uniquely immoral—so in the case of the status of non-human animals the topic is not so much a debate between two widely held positions as it is a challenge to the ideological status quo. Most of us assume, without further thought, that non-human animals are substantially less worthy of moral consideration than human beings—if they require moral consideration at all—and many of our social systems concerning food, clothing, recreation, transport, urban planning, and so on have that assumption of moral asymmetry built into them at their foundations. But are we really entitled to that presumption? Do our overall moral theories consistently allow us to ignore or radically de-prioritize the needs of non-human animals? Peter Singer, a well-known proponent of utilitarianism, argues forcefully that this is not so, and lays out the extensive social changes that are necessary if we take these moral commitments seriously. Mary Midgley, similarly, urges us to take animal rights seriously and does so by critiquing a notion of 'personhood' that would allow us to treat (some) human beings as persons while denying that any non-human could have an equivalent moral and legal status.

These four discussions—about abortion, immigration, terrorism, and non-human animals—are not separate and fragmentary debates, isolated and independent from the rest of moral philosophy. It is important to drill deep into the details—including the empirical details—of practical, pressing ethical questions, in order to make sure that discussion of them is rich, subtle, and grounded—and perhaps to challenge our abstract moral principles by testing them against difficult real-world cases. But it is also important to value intellectual consistency across different issues; to underpin judgments in particular cases with more general, principled moral views; and in the end, hopefully, to bring all our considered moral judgments under the umbrella of an overall theory of what makes those judgments true—a theory like Kant's deontology, or Mill's consequentialism, or some other. Some general philosophical themes can be traced through several of the readings in this chapter, including: the disputed normative notion of being a person (as opposed, say, to a biological human, or to a mere 'thing'); the tension between moral theories that tend to prioritize the good (good outcomes) versus the right (rights and duties); the tension that can exist between conflicting moral principles, such as competing rights; and the sometimes controversial role of thought experiments in moral reasoning.

Applied ethics is a philosophical field in its own right, with its own literature. Some useful resources to follow the debates introduced here further, or explore other practical moral questions, include *Contemporary Debates in Applied Ethics*, ed. Cohen and Wellman (Wiley-Blackwell, 2013); *Applied Ethics: A Multicultural Approach*, ed. May and Delston (Routledge, 2015); Robert L. Holmes, *Introduction to Applied Ethics* (Bloomsbury, 2018); Mike W. Martin, *Everyday Morality* (Wadsworth, 2007); and *A Companion to Applied Ethics*, ed. Frey and Wellman (Blackwell, 2008). The Cambridge Applied Ethics series from Cambridge University Press includes *Ethics and Animals* (Gruen, 2011); *Ethics and the Environment* (Jamieson, 2008); *Ethics and War* (Lee, 2011); *Ethics and Health Care* (Moskop, 2016); *Ethics and Science* (Briggle and Mitcham, 2012); *Ethics and Business* (Gibson, 2007); *Ethics and Criminal Justice* (Kleinig, 2008); *Ethics and Finance* (Hendry, 2013); *Ethics and the Media* (Ward, 2012); and *Ethics and Law* (Wendel, 2014).

DON MARQUIS

Why Abortion Is Immoral

Who Is Don Marquis?

Born in 1935, Donald Marquis is an American philosopher and professor emeritus at the University of Kansas. Marquis earned an AB in Anatomy and Physiology from Indiana University in 1957, an MA in History from the University of Pittsburgh in 1962, then an MA in History and Philosophy of Science from Indiana in 1964 and a PhD in Philosophy there in 1970. He spent his career teaching at the University of Kansas. He is best known for his work on the philosophy of science and medical ethics, particularly on issues of abortion, physician-assisted suicide, and the concept of clinical death.

What Is the Structure of This Reading?

Marquis leads off by noting that contemporary philosophers rarely defend the position that abortion is immoral. Bucking this trend, he asserts that, with few exceptions, deliberate abortion is an indefensible act. To begin, Marquis provides an overview of conventional arguments for and against the morality of abortion. Many anti-abortionists attempt to establish that fetuses are persons from conception, and thereby demonstrate that abortion is murder. Many pro-choicers argue that fetuses are not persons—that is, they lack some important capacity that makes grown humans morally considerable—and that abortion is therefore not murder. Both positions rely on generalizations that aren't shared by the other side and which lead to other morally unappealing conclusions. What both sides miss, according to Marquis, is an understanding of the central fact that makes killing immoral.

Marquis seeks to uncover this essence of the wrongness of killing by asking why it is wrong to kill *us* (as in, grown human beings). He claims that killing us is wrong because it causes the victim to lose "all the experiences, activities, projects and enjoyments that would otherwise have constituted [their] future." And since abortion deprives a fetus of a valuable future like ours, abortion is wrong for the same reasons that killing us is wrong. Marquis then considers alternative explanations of the wrongness of killing—the "discontinuation account" and the "desire account"—denying that either of these is as plausible as the "future-like-ours" account.* He argues that neither of these offers as convincing an explanation of the wrongness of killing.

If Marquis is right, then any killing that deprives an entity of a future like ours is wrong, including abortion. By focusing on the question of why killing is wrong rather than that of whether a fetus is a person, Marquis's argument doesn't hinge on the contentious point of dispute that has traditionally led to an impasse in the abortion debate.

Some Useful Background Information

Marquis makes use of a subtle terminological distinction between 'person' and 'human being.' Though we often use these terms interchangeably in ordinary speech, they are sometimes used quite differently in the academic literature. 'Human being' is, on this usage, a biological category inclusive of adults as well as infant children and perhaps other groups (possibly including fetuses). 'Person' is used in both a narrower and a broader sense to refer to a being with a certain set of psychological or social traits shared by most adult human beings—which might possibly include non-humans such as the great apes or hypothetical intelligent aliens, and might possibly categorize some humans as non-persons, such as those in permanent comas. This terminology is contentious, and Marquis examines some of the complexities of the distinction while pointing to it as one of the sticking points between pro-choice advocates and anti-abortion advocates.

---

* In the years since Marquis's paper was published, this has come to be known more standardly as the "deprivation" account.

Why Abortion Is Immoral*

The view that abortion is, with rare exceptions, seriously immoral has received little support in the recent philosophical literature. No doubt most philosophers affiliated with secular institutions of higher education believe that the anti-abortion position is either a symptom of irrational religious dogma or a conclusion generated by seriously confused philosophical argument. The purpose of this essay is to undermine this general belief. This essay sets out an argument that purports to show, as well as any argument in ethics can show, that abortion is, except possibly in rare cases, seriously immoral, that it is in the same moral category as killing an innocent adult human being.

The argument is based on a major assumption. Many of the most insightful and careful writers on the ethics of abortion—such as Joel Feinberg, Michael Tooley, Mary Anne Warren, H. Tristram Engelhardt, Jr., L.W. Sumner, John T. Noonan, Jr., and Philip Devine[1]—believe that whether or not abortion is morally permissible stands or falls on whether or not a fetus is the sort of being whose life it is seriously wrong to end. The argument of this essay will assume, but not argue, that they are correct.

Also, this essay will neglect issues of great importance to a complete ethics of abortion. Some anti-abortionists will allow that certain abortions, such as abortion before implantation or abortion when the life of a woman is threatened by a pregnancy or abortion after rape, may be morally permissible. This essay will not explore the casuistry† of these hard cases. The purpose of this essay is to develop a general argument for the claim that the overwhelming majority of deliberate abortions are seriously immoral.

I.

A sketch of standard anti-abortion and pro-choice arguments exhibits how those arguments possess certain symmetries that explain why partisans of those positions are so convinced of the correctness of their own positions, why they are not successful in convincing their opponents, and why, to others, this issue seems to be unresolvable. An analysis of the nature of this standoff suggests a strategy for surmounting it.

Consider the way a typical anti-abortionist argues. She will argue or assert that life is present from the moment of conception or that fetuses look like babies or that fetuses possess a characteristic such as a genetic code that is both necessary and sufficient for being human. Anti-abortionists seem to believe that (1) the truth of all of these claims is quite obvious, and (2) establishing any of these claims is sufficient to show that abortion is morally akin to murder.

A standard pro-choice strategy exhibits similarities. The prochoicer will argue or assert that fetuses are not persons or that fetuses are not rational agents or that fetuses are not social beings. Pro-choicers seem to believe that (1) the truth of any of these claims is quite obvious, and (2) establishing any of these claims is sufficient to show that an abortion is not a wrongful killing.

In fact, both the pro-choice and the anti-abortion claims do seem to be true, although the "it looks like a baby" claim is more difficult to establish the earlier the pregnancy. We seem to have a standoff. How can it be resolved?

As everyone who has taken a bit of logic knows, if any of these arguments concerning abortion is a good argument, it requires not only some claim characterizing fetuses, but also some general moral principle that ties a characteristic of fetuses to having or not having the right to life or to some other moral characteristic that will generate the obligation or the lack of obligation not to end the life of a fetus. Accordingly, the arguments of the anti-abortionist and the pro-choicer need a bit of filling in to be regarded as adequate.

Note what each partisan will say. The anti-abortionist will claim that her position is supported by

---

* Don Marquis, "Why Abortion Is Immoral," *The Journal of Philosophy* 86, 4 (April 1989): 183–202.

† Case-based reasoning, that is, reasoning about individual cases rather than general principles. In other contexts, "casuistry" sometimes refers to specious or unsound reasoning.

such generally accepted moral principles as "It is always prima facie* seriously wrong to take a human life" or "It is always prima facie seriously wrong to end the life of a baby." Since these are generally accepted moral principles, her position is certainly not obviously wrong. The pro-choicer will claim that her position is supported by such plausible moral principles as "Being a person is what gives an individual intrinsic moral worth" or "It is only seriously prima facie wrong to take the life of a member of the human community." Since these are generally accepted moral principles, the pro-choice position is certainly not obviously wrong. Unfortunately, we have again arrived at a standoff.

Now, how might one deal with this standoff? The standard approach is to try to show how the moral principles of one's opponent lose their plausibility under analysis. It is easy to see how this is possible. On the one hand, the anti-abortionist will defend a moral principle concerning the wrongness of killing which tends to be broad in scope in order that even fetuses at an early stage of pregnancy will fall under it. The problem with broad principles is that they often embrace too much. In this particular instance, the principle "It is always prima facie wrong to take a human life" seems to entail that it is wrong to end the existence of a living human cancer-cell culture, on the grounds that the culture is both living and human. Therefore, it seems that the anti-abortionist's favored principle is too broad.

On the other hand, the pro-choicer wants to find a moral principle concerning the wrongness of killing which tends to be narrow in scope in order that fetuses will *not* fall under it. The problem with narrow principles is that they often do not embrace enough. Hence, the needed principles such as "It is prima facie seriously wrong to kill only persons" or "It is prima facie wrong to kill only rational agents" do not explain why it is wrong to kill infants or young children or the severely retarded or even perhaps the severely mentally ill. Therefore, we seem again to have a standoff. The anti-abortionist charges, not unreasonably, that pro-choice principles concerning killing are too narrow to

be acceptable; the pro-choicer charges, not unreasonably, that anti-abortionist principles concerning killing are too broad to be acceptable.

Attempts by both sides to patch up the difficulties in their positions run into further difficulties. The anti-abortionist will try to remove the problem in her position by reformulating her principle concerning killing in terms of human beings. Now we end up with: "It is always prima facie seriously wrong to end the life of a human being." This principle has the advantage of avoiding the problem of the human cancer-cell culture counterexample. But this advantage is purchased at a high price. For although it is clear that a fetus is both human and alive, it is not at all clear that a fetus is a human *being*. There is at least something to be said for the view that something becomes a human being only after a process of development, and that therefore first trimester fetuses and perhaps all fetuses are not yet human beings. Hence, the anti-abortionist, by this move, has merely exchanged one problem for another.[2]

The pro-choicer fares no better. She may attempt to find reasons why killing infants, young children, and the severely retarded is wrong which are independent of her major principle that is supposed to explain the wrongness of taking human life, but which will not also make abortion immoral. This is no easy task. Appeals to social utility will seem satisfactory only to those who resolve not to think of the enormous difficulties with a utilitarian account† of the wrongness of killing and the significant social costs of preserving the lives of the unproductive.[3] A pro-choice strategy that extends the definition of 'person' to infants or even to young children seems just as arbitrary as an anti-abortion strategy that extends the definition of 'human being' to fetuses. Again, we find symmetries in the two positions and we arrive at a standoff.

There are even further problems that reflect symmetries in the two positions. In addition to counterexample problems, or the arbitrary application problems that can be exchanged for them, the standard anti-abortionist principle "It is prima facie seriously wrong to kill a human being," or one of its variants,

---

* Latin: "first impression"; a *prima facie* claim is one that is true in the absence of evidence to the contrary.

† An account that emphasizes the consequences of our actions (especially in connection with happiness or pleasure). See the reading from Mill's *Utilitarianism* in the Ethical Theory chapter.

can be objected to on the grounds of ambiguity. If 'human being' is taken to be a *biological* category, then the anti-abortionist is left with the problem of explaining why a merely biological category should make a moral difference. Why, it is asked, is it any more reasonable to base a moral conclusion on the number of chromosomes in one's cells than on the color of one's skin?[4] If 'human being', on the other hand, is taken to be a *moral* category, then the claim that a fetus is a human being cannot be taken to be a premise in the anti-abortion argument, for it is precisely what needs to be established. Hence, either the anti-abortionist's main category is a morally irrelevant, merely biological category, or it is of no use to the anti-abortionist in establishing (noncircularly,* of course) that abortion is wrong.

Although this problem with the anti-abortionist position is often noticed, it is less often noticed that the pro-choice position suffers from an analogous problem. The principle "Only persons have the right to life" also suffers from an ambiguity. The term 'person' is typically defined in terms of psychological characteristics, although there will certainly be disagreement concerning which characteristics are most important. Supposing that this matter can be settled, the pro-choicer is left with the problem of explaining why *psychological* characteristics should make a *moral* difference. If the pro-choicer should attempt to deal with this problem by claiming that an explanation is not necessary, that in fact we do treat such a cluster of psychological properties as having moral significance, the sharp-witted anti-abortionist should have a ready response. We do treat being both living and human as having moral significance. If it is legitimate for the pro-choicer to demand that the anti-abortionist provide an explanation of the connection between the biological character of being a human being and the wrongness of being killed (even though people accept this connection), then it is legitimate for the anti-abortionist to demand that the pro-choicer provide an explanation of the connection between psychological criteria for being a person and the wrongness of being killed (even though that connection is accepted).[5]

Feinberg has attempted to meet this objection (he calls psychological personhood "commonsense personhood"):

The characteristics that confer commonsense personhood are not arbitrary bases for rights and duties, such as race, sex or species membership; rather they are traits that make sense out of rights and duties and without which those moral attributes would have no point or function. It is because people are conscious; have a sense of their personal identities; have plans, goals, and projects; experience emotions; are liable to pains, anxieties, and frustrations; can reason and bargain, and so on—it is because of these attributes that people have values and interests, desires and expectations of their own, including a stake in their own futures, and a personal well-being of a sort we cannot ascribe to unconscious or nonrational beings. Because of their developed capacities they can assume duties and responsibilities and can have and make claims on one another. Only because of their sense of self, their life plans, their value hierarchies, and their stakes in their own futures can they be ascribed fundamental rights. There is nothing arbitrary about these linkages (*op. cit.*, p. 270).

The plausible aspects of this attempt should not be taken to obscure its implausible features. There is a great deal to be said for the view that being a psychological person under some description is a necessary condition for having duties. One cannot have a duty unless one is capable of behaving morally, and a being's capability of behaving morally will require having a certain psychology. It is far from obvious, however, that having rights entails consciousness or rationality, as Feinberg suggests. We speak of the rights of the severely retarded or the severely mentally ill, yet some of these persons are not rational. We speak of the rights of the temporarily unconscious. The New Jersey Supreme Court based their decision in the Quinlan case on Karen Ann Quinlan's right to privacy,

---

* A circular argument is one that in some way assumes the truth of its own conclusion. Marquis is saying that if the anti-abortionist *defines* 'human being' such that all human beings (including fetuses) have moral worth, that definition will only be agreeable to those who already believe that it's wrong to kill a fetus.

and she was known to be permanently unconscious at that time.* Hence, Feinberg's claim that having rights entails being conscious is, on its face, obviously false.

Of course, it might not make sense to attribute rights to a being that would never in its natural history have certain psychological traits. This modest connection between psychological personhood and moral personhood will create a place for Karen Ann Quinlan and the temporarily unconscious. But then it makes a place for fetuses also. Hence, it does not serve Feinberg's pro-choice purposes. Accordingly, it seems that the pro-choicer will have as much difficulty bridging the gap between psychological personhood and personhood in the moral sense as the anti-abortionist has bridging the gap between being a biological human being and being a human being in the moral sense.

Furthermore, the pro-choicer cannot any more escape her problem by making person a purely moral category than the anti-abortionist could escape by the analogous move. For if person is a moral category, then the pro-choicer is left without the resources for establishing (noncircularly, of course) the claim that a fetus is not a person, which is an essential premise in her argument. Again, we have both a symmetry and a standoff between pro-choice and anti-abortion views.

Passions in the abortion debate run high. There are both plausibilities and difficulties with the standard positions. Accordingly, it is hardly surprising that partisans of either side embrace with fervor the moral generalizations that support the conclusions they preanalytically† favor, and reject with disdain the moral generalizations of their opponents as being subject to inescapable difficulties. It is easy to believe that the counterexamples to one's own moral principles are merely temporary difficulties that will dissolve in the wake of further philosophical research, and that the counterexamples to the principles of one's opponents are as straightforward as the contradiction between *A* and *O* propositions in traditional logic.‡ This might suggest to an impartial observer (if there are any) that the abortion issue is unresolvable.

There is a way out of this apparent dialectical quandary. The moral generalizations of both sides are not quite correct. The generalizations hold for the most part, for the usual cases. This suggests that they are all *accidental* generalizations, that the moral claims made by those on both sides of the dispute do not touch on the *essence* of the matter.§

This use of the distinction between essence and accident is not meant to invoke obscure metaphysical categories. Rather, it is intended to reflect the rather atheoretical nature of the abortion discussion. If the generalization a partisan in the abortion dispute adopts were derived from the reason why ending the life of a human being is wrong, then there could not be exceptions to that generalization unless some special case obtains in which there are even more powerful countervailing reasons. Such generalizations would not be merely accidental generalizations; they would point to, or be based upon, the essence of the wrongness of killing, what it is that makes killing wrong. All this suggests that a necessary condition of resolving the abortion controversy is a more theoretical account of the wrongness of killing. After all, if we merely believe, but do not understand, why killing adult human beings such as ourselves is wrong, how could we conceivably show that abortion is either immoral or permissible?

---

* In 1975, Karen Ann Quinlan fell into a coma at the age of 21, suffering irreversible brain damage that left her in a persistent vegetative state. After several months, Quinlan's parents filed a suit requesting that she be disconnected from the ventilator which they believed was keeping her alive, as they felt it was causing her pain (and there was no hope for her recovery). The New Jersey Superior Court initially denied this request; however, the decision was reversed on appeal, and in 1976 Quinlan's ventilator was removed. Surprisingly, Quinlan survived the removal of her ventilator and continued to live, unconscious, until her death in 1985.

† Before analysis.

‡ In traditional categorical logic, "A" propositions are those of the form "All S are P," while "O" propositions are those of the form "Some S are not P." It's clear that both of those propositions can't be true at the same time.

§ In philosophy, the "essence" or "essential property" is a feature that a given thing must have, in order to be what it is. An "accidental property," by contrast, is a characteristic that a thing may or may not have.

II.

In order to develop such an account, we can start from the following unproblematic assumption concerning our own case: it is wrong to kill *us*. Why is it wrong? Some answers can be easily eliminated. It might be said that what makes killing us wrong is that a killing brutalizes the one who kills. But the brutalization consists of being inured to the performance of an act that is hideously immoral; hence, the brutalization does not explain the immorality. It might be said that what makes killing us wrong is the great loss others would experience due to our absence. Although such hubris* is understandable, such an explanation does not account for the wrongness of killing hermits, or those whose lives are relatively independent and whose friends find it easy to make new friends.

A more obvious answer is better. What primarily makes killing wrong is neither its effect on the murderer nor its effect on the victim's friends and relatives, but its effect on the victim. The loss of one's life is one of the greatest losses one can suffer. The loss of one's life deprives one of all the experiences, activities, projects, and enjoyments that would otherwise have constituted one's future. Therefore, killing someone is wrong, primarily because the killing inflicts (one of) the greatest possible losses on the victim. To describe this as the loss of life can be misleading, however. The change in my biological state does not by itself make killing me wrong. The effect of the loss of my biological life is the loss to me of all those activities, projects, experiences, and enjoyments which would otherwise have constituted my future personal life. These activities, projects, experiences, and enjoyments are either valuable for their own sakes or are means to something else that is valuable for its own sake. Some parts of my future are not valued by me now, but will come to be valued by me as I grow older and as my values and capacities change. When I am killed, I am deprived both of what I now value which would have been part of my future personal life, but also what I would come to value. Therefore, when I die, I am deprived of all of the value of my future. Inflicting this loss on me is ultimately what makes killing me wrong. This being the case, it would seem that what makes killing *any* adult human being prima facie seriously wrong is the loss of his or her future.[6]

How should this rudimentary theory of the wrongness of killing be evaluated? It cannot be faulted for deriving an 'ought' from an 'is',† for it does not. The analysis assumes that killing me (or you, reader) is prima facie seriously wrong. The point of the analysis is to establish which natural property ultimately explains the wrongness of the killing, given that it is wrong. A natural property will ultimately explain the wrongness of killing, only if (1) the explanation fits with our intuitions about the matter and (2) there is no other natural property that provides the basis for a better explanation of the wrongness of killing. This analysis rests on the intuition that what makes killing a particular human or animal wrong is what it does to that particular human or animal. What makes killing wrong is some natural effect or other of the killing. Some would deny this. For instance, a divine-command theorist‡ in ethics would deny it. Surely this denial is, however, one of those features of divine-command theory which renders it so implausible.

The claim that what makes killing wrong is the loss of the victim's future is directly supported by two considerations. In the first place, this theory explains why we regard killing as one of the worst of crimes.

---

* Excessive pride.

† "In every system of morality, which I have hitherto met with, I have always remarked, that the author proceeds for some time in the ordinary way of reasoning, and establishes the being of a God, or makes observations concerning human affairs; when of a sudden I am surprised to find, that instead of the usual copulations of propositions, is, and is not, I meet with no proposition that is not connected with an ought, or an ought not. This change is imperceptible; but is, however, of the last consequence. For as this ought, or ought not, expresses some new relation or affirmation, 'tis necessary that it should be observed and explained; and at the same time that a reason should be given, for what seems altogether inconceivable, how this new relation can be a deduction from others, which are entirely different from it."—David Hume, Book III, Part I, Section I, *A Treatise of Human Nature* (1739).

‡ A divine command theory of ethics holds that ethical truths are determined by the will of God or some other divine entity—and hence are made true solely by that divine decision, rather than by some other (natural) fact.

Killing is especially wrong, because it deprives the victim of more than perhaps any other crime. In the second place, people with AIDS or cancer who know they are dying believe, of course, that dying is a very bad thing for them. They believe that the loss of a future to them that they would otherwise have experienced is what makes their premature death a very bad thing for them. A better theory of the wrongness of killing would require a different natural property associated with killing which better fits with the attitudes of the dying. What could it be?

The view that what makes killing wrong is the loss to the victim of the value of the victim's future gains additional support when some of its implications are examined. In the first place, it is incompatible with the view that it is wrong to kill only beings who are biologically human. It is possible that there exists a different species from another planet whose members have a future like ours. Since having a future like that is what makes killing someone wrong, this theory entails that it would be wrong to kill members of such a species. Hence, this theory is opposed to the claim that only life that is biologically human has great moral worth, a claim which many anti-abortionists have seemed to adopt. This opposition, which this theory has in common with personhood theories, seems to be a merit of the theory.

In the second place, the claim that the loss of one's future is the wrong-making feature of one's being killed entails the possibility that the futures of some actual non-human mammals on our own planet are sufficiently like ours that it is seriously wrong to kill them also. Whether some animals do have the same right to life as human beings depends on adding to the account of the wrongness of killing some additional account of just what it is about my future or the futures of other adult human beings which makes it wrong to kill us. No such additional account will be offered in this essay. Undoubtedly, the provision of such an account would be a very difficult matter. Undoubtedly, any such account would be quite controversial. Hence, it surely should not reflect badly on this sketch of an elementary theory of the wrongness of killing that it is indeterminate with respect to some very difficult issues regarding animal rights.

In the third place, the claim that the loss of one's future is the wrong-making feature of one's being killed

does not entail, as sanctity of human life theories do, that active euthanasia is wrong. Persons who are severely and incurably ill, who face a future of pain and despair, and who wish to die will not have suffered a loss if they are killed. It is, strictly speaking, the value of a human's future which makes killing wrong in this theory. This being so, killing does not necessarily wrong some persons who are sick and dying. Of course, there may be other reasons for a prohibition of active euthanasia, but that is another matter. Sanctity-of-human-life theories seem to hold that active euthanasia is seriously wrong even in an individual case where there seems to be good reason for it independently of public policy considerations. This consequence is most implausible, and it is a plus for the claim that the loss of a future of value is what makes killing wrong that it does not share this consequence.

In the fourth place, the account of the wrongness of killing defended in this essay does straightforwardly entail that it is prima facie seriously wrong to kill children and infants, for we do presume that they have futures of value. Since we do believe that it is wrong to kill defenseless little babies, it is important that a theory of the wrongness of killing easily account for this. Personhood theories of the wrongness of killing, on the other hand, cannot straightforwardly account for the wrongness of killing infants and young children.[7] Hence, such theories must add special ad hoc* accounts of the wrongness of killing the young. The plausibility of such ad hoc theories seems to be a function of how desperately one wants such theories to work. The claim that the primary wrong-making feature of a killing is the loss to the victim of the value of its future accounts for the wrongness of killing young children and infants directly; it makes the wrongness of such acts as obvious as we actually think it is. This is a further merit of this theory. Accordingly, it seems that this value of a future-like-ours theory of the wrongness of killing shares strengths of both sanctity-of-life and personhood accounts while avoiding weaknesses of both. In addition, it meshes with a central intuition concerning what makes killing wrong.

The claim that the primary wrong-making feature of a killing is the loss to the victim of the value of its future has obvious consequences for the ethics of

---

* *Ad hoc* means "for the particular situation or case at hand and for no other" (Latin for "to this").

abortion. The future of a standard fetus includes a set of experiences, projects, activities, and such which are identical with the futures of adult human beings and are identical with the futures of young children. Since the reason that is sufficient to explain why it is wrong to kill human beings after the time of birth is a reason that also applies to fetuses, it follows that abortion is prima facie seriously morally wrong.

This argument does not rely on the invalid inference that, since it is wrong to kill persons, it is wrong to kill potential persons also. The category that is morally central to this analysis is the category of having a valuable future like ours; it is not the category of personhood. The argument to the conclusion that abortion is prima facie seriously morally wrong proceeded independently of the notion of person or potential person or any equivalent. Someone may wish to start with this analysis in terms of the value of a human future, conclude that abortion is, except perhaps in rare circumstances, seriously morally wrong, infer that fetuses have the right to life, and then call fetuses "persons" as a result of their having the right to life. Clearly, in this case, the category of person is being used to state the *conclusion* of the analysis rather than to generate the *argument* of the analysis.

The structure of this anti-abortion argument can be both illuminated and defended by comparing it to what appears to be the best argument for the wrongness of the wanton infliction of pain on animals. This latter argument is based on the assumption that it is prima facie wrong to inflict pain on me (or you, reader). What is the natural property associated with the infliction of pain which makes such infliction wrong? The obvious answer seems to be that the infliction of pain causes suffering and that suffering is a misfortune. The suffering caused by the infliction of pain is what makes the wanton infliction of pain on me wrong. The wanton infliction of pain on other adult humans causes suffering. The wanton infliction of pain on animals causes suffering. Since causing suffering is what makes the wanton infliction of pain wrong and since the wanton infliction of pain on animals causes suffering, it follows that the wanton infliction of pain on animals is wrong.

This argument for the wrongness of the wanton infliction of pain on animals shares a number of structural features with the argument for the serious prima facie wrongness of abortion. Both arguments start with an obvious assumption concerning what it is wrong to do to me (or you, reader). Both then look for the characteristic or the consequence of the wrong action which makes the action wrong. Both recognize that the wrong-making feature of these immoral actions is a property of actions sometimes directed at individuals other than postnatal human beings. If the structure of the argument for the wrongness of the wanton infliction of pain on animals is sound, then the structure of the argument for the prima facie serious wrongness of abortion is also sound, for the structure of the two arguments is the same. The structure common to both is the key to the explanation of how the wrongness of abortion can be demonstrated without recourse to the category of person. In neither argument is that category crucial.

This defense of an argument for the wrongness of abortion in terms of a structurally similar argument for the wrongness of the wanton infliction of pain on animals succeeds only if the account regarding animals is the correct account. Is it? In the first place, it seems plausible. In the second place, its major competition is Kant's account.* Kant believed that we do not have direct duties to animals at all, because they are not persons. Hence, Kant had to explain and justify the wrongness of inflicting pain on animals on the grounds that "he who is hard in his dealings with animals becomes hard also in his dealing with men."[8] The problem with Kant's account is that there seems to be no reason for accepting this latter claim unless Kant's account is rejected. If the alternative to Kant's account is accepted, then it is easy to understand why someone who is indifferent to inflicting pain on animals is also indifferent to inflicting pain on humans, for one is indifferent to what makes inflicting pain wrong in both cases. But, if Kant's account is accepted, there is no intelligible reason why one who is hard in his dealings with animals (or crabgrass or stones) should also be hard in his dealings with men. After all, men are persons: animals are no more persons than crabgrass or stones. Persons are Kant's

---

* Immanuel Kant (1724–1804) was an influential German philosopher. See the readings from Kant elsewhere in this volume.

crucial moral category. Why, in short, should a Kantian accept the basic claim in Kant's argument?

Hence, Kant's argument for the wrongness of inflicting pain on animals rests on a claim that, in a world of Kantian moral agents, is demonstrably false. Therefore, the alternative analysis, being more plausible anyway, should be accepted. Since this alternative analysis has the same structure as the anti-abortion argument being defended here, we have further support for the argument for the immorality of abortion being defended in this essay.

Of course, this value of a future-like-ours argument, if sound, shows only that abortion is prima facie wrong, not that it is wrong in any and all circumstances. Since the loss of the future to a standard fetus, if killed, is, however, at least as great a loss as the loss of the future to a standard adult human being who is killed, abortion, like ordinary killing, could be justified only by the most compelling reasons. The loss of one's life is almost the greatest misfortune that can happen to one. Presumably abortion could be justified in some circumstances, only if the loss consequent on failing to abort would be at least as great. Accordingly, morally permissible abortions will be rare indeed unless, perhaps, they occur so early in pregnancy that a fetus is not yet definitely an individual. Hence, this argument should be taken as showing that abortion is presumptively very seriously wrong, where the presumption is very strong—as strong as the presumption that killing another adult human being is wrong.

III.

How complete an account of the wrongness of killing does the value of a future-like-ours account have to be in order that the wrongness of abortion is a consequence? This account does not have to be an account of the necessary conditions for the wrongness of killing. Some persons in nursing homes may lack valuable human futures, yet it may be wrong to kill them for other reasons. Furthermore, this account does not obviously have to be the sole reason killing is wrong where the victim did have a valuable future. This analysis claims only that, for any killing where the victim did have a valuable future like ours, having that future by itself is sufficient to create the strong presumption that the killing is seriously wrong.

One way to overturn the value of a future-like-ours argument would be to find some account of the wrongness of killing which is at least as intelligible and which has different implications for the ethics of abortion. Two rival accounts possess at least some degree of plausibility. One account is based on the obvious fact that people value the experience of living and wish for that valuable experience to continue. Therefore, it might be said, what makes killing wrong is the discontinuation of that experience for the victim. Let us call this the *discontinuation account*.[9] Another rival account is based upon the obvious fact that people strongly desire to continue to live. This suggests that what makes killing us so wrong is that it interferes with the fulfillment of a strong and fundamental desire, the fulfillment of which is necessary for the fulfillment of any other desires we might have. Let us call this the *desire account*.[10]

Consider first the desire account as a rival account of the ethics of killing which would provide the basis for rejecting the anti-abortion position. Such an account will have to be stronger than the value of a future-like-ours account of the wrongness of abortion if it is to do the job expected of it. To entail the wrongness of abortion, the value of a future-like-ours account has only to provide a sufficient, but not a necessary, condition for the wrongness of killing. The desire account, on the other hand, must provide us also with a necessary condition for the wrongness of killing in order to generate a pro-choice conclusion on abortion. The reason for this is that presumably the argument from the desire account moves from the claim that what makes killing wrong is interference with a very strong desire to the claim that abortion is not wrong because the fetus lacks a strong desire to live. Obviously, this inference fails if someone's having the desire to live is not a necessary condition of its being wrong to kill that individual.

One problem with the desire account is that we do regard it as seriously wrong to kill persons who have little desire to live or who have no desire to live or, indeed, have a desire not to live. We believe it is seriously wrong to kill the unconscious, the sleeping, those who are tired of life, and those who are suicidal. The value-of-a-human-future account renders standard morality intelligible in these cases; these cases appear to be incompatible with the desire account.

The desire account is subject to a deeper difficulty. We desire life, because we value the goods of this life. The goodness of life is not secondary to our desire for it. If this were not so, the pain of one's own premature death could be done away with merely by an appropriate alteration in the configuration of one's desires. This is absurd. Hence, it would seem that it is the loss of the goods of one's future, not the interference with the fulfillment of a strong desire to live, which accounts ultimately for the wrongness of killing.

It is worth noting that, if the desire account is modified so that it does not provide a necessary, but only a sufficient, condition for the wrongness of killing, the desire account is compatible with the value of a future-like-ours account. The combined accounts will yield an anti-abortion ethic. This suggests that one can retain what is intuitively plausible about the desire account without a challenge to the basic argument of this paper.

It is also worth noting that, if future desires have moral force in a modified desire account of the wrongness of killing, one can find support for an anti-abortion ethic even in the absence of a value of a future-like-ours account. If one decides that a morally relevant property, the possession of which is sufficient to make it wrong to kill some individual, is the desire at some future time to live—one might decide to justify one's refusal to kill suicidal teenagers on these grounds, for example—then, since typical fetuses will have the desire in the future to live, it is wrong to kill typical fetuses. Accordingly, it does not seem that a desire account of the wrongness of killing can provide a justification of a pro-choice ethic of abortion which is nearly as adequate as the value of a human-future justification of an anti-abortion ethic.

The discontinuation account looks more promising as an account of the wrongness of killing. It seems just as intelligible as the value of a future-like-ours account, but it does not justify an anti-abortion position. Obviously, if it is the continuation of one's activities, experiences, and projects, the loss of which makes killing wrong, then it is not wrong to kill fetuses for that reason, for fetuses do not have experiences, activities, and projects to be continued or discontinued. Accordingly, the discontinuation account does not have the anti-abortion consequences that the value of a future-like-ours account has. Yet, it seems as intelligible as the value of a future-like-ours account, for when we think of what would be wrong with our being killed, it does seem as if it is the discontinuation of what makes our lives worthwhile which makes killing us wrong.

Is the discontinuation account just as good an account as the value of a future-like-ours account? The discontinuation account will not be adequate at all, if it does not refer to the *value* of the experience that may be discontinued. One does not want the discontinuation account to make it wrong to kill a patient who begs for death and who is in severe pain that cannot be relieved short of killing. (I leave open the question of whether it is wrong for other reasons.) Accordingly, the discontinuation account must be more than a bare discontinuation account. It must make some reference to the positive value of the patient's experiences. But, by the same token, the value of a future-like-ours account cannot be a bare future account either. Just having a future surely does not itself rule out killing the above patient. This account must make some reference to the value of the patient's future experiences and projects also. Hence, both accounts involve the value of experiences, projects, and activities. So far we still have symmetry between the accounts.

The symmetry fades, however, when we focus on the time period of the value of the experiences, etc., which has moral consequences. Although both accounts leave open the possibility that the patient in our example may be killed, this possibility is left open only in virtue of the utterly bleak future for the patient. It makes no difference whether the patient's immediate past contains intolerable pain, or consists in being in a coma (which we can imagine is a situation of indifference), or consists in a life of value. If the patient's future is a future of value, we want our account to make it wrong to kill the patient. If the patient's future is intolerable, whatever his or her immediate past, we want our account to allow killing the patient. Obviously, then, it is the value of that patient's future which is doing the work in rendering the morality of killing the patient intelligible.

This being the case, it seems clear that whether one has immediate past experiences or not does no work in the explanation of what makes killing wrong.

The addition the discontinuation account makes to the value of a human future account is otiose.* Its addition to the value-of-a-future account plays no role at all in rendering intelligible the wrongness of killing. Therefore, it can be discarded with the discontinuation account of which it is a part.

IV.

The analysis of the previous section suggests that alternative general accounts of the wrongness of killing are either inadequate or unsuccessful in getting around the anti-abortion consequences of the value of a future-like-ours argument. A different strategy for avoiding these anti-abortion consequences involves limiting the scope of the value of a future argument. More precisely, the strategy involves arguing that fetuses lack a property that is essential for the value-of-a-future argument (or for any anti-abortion argument) to apply to them.

One move of this sort is based upon the claim that a necessary condition of one's future being valuable is that one values it. Value implies a valuer. Given this one might argue that, since fetuses cannot value their futures, their futures are not valuable to them. Hence, it does not seriously wrong them deliberately to end their lives.

This move fails, however, because of some ambiguities. Let us assume that something cannot be of value unless it is valued by someone. This does not entail that my life is of no value unless it is valued by me. I may think, in a period of despair, that my future is of no worth whatsoever, but I may be wrong because others rightly see value—even great value—in it. Furthermore, my future can be valuable to me even if I do not value it. This is the case when a young person attempts suicide, but is rescued and goes on to significant human achievements. Such young people's futures are ultimately valuable to them, even though such futures do not seem to be valuable to them at the moment of attempted suicide. A fetus's future can be valuable to it in the same way. Accordingly, this attempt to limit the anti-abortion argument fails.

Another similar attempt to reject the anti-abortion position is based on Tooley's claim that an entity cannot possess the right to life unless it has the capacity to desire its continued existence. It follows that, since fetuses lack the conceptual capacity to desire to continue to live, they lack the right to life. Accordingly, Tooley concludes that abortion cannot be seriously prima facie wrong (*op. cit.*, pp. 46–47).

What could be the evidence for Tooley's basic claim? Tooley once argued that individuals have a prima facie right to what they desire and that the lack of the capacity to desire something undercuts the basis of one's right to it (*op. cit.*, pp. 44–45). This argument plainly will not succeed in the context of the analysis of this essay, however, since the point here is to establish the fetus's right to life on other grounds. Tooley's argument assumes that the right to life cannot be established in general on some basis other than the desire for life. This position was considered and rejected in the preceding section of this paper.

One might attempt to defend Tooley's basic claim on the grounds that, because a fetus cannot apprehend continued life as a benefit, its continued life cannot be a benefit or cannot be something it has a right to or cannot be something that is in its interest. This might be defended in terms of the general proposition that, if an individual is literally incapable of caring about or taking an interest in some X, then one does not have a right to X or X is not a benefit or X is not something that is in one's interest.[11]

Each member of this family of claims seems to be open to objections. As John C. Stevens[12] has pointed out, one may have a right to be treated with a certain medical procedure (because of a health insurance policy one has purchased), even though one cannot conceive of the nature of the procedure. And, as Tooley himself has pointed out, persons who have been indoctrinated, or drugged, or rendered temporarily unconscious may be literally incapable of caring about or taking an interest in something that is in their interest or is something to which they have a right, or is something that benefits them. Hence, the Tooley claim that would restrict the scope of the value of a future-like-ours argument is undermined by counterexamples.[13]

Finally, Paul Bassen[14] has argued that, even though the prospects of an embryo might seem to be

---

* Worthless, ineffective.

a basis for the wrongness of abortion, an embryo cannot be a victim and therefore cannot be wronged. An embryo cannot be a victim, he says, because it lacks sentience. His central argument for this seems to be that, even though plants and the permanently unconscious are alive, they clearly cannot be victims. What is the explanation of this? Bassen claims that the explanation is that their lives consist of mere metabolism and mere metabolism is not enough to ground victimizability. Mentation* is required.

The problem with this attempt to establish the absence of victimizability is that both plants and the permanently unconscious clearly lack what Bassen calls "prospects" or what I have called "a future life like ours." Hence, it is surely open to one to argue that the real reason we believe plants and the permanently unconscious cannot be victims is that killing them cannot deprive them of a future life like ours; the real reason is not their absence of present mentation.

Bassen recognizes that his view is subject to this difficulty, and he recognizes that the case of children seems to support this difficulty, for "much of what we do for children is based on prospects." He argues, however, that, in the case of children and in other such cases, "potentiality comes into play only where victimizability has been secured on other grounds" (*ibid.*, p. 333).

Bassen's defense of his view is patently question-begging, since what is adequate to secure victimizability is exactly what is at issue. His examples do not support his own view against the thesis of this essay. Of course, embryos can be victims: when their lives are deliberately terminated, they are deprived of their futures of value, their prospects. This makes them victims, for it directly wrongs them.

The seeming plausibility of Bassen's view stems from the fact that paradigmatic cases of imagining someone as a victim involve empathy, and empathy requires mentation of the victim. The victims of flood, famine, rape, or child abuse are all persons with whom we can empathize. That empathy seems to be part of seeing them as victims.[15]

In spite of the strength of these examples, the attractive intuition that a situation in which there is victimization requires the possibility of empathy is subject

to counterexamples. Consider a case that Bassen himself offers: "Posthumous obliteration of an author's work constitutes a misfortune for him only if he had wished his work to endure" (*op cit.*, p. 318). The conditions Bassen wishes to impose upon the possibility of being victimized here seem far too strong. Perhaps this author, due to his unrealistic standards of excellence and his low self-esteem, regarded his work as unworthy of survival, even though it possessed genuine literary merit. Destruction of such work would surely victimize its author. In such a case, empathy with the victim concerning the loss is clearly impossible.

Of course, Bassen does not make the possibility of empathy a necessary condition of victimizability; he requires only mentation. Hence, on Bassen's actual view, this author, as I have described him, can be a victim. The problem is that the basic intuition that renders Bassen's view plausible is missing in the author's case. In order to attempt to avoid counterexamples, Bassen has made his thesis too weak to be supported by the intuitions that suggested it.

Even so, the mentation requirement on victimizability is still subject to counterexamples. Suppose a severe accident renders me totally unconscious for a month, after which I recover. Surely killing me while I am unconscious victimizes me, even though I am incapable of mentation during that time. It follows that Bassen's thesis fails. Apparently, attempts to restrict the value of a future-like-ours argument so that fetuses do not fall within its scope do not succeed.

V.

In this essay, it has been argued that the correct ethic of the wrongness of killing can be extended to fetal life and used to show that there is a strong presumption that any abortion is morally impermissible. If the ethic of killing adopted here entails, however, that contraception is also seriously immoral, then there would appear to be a difficulty with the analysis of this essay.

But this analysis does not entail that contraception is wrong. Of course, contraception prevents the actualization of a possible future of value. Hence, it follows from the claim that futures of value should be maximized that contraception is prima facie immoral. This obligation to

---

* Mental activity.

maximize does not exist, however; furthermore, nothing in the ethics of killing in this paper entails that it does. The ethics of killing in this essay would entail that contraception is wrong only if something were denied a human future of value by contraception. Nothing at all is denied such a future by contraception, however.

Candidates for a subject of harm by contraception fall into four categories: (1) some sperm or other, (2) some ovum or other, (3) a sperm and an ovum separately, and (4) a sperm and an ovum together. Assigning the harm to some sperm is utterly arbitrary, for no reason can be given for making a sperm the subject of harm rather than an ovum. Assigning the harm to some ovum is utterly arbitrary, for no reason can be given for making an ovum the subject of harm rather than a sperm. One might attempt to avoid these problems by insisting that contraception deprives both the sperm and the ovum separately of a valuable future like ours. On this alternative, too many futures are lost. Contraception was supposed to be wrong, because it deprived us of one future of value, not two. One might attempt to avoid this problem by holding that contraception deprives the combination of sperm and ovum of a valuable future like ours. But here the definite article misleads. At the time of contraception, there are hundreds of millions of sperm, one (released) ovum and millions of possible combinations of all of these. There is no actual combination at all. Is the subject of the loss to be a merely possible combination? Which one? This alternative does not yield an actual subject of harm either. Accordingly, the immorality of contraception is not entailed by the loss of a future-like-ours argument simply because there is no nonarbitrarily identifiable subject of the loss in the case of contraception.

VI.

The purpose of this essay has been to set out an argument for the serious presumptive wrongness of abortion subject to the assumption that the moral permissibility of abortion stands or falls on the moral status of the fetus. Since a fetus possesses a property, the possession of which in adult human beings is sufficient to make killing an adult human being wrong, abortion is wrong. This way of dealing with the problem of abortion seems superior to other approaches to the ethics of abortion, because it rests on an ethics of killing which is close to self-evident, because the crucial morally relevant property clearly applies to fetuses, and because the argument avoids the usual equivocations on 'human life', 'human being', or 'person'. The argument rests neither on religious claims nor on Papal dogma. It is not subject to the objection of "speciesism."* Its soundness is compatible with the moral permissibility of euthanasia and contraception. It deals with our intuitions concerning young children.

Finally, this analysis can be viewed as resolving a standard problem—indeed, *the* standard problem—concerning the ethics of abortion. Clearly, it is wrong to kill adult human beings. Clearly, it is not wrong to end the life of some arbitrarily chosen single human cell. Fetuses seem to be like arbitrarily chosen human cells in some respects and like adult humans in other respects. The problem of the ethics of abortion is the problem of determining the fetal property that settles this moral controversy. The thesis of this essay is that the problem of the ethics of abortion, so understood, is solvable. ■

Suggestions for Critical Reflection

1. Marquis argues that participants in the traditional abortion debate cannot hope to convince one another because they rely on principles that are not shared. Do you agree? Why or why not?
2. Is Marquis correct in suggesting that deliberation about the moral permissibility of abortion ought to focus on standard cases rather than more complex ones in which, for example, the life of the mother is threatened by the pregnancy? In what circumstances should these "hard cases" be taken into account?

---

* Discrimination against the members of another species of animal.

3. Should there be a distinction between debates about the *morality* of abortion and debates about the *legality* of abortion? What different considerations should be taken into account when evaluating whether abortion should be legal, as opposed to determining if abortion is immoral? Is it possible to believe that abortion should be legal, yet still to consider it immoral? Why or why not?

4. Do you agree that the reason killing is ordinarily wrong is that it deprives us of a valuable future? Why or why not? If not, what other account would you support—and what would be its implications for the question of abortion?

5. Marquis argues that the important value of a fetus's potential future is the value to the fetus (i.e., not to others). But if it's true that fetuses have insufficient mental power to envision a future, how can they value it? Can something be of value to a being who doesn't value it? Explain and evaluate Marquis's argument here.

6. Marquis says "Morally permissible abortions will be rare indeed unless, perhaps, they occur so early in pregnancy that a fetus is not yet definitely an individual." Is this bringing back the debate about when a fetus becomes a "person," the argument that Marquis dismisses?

Notes

1   Feinberg, "Abortion," in *Matters of Life and Death: New Introductory Essays in Moral Philosophy*, Tom Regan, ed. (New York: Random House, 1986), pp. 256–293; Tooley, "Abortion and Infanticide," *Philosophy and Public Affairs*, II, 1 (1972): 37–65, Tooley, *Abortion and Infanticide* (New York: Oxford, 1984); Warren, "On the Moral and Legal Status of Abortion," *The Monist*, LVII, 1 (1973): 43–61; Engelhardt, "The Ontology of Abortion," *Ethics*, LXXXIV, 3 (1974): 217–234; Sumner, *Abortion and Moral Theory* (Princeton: University Press, 1981); Noonan, "An Almost Absolute Value in History," in *The Morality of Abortion: Legal and Historical Perspectives*, Noonan, ed. (Cambridge: Harvard, 1970); and Devine, *The Ethics of Homicide* (Ithaca: Cornell, 1978).

2   For interesting discussions of this issue, see Warren Quinn, "Abortion: Identity and Loss," *Philosophy and Public Affairs*, XIII, 1 (1984): 24–54; and Lawrence C. Becker, "Human Being: The Boundaries of the Concept," *Philosophy and Public Affairs*, IV, 4 (1975): 334–359.

3   For example, see my "Ethics and The Elderly: Some Problems," in Stuart Spieker, Kathleen Woodward, and David Van Tassel, eds., *Aging and the Elderly: Humanistic Perspectives in Gerontology* (Atlantic Highlands, NJ: Humanities, 1978), pp. 341–355.

4   See Warren, *op. cit.*, and Tooley, "Abortion and Infanticide."

5   This seems to be the fatal flaw in Warren's treatment of this issue.

6   I have been most influenced on this matter by Jonathan Glover, *Causing Death and Saving Lives* (New York: Penguin, 1977), ch. 3; and Robert Young, "What Is So Wrong with Killing People?" *Philosophy*, LIV, 210 (1979): 515–528.

7   Feinberg, Tooley, Warren, and Engelhardt have all dealt with this problem.

8   "Duties to Animals and Spirits," in *Lectures on Ethics*, Louis Infeld, trans. (New York: Harper, 1963), p. 239.

9   I am indebted to Jack Bricke for raising this objection.

10 Presumably a preference utilitarian would press such an objection. Tooley once suggested that his account has such a theoretical underpinning. See his "Abortion and Infanticide," pp. 44–45.

11 Donald VanDeVeer seems to think this is self-evident. See his "Whither Baby Doe?" in *Matters of Life and Death*, p. 233.

12 "Must the Bearer of a Right Have the Concept of That to Which He Has a Right?" *Ethics*, XCV, 1 (1984): 68–74.

13 See Tooley again in "Abortion and Infanticide," pp. 47–49.

14 "Present Sakes and Future Prospects: The Status of Early Abortion," *Philosophy and Public Affairs*, XI, 4 (1982): 322–326.

15 Note carefully the reasons he gives on the bottom of p. 316.

JUDITH JARVIS THOMSON

A Defense of Abortion

Who Is Judith Jarvis Thomson?

A distinguished philosopher of ethics and metaphysics, Judith Jarvis Thomson was born in New York City in 1929. The descendent of a long line of Eastern European rabbis, Thomson officially converted to Judaism when she was fourteen years old. After obtaining two BA degrees, one from Barnard College and one from Cambridge University, Thomson completed her PhD in philosophy at Columbia in 1959. She taught at Barnard College from 1956 to 1962 and briefly served as a professor at Boston University before securing a permanent professorship at MIT in 1964. Thomson has published numerous influential papers and several books, including *Acts and Other Events* (1977), *The Realm of Rights* (1990), and *Normativity* (2008). She received a prestigious Guggenheim Fellowship in 1986, and was awarded an honorary Doctor of Letters degree from Cambridge in 2015 and from Harvard in 2016.

What Is the Structure of This Reading?

Many arguments against abortion begin with the premise that human fetuses are persons from the moment of conception, on the grounds that it would be arbitrary to identify any other point in prenatal development as the beginning of personhood. From this, those arguments typically claim that, since all people have a right to life, a newly conceived fetus has a right to life, and therefore abortion must be morally impermissible. Thomson disagrees with the premise that personhood begins at conception; however, for the purposes of this paper, she supposes that the premise is true and asks whether it follows that abortion is wrong.

Thomson proposes a thought experiment. She asks you to imagine being connected to a famous but sickly violinist, whose life depends on being attached to your body for nine months. In this circumstance, she claims, remaining attached to the violinist is commendable, but not morally obligatory. The violinist may have a right to life, but this right does not overturn your right to decide what happens to your body. The case of a fetus is similar: supposing we grant that the fetus is a person and has a right to life (as does the violinist), this still wouldn't establish that the fetus's rights override the rights of the pregnant woman to control her body. Again, it *may*, at least in certain circumstances, be commendable for a pregnant woman to allow the fetus to develop, but it's not morally required of her, nor is it wrong for her to obtain an abortion. To further explain this position, Thomson distinguishes between two different conceptions of our moral obligations to each other: "Minimally Decent Samaritanism" and a more demanding standard of "Good Samaritanism." Thomson notes that abortion opponents demand pregnant women act as Good Samaritans towards unborn fetuses, even though current laws do not generally require people to act even as Minimally Decent Samaritans.

Thomson's argument aims to demonstrate that neither personhood nor a general "right to life" is enough to establish the morality of abortion. Such rights must always be weighed against a pregnant woman's own rights. And in most circumstances (though Thomson allows that there may be some exceptions), the pregnant woman's rights allow her to obtain an abortion.

A Defense of Abortion[*1]

Most opposition to abortion relies on the premise that the fetus is a human being, a person, from the moment of conception. The premise is argued for, but, as I think, not well. Take, for example, the most common argument. We are asked to notice that the development of a human being from conception through birth into childhood is continuous; then it is said that to draw a line, to choose a point in this development and say "before this point the thing is not a person, after this point it is a person" is to make an arbitrary choice, a choice for which in the nature of things no good reason can be given. It is concluded that the fetus is, or anyway that we had better say it is, a person from the moment of conception. But this conclusion does not follow. Similar things might be said about the development of an acorn into an oak tree, and it does not follow that acorns are oak trees, or that we had better say they are. Arguments of this form are sometimes called "slippery slope arguments"[†]—the phrase is perhaps self-explanatory—and it is dismaying that opponents of abortion rely on them so heavily and uncritically.

I am inclined to agree, however, that the prospects for "drawing a line" in the development of the fetus look dim. I am inclined to think also that we shall probably have to agree that the fetus has already become a human person well before birth. Indeed, it comes as a surprise when one first learns how early in its life it begins to acquire human characteristics. By the tenth week, for example, it already has a face, arms and legs, fingers and toes; it has internal organs, and brain activity is detectable.[2] On the other hand, I think that the premise is false, that the fetus is not a person from the moment of conception. A newly fertilized ovum, a newly implanted clump of cells, is no more a person than an acorn is an oak tree. But I shall not discuss any of this. For it seems to me to be of great interest to ask what happens if, for the sake of argument, we allow the premise. How, precisely,

are we supposed to get from there to the conclusion that abortion is morally impermissible? Opponents of abortion commonly spend most of their time establishing that the fetus is a person, and hardly any time explaining the step from there to the impermissibility of abortion. Perhaps they think the step too simple and obvious to require much comment. Or perhaps instead they are simply being economical in argument. Many of those who defend abortion rely on the premise that the fetus is not a person, but only a bit of tissue that will become a person at birth; and why pay out more arguments than you have to? Whatever the explanation, I suggest that the step they take is neither easy nor obvious, that it calls for closer examination than it is commonly given, and that when we do give it this closer examination we shall feel inclined to reject it.

I propose, then, that we grant that the fetus is a person from the moment of conception. How does the argument go from here? Something like this, I take it. Every person has a right to life. So the fetus has a right to life. No doubt the mother has a right to decide what shall happen in and to her body; everyone would grant that. But surely a person's right to life is stronger and more stringent than the mother's right to decide what happens in and to her body, and so outweighs it. So the fetus may not be killed; an abortion may not be performed.

It sounds plausible. But now let me ask you to imagine this. You wake up in the morning and find yourself back to back in bed with an unconscious violinist. A famous unconscious violinist. He has been found to have a fatal kidney ailment, and the Society of Music Lovers has canvassed all the available medical records and found that you alone have the right blood type to help. They have therefore kidnapped you, and last night the violinist's circulatory system was plugged into yours, so that your kidneys can be used to extract poisons from his blood as well as your own. The director of the hospital now tells you, "Look,

*   Judith Jarvis Thomson, "A Defense of Abortion," *Philosophy and Public Affairs* I, I (Autumn 1971): 47–66.

†   A slippery slope argument maintains that if we take one step X, then other undesired steps Y and Z will follow. E.g., "If marijuana is legalized, soon heroin and other hard drugs will be legal as well." Slippery slope arguments are fallacious if they fail to effectively argue for the likelihood of each step in the process.

we're sorry the Society of Music Lovers did this to you—we would never have permitted it if we had known. But still, they did it, and the violinist now is plugged into you. To unplug you would be to kill him. But never mind, it's only for nine months. By then he will have recovered from his ailment, and can safely be unplugged from you." Is it morally incumbent on you to accede to this situation? No doubt it would be very nice of you if you did, a great kindness. But do you *have* to accede to it? What if it were not nine months, but nine years? Or longer still? What if the director of the hospital says, "Tough luck, I agree, but you've now got to stay in bed, with the violinist plugged into you, for the rest of your life. Because remember this. All persons have a right to life, and violinists are persons. Granted you have a right to decide what happens in and to your body, but a person's right to life outweighs your right to decide what happens in and to your body. So you cannot ever be unplugged from him." I imagine you would regard this as outrageous, which suggests that something really is wrong with that plausible-sounding argument I mentioned a moment ago.

In this case, of course, you were kidnapped; you didn't volunteer for the operation that plugged the violinist into your kidneys. Can those who oppose abortion on the ground I mentioned make an exception for a pregnancy due to rape? Certainly. They can say that persons have a right to life only if they didn't come into existence because of rape; or they can say that all persons have a right to life, but that some have less of a right to life than others, in particular, that those who came into existence because of rape have less. But these statements have a rather unpleasant sound. Surely the question of whether you have a right to life at all, or how much of it you have, shouldn't turn on the question of whether or not you are the product of a rape. And in fact the people who oppose abortion on the ground I mentioned do not make this distinction, and hence do not make an exception in case of rape.

Nor do they make an exception for a case in which the mother has to spend the nine months of her pregnancy in bed. They would agree that would be a great pity, and hard on the mother; but all the same, all persons have a right to life, the fetus is a person, and so on. I suspect, in fact, that they would not make an exception for a case in which, miraculously enough, the pregnancy went on for nine years, or even the rest of the mother's life.

Some won't even make an exception for a case in which continuation of the pregnancy is likely to shorten the mother's life; they regard abortion as impermissible even to save the mother's life. Such cases are nowadays very rare, and many opponents of abortion do not accept this extreme view. All the same, it is a good place to begin: a number of points of interest come out in respect to it.

1. Let us call the view that abortion is impermissible even to save the mother's life "the extreme view." I want to suggest first that it does not issue from the argument I mentioned earlier without the addition of some fairly powerful premises. Suppose a woman has become pregnant, and now learns that she has a cardiac condition such that she will die if she carries the baby to term. What may be done for her? The fetus, being a person, has a right to life, but as the mother is a person too, so has she a right to life. Presumably they have an equal right to life. How is it supposed to come out that an abortion may not be performed? If mother and child have an equal right to life, shouldn't we perhaps flip a coin? Or should we add to the mother's right to life her right to decide what happens in and to her body, which everybody seems to be ready to grant—the sum of her rights now outweighing the fetus' right to life?

The most familiar argument here is the following. We are told that performing the abortion would be directly killing[3] the child, whereas doing nothing would not be killing the mother, but only letting her die. Moreover, in killing the child, one would be killing an innocent person, for the child has committed no crime, and is not aiming at his mother's death. And then there are a variety of ways in which this might be continued. (1) But as directly killing an innocent person is always and absolutely impermissible, an abortion may not be performed. Or, (2) as directly killing an innocent person is murder, and murder is always and absolutely impermissible, an abortion may not be performed.[4] Or, (3) as one's duty to refrain from directly killing an innocent person is more stringent than one's duty to keep a person from dying, an abortion may not be performed. Or, (4) if one's only options are directly killing an innocent person or letting a person die, one must prefer letting the person die, and thus an abortion may not be performed.[5]

Some people seem to have thought that these are not further premises which must be added if the conclusion is to be reached, but that they follow from the very fact that an innocent person has a right to life.[6] But this seems to me to be a mistake, and perhaps the simplest way to show this is to bring out that while we must certainly grant that innocent persons have a right to life, the theses in (1) through (4) are all false. Take (2), for example. If directly killing an innocent person is murder, and thus is impermissible, then the mother's directly killing the innocent person inside her is murder, and thus is impermissible. But it cannot seriously be thought to be murder if the mother performs an abortion on herself to save her life. It cannot seriously be said that she *must* refrain, that she *must* sit passively by and wait for her death. Let us look again at the case of you and the violinist. There you are, in bed with the violinist, and the director of the hospital says to you, "It's all most distressing, and I deeply sympathize, but you see this is putting an additional strain on your kidneys, and you'll be dead within the month. But you have to stay where you are all the same. Because unplugging you would be directly killing an innocent violinist, and that's murder, and that's impermissible." If anything in the world is true, it is that you do not commit murder, you do not do what is impermissible, if you reach around to your back and unplug yourself from that violinist to save your life.

The main focus of attention in writings on abortion has been on what a third party may or may not do in answer to a request from a woman for an abortion. This is in a way understandable. Things being as they are, there isn't much a woman can safely do to abort herself. So the question asked is what a third party may do, and what the mother may do, if it is mentioned at all, is deduced, almost as an afterthought, from what it is concluded that third parties may do. But it seems to me that to treat the matter in this way is to refuse to grant to the mother that very status of person which is so firmly insisted on for the fetus. For we cannot simply read off what a person may do from what a third party may do. Suppose you find yourself trapped in a tiny house with a growing child. I mean a very tiny house, and a rapidly growing child—you are already up against the wall of the house and in a few minutes you'll be crushed to death. The child on the other hand won't be crushed to death; if nothing is done to stop him from growing he'll be hurt, but in the end he'll simply burst open the house and walk out a free man. Now I could well understand it if a

bystander were to say, "There's nothing we can do for you. We cannot choose between your life and his, we cannot be the ones to decide who is to live, we cannot intervene." But it cannot be concluded that you too can do nothing, that you cannot attack it to save your life. However innocent the child may be, you do not have to wait passively while it crushes you to death. Perhaps a pregnant woman is vaguely felt to have the status of house, to which we don't allow the right of self-defense. But if the woman houses the child, it should be remembered that she is a person who houses it.

I should perhaps stop to say explicitly that I am not claiming that people have a right to do anything whatever to save their lives. I think, rather, that there are drastic limits to the right of self-defense. If someone threatens you with death unless you torture someone else to death, I think you have not the right, even to save your life, to do so. But the case under consideration here is very different. In our case there are only two people involved, one whose life is threatened, and one who threatens it. Both are innocent: the one who is threatened is not threatened because of any fault, the one who threatens does not threaten because of any fault. For this reason we may feel that we bystanders cannot intervene. But the person threatened can.

In sum, a woman surely can defend her life against the threat to it posed by the unborn child, even if doing so involves its death. And this shows not merely that the theses in (1) through (4) are false; it shows also that the extreme view of abortion is false, and so we need not canvass any other possible ways of arriving at it from the argument I mentioned at the outset.

2. The extreme view could of course be weakened to say that while abortion is permissible to save the mother's life, it may not be performed by a third party, but only by the mother herself. But this cannot be right either. For what we have to keep in mind is that the mother and the unborn child are not like two tenants in a small house which has, by an unfortunate mistake, been rented to both: the mother *owns* the house. The fact that she does adds to the offensiveness of deducing that the mother can do nothing from the supposition that third parties can do nothing. But it does more than this: it casts a bright light on the supposition that third parties can do nothing. Certainly it lets us see that a third party who says "I cannot choose between you" is fooling himself if he thinks this is impartiality. If Jones has found and fastened on a certain coat,

which he needs to keep him from freezing, but which Smith also needs to keep him from freezing, then it is not impartiality that says "I cannot choose between you" when Smith owns the coat. Women have said again and again "This body is *my* body!" and they have reason to feel angry, reason to feel that it has been like shouting into the wind. Smith, after all, is hardly likely to bless us if we say to him, "Of course it's your coat, anybody would grant that it is. But no one may choose between you and Jones who is to have it."

We should really ask what it is that says "no one may choose" in the face of the fact that the body that houses the child is the mother's body. It may be simply a failure to appreciate this fact. But it may be something more interesting, namely the sense that one has a right to refuse to lay hands on people, even where it would be just and fair to do so, even where justice seems to require that somebody do so. Thus justice might call for somebody to get Smith's coat back from Jones, and yet you have a right to refuse to be the one to lay hands on Jones, a right to refuse to do physical violence to him. This, I think, must be granted. But then what should be said is not "no one may choose," but only "*I* cannot choose," and indeed not even this, but "*I* will not *act*," leaving it open that somebody else can or should, and in particular that anyone in a position of authority, with the job of securing people's rights, both can and should. So this is no difficulty. I have not been arguing that any given third party must accede to the mother's request that he perform an abortion to save her life, but only that he may.

I suppose that in some views of human life the mother's body is only on loan to her, the loan not being one which gives her any prior claim to it. One who held this view might well think it impartiality to say "I cannot choose." But I shall simply ignore this possibility. My own view is that if a human being has any just, prior claim to anything at all, he has a just, prior claim to his own body. And perhaps this needn't be argued for here anyway, since, as I mentioned, the arguments against abortion we are looking at do grant that the woman has a right to decide what happens in and to her body.

But although they do grant it, I have tried to show that they do not take seriously what is done in granting it. I suggest the same thing will reappear even more clearly when we turn away from cases in which the mother's life is at stake, and attend, as I propose we now do, to the vastly more common cases in which a woman wants an abortion for some less weighty reason than preserving her own life.

3. Where the mother's life is not at stake, the argument I mentioned at the outset seems to have a much stronger pull. "Everyone has a right to life, so the unborn person has a right to life." And isn't the child's right to life weightier than anything other than the mother's own right to life, which she might put forward as ground for an abortion?

This argument treats the right to life as if it were unproblematic. It is not, and this seems to me to be precisely the source of the mistake.

For we should now, at long last, ask what it comes to, to have a right to life. In some views having a right to life includes having a right to be given at least the bare minimum one needs for continued life. But suppose that what in fact *is* the bare minimum a man needs for continued life is something he has no right at all to be given? If I am sick unto death, and the only thing that will save my life is the touch of Henry Fonda's* cool hand on my fevered brow, then all the same, I have no right to be given the touch of Henry Fonda's cool hand on my fevered brow. It would be frightfully nice of him to fly in from the West Coast to provide it. It would be less nice, though no doubt well meant, if my friends flew out to the West Coast and carried Henry Fonda back with them. But I have no right at all against anybody that he should do this for me. Or again, to return to the story I told earlier, the fact that for continued life that violinist needs the continued use of your kidneys does not establish that he has a right to be given the continued use of your kidneys. He certainly has no right against you that *you* should give him continued use of your kidneys. For nobody has any right to use your kidneys unless you give him such a right; and nobody has the right against you that you shall give him this right—if you do allow him to go on using your kidneys, this

---

* Henry Fonda (1905–82) was an American film and stage actor, best known for his performances in *The Grapes of Wrath* (1940), *12 Angry Men* (1957), and *Once Upon a Time in the West* (1968).

is a kindness on your part, and not something he can claim from you as his due. Nor has he any right against anybody else that *they* should give him continued use of your kidneys. Certainly he had no right against the Society of Music Lovers that they should plug him into you in the first place. And if you now start to unplug yourself, having learned that you will otherwise have to spend nine years in bed with him, there is nobody in the world who must try to prevent you, in order to see to it that he is given something he has a right to be given.

Some people are rather stricter about the right to life. In their view, it does not include the right to be given anything, but amounts to, and only to, the right not to be killed by anybody. But here a related difficulty arises. If everybody is to refrain from killing that violinist, then everybody must refrain from doing a great many different sorts of things. Everybody must refrain from slitting his throat, everybody must refrain from shooting him, and everybody must refrain from unplugging you from him. But does he have a right against everybody that they shall refrain from unplugging you from him? To refrain from doing this is to allow him to continue to use your kidneys. It could be argued that he has a right against us that *we* should allow him to continue to use your kidneys. That is, while he had no right against us that we should give him the use of your kidneys, it might be argued that he anyway has a right against us that we shall not now intervene and deprive him of the use of your kidneys. I shall come back to third-party interventions later. But certainly the violinist has no right against you that *you* shall allow him to continue to use your kidneys. As I said, if you do allow him to use them, it is a kindness on your part, and not something you owe him.

The difficulty I point to here is not peculiar to the right to life. It reappears in connection with all the other natural rights;* and it is something which an adequate account of rights must deal with. For present purposes it is enough just to draw attention to it. But I would stress that I am not arguing that people do not have a right to life—quite to the contrary, it seems to me that the primary control we must place on the acceptability of an account of rights is that it should turn out in that account to be a truth that all persons have a right to life. I am arguing only that having a right to life does not guarantee having either a right to be given the use of or a right to be allowed continued use of another person's body—even if one needs it for life itself. So the right to life will not serve the opponents of abortion in the very simple and clear way in which they seem to have thought it would.

4. There is another way to bring out the difficulty. In the most ordinary sort of case, to deprive someone of what he has a right to is to treat him unjustly. Suppose a boy and his small brother are jointly given a box of chocolates for Christmas. If the older boy takes the box and refuses to give his brother any of the chocolates, he is unjust to him, for the brother has been given a right to half of them. But suppose that, having learned that otherwise it means nine years in bed with that violinist, you unplug yourself from him. You surely are not being unjust to him, for you gave him no right to use your kidneys, and no one else can have given him any such right. But we have to notice that in unplugging yourself, you are killing him; and violinists, like everybody else, have a right to life, and thus in the view we were considering just now, the right not to be killed. So here you do what he supposedly has a right you shall not do, but you do not act unjustly to him in doing it.

The emendation which may be made at this point is this: the right to life consists not in the right not to be killed, but rather in the right not to be killed unjustly. This runs a risk of circularity, but never mind: it would enable us to square the fact that the violinist has a right to life with the fact that you do not act unjustly toward him in unplugging yourself, thereby killing him. For if you do not kill him unjustly, you do not violate his right to life, and so it is no wonder you do him no injustice.

But if this emendation is accepted, the gap in the argument against abortion stares us plainly in the face: it is by no means enough to show that the fetus is a person, and to remind us that all persons have a right to life—we need to be shown also that killing the fetus violates its right to life, i.e., that abortion is unjust killing. And is it?

---

* Natural rights (as opposed to legal rights) are rights that every human being has—which do not depend on, and which have precedence over, the laws or customs of any social institution.

I suppose we may take it as a datum* that in a case of pregnancy due to rape the mother has not given the unborn person a right to the use of her body for food and shelter. Indeed, in what pregnancy could it be supposed that the mother has given the unborn person such a right? It is not as if there were unborn persons drifting about the world, to whom a woman who wants a child says "I invite you in."

But it might be argued that there are other ways one can have acquired a right to the use of another person's body than by having been invited to use it by that person. Suppose a woman voluntarily indulges in intercourse, knowing of the chance it will issue in pregnancy, and then she does become pregnant; is she not in part responsible for the presence, in fact the very existence, of the unborn person inside her? No doubt she did not invite it in. But doesn't her partial responsibility for its being there itself give it a right to the use of her body?[7] If so, then her aborting it would be more like the boy's taking away the chocolates, and less like your unplugging yourself from the violinist—doing so would be depriving it of what it does have a right to, and thus would be doing it an injustice.

And then, too, it might be asked whether or not she can kill it even to save her own life: If she voluntarily called it into existence, how can she now kill it, even in self-defense?

The first thing to be said about this is that it is something new. Opponents of abortion have been so concerned to make out the independence of the fetus, in order to establish that it has a right to life, just as its mother does, that they have tended to overlook the possible support they might gain from making out that the fetus is *dependent* on the mother, in order to establish that she has a special kind of responsibility for it, a responsibility that gives it rights against her which are not possessed by any independent person—such as an ailing violinist who is a stranger to her.

On the other hand, this argument would give the unborn person a right to its mother's body only if her pregnancy resulted from a voluntary act, undertaken in full knowledge of the chance a pregnancy might result from it. It would leave out entirely the unborn person whose existence is due to rape. Pending the availability of some further argument, then, we would be left with the conclusion that unborn persons whose existence is due to rape have no right to the use of their mothers' bodies, and thus that aborting them is not depriving them of anything they have a right to and hence is not unjust killing.

And we should also notice that it is not at all plain that this argument really does go even as far as it purports to. For there are cases and cases, and the details make a difference. If the room is stuffy, and I therefore open a window to air it, and a burglar climbs in, it would be absurd to say, "Ah, now he can stay, she's given him a right to the use of her house—for she is partially responsible for his presence there, having voluntarily done what enabled him to get in, in full knowledge that there are such things as burglars, and that burglars burgle." It would be still more absurd to say this if I had had bars installed outside my windows, precisely to prevent burglars from getting in, and a burglar got in only because of a defect in the bars. It remains equally absurd if we imagine it is not a burglar who climbs in, but an innocent person who blunders or falls in. Again, suppose it were like this: people-seeds drift about in the air like pollen, and if you open your windows, one may drift in and take root in your carpets or upholstery. You don't want children, so you fix up your windows with fine mesh screens, the very best you can buy. As can happen, however, and on very, very rare occasions does happen, one of the screens is defective; and a seed drifts in and takes root. Does the person-plant who now develops have a right to the use of your house? Surely not—despite the fact that you voluntarily opened your windows, you knowingly kept carpets and upholstered furniture, and you knew that screens were sometimes defective. Someone may argue that you are responsible for its rooting, that it does have a right to your house, because after all you *could* have lived out your life with bare floors and furniture, or with sealed windows and doors. But this won't do—for by the same token anyone can avoid a pregnancy due to rape by having a hysterectomy, or anyway by never leaving home without a (reliable!) army.

It seems to me that the argument we are looking at can establish at most that there are *some* cases in which the unborn person has a right to the use of its mother's body, and therefore *some* cases in which

---

* Singular of "data"—in this case, meaning something we are entitled to assume as true.

abortion is unjust killing. There is room for much discussion and argument as to precisely which, if any. But I think we should sidestep this issue and leave it open, for at any rate the argument certainly does not establish that all abortion is unjust killing.

5. There is room for yet another argument here, however. We surely must all grant that there may be cases in which it would be morally indecent to detach a person from your body at the cost of his life. Suppose you learn that what the violinist needs is not nine years of your life, but only one hour: all you need do to save his life is to spend one hour in that bed with him. Suppose also that letting him use your kidneys for that one hour would not affect your health in the slightest. Admittedly you were kidnapped. Admittedly you did not give anyone permission to plug him into you. Nevertheless it seems to me plain you *ought* to allow him to use your kidneys for that hour—it would be indecent to refuse.

Again, suppose pregnancy lasted only an hour, and constituted no threat to life or health. And suppose that a woman becomes pregnant as a result of rape. Admittedly she did not voluntarily do anything to bring about the existence of a child. Admittedly she did nothing at all which would give the unborn person a right to the use of her body. All the same it might well be said, as in the newly emended violinist story, that she *ought* to allow it to remain for that hour—that it would be indecent of her to refuse.

Now some people are inclined to use the term "right" in such a way that it follows from the fact that you ought to allow a person to use your body for the hour he needs, that he has a right to use your body for the hour he needs, even though he has not been given that right by any person or act. They may say that it follows also that if you refuse, you act unjustly toward him. This use of the term is perhaps so common that it cannot be called wrong; nevertheless it seems to me to be an unfortunate loosening of what we would do better to keep a tight rein on. Suppose that box of chocolates I mentioned earlier has not been given to both boys jointly, but was given only to the older boy. There he sits, stolidly eating his way through the box, his small brother watching enviously. Here we are likely to say "You ought not to be so mean. You ought to give your brother some of those chocolates." My own view is that it just does not follow from the truth of this that the brother has any right to any of the chocolates. If the

boy refuses to give his brother any, he is greedy, stingy, callous—but not unjust. I suppose that the people I have in mind will say it does follow that the brother has a right to some of the chocolates, and thus that the boy does act unjustly if he refuses to give his brother any. But the effect of saying this is to obscure what we should keep distinct, namely the difference between the boy's refusal in this case and the boy's refusal in the earlier case, in which the box was given to both boys jointly, and in which the small brother thus had what was from any point of view clear title to half.

A further objection to so using the term "right" that from the fact that A ought to do a thing for B, it follows that B has a right against A that A do it for him, is that it is going to make the question of whether or not a man has a right to a thing turn on how easy it is to provide him with it; and this seems not merely unfortunate, but morally unacceptable. Take the case of Henry Fonda again. I said earlier that I had no right to the touch of his cool hand on my fevered brow, even though I needed it to save my life. I said it would be frightfully nice of him to fly in from the West Coast to provide me with it, but that I had no right against him that he should do so. But suppose he isn't on the West Coast. Suppose he has only to walk across the room, place a hand briefly on my brow—and lo, my life is saved. Then surely he ought to do it, it would be indecent to refuse. Is it to be said "Ah, well, it follows that in this case she has a right to the touch of his hand on her brow, and so it would be an injustice in him to refuse"? So that I have a right to it when it is easy for him to provide it, though no right when it's hard? It's rather a shocking idea that anyone's rights should fade away and disappear as it gets harder and harder to accord them to him.

So my own view is that even though you ought to let the violinist use your kidneys for the one hour he needs, we should not conclude that he has a right to do so—we should say that if you refuse, you are, like the boy who owns all the chocolates and will give none away, self-centered and callous, indecent in fact, but not unjust. And similarly, that even supposing a case in which a woman pregnant due to rape ought to allow the unborn person to use her body for the hour he needs, we should not conclude that he has a right to do so; we should conclude that she is self-centered, callous, indecent, but not unjust, if she refuses. The complaints are no less grave; they are just different. However, there is no need to insist on this point.

If anyone does wish to deduce "he has a right" from "you ought," then all the same he must surely grant that there are cases in which it is not morally required of you that you allow that violinist to use your kidneys, and in which he does not have a right to use them, and in which you do not do him an injustice if you refuse. And so also for mother and unborn child. Except in such cases as the unborn person has a right to demand it—and we were leaving open the possibility that there may be such cases—nobody is morally *required* to make large sacrifices, of health, of all other interests and concerns, of all other duties and commitments, for nine years, or even for nine months, in order to keep another person alive.

6. We have in fact to distinguish between two kinds of Samaritan: the Good Samaritan* and what we might call the Minimally Decent Samaritan. The story of the Good Samaritan, you will remember, goes like this:

A certain man went down from Jerusalem to Jericho, and fell among thieves, which stripped him of his raiment, and wounded him, and departed, leaving him half dead.

And by chance there came down a certain priest that way; and when he saw him, he passed by on the other side.

And likewise a Levite, when he was at the place, came and looked on him, and passed by on the other side.

But a certain Samaritan, as he journeyed, came where he was; and when he saw him he had compassion on him.

And went to him, and bound up his wounds, pouring in oil and wine, and set him on his own beast, and brought him to an inn, and took care of him.

And on the morrow, when he departed, he took out two pence, and gave them to the host,

and said unto him, "Take care of him; and whatsoever thou spendest more, when I come again, I will repay thee." (Luke 10:30–35)

The Good Samaritan went out of his way, at some cost to himself, to help one in need of it. We are not told what the options were, that is, whether or not the priest and the Levite could have helped by doing less than the Good Samaritan did, but assuming they could have, then the fact they did nothing at all shows they were not even Minimally Decent Samaritans, not because they were not Samaritans, but because they were not even minimally decent.

These things are a matter of degree, of course, but there is a difference, and it comes out perhaps most clearly in the story of Kitty Genovese,† who, as you will remember, was murdered while thirty-eight people watched or listened, and did nothing at all to help her. A Good Samaritan would have rushed out to give direct assistance against the murderer. Or perhaps we had better allow that it would have been a Splendid Samaritan who did this, on the ground that it would have involved a risk of death for himself. But the thirty-eight not only did not do this, they did not even trouble to pick up a phone to call the police. Minimally Decent Samaritanism would call for doing at least that, and their not having done it was monstrous.

After telling the story of the Good Samaritan, Jesus said "Go, and do thou likewise." Perhaps he meant that we are morally required to act as the Good Samaritan did. Perhaps he was urging people to do more than is morally required of them. At all events it seems plain that it was not morally required of any of the thirty-eight that he rush out to give direct assistance at the risk of his own life, and that it is not morally required of anyone that he give long stretches of his life—nine years or nine months—to sustaining the life of a person who has no special right (we were leaving open the possibility of this) to demand it.

---

* Samaritans are an ethnoreligious group that descended from the ancient Hebrews. In ancient times, Jews and Samaritans were prohibited from interacting with one another. In a famous parable, or morality tale, in the New Testament of the Bible, Jesus tells of a Good Samaritan who helped an injured Jew, and overlooked the traditional conflict between their peoples. In English, the term "Good Samaritan" colloquially refers to a person who displays exceptional morality by helping a stranger.

† In 1964, Kitty Genovese was stabbed to death outside her apartment building. The *New York Times* reported that 38 people claimed to have seen or heard the event take place but that none had helped or called the police. In more recent years, the accuracy of the *Times* article has been called into question.

Indeed, with one rather striking class of exceptions, no one in any country in the world is *legally* required to do anywhere near as much as this for anyone else. The class of exceptions is obvious. My main concern here is not the state of the law in respect to abortion, but it is worth drawing attention to the fact that in no state in this country is any man compelled by law to be even a Minimally Decent Samaritan to any person; there is no law under which charges could be brought against the thirty-eight who stood by while Kitty Genovese died. By contrast, in most states in this country women are compelled by law to be not merely Minimally Decent Samaritans, but Good Samaritans to unborn persons inside them. This doesn't by itself settle anything one way or the other, because it may well be argued that there should be laws in this country—as there are in many European countries—compelling at least Minimally Decent Samaritanism.[8] But it does show that there is a gross injustice in the existing state of the law. And it shows also that the groups currently working against liberalization of abortion laws, in fact working toward having it declared unconstitutional for a state to permit abortion, had better start working for the adoption of Good Samaritan laws generally, or earn the charge that they are acting in bad faith.

I should think, myself, that Minimally Decent Samaritan laws would be one thing, Good Samaritan laws quite another, and in fact highly improper. But we are not here concerned with the law. What we should ask is not whether anybody should be compelled by law to be a Good Samaritan, but whether we must accede to a situation in which somebody is being compelled—by nature, perhaps—to be a Good Samaritan. We have, in other words, to look now at third-party interventions. I have been arguing that no person is morally required to make large sacrifices to sustain the life of another who has no right to demand them, and this even where the sacrifices do not include life itself; we are not morally required to be Good Samaritans or anyway Very Good Samaritans to one another. But what if a man cannot extricate himself from such a situation? What if he appeals to us to extricate him? It seems to me plain that there are cases in which we can, cases in which a Good Samaritan would extricate him. There you are, you were kidnapped, and nine years in bed with that violinist lie ahead of you. You have your own life to lead. You are sorry, but you simply cannot see giving up so much of your life to the sustaining of

his. You cannot extricate yourself, and ask us to do so. I should have thought that—in light of his having no right to the use of your body—it was obvious that we do not have to accede to your being forced to give up so much. We can do what you ask. There is no injustice to the violinist in our doing so.

7. Following the lead of the opponents of abortion, I have throughout been speaking of the fetus merely as a person, and what I have been asking is whether or not the argument we began with, which proceeds only from the fetus' being a person, really does establish its conclusion. I have argued that it does not.

But of course there are arguments and arguments, and it may be said that I have simply fastened on the wrong one. It may be said that what is important is not merely the fact that the fetus is a person, but that it is a person for whom the woman has a special kind of responsibility issuing from the fact that she is its mother. And it might be argued that all my analogies are therefore irrelevant—for you do not have that special kind of responsibility for that violinist, Henry Fonda does not have that special kind of responsibility for me. And our attention might be drawn to the fact that men and women both *are* compelled by law to provide support for their children.

I have in effect dealt (briefly) with this argument in section 4 above; but a (still briefer) recapitulation now may be in order. Surely we do not have any such "special responsibility" for a person unless we have assumed it, explicitly or implicitly. If a set of parents do not try to prevent pregnancy, do not obtain an abortion, and then at the time of birth of the child do not put it out for adoption, but rather take it home with them, then they have assumed responsibility for it, they have given it rights, and they cannot *now* withdraw support from it at the cost of its life because they now find it difficult to go on providing for it. But if they have taken all reasonable precautions against having a child, they do not simply by virtue of their biological relationship to the child who comes into existence have a special responsibility for it. They may wish to assume responsibility for it, or they may not wish to. And I am suggesting that if assuming responsibility for it would require large sacrifices, then they may refuse. A Good Samaritan would not refuse—or anyway, a Splendid Samaritan, if the sacrifices that had to be made were enormous. But then so would a Good Samaritan assume responsibility for that violinist; so would Henry Fonda, if he is a Good Samaritan, fly in from the West Coast and assume responsibility for me.

8. My argument will be found unsatisfactory on two counts by many of those who want to regard abortion as morally permissible. First, while I do argue that abortion is not impermissible, I do not argue that it is always permissible. There may well be cases in which carrying the child to term requires only Minimally Decent Samaritanism of the mother, and this is a standard we must not fall below. I am inclined to think it a merit of my account precisely that it does *not* give a general yes or a general no. It allows for and supports our sense that, for example, a sick and desperately frightened fourteen-year-old schoolgirl, pregnant due to rape, may *of course* choose abortion, and that any law which rules this out is an insane law. And it also allows for and supports our sense that in other cases resort to abortion is even positively indecent. It would be indecent in the woman to request an abortion, and indecent in a doctor to perform it, if she is in her seventh month, and wants the abortion just to avoid the nuisance of postponing a trip abroad. The very fact that the arguments I have been drawing attention to treat all cases of abortion, or even all cases of abortion in which the mother's life is not at stake, as morally on a par ought to have made them suspect at the outset.

Secondly, while I am arguing for the permissibility of abortion in some cases, I am not arguing for the right to secure the death of the unborn child. It is easy to confuse these two things in that up to a certain point in the life of the fetus it is not able to survive outside the mother's body; hence removing it from her body guarantees its death. But they are importantly different. I have argued that you are not morally required to spend nine months in bed, sustaining the life of that violinist; but to say this is by no means to say that if, when you unplug yourself, there is a miracle and he survives, you then have a right to turn round and slit his throat. You may detach yourself even if this costs him his life; you have no right to be guaranteed his death, by some other means, if unplugging yourself does not kill him. There are some people who will feel dissatisfied by this feature of my argument. A woman may be utterly devastated by the thought of a child, a bit of herself, put out for adoption and never seen or heard of again. She may therefore want not merely that the child be detached from her, but more, that it die. Some opponents of abortion are inclined to regard this as beneath contempt—thereby showing insensitivity to what is surely a powerful source of despair. All the same, I agree that the desire for the child's death is not one which anybody may gratify, should it turn out to be possible to detach the child alive.

At this place, however, it should be remembered that we have only been pretending throughout that the fetus is a human being from the moment of conception. A very early abortion is surely not the killing of a person, and so is not dealt with by anything I have said here. ■

Suggestions for Critical Reflection

1. Appraise the effectiveness of Thomson's violinist thought experiment. In what ways does it parallel the case of abortion? In what ways does it differ?

2. Thomson considers a variation of the violinist scenario in which the woman will die if she remains connected to the violinist. She states: "If anything in the world is true, it is that you do not commit murder ... if you reach around to your back and unplug yourself from that violinist to save your life." Do you agree? Why or why not?

3. Thomson claims that her argument establishes the permissibility of abortion, but not "the right to secure the death of the unborn child." Does this suggest that some techniques of abortion are permissible while others are not?

4. Thomson states her view is that "if a human being has any just, prior claim to anything at all, he has a just, prior claim to his own body." Assess this position. Does this imply that we relate to our own bodies as something like property owners (consider also Thomson's analogies to home burglary in section 4)? Are there other ways in which we might conceptualize the relationship of a person to their body?

5. Is there a certain level of samaritanism that is not just exemplary but morally required of us (even if it is not legally required)? To what degree are we obligated to help others?

Notes

1 I am very much indebted to James Thomson for discussion, criticism, and many helpful suggestions.

2 Daniel Callahan, *Abortion: Law, Choice and Morality* (New York, 1970), p. 373. This book gives a fascinating survey of the available information on abortion. The Jewish tradition is surveyed in David M. Feldman, *Birth Control in Jewish Law* (New York, 1968), Part 5; the Catholic tradition in John T. Noonan, Jr., "An Almost Absolute Value in History," in *The Morality of Abortion*, ed. John T. Noonan, Jr. (Cambridge, Mass., 1970).

3 The term "direct" in the arguments I refer to is a technical one. Roughly, what is meant by "direct killing" is either killing as an end in itself, or killing as a means of some end, for example, the end of saving someone else's life. See footnote 6 for an example of its use.

4 Cf. *Encyclical Letter of Pope Pius XI on Christian Marriage*, St. Paul Editions (Boston, n.d.), p. 32: "however much we may pity the mother whose health and even life is gravely imperiled in the performance of the duty allotted to her by nature, nevertheless what could ever be a sufficient reason for excusing in any way the direct murder of the innocent? This is precisely what we are dealing with here." Noonan (*The Morality of Abortion*, p. 43) reads this as follows: "What cause can ever avail to excuse in any way the direct killing of the innocent? For it is a question of that."

5 The thesis in (4) is in an interesting way weaker than those in (1), (2), and (3): they rule out abortion even in cases in which both mother and child will die if the abortion is not performed. By contrast, one who held the view expressed in (4) could consistently say that one needn't prefer letting two persons die to killing one.

6 Cf. the following passage from Pius XII, *Address to the Italian Catholic Society of Midwives*: "The baby in the maternal breast has the right to life immediately from God.—Hence there is no man, no human authority, no science, no medical, eugenic, social, economic or moral 'indication' which can establish or grant a valid juridical ground for a direct deliberate disposition of an innocent human life, that is a disposition which looks to its destruction either as an end or as a means to another end perhaps in itself not illicit.—The baby, still not born, is a man in the same degree and for the same reason as the mother" (quoted in Noonan, *The Morality of Abortion*, p. 45).

7 The need for a discussion of this argument was brought home to me by members of the Society for Ethical and Legal Philosophy, to whom this paper was originally presented.

8 For a discussion of the difficulties involved, and a survey of the European experience with such laws, see *The Good Samaritan and the Law*, ed. James M. Ratcliffe (New York, 1966).

CHRISTOPHER HEATH WELLMAN

Immigration and Freedom of Association

Who Is Christopher Heath Wellman?

Christopher Heath "Kit" Wellman (b. 1967) earned a PhD from the University of Arizona in 1994; he is currently a Professor of Philosophy at Washington University in St. Louis. He specializes in ethics and legal and political philosophy, and has published on issues of political legitimacy, the rights and obligations of citizens and states, and the permissibility of punishment. Wellman's books include *Rights Forfeiture and Punishment* (2017), *Debating the Ethics of Immigration*, co-authored with Phillip Cole (2011), and *A Theory of Secession* (2005).

What Is the Structure of This Reading?

In recent years philosophers have been paying more attention to the role that immigration plays in political and moral theories of statehood and to how political communities are constituted. Much debate centers on arguments that either support open borders or defend the right to closed borders. Related questions include: What criteria should a state use in setting an immigration admission policy? What duties do we owe to individuals of other states? Do states have a right to preserve distinctive identities and cultures that may be affected by immigration? Is it morally permissible to allow guest workers to reside in a country over the long term without granting them the rights and privileges of citizenship? How should irregular or undocumented migrants be addressed? Are refugees a special type of migrant?

Wellman offers a provocative defense of a state's right to control immigration. His argument follows this basic structure:

1. Legitimate states are entitled to political self-determination (that is, they have the right to choose their own political policies).
2. Freedom of association, including the freedom *not* to associate with others, is an integral component of self-determination.

3. Therefore, legitimate states have the right not to associate with others, including through restrictions on immigration.

He draws analogies to other types of association, such as marriage and membership in social groups like golf clubs. Just as individuals have the right to choose their spouses, and just as social groups have the right to choose their members, so does the state have the right to choose which people it allows in.

Wellman considers several objections, including egalitarian arguments—that is, arguments grounded in the idea that all people are deserving of equal rights and treatment. An egalitarian might claim that the country in which one is born is a matter of luck, and the dramatically unequal life prospects of people who are born in different countries is an injustice. Therefore, it would arguably be wrong to employ a policy of restricted immigration that enforces those injustices by preventing people from moving from one state to another. Another form of egalitarianism—the "relational egalitarianism" championed by philosopher Elizabeth Anderson—might further hold that, whether or not goods and rights are distributed equally, the relationships between states (including immigration policies) can cause and perpetuate oppression and inequality.

In response to these egalitarian objections, Wellman claims that "luck equality matters, but it matters considerably less than relational equality ... [and] realizing luck equality is not important enough to deny people their rights to self-determination." Wellman does not deny that a state or its members may have obligations toward the members of other states. Indeed, he claims that members of wealthy nations have a natural samaritan duty to help those in extreme poverty, particularly when this could be done at no unreasonable cost to themselves. And furthermore, given the increasing globalization of international trade and the history of colonialism, it is clear that members of distant countries are connected, and that their relationships may result in inequalities. Nonetheless, Wellman maintains that the relationships between fellow-citizens are particularly important and entail obligations that don't hold between citizens of different countries.

Wellman further argues that even if wealthy nations have obligations toward less wealthy nations, it's possible to satisfy those obligations without an open-border immigration policy. Here again Wellman draws a comparison to marriage. One wouldn't, he claims, argue that the inequality of a wealthy married couple living within an impoverished society could only be addressed by either banning marriage or by forcing the wealthy couple to allow the poor to enter into their marriage. Likewise, Wellman holds that wealthy countries are not required to allow entry, and can instead address their obligations by sending their wealth and resources to other countries. In reality, most countries may not be living up to the full extent of their obligations, but that doesn't mean that it is not possible for them to do so without an open-door immigration policy.

Some Useful Background Information

1. Wellman also considers two libertarian arguments against his position (not included in this reading). These arguments appeal to the importance of individual freedom of movement and property rights. A libertarian may hold that private property owners who wish to invite foreigners to live on their land indefinitely should not have their individual rights trumped by the state's control over immigration. To this, Wellman responds that in such conflicts the claims of the state take precedence because "one cannot consistently insist that property rights are totally unlimited without committing oneself to anarchism." A libertarian might also argue that individuals should have the right to freedom of movement, and any government intervention restricting that movement—such as a limitation on immigration—is a violation of rights. Wellman counters that such rights are not absolute, and that just as our freedom of movement does not entitle us to enter other people's homes without their permission, likewise it does not entitle us to enter a foreign state without that state's permission.

2. Note that Wellman is not arguing that states ought to close their borders to immigrants; he is arguing that states have the right to determine their immigration policies. In a passage from this paper not included here, Wellman writes: "if anything, I am personally inclined toward more open borders.... I believe that, just as few individuals flourish in personal isolation, open borders are typically (and within limits) best for political communities and their constituents."

Immigration and Freedom of Association[*1]

In this article I appeal to freedom of association to defend a state's right to control immigration over its territorial borders. Without denying that those of us in wealthy societies may have extremely demanding duties of global distributive justice, I ultimately reach the stark conclusion that every legitimate state has the right to close its doors to all potential immigrants, even refugees desperately seeking asylum from incompetent or corrupt political regimes that are either unable or unwilling to protect their citizens' basic moral rights....

I. The Case for the Right to Closed Borders

To appreciate the presumptive case in favor of a state's right to control its borders that can be built upon the right to freedom of association, notice both that (1) freedom of association is widely thought to be important and that (2) it includes the right not to associate and even, in many cases, the right to disassociate.

That freedom of association is highly valued is evident from our views on marriage and religion. In the past, it was thought appropriate for one's father to

* Originally published in *Ethics* 119, 1 (October 2008): 109–41.

select one's marital partner or for one's state to determine the religion one practiced, but, thankfully, those times have (largely) passed. Today, virtually everyone agrees that we are entitled to marital and religious freedom of association; we take it for granted that each individual has a right to choose his or her marital partner and the associates with whom he or she practices his or her religion. Put plainly, among our most firmly settled convictions is the belief that each of us enjoys a morally privileged position of dominion over our self-regarding affairs,* a position which entitles us to freedom of association in the marital and religious realms.

Second, notice that freedom of association includes a right to reject a potential association and (often) a right to disassociate. As Stuart White explains: "Freedom of association is widely seen as one of those basic freedoms which is fundamental to a genuinely free society. With the freedom to associate, however, there comes the freedom to refuse association. When a group of people get together to form an association of some kind (e.g., a religious association, a trade union, a sports club), they will frequently wish to exclude some people from joining their association. What makes it *their* association, serving their purposes, is that they can exercise this 'right to exclude.'"[2]

In the case of matrimony, for instance, this freedom involves more than merely having the right to get married. One fully enjoys freedom of association only if one may choose whether or not to marry a second party who would have one as a partner. Thus, one must not only be permitted to marry a willing partner whom one accepts; one must also have the discretion to reject the proposal of any given suitor and even to remain single indefinitely if one so chooses. As David Gauthier puts it, "I may have the right to choose the woman of my choice who also chooses me, but not the woman of my choice who rejects me."[3] We understand religious self-determination similarly: whether, how, and with whom I attend to my humanity is up to me as an individual. If I elect to explore my religious nature in community with others, I have no duty to do so with anyone in particular, and I have no right to force others to allow me to join them in worship.

In light of our views on marriage and religious self-determination, the case for a state's right to control immigration might seem straightforward: just as an individual has a right to determine whom (if anyone) he or she would like to marry, a group of fellow-citizens has a right to determine whom (if anyone) it would like to invite into its political community. And just as an individual's freedom of association entitles one to remain single, a state's freedom of association entitles it to exclude all foreigners from its political community. There are at least two reasons that this inference from an individual's to a state's right to freedom of association might strike some as problematic, however. First, presumably there are morally relevant differences between individuals and groups, and these differences might explain why only individuals can have a right to self-determination. Second, even if it is possible for groups to have rights, presumably the interests a group of citizens might have in controlling immigration are nowhere near as important as an individual's interest in having a decisive say regarding whom he or she marries. Let us consider these two issues in turn.

In response to concerns about the differences between individuals and groups, let me begin by highlighting some commonly held convictions which illustrate that we typically posit at least a presumptive group right to freedom of association. Think, for instance, of the controversy that has surrounded groups like the Boy Scouts of America or the Augusta National Golf Club, both of which have faced considerable public pressure and even legal challenges regarding their rights to freedom of association. In particular, some have contested the Boy Scouts' right to exclude homosexuals and atheists, while others have criticized Augusta National's exclusion of women.[4] These cases raise a number of thorny issues. We need not adjudicate either of these conflicts here, however, because the requisite point for our purposes is a minimal one. Specifically, notice that even those who insist that the Boy Scouts should be legally forced to include gays and atheists or that Augusta National cannot justify their continued exclusion of women typically concede that there are weighty reasons in favor of allowing these groups to determine their own

---

* Things we do that affect us but not other people.

membership. That is, even activists lobbying for intervention usually acknowledge that there are reasons to respect these groups' rights to autonomy; the activists claim only that the *prima facie** case in favor of group self-determination is liable to be outweighed in sufficiently compelling instances (e.g., when society as a whole discriminates against women or privileges theism and heterosexuality over atheism and homosexuality). The key point, of course, is that questioning Augusta National's group right to determine its own membership does not require one to deny that groups have a presumptive right to freedom of association because one could simply assert that this presumptive right is vulnerable to being overridden. And because I seek at this stage to defend only a presumptive case in favor of a state's right to control its own borders, it is enough to note how uncontroversial it is to posit a group's right to freedom of association.

There is still room to question my slide from an individual's to a state's right to freedom of association, however, because, unlike the Boy Scouts and the Augusta National Golf Club, political states do not owe their membership to the autonomous choices of their constituents. The nonvoluntary nature of political states can raise complex problems for those who would defend a state's right to political self-determination (problems I address at length elsewhere), but here I would like merely to highlight some of the unpalatable implications that follow from denying a country's right to freedom of association.[5] In particular, consider the moral dynamics of regional associations like the North American Free Trade Agreement (NAFTA) or the European Union (EU). If legitimate states did not enjoy a right to freedom of association—a right which entitles them to decline invitations to associate with others—then they would not be in a position to either accept or reject the terms of these regional associations. Think of Canada's choice to join NAFTA, or Slovenia's decision to enter the EU, for instance. No one believes that it would be permissible to force Canada into NAFTA or to coerce Slovenia to join the EU. (Of course, nor may Canada or Slovenia unilaterally insert themselves into these associations!) And the reason it is wrong to forcibly include these countries is because Canada's and Slovenia's rights to self-determination entitle them to associate (or not) with other countries as they see fit. Put plainly, if one denies that legitimate states like Canada and Slovenia have a right to freedom of association, one could not explain why they would be righteously aggrieved at being forced into these mergers.

Indeed, there would be even more awkward implications because, without positing a right to freedom of association, we could not satisfactorily explain what is wrong with one country forcibly annexing another. Imagine, for instance, that a series of plebiscites† revealed both that an overwhelming majority of Americans wanted to merge with Canada and that an equally high proportion of Canadians preferred to maintain their independence. Would it be permissible for the United States to forcibly annex Canada? I assume without argument that, even if the United States could execute this unilateral merger without disrupting the peace or violating the individual rights of any Canadians, this hostile takeover would be impermissible. The crucial point for our purposes is that one cannot explain the wrongness of unilateral annexations like this unless one supposes that countries like Canada enjoy a right to autonomy, a right which accords Canadians the freedom to associate with others as they see fit.[6]

If the analysis to this point has been sound, then there is no reason to doubt that groups, even political states, can have rights to autonomy analogous to those enjoyed by individuals. Even if one agrees that legitimate states can have rights to self-determination, though, one might still question the argument sketched above on the grounds that the intimacy of marriage makes freedom of association immeasurably more important in the marital context than in the political realm. After all, in the vast majority of cases, fellow citizens will never even meet one another. On this point, consider Stuart White's contention that "if the formation of a specific association is essential to the individual's ability to exercise properly his/her liberties of conscience and expression, *or to his/her ability to form and enjoy intimate attachments*, then exclusion rules which are genuinely necessary to protect the association's primary purposes have an especially

---

* Latin: "first impression"; a *prima facie* case is one that is true in the absence of evidence to the contrary.
† A vote on an important matter, such as a change in the constitution, that is open to all members of an electorate.

strong presumption of legitimacy."[7] Transposing White's reasoning, one might insist that, since there is no intimacy among compatriots, it is not at all clear why we need to respect freedom of association for groups of citizens.[8]

I concede that freedom of association is much more important for individuals in the marital context than for groups of citizens in the political realm, but my argument does not rely upon these two types of freedom of association being equally important. Notice, for instance, that being able to choose the associates with whom one worships is also less important than having discretion over one's marital partner, but no one concludes from this that we need not respect freedom of association in the religious realm. It is important to recognize that I seek at this stage to establish only that there is a *prima facie* case in favor of each legitimate state's right to control immigration (it will be the burden of the remainder of this article to show that competing considerations are not as weighty as one might think). Nonetheless, let me say a bit more about this presumptive case.

In my view, autonomous individuals and legitimate states both have rights to autonomy. This means that they occupy morally privileged positions of dominion over their self-regarding affairs. Such a position can be outweighed by sufficiently compelling considerations, of course, but in general people and states have a right to order their own affairs as they please. Freedom of association is not something that requires an elaborate justification, then, since it is simply one component of the self-determination which is owed to all autonomous individuals and legitimate states. As a consequence, I think that there is a very natural and straightforward case to be made in favor of freedom of association in all realms. Just as one need not explain how playing golf is inextricably related to the development of one's moral personality, say, in order to justify one's right to play golf, neither must one show that one's membership in a golf club is crucial to one's basic interests to establish the club members' right to freedom of association. And if no one doubts that golf clubs have a presumptive right to exclude others, then there seems no reason to suspect that a group of citizens cannot also have the right to freedom of association, even if control over membership in a country is not nearly as significant as control regarding one's potential spouse.

What is more, for several reasons it seems clear that control over membership in one's state is extremely important. To see this, think about why people might care about the membership rules for their golf club. It is tempting to think that club members would be irrational to care about who else are (or could become) members; after all, they are not forced to actually play golf with those members they dislike. But this perspective misses something important. Members of golf clubs typically care about the membership rules because they care about how the club is organized and the new members have a say in how the club is organized. Some members might want to dramatically increase the number of members, for instance, because the increased numbers will mean that each individual is required to pay less. Other members might oppose expanding the membership because of concerns about the difficulty of securing desirable tee times, the wear and tear on the course, and the increased time it takes to play a round if there are more people on the course at any given time.

And if there is nothing mysterious about people caring about who are (or could become) members of their golf clubs, there is certainly nothing irrational about people being heavily invested in their country's immigration policy. Again, to note the lack of intimacy among compatriots is to miss an important part of the story. It is no good to tell citizens that they need not personally (let alone intimately) associate with any fellow citizens they happen to dislike because fellow citizens nonetheless remain political associates; the country's course will be charted by the members of this civic association. The point is that people rightly care very deeply about their countries, and, as a consequence, they rightly care about those policies which will affect how these political communities evolve. And since a country's immigration policy affects who will share in controlling the country's future, it is a matter of considerable importance.

These examples of the golf club and the political state point toward a more general lesson that is worth emphasizing: because the members of a group can change, an important part of group self-determination is having control over what the "self" is. In other words, unlike individual self-determination, a significant component of group self-determination is having control over the group which in turn gets to be self-determining. It stands to reason, then, that if there is any group whose self-determination we care about, we should be concerned about its rules for membership. This explains why freedom of association is such an integral part of the self-determination to which some groups (including legitimate states) are entitled. If so, then anyone who denies that we should care about the freedom of association of nonintimate groups would seem to be committed to the more sweeping claim that we should not care about the self-determination of any nonintimate groups. But, unless one implausibly believes that we should care only about intimate groups, then why should we suppose that only the self-determination of intimate groups matters? Thus, people rightly care deeply about their political states, despite these states being large, anonymous, and multicultural, and, as a consequence, people rightly care about the rules for gaining membership in these states. Or, put another way, the very same reasoning which understandably leads people to jealously guard their state's sovereignty also motivates them to keep an eye on who can gain membership in this sovereign state.

A second, less obvious, reason to care about immigration policy has to do with one's duties of distributive justice. As I will argue in the next section, it seems reasonable to think that we have special distributive responsibilities to our fellow citizens. If this is right, then in the same way that one might be reluctant to form intimate relationships because of the moral freight attached, one might want to limit the number of people with whom one shares a morally significant political relationship. Thus, just as golf club members can disagree about the costs and benefits of adding new members, some citizens might want to open the doors to new immigrants (e.g., in order to expand the labor force), while others would much rather forgo these advantages than incur special obligations to a greater number of people.

Finally, rather than continue to list reasons why citizens ought to care about issues of political membership, let me merely point out that citizens today obviously do care passionately about immigration. I do not insist that the current fervor over political membership is entirely rational, but it is worth noting that anyone who submits that freedom of association in this context is of no real importance is committed to labeling all those who care about this issue as patently irrational. Thus, even though the relationship among citizens does not involve the morally relevant intimacy

of that between marital partners, the considerations quickly canvassed above, as well as the behavior of actual citizens, indicate that we need not conclude that control over immigration is therefore of negligible significance. If so, then neither the observation that (1) individual persons are importantly disanalogous to political states nor the fact that (2) freedom of association is much more important for individuals in the marital context than for groups of citizens in the political realm should lead us to abandon our initial comparison between marriage and immigration. As a consequence, we have no reason to abandon the claim that, like autonomous individuals, legitimate political regimes are entitled to a degree of self-determination, one important component of which is freedom of association. In sum, the conclusion initially offered only tentatively can now be endorsed with greater conviction: just as an individual has a right to determine whom (if anyone) he or she would like to marry, a group of fellow-citizens has a right to determine whom (if anyone) it would like to invite into its political community. And just as an individual's freedom of association entitles him or her to remain single, a state's freedom of association entitles it to exclude all foreigners from its political community.

...

In sum, the commonly prized value of freedom of association provides the basic normative building blocks for a presumptive case in favor of each legitimate state's right to exclude others from its territory. But, while freedom of association provides a weighty consideration in favor of a state's right to limit immigration, it is obviously not the only value of importance. Thus, even if my reasoning to this point has been sound, the case in favor of a state's dominion is only presumptive and may be outweighed by competing considerations. With this in mind, let us now review the arguments in favor of open borders to see if they defeat a state's right to limit immigration.

II. The Egalitarian Case for Open Borders

Egalitarians survey the vast inequalities among states and then allege that it is horribly unjust that people should have such dramatically different life prospects simply because they are born in different countries. The force of this view is not difficult to appreciate. Given that one's country of birth is a function of brute luck, it seems grossly unfair that one's place of birth would so profoundly affect one's life prospects. Some believe that the solution is clear: political borders must be opened, so that no one is denied access to the benefits of wealthy societies. Although he couches his argument in terms of a principle of humanity rather than equality, Chandran Kukathas makes this point particularly forcefully: "A principle of humanity suggests that very good reasons must be offered to justify turning the disadvantaged away. It would be bad enough to meet such people with indifference and to deny them positive assistance. It would be even worse to deny them the opportunity to help themselves. To go to the length of denying one's fellow citizens the right to help those who are badly off, whether by employing them or by simply taking them in, seems even more difficult to justify—if, indeed, it is not entirely perverse."[9]

For several reasons, this case for open borders presents an especially imposing obstacle to the *prima facie* case for the right to restrict immigration outlined above. For starters, both its moral and empirical premises appear unexceptionable. How could one plausibly deny either that all humans are in some fundamental sense equally deserving of moral consideration or that the staggering inequalities across the globe dramatically affect people's prospects for living a decent life? Indeed, looked at from this perspective, sorting humans according to the countries in which they were born appears tantamount to a geographical caste system. As Joseph Carens famously argues: "Citizenship in Western liberal democracies is the modern equivalent to feudal privilege—an inherited status that greatly enhances one's life chances. Like feudal birthright privileges, restrictive citizenship is hard to justify when one thinks about it closely."[10] What is more, notice that advocating this position does not require one to deny the importance of freedom of association: an egalitarian who presses this objection can agree that we should generally be free to choose our associates, as long as the resulting associations do not lead to unjust arrangements. Thus, allowing states to limit immigration is regarded as problematic on this view only because countries cannot enjoy this form of freedom of association without people's life prospects being seriously affected by morally irrelevant matters, that is, factors entirely beyond their control.

Despite the intuitive appeal of this line of reasoning, I will counter this objection with two arguments. First, I suggest that the most compelling understanding of equality does not require us to guarantee that no one's life prospects are affected by matters of luck; more minimally, equality demands that we address those inequalities that render people vulnerable to oppressive relationships. If this is correct, then the particular theory of equality required to motivate the egalitarian case for open borders is suspect and should be rejected in favor of a theory of relational equality. Second, even if luck egalitarianism is the best theory of equality, it would not generate a duty to leave borders open, because a wealthy state's redistributive responsibilities can be discharged without including the recipients in the union. Consider each of these responses in turn.

I should begin by acknowledging the obvious appeal of luck egalitarianism. After all, it does seem unfair that some people's life prospects are dramatically worse than others when neither the poorly off nor the well off did anything to deserve their initial starting points. And it is hard to deny that the world would be better if everyone enjoyed roughly equal prospects for a rewarding life. It is important to recognize, though, that luck egalitarianism is not the only game in town. In *Political Philosophy*, for instance, Jean Hampton recommends an approach she ascribes to Aristotle: "We want, he says, a society in which people treat each other as equals (no one should be allowed to be the master of another or the slave of another) and in which these equals treat each other as partners—or 'civic friends.' The way to get that is to pursue not exact equality of resources but sufficient equality to ensure that no one is able to use his greater wealth to gain political advantage over others in a way that damages their partnership."[11]

Now, one might be struck by Hampton's suggestion that we need not pursue "exact" equality, but I want to call attention to another, related feature of her view: its relational nature. As Hampton emphasizes, Aristotle is concerned with equality because he sees it as necessary to sustain the desired relationships among fellow citizens. We need not concern ourselves with securing exact equality, then, because (political) relationships are not undermined by slight disparities in wealth; clearly, compatriots can interact as political equals even if some have more than others, regardless of whether or not their unequal resources are deserved.

Others share Hampton's preference for relational theories of equality, but no one, to my knowledge, has better motivated this approach than Elizabeth Anderson.[12] Key to Anderson's defense of relational equality is the question: "What is the point of equality?" In her view, answering this question reveals most clearly why relational theories are preferable to those which fixate on luck. The crucial point is that we should care about inequality principally to the extent that subordinates are dominated in oppressive relationships. For this reason, Anderson insists that we should be "fundamentally concerned with the relationships within which the goods are distributed, not only the distribution of goods themselves."[13]

To appreciate the force of this point, compare two possible inequalities. The first exists between two societies, A and B. Assume that everyone in A is equally well off; everyone in B is doing equally poorly; and no one in either A or B knows anything of the other society's existence, since they are on opposite sides of the earth and have never had any contact. The second inequality mirrors the disparity between the As and Bs, except that it exists within a single society C. And because the Cs share a single political community, not only are they aware that others are faring considerably better/worse but also their relationships are affected by these inequalities. I take it as uncontroversial that the inequality among the Cs is much more worrisome than the same inequality between the As and Bs. In other words, whether or not we should care about the inequality between the As and Bs, clearly we should be much more concerned to eliminate the inequality among the Cs. Based in part upon reasoning like this, Anderson concludes: "Negatively, people are entitled to whatever capabilities are necessary to enable them to avoid or escape entanglement in oppressive relationships. Positively, they are entitled to the capabilities necessary for functioning as an equal citizen in a democratic state."[14]

Arguments like Anderson's convince me that we should be keenly aware of the relationships within which the goods are distributed, but I stop short of concluding that relational equality is the one correct theory of equality. In my view, luck equality matters, but it matters considerably less than relational equality. In other words, although I would not hesitate to eliminate the inequality between the As and Bs if I could do so by waving a magic wand, this inequality is not sufficiently worrisome that I would necessarily interfere in the internal affairs of the As in order to eliminate the inequality between them and the Bs. However, because I am much more concerned about the inequality among the Cs, I would be correspondingly less reluctant to demand that the wealthy Cs take measures to ensure that the less well off Cs are not entangled in oppressive relationships.

As a consequence, while I do not think that there is nothing of moral consequence to be gained from realizing luck equality, I do accept a more modest claim: even if achieving relational equality is important enough to trump other values like freedom of association, realizing luck equality is not important enough to deny people their rights to self-determination. And this more modest conclusion has important implications for the morality of immigration. Most obviously, even if we would prefer a world with no inequality between the As and the Bs, eliminating this inequality is not important enough to justify limiting the As' right to freedom of association. In short, given that the moral importance of any particular inequality is a function of the relationship in which the goods are distributed, the lack of a robust relationship between the constituents of a wealthy state and the citizens of a poorer country implies that this admittedly lamentable inequality does not generate sufficient moral reasons to obligate the wealthy state to open its borders, even if nothing but luck explains why those living outside of the territorial borders have dramatically worse prospects of living a rewarding life.

Here two potential objections present themselves. First, although it is not false to say that the citizens of some countries are relatively well off while the constituents of others are relatively poorly off (as I do in my example of the As and Bs), this cryptic description is nonetheless misleading insofar as it fails to capture that, in the real world, those in the developed countries are staggeringly wealthy in comparison to the masses who are imperiled (when not outright killed) by eviscerating poverty. In short, given the radical inequality and objective plight that make Carens's reference to "feudal privilege" apt, it is not so easy to dismiss global inequality merely because it does not exist between compatriots. Second, because of the history of colonization, as well as the current levels of international trade (among other things), it is simply not the case that the world's wealthy and poor are unconnected and unaware of each other (as I stipulate in my example of the As and Bs). On the contrary, one consequence of the emerging global basic structure is that virtually all of the world's people now share some type of relationship, so presumably even relational egalitarians cannot dismiss the moral significance of global inequality. I think there are important truths in both of these objections, so I will consider each in turn.

To begin, the twin facts that the world's poor are so desperately needy and the world's wealthy are so spectacularly well off that they could effectively help the impoverished without sacrificing anything of real consequence is unquestionably morally significant, but in my mind these facts indicate that the real issue is not about equality. Rather than being exercised merely because some are relatively worse off through no fault of their own, we are (or at least should be) concerned simply because others are suffering in objectively horrible circumstances.[15]

What is more, the reason that we may have a duty to help is not because mere luck explains why we are doing better than they (presumably we would be obligated to relieve their suffering even if our relative standing was fully attributable to morally relevant factors like our hard work). Instead, our duty to help stems most straightforwardly from samaritanism: one has a natural duty to assist others when they are sufficiently imperiled and one can help them at no unreasonable cost to oneself.[16] As a result, I am inclined to respond to the first objection in disjunctive fashion: if the less well off Bs are not doing terribly badly in objective terms, then the inequality between the As and Bs does not generate a duty on the part of the As to help the Bs. If the Bs are clearly suffering in absolute poverty, on the other hand, then the As may indeed have stringent duties to help, but these duties spring from a samaritan source rather than from the mere fact that the As are (for morally arbitrary reasons) doing better than the Bs.[17] If this is right, then even the previously unfathomable inequalities we now see in the real world do not sufficiently buttress the luck egalitarian's case for open borders.

Regarding the second objection, I am inclined to agree that the emerging global infrastructure entails that virtually all of us have increasingly substantial relationships with people all over the world. And as a relational egalitarian, it seems to follow that the more robust these relationships become, the more concerned we should be about the inequalities within them. But I can concede all of this without jettisoning my response to the egalitarian case for open borders because my account has never relied upon the claim that being fellow citizens of a country is the only morally relevant relationship.[18] On the contrary, my account requires only that the less ambitious (and more plausible) claim that the relationship among compatriots is one relationship with morally relevant implications for inequality. To see the significance of this point, notice what I would say about inequalities within a particular state. Even though I think that the relationship shared among compatriots is relevant when assessing the inequalities among two people, I would never allege that no relationships within a state are morally relevant. Because familial relations are particularly liable to oppression, for instance, we might worry about the inequalities between wife and husband, between the parents and children, or among the children in a way that we would not among compatriots who are not members of the same family. For example, we would likely be less comfortable with a scenario in which a family paid for the sons but not the daughters to go to college than one in which one set of parents paid for the children's college expenses and another set of parents did not. Thus, there is nothing about my insistence on the moral relevance of the relationship among compatriots that forces me to deny the possibility of other relationships within the states which are significant for the purposes of inequality. And if I can acknowledge important relationships within a state, there seems no reason why I cannot accept that citizens of separate states can stand in relationships which matter from the point of equality. Most important, notice that conceding this last point does not undermine my response to the egalitarian case for open borders, because I can still insist that (whatever other relationships there are which matter from the standpoint of equality) the relationship between fellow citizens is one particularly important relationship which explains why we need not necessarily restrict the liberty of the better-off citizens in one country merely because nothing but luck explains why they are faring so much better than the citizens of a foreign state.

Finally, a persistent critic might counter that, even if the case based on luck egalitarianism fails, both samaritanism and the morally relevant relationships among foreigners explain why we have duties to those outside of our borders. In response, I suggest that these duties, even if stringent, can be fully satisfied without necessarily allowing those to whom we are duty bound entry to our country....

Even the most zealous critics of inequality typically recommend neither that we must abolish marriage nor that wealthy couples must literally open up their marriages to the less well off. Instead, it is standard to keep separate our rights to freedom of association and our duties of distributive justice, so that wealthy people are able to marry whomever they choose and then are required to transfer a portion of their wealth to others no matter whom (or even whether) they marry. Admittedly, history includes radical movements like the Khmer Rouge,* who abolished marriage because it was thought to be inconsistent with their quest for complete equality, but most egalitarians rightly shy away from this degree of fanaticism.[19] Indeed, consider this: despite the enormous disagreement about what type of responsibilities the likes of Bill Gates and Warren Buffet have in virtue of their staggering wealth, no one alleges that, unlike the rest of us, these billionaires are required to marry poor spouses. And just as our domestic redistribution of wealth among individuals has not led us to prohibit marriage, global redistribution does not require us to open all political borders. Instead, even if we presume that wealthy societies have extensive distributive duties, these duties are distinct and can be kept separate from the societies' rights to freedom of association. To reiterate: if wealthy couples need not open up their marriages to those less well off, why think that wealthy countries must open their borders to less fortunate immigrants? Just as relatively wealthy families are required merely to transfer some of their wealth to others, why cannot wealthy countries fully discharge their global distributive duties without including the recipients in their political union, simply by transferring the required level of funds abroad?[20]

Thus, no matter how substantial their duties of distributive justice, wealthier countries need not open their borders. At most, affluent societies are duty bound to choose between allowing needy foreigners to enter their society or sending some of their wealth to those less fortunate. In fact, David Miller has pressed this point even further, suggesting that it would be better if wealthier countries sent resources abroad. He puts it as follows:

> People everywhere have a right to a decent life. But before jumping to the conclusion that the way to respond to global injustice is to encourage people whose lives are less than decent to migrate elsewhere, we should consider the fact that this policy will do little to help the very poor, who are unlikely to have the resources to move to a richer country. Indeed, a policy of open migration may make such people worse off still, if it allows doctors, engineers, and other professionals to move from economically undeveloped to economically developed societies in search of higher incomes, thereby depriving their countries of origin of vital skills. Equalizing opportunity for the few may diminish opportunities for the many.[21]

If Miller is right about this, then the ardent egalitarian not only may be in no position to demand that affluent societies open their borders but she also may be forced to insist that states not do so, since sending aid abroad is a better way to rescue those most imperiled by poverty.

Even if legitimate states have no duty to open their borders to the world's poor, however, surely it would be unconscionable for a state to slam its doors on people desperately fleeing unjust regimes. After all, even authors like [Michael] Walzer, who are in general prepared to defend a state's right to control its membership, make an exception for refugees.[22] The core idea behind this exception is that, unlike those who merely lack exportable resources, some asylum seekers are actively threatened by their states, and thus they cannot be helped by an international transfer of goods; their only escape from peril is to be granted asylum.

---

* A communist regime that ruled Cambodia and committed genocide in the late twentieth century by murdering almost a quarter of their own population, largely by forcibly relocating the urban population to the countryside to work on collective farms.

As implausible as it might initially seem, I suggest that, even in cases of asylum seekers desperately in need of a political safe haven, a state is not required to take them in. I adopt this stance not because I am unmoved by the plight of asylum seekers but because I am not convinced that the only way to help victims of political injustice is by sheltering them in one's political territory. In my view, these people might also be helped in something like the fashion in which wealthy societies could choose to assist impoverished foreigners: by, as it were, exporting justice. Admittedly, one cannot ship justice in a box, but one can intervene, militarily if necessary, in an unjust political environment to ensure that those currently vulnerable to the state are made safe in their homelands.[23] Let me be clear: I am not suggesting that this is always easy or even advisable, nor do I assert that states are necessarily obligated to take this course of action. I claim instead that where asylum seekers are genuinely left vulnerable because their government is either unable or unwilling to protect their basic rights, then their government is illegitimate, it has no claim to political self-determination, and thus it stands in no position to protest if a third party were to intervene on behalf of (some of) its constituents. Think, for instance, of the Kurds* in Iraq. One way to help them is to allow them to emigrate en masse. Another option, though, is to use military force to create a safe haven and no-fly zone in Northern Iraq. And since the Iraqi government was the party threatening the Kurds, it had no right to object to this interference with its sovereignty. I suspect that Walzer stops short of this conclusion only because he wrongly, I think, respects the political self-determination of virtually all states, even those persecuting asylum seekers.[24]

Walzer and I diverge on this point, then, not because I am less impressed than he by the plight of asylum seekers but because he is more impressed than I by the claims to political self-determination of failed and rogue states, those regimes either unable or unwilling to secure their citizens' basic moral rights. Thus, I once again conclude that affluent societies have a duty to help but that it is a disjunctive duty: just as global poverty requires wealthy states to either export aid or import unfortunate people, the presence of those desperately seeking political asylum renders those of us in just political communities duty bound either to grant asylum or to ensure that these refugees no longer need fear their domestic regimes. Miller seems to me to get it just right when he suggests: "The lesson for other states, confronted with people whose lives are less than decent, is that they have a choice: they must either ensure that the basic rights of such people are protected in the places where they live—by aid, by intervention, or by some other means—or they must help them to move to other communities where their lives will go better. Simply shutting one's borders and doing nothing else is not a morally defensible option here."[25]

... I would like to emphasize that nothing in the preceding critique of the egalitarian case for open borders is intended as a rejection of egalitarianism or as a defense of the status quo. On the contrary, I believe that most of us in affluent societies have pressing restitutive, samaritan, and egalitarian duties to do considerably more to help the masses of people in the world tragically imperiled by poverty, and I even think that one good way to provide this assistance is to allow more immigrants from poorer countries. If sound, the arguments of this section establish merely that egalitarian considerations do not by themselves generate a moral duty which requires wealthy countries to open their borders, in part because the egalitarian case for open borders depends upon a suspect theory of equality, but also because wealthy countries have the discretion to discharge their distributive responsibilities in other manners....

Conclusion

In this article I have tried first to construct a presumptive case in favor of a state's right to set its own immigration policy and then to defend this *prima facie* case against the formidable arguments that have been made on behalf of open borders. If my arguments are sound, then we should conclude that, even if egalitarians are right that those of us in wealthy societies have demanding duties of global distributive justice and even if libertarians are correct that individuals have rights both to freedom of movement and to control their private property, legitimate states are entitled to reject all potential immigrants, even those desperately seeking asylum from corrupt governments. ■

---

*   A Middle Eastern ethnic group residing in parts of Iraq, Iran, Turkey, and Syria.

Suggestions for Critical Reflection

1. Does Wellman's use of analogies to marriage and other types of association (the Boy Scouts and the Augusta National Golf Club) properly support his argument? Are there important differences between those cases and the issues of immigration? If so, does he deal adequately with these differences?

2. Do the messiness and complications of real-world immigration and global relations have any bearing on Wellman's arguments? For example, do close economic and historical relations between neighboring states such as Mexico and the US entail any special obligations when it comes to migrants? Does the high mortality risk for migrants crossing the Mediterranean to Europe by boat imply any special obligations on the part of European states?

3. Are legitimate states entitled to political self-determination? If so, why?

4. "If wealthy couples need not open up their marriages to those less well off, why think that wealthy countries must open their borders to less fortunate immigrants?" How persuasive do you find this argument? What are its implications?

5. Why does Wellman argue that some inequalities between foreigners might be benign even though the same inequalities between citizens of the same state would be harmful? Explain and evaluate his argument.

6. Wellman argues that "affluent societies are duty-bound to choose between allowing needy foreigners to enter their society or sending some of their wealth to those less fortunate" and indeed intervening militarily in other countries with "regimes either unable or unwilling to secure their citizens' basic moral rights." How does Wellman argue for this? Suppose wealthy countries do not adequately do the latter (i.e., improve the lot of poor people in their own home countries); does this change their responsibility to do the former (i.e., open their borders to those poor people), on Wellman's account?

7. It might be argued that a substantial amount of opposition to immigration is racist rather than economic in origin, and that governments should not allow potentially racist attitudes to determine *any* of their policies—domestic or international. If so, does this have bearing on the question of whether or not a state should have the right to restrict immigration, or on the related question of *how* a state should make decisions about immigration policy?

Notes

1 I am extremely grateful for the constructive criticism I received from two anonymous reviewers and the editors of this journal. In addition to audiences at Washington University, University of Missouri, and Australian National University, I am indebted to Andrew Altman, Michael Blake, Joseph Carens, Thomas Christiano, Andrew I. Cohen, Robert Goodin, John Kleinig, Chandran Kukathas, David Lefkowitz, Matt Lister, Larry May, David Miller, Mathias Risse, Alex Sager, Fernando Teson, Andrew Valls, and Carl Wellman for their written comments on earlier drafts of this essay. Above all, I would like to thank the Earhart Foundation for generously supporting my work on this project.

2 Stuart White, "Freedom of Association and the Right to Exclude," *Journal of Political Philosophy* 5 (1997): 373–91, 373.

3 David Gauthier, "Breaking Up: An Essay on Secession," *Canadian Journal of Philosophy* 24 (1994): 357–92, 360–61.

4 Some also object to the Boy Scouts' refusal to admit girls.

5 For an extended discussion of some of the issues associated with group autonomy, see chap. 3 of my book *A Theory of Secession* (New York: Cambridge University Press, 2005).

6 Here one might be tempted to object that Canada's right to independence is more straightforwardly accounted for in terms of its right to self-determination. But, as I shall argue below, it is misleading to contrast freedom of association with self-determination because freedom of association is actually a central component of the more general right to self-determination. In the case of political states, for instance, a state cannot fully enjoy the right to political self-determination unless its rights to freedom of association are respected.

7 White, "Freedom of Association and the Right to Exclude," 381 (emphasis added).

8 It should be noted White is not necessarily committed to this line of argument because his analysis is explicitly restricted to "secondary" groups (which I take to be groups within states) which adopt "categorical" exclusion (i.e., exclusion based upon an individual's race, gender, sexuality, or religion).

9 Chandran Kukathas, "The Case for Open Immigration," in Cohen and Wellman, *Contemporary Debates in Applied Ethics*, 207–20, 211.

10 Joseph H. Carens, "Aliens and Citizens: The Case for Open Borders," *Review of Politics* 49 (1987): 251–73, 252.

11 Jean Hampton, *Political Philosophy* (Boulder, CO: Westview, 1996), 158.

12 Other prominent defenses include David Miller, "What Kind of Equality Should the Left Pursue?" in *Equality*, ed. Jane Franklin (London: Institute for Public Policy Research, 1997), 83–99; Jonathan Wolff, "Fairness, Respect, and the Egalitarian Ethos," *Philosophy & Public Affairs* 27 (1998): 97–122; Andrew Mason, "Equality, Personal Responsibility, and Gender Socialisation," *Proceedings of Aristotelian Society* 100 (1999–2000): 227–46; and Samuel Scheffler, "What Is Egalitarianism?" *Philosophy & Public Affairs* 31 (2003): 5–39.

13 Elizabeth S. Anderson, "What Is the Point of Equality?" *Ethics* 109 (1999): 287–337, 314.

14 Ibid., 316.

15 Harry Frankfurt makes a similar point in "Equality as a Moral Ideal," *Ethics* 98 (1987): 21–43.

16 Incidentally, this point both explains, and is confirmed by, the fact that Chandran Kukathas's quote listed earlier is offered under the banner of a principle of "humanity" rather than one of equality.

17 I do not claim that Michael Blake would follow me in putting this point in terms of samaritanism, but in some important respects the position I outline here squares well with what he says about international distributive justice in his excellent article "Distributive Justice, State Coercion, and Autonomy," *Philosophy & Public Affairs* 30 (2001): 257–96.

18 This appears to be another respect in which my views diverge from those which Blake develops in "Distributive Justice, State Coercion, and Autonomy." According to Blake, the relationship among compatriots is singled out because the state's coercion is key to determining when relative equality is important.

19 As Jonathan Glover explains in his book *Humanity* (New Haven, CT: Yale University Press, 2001): "The idea of the family was attacked. People who were allowed to stay in their villages had to share everything, down to pots and pans. Communal meals for hundreds of families together were compulsory. Many families were split up, with men and women being forced to sleep in segregated communal dormitories" (303).

20 Here one might reassert the objection to my analogy between immigration and marriage. In particular, because political unions are not nearly as intimate as marriages, an egalitarian might consistently protect freedom of association in the marital realm without being similarly impressed with a state's right to craft its own immigration policy. I agree that it would be more of an imposition to restrict one's discretion to select one's spouse, but this concession does not trouble me because I need not press the marriage analogy as far as this objection presumes. My limited hope is that our firmly held and familiar views on marriage will confirm my contention that a state's right to control its territorial borders need not conflict with its duties of distributive justice, even when the latter are cashed out in starkly luck egalitarian terms. If this is right, then arguments like Peter Singer's (which compares refugees to people desperately clamoring for shelter from the fallout of a nuclear bomb) are fallacious because, unlike those exposed to the fallout (whose only hope is to be admitted to the shelter), potential immigrants can be effectively helped without being admitted into one's country. See Peter Singer, "Insiders and Outsiders," in *Practical Ethics* (Cambridge: Cambridge University Press, 1993), 247–63.

21 Miller, "Immigration: The Case for Limits," 198–99. Thomas Pogge and Eric Cavallero have offered similar arguments. See Pogge's "Migration and Poverty," in *Citizenship and Exclusion*, ed. Veit M. Bader (Houndmills: Macmillan, 1997), 12–27; and Cavallero's "An Immigration-Pressure Model of Global Distributive Justice," *Politics, Philosophy and Economics* 5 (2006): 97–127.

22 It is important to note, though, that those who make an exception for refugees (as defined by international law) apparently cannot do so on principled grounds. As theorists like Andrew Shacknove and Michael Dummett have pointed out, restricting the status of refugees to those who have crossed an international border because of a well-founded fear of persecution is morally arbitrary. See Andrew Shacknove, "Who Is a Refugee?" *Ethics* 95 (1985): 274–84; and Michael Dummett, *On Immigration and Refugees* (New York: Routledge, 2001).

23 Of course, interventions will typically take time, and in these cases the intervening state should not return the refugees to their home state (at least without protecting them) until the intervention is successfully completed.

24 For more on the permissibility of armed humanitarian intervention (as well as a more expanded critique of Walzer's position), see Andrew Altman and Christopher Heath Wellman, "From Humanitarian Intervention to Assassination," *Ethics* 118 (2008): 228–57.

25 Miller, "Immigration: The Case for Limits," 198.

JOSÉ JORGE MENDOZA

The Ethics of Immigration Enforcement

Who Is José Jorge Mendoza?

Mendoza earned his PhD in Philosophy from the University of Oregon in 2012 and currently teaches in the philosophy department of the University of Massachusetts Lowell. He specializes in moral and political philosophy (especially issues of global justice), as well as philosophy of race and Latin American philosophy, and is co-editor of the journal *Radical Philosophy Review*. Mendoza's first book, from which this reading is drawn, is *The Moral and Political Philosophy of Immigration: Liberty, Security, and Equality* (2017).

What Is the Structure of This Reading?

Mendoza calls into question the idea that we can assess the ethics of an immigration policy without looking into how that policy is implemented. In this way, he reverses the typical order of the debate: instead of deciding on strategies for immigration enforcement on the basis of policy, he argues that we must examine the morality of those strategies in order to see what kinds of policies are morally permissible. If Mendoza is correct, the state must demonstrate that there is a legally and morally permissible way to restrict immigration before it can claim a right to implement such restrictions.

The first parts of this reading address issues of border control. Here, Mendoza is responding primarily to Christopher Heath Wellman, who argues for a "presumptive case in favor of a state's right to set its own immigration policy" (see the previous reading in this book). If such a right exists, Mendoza argues, then its implementations are clearly limited in at least some ways. Moral requirements of equality and liberty—requirements that Wellman himself is committed to—entail that some acts of border enforcement are prohibited. The question, then, is "what could a legitimate state do to enforce its immigration policy in a morally acceptable way?" Mendoza considers four possible responses, rejecting each of them on the grounds that they will either be ineffective or that they will entail breaches of moral and political commitments.

In the second half of this reading, Mendoza turns from questions of border control to those of internal enforcement. He asks what limits exist on a state's ability to enforce immigration laws with regard to those who have already crossed the border, arguing that moral obligations to ensure "equality of burdens" and "universal protection" entail strict limitations on internal enforcement strategies. If Mendoza is right about this, then it may be immoral for most states to use certain methods to identify and deport immigrants and refugees, even when their entrance is in violation of policy.

Some Useful Background Information

For decades, the US-Mexico border has been a regular site of undocumented crossings. In recent years, American strategies of immigration enforcement have been the subject of much political dispute, especially in connection with the treatment of those who successfully cross the border. In mid-2018, well after the first publication of this reading, it came to public attention that US border agencies were forcibly separating members of families crossing over from Mexico. Children were put in holding facilities separated from their parents, often with little or no relevant information conveyed to either parent or child. Some government officials claimed that these practices did not constitute a change in the law, but were merely the implementation of existing policies. Indeed, earlier US laws and court decisions, including the 1997 *Flores v. Reno* case in which specific conditions were set on the detention and treatment of immigrant children, arguably offered explanation (if not justification) for those practices.

The Ethics of Immigration Enforcement*

... [P]hilosophers working on the issue of immigration have primarily focused their attention on questions of admission and exclusion (i.e., *who* may be let into a political community and *who* may be kept out), so a criticism that focuses on enforcement (i.e., *how* and through *what* means a legitimate state† can keep unwanted foreigners out) might seem a little out of bounds. After all, philosophers often bracket questions of enforcement, at least initially, when attempting to determine who is entitled to certain rights and who is bound by certain duties. For example, in just war theory it is not uncommon to separate discussions about whether to go to war (i.e., *jus ad bellum*) from discussions about what kind of conduct is proper while fighting a war (i.e., *jus in bello*). This chapter therefore challenges the way the immigration debate has been framed within the ethics of immigration literature by showing that enforcement does matter in determining the presumptive rights or duties of immigrants.

The first section of this chapter will make the case that there are presumptive moral limitations on what a legitimate state can do to enforce its border. It will argue that in order to properly adhere to those limitations a legitimate state's immigration policy cannot be discretionary, but must instead be circumvented by such factors as economic realities, family relationships, and socio-historical circumstances. The second section of this chapter then turns to the issue of internal enforcement and the concern for political equality. That section argues that when minority communities are forced to bear a disproportionate amount of the surveying, identifying, interrogating, and apprehending that comes along with internal immigration enforcement, members of those particular minority communities become socially and civically ostracized. In other words, they are not given equal political consideration. In order to avoid such an outcome, internal immigration enforcement must be constrained so that no citizen (or group of citizens) comes to bear a disproportionate amount of the negative externalities‡ that come with enforcement (e.g., an "equality of burdens" standard) and certain protections must be put in place that shield all citizens from the excesses of immigration enforcement (e.g., "universal protections" standard). Together these two standards create a canopy that provides all persons, including undocumented immigrants, with certain presumptive protections against a legitimate state's internal enforcement apparatus.

If the arguments in either section are convincing, then they will show that when enforcement is taken into consideration a commitment to universal equality (e.g., moral or political equality) cannot be reconciled with a legitimate state having a presumptive right to control immigration. Instead, a commitment to universal equality entails that a legitimate state's right to control immigration should be limited by presumptive duties (e.g., *equality of burdens* and *universal protections* standards) and its admissions and exclusions criteria must be determined, at least in part, by *external* factors such as social, historical, and economic circumstances. In short, when an ethics of immigration is considered in its entirety—admission, exclusion, and enforcement—the only way to consistently reconcile democratic self-determination with a commitment to human rights (e.g., individual freedom and universal equality) is for the burden of proof§ (i.e., the presumptive duty) to be on legitimate states and not immigrants.

---

* Chapter 5 of José Jorge Mendoza's book, *The Moral and Political Philosophy of Immigration* (Lexington Books, 2016): 95–113, 117–19. The editors of this volume have taken the liberty of silently correcting minor typographical errors.

† By a "legitimate state," Mendoza means one that adequately *protects* the human rights of its citizens and *respects* the rights of everyone, whether a citizen or not. (If a state is not legitimate, then all bets are off when that state uses coercion in any form, including by restricting its borders, because it is not entitled to its power, so the moral questions we are interested in here do not arise.)

‡ A term from economics meaning a cost that affects someone who did not choose to incur it; usually what users of the term have in mind are social costs, such as the cost to all of us of the pollution emitted by cars and trucks.

§ An obligation to show the truth of one's claim. If A and B are parties in a dispute, and party A holds the burden of proof, then A needs to demonstrate the truth of their claim (through argument or evidence); in the absence of such a

Justified Limits on Border Enforcement

In 1994 the US began to employ a military-style border enforcement strategy along its southern border dubbed "prevention through deterrence."[1] This strategy was put in place in response to the increased number of undocumented immigrants living in the US and in particular to the unauthorized crossing of migrants at easily accessible points of entry (e.g., urban areas along the US/Mexico border). The idea behind *prevention through deterrence* was simple. Given that the personnel and resources at the disposal of the US Border Patrol is finite and that not all areas along the border are as easily accessible, the inhospitable parts along the border (e.g., deserts, mountains, and rivers) would be used as natural barriers to prevent unauthorized entry. This strategy therefore concentrated personnel and resources at easily accessible points of entry, while at the same time paying less attention to the more inhospitable (and less easy to patrol) areas. The assumption was that the risk posed by the inhospitable terrain would deter unlawfully entry in those areas of the border. At the same time, a strong show of force at more easily accessible points of entry would deter unauthorized crossing at those points as well.

The architects of this strategy were well aware that the number of migrant deaths along the border would likely increase during the first few years of this strategy's implementation. Unauthorized crossings would obviously get funneled away from the safer, but now more heavily patrolled, urban areas toward the more dangerous, but less patrolled, mountainous and desert regions. They believed, however, that the number of undocumented immigrants, as well as the death toll along these regions of the border, would begin to decrease as word got out about the dangers of trying to unlawfully enter the US through these areas. Hence the name: *prevention through deterrence*.

Unfortunately, their prediction was wrong on both accounts. Unauthorized crossings through these inhospitable terrains, along with the exposure deaths that come with it, have remained unabated. To put this in perspective, migration expert, Wayne Cornelius,

made the following observations ten years after the implementation of *prevention through deterrence*:

> the fortified US border with Mexico has been more than 10 times deadlier to migrants from Mexico during [1995–2004] than the Berlin Wall was to East Germans throughout its 28-year existence. More migrants (at least 3,218) have died trying to cross the US/Mexico border since 1995 than people—2,752—were killed in the World Trade Center attacks on 11 September 2001.[2]

According to an even more recent report, close to 6,000 migrants have died trying to cross into the US between the years 2000 and 2014 with most of these deaths being directly attributed to the *prevention through deterrence* strategy.[3]

To add insult to injury, this strategy has also been both very expensive and ineffective at reducing the number of undocumented immigrants. In 1993—the year before *prevention through deterrence* strategy went into effect—the budget for US border enforcement was close to 1.5 billion dollars,[4] while the requested budget for border enforcement for 2016 was close to 19 billion dollars. This is almost a 1300% increase![5] Yet before 1994 the estimated number of undocumented immigrants living in the US was believed to be about 3.5 million. In 2007—so thirteen years into the strategy—the number of undocumented immigrants living in the US was estimated to be about 12 million.[6] The *prevention through deterrence* strategy has therefore proven itself to be an absolute humanitarian, economic, and practical failure.

Part of the reason for this strategy's failure was its misguided understanding of migration to the US. Before 1994, most undocumented immigrants who came to the US followed a pattern of circular migration. They would work in the US for a few days, weeks, months, or even years and then return home. Few migrant workers came to the US with the intention of remaining permanently. The *prevention through deterrence* strategy disrupted this pattern of migration. As it became more dangerous and more expensive to

---

demonstration, B's claim prevails. Many philosophical disputes hinge on the question of which position bears the burden of proof.

enter the US without proper documentation, more undocumented immigrants simply began staying in the US instead of returning home. As migrants began to stay permanently they did what most people do, they set down roots in the US, made a life for themselves, and began to bring their family. So this is why instead of keeping undocumented immigrants out, the *prevention through deterrence* strategy actually had the unintended consequence of sealing many undocumented immigrants in. On top of that, it appears that the US economy needed these undocumented immigrants. This changed, however, after the 2008 financial crisis. During this crisis demand for migrant labor dropped and with it came a corresponding drop of about one million undocumented migrants. This signaled the first drop in the number of undocumented immigrants in the US in almost twenty years.[7]

The ineffectiveness and morally questionable consequences of *prevention through deterrence* are damning and they raise an issue to which few philosophers have given much consideration: what, if any, are the limits to the coercion a legitimate state may use to enforce its immigration policies and could these limits be weighty enough to circumvent the discretion legitimate states have in determining admissions and exclusions criteria?

...

[Christopher Heath] Wellman acknowledged* that legitimate states have an obligation to respect individual liberty and universal equality. In doing so, legitimate states amassed some fairly onerous moral obligations. For this reason, Wellman proposed various, and at times very ingenious, ways for legitimate states to discharge those obligations without, at the same time, accruing any limits on their right to exclude unwanted immigrants. It therefore seems safe to assume that in assessing the morality of border enforcement, Wellman would continue to accept that legitimate states must respect commitments to individual liberty and universal equality.

If we begin from the assumption that there is nothing inherently unjust about the boundaries that exist between political communities (which is an assumption that can and should be challenged, especially in non-ideal circumstances), then border enforcement does not on its face appear to be a violation of individual liberty or universal equality. Border enforcement becomes unjust only when it uses certain intrusive methods or practices that infringe on the liberties of individuals in morally objectionable ways.[8] For example, imagine a case where everyone attempting to enter a country, including citizens, were subjected to extensive interrogation without counsel or indefinite detention until their legal status could be positively confirmed. One does not necessarily need to have strong libertarian[†] tendencies to see that such practices, even if everyone were equally subjected to them, run counter to a commitment to individual liberty. Under normal circumstances, justice requires that legitimate states not deploy such harsh and invasive measures—even when they are the only way to prevent undocumented immigration.

A concern for individual liberty therefore places certain moral limits on the kinds of enforcement a legitimate state may properly implement at its border. This means that the need for border enforcement is not a moral blank check for legitimate states to do anything they want. These limits, however, are still not yet limits on the discretion legitimate states are thought to have in granting or denying immigrants admission. Even if legitimate states are limited in what they can do to enforce their immigration policy at the border, it does not mean they must therefore admit immigrants they would rather not associate with.

A concern for universal equality, however, might prove to be a different story. Recall the earlier example of *prevention through deterrence*. In that case, the US government deployed a border enforcement strategy that has been responsible for an increase in migrant deaths. The dire consequence of this strategy was both foreseeable and confirmed by over twenty years of experience. In this case the border enforcement strategy was also ineffective, but what if that had not been the case? Could legitimate states be free to implement

---

* Mendoza describes Wellman's arguments in the previous chapter of his book. See the previous reading of this volume for more information on Wellman's position.

† Political libertarianism is, in general terms, the view that freedom and liberty are of central importance and outweigh other goods such as social well-being.

a border enforcement strategy that fails to give foreigners adequate moral consideration, if it is the only effective way to enforce their democratically supported immigration policy? If not, as I think an account like Wellman's must concede, then what could a legitimate state do to enforce its immigration policy in a morally acceptable way?

In such a case, a legitimate state seems to have four options at its disposal. First, (1) it could try to entice precluded immigrants either to remain in their home countries or to migrate to a different country. This option might alleviate enough pressure on border enforcement and thereby make it possible for a legitimate state to enforce its preferred immigration policy without having to resort to any morally problematic means (e.g., *prevention through deterrence*). Second (2), and likely in conjunction with the first, it could modify the internal "pull" factors* that are attracting precluded immigrants to its territory and in that way alleviate some of the pressure on border enforcement. Third, (3) it can limit its border enforcement to morally acceptable levels while at the same time tacitly accepting that some precluded immigrants will gain unauthorized (i.e., not official) entry into its territory. Finally, (4) it can limit its border enforcement to morally acceptable levels and at the same time change its immigration policy to better reflect internal "pull" factors that are attracting precluded immigrants to its territory, thereby alleviating the pressure on border enforcement that make morally problematic means of enforcement necessary.

...Wellman faced a similar difficulty as the one we are facing here, but he was able to overcome it by suggesting that legitimate states could discharge their egalitarian duties by "exporting justice" (e.g., supplying humanitarian aid, providing restitution, intervening in unjust societies, or paying other countries to take in needy immigrants). In the case of morally problematic border enforcement—when the implementation of a political community's preferred immigration policy would require not giving foreigners full moral consideration—could a similar tactic of "exporting justice" be possible? If it is, then the closest thing to such an approach would be something along the lines of options (1) and (2).

On its face, there seems nothing wrong with legitimate states trying to entice precluded immigrants to either remain where they are or to migrate to a different country. This could be accomplished in a variety of creative and non-coercive ways. A legitimate state could provide various forms of assistance or reparations to make where precluded immigrants currently reside a much more attractive option for them to remain. A legitimate state could also work with other countries, either by offering them money or other incentives, to be both receptive to and also more attractive destinations for precluded immigrants.

The problem, however, is that this tactic will only alleviate pressure from precluded immigrants whose primary impetus for migrating are "push" factors. In other words, this will only address the issue of precluded immigrants who are simply trying to escape the situation they are currently in and do not care so much where they eventually end up, so long as it is better than where they are now. Enticements to remain in place or to migrate to a different country are much less effective when the primary motivation for migration are "pull" factors. Pull factors can include, but are not limited to, economic conditions where wages are higher and the current domestic labor pool is not or cannot adequately satisfy demand, where close family relations exist (e.g., young children trying to reunite with parents and vice versa), or where migration patterns have a long and established history (e.g., circular migration, colonialism, and military interventions). In these sorts of cases, enticements are not usually enough to override the strong impetus precluded immigrants have to enter a particular country.

A legitimate state could therefore supplement option (1) with something like option (2), which is to modify the internal factors that are attracting precluded immigrants to their particular territory. This option, however, raises a whole host of other serious problems. If these internal factors are primarily things

---

* "Pull" factors are the aspects of a destination state that encourage an immigrant to move to that state, such as job opportunities, fertile land, or a high quality of life. "Push" factors, by contrast, are aspects of an immigrant's state of origin that compel them to leave that state, such as war, famine, or a lack of job opportunities.

such as the economy, family relationships, and history, it is unclear what a liberal* (as opposed to say a totalitarian) state could do to significantly modify these factors. The economies of liberal states are increasingly becoming more globalized and more market-based than command-based. This means that while government intervention is not necessarily inconsistent with a globalized free(ish) market economy, liberal governments do not enjoy the same kind of control over their economy as totalitarian regimes do with a command-based economic system. In short, there is not much a liberal government can do to alter the economic factors that create the demand for immigrant labor (e.g., domestic labor's inability, unattractiveness, or unwillingness to satisfy domestic demand) since these factors are largely outside of government control.

The same can also be said for family and socio-historical relationships. Once these relationships are established it is not easy (and at times might even be immoral) for a liberal government to try to sever them. For example, it would be naive to expect that a parent would allow a lack of immigration status to prevent him or her from being with their child. In such cases, deporting a citizen child (or any other close family member) might be the only way to effectively end the attraction a precluded immigrant has with a particular territory, but deporting citizens is inconsistent with a commitment to political equality, so again this is not an option open for liberal states. There are also cases where circular migration, colonialism, and military involvement have had the effect of creating close relationships between certain countries and foreigners. In these sorts of cases a legitimate state can do some things to try and sever the relationship, but the inertia of these types of relationships is not easily or instantaneously brought to a halt. For these reasons, options (1) and (2) do not provide a sufficient enough response for how legitimate states can [maintain] their legitimacy (e.g., not employ morally problematic border enforcement) while implementing an immigration policy that runs counter to global realities.

Option (3) seems to split the difference: limit border enforcement to morally acceptable levels, while at the same time accepting that there will be some degree of unauthorized entry by precluded immigrants. This option, however, starts to take us away from an account like Wellman's. While this option does not deny that a legitimate state may attempt to deter unlawful border crossings, it does limit what a legitimate state can do in its attempts to not associate itself with precluded immigrants. So while it is true that these limits do not necessarily generate a positive right to be admitted, they do seem to generate a presumptive right in the negative sense: it accepts that there are some things that a legitimate state may not do in preventing unauthorized entry into its territory. Furthermore, these limits are in place not to ensure the civic standing of citizens, but for the sake of noncitizens.

This option therefore offers a slight departure from Wellman's earlier position, where fulfilling moral obligations to foreigners did not entail limits on a legitimate state's right to control immigration. This option, however, can still be made compatible with an account like Wellman's. After all, it does allow legitimate states to maintain their discretion over official admissions policy and immigrants who enter through unauthorized means have not officially been "admitted" by the state. In other words, even though unauthorized entry of precluded immigrants is tacitly accepted on this option, those precluded immigrants have technically not been allowed in.

The problem with this option, besides the apparent hypocrisy, is that it enables conditions of exploitation, oppression, and discrimination. Undocumented immigrants, because of their susceptibility to automatic deportation, are some of the most vulnerable people in society. Their precarious situation leaves them virtually unprotected against various forms of exploitation, oppression, and discrimination by both public (e.g., tax collectors and police) and private (e.g., private employers and landlords) entities. This kind of treatment is a violation of moral equality because, even if undocumented immigrants do not have the political right to be present, they are nonetheless still entitled to have their basic human rights respected.

---

* In this context, a "liberal" state is one in which citizens are granted a high degree of individual freedom, as opposed to a "totalitarian" state, in which individual freedoms are limited and the state has a high degree of control over the lives of its citizens. Most Western democracies qualify as liberal states in this broad sense.

Some might argue that the situation undocumented immigrants find themselves in is of their own making, so a political community is not morally required to ameliorate it. A view like this is mistaken for two reasons. First, it is not clear that even those who knowingly put themselves in bad situations deserve to lose or have their basic human rights ignored. Second, even if there are such cases, the case in question is not of this kind. In the case we are considering, the political community has tacitly accepted some degree of unauthorized entry and to that extent is at least partially responsible for the presence of undocumented immigrants and whatever injustices befall them due to their unlawful status. A legitimate state could remedy this situation simply by lifting the threat of deportation, and thereby bringing undocumented immigrants out of the proverbial shadows, but this would then undermine the very discretion option (3) was supposed to be ensuring. This is because if the threat of deportation were lifted, legitimate states would find themselves associating with foreigners they would rather not associate with. Therefore, option (3) does not appear to be a viable option either.

The fourth and final option (4) is for legitimate states to limit their border enforcement to morally acceptable levels while at the same time changing their immigration policy to better reflect internal "pull" factors. The upside of this option is that, if successfully implemented, it should reduce the demand for unauthorized entry. Undocumented immigrants who currently migrate mainly due to "pull" factors will now have legal means by which to enter. This in turn would reduce the pressure on border enforcement such that morally acceptable levels of deterrence and screening would be sufficient to reduce unauthorized entries to a bare minimum.

This option marks a significant upgrade over option (3) in that it would prevent legitimate states from being implicated in the creation of an underclass susceptible to various forms of exploitation, oppression, and discrimination. It also presents an improvement over options (1) and (2) because it would deal not only with "push" but also with "pull" factors and do so in a way that would not ask government to intrude into the economy or the lives of its citizens in illiberal ways. At the same time, option (1), which entices immigrants either to remain where they are or to migrate to a different country, would not be inconsistent (and could

be used in conjunction) with option (4). For these reasons, something like option (4) seems to be the best and most effective option for guarding against morality excessive border enforcement.

Option (4), however, seems to be at odds with a position like Wellman's and there does not seem to be a way to reconcile the two. Option (4) not only limits what a legitimate state can do with regard to border enforcement, but it also circumvents the discretion it has in determining for itself its own admissions and exclusions criteria. On this option, admissions and exclusions criteria have to take into account internal "pull" factors, such as economic realities, family relationships, and even socio-historical circumstances. These limitations are problematic for an account like Wellman's because they present presumptive duties that cannot be exported, but can only be discharged by conceding that there are at least some foreigners who must be granted admission (i.e., those who are pulled in by economic realities, family relationships, and socio-historical circumstances) even when the vast majority of citizens within that state would rather not associate with them.

If the preceding argument is correct, it provides an indirect argument against legitimate states having a presumptive right to control immigration. It shows that when border enforcement is factored into an ethics of immigration the only way to remain committed to democratic self-determination, individual liberty, and universal equality is for the burden of proof to be on the political community to justify any restrictions it wishes to place on immigration. This is because restrictions on immigration must be enforced and enforcing these restrictions always runs the risk of violating commitments to individual liberty and universal equality. For this reason, border enforcement must be limited, but limits on border enforcement are also what make undocumented immigration possible and sometimes necessary. While some forms of undocumented immigration can be alleviated by attending to the "push" factors in immigrant-sending countries (e.g., lack of opportunity, poverty, crime, and violence) and by diverting some of those immigrants to other more receptive countries, these actions will not be sufficient on their own. A lot of undocumented immigration is primarily driven by "pull" factors and there is little that liberal states can do to alter those factors. Therefore, an account like Wellman's must either abandon its claim to liberalism or make the concession that the immigration policy of legitimate states should not be discretionary but dictated by the "pull" factors that are drawing in immigrants.

Justified Limits on Internal Enforcement

In 2008, Roberto Lovato wrote an article for *The Nation* magazine entitled "Juan Crow in Georgia." Lovato's article featured a sympathetic young girl living in less-than-ideal circumstances, who nonetheless had big dreams of one day going to college and becoming a clinical psychologist. The young girl in question was fifteen-year-old Marie Justeen Mancha. Mancha and her mother were living in Reidsville, Georgia, where the two of them had recently migrated, and were eking out a meager existence by working in onion fields and living out of what Lovato described as a battered old trailer.

In September of 2006, Mancha's dreams were put in jeopardy. As she was getting ready to go to school, armed Immigration and Customs Enforcement agents (ICE) raided her trailer. These agents had neither warrants, probable cause, nor permission to enter Mancha's residence, but they entered anyway and interrogated Mancha over her and her mother's immigration status. At the end of this interrogation the agents simply left. Mancha and her mother were not deported. Tragedy was averted because, as Lovato informs us, Mancha and her mother were: "... the wrong kind of 'Mexicans'; they were US citizens."[9]

The story of Mancha is instructive because it highlights the fact that not everyone who is ensnared in the dragnets of internal immigration enforcement are undocumented immigrants or even noncitizens. It also shows that in practice not all citizens are affected by internal immigration enforcement in the same way. Some citizens (e.g., Latino/as, Middle Eastern Americans, and Asian-Americans) are more likely than other citizens (e.g., white Americans) to have their day-to-day lives disrupted by internal immigration enforcement. In this regard, it seems that philosophers inquiring about immigration justice have another thing to consider. Moral and political philosophers also need to look into how political regimes locate, identify, treat, detain, and remove noncitizens within [their] territory and what (if any) limits ought to be placed on this exercise of power.

This concern is underscored by the fact that in places like the US almost 50% of the undocumented immigrant population entered the country through *legal* channels.[10] In other words, these immigrants went out-of-status (i.e., became undocumented) only after overstaying or not renewing their entry visa. This means that for nearly half the cases of undocumented immigration, stricter enforcement at the border would have made no difference. This point has also not been lost on many anti-immigration groups in the US and for that reason many have begun to support a strategy dubbed "attrition through enforcement."[11]

According to Mark Krikorian, one of this strategy's principal architects, *attrition through enforcement* is "... designed to reduce the number of new illegal arrivals and persuade a large share of illegals already here to give up and deport themselves."[12] According to folks like Krikorian, self-deportation can be accomplished by extending immigration enforcement into areas that have very little to do with immigration itself, such as commandeering local police officials to perform immigration enforcement tasks, requiring employers to verify the immigration status of their employees, and similarly landlords with potential renters, doctors with their patients, and school officials with the parents of children seeking to enroll in their schools. The idea is that if undocumented immigrants are too afraid to look for work, housing, schooling or even to see a doctor or call the police, they will eventually grow tired of living this way and will leave the country voluntarily.

As was briefly mentioned in the section above, a strategy like this can be problematic in that it runs the risk of not respecting the human rights that are due to all persons, regardless of their immigration status. A further problem, as we saw with the case of Mancha, is that strategies like *attrition through enforcement* do not just affect the lives of undocumented immigrants; they also come to affect the lives of citizens and also lawfully present immigrants in very illiberal ways. And while Wellman's account never specifically engages with issues of internal immigration enforcement, we might still be able to glean what an account like his would have to say about means for internal enforcement by looking at how it dealt with a similar case. In particular, how it responded to the criticism that an account like [his would] be unable to reject discriminatory immigration policies (i.e., immigration policies that fail to give citizens equal political consideration)....

Unlike the kinds of cases considered so far, where foreigners are thought of as existing outside the state's territory and seeking to enter, the case of internal immigration enforcement deals with foreigners who are already inside the territory (whether lawfully or not) and are seeking to remain. This latter case is more difficult to deal with because citizens and immigrants (both documented and undocumented) are not living in isolation from one another but often intermingle and live with and among each other. The task of internal immigration enforcement is to somehow disentangle these two groups without at the same time violating the rights of persons or undermining the standing of citizens. This presents a problem for an account like Wellman's because, as the rest of this section will show, the only way to ensure that such illiberal practices do not take place is to create a canopy of protections which will not only shield citizens but will also cover noncitizens (including undocumented immigrants) from the excesses of internal immigration enforcement. In short, one of the consequences of having internal enforcement respect the basic rights of everyone and preserve the equal standing of citizens is that legitimate states must forgo some of the discretion they normally are thought to have over immigration.

If we return to the earlier case of Mancha, we can see that one of the problems that arise with internal immigration enforcement is that the collateral effects of such enforcement are not distributed equally among the citizenry. These collateral effects typically and disproportionately fall on certain racial, cultural, and ethnic minorities, which in turn degrade their standing as full and equal citizens. It is therefore necessary that internal immigration enforcement adhere to something like an "equality of burdens" standard. This standard would require that any collateral effects that result from internal immigration enforcement be allocated as equally as possible among the citizenry. For example, if agents are allowed to conduct raids of private homes or places of work, then *every* citizen's home or place of work should be as likely as any other citizen's to be raided. Abiding by such an onerous standard will undoubtedly make enforcement much less efficient and will also inconvenience many more citizens, but there are at least two good reasons for why a legitimate state's internal immigration enforcement should have to adhere to such a standard.

First, adhering to this standard would make citizens in a democracy much more reflective about the kind of enforcement they are willing to let their government deploy internally. This is especially important in a democracy, where decisions are made by the will of the majority. As things currently stand in places like the US, a majority of citizens are unaware of stories like Mancha's because this kind of enforcement rarely impacts their own lives. This disconnection between what the majority experience in their own daily lives and how the collateral effects of internal immigration enforcement affect the lives of minorities, hides the true cost of enforcement. It is therefore easier for the majority to vote for stricter internal enforcement measures that violate the rights and liberties of minorities, because they are either unaware or do not care about this cost and also they do not perceive stricter enforcement as in itself unjust.

An *equality of burdens* standard would reverse this situation. While the American public has shown itself willing to accept stricter internal enforcement when minorities foot the bill (as is evidenced by the fact that most legislation proposed in recent years that follows an *attrition through enforcement* strategy has enjoyed tremendous public support in the US), it would be interesting to see if such support remained strong when all citizens had to share in the costs. An *equality of burdens* standard would therefore distribute the costs of enforcement in a fairer manner and at the same time give the voters in a democracy a more accurate assessment of what stricter internal immigration enforcement entails.

Second, while meeting this standard might not change deeply entrenched social attitudes on race, ethnicity, or culture, it would prevent those attitudes (e.g., implicit biases* or institutionalized discrimination) from unduly influencing the course of immigration enforcement. An *equality of burdens* standard would prohibit selective enforcement that disproportionately

---

* An implicit bias is an unconscious belief that influences one's attitudes and actions toward other individuals, especially toward members of other social groups. Some have suggested that implicit biases are an important cause of discrimination and social inequality.

targets some citizens for morally arbitrary reasons (i.e., facts about them that should garner neither praise nor blame). In other words, even if increased scrutiny on people who are identified with a particular religion (e.g., wearing a headscarf or turban) or with a particular part of the world (e.g., looking Latin American or Asian) would yield better immigration enforcement results, these sorts of practices should be prohibited on account that they diminish the political standing of minority citizens who happen to share those features. In short, a commitment to political equality should never be traded away for any supposed benefits to enforcement.

But while something like an *equality of burdens* standard would be a necessary part of a just internal immigration enforcement scheme, it would not itself be sufficient—at least not to insure that basic liberties (i.e., individual freedom) are not violated. For example, certain intrusive inspections might be okay at points of entry, but when conducted internally or done too frequently could easily constitute a rights violation. For example, routine car inspections might be acceptable at points of entry, but random car inspections on the highway (especially if done frequently) might prove to be too excessive in a liberal democracy. Similarly, standard requests to verify one's immigration status might be okay at points of entry, but excessive when applied often on the streets of a liberal democracy and especially at one's home. The idea here is that even when citizens are asked to share equally in the burdens of enforcement, there are some costs that no legitimate state should ask their citizens to bear. In other words, government actions such as indefinite detention and unreasonable searches and seizures are not simply unjust when the burdens are not shared equally. Those sorts of actions are always and in-themselves unjust. Another way of putting the same point is that even if citizens shared equally all the burdens of internal immigration enforcement, some forms of enforcement would still be too excessive and should always remain off the table.

So along with an *equality of burdens* standard, it would be necessary for legitimate states to meet a "universal protections" standard. Meeting this standard would require that all persons be reasonably protected from excessive internal immigration

enforcement. This standard would complement the *equality of burdens* standard by putting in place certain mechanisms for oversight against excessive enforcement. Specifying what particular type of oversight or which particular restrictions would be demanded by a *universal protections* standard, is difficult to pinpoint exactly given that different political communities have their own unique set of circumstances and challenges.

With that being said, there seems to be at least one general oversight that a *universal protections* standard should always adhere to: there must always be a presumption of innocence. In the immigration context this would mean that all persons present should initially be treated as though they are lawfully present until their status has been confirmed to be irregular and even then should still have their dignity and rights respected as human beings. This general oversight is based on the same idea that people should be considered innocent until proven guilty; the famous Blackstone formulation that it is better to let many guilty people to go free than for one innocent person to be found guilty.* This is an important point to keep in mind when we consider that places like the US have in the past wrongfully deported some of its own citizens and people who otherwise were eligible to remain in the country. In one case, the wrongfully deported citizen was a developmentally disabled man, whose return trip was traumatic and very easily could have ended in tragedy.[13] Another case did end in tragedy, when the wrongfully deported person died in a fire inside a Honduran jail where the Honduran immigration agency was holding him.[14]

So if a legitimate state's immigration enforcement were to adhere to something like a *universal protections* standard and the presumption of innocence that such a standard always entails, it would need to give all persons present, regardless of their immigration status, such basic protections as the right to due process, equal protection under the law, freedom from unreasonable searches and seizures, a right to a court appointed attorney, and protection from indefinite detention.[15] Protections like these are essential in immigration cases because without them immigration controls could easily infringe on the basic liberties

---

* "It is better that ten guilty persons escape, than that one innocent suffer," from *Commentaries on the Laws of England* by Sir William Blackstone (1723–80).

of persons and could also lead to accidental deportations. These protections are not the only ones that would satisfy the *universal protections* standard, and it is likely that more, rather than less, protections would be necessary in order to adequately meet this standard in most cases. But even just the protections mentioned here are enough to illustrate the following point: protecting basic liberties from potential governmental excesses puts the burden on legitimate states to insure that their immigration enforcement practices do not overreach, especially internally, and this can be done only by putting adequate protections in place.

When taken together, the two standards outlined above form a canopy of protections that ameliorate, if not eliminate, the threat of internal immigration enforcement infringing on the basic liberties of persons or undermining the standing of citizens. For example, the raid that took place in Mancha's home would have been prohibited under these two standards. In that case, ICE agents would have (1) needed to have a warrant in order to enter Mancha's home, as would be demanded by something like a *universal protections* standard and (2) such a warrant could not have been obtained by ICE, under an *equality of burdens* standard, if its only reason for targeting Mancha and her mother was their ethnicity or occupation.

Similarly, this canopy of protections would prohibit most other nefarious aspects of strategies like *attrition through enforcement*. For example, the commandeering of police officers to perform immigration enforcement duties, a common feature of many recent internal immigration enforcement strategies,[16] would be prohibited under this canopy of protections. There are at least two reasons as to why. First, when police are required or have the power to enforce immigration laws, certain citizens are less likely to come forward to report crimes. Currently, many households are of "mixed status," that is households where the immigration status of individual household members can vary from undocumented to full citizen. Victims of crimes who happen to be living in mixed-status households are often hesitant to call police when they believe that the police will or has the power to deport members of their household. This indirect consequence of internal enforcement is not only a violation of the *universal protections* standard, but also the *equality of burdens* standard, since it affects only certain citizens and usually for morally arbitrary reasons.

A second reason is that the safety of a community is dependent on the lawful cooperation of all persons present, regardless of their immigration status. It is not uncommon, for example, that undocumented immigrants are themselves the victims of crime or are witnesses to crimes. In either case it is important that all persons present be assumed to be lawfully present by police in order for officers to adequately perform their primary function which is to protect, serve, and fulfill the rights of everybody in the community. In this case the *universal protections* standard would apply and prohibit police from performing immigration enforcement duties, even when that prohibition would undermine the effectiveness of the current immigration policy.

These sorts of arguments can be extended to cases of employment, renting a home, enrolling children in school, and many other everyday activities that have recently been incorporated as part of internal immigration enforcement strategies.[17] What each of these prohibitions on internal enforcement show is that the kinds of protections needed to avoid the potentially pernicious aspects of enforcement are ones that not only cover citizens, but also extends to everyone present, including undocumented immigrants. This canopy of protections is therefore a presumptive check on a legitimate state's ability to control immigration. It makes it such that there are certain things a legitimate state, all things being equal, is prohibited from doing even when failing to do so negatively impacts its ability to control immigration. In the examples just provided, we see that a legitimate state is *prima facie* prohibited from using its own police force as part of its immigration enforcement scheme and also that the power immigration enforcement officers have must be curtailed in ways that inhibit their ability to control immigration (e.g., they must get warrants and have substantial probable cause). These sorts of protections do not necessarily generate positive rights to admission, but they are nonetheless overriding negative prohibitions that, all things being equal, protect undocumented immigrants from a legitimate state's enforcement mechanism....

If the argument provided above is correct, a legitimate state will at times have to associate with undocumented immigrants (e.g., either through its police force or public schools), but its liberal commitments—enshrined in the *equality of burdens* and *universal protections* standards—will prohibit it from using those particular interactions as occasions to remove them. A legitimate state will be in a bizarre position of having to actively restrict itself, because of its liberal commitments, from fully enforcing its own immigration laws. And while this does not necessarily generate a positive right to immigrate, it nonetheless provides presumptive negative rights that shield immigrants from internal immigration enforcement....

Conclusion

The arguments presented in the first two sections of this chapter focused on Christopher Heath Wellman's freedom of association argument.... My objection to Wellman's argument, which is different from other criticisms that have already been leveled against it, is that when immigration enforcement is taken into consideration his argument cannot hold up. Border and internal enforcement present threats to individual freedom and universal equality that legitimate states must guard against. In order to develop a principled way of guarding against these threats, the control legitimate states are normally thought to have over designing and implementing their immigration policy will be bounded and not discretionary. This is a position that I call a minimalist defense of immigrant rights.... ■

Suggestions for Critical Reflection

1. Mendoza does not, in this reading, argue for the stronger claim that states lack the right to self-determination, a right which Wellman has argued serves as the basis for the freedom to restrict immigration. Rather, he holds that the right to self-determination conflicts with other moral and political commitments. How should we weigh those competing obligations? Does a commitment to liberty and universal equality necessarily override a state's right to self-determination?

2. Many of Mendoza's arguments focus on concrete examples, most of them from current or recent American history. Do Mendoza's arguments apply equally to other countries?

3. Do circumstances matter? Would it make a difference if, for example, high levels of immigration were exceeding the limits of the infrastructure needed to support rapid population increases, such as housing and social services? To what extent, if any, do such considerations bear on this issue?

4. Many municipalities in the US identify as "sanctuary cities," meaning that they do not enforce immigration laws or they enforce them in only limited ways. Is this a reasonable means of compromise, in that it enables the state's right to determine immigration policy without applying the harmful enforcement strategies Mendoza discusses? In what sense does a law or policy exist if it is not enforced by police or other state authorities?

Notes

1 "Immigration Enforcement Within the United States," Congressional Research Service, *The Library of Congress*, April 6, 2006. Accessed December 21, 2014. http://www.fas.org/sgp/crs/misc/RL33351.pdf

2 Wayne A. Cornelius, "Controlling 'Unwanted' Immigration: Lessons from the United States, 1993–2004," *Journal of Ethnic and Migration Studies* 31.4 (2005): 783.

3 Tara Brian and Frank Laczko, ed., "Fatal Journeys: Tracking Lives Lost during Migration," *International Organization for Migration* 1.1 (2014): 54.

4 "Immigration and Naturalization Service," *Department of Justice*. Accessed November 19, 2015. http://www.justice.gov/archive/jmd/1975_2002/2002/html/page104-108.htm

5 "Budget-in-Brief Fiscal-Year 2016," *Department of Homeland Security* pdf. Accessed November 19, 2015. http://www.dhs.gov/sites/default/files/publications/FY_2016_DHS_Budget_in_Brief

6 "Unauthorized Immigrant Population Trends for States, Birth Countries and Regions," *Pew Research Center*, December 11, 2014. Accessed

November 19, 2015. http://www.pewhispanic.org/2014/12/11/unauthorized-trends/#All

7   Ibid.

8   For a different, but compatible, account of how political boundaries can become unjust see Grant J. Silva, "On the Militarization of Borders and the Juridical Right to Exclude," *Public Affairs Quarterly* 29.2 (2015).

9   Roberto Lovato, "Juan Crow in Georgia" *The Nation*, May 26, 2008. Accessed December 21, 2014. http://www.thenation.com/article/juan-crow-georgia.

10 See Ted Robbins, "Nearly Half of Illegal Immigrants Overstay Visas," *NPR*, June 14, 2006. Accessed September 15, 2011. http://www.npr.org/templates/story/story.php?storyId=5485917

11 Jessica Vaughan, "Attrition Through Enforcement: A Cost-Effective Strategy to Shrink the Illegal Population," *Center for Immigration Studies*, April 2006. Accessed September 15, 2011. http://www.cis.org/Enforcement-IllegalPopulation

12 Mark Krikorian, "Attrition Through Enforcement Will Work," *San Diego Union Tribune*, April 2, 2006. Accessed May 23, 2015. http://www.utsandiego.com/uniontrib/20060402/news_mz1e02krikor.html

13 Kemp Powers, "Group Says U.S. Citizen Wrongly Deported to Mexico" *Reuters*, June 11, 2007. Accessed May 10, 2012. http://www.reuters.com/article/2007/06/11/us-usa-immigration-deportation-idUSN1118919320070611

14 Ruxandra Guidi, "Honduran LA Resident Accidentally Deported, then Dies in Prison Fire," *Southern California Public Radio*, March 2, 2012. Accessed May 10, 2012. http://www.scpr.org/news/2012/03/02/31481/honduran-resident-los-angeles-wrongfully-deported

15 For an excellent argument on how the detention of undocumented immigrants constitutes a rights violation see Stephanie J. Silverman, "Detaining Immigrants and Asylum Seekers: A Normative Introduction," *Critical Review of International Social and Political Philosophy* 17.5 (2014).

16 In the US, federal law currently allows for immigration enforcement and local law enforcement to form a partnership under a program called "Secure Communities." For more information on this specific program see http://www.ice.gov/secure_communities/. Also, this linking up of local law enforcement with immigration enforcement has appeared in various state immigration bills. The most notorious of these being Arizona's SB 1070. See State of Arizona Senate, Forty-Ninth Legislature, Second Regular Session 2010, Senate Bill 1070.

17 For a more detailed argument along these lines see Joseph H. Carens, "The Rights of Irregular Migrants," *Ethics & International Affairs* 22.2 (2008).

VIRGINIA HELD

Terrorism and War

Who Is Virginia Held?

Virginia P. Held (b. 1929) is an influential ethicist and social-political philosopher, known especially as one of the central figures in the development of the "ethics of care," along with Carol Gilligan, Sara Ruddick, Nel Noddings, and others. Before becoming a professional philosopher she was a reporter, working for *The Reporter* magazine and other publications. She obtained her PhD from Columbia University in 1968, going on to spend much of her career teaching at Hunter College in New York. A past President of the Eastern Division of the American Philosophical Society, she is now a Distinguished Professor Emerita in the philosophy program of the Graduate Center at the City University of New York. She is the author of several books, including *Feminist Morality: Transforming Culture, Society and Politics* (1993), *Rights and Goods: Justifying Social Action* (1984), and *The Ethics of Care: Personal, Political, and Global* (2006)—and many articles on social and political philosophy, ethics, and feminist philosophy.

What Is the Structure of This Reading?

Many people would agree that not all wars, and not all participants in war, are on an equal moral footing. While we may hold, as Held does, that all wars are awful, and some believe it is always immoral to enter into war, few would claim that there is moral equivalence between, say, a war of genocidal conquest and a civil war meant to overthrow a regime that has repeatedly violated human rights. The long-standing doctrine of just war theory, which dates back at least as far as Saint Thomas Aquinas in the thirteenth century and continues to have a central role in political and academic discussions, holds that some acts of war are morally justified while others are not.

With terrorism, however, it's not uncommon for politicians, military leaders, and the media to speak and write as though all terrorist acts fall into one category, and as though we can't or shouldn't attempt to make moral distinctions. In this paper, Held argues that this purported "moral clarity" can mislead us into treating all terrorist acts as equivalent, when in fact they are as varied in purposes and moral justification as conventional acts of war.

Held's essay examines three aspects of terrorism: its definition, its potential justification, and its causes. On each of these points, Held aims to show that certain widely-held and publicly advocated positions fail to hold up to scrutiny. Most standard definitions of terrorism fail to distinguish between acts of genuine terrorism and other acts, for example, acts of conventional war. This may be unavoidable, given that terrorism is so varied: some terrorist acts are caused by independent groups and individuals, while others are state-sanctioned; some inflict harm on non-combatants, while others do not. As Held points out, the same is true of conventional acts of war: some involve non-governmental groups while other wars are between states, and some acts of war inflict harm on non-combatants while others do not.

Held also examines the so-called war on terrorism, questioning both its moral justification and its effectiveness as a strategy for reducing terrorist activity. She notes that to try to understand terrorism is not to excuse it. A more nuanced understanding of the varied motivations and purported justifications of terrorist acts may lead to non-violent strategies of countering terrorism that are more effective than military intervention. In the final section of this reading, Held posits that one of the main causes of terrorism may be a feeling of humiliation; accordingly, she suggests that preventing others from feeling humiliated may be one effective way of preventing terrorism.

A Common Misconception

Held is not setting out to argue that terrorism is ever a good thing, or even that it can in some cases be justified. Her stated goal is "to compare war and terrorism, and to show how war can be morally worse." This position is consistent with a belief that all acts of terrorism (and all acts of war) are morally unjustifiable.

Terrorism and War[*]

There are different kinds of war: world wars, small wars, civil wars, revolutions, wars of liberation. A serious mistake to be avoided, in current discussions of terrorism, is to suppose that all terrorism is alike. There are different kinds of terrorism as there are of war.

The United States Right is currently asserting that to hold anything else than that all terrorism is the same is to undermine the "moral clarity" needed to pursue the war on terrorism. U.S. neo-conservatives, Christian fundamentalists, and the Israeli Right[†] are especially intent on arguing that the terrorism carried out by Palestinians is the same as the terrorism carried out by Osama bin Laden[‡] and the Al Qaeda network,[1] agreeing with Israeli prime minister Ariel Sharon that "terrorism is terrorism is terrorism anywhere in the world."[2] Sharon has asserted that Israel is battling the same enemy as the U.S., saying that "the cultured world is under a cruel attack by radical Islam. It is an enemy composed of lunatic individuals, lunatic regimes and lunatic countries."[3]

Those holding that all terrorism is the same argue that the same countermeasures, such as military obliteration and preventive attack, should be used against all terrorists, and the same principles, such as "never negotiate with terrorists or with those who support them" should be applied. To U.S. vice president Dick Cheney,[§] with terrorists "no policy of containment or deterrence will prove effective. The only way to deal with this threat is to destroy it, completely and utterly."[4] Those who share these views are intent on rejecting any comparisons between deaths caused by terrorists and deaths caused by their opponents, on the grounds that there is "no moral equivalence" between terrorism and fighting against terrorism.

It is not only the Right, however, that seeks a simple, all-purpose moral condemnation of all terrorism.

The New York Times correspondent Nicholas Kristof, while acknowledging the difficulties in seeking "moral clarity," nevertheless advocates it with respect to terrorism.[5] He suggests that a moral revulsion against killing civilians could develop akin to the moral revulsion that developed after World War I delegitimizing the use of poison gas. But this assumes we can clearly distinguish "civilians" from "legitimate targets," and this is among the issues that can be contested. It is voting publics that often put in power the governmental leaders, and support the policies, that terrorists oppose. *If* other means have failed and *if* violence against the members of a state's armed services is justified, it is unclear why those who bring about that state's policies and give its armed services their orders should be exempt. At least such an argument could muddy the moral clarity of the moral revulsion against terrorism the proponents of such revulsion seek.

Furthermore, the occasions for moral revulsion are unlikely to be limited in the way suggested. Ted Honderich, for instance, shares the moral revulsion of so many others at the carnage of 11 September 2001.[6] But he is also greatly outraged by the many millions of lives cut short and made miserable in the poor countries of the world by the global economic forces promoted by the U.S. He sees enough of a connection between such misery and the appeal of terrorism to its potential recruits that he finds the U.S. partly responsible for the terrorism practiced against it. Moral revulsion can thus be so appropriately multiplied that the uniqueness of terrorism is undermined, and with this goes the sought-for moral clarity. We seem to be left, then, with needing to make complex and disputable moral judgments, here as everywhere else. This is not at all to suggest that persuasive judgments are impossible, but they are unlikely to plausibly focus as

---

[*] Virginia Held, "Terrorism and War," *The Journal of Ethics* 8, 1 (2004): 59–75.

[†] Here and elsewhere in this reading, Held refers to the Israeli-Palestinian conflict. Since the mid-twentieth century, violent interactions, some of them widely classified as terrorism, have frequently broken out between Israel and the Palestinian people. Ariel Sharon (1928–2014) was prime minister of Israel from 2001 to 2006.

[‡] Osama bin Laden (1957–2011) was co-founder of Al Qaeda, a militant organization of Islamic extremists that claimed responsibility for a number of terrorist attacks, including the September 11, 2001 attacks on the World Trade Center and Pentagon.

[§] Dick Cheney was US vice president from 2001 to 2009.

exclusively on terrorism as the proponents of moral clarity about it in particular wish.

Persuasive judgments should, for instance, consider how the actions of states opposing terrorist groups have frequently killed far more civilians than have terrorists. The Reagan administration's "War on Terror" in Central America in the 1980's killed approximately 200,000 people and produced over a million refugees.[7] A frequently used argument of states engaged in what they call "countering terrorism," but which the recipients of their violence often consider terrorism, is that they do not "target" civilians; if civilians are killed it is by accident, even though foreseeable. But such states' possession of weapons of precision capable of attacking, when they choose to, targeted persons intentionally and civilians only unintentionally is just another way in which their superior power allows them to be dominant. It may be that such domination is what a group engaging in terrorism is resisting. It will in any case be unpersuasive to hold that such a group ought to use means of which it is incapable. If such groups had the means to challenge the armed forces of the states whose domination they oppose they might well do so, but their lack of power is often the reason why terrorism is their weapon in the first place. As any number of commentators have noted, terrorism is the weapon of the weak.[8] Moreover, as war is increasingly "riskless" for armed forces with overwhelming power who, understandably, try to minimize their own casualties as much as possible, there may be less and less possibility for opposing groups to attack the actual combatants of powerful countries.[9] For an argument that terrorism should never be used to be persuasive, it would have to be assumed that the weapons used against it and against those who support it are always used for morally justifiable goals and in morally justifiable ways, and moral clarity about such an assumption is impossible for any reasonable person.

Those of us who are engaged year after year in slogging through arguments seeking moral clarity can reject the U.S. and Israeli Right's versions of it with respect to terrorism. But we are far from agreeing on what terrorism is and how to understand it, let alone on how to respond to it and what to do about it.

My judgments in this paper will be comparative. I will not argue that terrorism can be justified or that war can be justified, but that terrorism is not necessarily worse than war. The direction of a great deal of recent discussion of terrorism is that terrorism is so morally unacceptable as a means that we do not need even to consider the political objectives of those who engage in terrorism. War, on the other hand, is seen as quite possibly justified. My intent will be to compare war and terrorism, and to show how war can be morally worse.

Defining "Terrorism"

Understanding how "terrorism" should be defined is notoriously difficult. It is one of the *most* contested concepts and obviously difficult to be clear about.

Governments characteristically define "terrorism" as something only their opponents can commit, as something only those who seek to change policies, or to attack a given political system or status quo can engage in.[10] The definition used by the U.S. State Department, for instance, includes the claim that it is carried out by "subnational groups or clandestine agents."[11] And international law seems to concur.[12] This is obviously unsatisfactory. When the military rulers of Argentina caused thousands of their suspected opponents to "disappear" in order to spread fear among other potential dissidents, this was state terrorism. And as the Israeli and U.S. political scientists Neve Gordon and George Lopez say, "Israel's practice of state-sanctioned torture also qualifies as political terrorism. It is well known that torture is not only used to extract information or to control the victim; it is also used to control the population as a whole."[13] They conclude, and I agree, "that states can terrorize and can use soldiers, airplanes, and tanks to do so ... terror should not be reduced to the difference between nonstate and state action."[14]

There can also be state sponsored terrorism as when the government of one state funds and supports terrorism carried out by members of groups or states not under its control. The U.S. routinely lists a number of countries such as Iran and Syria which, it claims, support terrorist groups elsewhere. And U.S. support in the 1980's for the Contras in Nicaragua who spread fear of what would happen to people if they joined or supported the Sandanista rebels would fall also into this category. This is a kind of terrorism most states recognize when engaged in by their adversaries, if not when they themselves aid such terrorists.

Terrorism is certainly violence, and it is political violence. One can doubt that Al Qaeda has a *political* objective in the sense in which most of us understand politics, but since it aims at the religious domination of the political, its violence is itself political, though perhaps not open to the usual responses to political aims through dialogue and compromise. War is also political violence, on a larger scale, though if the most alarming plans of current terrorist groups would be successful, they would often amount to war as currently understood. And political violence can also be more limited than most terrorism, as in the assassination of a particular political leader. Terrorism usually seeks to terrorize, to spread fear among a wider group than those directly harmed or killed.

An important definitional question to which I would like to devote some attention is whether the targeting of civilians must be part of the definition of "terrorism," and whether such targeting turns other political violence into terrorism. Many of those writing on terrorism build the targeting of civilians into their definitions, among them Michael Walzer,[15] C.A.J. Coady,[16] and in recent work Carol Gould and Alison Jaggar.[17] It should be pointed out that this is the meaning of "terrorism" that may be emerging in international law. Since the development of international law is something to which progressives must attach great importance, we should certainly hesitate to challenge its positions. But international law is itself evolving, and has serious limitations. As currently formulated, it is highly biased in favor of existing states and against non-state groups. This may be a bias we should accept in a dangerous world, but considering the moral issues involved is surely appropriate.

I think there are serious problems with a definition of "terrorism" that sees "the deliberate killing of innocent people" as Walzer puts it, to be its defining characteristic, or what distinguishes it from other kinds of political violence and war, and makes it automatically morally unjustifiable in the same way that murder is.

First, consider some of the descriptive implications. If targeting civilians must be part of terrorism, then blowing up the U.S. Marine barracks in Lebanon in 1983 and killing hundreds of marines, and blowing a hole in the U.S. destroyer USS Cole and killing 17 sailors in Yemen in October of 2000, would not be instances of terrorism, and yet they are routinely

described as examples of terrorism. Although we might say that such descriptions are simply wrong, I am inclined to think they are not.

Even more awkward for the proposed definition that killing civilians is the defining characteristic of terrorism is that we would have to make a very sharp distinction between the September 11th attack on the World Trade Center, which was certainly terrorism, and the attack that same day and with entirely similar means, on the U.S. Pentagon building, which on this definition would not be (although some civilians work at the Pentagon, it is certainly primarily a military target).[18] And this seems very peculiar.

If one tries with this definition to include rather than exclude these cases as instances of terrorism, and thinks that instead of those who are technically "civilians" one simply means those who are not now shooting at one, like the Marines when they were asleep or the colonels in the Pentagon at their desks, and suggests that only those actually presently engaged in combat are legitimate targets, one will make it illegitimate for the opponents of terrorism to target terrorists when they are not actually engaged in bombings and the like. And distinguishing when members of the armed forces are actual present threats that may be targeted, as distinct from only potential threats because now resting, has not been part of the distinctions worked out asserting that noncombatants should not be targeted. As Robert Fullinwider writes, "combatants are first of all those in a warring country's military service. They are ... fair targets of lethal response ... even when they are in areas to the rear of active fighting and even when they are sleeping."[19] What counts is whether they are members of the armed forces or fighting group, or not.

An even more serious problem with a proposal to tie the definition of "terrorism" to the targeting of civilians (but to include the attack on the Pentagon among instances of terrorism because members of the armed forces working at the Pentagon should be thought of as if they were civilians) is that it puts the burden of being a "legitimate target" on the lowest levels of the military hierarchy, the ordinary soldiers and sailors and pilots and support personnel, and exempts the persons who give them their orders, send them into combat, and make them instruments of violence.

Furthermore, if attacking civilians *is* the defining characteristic of terrorism, a great many actions that are standardly *not* called terrorism would have to be considered to be: the bombings of Hiroshima, Nagasaki, Dresden, London, and all those other bombings of places where people live and where civilians become targets, and where the aim to spread fear and demoralization among wider groups was surely present. U.S. bombings in the war in Vietnam would be prime examples. Perhaps we should just get used to calling all these "acts of terrorism." But perhaps we should find a definition of "terrorism" that does not ask us to.

What a lot of discussions of terrorism try of course to do is to come up with a definition such that what *they* do is terrorism and is *unjustified*, whereas what *we* and our friends do is not terrorism but a justified response to it, or is justified self-defense. Building the targeting of civilians into the definition of "terrorism" is often used to accomplish this, since "intentionally killing innocent people" seems by definition wrong and unjustified. However, the net then catches not only the usual miscreants of terrorism, but also much bombing carried out by, for instance, the U.S. and its allies, bombing that proponents are very reluctant to consider unjustified. And they end up with the kind of double standard that moral discussion ought to avoid. Walzer, for instance, has argued that terrorism is never justified, even in a just cause, because it deliberately kills innocents, but that at least some allied bombing of German cities in World War II was justified even though many innocent civilians were deliberately killed.[20]

Of course, there has been a great deal of discussion of what "deliberately" amounts to. The claim is often made that terrorism intentionally targets civilians, while the violence of governments seeking to suppress it only accidentally causes comparable loss of life among civilians, and that this makes all the moral difference. I find this a dubious claim. Only governments with highly sophisticated weaponry can afford to be highly selective in their targets—the Allies in World War II, for instance, could not afford to be—and we know that even "smart bombs" often make mistakes. So the relevant comparison with respect to civilians seems to me to be: in the pursuit of their political goals, which side is causing the greater loss of civilian life. And if the deaths caused by both sides of a political conflict in which terrorism is used by at least one side are roughly equivalent, the argument may appropriately focus especially on the justice, or lack of it, of the political goals involved.

It is not a popular point to make in the wake of September 11th, but we might keep in mind that the actual loss of life caused by terrorism in comparison with conventional warfare remains relatively modest. It is the fear that is large rather than the actual numbers killed. Of course this may change if nuclear weapons come to be used by terrorists; but the *comparative* figures may easily not change if the Pentagon has its way and nuclear weapons become a much more standard and routine part of the arsenal of "defense."

Another difficulty with building the killing of civilians, or noncombatants, or "the innocent," into the definition of "terrorism" is that, as previously mentioned, it is not at all clear who the "innocent" are as distinct from the "legitimate" targets. Let us explore this issue somewhat further.

We can agree, perhaps, that small children are innocent, but beyond this, there is little moral clarity. First of all, many members of the armed forces are conscripts who have no choice but to be combatants. Many conscripts in the Israeli army, for instance, may disapprove of their government's policies. Many others of those who participate in armed conflict, in the U.S. armed forces for instance, have been pressed into service by economic necessity and social oppression. Many other combatants around the world are themselves children, pulled into combat at age 12, 13, or 14, for instance. Studies by international inquiries put the numbers of children in combat in the hundreds of thousands.

More complicatedly, many civilians, the so-called "innocents," may have demanded of their governments the very policies that opponents are resisting, sometimes using terrorism to do so. A political analyst for an Israeli newspaper, for instance, said that even more than Sharon's inclinations, it was the Israeli public's demands that caused the recent violent reoccupation of Palestinian territories and massive destruction there,[21] though Sharon may not have needed much help in deciding on these actions. In January of 2003, the Israeli public had the chance to accept or reject the policies of the Sharon government: voters returned Sharon and his Likud party to power with double the number of seats in parliament they had before.[22] Unfortunately, terrorism that kills civilians to oppose a government's policies does not distinguish between those who support and those who oppose that government.[23] But neither does counter-terrorism that kills civilians distinguish between those who support and those who do not support terrorist groups.

Especially in the case of a democracy, where citizens elect their leaders and are ultimately responsible for their government's policies, it is not clear that citizens should be exempt from the violence those policies may lead to while the members of their armed services are legitimate targets. *If* a government's policies are *unjustifiable*, and *if* political violence to resist them is *justifiable* (these are very large "ifs," but not at all unimaginable) then it is not clear why the political violence should not be directed at those responsible for these policies. As one lawyer and political scientist asks, "In the history of modern democracy, a history that includes racial and colonial terrorism, was the use of terrorism by others *never* justified?"[24]

We are so accustomed to associate suicide bombings with Palestinians and with Al Qaeda members that it may come as a surprise to learn that suicide bombings were used extensively in the 1980's by the Liberation Tigers struggling for a homeland in Sri Lanka for their Tamil ethnic minority. Prior to September 11th they had carried out about 220 suicide attacks, killing a Sri Lankan president, a former Indian prime minister, various government ministers, and mayors. Hundreds, perhaps thousands, of civilians were killed in these attacks "though civilians were never their explicit target."[25] According to the Tigers' political leader, S. Thamilchelvam, suicide bombings were used to make up for the Tamils' numerical disadvantage; the goal was "to ensure maximum damage done with minimum loss of life."[26]

I do not mean to suggest that no distinction at all can be made between combatants and civilians, or that the restraints on the conduct of war demanding that civilians be spared to the extent possible be abandoned. Rather, I am suggesting that the distinction cannot do nearly as much moral work as its advocates assign it. I reject the view that terrorism is inevitably and necessarily morally worse than war, which many assert

because they declare that, by definition, terrorism targets civilians.

In sum, then, I decline to make targeting civilians a defining feature of terrorism. Terrorism is political violence that usually spreads fear beyond those attacked, as others recognize themselves as potential targets. This is also true of much war. The "Shock and Awe"* phase of the U.S.'s war against Iraq in March of 2003 was a clear example. Terrorism's political objectives distinguish it from ordinary crime. Perhaps more than anything else, terrorism resembles small-scale war. It can consist of single events such as (in the U.S.) the Oklahoma City bombing,† whereas war is composed of a series of violent events. And there are many kinds of terrorism, as there are many kinds of war.

Terrorism and Justification

Governments try hard to portray groups that use terrorism as those who cause violence that would otherwise not exist, and to portray their own efforts to suppress that violence, however violently they do so, as a justified response to provocation. But if the governments would agree to what the groups seek—independence for Chechnya‡ for instance—the violence of the terrorists would not take place. So the violence used to suppress terrorism is the price paid to maintain the status quo, as the violence used by the dissatisfied group is the price paid to pursue its goal. From a moral point of view, it is entirely appropriate to compare these levels of violence. The status quo is not in itself morally superior; it may include grievous violations of rights or denials of legitimate aims. Whether the goals of a dissatisfied group are morally defensible or not needs to be examined, as does whether a government's refusal to accede to these goals is morally defensible. Using violence to bring about change is not inherently worse from a moral point of view than using violence to prevent such change. No doubt stability has value, but its costs need to be assessed.

---

* To employ a "shock and awe" tactic is to use an overwhelming display of military superiority in order to intimidate and weaken an enemy. In 2003, American military leaders publicly described their approach to the invasion of Iraq as employing shock and awe.

† In 1995, Timothy McVeigh and Terry Nichols detonated explosive materials in a truck outside of a federal government building in Oklahoma City. At least 168 people were killed and hundreds of others were injured.

‡ A small "republic" located inside south west Russia. Two very violent wars, the last one ending in 2000, were the most recent examples of centuries of conflict between Russians and Chechens fighting for independence.

A more promising argument against terrorism is that it does not achieve what its advocates seek, that other means are not only more justifiable but more successful. But then the burden of making them more successful is on governments and those with power. When nonviolent protest is met with violence and fails consistently to change the policies protested against even when such policies are unjustifiable, it will be hard to argue that nonviolence works where terrorism does not. The terrorist Leila Khaled said about Palestinian hijackings in the 1970's that they "were used as a kind of struggle to put the question— who are the Palestinians—before the world. Before we were dealt with as refugees. We yelled and screamed, but the whole world answered with more tents and did nothing."[27] Terrorists often believe, whether mistakenly or not, that violence is the only course of action open to them that can advance their political objectives. It is the responsibility of those who are able to do so to make this assessment untrue.

As many have noted, one of the most effective ways to reduce the appeal of terrorism to the disaffected is to enable them to participate in the political processes that affect them. Democracy is more effective than counter-terrorism. As Benjamin Barber writes,

> Violence is not the instrument of choice even under tyrannical governments because confrontations based on force usually favor the powerful ... But it can become the choice of those so disempowered by a political order (or a political disorder) that they have no other options.... To create a just and inclusive world in which all citizens are stakeholders is the first objective of a rational strategy against terrorism ...[28]

Lloyd Dumas examines the ineffectiveness of violent counter-terrorism, noting that "for decades, Israel has doggedly followed a policy of responding to any act of terrorism with violent military retaliation."[29] The result has been that "there exists today more terrorism directed against Israel than ever before ... Israelis live in fear and Palestinians live in misery."[30] He concludes that "in the long run, encouraging economic and political development is the single most effective counter-terrorist approach."[31]

Claiming that all terrorism is the same and necessarily evil and that the so-called "war on terrorism" must *end* terrorism, or must stamp it out once and for all, or claiming that all responses to terrorism should be the same, is worse than unrealistic and misleading. It invites those who set up the eradication of terrorism as a goal to be humiliated when it is not achieved, and to be thus provoked into even more unjustified violence.

Of course there is no good terrorism. All terrorism is awful, just as all war is awful, and it is outrageous that human beings have not yet managed to avoid, head off, control, and put an end to war (and to terrorism).

But this said, we can recognize that some war is worse than other war, that moral judgments are possible of its purposes and of the way it is carried out. We are accustomed to making such judgments with respect to war; we should become accustomed to making them with respect to terrorism.

One may have grave doubts whether the criteria for a just war offered by just war theory can *ever* be satisfied, especially in the case of wars fought with contemporary weaponry. But one can still agree that some wars carried out by some states or groups and fought in some ways for some purposes are *more unjustifiable* than others. And *if* war can be justified, so can some terrorism be. As Andrew Valls argues, "if just war theory can justify violence committed by states, then terrorism committed by nonstate actors can also, under certain circumstances, be justified by it as well."[32]

The United Nations, and most states, are intent on holding that to be legitimate, violence must be carried out by states, not non-state groups. But the UN also recognizes a fundamental right to self-determination which includes rights to resist "colonial, foreign and alien domination." As Fullinwider notes, "since the United States is a country founded on violent rebellion against lawful authority, we can hardly endorse a blanket disavowal of the right by others violently to rebel against their own oppressors."[33] What is so disturbing about terrorists, he concludes, is that they appeal to morality directly without appealing to law; they rely on "private judgment." But private judgment is not only a menace when exercised by non-state groups. When states put private judgment ahead of international law, as the U.S. has been doing increasingly under the George W. Bush presidency, the chances of escaping Hobbesian chaos* are undermined.

It is very important to be able to make some relevant distinctions about terrorism. If its purpose is to impose a religious tyranny on unwilling citizens, it is worse than if it seeks a legitimate purpose. If its success would bring about the end of democratic discourse and the violation of its subjects' human rights, it is more unjustifiable than if its success would create acceptable political outcomes. Judgments of the purposes aimed at are of great, though of course not conclusive importance, as they are in judging war. Judgments of the kinds of violence used to try to achieve or to prevent political purposes are also of great importance. Terrorism that kills large numbers of children and relatively non-responsible persons is obviously worse than terrorism that largely targets property, or that kills only small numbers of persons responsible for an unjustifiable policy. Terrorism that kills many civilians is worse than that which does not, as is war that does so.

No form of violence can be justified unless other means of achieving a legitimate political objective have failed. But this is *also* a moral requirement on the governments that oppose change and that seek to suppress terrorism. And those with greater power have a greater obligation to avoid violence and to pursue other means of obtaining political objectives.

It is not only potential terrorists who should find non-violent means to press their demands; those resisting these demands should find non-violent means to oppose terrorism—to give a voice to opponents, and not just an empty voice, but to respond to legitimate demands to, for instance, end an occupation, cease a colonization, and stop imperialistic impositions. Governments that use violence—military and police forces—to suppress their opponents are often as guilty of using unjustified violence as are those struggling for a hearing for their legitimate grievances. And

sometimes they are more at fault because alternative courses of action were more open to them.

Understanding and judging terrorists as distinct from terrorism involves attention to their motives. In 1986, Benjamin Netanyahu, a former prime minister of Israel, described the terrorist as "a new breed of man which takes humanity back to prehistoric times, to the times when morality was not yet born."[34] In 2002, he repeated nearly the same words, calling terrorists "an enemy that knows no boundaries," and saying "we are at the beginning of a war of worlds"—Israel and other democracies against "a world of fanatic murder[ers] trying to throw on us inhuman terror, to take us back to the worst days of history."[35]

On this view there is absolutely no justification for considering the arguments of terrorists; they are not within the same realm of discourse or circle of humanity. In contrast, those who actually talk with and study many terrorists are often amazed at how "normal" they seem, how articulate and rational.[36] They may be misguided but they are not necessarily more morally depraved than many members of the armed forces of established states who speak in terms of the costs of weaponry and personnel and of the military gains they can achieve with them. On both sides, there may be a gross lack of feeling for the victims of their violence, or, if there is feeling it is overridden by the calculations of necessity. So, in preventing terrorism, we might often achieve much more by engaging in moral argument with its potential recruits than by declaring that terrorists and their supporters are, *a priori*,† beyond the moral pale.

There are many, not only in the current U.S. administration and on the U.S. Right, but even among liberals, who equate trying to understand terrorism with excusing it. Perhaps philosophers can resist such mistakes; especially if we are ethical non-naturalists we can persuasively distinguish between causal explanations and normative evaluations.‡ We are all in need

---

* This refers to the ideas of Thomas Hobbes (1588–1679), as expressed primarily in *Leviathan* (see elsewhere in this volume). Hobbes argued that people are protected from a "nasty, brutish, and short" existence by means of an implicit social contract prohibiting certain behaviors. When individuals (or, as Held is arguing, states) act without regard for such agreements, they run the risk of anarchy and chaos.

† In this context, 'a priori' means, roughly, "knowable even without evidence."

‡ Roughly speaking, ethical non-naturalism is the view that ethical properties (such as goodness) are not the same as non-ethical properties (such as pleasure). For the non-naturalist, to say that something is pleasurable is not the same as saying that it is good. And, presumably, to offer a causal explanation of terrorism is not to say anything about the

of both sorts of inquiries. We need to understand terrorism in a way that includes understanding how terrorists think and feel and the arguments they find persuasive. This is not to excuse terrorism. But it may well involve also not excusing those who willfully fail to understand it.

The Causes of Terrorism

Suppose we look for causes more immediate than the despair that may be best addressed in the long run by democracy and development. I would like to take up very briefly the question of the causes of terrorism.

There is some agreement that it is not poverty, *per se*, that causes terrorism.[37] By this claim the point is not that individual terrorists themselves are not usually from impoverished families, since it is well known that the leaders of revolutions and political movements are usually from the middle class. But if such leaders represent (and struggle in behalf of) others who are impoverished and with whom they identify, one could say that poverty was the cause of the movement. In the case of terrorism, however, we often do not seem to be able to say exactly this. Many places in the world suffer more severe poverty than those from which many terrorists arise. So other causes can be looked to. Religious zealotry has become primary among them. This is the main direction of Walter Laqueur's latest dissection of terrorism.[38] He recognizes that some terrorists have had good reasons for their violent acts: Russian revolutionaries in the 19th century and Irish Patriots in the early 20th century are his examples. But he comes close to denying this in anyone who is Muslim. What is new about terrorism, he thinks, is that it is largely motivated by Islamic fanaticism added to psychological predisposition.

Many terrorists are not religious zealots, however, so religious fervor is at most a partial explanation. Certainly the factors of gender play a causal role. That masculinity is constructed in terms of the willingness to use violence, and that he who does so can thereby become a hero, enter fundamentally into the causal

story.[39] But these factors affect men who do and men who do not become terrorists, and more is needed to ignite them. Some time ago, on the basis of what I had read, I ventured the suggestion that the most salient factor in causing terrorism seemed to me to be *humiliation*. Since then I have been on the lookout for supporting evidence or counter-evidence, and I find much to support this view, though no single-cause explanation is likely to be helpful here or elsewhere in human affairs.

Support for paying special attention to humiliation comes from an inquiry by Laura Blumenfeld, who went to Israel seeking revenge for the wounding of her father in a terrorist attack by a Palestinian.[40] Her goal was to make her father's attacker see him as a human person, and she succeeded. In an interview, she says that "humiliation drives revenge more than anything else.... I think for the Palestinians, they feel honor and pride are very important in their culture, and they feel utterly humiliated.... I found that feelings of humiliation and shame fuel revenge more than anything else."[41] Nasra Hasson, a UN relief worker, interviewed nearly 250 Palestinian militants and their associates, and found that there is an ample supply of willing suicide bombers. "Over and over," he reports, he "heard them say, 'The Israelis humiliate us. They occupy our land, and deny our history.'"[42]

It is not hard to understand the humiliation felt by Palestinians: The continued and expanded settlement activity that eats up their land, the constant checkpoints, the confinement of Arafat,* the destruction of one symbol after another of Palestinian self-rule, and lately the destruction of not just the symbols but the reality of the Palestinian Authority.[43] And one can understand the humiliation of Israelis, whose overwhelming military superiority is so unable to stop the suicide bombings, and whose government engages in its own kind of terrorism as in the scores of assassinations of suspected Palestinian militants, several of which have occurred *after* periods in which Palestinians refrained from violence as Israel had demanded.

---

morality of terrorism. A normative explanation, on the other hand, is one that is already couched in the vocabulary of morality—it is about what ought to be the case.

* Palestinian political leader Yasser Arafat (1929–2004) was confined to a limited compound by the Israeli government from 2002 until his death.

But why so much of the rest of the Islamic world feels humiliation, if it does, is much less clear. In addition to sympathy with the Palestinians it seems in part the result of the economic disadvantage affecting much of the region. With its quite glorious intellectual and artistic past and substantial resources, the region's current economic weakness may well be somewhat galling. And as many have pointed out, the lack of openings for political expression engenders frustration. But what seems to be the most serious source of felt humiliation is cultural. The inability of traditional Islamic patterns of life to withstand the onslaught of capitalist culture and Western images may well be experienced as humiliating. Barber considers "the aggressively secular and shamelessly materialistic tendencies of modernity's global markets and its pervasive, privatizing attachment to consumerism."[44] Though fundamentalism is an invention of the West, he notes—"the Crusaders were the first great Jihadic warriors"—it should not be a surprise that "a handful of the children of Islam imagine that the new global disorder [brought about by the global market] spells the death of their children, their values, and their religion."[45]

What is humiliation? It has not received adequate philosophical attention.[46] Avishai Margalit is one of the few philosophers who has written about humiliation. He sees it as "any sort of behavior or condition that constitutes a sound reason for a person to consider his or her self-respect injured."[47] He sees the decent society as one "whose institutions do not humiliate people."[48] This is a normative sense of humiliation rather than an account of how it is experienced, but he later describes it as "a loss of human dignity"[49] and makes the interesting claim that when we remember being humiliated we relive the emotion. I am skeptical that this is more true of humiliation than of some other strongly felt emotions, but the claim merits investigation.

I will here only suggest that I think humiliation is not the same as shame. One feels shame because of some felt deficiency in oneself. One feels humiliation because of what someone else has done to diminish one or to show disrespect. Certainly shame and humiliation are related; if one did not have the deficiency one is ashamed of, the other would perhaps not be able to humiliate one. But one could have the deficiency and still not be humiliated by that other if that other was considerate, sensitive, and respectful. If, on the other hand, one *is* humiliated, and especially if one is intentionally humiliated, the result is often anger, as well as and perhaps even more than shame. And the response may quite easily be violent.

Some humiliation is caused intentionally. It is hard to believe that many of Sharon's policies and actions toward the Palestinians are not intentionally humiliating. But the kind of humiliation that the U.S. may be causing in the Islamic world seems often unintentional, more like the blustering of the huckster who cannot imagine that anyone does not want his touted new product or promoted new service. But if the U.S. cultural onslaught does produce humiliation, whether intentional or not, it behooves us all to develop more sensitivity and to be more considerate and respectful.

Feminist approaches to morality can certainly contribute here. Feminists may be especially helpful in understanding humiliation and how to deal with it in ways that do not lead to self-defeating spasms of violence. There seems to be a connection in men between adopting a macho posture, and feeling humiliation when it is challenged or shaken. Women have had much and rich experience with humiliation, but seldom respond with violence (or terrorism).[50] Understanding why could be highly relevant. ∎

Suggestions for Critical Reflection

1. Though Held rejects some commonly used definitions of terrorism, she does not in this paper present her own definition. Is there a definition of terrorism that would escape Held's worries and accurately capture all acts of terrorism without being so broad as to include other non-terrorist acts?

2. Is it possible for a government to commit an act of terrorism, or is this a contradiction in terms?

3. Held suggests that humiliation may be one of the central causes of terrorism. Are there other contexts in which humiliation may be a central cause of harmful actions and attitudes? (Consider online

discussion forums, bullying, or voter disenfran-
chisement.) If so, does this tell us anything about
how we should combat such actions and attitudes?

4. This paper was first published in 2004. Does Held's
account of the position of the "United States Right"
and of other Western governmental institutions
remain accurate today? Do any subsequent
political developments, or any particular terrorist
actions in the succeeding years, have bearing on
the strength of her argument?

5. "War" is often defined in a morally neutral way;
the *Oxford English Dictionary*, for example, offers
this primary definition: "a state of armed conflict
between different countries or different groups
within a country." On this definition, the question of whether a war is taking place is distinct

from the question of whether that war is morally
justified. On the other hand, standard definitions
of "murder"—"the *unjustified* killing of one human
being by another"—imply that all murder is by
definition immoral. Would it be better to define
"terrorism" such that all terrorist acts are immoral
by definition (as with "murder"), or would it be
better to seek a morally neutral definition (as with
"war")? Why?

6. If you have read the Held article in the section on
Ethical Theory in this volume, you might like to
try and put that piece together with this one and
examine what light, if any, each might shed on the
other. For example, does Held's general stance on
ethical theory support or influence her position on
terrorism, or are the two entirely separable?

Notes

1 Alison Mitchell, "Israel Winning Broad Support from
U.S. Right," *The New York Times* (21 April 2002), pp.
A1, 13.

2 *The New York Times* (19 March 2002), p. A12.

3 James Bennet, "Israelis Storm a Gaza Camp; 11
Palestinians Are Killed," *The New York Times* (7 March
2003), p. A10.

4 Sam Dillon, "Reflections on War, Peace, and How to
Live Vitally and Act Globally," *The New York Times* (1
June 2003), p. A28. A response to this way of thinking
is offered by Benjamin R. Barber: "Do we think we can
bomb into submission the millions who resent, fear and
sometimes detest what they think America means?"
[Benjamin R. Barber, "Beyond Jihad vs. McWorld," *The
Nation* (21 January 2002), p. 12.]

5 Nicholas D. Kristof, "A Toast to Moral Clarity," *The
New York Times* (27 December 2002), Op-ed page.

6 Ted Honderich, *After the Terror* (Edinburgh:
Edinburgh University Press, 2002).

7 Noam Chomsky, *Power and Terror* (New York: Seven
Stories Press, 2003), p. 49.

8 See Walter Laqueur, *No End to War: Terrorism in the
Twenty-First Century* (New York: Continuum, 2003), p.
113.

9 See Paul W. Kahn, "The Paradox of Riskless Warfare,"
in Verna V. Gehring (ed.), *War after September 11*
(Lanham: Rowman & Littlefield Publishers, 2003).

10 See Virginia Held, "Terrorism, Rights, and Political
Goals," in R.G. Frey and Christopher W. Morris (eds.),

Violence, Terrorism, and Justice (Cambridge: Cambridge
University Press, 1991), pp. 59–85.

11 US Department of State, *Patterns of Global Terrorism
1997*, Department of State Publications, 10321
(Washington, DC: United States Department of State,
1998), p. vi.

12 "Under international law, terrorism cannot be com-
mitted by states qua states. State sponsored terrorism,
however, is another matter ...," John Alan Cohan,
"Formulation of a State's Response to Terrorism and
State-Sponsored Terrorism," *Pace International Law
Review* XIV (2001), pp. 77–119, 88–89.

13 Neve Gordon and George A. Lopez, "Terrorism in the
Arab-Israeli Conflict," in Andrew Valls (ed.), *Ethics in
International Affairs* (Lanham: Rowman & Littlefield
Publishers, 2000), p. 110.

14 Gordon and Lopez, "Terrorism in the Arab-Israeli
Conflict," p. 110.

15 Michael Walzer, "Five Questions about Terrorism,"
Dissent 49 (2002), pp. 5–10.

16 C.A.J. Coady, "Terrorism and Innocence," in this issue
of *The Journal of Ethics*.

17 Carol C. Gould at the "Gender and Terrorism" panel
discussion, American Philosophical Association
(Pacific Division), Seattle, Washington, 30 March
2002; Alison M. Jaggar, "Responding to the Evil of
Terrorism," *Hypatia* 18 (2003), pp. 175–182.

18 C.A.J. Coady has suggested in discussion that what
makes the attack on the U.S. Pentagon an attack
on civilians and thus terrorism is that a plane with

civilians on board was hijacked and civilians killed in attacking the Pentagon. But if we pursue this line of argument, we would need to separate the two events of hijacking the plane and then crashing it into the Pentagon rather than some other target, and it would be the latter that I would point to as causing a problem for the definition in question.

19 Robert Fullinwider, "Terrorism, Innocence, and War," in Verna V. Gehring (ed.), *War after September 11* (Lanham: Rowman & Littlefield Publishers, 2003), p. 22.

20 Michael Walzer, *Just and Unjust Wars*, 3rd edition (New York: Basic Books, 2003), Chapter 16.

21 Serge Schmemann, "Not Quite an Arab-Israeli War, But a Long Descent into Hatred," *The New York Times* (22 April 2002), pp. A1, A11.

22 James Bennet, "Israeli Voters Hand Sharon Strong Victory," *The New York Times* (29 January 2003), pp. A1, A8.

23 This point was made by Sigal Benporath.

24 Angelia Means, "The Idea of the Enemy," typescript, p. 4. Quoted with permission.

25 Amy Waldman, "Masters of Suicide Bombing: Tamil Guerrillas of Sri Lanka," *The New York Times* (14 January 2003), pp. A1, A6.

26 Waldman, "Masters of Suicide Bombing: Tamil Guerrillas of Sri Lanka," pp. A1, A6.

27 Kamel B. Nasr, *Arab and Israeli Terrorism* (Jefferson: McFarland & Co., 1997), p. 57.

28 Benjamin R. Barber, "The War of All against All," in Verna V. Gehring (ed.), *War after September 11* (Lanham: Rowman & Littlefield Publishers, 2003), pp. 77, 88.

29 Lloyd J. Dumas, "Is Development an Effective Way to Fight Terrorism," in Verna V. Gehring (ed.), *War after September 11* (Lanham: Rowman & Littlefield Publishers, 2003), p. 73.

30 Dumas, "Is Development an Effective Way to Fight Terrorism," p. 73.

31 Dumas, "Is Development an Effective Way to Fight Terrorism," p. 73.

32 Andrew Valls, "Can Terrorism Be Justified?" in Andrew Valls (ed.), *Ethics in International Affairs* (Lanham: Rowman & Littlefield Publishers, 2000), p. 66.

33 Fullinwider, "Terrorism, Innocence, and War," p. 24.

34 Benjamin Netanyahu (ed.), *Terrorism: How the West Can Win* (New York: Farrar, Straus & Giroux, 1986), pp. 29–30.

35 Michael Wines, "Mourners at Israeli Boys' Funeral Lament a Conflict with No Bounds," *The New York Times* (2 December 2002).

36 Bruce Hoffman, *Inside Terrorism* (New York: Columbia University Press, 1998), "Preface."

37 See, e.g., Alan B. Krueger and Jitka Maleckova, "Seeking the Roots of Terrorism," *The Chronicle of Higher Education* (6 June 2003), B10–11.

38 Laqueur, *No End to War*.

39 See, e.g., Robin Morgan, *The Demon Lover: The Roots of Terrorism* (New York: Washington Square Press, 2001); and Virginia Held, *Feminist Morality: Transforming Culture, Society, and Politics* (Chicago: University of Chicago Press, 1993), Chapter 7.

40 Laura Blumenfeld, *Revenge: A Story of Hope* (New York: Simon and Schuster, 2002).

41 "Q & A," *The New York Times* (6 April 2002), Section B, p. 9.

42 Krueger and Maleckova, "Seeking the Roots of Terrorism," B11.

43 See, e.g., Richard Falk, "Ending the Death Dance," *The Nation* (29 April 2002), pp. 11–13.

44 Benjamin Barber, "The War of All against All," p. 78.

45 Benjamin Barber, "The War of All against All," pp. 79–80.

46 *The Philosopher's Index* for the entire period 1940–2002 lists only six articles or reviews that deal substantially with humiliation, and none for which it is the major topic.

47 Avishai Margalit, *The Decent Society* (Cambridge: Harvard University Press, 1996), p. 9.

48 Margalit, *The Decent Society*, p. 1.

49 Avishai Margalit, *The Ethics of Memory* (Cambridge: Harvard University Press, 2002), p. 118.

50 Of course, a few suicide bombers have been women, as a few rulers of states have been women, but the numbers are comparatively small.

CLAUDIA CARD

Recognizing Terrorism

Who Was Claudia Card?

Claudia Card (1940–2015) was a prolific philosopher known for her willingness to explore and advocate uncommon and provocative positions on issues of sexism, racism, and oppression. She received a PhD in philosophy from Harvard University, under the supervision of John Rawls. Soon after, she became a member of the philosophy department at the University of Wisconsin, where she was the Emma Goldman Professor of Philosophy until her death from cancer in 2015. Card worked primarily in ethics, LGBT philosophy, and social-political philosophy. In more recent years, she is perhaps best known for her work on the concept of evil, as articulated in her final books, *The Atrocity Paradigm: A Theory of Evil* (2002) and *Confronting Evils: Terrorism, Torture, Genocide* (2010).

What Is the Structure of This Reading?

Card offers a number of related and overlapping observations, including comments on the nature of terrorism, remarks on how terrorism functions, and arguments as to how we should understand and react to acts of terrorism. Card advocates a broadened conception, inclusive not only of those acts that are considered paradigmatic examples of terrorism—such as the World Trade Center attacks of 9/11 or the Manchester Arena Bombing of 2017—but also of assassinations, mistreatments of prisoners of war, acts of witness intimidation, sexual violence, and other more common events.

In making this case, Card examines the application of two separate models of terrorism:

1. The coercion model, according to which terrorists aim to coerce another party to act (or refrain from acting) in some way, through the threat of violence.
2. The group target model, according to which terrorists target a group or class of people on the grounds of their membership in that group.

Both models are limited, according to Card, insofar as neither of them fits comfortably with all cases of terrorism. Yet, both can shed light on central features of terrorism and so are worth exploring in depth.

Some Useful Background Information

1. Note that Card's analysis is not meant to provide a specific definition of terrorism, nor is it primarily a critique of existing definitions. She invokes the idea of "family resemblance" as a way of understanding and exploring terrorism. Consider the facial features of the members of a family: it is rare that any one physical trait is shared by all members. Even siblings with the same parents don't typically have all of their facial features in common. And yet, the members of a family may be said to share a resemblance: some (but not all) have the same deep-set eyes, some have the same cleft chin, some have the same widow's peak, and so on. Similarly, in this reading Card does not argue that there is a single defining trait shared by all cases of terrorism, but instead examines various shared features, each of which fits with some acts of terrorism and helps us to better understand the concept.

2. Card also makes reference to "reflective equilibrium," a concept employed by John Rawls. The basic idea here is that moral inquiry should aim for a balance in which our general principles and concepts align with our judgments about particular cases. So, rather than beginning from principles and applying them to specific cases *or* beginning from our judgments about specific cases and using those to determine our principles, we should be willing to go back and forth, revising both our judgments about cases and our principles in order to bring them into alignment. In combination with the "family resemblance" approach described above, this method means that a single example of terrorism that appears to fall outside of a particular

model doesn't necessarily invalidate the model—it may only mean that the model needs to be extended, or that our judgment about the example should be revised.

3. Not included in the selection below is a more detailed discussion of what Card calls "rape terrorism." This kind of terrorism shares many similarities with other more familiar forms of terrorism, especially when perpetrated as a weapon of war intended to coerce certain groups to abandon a territory or cause. Card argues that "civilian rape"—domestic, and not part of a military conflict—is also coercive and targets a group of people rather than individuals; it harms women and girls by causing fear, even among those who are not directly victimized. "It is only at the level of rules mandating female attachment to male protectors that it becomes possible to see rape as a coercive practice creating an atmosphere of terror for women who would, or who might, violate the rules."

*Recognizing Terrorism**

It has been observed that "most of the preventable suffering and death in the world is not caused by terrorism" but "by malnutrition, and lack of education, and all the ills connected to poverty."[1] That claim, if true, could be difficult to substantiate. For most terrorism is not documented as such, and it is far commoner than paradigms of the usual suspects suggest. Everyday lives under oppressive regimes, in racist environments, and of women, children, and elders everywhere who suffer violence in their homes seldom capture public attention as high drama. But there is real terrorism in many of these lives. A genuine war on terrorism might well begin with such domestic issues. But first it is necessary to be able to recognize terrorism.

To recognize terrorism in the everyday lives of people who may never make headlines, and at the same time deepen our appreciation of terrorism in more high profile cases, it is helpful to be able to identify imaginatively with not only potential targets but also potential terrorists. In an early essay on method, John Rawls[†] included in his definition of a "competent moral judge" the capacity to identify with persons in a variety of positions.[2] Identifying with others does not mean endorsing their judgments. It does not even mean being favorably disposed toward them. It means entering imaginatively into their situations, which can yield a livelier and truer appreciation of their perceptions, feelings, options, reasoning, and motives.

My aim in adopting this strategy of identification is to justify an expanded range of paradigms of terrorism that is not limited to high-profile cases and to do this without diluting the moral seriousness of the concept. The importance of this project is twofold. On one hand, we gain greater insight into what is distinctive about terrorism and what kind of moral significance it has. On the other, we realize that many cases of publicly invisible terrorism deserve to be taken as seriously as the widely recognized high-profile cases involving governments and other public policy-makers.

I neither begin nor conclude this project with a definition of terrorism in the sense of a set of necessary and sufficient conditions. Nor do I take a final position on whether terrorism is ever justifiable. The conception of terrorism that emerges from this investigation suggests, however, that for the relatively powerless oppressed, and especially for those who are coerced into a relationship from which they cannot extricate themselves by ordinary lawful means, the question of justification is a serious one, and its answer is not obvious.

Terrorism's varied history and uses invite a Wittgensteinian[‡] family resemblance approach to its meaning, developed with something like a

---

* Claudia Card, "Recognizing Terrorism," *The Journal of Ethics* 11, 1 (March 2007): 1–12, 17–20, 28–29.

† See the introduction to John Rawls in the Justice section in this volume for more information on this philosopher.

‡ Ludwig Wittgenstein (1889–1951) was an Austrian philosopher who contributed to the philosophy of language, formal logic, and other subjects. In his *Philosophical Investigations*, Wittgenstein proposes that there are some categories of things, such as "games," that are best understood as connected by various overlapping similarities rather than any set of defining traits shared by all members of the category. See the introduction to this reading.

Nietzschean* perspectivism.[3] Accordingly, I begin with two models of terrorism that fit high-profile paradigms. Let us call them the "the coercion model" and the "group target model." Each model has appealed to philosophers. Each emerges from important histories. Even if, ultimately, one model might absorb the other, both are useful in that they encourage identification with different parties.

1. Two Models of Terrorism

One test of a satisfactory conception of terrorism is whether it makes sense of a wide range of paradigm instances. A paradigm is an instance that appears, to relevantly informed and clear-headed thinkers, indisputably an instance, a non-controversial case.[4] There need be no consensus on what *makes* something an instance, only on whether it is. Like Rawls' "considered moral judgments," these non-controversial judgments are firm but also revisable.[5] Our paradigms are cases about which we are most confident now, based on what we think we know now.

Another test of a satisfactory conception is whether it enables us to recognize instances we had failed to appreciate before and understand why we should have. Something like Rawls' idea of "reflective equilibrium," which he applies to moral theory, can apply to more specific moral and political concepts, such as terrorism.[6] Thus, to arrive at a satisfactory conception, we may go back and forth between an abstract conception and paradigm cases, now revising the conception, now rejecting or modifying old paradigms or admitting new ones. A satisfactory conception will make sense of a significant body of uncontroversial cases, help us see instances that are not so widely recognized, and provide bases for arguing about controversial and borderline ones.

Think of a model as a blueprint for a definition or conception, an abstraction that highlights elements or

relationships in what it models. Different models suggest different ways to conceive of terrorism by encouraging us to approach it from different perspectives. The coercion model highlights elements that suggest the projects of terrorists, who may not appreciate fully the impact on victims. The group target model, in contrast, highlights elements that suggest the perceptions of victims, who may not fully appreciate terrorists' intentions. Each model is limited. Yet each also points beyond its limits.

The coercion model was persuasively developed by Carl Wellman[†] nearly three decades ago.[7] It focuses on the logic of terrorism, how the terrorist thinks, what the terrorist hopes to achieve. Ultimately, it encourages inquiry into why such drastic means would be chosen to achieve those objectives. On this model, terrorism typically has two targets. One target is direct but secondary in importance. The indirect target is primary in that it is the intended recipient of a message containing the terrorist's demands, which are sent by way of violence (or the threat of violence) to the direct target. Direct targets can be people, property, or both. An example captured by this model is bombing a public building (direct but secondary target) to pressure a government (indirect but primary target) to release prisoners or alter policies. The message, often implicit, is "accede to our demands, or there will be further bombings." The building and any occupants may be treated as "throwaways." Their survival may not matter to achievement of the terrorist's objective, whereas survival of the primary target can be essential to that end.

Other examples, arguably captured by the coercion model, include hostage-taking (Munich, 1972[‡]), kidnap for ransom (the Lindbergh baby[§]), airplane hijackings (or car-jackings), some forms of witness intimidation, some forms of extortion practiced by organized crime (the Godfather's "offers one cannot refuse" and the horse-beheading response to a man

---

* Friedrich Nietzsche (1844–1900) was an influential German philosopher. His "perspectivism" entails, very roughly, that there is no independent truth and that knowledge and value depends on one's perspective.

† Father of Kit Wellman, author of one of the articles in this volume.

‡ During the 1972 Summer Olympics in Munich, West Germany, the Palestinian group Black September took 11 Israeli Olympic team members hostage and ultimately killed them along with a West German police officer.

§ The 20-month-old son of famous aviator Charles Lindbergh and Anne Morrow Lindbergh was kidnapped from his New Jersey home in 1932, and a ransom note was left demanding $50,000. The ransom was paid, but the toddler's dead body was found a couple of weeks afterwards. The case, and subsequent trial and execution, transfixed America.

who thought he could),[8] some drive-by shootings by inner city gangs, and cross-burnings by the Ku Klux Klan. Wellman gives armed hold-ups as an example of terrorist coercion. But that example requires a little tampering with the model, since the same person is ordinarily both the primary and secondary target, a matter to which I return. Likewise, hijacking methods are typically coercive (armed hold-ups), even if the plane or vehicle is not used for further coercion.

A shortcoming of the coercion model is that it restricts terrorist objectives to coercion to comply with demands. But the same basic pattern characteristic of the coercion model, namely, two targets (direct and indirect) and a message (to the indirect but primary target), is compatible with objectives other than coercion and messages other than demands. Other objectives might be, for example, those of demonstration, protest, revenge, or disruption.

Actions of partisans and of resistance fighters in World War II, such as bombing trains headed for Poland, are often cited in raising the question whether terrorism can be justified.[9] Such actions appear not to fit the coercion model in that they do not present the primary target with a demand or offer a choice. Still, they send messages: to the Allies, "watch these trains" and to Nazis, "we will not just stand by but will do all in our power to stop you," an urgent message in the context of widespread acquiescence to Nazi policies. The pattern of a direct and indirect target and a message remains, even if coercion drops out. Coercion may not be an option for those extremely lacking in power. But some can still use terrorist means to send messages.

Not only is coercive terrorism limited to those with enough power to coerce, but also it carries certain risks for the terrorist. As with interrogational torture, it is possible to go too far and defeat one's purposes. The primary target may be too devastated by harm to the direct target to care about the message or may be unable to comply with demands. Or the message may not get across successfully. When a message fails to get across, there may appear to be none. But that conjecture gets ahead of our story, anticipating how targets may perceive matters.

In presenting the coercion model, Wellman did not defend terrorism. Yet it may be no accident that he found that model apt in the 1970s. Popular paradigms of terrorism in the U.S. then included an array of morally and politically motivated non-lethal violent crimes (mainly property destruction) committed by otherwise ordinary citizens, some from well-off and highly respected families.[10] These crimes ranged from bombings by members of the Weather Underground* to "monkey-wrenching" by environmental activists (such as sabotage of off-road vehicles used in projects destructive of natural habitats).[11] Many sent clear demands to stop specific activities. Their objectives evoked some sympathy from social critics on the left.[12]

If the coercion model gets us to focus on terrorist reasoning, the group target model, in contrast, gets us to focus on target predicaments. The group target model appears to be at work in Michael Walzer's widely cited chapter on terrorism in *Just and Unjust Wars*.[13] Although Walzer describes terrorist violence as targeting victims randomly ("its method is the random murder of innocent people"), what he appears to have in mind is randomness within a group, as he also characterizes terrorism as "the systematic terrorizing of whole populations" in order "to destroy the morale of a nation or a class."[14] Again there is a primary target, often less obvious than the immediate (direct) targets. The primary target here is a group, a "class," which presumably might be racial, ethnic, or religious, not only national. Immediate targets appear (at least, to members of the target group) to be randomly chosen members of the group, vulnerable not for their conduct (in that sense "innocent") but simply on account of their identity as members of the group. Immediate targets could also be persons or property presumed to be of value to the group, targeted for that reason. The apparent objective is to hurt the group (demoralization, as Walzer puts it); harm to immediate targets is part of or

---

* The Weather Underground was a radical left-wing student organization, founded in 1969, that—among other militant activities—conducted a campaign of bombings through the mid-1970s targeting mostly government buildings and banks and primarily objecting to US involvement in the Vietnam War. Nobody was killed in any of their acts of property destruction, although three members of the group were killed in an accidental explosion when they were assembling a bomb.

a means to that end. Terrorism so understood fits what have come to be (long since Walzer's book appeared) common definitions of hate crime, according to which victims are selected at least partly on the basis of their membership in an ethnic, racial, religious, or national group. In contrast, terrorism understood on the coercion model need not be a hate crime.

The group target model makes sense of some ethnic, racist, and religious harassment that apparently goes beyond coercion. An example might be the physical beating of Jewish students on their way to school by groups of Christian students on examination days, as recounted by Simon Wiesenthal in his memoir *The Sunflower*.[15] The immediate aim was to hinder Jewish students from passing examinations. Yet there was no evident demand satisfaction of which would have ended the harassment. Were it not exams, it would likely have been something else. The aim seemed to be to harm the Jewish community; coercion, a means. Other examples that seem to fit the group target model are vendettas that sanction indiscriminate targeting of members of an offending family and comparably indiscriminate vigilante activities.

The coercion model might be made compatible with the group target model by the supposition that there is at least an implicit coercive demand for the entire group to get out. But terrorists can be expected to know that the demand is unrealistic when there is no place for those expelled to go. Demoralization may be a more realistic goal of terrorism that targets a group.

A shortcoming of the group target model is that it does not encourage inquiry into why assailants wish to harm the group. Perhaps the assumption is that it does not matter: people should not be harmed on the basis of their identity as members of such groups, whatever the reason. But failure to look for a rationale can mislead us about who the primary target is. When we discover animating objectives, we sometimes identify the primary target differently, often more (or less) specifically....

Even if neither model entirely absorbs the other, many terrorist deeds seem to fit both. On both, individuals may be deliberately harmed regardless of whether they have done anything to provoke attack. Yet neither a lack of scruple regarding who is harmed nor the actual infliction of harm is central to the coercion model (threats may suffice). On both, targets may be coerced into acceding to terrorists' demands. Yet that aim is not central to the group target model (terrorism may continue even though some demands are met). The two models also incorporate some of the same features. On both, there is an absence of procedural justice in target selection. On both, there is, if not major harm or an attempt at it, at least a credible threat of major harm.

Yet there are also important differences. On the group target model, terrorism lies on a continuum of hate crime, at one extreme end of which is genocide. The coercion model does not put terrorism on that continuum. On the contrary, the coercion model suggests grounds for relative optimism regarding terrorists' potential amenability to dialogue and argument. Coercive terrorists may hope to succeed in relying on threats and avoid ever having to carry them out.

It is the group target model, however, that makes sense of much popular thinking about terrorism in the United States today, which would have us identify not only *with* but *as* potential direct targets who have done nothing to provoke attack. It is no accident that this model enjoys popularity now, following the 1993 bombing of the World Trade Center[*] and the massively lethal attacks of the Oklahoma City[†] and 9/11 bombings. These deeds' objectives have not been made specific and explicit. They appear somewhat mysterious, perpetrated by persons unauthorized by any state. And they do not evoke widespread sympathy in the U.S. from left or right, although they have elicited many questions.[16] These deeds, along with recent bombings of embassies and ships, are the paradigms that underlie and inform the current G.W. Bush administration's "war on terrorism."

---

[*] Islamic extremists drove a truck loaded with explosives into one of the Twin Towers, hoping to bring them both down. This failed, but six people were killed and over 1,000 injured.

[†] Right-wing terrorists opposed to government policies bombed a federal building in Oklahoma City in 1995, killing 68 people and injuring 10 times that many.

2. War on Terrorism

The Bush administration's war on terrorism appears not only to *invoke* the group target model as applicable to the enemy, it also appears to *exemplify* that model in the way it treats those it regards as the enemy. It views terrorism as a special form of combat or violence, distinguishable on one hand from conventional warfare (terrorists need not be agents of states bound by treaties or international conventions) and on the other from ordinary violent civilian crime (terrorist harm is often on a greater scale and for larger purposes). The upshot is that restrictions applying to conventional warfare and to the treatment of civilian criminals are bypassed. As noted by David Luban, persons arrested and detained as suspected terrorists enjoy neither Prisoner of War (POW) protections nor civil rights.[17] This situation leaves them vulnerable to suffering many forms of terrorism.

It can easily seem right, however, to distinguish terrorism from both conventional warfare and ordinary crime and to treat terrorists differently from POWs and from civilian criminals. First, the discrimination principle (from the "*jus in bello*" part of "just war theory"[*]), which prohibits direct targeting of non-combatants, appears to be increasingly a scruple that is not recognized by terrorists.[18] Second, criminal violence is usually motivated by personal, family, or business interests rather than by political concerns, whereas terrorists are more often politically motivated. Third, criminal violence is also commonly clandestine, whereas terrorists are often politically motivated and sometimes take responsibility publicly.

Yet these distinctions are not firm. On both models, terrorism overlaps substantially with conventional warfare and with ordinary crime. First, in the 20th century, conventional warfare also increasingly departed from the *jus in bello* discrimination principle until by its end, over 80% of war casualties were civilians.[19] That statistic makes dubious whether the old *jus in bello* discrimination principle is any longer

even *governing* such warfare. The World War II saturation bombings of Dresden and Tokyo, for example, directly targeted civilians with conventional weapons, aiming to coerce German and Japanese capitulation, sending the message that otherwise more cities would be destroyed.[20]

Second, domestic hate crimes do have political motives, whereas terrorism is often *not* political. Hostages are often taken for private gain, for example, as in the Lindbergh kidnapping and the 1974 holdup of a Stockholm bank (which bequeathed us the concept of the "Stockholm syndrome"[†]).[21] Taking tellers as hostages is criminal terrorism to coerce law enforcement into letting robbers escape with their loot.

Finally, ordinary crime need not be clandestine. Some bank robbers act in broad daylight, as the Stockholm robbers did. The Tokyo and Dresden fire bombings were not isolated incidents in the Allied conduct of the war. Less well known than it deserves to be is the massive area bombing by British forces throughout Germany and by U.S. forces in the Pacific.[22] This is terrorism in modern conventional war. Closer to the present, the conduct of U.S. soldiers in Iraq in rounding up detainees indiscriminately as "insurgents" illustrates routine military terrorism. Mark Danner in *Torture and Truth: America, Abu Ghraib, and the War on Terror* quotes a Red Cross report:

> Arresting authorities entered houses usually after dark, breaking down doors, waking up residents roughly, yelling orders, forcing family members into one room under military guard while searching the rest of the house and further breaking doors, cabinets, and other property. They arrested suspects, tying their hands in the back with flexi-cuffs, hooding them, and taking them away. Sometimes they arrested all adult males present in a house, including elderly, handicapped or sick people ... pushing people around, insulting, taking aim with rifles, punching and kicking and striking with rifles.[23]

---

[*] A historical and contemporary doctrine holding that some acts of war are morally justified while others are not. The doctrine has traditionally focused on two categories of action: the right to go to war (in Latin, "*jus ad bellum*") and right conduct in war ("*jus in bello*"); in more recent years, it has also addressed issues of justice after war ("*jus post bellum*").

[†] A psychological condition in which a hostage or kidnapping victim comes to sympathize with his or her captors.

He quotes further:

> In almost all instances..., arresting authorities provided no information about who they were, where their base was located, nor did they explain the cause of arrest. Similarly, they rarely informed the arrestee or his family where he was being taken and for how long, resulting in the de facto 'disappearance' of the arrestee.... Many families were left without news for months, often fearing that their relatives were dead.[24]

The Red Cross then notes that military intelligence officers said that "in their estimate between *70 percent and 90 percent of the persons deprived of their liberty in Iraq had been arrested by mistake* [emphasis added by Danner]."[25]

"Mistakes" that occur 90% of the time are not mistakes. This is terrorism. The group target model appears to fit. The ostensible purpose was to coerce information from detainees. But people were selected for round-up on the basis of their identity, not on the basis of prior evidence that they had information. Terrorism was an expedient and a weapon. It may not be clear whether the message-to-others aspect of the coercion model also fits. There could be an implied message in the disappearances—a possible form of hostage-taking—that anyone else who knows anything had better come forward, or their families would be subjected to similar treatment. But even without that message, this activity fits the group target model.

Active opposition to terrorism *as such* would reject not only saturation bombing of cities but tactics described in this Red Cross report. Such a campaign would also publicly expose and aggressively oppose *as terrorist* many kinds of domestic criminal violence: disappearances engineered by oppressive regimes, witness intimidation, drive-by shootings, and even stalking, rape, and intimate relationship violence. I select for special attention... the cases of oppressive regimes and the often doubly domestic crimes of rape and relationship violence, which have in common that their targets tend to be relatively low-profile.

Perhaps it will be objected that because domestic violence is small-scale compared with mass killings in the bombing of buildings or even ships, calling them "terrorist" alters the meaning and dilutes the seriousness of the concept of terrorism. Yet the appearance of a small scale comes from looking only at individual episodes or at episodes with a single victim. Victims of domestic violence are more spread out in time and space than victims in bombed buildings. Collectively, domestic violence victims are not less numerous. Individually, many of them suffer equally serious harms and fatalities. Because those who suffer violence in the home need not be prominent individuals, such as government officials, or even individuals about whom prominent people can be expected to care particularly, their cases are better described as "low-profile" than as "small-scale."

Similar points, however, can be made about easily preventable harms of poverty: collectively, poverty victims are hardly less numerous than bombing victims, and individually, many suffer harms at least as serious. Yet preventable poverty does not thereby become terrorism. To sustain the case that real terrorism is present not only in high-profile bombings but also in much rape, stalking, domestic violence, and oppressive government, it is necessary to show relevant similarities to the high-profile cases and bring out relevant differences from other sources of harm, such as poverty.....

The *group* target model appears inapt to make the case that stalking and intimate relationship violence (relationship violence, for short) can be terrorist, as their *primary* targets are specific individuals. And for the coercion model to fit, as in the case of hold-ups, we need to collapse the two targets....

4. Beyond the Two Models

Restricting terrorism to political violence aimed at groups seems arbitrary, as does restricting it to political violence with a coercive aim. Emma Goldman and Michael Walzer have discussed instances of political violence, including assassinations, that were not aimed at groups.[26] Were they not terrorist? Many 19th and early 20th Century political activists aimed their violence at specific individuals who occupied positions of public trust and could affect public policy. Walzer notes that some assassins who killed in public apparently had scruples against allowing children to be killed, even as "collateral damage." The lack of randomness leads Walzer to distinguish such political violence from terrorism.

And yet, assassinations share morally very significant features with less focused terrorist violence.

Bystanders predictably get caught in the crossfire when assassinations are carried out in public places. Because the killings are preceded by no public and fair trials justifying the selection of one target rather than another, there also may be nothing to restrain even assassins who are protective of children from continually moving on to additional adult targets. It may also be impossible to prevent others from using the assassination as a cover for their own killings, done for their own less principled reasons. Thus, in practice, assassination is apt to be less focused in its impact and more arbitrary than one might have thought.

Like many rapists, stalkers and abusers in intimate relationships target specific individuals. Still, it might seem that the group target model captures these cases. For it appears that most victims are female. A good case can be made for the view that women who suffer domestic abuse are targeted not for who they are or for what they are like as individuals but because they are female, because they are easily accessible by their partners, and because any penalty for the abuse is likely not to be high.

Crime reporting in this area, however, is problematic. Statistics tend to overlook same-sex relationships and probably underestimate women's effective abuse of men. Relationship violence—"family violence" in sociologists' parlance—includes, in addition, child abuse, sibling violence, violence against elders, and violence against parents by teenaged children. Victims include both genders. Stalking, defined as a crime in the early 1990s throughout the U.S., has much in common with relationship violence and can be an element of it. Stalkers can easily be female.[27] Further, targets are not always known personally, let alone intimately, to stalkers (celebrity stalkers, for example), although the stalkers—at any rate, those commonly identified as such—characteristically have a passionate attachment to or emotional involvement with their targets, even if the passion is never reciprocated.[28]

Although the group target model is not clearly apt, many cases of relationship violence and stalking do appear to fit the coercion model, at least somewhat. As Wellman noted long ago in the case of armed hold-ups by robbers, we have to tamper with the model a little to make it fit. First, both the direct and the indirect targets are usually the same person, whom it is more natural to call "the target." In intimate relationships, as in punishment by the state, the message "do this or else" is usually sent to the same person who will suffer the "or else" if the demand is not met.

Second, what is coercive is more the whole relationship than a series of specific demands, and even the demands are often implicit and vague or general rather than explicit and clear or specific.[29] There are, of course, coercive episodes: batterers escalate violence when a partner attempts to leave, or to get a restraining order, or to report prior violence to friends, doctors, or police. But not every threat, act of violence, or other deed that contributes to a coercive pattern need come with its own demand. Some threats and violent episodes display dominance—show who is boss or demonstrate the futility of resistance—rather than manipulate particular choices.[30] Yet they are part of a pattern that manipulates a partner's attitudes toward the batterer and toward possibilities of resistance. Many episodes that pretend to be punishments (coercive) are better construed as dominance displays, since the "offense" that ostensibly provoked them could not reasonably have been predicted in advance to be an offense and will not necessarily provoke "punishment" next time. Abused partners are often forced to use imagination and ingenuity to anticipate what will displease or provoke and what will please or pacify.

If assassinations, stalkings, and relationship violence have primary targets that are more focused than groups, terrorist *regimes* can be less discriminating than even the group target model ordinarily allows. In oppressive regimes, harm is aimed by a ruling body, or its representatives, against its own people, or rather against a subset of them that defies definition.[31] Oppressive regimes are notorious for cannibalizing themselves. The French Revolution and ensuing Terror of 1793–1794 (which bequeathed us the concept of terrorism) ostensibly targeted the privileged—royalty, nobility, and clergy who supported them. In practice, however, it targeted *anyone who was perceived as insufficiently supportive of the revolution*, which included former leaders of the revolution. Likewise,

Joseph Stalin and Pol Pot* (and closer to home, former U.S. Senator Joseph McCarthy and former FBI Director J. Edgar Hoover†) targeted anyone who fell into political disfavor.

For terrorist regimes, the group target model is both unhelpful and misleading. The regime's alleged principles do not really explain why many individuals are targeted. They do not yield a group the members of which could have been identified in advance. It may appear that primary targets are certain groups—homosexuals, Communists, Capitalists. In practice, however, those groups are like the targets of the French Terror: anyone who falls into political disfavor. Victims may come to be branded "queer," "Communists," or "Capitalists" *after* the fact (after they have been targeted). People who never identified themselves as members of such groups may be so "identified" by others, for any number of reasons, and treated accordingly. Hence, the terror.

The message not to do anything that would bring one into political disfavor is unhelpful, as there is no reliable way to predict what would stave off political disfavor. Regime violence is often better understood as a dominance display and as coercive in many of the same ways as relationship violence. Some demands, such as "do not even attempt to leave," are specific. Citizens who tried to escape the Soviet Union by going over the Berlin Wall were shot, as are many battered women who try to leave a partner. But targets must often use imagination and ingenuity to avoid being harmed. What they are coerced into is, basically,

maintaining a relationship, just as abused intimate partners are, although the relationship is a different one.

Neither model is an entirely satisfactory fit for the cases of oppressive regimes and relationship violence. But the coercion and group target models are best treated not as *definitive* of terrorism but as invitations to *understand* terrorism by identifying with different parties to a relationship that at least one of them perceives as terrorist....

The current U.S. war on terrorism is philosophically misleading with respect to the project of arriving at an adequate, realistic understanding of terrorism because that war was never meant to target terrorists in general. It ignores the terrorism of rape, of violence in intimate relationships, and of terrorist regimes and military policies, such as those described by the Red Cross regarding the U.S. treatment of Arab detainees. A conception of terrorism guided solely by the objective of making sense of the usual suspects, or of the war on terrorism, risks leaving out the commonest, most pervasive forms of terrorism in the world, perpetuating their public invisibility. Even if it remains true that most preventable suffering and death are caused not by terrorism but "by malnutrition, lack of education, and all the ills connected to poverty," an enormous amount of preventable suffering and death, globally, is caused by terrorism against targets who have lacked a public voice.

And how much suicidal terrorism directed against those in positions of power is a desperate, last-ditch attempt also to gain a public voice?[32] ∎

Suggestions for Critical Reflection

1. Card holds that neither the coercive model nor the group model functions adequately as a definition of terrorism, but nonetheless she makes use of them in attempting to understand terrorism. Do you believe that either of those models serves as a definition of "terrorism," or do both admit of exceptions? Is there another definition that would better fit with all cases of terrorism?

2. Card argues that acts of relationship violence and stalking share some important features with more

---

* Joseph Stalin (1878–1953) and Pol Pot (1925–98) were dictatorial rulers of the Soviet Union and Cambodia, respectively, known for their brutal treatment of citizens and political opponents.

† Joseph McCarthy (1908–57) and J. Edgar Hoover (1895–1972) were prominent figures in the "Red Scare" of the mid-twentieth century, during which paranoia about the spread of communism in the United States led to civil rights abuses and unwarranted accusations of communist sympathy.

conventional terrorist acts and yet have been excluded from discussions of terrorism. Is there a plausible explanation for why such acts have been excluded? Is this exclusion politically motivated?

3. If it's true that domestic violence and other kinds of harm share much in common with more conventional acts of terrorism, should our understanding of the term "terrorism" be broadened accordingly? Or would it be more practical to limit the term "terrorism" to some narrower category of actions for the purpose of setting policies and law, while using another term to describe the harms of domestic violence, etc.?

4. If taken literally, what would it mean to engage in a "war on terrorism"? Would the goals and methods of this war change if we adopted Card's broadened understanding of what counts as terrorism?

Notes

1 Martha Nussbaum, "Compassion and Terror," in James P. Sterba (ed.), *Terrorism and International Justice* (Oxford: Oxford University Press, 2003), p. 248.

2 John Rawls, *Collected Papers*, Samuel Freeman (ed.), (Cambridge: Harvard University Press, 1999), pp. 2–3.

3 See Ludwig Wittgenstein, *Philosophical Investigations*, G.E.M. Anscombe (trans.) (London: Blackwell, 1958), pp. 31–33 on "family resemblance"; see Friedrich Nietzsche, *On the Genealogy of Morals*, in Walter Kaufmann (trans.) *Basic Writings of Nietzsche*, (New York: Modern Library, 1966), pp. 460–492, for illustration of Nietzsche's perspectivism in his speculations regarding the noble and slave modes of valuation.

4 This is the sense of "paradigm" that Eric Reitan employs in his insightful paper; "Rape as an Essentially Contested Concept," *Hypatia* 16 (2001), pp. 43–66.

5 See Rawls, *Collected Papers*, pp. 5–6 on "considered moral judgments."

6 See Rawls' discussion of "reflective equilibrium" in John Rawls, *A Theory of Justice*, Revised Edition (Cambridge: Harvard University Press, 1999), pp. 18–19 and elsewhere.

7 Carl Wellman, "On Terrorism Itself," *Journal of Value Inquiry* 13 (1978), pp. 250–258. This is a model I have relied on and found useful in the past.

8 See Mario Puzo, *The Godfather* (New York: New American Library, 1978) or *The Godfather*, 1973 Paramount, Frances Ford Coppola. (dir.), (Volume 1, DVD 2004).

9 See, for example, R.M. Hare, "Terrorism," *Journal of Value Inquiry* 13 (1978), pp. 241–249.

10 Susan Braudy, *Family Circle: The Boudins and the Aristocracy of the Left* (New York: Knopf, 2003) details the career and background of Kathy Braudy, member of the Weather Underground, who eventually served twenty-two and a half years in prison for complicity in a bank hold-up.

11 See Edward Abbey, *The Monkey Wrench Gang* (Philadelphia: Lippincott, 1975).

12 See documentary film *The Weather Underground*, Bill Seigel and Sam Green (JI), (dirs.), 2003 (DVD 2004) and Abbey, *The Monkey Wrench Gang*.

13 Michael Walzer, *Just and Unjust Wars: A Moral Argument with Historical Illustrations* (New York: Basic Books, 1977), pp. 197–206. A version of the coercion model is also currently being developed persuasively by Reitan in "Defining Terrorism," unpublished paper presented at the Pacific Division meetings of the American Philosophical Society, March 2004; cited with permission.

14 Walzer, *Just and Unjust Wars*, p. 197.

15 Simon Wiesenthal, *The Sunflower: On the Possibilities and Limits of Forgiveness*, Revised and Expanded Edition, H.A. Pichler (trans.) (New York: Schocken, 1997), pp. 18–20.

16 For details on some very disturbing questions, see David Ray Griffin, *The New Pearl Harbor: Disturbing Questions about the Bush Administration and 9/11* (Northampton: Olive Branch Press, 2004); he summarizes the book's concerns in forty questions, pp. 197–201. Further materials (books, videos, websites) raising and pursuing questions regarding what happened on 9/11 are listed in *Global Outlook: The Magazine of 9/11 Truth*, Issue #10 (Spring/Summer 2005), a periodical given to me by an anonymous member of the audience at the University of Victoria, where I presented an earlier draft of the present essay. A more recent documentary DVD "Loose Change 2," shown on my campus in May 2006, raises still further questions.

17 David Luban, "The War on Terrorism and the End of Human Rights," *Philosophy and Public Policy Quarterly* 22 (2002), pp. 9–14.

18 Reitan argues that terrorism is distinguished from conventional war in being governed by a variant principle of target selection: target directly only members of the

target group ("Defining Terrorism"). A useful introduction to just war theory is William V. O'Brien, *The
Conduct of Just and Limited War* (New York: Praeger,
1981).

19 Mary Kaldor, *New and Old Wars: Organized Violence in
a Global Era, with an Afterword January 2001* (Stanford:
Stanford University Press, 1999, 2001), p. 100.

20 There is in addition the claim made by some critics of
the bombings of Hiroshima and Nagasaki that a deterrent message was also intended for the Soviet Union.

21 See Irka Kulshnyk, "The Stockholm Syndrome:
Toward an Understanding," *Social Action and the Law* 10
(1984), pp. 37–42 and Thomas Strentz, "The Stockholm
Syndrome: Law Enforcement Policy and Hostage
Behavior," in Frank M. Ochberg and David A. Soskis
(eds.), *Victims of Terrorism* (Boulder: Westview, 1982),
pp. 149–161.

22 See A.C. Grayling, *Among the Dead Cities: The History
and Moral Legacy of the WWII Bombing of Civilians in
Germany and Japan* (New York: Walker and Company,
2006).

23 Mark Danner, *Torture and Truth: America, Abu Ghraib,
and the War on Terror* (New York: New York Review
Books, 2004), p. 2.

24 Danner, *Torture and Truth*, p. 2.

25 Danner, *Torture and Truth*, p. 3.

26 Walzer, *Just and Unjust Wars*, pp. 197–206; Emma
Goldman, *Anarchism and Other Essays* (New York:
Dover, 1969), pp. 79–108. See, also, Goldman's
autobiography, *Living My Life*, 2 volumes (New York:
Knopf, 1931). Goldman was vilified as a terrorist on the
basis of her alleged connections with an assassination
(President McKinley) and an attempted assassination
(Henry Clay Frick).

27 Between 1990 and 1993, most states in the U.S. passed
anti-stalking laws. Similar laws were soon passed in
the rest and in the District of Columbia. Discussions
appeared in popular magazines, such as *Newsweek* (13
July 1992) and *Good Housekeeping* (August, 1993).

28 Are police detectives stalkers? They do many of the
same things as stalkers with many of the same consequences in emotional stress to their targets. But given
what they are legally authorized to do, their trailing
does not count as the crime of stalking. I imagine that
private detectives walk a thin line. When they become
stalkers, they need, of course, have no emotional
engagement with or attachment to their targets.

29 I have discussed this issue at greater length in Claudia
Card, *Lesbian Choices* (New York: Columbia University
Press, 1995), pp. 110–115.

30 For an excellent discussion that makes this point, using
Amnesty International's Chart of Coercion, see Ann
Jones, *Next Time She'll Be Dead: Battering and How to
Stop It* (Boston: Beacon, 1994), pp. 90–91.

31 For accounts of the French Revolution and the Terror
of 1793–1794, I have relied on Will and Ariel Durant,
The Age of Napoleon (New York: Simon & Schuster,
1975), pp. 13–87, and Thomas Carlyle, *The French
Revolution*, Volume 3 (London: J. Fraser, 1837).

32 Thanks to Alison Jaggar, Paula Gottlieb, Mohammed
Abed, Vivi Atkin, Sara Gavrell, Fred Harrington,
Alan Rubell, and to audiences at the Rocky Mountain
Philosophy Conference in Boulder (2006) and at the
University of Victoria Lansdowne lecture (2006) for
helpful comments, reflections, and suggestions.

PETER SINGER

Equality for Animals?

Who Is Peter Singer?

Singer was born in Melbourne, Australia in 1946, the son of Jewish parents who left Austria shortly before World War II. He received a BA and an MA from the University of Melbourne, as well as a BPhil degree from Oxford. Several of Singer's most well-known and influential works were published early in his career, including "Famine, Affluence, and Morality" in 1971, and a 1973 article in *The New York Review of Books* titled "Animal Liberation." The latter was the germ of his 1975 book of the same name, which quickly became a central text in discussions regarding the welfare of non-human animals. Over his career, Singer has published numerous academic and non-academic books, including *Practical Ethics* (1979), *The Life You Can Save: Acting Now to End World Poverty* (2009), and *The Most Good You Can Do* (2015). One of the most well-known living philosophers, Singer has in recent years become a central figure in the "effective altruism" movement, which advocates the use of evidence-based reasoning in our philanthropic practices.

What Is Singer's Overall Philosophical Project?

Singer identifies as a utilitarian and is arguably the most well-known present day advocate of this philosophical approach. Utilitarianism is the view that we should act so as to maximize "utility," where utility is defined as happiness, pleasure, the satisfaction of preferences, or some other form of positive outcome (depending on the particular species of utilitarianism). See the reading from John Stuart Mill for a more detailed description and defense of this approach.

Much of Singer's work applies utilitarian reasoning to particular issues of moral concern, including the treatment of non-human animals, global poverty, and topics in medical ethics such as abortion and euthanasia. Singer is perhaps most widely known for his arguments against the consumption and inhumane treatment of animals, as well as his claims about the obligations of the wealthy toward those who live in poverty. In his influential 1971 article, "Famine, Affluence, and Morality," Singer argues that our moral obligations toward other people are not limited by geographical boundaries:

> It makes no difference whether the person I can help is a neighbor's child ten yards away from me or a Bengali whose name I shall never know, ten thousand miles away.*

Though some of the particulars of Singer's arguments and positions have changed over the years, his general utilitarian outlook has been remarkably consistent throughout his career. This consistency, and the accessibility and clarity of his writing, have likely contributed to the continuing popularity of Singer's work.

What Is the Structure of This Reading?

Singer grounds his argument in what he calls "the principle of equal consideration of interests," according to which we ought to treat equal interests equally regardless of which creature holds those interests. This principle, or something like it, seems widely agreeable with respect to human beings. We ought not to favor the interests of men over those of women, or the interests of members of one race over those of another, and so on. Belief that we are all equally deserving of moral consideration is known as *egalitarianism*.

What distinguishes Singer's view from more conventional forms of egalitarianism is that he extends the consideration of interests to include non-human animals. Many other animals experience pleasure and pain,

---

* Peter Singer, "Famine, Affluence, and Morality," *Philosophy and Public Affairs* 1, 3 (Spring, 1972): 231–32.

and this is enough to establish that they have interests of their own, argues Singer. If we're committed to the principle of equal consideration of interests, we should therefore take their interests into consideration in our moral decision-making. We don't allow differences in intelligence, size, etc., to justify the unequal treatment of people, and so the fact that humans differ from other animals in these ways doesn't justify the privileging of humans over non-human animals. To favor human interests is "speciesist," Singer claims.

The practical implications of this conclusion are significant, given that a great many of our society's practices—from the consumption of meat to scientific and pharmaceutical experimentation—largely neglect the interests of non-human animals. Singer examines several of these implications, arguing that a consistent application of the principle of equal consideration of interests would require drastic changes in our behavior.

Some Common Misconceptions

1. Singer is not arguing that we need to take into consideration the interests of *all* living organisms. Though he makes only a few references to "utility" in this selection, Singer describes the possession of interests in largely utilitarian terms. He states that "if a being is not capable of suffering, or of experiencing enjoyment or happiness, there is nothing to be taken into account." Humans and many non-human animals such as cattle and fish have the capacity for pain and pleasure, and so they have interests to be taken into account. However, some other kinds of organisms, such as plants and protozoa, lack this capacity and so don't have interests that need to be considered, in Singer's view.

2. Though Singer argues that the vast majority of our meat-eating practices are morally wrong, he does not claim that it is never right to kill or consume animals. He suggests that some people in remote regions may have no alternative but to eat non-human animals or die of starvation, in which case their interests may outweigh the interests of the animals they consume. More generally, any person's interests could *potentially* justify the killing or consumption of another animal in certain dire circumstances. However, as the vast majority of people are not in those situations and likely never will be, most meat consumption is morally wrong.

Equality for Animals?*

Racism and Speciesism

... Many philosophers have advocated equal consideration of interests, in some form or another, as a basic moral principle. Few recognized that the principle has applications beyond our own species. One of those few was Jeremy Bentham, the founding father of modern utilitarianism. In a forward-looking passage, written at a time when African slaves in the British dominions were still being treated much as we now treat nonhuman animals, Bentham wrote:

The day may come when the rest of the animal creation may acquire those rights which never could have been withholden from them but by the hand of tyranny. The French have already discovered that the blackness of the skin is no reason why a human being should be abandoned without redress to the caprice of a tormentor. It may one day come to be recognised that the number of the legs, the villosity[†] of the skin, or the termination of the *os sacrum*,[‡] are reasons equally insufficient for abandoning a sensitive being to the same fate. What else is it that should trace the insuperable line? Is it the faculty

---

* From Peter Singer, *Practical Ethics*, 3rd ed. (Cambridge University Press, 2011), 49–61.

† Hairiness.

‡ "Termination of the *os sacrum*": i.e., whether or not one has a tail.

of reason, or perhaps the faculty of discourse? But a full-grown horse or dog is beyond comparison a more rational, as well as a more conversable animal, than an infant of a day, or a week, or even a month, old. But suppose they were otherwise, what would it avail? The question is not, Can they *reason*? nor Can they *talk*? but, *Can they suffer*?

In this passage, Bentham points to the capacity for suffering as the vital characteristic that entitles a being to equal consideration. The capacity for suffering—or more strictly, for suffering and/or enjoyment or happiness—is not just another characteristic like the capacity for language or for higher mathematics. Bentham is not saying that those who try to mark 'the insuperable line' that determines whether the interests of a being should be considered happen to have selected the wrong characteristic. The capacity for suffering and enjoying things is a prerequisite for having interests at all, a condition that must be satisfied before we can speak of interests in any meaningful way. It would be nonsense to say that it was not in the interests of a stone to be kicked along the road by a child. A stone does not have interests because it cannot suffer. Nothing that we can do to it could possibly make any difference to its welfare. A mouse, on the other hand, does have an interest in not being tormented, because mice will suffer if they are treated in this way.

If a being suffers, there can be no moral justification for refusing to take that suffering into consideration. No matter what the nature of the being, the principle of equality requires that the suffering be counted equally with the like suffering—in so far as rough comparisons can be made—of any other being. If a being is not capable of suffering, or of experiencing enjoyment or happiness, there is nothing to be taken into account. This is why the limit of sentience (using the term as convenient, if not strictly accurate, shorthand for the capacity to suffer or experience enjoyment or happiness) is the only defensible boundary of concern for the interests of others. To mark this boundary by some characteristic like intelligence or rationality would be to mark it in an arbitrary way. Why not choose some other characteristic, like skin colour?

Racists violate the principle of equality by giving greater weight to the interests of members of their own race when there is a clash between their interests and the interests of those of another race. The white racists who supported slavery typically did not give the suffering of Africans as much weight as they gave to the suffering of Europeans. Similarly, speciesists give greater weight to the interests of members of their own species when there is a clash between their interests and the interests of those of other species. Human speciesists do not accept that pain is as bad when it is felt by pigs or mice as when it is felt by humans.

That, then, is really the whole of the argument for extending the principle of equality to nonhuman animals, but there may be some doubts about what this equality amounts to in practice. In particular, the last sentence of the previous paragraph may prompt some people to reply: 'Surely pain felt by a mouse just is not as bad as pain felt by a human. Humans have much greater awareness of what is happening to them, and this makes their suffering worse. You can't equate the suffering of, say, a person dying slowly from cancer and a laboratory mouse undergoing the same fate.'

I fully accept that in the case described, the human cancer victim normally suffers more than the nonhuman cancer victim. This in no way undermines the extension of equal consideration of interests to nonhumans. It means, rather, that we must take care when we compare the interests of different species. In some situations, a member of one species will suffer more than a member of another species. In this case, we should still apply the principle of equal consideration of interests but the result of so doing is, of course, to give priority to relieving the greater suffering. A simpler case may help to make this clear.

If I give a horse a hard slap across its rump with my open hand, the horse may start, but it presumably feels little pain. Its skin is thick enough to protect it against a mere slap. If I slap a baby in the same way, however, the baby will cry and presumably does feel pain, for the baby's skin is more sensitive. So it is worse to slap a baby than a horse, if both slaps are administered with equal force. But there must be some kind of blow—I don't know exactly what it would be, but perhaps a blow with a heavy stick—that would cause the horse as much pain as we cause a baby by a simple slap. That is what I mean by 'the same amount of pain', and if we consider it wrong to inflict that much pain on a baby for no good reason then we must, unless we are speciesists, consider it equally wrong to inflict the same amount of pain on a horse for no good reason.

There are other differences between humans and animals that cause other complications. Normal adult human beings have mental capacities that will, in certain circumstances, lead them to suffer more than animals would in the same circumstances. If, for instance, we decided to perform extremely painful or lethal scientific experiments on normal adult humans, kidnapped at random from public parks for this purpose, adults who entered parks would become fearful that they would be kidnapped. The resultant terror would be a form of suffering additional to the pain of the experiment. The same experiments performed on nonhuman animals would cause less suffering because the animals would not have the anticipatory dread of being kidnapped and experimented on. This does not mean, of course, that it would be *right* to perform the experiment on animals, but only that there is a reason, and one that is not speciesist, for preferring to use animals rather than normal adult humans, if the experiment is to be done at all. Note, however, that this same argument gives us a reason for preferring to use human infants—orphans perhaps—or severely intellectually disabled humans for experiments, rather than adults, because infants and severely intellectually disabled humans would also have no idea of what was going to happen to them. So far as this argument is concerned, nonhuman animals and infants and severely intellectually disabled humans are in the same category; and if we use this argument to justify experiments on nonhuman animals, we have to ask ourselves whether we are also prepared to allow experiments on human infants and severely intellectually disabled adults. If we make a distinction between animals and these humans, how can we do it, other than on the basis of a morally indefensible preference for members of our own species?

There are many areas in which the superior mental powers of normal adult humans make a difference: anticipation, more detailed memory, greater knowledge of what is happening and so on. These differences explain why a human dying from cancer is likely to suffer more than a mouse. It is the mental anguish that makes the human's position so much harder to bear. Yet these differences do not all point to greater suffering on the part of the normal human being. Sometimes animals may suffer more because of their more limited understanding. If, for instance, we are taking prisoners in wartime, we can explain to them that although they must submit to capture, search and confinement, they will not otherwise be harmed and

will be set free at the conclusion of hostilities. If we capture wild animals, however, we cannot explain that we are not threatening their lives. Animals cannot distinguish attempts to overpower and confine from attempts to kill them; the one causes as much terror as the other.

It may be objected that comparisons of the sufferings of different species are impossible to make, and that for this reason when the interests of animals and humans clash, the principle of equality gives no guidance. It is true that comparisons of suffering between members of different species cannot be made precisely. Nor, for that matter, can comparisons of suffering between different human beings be made precisely. Precision is not essential. As we shall see shortly, even if we were to prevent the infliction of suffering on animals only when the interests of humans will not be affected to anything like the extent that animals are affected, we would be forced to make radical changes in our treatment of animals that would involve the food we eat, the farming methods we use, experimental procedures in any fields of science, our approach to wildlife and to hunting, trapping and the wearing of furs, and areas of entertainment like circuses, rodeos and zoos. As a result, the total quantity of suffering we cause would be hugely reduced.

So far, I have said a lot about the infliction of suffering on animals but nothing about killing them. This omission has been deliberate. The application of the principle of equality to the infliction of suffering is, in theory at least, fairly straightforward. Pain and suffering are bad and should be prevented or minimized, irrespective of the race, sex or species of the being that suffers. How bad a pain is depends on how intense it is and how long it lasts, but pains of the same intensity and duration are equally bad, whether felt by humans or animals. When we come to consider the value of life, we cannot say quite so confidently that a life is a life and equally valuable, whether it is a human life or an animal life. It would not be speciesist to hold that the life of a self-aware being, capable of abstract thought, of planning for the future, of complex acts of communication and so on, is more valuable than the life of a being without these capacities. (I am not saying, at this stage, whether this view is justifiable or not; I am saying only that it cannot simply be rejected as speciesist, because it is not on the basis of species itself that one life is held to be more valuable than another.) The value of life is a notoriously difficult ethical question, and we can only arrive at a reasoned conclusion about the comparative value of human and animal life after we have discussed the value of life in general.... Meanwhile, there are important conclusions to be derived from the extension beyond our own species of the principle of equal consideration of interests, irrespective of our conclusions about the value of life.

Speciesism in Practice

ANIMALS AS FOOD

For most people in modern, urbanized societies, the principal form of contact with nonhuman animals is at meal times. The use of animals for food is probably the oldest and the most widespread form of animal use. There is also a sense in which it is the most basic form of animal use, the foundation stone of an ethic that sees animals as things for us to use to meet our needs and interests.

If animals count in their own right, our use of animals for food becomes questionable. Inuit living a traditional lifestyle in the far north where they must eat animals or starve can reasonably claim that their interest in surviving overrides that of the animals they kill. Most of us cannot defend our diet in this way. People living in industrialized societies can easily obtain an adequate diet without the use of animal flesh. Meat is not necessary for good health or longevity. Indeed, humans can live healthy lives without eating any animal products at all, although a vegan diet requires greater care, especially for young children, and a B12 vitamin supplement should be taken. Nor is animal production in industrialized societies an efficient way of producing food, because most of the animals consumed have been fattened on grains and other foods that we could have eaten directly. When we feed these grains to animals, only about one-quarter—and in some cases, as little as one-tenth—of the nutritional value remains as meat for human consumption. So, with the exception of animals raised entirely on grazing land unsuitable for crops, animals are eaten neither for health nor to increase our food supply. Their flesh is a luxury, consumed because people like its taste. (The livestock industry also contributes more to global warming than the entire transport sector.)

In considering the ethics of the use of animal products for human food in industrialized societies, we are considering a situation in which a relatively minor human interest must be balanced against the lives and welfare of the animals involved. The principle of equal consideration of interests does not allow major interests to be sacrificed for minor interests.

The case against using animals for food is at its strongest when animals are made to lead miserable lives so that their flesh can be made available to humans at the lowest possible cost. Modern forms of intensive farming apply science and technology to the attitude that animals are objects for us to use. Competition in the marketplace forces meat producers to copy rivals who are prepared to cut costs by giving animals more miserable lives. In buying the meat, eggs or milk produced in these ways, we tolerate methods of meat production that confine sentient animals in cramped, unsuitable conditions for the entire duration of their lives. They are treated like machines that convert fodder into flesh, and any innovation that results in a higher 'conversion ratio' is liable to be adopted. As one authority on the subject has said, 'cruelty is acknowledged only when profitability ceases'. To avoid speciesism, we must stop these practices. Our custom is all the support that factory farmers need. The decision to cease giving them that support may be difficult, but it is less difficult than it would have been for a white Southerner to go against the values of his community and free his slaves. If we do not change our dietary habits, how can we censure those slave holders who would not change their own way of living?

These arguments apply to animals reared in factory farms—which means that we should not eat chicken, pork or veal unless we know that the meat we are eating was not produced by factory farm-methods. The same is true of beef that has come from cattle kept in crowded feedlots (as most beef does in the United States). Eggs come from hens kept in small wire cages, too small even to allow them to stretch their wings, unless the eggs are specifically sold as 'cage-free' or 'free range'. (At the time of writing, Switzerland has banned the battery cage, and the European Union is in the process of phasing it out. In the United States, California voted in 2008 to ban it, and that ban will come into effect in 2015. A law passed in Michigan in 2009 requires battery cages to be phased out over ten years.) Dairy products also often come from cows confined to a barn, unable to go out to pasture. Moreover, to continue to give milk, dairy cows have to be made pregnant every year, and their calf then taken away from them shortly after birth, so we can have the milk. This causes distress to both the cow and the calf.

Concern about the suffering of animals in factory farms does not take us all the way to a vegan diet, because it is possible to buy animal products from animals allowed to graze outside. (When animal products are labeled 'organic', this should mean that the animals have access to the outdoors, but the interpretation of this rule is sometimes loose.) The lives of free-ranging animals are undoubtedly better than those of animals reared in factory farms. It is still doubtful if using them for food is compatible with equal consideration of interests. One problem is, of course, that using them for food involves killing them (even laying hens and dairy cows are killed when their productivity starts to drop, which is far short of their natural life span).... Apart from killing them, there are also many other things done to animals in order to bring them cheaply to our dinner table. Castration, the separation of mother and young, the breaking up of herds, branding, transporting, slaughterhouse handling and finally the moment of slaughter itself—all of these are likely to involve suffering and do not take the animals' interests into account. Perhaps animals can be reared on a small scale without suffering in these ways. Some farmers take pride in producing 'humanely raised' animal products, but the standards of what is regarded as 'humane' vary widely. Any shift towards more humane treatment of animals is welcome, but it seems unlikely that these methods could produce the vast quantity of animal products now consumed by our large urban populations. At the very least, we would have to considerably reduce the amount of meat, eggs and dairy products that we consume. In any case, the important question is not whether animal products *could* be produced without suffering, but whether those we are considering buying *were* produced without suffering. Unless we can be confident that they were, the principle of equal consideration of interests implies that their production wrongly sacrificed important interests of the animals to satisfy less important interests of our own. To buy the results of this process of production is to

support it and encourage producers to continue to do it. Because those of us living in developed societies have a wide range of food choices and do not need to eat these products, encouraging the continuation of a cruel system of producing animal products is wrong.

For those of us living in cities where it is difficult to know how the animals we might eat have lived and died, this conclusion brings us very close to a vegan way of life....

EXPERIMENTING ON ANIMALS

Perhaps the area in which speciesism can most clearly be observed is the use of animals in experiments. Here the issue stands out starkly, because experimenters often seek to justify experimenting on animals by claiming that the experiments lead us to discoveries about humans; if this is so, the experimenter must agree that human and nonhuman animals are similar in crucial respects. For instance, if forcing a rat to choose between starving to death and crossing an electrified grid to obtain food tells us anything about the reactions of humans to stress, we must assume that the rat feels stress in this kind of situation.

People sometimes think that all animal experiments serve vital medical purposes and can be justified on the grounds that they relieve more suffering than they cause. This comfortable belief is mistaken. The LD_{50}—a test designed in the 1920s to find the 'Lethal Dose', or level of consumption that will make 50 percent of a sample of animals die—is still used today for some purposes. It is, for example, used to test the popular anti-wrinkle treatment, Botox® Cosmetic. For this purpose, mice are given varying doses. Those given a high enough dose slowly suffocate as their respiratory muscles become paralyzed, undoubtedly after considerable suffering. These tests are not necessary to prevent human suffering: even if there were no alternative to the use of animals to test the safety of the products, it would be better to do without them, and learn to live with wrinkles, as most elderly people always have.

Nor can all university experiments be defended on the grounds that they relieve more suffering than they inflict. In a well-known series of experiments that went on for more than fifteen years, H.F. Harlow of the Primate Research Center, Madison, Wisconsin, reared monkeys under conditions of maternal deprivation and total isolation. He found that in this way he could reduce the monkeys to a state in which, when placed among normal monkeys, they sat huddled in a corner in a condition of persistent depression and fear. Harlow also produced female monkeys so neurotic that when they became mothers they smashed their infant's face into the floor and rubbed it back and forth. Although Harlow himself is no longer alive, some of his former students at other U.S. universities continued to perform variations of his experiments for many years after his death.

In these cases, and many others like them, the benefits to humans are either non-existent or very uncertain; while the losses to members of other species are certain and real. Hence, the experiments indicate a failure to give equal consideration to the interests of all beings, irrespective of species. In the past, argument about animal experimentation has often missed this point because it has been put in absolutist terms: would the opponent of experimentation be prepared to let thousands die from a terrible disease that could be cured only by experimenting on one animal? This is a purely hypothetical question, because no experiment could ever be predicted to have such dramatic results, but so long as its hypothetical nature is clear, I think the question should be answered affirmatively—in other words, if one, or even a dozen animals had to suffer experiments in order to save thousands, I would think it right and in accordance with equal consideration of interests that they should do so.

To the hypothetical question about saving thousands of people through experiments on a limited number of animals, opponents of speciesism can reply with a hypothetical question of their own: would experimenters be prepared to perform their experiments on orphaned humans with severe and irreversible brain damage if that were the only way to save thousands? (I say 'orphaned' in order to avoid the complication of the feelings of the human parents.) If experimenters are not prepared to use orphaned humans with severe and irreversible brain damage, their readiness to use nonhuman animals seems to discriminate on the basis of species alone, because apes, monkeys, dogs, cats and even mice and rats are more intelligent, more aware of what is happening to them, more sensitive to pain and so on than many severely brain-damaged humans barely surviving in hospital wards and other

institutions. There seems to be no morally relevant characteristic that such humans have that nonhuman animals lack. Experimenters, then, show bias in favour of their own species whenever they carry out experiments on nonhuman animals for purposes that they would not think justified them in using human beings at an equal or lower level of sentience, awareness, sensitivity and so on. If this bias were eliminated, the number of experiments performed on animals would be greatly reduced.

It is possible that a small number of actual experiments on animals could be justified along the lines of the hypothetical justification I accepted previously, that is, without violating the principle of equal consideration of interests. Although the gains from an actual experiment would never be as certain as in the hypothetical example, if the benefit were sufficiently great, the probability of achieving that benefit high enough and the suffering to the animals sufficiently small, a utilitarian could not say that it is wrong to do it. That would also be true if the experiment were to be done on an orphaned, brain-damaged human being. Whether or not the occasional experiment on animals is defensible, current institutional practices of using animals in research are not because, despite some improvements during the past thirty years, these practices still come nowhere near to giving equal consideration to the interests of animals. It would therefore be better to shift funds now going into research on animals to clinical research involving consenting patients and to developing other methods of research that do not make anyone, animal or human, suffer.

OTHER FORMS OF SPECIESISM

I have concentrated on the use of animals as food and in research, because these are examples of large-scale, systematic speciesism. They are not, of course, the only areas in which the principle of equal consideration of interests, extended beyond the human species, has practical implications. There are many other areas that raise similar issues, including the fur trade, hunting in all its different forms, circuses, rodeos, zoos and the pet business. Because the philosophical questions raised by these issues are not very different from those raised by the use of animals as food and in research, I shall leave it to the reader to apply the appropriate ethical principles to them.

Some Objections

When I first put forward the views outlined in this chapter, in 1973, there was no animal liberation or animal rights movement. Now there is, and the hard work of countless animal activists has paid off, not only in greater public awareness of animal abuse, but also in concrete benefits for animals in many different areas. Despite this increasing acceptance of many aspects of the case for equal consideration for the interests of animals and the slow but tangible progress made on behalf of animals in many different areas, a number of objections keep coming up. In this final section ... I shall attempt to answer the most important of these objections.

HOW DO WE KNOW THAT ANIMALS CAN FEEL PAIN?

We can never directly experience the pain of another being, whether that being is human or not. When I see a child fall and scrape her knee, I know that she feels pain because of the way she behaves—she cries, she tells me her knee hurts, she rubs the sore spot and so on. I know that I myself behave in a somewhat similar—if more inhibited—way when I feel pain, and so I accept that the child feels something like what I feel when I scrape my knee.

The basis of my belief that animals can feel pain is similar to the basis of my belief that children can feel pain. Animals in pain behave in much the same way as humans do, and their behaviour is sufficient justification for the belief that they feel pain. It is true that, with the exception of a few animals who have learned to communicate with us in a human language, they cannot actually say that they are feeling pain—but babies and toddlers cannot talk either. They find other ways to make their inner states apparent, however, demonstrating that we can be sure that a being is feeling pain even if the being cannot use language.

To back up our inference from animal behaviour, we can point to the fact that the nervous systems of all vertebrates, and especially of birds and mammals, are fundamentally similar. Those parts of the human nervous system that are concerned with feeling pain are relatively old, in evolutionary terms. Unlike the cerebral cortex, which developed only after our ancestors diverged from other mammals, the basic nervous system evolved in more distant ancestors and so is common to all of the other 'higher' animals, including humans. This anatomical parallel makes it likely that the capacity of vertebrate animals to feel is similar to our own.

The nervous systems of invertebrates are less like our own, and perhaps for that reason we are not justified in having quite the same confidence that they can feel pain. In the case of bivalves like oysters, mussels and clams, a capacity for pain or any other form of consciousness seems unlikely, and if that is so, the principle of equal consideration of interests will not apply to them. On the other hand, scientists studying the responses of crabs and prawns to stimuli like electric shock or a pinch on an antenna have found evidence that does suggest pain. Moreover, the behaviour of some invertebrates—especially the octopus, who can learn to solve novel problems like opening a screw-top glass jar to get at a tasty morsel inside—is difficult to explain without accepting that consciousness has also evolved in at least some invertebrates.

It is significant that none of the grounds we have for believing that animals feel pain hold for plants. We cannot observe behaviour suggesting pain—sensational claims to have detected feelings in plants by attaching lie detectors to them proved impossible to replicate—and plants do not have a centrally organized nervous system like ours.

ANIMALS EAT EACH OTHER, SO WHY SHOULDN'T WE EAT THEM?

This might be called the Benjamin Franklin Objection because Franklin recounts in his *Autobiography* that he was for a time a vegetarian, but his abstinence from animal flesh came to an end when he was watching some friends prepare to fry a fish they had just caught. When the fish was cut open, it was found to have a smaller fish in its stomach. 'Well', Franklin said to himself, 'if you eat one another, I don't see why we may not eat you', and he proceeded to do so.

Franklin was at least honest. In telling this story, he confesses that he convinced himself of the validity of the objection only after the fish was already in the frying pan and smelling 'admirably well'; and he remarks that one of the advantages of being a 'reasonable creature' is that one can find a reason for whatever one wants to do. The replies that can be made to this objection are so obvious that Franklin's acceptance of it does testify more to his hunger on that occasion than to his powers of reason. For a start, most animals who kill for food would not be able to survive if they did not, whereas we have no need to eat animal flesh. Next, it is odd that humans, who normally think of the behaviour of animals as 'beastly' should, when it suits them, use an argument that implies that we ought to look to animals for moral guidance. The most decisive point, however, is that nonhuman animals are not capable of considering the alternatives open to them or of reflecting on the ethics of their diet. Hence, it is impossible to hold the animals responsible for what they do or to judge that because of their killing they 'deserve' to be treated in a similar way. Those who read these lines, on the other hand, must consider the justifiability of their dietary habits. You cannot evade responsibility by imitating beings who are incapable of making this choice.

Sometimes people draw a slightly different conclusion from the fact that animals eat each other. This suggests, they think, not that animals deserve to be eaten, but rather that there is a natural law according to which the stronger prey on the weaker, a kind of Darwinian 'survival of the fittest' in which by eating animals we are merely playing our part.

This interpretation of the objection makes two basic mistakes, one of fact and the other of reasoning. The factual mistake lies in the assumption that our own consumption of animals is part of some natural evolutionary process. This might be true of those who still hunt for food, but it has nothing to do with the mass production of domestic animals in factory farms.

Suppose that we did hunt for our food, though, and this was part of some natural evolutionary process. There would still be an error of reasoning in the assumption that because this process is natural it is right. It is, no doubt, 'natural' for women to produce an infant every year or two from puberty to menopause, but this does not mean that it is wrong to interfere with this process. We need to understand nature and develop the best theories we can to explain why things are as they are, because only in that way can we work out what the consequences of our actions are likely to be; but it would be a serious mistake to assume that natural ways of doing things are incapable of improvement....

DEFENDING SPECIESISM

... Shortly before he died in 2003, the British philosopher Bernard Williams defended speciesism in an article entitled, appropriately enough, "The Human Prejudice." Williams started from the claim that all our values are necessarily 'human values'. In one sense, of course, they are. Because we have yet to encounter any nonhumans who articulate, reflect on and discuss their values, all the values up for discussions are human in the sense that they have been formulated and articulated by human beings. The fact that our values are human in this sense does not exclude the possibility of developing values that would be accepted by any rational being capable of empathy with other beings. Nor—and this is the most important point—does the human nature of our values tell us anything about what our values can or should be and, in particular, whether we should value the pains, pleasures and lives of nonhuman animals less highly than we value our own pains, pleasures and lives. Williams, to his credit, acknowledged that 'it is itself part of a human, or humane, outlook to be concerned with how animals should be treated, and there is nothing in what I have said to suggest that we should not be concerned with that'. What, then, is the significance of the fact that our values are human values? Williams' ultimate defence of 'the human prejudice' is surprisingly crude. He asks us to imagine that our planet has been colonized by benevolent, fair-minded and far-sighted aliens who judge it necessary to remove us. He then says that no matter how fair-minded and well-informed that decision was (we can imagine, perhaps, that our incorrigible aggression was likely, sooner or later, to destroy the planet), we would be right to side with our own species against these aliens. The ultimate question, Williams says, is 'Which side are you on?'

We have heard that question before. In times of war, or racial, ethnic, religious or ideological conflict, 'which side are you on?' is used to evoke group solidarity and suggest that any questioning of the struggle is treason. In the United States in the 1950s, followers of Senator Joseph McCarthy asked it of those who opposed their methods of fighting communism. Senior figures in the administration of President George W. Bush used it to imply that their critics were giving support to terrorists. The question divides the world into 'us' and 'them' and demands that the mere fact of this division transcends the very different question: 'What is the right thing to do?' In these circumstances, the right and courageous thing to do is not to side with the tribal instincts that prompt us to say, 'My tribe (country, race, ethnic group, religion, etc.) right or wrong' but to say, 'I'm on the side that does what is right'. Although it is fantastic to imagine that a fair-minded, well-informed, far-sighted judge could ever decide that there was no alternative to the 'removal' of our species in order to avoid much greater injustice and misery, if this really were the case, we should reject the tribal—or species—instinct and answer Williams' question in the same way. ■

Suggestions for Critical Reflection

1. Do humans and other animals hold equal interests? Is it best to think of interests in terms of pleasure and pain, or are interests better understood as relating to more complex desires and life goals, such as a person's interest in having a successful career or in having good relationships with friends and family? John Stuart Mill famously wrote that "it is better to be a human being dissatisfied than a pig satisfied." Is Mill correct, or is this a speciesist attitude?

2. Singer asserts that "[t]here seems to be no morally relevant characteristic that [orphaned humans with severe and irreversible brain damage] ... have that nonhuman animals lack." Why does Singer say this? How important is it to his overall position that this is true? Do you think it is true, and if not, exactly why not?

3. The majority of meat-eating North Americans rarely if ever kill the animals they personally consume. Rather, it is common for meat and other animal products to proceed through a series of people and processes: farmers, slaughterhouse workers, butchers, retailers, cooks, and finally the person who purchases and eats the resulting product. If Singer is correct in his claim that it is usually wrong to consume non-human animals, are all of these parties equally morally responsible, or are some more responsible than others?

4. Philosopher Roger Crisp agrees with Singer that if we aim to maximize utility we should abstain from eating animals raised in excessively harmful conditions (what he calls "intensively reared animals"). However, he claims that we *should* eat animals raised in less harmful conditions, since those animals have lives of positive overall utility and they would never be born or raised in the absence of a human demand for animal meat. Crisp writes:

> The worthwhileness of [the lives of non-intensively-reared animals], and the pleasure we gain from eating them, justify the practice of rearing them, although it inevitably involves causing suffering. And if we were not to eat them, both of these sources of utility would disappear.*

How does this contrast with Singer's position? Both Singer and Crisp apply utilitarian reasoning, and yet their conclusions differ—does one offer a more plausible interpretation of utilitarianism than the other?

5. Singer draws an analogy between the history of slavery, which was widely accepted by some cultures at certain points in human history, and the current widespread acceptance of meat consumption and animal mistreatment. Is this comparison apt? Why or why not? At one point he writes, "If we do not change our dietary habits, how can we censure those slave holders who would not change their own way of living?" This is a striking claim— what do you think about it?

6. Recent research seems to show that plants can respond to their environment in much more

---

* Roger Crisp, "Utilitarianism and Vegetarianism," *International Journal of Applied Philosophy* 4, 1 (1988): 44.

complicated ways than was previously assumed.* This includes 'seeing,' 'hearing' and otherwise perceiving and responding to threats, communicating with other plants, recognizing and behaving differently towards conspecifics that are more closely genetically related, and even learning to associate one stimulus with another unrelated stimulus (e.g., young pea plants can be 'taught' to associate the wind from a fan at one time with blue light—which helps them grow—at a later time, and their tendrils will 'choose' routes to climb in the direction of the fan). If plants turn out to be aware, even in some sense to be able to think, how might this affect Singer's arguments or his conclusions?

7. In an earlier reading in this volume, Virginia Held argues that one is justified in giving special ethical consideration to—"care" more for—those with whom we have relationships, such as members of one's own family and possibly members of the same neighborhood, etc. Could Held's arguments also justify the extension of special ethical consideration to members of one's own species? If so, would this serve as a convincing objection to Singer?

---

* For example, Monica Gagliano, "The Mind of Plants: Thinking the Unthinkable," *Communicative & Integrative Biology* 10, 2 (2017): e1288333.

MARY MIDGLEY

Is a Dolphin a Person?

Who Was Mary Midgley?

Mary Beatrice Midgley (1919–2018) was a moral philosopher renowned for her no-nonsense, highly practical approach to fundamental human issues. She wrote mainly on religion, science, and ethics. Although no foe of science in general, she strongly opposed any attempt by science to enter the domain of the humanities and supplant it. She also wrote extensively about what human beings can learn from nature, particularly from animals. A professor of philosophy at the University of Newcastle until her retirement, she was one of Britain's most popular and well-known philosophical figures. Although known for her commitment to collegial encouragement and collaborative enquiry, she could be fiercely combative when provoked by her peers; she was once described as possibly "the most frightening philosopher in the country: the one before whom it is least pleasant to appear a fool."[*] Between 1979 and 1983 Midgley was involved in a highly public, very heated exchange of articles after she attacked Richard Dawkins's "selfish gene" thesis.

Midgley studied Classics at Somerville College, Oxford, and graduated with a First Class Honours degree, but despite returning for graduate studies at Oxford never completed a PhD (which was not all that unusual for academics at the time). In 2005 she published a newspaper article called "Proud not to be a doctor," in which she argued that a PhD may give you the skills of a lawyer, but it can also obscure the big issues in a mass of detail. She was at Oxford during World War II and later wrote that she—along with several other prominent female British philosophers of her genera-

tion—might have owed her start in philosophy to the fact that many male undergraduates left after a year to fight in the war and so left a space in which women students could make more of an impact. "I do think that in normal times a lot of good female thinking is wasted because it simply doesn't get heard."[†]

She wrote her first book in her fifties, after raising a family,[‡] but then went on to produce more than 18 volumes including *Beast and Man* (1978); *Animals and Why They Matter* (1983); *Wickedness* (1984); *Evolution as a Religion* (1985); *The Ethical Primate* (1994); *Science and Poetry* (2001); and *What Is Philosophy For?* (2018).

What Is the Structure of This Reading?

Though in everyday speech we may think of the terms "human being" and "person" as largely interchangeable, their meaning in moral philosophy and the law is distinct. For example, many arguments as to the ethics of abortion hinge on whether an unborn fetus (a human being of sorts) counts as a person. Since persons have certain rights, the question of a fetus's personhood presumably has bearing on our obligations toward it (see the readings on abortion earlier in this section for more). Likewise, with non-human animals such as dolphins, some argue that the morality of our treatment toward them depends at least in part on whether we count them as persons. In this article, Midgley argues that we need to develop a more flexible notion of moral personhood that will allow us to treat non-human animals as morally important in their own right.

---

[*]   Andrew Brown, "Mary, Mary, quite contrary," *The Guardian*, Saturday, 13 January 2001.

[†]   *The Owl of Minerva* (Routledge, 2005), 123.

[‡]   As she once put it: "I wrote no books until I was a good 50, and I'm jolly glad because I didn't know what I thought before then."

Is a Dolphin a Person?*

The Undoubting Judge

This question came up during the trial of the two people who, in May 1977, set free two bottle-nosed dolphins used for experimental purposes by the University of Hawaii's Institute of Marine Biology. It is an interesting question for a number of reasons, and I want to use most of this discussion in interpreting it, and tracing its connexion with several others which may already be of concern to us. I shall not go into details of the actual case, but shall rely on the very clear and thoughtful account which Gavin Daws gives in his paper, '"Animal Liberation" as Crime'.[1]

Kenneth le Vasseur, the first of the two men to be tried, attempted through his counsel what is called a 'choice of evils' defence. In principle the law allows this in cases where an act, otherwise objectionable, is necessary to avoid a greater evil. For this defence to succeed, the act has to be (as far as the defendant knows) the only way of avoiding an imminent, and more serious, harm or evil to himself or to 'another'.

Le Vasseur, who had been involved in the care of the dolphins, believed that their captivity, with the conditions then prevailing in it, actually endangered their lives. His counsel, in his opening statement for the defence, spoke of the exceptional nature of dolphins as animals; bad and rapidly deteriorating physical conditions at the laboratory; a punishing regimen for the dolphins, involving overwork, reductions in their food rations, the total isolation they endured, deprived of the company of other dolphins, even of contact with humans in the tank, deprived of all toys which they had formerly enjoyed playing with—to the point where Puka, having refused to take part consistently in experimental sessions, developed self-destructive behaviours symptomatic of deep disturbance, and finally became lethargic—'comatose'. Le Vasseur, seeing this, fearing that death would be the outcome, and knowing that there was no law that

he could turn to, believed himself authorized, in the interests of the dolphins' well-being, to release them. The release was not a theft in that Le Vasseur did not intend to gain anything for himself. It was intended to highlight conditions in the laboratory. (Daws: 356–67)

But was a dolphin 'another'? The judge thought not. He said that 'another' would have to be another person, and he defined dolphins as property, not as persons, as a matter of law. A dolphin could not be 'another person' under the penal code. The defence tried and failed to get the judge disqualified for prejudice. It then asked leave to go to Federal Court in order to claim that Thirteenth Amendment rights in respect of involuntary servitude might be extended to dolphins. This plea the judge rejected:

Judge Doi said, 'We get to dolphins, we get to orangutans, chimpanzees, dogs, cats. I don't know at what level you say intelligence is insufficient to have that animal or thing, or whatever you want to call it, a human being under the penal code. I'm saying that they're not under the penal code and that's my answer.' (Daws: 365)

At this point—which determined the whole outcome of the trial—something seemed perfectly obvious to the judge about the meaning of the words 'other' and 'person'. What was it? And how obvious is it to everybody else? In the answer just given, he raises the possibility that it might be a matter of intelligence, but he rejects it. That consideration, he says, is not needed. The question is quite a simple one; no tests are called for. The word 'person' just means a human being.

What Are Persons?

I think that this is a very natural view, but not actually a true one, and the complications which we find when we look into the use of this interesting word are instructive. In the first place, there are several well-established and

---

* This article was first published under the title "Persons and Non-Persons," in *In Defence of Animals*, ed. Peter Singer (Basil Blackwell, 1985), 52–62. Copyright © 1985. The version reprinted here appeared as Chapter Nine of *Utopias, Dolphins and Computers* (Routledge, 1996).

indeed venerable precedents for calling non-human beings 'persons'.

One concerns the persons of the Trinity, and indeed the personhood of God. Another is the case of 'legal persons'—corporate bodies such as cities or colleges, which count as persons for various purposes, such as sueing and being sued. As Blackstone says, these 'corporations or bodies politic ... are formed and created by human laws for the purposes of society and government'; unlike 'natural persons', who can only be created by God.* The law, then, can if it chooses create persons; it is not a mere passive recorder of their presence (as indeed Judge Doi implied in making his ruling a matter of law and not of fact). Thirdly, what may look nearer to the dolphins, the word is used by zoologists to describe the individual members of a compound or colonial organism, such as jellyfish or coral, each having (as the dictionary reasonably puts it) 'a more or less independent life'.[2]

There is nothing stretched or paradoxical about these uses, for the word does not in origin mean 'human being' or anything like it. It means a mask, and its basic general sense comes from the drama. The 'masks' in a play are the characters who appear in it. Thus, to quote the Oxford Dictionary again, after 'a mask', it means 'a character or personage acted, one who plays or performs any part, a character, relation or capacity in which one acts, a being having legal rights, a juridical person'.

The last two meanings throw a sharp light on the difference between this notion and that of being human. Not all human beings need be persons. The word *persona* in Latin does not apply to slaves, though it does apply to the State as a corporate person. Slaves have, so to speak, no speaking part in the drama; they do not figure in it; they are extras.

There are some entertaining similar examples about women. Thus:

One case, brought before the US Supreme Court in the 1890s, concerned Virginia's exclusion of

a woman from the practice of the law, although the pertinent statute was worded in terms of 'persons'. The Court argued that it was indeed up to the State's Supreme Court 'to determine whether the word 'person' as used (in the Statute) is confined to males, and whether women are admitted to practise law in that Commonwealth'. The issue of whether women must be understood as included by the word 'persons' continued even into the twentieth century ... In a Massachusetts case in 1931 ... women were denied eligibility for jury service, although the statute stated that every 'person qualified to vote' was so eligible. The Massachusetts Supreme Court asserted: 'No intention to include women can be deduced from the omission of the word male.'[3]

Finding the Right Drama

What is going on here? We shall not understand it, I think, unless we grasp how deeply drama is interwoven with our thinking, how intimately its categories shape our ideas. People who talk like this have a clear notion of the drama which they think is going on around them. They know who is supposed to count in it and who is not. Attempts to introduce fresh characters irritate them. They are inclined to dismiss these attempts sharply as obviously absurd and paradoxical. The question who is and who is not a person seems at this point a quite simple and clear-cut one. Bertie Wooster simply is not a character in *Macbeth* and that is the end of the matter.[†]

It is my main business here to point out that this attitude is too crude. The question is actually a very complex one, much more like 'who is important?' than 'who has got two legs?' If we asked 'who is important?' we would know that we needed to ask further questions, beginning with 'important for what?' Life does not contain just one purpose or one drama, but many interwoven ones. Different characters matter in

---

* Sir William Blackstone's *Commentaries on the Laws of England*, published in four volumes between 1765 and 1767, codified the common law—law based on judicial custom and precedent—which today forms a major part of the law of many countries which were once British territories or colonies.

† Bertie Wooster is a fictional character in the *Jeeves* stories written by P.G. Wodehouse (1881–1975). *Macbeth* is a play by William Shakespeare (1564–1616).

different ways. Beings figure in some who are absent from others, and we all play different parts in different scripts.

Even in ordinary human life, it is fatal to ignore this. To insist on reducing all relationships to those prescribed by a single drama—such, for instance, as the Social Contract*—is disastrous. Intellectuals are prone to such errors, and need to watch out for them. But when we come to harder cases, where the variation is greater—cases such as abortion, euthanasia or the treatment of other species—this sort of mistake is still more paralysing. That is why these cases are so helpful in illuminating the more central ones.

It is clear that, over women, those who limited the use of the concept 'person' felt this difficulty. They did not want to deny altogether that women were persons, since in the dramas of private life women figured prominently. Public life, however, was a different stage, whose rules and conventions excluded them (queens apart) as completely as elephants or angels. The fact that private life often impinges on public was an informal matter and could not affect this ruling. Similarly at Rome, it is clear that slaves actually played a considerable part in life. In Greek and Roman comedy ingenious slaves, both male and female, often figure as central characters, organizing the intrigue and supplying the brains which the hero and heroine themselves unfortunately lack. This, however, was not going to get them legal rights. The boundaries of particular situations and institutions served to compartmentalize thought and to stop people raising questions about the rights and status of those who were for central purposes currently disregarded.

I think it will be helpful here to follow out a little further the accepted lines of usage for the word person. How complete is its link with the human bodily form? What, for instance, about intelligent alien beings? Could we call them persons? If not,

then contact with them—which is certainly conceivable—would surely require us to coin a new word to do the quite subtle moral job which is done at present by 'person'. The idea of a person in the almost technical sense required by morality today is the one worked out by Kant.[†] It is the idea of a rational being, capable of choice and therefore endowed with dignity, worthy of respect, having rights; one that must be regarded always as an end in itself, not only as a means to the ends of others.

Because this definition deals solely with rational qualities, it makes no mention of human form or human descent, and the spirit behind it would certainly not license us to exclude intelligent aliens, any more than disembodied spirits. The moral implications of the word 'person' would therefore, on our current Kantian principles, surely still have to attach to whatever word we might coin to include aliens. C.S. Lewis,[‡] describing a planet where there are three distinct rational species, has them use the word *hnau* for the condition which they all share, and this term is naturally central to the morality of all of them.[5]

Now if intelligence is really so important to the issue, a certain vertigo descends when we ask 'where do we draw the line?' because intelligence is a matter of degree. Some inhabitants of our own planet, including whales and dolphins, have turned out to be a lot brighter than was once thought. Quite how bright they are is not yet really clear to us. Indeed it may never become so, because of the difference in the kind of brightness appropriate to beings with very different sorts of life. How can we deal with such a situation?

Attending to the Middle Ground

The first thing needed is undoubtedly to get away from the single, simple, black-and-white antithesis with which Kant started, the antithesis between persons and

---

* The idea of a *social contract* is typically appealed to in order to justify constraints on people's individual freedom, on the basis that people voluntarily agree (or would agree, or ought to agree) to these restrictions because in the long run they make everybody better off. For example, one might argue, we tacitly agree to submit appropriately to the authority of the police because we are better off living in a society where there is a police force than one where there is not. See the reading from Hobbes and the other readings in the Justice section of this volume for more.

† Immanuel Kant (1724–1804) was an important German philosopher. See the reading from Kant in the Ethical Theory section of this volume.

‡ C.S. Lewis (1898–1963) was a British novelist and philosopher best known today for his series of fantasy novels, *The Chronicles of Narnia*.

things. Most of Kant's argument is occupied with this, and while it remains so he does not need to make finer distinctions. *Things* (he says) can properly be used as means to human ends in a way in which *people* cannot. Things have no aims of their own; they are not subjects but objects.

Thing-treatment given to people is exploitation and oppression. It is an outrage, because, as Kant exclaims, 'a man is not a thing'. Masters sell slaves; rulers deceive and manipulate their subjects; employers treat their secretaries as part of the wallpaper. By dwelling on the simple, stark contrast involved here, Kant was able to make some splendid moral points which are still vital to us today, about the thorough-going respect which is due to every free and rational human being. But the harsh, bright light which he turned on these situations entirely obscured the intermediate cases. A mouse is not a thing either, before we even start to think about a dolphin.

I find it interesting that, just as the American courts could not quite bring themselves to say that women were not persons, so Kant cannot quite get around to saying what his theory certainly implies, that animals are things. He does say that they 'are not self-conscious and are there merely as a means to an end',[6] that end being ours. But he does not actually call them things, nor does he write off their interests. In fact he emphatically condemns cruel and mean treatment of them. But, like many other humane people who have got stuck with an inadequate moral theory, he gives ingeniously unconvincing reasons for this. He says—what has gone on being said ever since—that it is only because cruelty to animals may lead on to cruelty to humans, or degrade us, or be a sign of a bad moral character, that we have to avoid it.

This means that if we can show that, for instance, venting our ill-temper on the dog will prevent our doing it on our families, or if we can produce certificates to show that we are in general people of firm moral character, not easily degraded, we can go ahead with a clear conscience. Dog-bashing, properly managed, could count as a legitimate form of therapy, along with gardening, pottery and raffia-work. In no case would the physical materials involved be directly considered, because all equally would be only objects, not

subjects. And there is nothing degrading about simply hitting an object.

In spite of the appalling cruelty which human beings show towards animals the world over, it does not seem likely that anyone regards them consistently in this light, as objects. Spasms of regard, tenderness, comradeship and even veneration, alternating with unthinking callousness, seem to make up the typical human attitude to them. And towards fellow-human-beings too, a rather similar alternation is often found. So this cannot really be an attitude confined to things. Actually even cruelty itself, when it is deliberate, seems to require that its objects should not be mere physical objects, but should be capable of minding what is done to them, of responding as separate characters in the drama.

More widely, the appeal of hunting, and also of sports such as bullfighting, seems to depend on the sense of outwitting and defeating a conscious quarry or opponent, 'another', able to be one's opposite in the game or drama. The script distinctly requires non-human characters, who can play their parts well or badly. Moby Dick* is not an extra. And the degradingness of deliberate cruelty itself surely requires this other-regarding element. 'Another' is not always another human being.

Indirect Justifications

The degradingness of cruelty is of course widely admitted, and le Vasseur's counsel used this admission as the ground of an alternative defence. He drew attention to his client's status as a state employee, which conferred authority on him to act as he did in coming to the defence of 'another', in this case the United States, whose social values were injured by what was being done to the dolphins. This argument was rejected, on the ground that, in the eyes of the law, cruelty to animals is merely a misdemeanour, whereas theft is a felony. Accordingly the choice of evils could not properly be resolved in such a way as to make theft the less serious offence. It is interesting that this argument makes no objection to treating the United States as 'another' or 'another person'—it does not insist that a person

---

* Herman Melville's famous 1851 novel is about the obsessive quest of Ahab, captain of a whaling ship, to kill Moby Dick, the white whale that, on the ship's previous voyage, bit his leg off.

simply means a human being—but rests instead on contending that this 'other' finds its values more seriously attacked by theft than by cruelty to dolphins.

This sort of argument is not easy to come to grips with, even in the case of an ordinary individual person, still less in that of a nation. How serious an evil is cruelty? Once it is conceded that the victim's point of view does not count, that the injury is only to the offender or some body of which he is part, we seem to be cut off from the key considerations of the argument and forced to conduct it in a strained manner, from grounds which are not really central. Is cruelty necessarily depraving? On this approach, that seems partly to be a factual question about how easily people are depraved, and partly perhaps an aesthetic one about how far cruel acts are necessarily disgusting and repellent.

These acts seem to be assimilated now to others which are repellent without being clearly immoral, such as eating the bodies of people whom one has not killed, or watching atrocities over which one has no control. The topic becomes a neighbour of pornography rather than of abortion and euthanasia. (In the disputes about permissiveness in the 1960s, an overlap actually developed here at times, as when a London art gallery organized a happening in which some fish were to be electrocuted as part of the show, and efforts to ban this were attacked as censorious manifestations of aesthetic narrow-mindedness.)

Something seems to have gone wrong with the thinking here. The distinctive feature of actions attacked on purely aesthetic grounds should surely be that their effects are confined to those who actually perform them. No other sentient being is harmed by them. That is why they pose problems for libertarians, when bystanders object to them. But cruelty does not pose this kind of problem, since the presence of 'another' who is harmed is essential to it. In our case it is the dolphin, who does seem to be 'another'. Can we avoid thinking of it in this way? Can the central objection to cruelty really be something rather indirect, such as its being in bad taste?

Moral Change and the Law

The law seems to have ruled thus here. And in doing this, the law shows itself to be in a not uncommon difficulty, one that arises when public opinion is changing. Legal standards are not altogether independent of moral standards. They flow from them and crystallize in ways designed to express certain selected moral insights. When those insights change deeply enough, the law changes. But there are often jolts and discrepancies here, because the pace of change is different. New moral perceptions require the crystals to be broken up and reformed, and this process takes time. Changes of this kind have repeatedly altered the rules surrounding the central crux which concerns us here; the stark division of the world into persons and property. Changing attitudes to slavery are a central case, to which we must come back in a minute. But it is worth noticing first that plain factual discoveries too can make a difference.

When our civilization formed the views on the species barrier which it still largely holds, all the most highly-developed non-human animals were simply unknown. Legend apart, it was assumed that whales and dolphins were much like fish. The great apes were not even discovered till the eighteenth century and no real knowledge of their way of living was acquired until within the last few decades. About better-known creatures too, there was a very general ignorance and unthinking dismissal of available evidence; their sociality was not noticed or believed in. The central official intellectual tradition of our culture never expected to be forced to subtilize its crude, extreme, unshaded dichotomy between man and beast. In spite of the efforts of many concerned thinkers, from Plutarch to Montaigne and from Blake to John Stuart Mill, it did not develop other categories.*

If alien beings landed tomorrow, lawyers, philosophers and social scientists would certainly have to do some very quick thinking. (I don't expect the aliens myself, but they are part of the imaginative furniture of our age, and it is legitimate to use them to roust us

---

* Plutarch lived in Greece around 100 CE and Michel de Montaigne (1533–92) was French; both were famous essayists. William Blake (1757–1827) was a British Romantic poet, and John Stuart Mill (1806–73) was a British philosopher (see the readings from Mill in the Ethical Theory and Justice sections of this volume).

from our dogmatic slumbers.*) Science fiction, though sometimes helpful, has far too often side-tracked the problem by making its aliens just scientists with green antennae—beings whose 'intelligence' is of a kind to be instantly accepted at the Massachusetts Institute of Technology, only of course a little greater. Since neither dolphins nor gorillas write doctoral theses, this would still let us out as far as terrestrial non-human creatures were concerned. 'Persons' and their appropriate rights could still go on being defined in terms of this sort of intelligence, and we could quietly continue to poison the pigeons in the park any time that we felt like it.

The question is, why should this kind of intelligence be so important, and determine the limits of our moral concern? It is often assumed that we can only owe duties to beings capable of speech. Why this should be thought is not altogether clear. At a simple level, Bentham† surely got it right: 'The question is not *can they talk*? Nor *can they reason*? But *can they suffer?*'⁷ With chimps, gorillas and dolphins, however, there is now a further problem, because people have been trying, apparently with some degree of success, to teach them certain kinds of language. This project might have taught us a great deal about just what new categories we need in our attempt to classify beings more subtly. But unluckily it has been largely obscured by furious opposition from people who still have just the two categories, and who see the whole proceeding as an illicit attempt to smuggle contraband from one to the other.

This reaction is extremely interesting. What is the threat? Articulate apes and cetaceans‡ are scarcely likely to take over the government. What might happen, however, is that it would become much harder to exclude them from moral consideration. In particular, their use as experimental subjects might begin to look very different. Can the frontier be defended by a resolute and unbreakable refusal to admit that these animals can talk?

The Meaning of Fellowship

It is understandable that people have thought so, but this surely cannot really be the issue. What makes creatures our fellow-beings, entitled to basic consideration, is not intellectual capacity, but emotional fellowship. And if we ask what powers can give a higher claim, bringing some creatures nearer to the degree of consideration which is due to humans, what is most relevant seems to be sensibility, social and emotional complexity of the kind which is expressed by the forming of deep, subtle and lasting relationships. The gift of imitating certain intellectual skills which are important to humans is no doubt an indicator of this, but it cannot be central. We already know that both apes and dolphins have this kind of social and emotional complexity.

If we ask what elements in 'persons' are central in entitling them to moral consideration, we can, I think, get some light on the point by contrasting the claim of these sensitive social creatures with that of a computer of the present generation, programmed in a manner which entitles it, by current controversial usage, to be called 'intelligent' and certainly able to perform calculations impossible to human beings. That computer does not trouble our sleep with any moral claims, and would not do so however much more 'intelligent' it became, unless it eventually seemed to be conscious, sensitive and endowed with emotions.

If it did seem so, we should have the Frankenstein§ problem in an acute form. (The extraordinary eagerness with which Frankenstein drove his researches to this disastrous point is something which contemporary monster-makers might like to ponder.) But those who at present emphasize the intelligence of computers do not see any reason to want to call them persons, nor to allow for them as members of the moral community. Speech alone, then, would scarcely do this job

---

*   A reference to Kant's statement that Hume woke him from his "dogmatic slumber."

†   Jeremy Bentham (1748–1832), an English philosopher and advocate of legal reform, was an influential formulator of the principle of 'utilitarianism'—the principle that actions are right insofar as they contribute to general happiness, and wrong insofar as they contribute to unhappiness—and was a great influence on John Stuart Mill.

‡   Whales, dolphins, and porpoises.

§   The scientist in Mary Shelley's 1818 novel *Frankenstein* who builds and brings to life a hideous humanoid creature who, despite being intelligent and sensitive, is abandoned and hunted by his creator, and thereby driven to become a destructive murderer. (Note that this is the name of the scientist, Victor Frankenstein, not of his creature, which is nameless.)

for the apes. What is at issue is the already glaring fact, which speech would make it finally impossible to deny, that they mind what happens to them—that they are highly sensitive social beings.

These considerations are not, I think, ones confined to cranks or extremists. They seem fairly widespread today, and probably occur at times to all of us, however uncertain we may be what to do about them. If so, and if the law really allows them no possible weight, then we seem to have reached the situation where the law will have to be changed, because it shocks morality. There is an obvious precedent, to which the dolphin-liberators tried to appeal:

> When the dolphins were taken from the tanks, a message was left behind identifying the releasers as the 'Undersea Railroad', a reference to the Underground Railroad, the Abolitionists' slave-freeing network of pre–Civil War days. Along the Underground Railroad in the 1850s, it sometimes happened that juries refused to convict people charged with smuggling slaves to freedom.

That was the kind of vindication le Vasseur and Sipman were looking for ... They did not consider themselves to be criminals. In fact they took the view that, if there was a crime, it was the crime of keeping dolphins—intelligent, highly aware creatures with no criminal record of their own—in solitary confinement, in small, concrete tanks, made to do repetitious experiments, for life. (Daws: 362)

If we go back to the alien beings for a moment and consider whether even the most intelligent of them would have the right to keep any visiting human beings, however stupid, in these conditions, even those of us least partial to astronauts may begin to see the point which le Vasseur and Sipman were making. It surely cannot be dismissed merely by entrenching the law round the definition of the word 'person'. We need new thinking, new concepts and new words, not (of course) just about animals but about our whole relation to the non-human world. We are not less capable of providing these than people were in the 1850s, so we should get on with it. ∎

Suggestions for Critical Reflection

1. Can non-humans be persons? All non-humans, or only those with certain attributes?
2. Are all humans persons? How do we decide who is a person and what isn't?
3. What makes cruelty immoral? Is there a moral difference between cruelty to people and cruelty to animals?
4. How should we weigh human interests against those of non-humans? Should these considerations affect what we eat or wear? How we farm?
5. What is the relationship between law and morality? When and how should laws be revised to reflect the changing moral beliefs of a society? Are there cases in which laws should be revised in light of persuasive moral arguments, even if those revisions don't reflect the opinions of the majority of society?
6. If one disagrees with an existing law, under what circumstances (if any) is it morally permissible to break that law?
7. Peter Singer (in the reading preceding this one) argues that we ought to consider the interests of many non-human animals because they have the capacity for pleasure and pain. Supposing that we do have moral obligations towards non-human animals, does it make a difference whether we conceive of those obligations on utilitarian grounds (as Singer does) or in terms of personhood?
8. Jeremy Bentham says the important moral question is "can they suffer?" Midgley says that what matters is whether they have "social and emotional complexity of the kind which is expressed by the forming of deep, subtle and lasting relationships." In determining which entities deserve our moral consideration, is one of these conditions more important than the other? Why?

Notes

1   Gavin Daws, "'Animal Liberation' as Crime" in Harlan B. Miller and William H. Williams (eds.), *Ethics and Animals* (Totowa, NJ: Humana Press, 1983).

2   It is also interesting that 'personal identity' is commonly held to belong to continuity of consciousness rather than of bodily form, in stories where the two diverge. Science fiction strongly supports this view, which was first mooted by John Locke, *Essay Concerning Human Understanding*, bk. 2, ch. 27, sect. 15.

3   Susan Möller Okin, *Women in Western Political Thought* (Princeton, NJ, 1979), p. 251.

4   See Immanuel Kant, *Foundations of the Metaphysics of Morals* (tr. Lewis White Beck, Bobbs-Merrill, 1959), sect. 428–432, p. 46. In the UK a more available translation is that called *The Moral Law* (tr. H.J. Paton, Hutchinson, 1948), pp. 90–92.

5   C.S. Lewis, *Out of the Silent Planet* (London, John Lane, 1938).

6   Immanuel Kant, 'Duties towards Animals and Spirits' in his *Lectures on Ethics* (tr. Louis Infield, Methuen, London, 1930), p. 239.

7   Jeremy Bentham, *Introduction to the Principles of Morals and Legislation*, ch. 17.

Justice

WHAT IS JUSTICE?

Social and political philosophy is made up of our attempts to understand and map the basic categories of social life, and to ethically evaluate different forms of social organization. It has three closely interwoven strands: *conceptual analysis* of various important social dimensions, *normative assessment* of the ways society ought to be structured along these dimensions, and *empirical investigation* of issues relevant to the implementation of these social ideals. It includes social philosophy, political philosophy, philosophy of law, and philosophy of the social sciences (such as economics and sociology).

Among the central concepts studied within social and political philosophy are society, culture, human nature, political obligation, power, democracy, toleration, rights, equality, autonomy or freedom, justice, merit, welfare, property, social class, public interest, and social stability. Different analyses of these notions, and different emphases on some ideas (e.g., equality) over others (e.g., autonomy), give rise to differing political philosophies—differing ideological stances as to what the ideal society should look like, and thus different views on how current societies should be modified in order to move them closer to this ideal. Some of the main social-political ideologies (not all of which are mutually exclusive) are:

- *Anarchism*, which denies that any coercive government institutions are ever justified;
- *Libertarianism* (or "classical liberalism"), which holds that government infringements on individual liberty are always inappropriate, but accepts that a "minimal" state is consistent with this; libertarians also hold that failing to help people in need is not an infringement on their liberty, and that the state therefore has no duty to provide this form of support for its citizens;
- *Liberalism* (or "welfare liberalism"), which is also concerned with promoting individual liberty but holds that a guaranteed social minimum standard of living and enforced equal opportunity are necessary to provide citizens with genuinely substantive autonomy;
- *Communitarianism*, which denies that the rights of individuals are basic and asserts that collectives (states, cultures, communities) have moral claims that are prior to, and sometimes even opposed to, the rights which liberals ascribe to individuals; usually, this is because communitarians hold some version of the thesis that individual identity is constituted by one's social setting, and thus that the liberal notion of an "isolated individual" who exists independently of society is a mere myth;
- *Fascism*, which is an extreme communitarian view stressing the overriding importance of national culture and giving the state authority to control almost all aspects of social life;
- *Socialism*, which takes neither individual liberty nor community to be a fundamental ideal, but instead emphasizes the value of equality, and justifies coercive social institutions insofar as they promote social equality;
- *Communism*, which advocates a society in which private property is abolished in favor of communal ownership of all goods, in the belief that it is only in such conditions that human beings can truly flourish;
- *Conservatism*, which distrusts naked political power and is skeptical of social planning, and which therefore seeks to channel and constrain government within historically evolved, time-tested social institutions and relationships; and
- *Feminism*, which advocates, among other things, social reform (e.g., to the institution of the family) in order to take better account of the fact that women should have the same basic social rights as men.

In addition to conceptual and ethical analysis, there are also many substantive empirical questions which have an important bearing on the choice and implementation of social philosophies. For example, ethical analysis might lead us to decide on a particular set of principles of distributive justice (indicating the ideal distribution of benefits and burdens in society); then, however, it is still a substantial empirical problem to decide which social and economic arrangements will best instantiate those principles. A sampling of other important questions: What checks and balances on government power will be most effective without being inefficient? How can the self-interest of individuals best be harnessed for the public good? What is the most effective body of legislation for fostering social stability? Can equality of opportunity be preserved without infringing on personal autonomy (e.g., on people's choices about who to hire or rent to)? Which forms of punishment are the most effective deterrent of crime? How much is human nature shaped and changed by social circumstances? What is the relationship between free economic markets and democratic political structures? And so on.

The particular social-political issue which is the focus of this section is the problem of justice. The readings approach the topic in all three of the inter-connected ways identified above: they deal with the philosophical analysis of the concept of justice, make claims about how society should be organized in order to take proper account of justice, and touch on some of the empirical data relevant to the construction of a just society. They also deal with some of the different *aspects* of justice: justice as a property of a political system, a set of social relationships, of actions, or of individuals; and justice considered as a problem of specifying how social benefits and burdens should be distributed among the members of that society (*distributive justice*), and the problem of determining the appropriate way to correct injustices or compensate for illegitimate inequalities (*rectificatory justice*).

Aristotle provides an influential initial analysis of the notion of justice which sets some of the terms for the debate. The reading from Hobbes pursues similar questions and also introduces an additional theme: the pressing problem of justifying (and defining the limits of) coercive state power over individuals. Hobbes, famously, answers this question with the device of a "social contract," by which rationally self-interested individuals would agree to leave the "state of nature" and submit themselves to the authority of the state. Mill is also, in the reading reprinted here, concerned with the question of the justice of government intervention in the lives of citizens, and he formulates and defends the classical liberal position which limits government action to the prevention of harm. The following readings then present three of the most important modern political ideologies on justice, and particularly distributive justice. Marx and Engels argue for the inevitable ascendance of communism; Rawls carefully lays out the most influential contemporary version of welfare liberalism; and Nozick attempts to rebut Rawls with a lively and fast-moving defense of libertarianism. The final reading, by Susan Moller Okin, presents a feminist critique of contemporary liberal theory and raises deeper questions about gender and its relationship to justice.

There are a number of good books which will take you deeper into social and political philosophy. Perhaps the best place to start is with Will Kymlicka's excellent *Contemporary Political Philosophy* (Oxford University Press, 2001). Also good are John Christman, *Social and Political Philosophy: A Contemporary Introduction* (Routledge, 2017); Carl Cohen, *Communism, Fascism, and Democracy: The Theoretical Foundations* (McGraw-Hill, 1997); Iain Hampsher-Monk, *A History of Modern Political Thought, Major Political Thinkers from Hobbes to Marx* (Blackwell, 1993); J.R. Lucas, *The Principles of Politics* (Oxford University Press, 1986); Gerald MacCallum, *Political Philosophy* (Prentice Hall, 1987); Michael

J. Sandel, *Justice: What's the Right Thing to Do?* (Farrar, Strauss and Giroux, 2009); Adam Swift, *Political Philosophy* (Polity Press, 2013); and Jonathan Wolff, *An Introduction to Political Philosophy* (Oxford University Press, 2006). Goodin and Pettit, eds., *A Companion to Contemporary Political Philosophy* (Blackwell, 1996) and Gaus and D'Agostino, eds., *The Routledge Companion to Social and Political Philosophy* (Routledge, 2017) are both well worth consulting.

The modern literature on justice is rich and extensive. Here are some relevant books: Brian Barry, *Theories of Justice*, Volume 1 (University of California Press, 1991); G.A. Cohen, *Self-Ownership, Freedom, and Equality* (Cambridge University Press, 1995); Ronald Dworkin, *Taking Rights Seriously* (Harvard University Press, 1978); Friedrich A. Hayek, *The Constitution of Liberty* (Routledge and Kegan Paul, 1960); David Miller, *Principles of Social Justice* (Harvard University Press, 2001); Stephen Nathanson, *Economic Justice* (Prentice Hall, 1998); D.D. Raphael, *Concepts of Justice* (Oxford University Press, 2001); John Roemer, *Theories of Distributive Justice* (Harvard University Press, 1996); Michael Sandel, *Liberalism and the Limits of Justice* (Cambridge University Press, 1998); Amartya Sen, *The Idea of Justice* (Harvard University Press, 2009); Arthur and Shaw, eds., *Justice and Economic Distribution* (Prentice Hall, 1991); and Michael Walzer, *Spheres of Justice* (Basic Books, 1984).

ARISTOTLE

FROM *Nicomachean Ethics*

For information on Aristotle's life and his overall philosophical project, please see the introduction to Aristotle earlier in this volume.

What Is the Structure of This Reading?

The overall structure of the *Nicomachean Ethics* is described in the introduction to Aristotle from earlier in this volume. Book V, in which Aristotle discusses justice, comes after discussions of various moral virtues, such as courage, temperance, generosity, good temper, and truthfulness. It is fairly clear that Aristotle thinks justice is a particularly important virtue, however, since it is the one to which he devotes by far the most space.

The first five sections of Book V are reprinted here. After distinguishing between the particular virtue of justice and "the type of justice ... that accords with the whole of virtue," Aristotle goes on, in section two, to divide particular justice into two types: distributive justice and rectificatory justice. In the next three sections, however, he discusses, in turn, *three* varieties of justice—distributive justice in section three, rectificatory justice in section four, and "justice in exchange" in section five. The rest of Book V, which is not included here, deals with the difference between natural and legal justice and emphasizes the role of choice in the virtue of justice (roughly, that people are unjust, according to Aristotle, only if they deliberately *choose* to take unfair advantage of others).

Some Useful Background Information

1. The Greek words for "just" and "unjust" (*dikaios* and *adikos*) are ambiguous in a way which is much less evident in their English counterparts, and Aristotle begins by discussing this ambiguity. The Greek words apply not only to people or actions that we would call just or unjust—i.e., roughly, those that are fair or unfair—but also to moral rightness or wrongness *in general*. Thus what Aristotle calls "particular justice" is one virtue

(albeit a particularly important one) among others, while "general justice" corresponds to moral virtue in general (or at least, "complete virtue in relation to another").

2. For Aristotle, justice is not primarily a state of affairs (such as an even distribution of wealth) or a framework of social rules (such as a fair taxation system). Instead, justice is a *virtue*, just as courage and truthfulness are virtues—justice is, at bottom, a sort of *character trait*. Just actions, then, are (roughly) those performed by just people; a just society is one which is governed by just people; and just laws are those which prescribe moral virtue, and especially the particular virtue of justice.

3. Furthermore, the virtue of justice, for Aristotle, is defined not merely by one's disposition to *behave* in certain ways, but also by one's *motive* for that behavior. That is, unjust people, according to Aristotle, are motivated by what he calls *pleonexia*, usually translated as being "grasping," "greedy," or "overreaching." Literally, it means desiring to have more than other people or wanting more than one's share. (People who possess the particular virtue of justice, presumably, are those who are *not* motivated by *pleonexia*.)

4. At one point Aristotle refers to "members of a community who share in a political system," and this is a significant indicator of his view of the political dimension of distributive justice. For Aristotle, and in ancient Greek thought generally, the free citizens of a political state are like *shareholders* or *partners* in the state. Public property (such as the land of a new colony) or public rewards and honors (such as political office) are to be divided up among citizens in accordance with their merit (i.e., their wealth, nobility, or virtue). The question of just distribution of rewards is therefore, for Aristotle, fundamentally a question about how social goods should be divided up among the (free, male, landowning) members of the society—that is, of how people should fairly be rewarded for their contribution to a common political enterprise.

A Common Misconception

Aristotle's focus is on *acting* justly or unjustly, rather than on what it is to be *treated* justly or not. Thus, for example, in his discussion of rectificatory justice, his main focus is on how the judge or arbiter should act, and not on the 'injustice' of the state of affairs which the judge is concerned to redress. To put it another way, for Aristotle, justice is a virtue, and since being treated fairly or unfairly manifests neither virtue nor vice, Aristotle's real interest is in those who *do the treating*.

How Important and Influential Is This Passage?

The huge influence of Aristotle's *Nicomachean Ethics* as a whole has already been discussed in notes to the Aristotle reading in the Ethical Theory section of this volume. Many of the concepts introduced in Book V specifically have been particularly influential. For example, the distinction between the just *distribution and exchange of goods* and justice considered as *the redressing of wrongs*, has become a standard part of debates about justice since Aristotle's time. Also, Aristotle's analysis of reciprocal justice is one of the first discussions of political economy and is often hailed as an example of his visionary analytic genius. On the other hand, Aristotle's actual theories of justice—such as that distributive justice is a matter of geometrical proportion—are usually considered useful starting points for discussion but are often criticized as being too unsophisticated to be taken seriously today as complete accounts of justice.

FROM *Nicomachean Ethics**

BOOK V [JUSTICE], SECTIONS 1–5

1 [Varieties of Justice]

The questions we must examine about justice and injustice are these: What sorts of actions are they concerned with? What sort of mean is justice? What are the extremes between which justice is intermediate? Let us investigate them by the same line of inquiry as we used in the topics discussed before.

We see that the state everyone means in speaking of justice is the state that makes us just agents—[that is to say], the state that makes us do justice and wish what is just. In the same way they mean by injustice the state that makes us do injustice and wish what is unjust. That is why we also should first assume these things as an outline.

For what is true of sciences and capacities is not true of states. For while one and the same capacity or science† seems to have contrary activities,‡ a state that is a contrary has no contrary activities. Health, for instance, only makes us do healthy actions, not their contraries; for we say we are walking in a healthy way if [and only if] we are walking in the way a healthy person would.

Often one of a pair of contrary states is recognized from the other contrary; and often the states are recognized from their subjects. For if, for instance, the good state is evident, the bad state becomes evident too; and moreover the good state becomes evident from the things that have it, and the things from the state. For if, for instance, the good state is thickness of flesh, the

---

* The *Nicomachean Ethics* was probably written, as a series of lecture notes which would have undergone frequent revision, sometime between 334 and 322 BCE. This selection is reprinted from *Aristotle: Nicomachean Ethics*, 2nd ed., ed. and trans. Terence Irwin (Hackett, 1999). The section headings are not Aristotle's own, but are supplied by the translator.

† 'Sciences' are structured bodies of knowledge.

‡ For example, medicine deals with disease as well as health; an engineer has the skill necessary to either build or destroy a bridge.

bad state must be thinness of flesh, and the thing that produces the good state must be what produces thickness of flesh.

If one of a pair of contraries is spoken of in more ways than one, it follows, usually, that the other is too. If, for instance, the just is spoken of in more ways than one, so is the unjust.

Now it would seem that justice and injustice are both spoken of in more ways than one, but since their homonymy* is close, the difference is unnoticed, and is less clear than it is with distant homonyms where the distance in appearance is wide (for instance, the bone below an animal's neck and what we lock doors with are called keys homonymously†).

Let us, then, find the number of ways an unjust person is spoken of. Both the lawless person and the overreaching and unfair person seem to be unjust; and so, clearly, both the lawful and the fair person will be just. Hence the just will be both the lawful and what is fair, and the unjust will be both the lawless and the unfair.

Since the unjust person is an overreacher, he will be concerned with goods—not with all goods, but only with those involved in good and bad fortune, goods which are, [considered] without qualification, always good, but for this or that person not always good.‡ Though human beings pray for these and pursue them, they are wrong; the right thing is to pray that what is good without qualification will also be good for us, but to choose [only] what is good for us.

Now the unjust person [who chooses these goods] does not choose more in every case; in the case of what is bad without qualification he actually chooses less. But since what is less bad also seems to be good in a way, and overreaching aims at more of what is good, he seems to be an overreacher. In fact he is unfair; for

unfairness includes [all these actions], and is a common feature [of his choice of the greater good and of the lesser evil].

Since, as we saw, the lawless person is unjust and the lawful person is just, it clearly follows that whatever is lawful is in some way just; for the provisions of legislative science are lawful, and we say that each of them is just. In every matter that they deal with, the laws aim either at the common benefit of all, or at the benefit of those in control, whose control rests on virtue or on some other such basis. And so in one way what we call just is whatever produces and maintains happiness and its parts for a political community.

Now the law instructs us to do the actions of a brave person—for instance, not to leave the battle-line, or to flee, or to throw away our weapons; of a temperate person—not to commit adultery or wanton aggression; of a mild person—not to strike or revile another; and similarly requires actions in accord with the other virtues, and prohibits actions in accord with the vices. The correctly established law does this correctly, and the less carefully framed one does this worse.

This type of justice, then, is complete virtue, not complete virtue without qualification, but complete virtue in relation to another. And that is why justice often seems to be supreme among the virtues, and "neither the evening star nor the morning star is so marvelous,"§ and the proverb says, "And in justice all virtue is summed up."¶

Moreover, justice is complete virtue to the highest degree because it is the complete exercise of complete virtue. And it is the complete exercise because the person who has justice is able to exercise virtue in relation to another, not only in what concerns himself; for many are able to exercise virtue in their own concerns, but unable in what relates to another.

---

* Two words are homonyms if they look and sound the same written or spoken, but have different meanings. (For example, "current," which can mean the movement of a fluid, electrical charge, or something that is of the present.)

† The collarbone is called *kleis* in Greek, which is the same as the word for key.

‡ For example, wealth is something which can always contribute to a good life, but for people with defective characters—i.e., those who do not use money wisely—it can make them less happy.

§ According to some ancient commentaries, this is a quotation from Euripides' lost play *Melanippe* (of which just a fragment remains today).

¶ This saying is attributed to the poet Theognis of Megara and to another poet called Phocylides (both of whom lived around the middle of the sixth century BCE).

That is why Bias* seems to have been correct in saying that ruling will reveal the man; for a ruler is automatically related to another, and in a community. That is also why justice is the only virtue that seems to be another person's good; because it is related to another; for it does what benefits another, either the ruler or the fellow member of the community.

The worst person, therefore, is the one who exercises his vice toward himself and his friends as well [as toward others]. And the best person is not the one who exercises virtue [only] toward himself, but the one who [also] exercises it in relation to another, since this is a difficult task.

This type of justice, then, is the whole, not a part, of virtue, and the injustice contrary to it is the whole, not a part, of vice.

Our discussion makes clear the difference between virtue and this type of justice. For virtue is the same as justice, but what it is to be virtue is not the same as what it is to be justice. Rather, insofar as virtue is related to another, it is justice, and insofar as it is a certain sort of state without qualification, it is virtue.

2 [Special Justice Contrasted with General]

But we are looking for the type of justice, since we say there is one, that consists in a part of virtue, and correspondingly for the type of injustice that is a part of vice.

A sign that there is this type of justice and injustice is this: If someone's activities accord with the other vices—if, for instance, cowardice made him throw away his shield, or irritability made him revile someone, or ungenerosity made him fail to help someone with money—what he does is unjust, but not overreaching. But when someone acts from overreaching, in many cases his action accords with none of these vices—certainly not all of them; but it still accords with some type of wickedness, since we blame him, and [in particular] it accords with injustice. Hence there is another type of injustice that is a part of the whole, and a way of being unjust that is a part of the whole that is contrary to law.

Further, if A commits adultery for profit and makes a profit, but B commits adultery because of his appetite, and spends money on it to his own loss, B seems intemperate rather than overreaching, but A seems unjust, not intemperate. Clearly, then, this is because A acts to make a profit.

Further, we can refer every other unjust action to some vice—to intemperance if someone committed adultery, to cowardice if he deserted his comrade in the battle-line, to anger if he struck someone. But if he made an [unjust] profit, we can refer it to no other vice except injustice.

It is evident, then, that there is another type of injustice, special injustice, apart from injustice as a whole, and that it is synonymous with injustice as a whole, since the definition is in the same genus. For both have their area of competence in relation to another, but special injustice is concerned with honor or wealth or safety (or whatever single name will include all these), and aims at the pleasure that results from making a profit, whereas the concern of injustice as a whole is whatever concerns the excellent person.

Clearly, then, there is more than one type of justice, and there is another type besides [the type that is] the whole of virtue; but we must still grasp what it is, and what sort of thing it is.

The unjust is divided into the lawless and the unfair, and the just into the lawful and the fair. The injustice previously described, then, is concerned with the lawless. But the unfair is not the same as the lawless; it is related to it as part to whole, since whatever is unfair is lawless, but not everything lawless is unfair. Hence also the unfair type of injustice and the unfair way of being unjust are not the same as the lawless type, but differ as parts from wholes. For unfair injustice is a part of the whole of injustice, and, similarly, fair justice is a part of the whole of justice. Hence we must describe special as well as general justice and injustice, and equally this way of being just or unjust.

Let us, then, set aside the type of justice and injustice that accords with the whole of virtue, justice being the exercise of the whole of virtue, and injustice of the whole of vice, in relation to another. And it is evident how we must distinguish the way of being just or unjust that accords with this type of justice and injustice. For most lawful actions, we might say,

---

* Bias of Priene (who lived in the sixth century BCE) was one of the Seven Sages—a group of seventh- and sixth-century Greek politicians and philosophers renowned in later ages for their practical wisdom.

are those produced by virtue as a whole; for the law prescribes living in accord with each virtue, and forbids living in accord with each vice. Moreover, the actions producing the whole of virtue are the lawful actions that the laws prescribe for education promoting the common good. We must wait till later, however, to determine whether the education that makes an individual an unqualifiedly good man is a task for political science or for another science; for, presumably, being a good man is not the same as being every sort of good citizen.

Special justice, however, and the corresponding way of being just have one species that is found in the distribution of honors or wealth or anything else that can be divided among members of a community who share in a political system; for here it is possible for one member to have a share equal or unequal to another's.* A second species concerns rectification in transactions.

This second species has two parts, since one sort of transaction is voluntary, and one involuntary. Voluntary transactions (for instance, selling, buying, lending, pledging, renting, depositing, hiring out) are so called because their principle is voluntary. Among involuntary transactions some are secret (for instance, theft, adultery, poisoning, pimping, slave-deception, murder by treachery, false witness), whereas others involve force (for instance, imprisonment, murder, plunder, mutilation, slander, insult).

3 [Justice in Distribution]

Since the unjust person is unfair, and what is unjust is unfair, there is clearly an intermediate between the unfair [extremes]. This is the fair; for in any action where too much and too little are possible, the fair [amount] is also possible. And so, if the unjust is unfair, the just is fair (*ison*), as seems true to everyone even without argument. And since the equal (*ison*) [and fair] is intermediate, the just is some sort of intermediate.

Since the equal involves at least two things [equal to each other], it follows that the just must be intermediate and equal, and related to something, and for some people. Insofar as it is intermediate, it must be between too much and too little; insofar as it is equal, it involves two things; and insofar as it is just, it is just for some people. Hence the just requires four things at least; the people for whom it is just are two, and the [equal] things involved are two.

Equality for the people involved will be the same as for the things involved, since [in a just arrangement] the relation between the people will be the same as the relation between the things involved. For if the people involved are not equal, they will not [justly] receive equal shares; indeed, whenever equals receive unequal shares, or unequals equal shares, in a distribution, that is the source of quarrels and accusations.

This is also clear from considering what accords with worth. For all agree that the just in distributions must accord with some sort of worth, but what they call worth is not the same; supporters of democracy say it is free citizenship, some supporters of oligarchy say it is wealth, others good birth, while supporters of aristocracy say it is virtue.

Hence the just [since it requires equal shares for equal people] is in some way proportionate. For proportion is special to number as a whole, not only to numbers consisting of [abstract] units,† since it is equality of ratios and requires at least four terms. Now divided proportion clearly requires four terms. But so does continuous proportion,‡ since here we use one term as two, and mention it twice. If, for instance, line A is to line B as B is to C, B is mentioned twice; and so if B is introduced twice, the terms in the proportion will be four.

The just also requires at least four terms, with the same ratio [between the pairs], since the people [A and B] and the items [C and D] involved are divided in the same way. Term C, then, is to term D as A is to B, and, taking them alternately, B is to D as A is to C. Hence there will also be the same relation of whole

---

* The Greek words *anisos* and *isos*, translated here as "unequal" and "equal," have a wider meaning than their English equivalents. In particular, they can also be rendered as "unfair" and "fair."

† The contrast here is, roughly, between numbers considered as mathematical entities and numbers of *things*—between *the number two* and *two apples*, for example.

‡ An example of "divided proportion" would be A : B = C : D. An example of "continuous proportion" would be A : B = B : C. (Note that Aristotle uses the terms "discrete" and "continuous" in a way unrelated to their meanings in modern mathematics.)

[A and C] to whole [B and D];* this is the relation in which the distribution pairs them, and it pairs them justly if this is how they are combined.

Hence the combination of term A with C and of B with D is the just in distribution, and this way of being just is intermediate, whereas the unjust is contrary to the proportionate. For the proportionate is intermediate, and the just is proportionate.

This is the sort of proportion that mathematicians call geometrical, since in geometrical proportion the relation of whole to whole is the same as the relation of each [part] to each [part]. But this proportion [involved in justice] is not continuous, since there is no single term for both the person and the item. The just, then, is the proportionate, and the unjust is the counterproportionate. Hence [in an unjust action] one term becomes more and the other less; and this is indeed how it turns out in practice, since the one doing injustice has more of the good, and the victim has less.

With an evil the ratio is reversed, since the lesser evil, compared to the greater, counts as a good; for the lesser evil is more choiceworthy than the greater, what is choiceworthy is good, and what is more choiceworthy is a greater good.

This, then, is the first species of the just.

4 [Justice in Rectification]

The other species is rectificatory, found in transactions both voluntary and involuntary. This way of being just belongs to a different species from the first.

For the just in distribution of common assets will always accord with the proportion mentioned above; for [just] distribution from common funds will also accord with the ratio to one another of different people's deposits. Similarly, the way of being unjust that is opposed to this way of being just is what is counterproportionate.

The just in transactions, by contrast, though it is a sort of equality (and the unjust a sort of inequality), accords with numerical proportion,† not with the [geometrical] proportion of the other species. For here it does not matter if a decent person has taken from a base person, or a base person from a decent person, or if a decent or a base person has committed adultery. Rather, the law looks only at differences in the harm [inflicted], and treats the people involved as equals, if one does injustice while the other suffers it, and one has done the harm while the other has suffered it.

And so the judge tries to restore this unjust situation to equality, since it is unequal. For [not only when one steals from another but] also when one is wounded and the other wounds him, or one kills and the other is killed, the action and the suffering are unequally divided [with profit for the offender and loss for the victim]; and the judge tries to restore the [profit and] loss to a position of equality, by subtraction from [the offender's] profit.

For in such cases, stating it without qualification, we speak of profit for the attacker who wounded his victim, for instance, even if that is not the proper word for some cases; and we speak of loss for the victim who suffers the wound. At any rate, when what was suffered has been measured, one part is called the [victim's] loss, and the other the [offender's] profit. Hence the equal is intermediate between more and less. Profit and loss are more and less in contrary ways, since more good and less evil is profit, and the contrary is loss. The intermediate area between [profit and loss], we have found, is the equal, which we say is just. Hence the just in rectification is the intermediate between loss and profit.

That is why parties to a dispute resort to a judge, and an appeal to a judge is an appeal to the just; for the judge is intended to be a sort of living embodiment of the just. Moreover, they seek the judge as an

---

*   Suppose that A and B are people, and C and D are goods. The idea Aristotle expresses here is that if the ratios of A to B and C to D are the same, then the ratios of A to C and B to D will be the same, and therefore the ratio of (A + C) to (B + D) will be the same as that of A to B. In other words, the goods will be divided according to the same ratio as the difference in merit between the people.

†   A numerical proportion is, actually, not so much what we would call a "proportion" at all, but a series in a particular sort of mathematical progression. In such a series, the first term is larger than the second by the same amount by which the third term is larger than the fourth (and so on); thus, $A - B = C - D$. For example, the series 8, 6, 4, 2 would be an arithmetical proportion, since $8 - 6 = 4 - 2$. Aristotle calls this "a sort of equality" because in an arithmetical proportion the sum of the extremes is equal to the sum of the means, i.e., $A + D = B + C$.

intermediary, and in some cities* they actually call a judge a "mediator," assuming that if they are awarded an intermediate amount, the award will be just. If, then, the judge is an intermediary, the just is in some way intermediate.

The judge restores equality, as though a line [AB] had been cut into unequal parts [AC and CB], and he removed from the larger part [AC] the amount [DC] by which it exceeds the half [AD] of the line [AB], and added this amount [DC] to the smaller part [CB]. And when the whole [AB] has been halved [into AD and DB], then they say that each person has what is properly his own, when he has got an equal share.

The equal [in this case] is intermediate, by numerical proportion, between the larger [AC] and the smaller line [CB]. This is also why it is called just (*dikaion*), because it is a bisection (*dicha*), as though we said bisected (*dichaion*), and the judge (*dikastes*) is a bisector (*dichastes*).† For when [the same amount] is subtracted from one of two equal things and added to the other, then the one part exceeds the other by the two parts; for if a part had been subtracted from the one, but not added to the other, the larger part would have exceeded the smaller by just one part. Hence the larger part exceeds the intermediate by one part, and the intermediate from which [a part] was subtracted [exceeds the smaller] by one part.

In this way, then, we will recognize what we must subtract from the one who has more and add to the one who has less [to restore equality]; for to the one who has less we must add the amount by which the intermediate exceeds what he has, and from the greatest amount [held by the one who has more] we must subtract the amount by which it exceeds the intermediate. Let lines AA′, BB′, and CC′ be equal; let AE be subtracted from AA′ and CD‡ be added to CC′, so that the whole line DCC′ will exceed the line EA′ by the parts CD and CF [where CF equals AE]; it follows that DCC′ exceeds BB′ by CD.

These names "loss" and "profit" are derived from voluntary exchange. For having more than one's own share is called making a profit, and having less than what one had at the beginning is called suffering a loss, in buying and selling, for instance, and in other transactions permitted by law. And when people get neither more nor less, but precisely what belongs to them, they say they have their own share and make neither a loss nor a profit. Hence the just is intermediate between a certain kind of loss and profit, since it is having the equal amount both before and after [the transaction].

5 [Justice in Exchange]

Some people, however, think reciprocity§ is also just without qualification. This was the Pythagoreans'¶ view, since their definition stated without qualification that what is just is reciprocity with another.

The truth is that reciprocity suits neither distributive nor rectificatory justice, though people take even Rhadamanthys** [primitive] conception of justice to describe rectificatory justice: "If he suffered what he did, upright justice would be done." For in many cases reciprocity conflicts [with rectificatory justice]. If, for instance, a ruling official [exercising his office] wounded someone else, he must not be wounded in retaliation, but if someone wounded a ruling official, he must not only be wounded but also receive corrective treatment. Moreover, the voluntary or involuntary character of the action makes a great difference.

In communities for exchange, however, this way of being just, reciprocity that is proportionate rather than equal, holds people together; for a city is maintained by proportionate reciprocity. For people seek to return either evil for evil, since otherwise [their condition] seems to be slavery, or good for good, since otherwise there is no exchange; and they are maintained [in a community] by exchange. Indeed, that is why they

---

*   Such as Larissa (eastern Greece) or Abydos (on the Dardanelles Strait).

†   This is not the actual etymology of these words (Aristotle was mistaken if he thought it was).

‡   For the example to work, CD must be equal in length to AE. Aristotle would have used a diagram to make this clear.

§   The Greek term—*antipeponthos*—literally means "suffering in return for one's action."

¶   The followers of Pythagoras (c. 570–495 BCE), a philosopher who believed in reincarnation and defended the view that all of reality could be understood in numerical terms (*harmonia*).

**   A mythical king of the Minoans, said to be the son of Zeus and Europa. He was famous for his uncompromising sense of justice and as a reward he was made immortal and transported to Hades, the Greek afterworld, where he judges the souls of the dead. The quotation on the next line is probably from Hesiod.

make a temple of the Graces* prominent, so that there will be a return of benefits received. For this is what is special to grace;† when someone has been gracious to us, we must do a service for him in return, and also ourselves take the lead in being gracious again.

It is diagonal combination that produces proportionate exchange. Let A be a builder, B a shoemaker, C a house, D a shoe. The builder must receive the shoemaker's product from him, and give him the builder's own product in return. If, then, first of all, proportionate equality is found, and, next, reciprocity is also achieved, the proportionate return will be reached. Otherwise it is not equal, and the exchange will not be maintained, since the product of one may well be superior to the product of the other. These products, then, must be equalized.

This is true of the other crafts also; for they would have been destroyed unless the producer produced the same thing, of the same quantity and quality as the thing affected underwent. For no community [for exchange] is formed from two doctors. It is formed from a doctor and a farmer, and, in general, from people who are different and unequal and who must be equalized.

This is why all items for exchange must be comparable in some way. Currency came along to do exactly this, and in a way it becomes an intermediate, since it measures everything, and so measures excess and deficiency—[for instance,] how many shoes are equal to a house. Hence, as builder is to shoemaker, so must the number of shoes be to a house; for if this does not happen, there will be no exchange and no community. But proportionate equality will not be reached unless they are equal in some way. Everything, then, must be measured by some one measure, as we said before.

In reality, this measure is need, which holds everything together; for if people needed nothing, or needed things to different extents, there would be either no exchange or not the same exchange. And currency has become a sort of pledge of need, by convention; in fact it has its name (*nomisma*) because it is not by nature, but by the current law (*nomos*), and it is within our power to alter it and to make it useless.

Reciprocity will be secured, then, when things are equalized, so that the shoemaker's product is to the farmer's as the farmer is to the shoemaker. However, they must be introduced into the figure of proportion not when they have already exchanged and one extreme has both excesses, but when they still have their own; in that way they will be equals and members of a community, because this sort of equality can be produced in them. Let A be a farmer, C food, B a shoemaker, and D his product that has been equalized; if this sort of reciprocity were not possible, there would be no community.

Now clearly need holds [a community] together as a single unit, since people with no need of each other, both of them or either one, do not exchange, as they exchange whenever another requires what one has oneself, such as wine, when they allow the export of corn. This, then, must be equalized.

If an item is not required at the moment, currency serves to guarantee us a future exchange, guaranteeing that the item will be there for us if we need it; for it must be there for us to take if we pay. Now the same thing happens to currency [as other goods], and it does not always count for the same; still, it tends to be more stable. Hence everything must have a price; for in that way there will always be exchange, and then there will be community.

Currency, then, by making things commensurate‡ as a measure does, equalizes them; for there would be no community without exchange, no exchange without equality, no equality without commensuration. And so, though things so different cannot become commensurate in reality, they can become commensurate enough in relation to our needs.

Hence there must be some single unit fixed [as current] by a stipulation. This is why it is called currency; for this makes everything commensurate, since everything is measured by currency. Let A, for instance, be a house, B ten minae,§ C a bed. A is half of B if a house is worth five minae or equal to them; and C, the bed, is a tenth of B. It is clear, then, how many beds are equal to one house—five. This is clearly how exchange

---

* The three goddesses of joy, charm, and beauty.
† *Charis*, Greek for "grace," also suggests the notions of "gratitude" and "favor."
‡ Equivalent, comparable.
§ A unit of currency. One mina was worth 100 ancient drachmae.

was before there was currency; for it does not matter whether a house is exchanged for five beds or for the currency for which five beds are exchanged.

We have now said what it is that is unjust and just. And now that we have defined them, it is clear that doing justice is intermediate between doing injustice and suffering injustice, since doing injustice is having too much and suffering injustice is having too little.

Justice is a mean, not as the other virtues are, but because it is about an intermediate condition, whereas injustice is about the extremes. Justice is the virtue in accord with which the just person is said to do what is just in accord with his decision, distributing good things and bad, both between himself and others and between others. He does not award too much of what is choiceworthy to himself and too little to his neighbor (and the reverse with what is harmful), but awards what is proportionately equal; and he does the same in distributing between others.

Injustice, on the other hand, is related [in the same way] to the unjust. What is unjust is disproportionate excess and deficiency in what is beneficial or harmful; hence injustice is excess and deficiency because it concerns excess and deficiency. The unjust person awards himself an excess of what is beneficial, [considered] without qualification, and a deficiency of what is harmful, and, speaking as a whole, he acts similarly [in distributions between] others, but deviates from proportion in either direction. In an unjust action getting too little good is suffering injustice, and getting too much is doing injustice.

So much, then, for the nature of justice and the nature of injustice, and similarly for just and unjust in general. ■

Suggestions for Critical Reflection

1. Aristotle seems to suggest the law does (or at least, should) forbid any behavior that conflicts with the virtues—that a good system of law prescribes general justice. Is Aristotle right about this? For example, should the laws of the state attempt to ensure that I am exactly as generous, even-tempered, courageous, friendly, witty, truthful (and so on) as I ought to be?

2. Do you think people can behave unjustly even if they are not motivated by greed (*pleonexia*)? If so, can Aristotle take account of this, or is it a problem for his view of justice? Do you think he is entirely consistent throughout this reading in his view that injustice is always connected to *pleonexia*?

3. How adequate is Aristotle's account of distributive justice? If Aristotle is mainly thinking of the fairness of the distribution of goods *by the state*, can his theory of distributive justice work for other forms of distribution (e.g., by a parent to her children, or an employer to her staff)? Are all fair ways of dividing things up connected to the *worth* or *merit* of those receiving shares, as Aristotle seems to think? If so, should more worthy people get a bigger share of *every* good—more money, more food, more respect, and so on—than their less worthy counterparts?

4. How adequately can Aristotle's account of distributive justice deal with cases of goods that cannot be shared (such as, say, a political office like the Presidency of the United States)? Do cases like this cause problems for his theory?

5. Aristotle points out that people disagree about the sort of merit that is relevant to distributive justice: "supporters of democracy say it is free citizenship, some supporters of oligarchy say it is wealth, others good birth, while supporters of aristocracy say it is virtue." What does Aristotle have to say about the *proper* kind of merit? Do you think he has a view on this? If more than one kind of merit is relevant, does this cause problems for Aristotle's account of distributive justice?

6. How adequate is Aristotle's account of rectificatory justice? For example, is it always possible to take from the offender what has been stolen and restore it to the victim? (What about, for example, cases of adultery or murder?) Is it even *sufficient* merely to restore the situation to the previous status quo? For example, is it an adequate response to theft merely to require the thief to return exactly what has been stolen (no more and no less)?

7. How adequate is Aristotle's account of justice in exchange? How close to modern economic theory

is Aristotle's analysis? (For example, how does modern economics square with Aristotle's view of justice as a kind of *character trait*?)

8. What is the relationship between justice in exchange and the other two kinds of justice Aristotle deals with? Why do you think Aristotle announces there are *two* kinds of justice and then, apparently, describes three?

9. Does Aristotle have a theory of *criminal* justice (i.e., of just punishment for crimes)? If so, which of the three types of justice does it belong to? If not, then *why* do you think Aristotle neglects this sphere of justice?

10. How does Aristotle's account of the virtue of "particular justice" fit in with his general account of virtue (as presented in the selection from *Nicomachean Ethics* in the Ethical Theory section of this volume)? For example, is the virtue of justice really a mean between two vices?

THOMAS HOBBES

FROM *Leviathan*

Who Was Thomas Hobbes?

Thomas Hobbes was born, prematurely, in 1588* in the village of Westport near the small town of Malmesbury, in the southern English county of Wiltshire. Though several relatives had grown wealthy in the family's cloth-making business, Hobbes's father was a poor, ill-educated country clergyman, who frequently ran into trouble with the church authorities for disobedience and volatility. Young Thomas was apparently a studious, unhealthy, rather melancholy boy, who loved music. Because of his black hair, he was nicknamed "Crow" by his schoolfellows. When Hobbes was 16, his father's long-running feud with a nearby vicar, whom he had publicly slandered as "a knave† and an arrant knave and a drunken knave," came to a head when (probably drunk) he encountered his enemy in the churchyard at Malmesbury and set about him with his fists. Any act of violence in a church or churchyard was an excommunicable offense at that time, and laying hands on a clergyman was an even more serious crime, subject to corporal punishment and imprisonment. Hobbes's father was forced to flee. It is not known whether Thomas ever again saw his father, who died "in obscurity beyond London."

By the time of his father's disappearance, however, young Hobbes had already been plucked out of his family situation and sent off to Oxford (an education paid for by his uncle Francis, a prosperous glover). There, Hobbes attended Magdalen Hall, one of the poorer foundations at

Oxford and one which was renowned for its religious Puritanism.‡ He does not seem to have been impressed by the quality of the education he received. Later in life he was dismissive of the Aristotelian logic and metaphysics he was taught and claimed that, at the time, he was more interested in reading about explorations of newly discovered lands and poring over maps of the world and the stars, than in studying traditional philosophy.

As soon as Hobbes completed his BA, in 1608, he was lucky enough to be offered a job as tutor to the eldest son of William Cavendish, a rich and powerful Derbyshire landowner who owned the great stately home at Chatsworth (and who became the first Earl of Devonshire in 1618). Cavendish's son, also called William, was only a few years younger than Hobbes himself, and Hobbes's position quickly became that of a servant, secretary, and friend, rather than tutor. In 1614, Hobbes and Cavendish toured France and Italy, where they both learned Italian and encountered some of the currents of Italian intellectual thought, including the fiercely anti-Papal writings of several Venetian authors.

William Cavendish succeeded his father as the Earl of Devonshire in 1626, but died of disease just two years later. Hobbes, now 40 years old, signed on as tutor to the son of another rich landowner, Sir Gervase Clifton. During this period, he accompanied his charge on another trip to the continent (France and Switzerland), and it was in Geneva that he picked up a copy of Euclid's *Elements* and fell in love with its method of deductive

---

*   This was the year that the Catholic monarch of Spain, Philip II, dispatched a massive fleet of ships—the Armada—to invade Protestant England. Hobbes later wrote, in an autobiographical poem, that "hereupon it was my mother dear/ Did bring forth twins at once, both me and fear," and used to joke that this explained his timid nature. (In the event, however, the Armada was decisively defeated in the English Channel before it could rendezvous with the Spanish invasion force waiting in the Spanish Netherlands, an area comprising modern Belgium, Luxembourg, and part of northern France.) See Thomas Hobbes, *Verse Autobiography* (1670), lines 27–28. This poem is reprinted in the Curley edition of *Leviathan* (Hackett, 1994), liv–lxiv.

†   A well-known out-and-out dishonest person.

‡   The Puritans were a group of English Protestants who regarded the Protestant Reformation under Elizabeth I (1558–1603) as incomplete. Influenced by Protestant teachings from continental Europe, such as Calvinism, they advocated strict religious discipline and simplification of the ceremonies and creeds of the Church of England.

reasoning. A contemporary biographer wrote of the incident:

> Being in a gentleman's library, Euclid's *Elements* lay open, and 'twas the 47th Prop. of Book I. He read the proposition. "By G—," said he (he would now and then swear, by way of emphasis), "this is impossible!" So he reads the demonstration of it, which referred him back to such a proposition; which proposition he read. That referred him back to another, which he also read. And so on, until at last he was demonstratively convinced of that truth. This made him in love with geometry.*

After his return to England, Hobbes agreed to re-enter the service of the widowed countess of Devonshire as tutor to her 13-year-old son, the third earl. The 1630s were important years for Hobbes's intellectual development. His secure, and relatively undemanding, position allowed him time both to develop the main outlines of his political philosophy and also to pursue his interest in science (especially optics). His connection to a great noble house also gave him contacts with other intellectuals clustered around noble patrons, such as the mathematicians and scientists supported by the Earl of Newcastle, and the theologians, lawyers, and poets associated with the Viscount Falkland.

In 1634, Hobbes embarked on another European tour with his pupil, and spent over a year living in Paris where he met French scientists and mathematicians—and especially the influential and well-connected Marin Mersenne—and became finally and fully gripped by the intellectual excitement of the age. "The extreme pleasure I take in study overcomes in me all other appetites," he wrote at this time in a letter.† By 1636, when Hobbes had returned to England, he was devoting as much of his energies as possible to philosophical and scientific work:

the third earl turned 18 in 1637, so—although Hobbes remained in his service—he was no longer needed as a tutor and his time was largely his own.

His earliest surviving work is a treatise on the science of optics, in part of which Hobbes attacks Descartes's *Discourse on the Method* (published in 1637). Hobbes accused Descartes of inconsistency and of not taking seriously enough his own mechanistic physics. Since perception is caused entirely by physical motions or pressures, then the mind—that which does the perceiving—must also be a physical object, capable of being affected by motion, Hobbes argued.‡ Hobbes, therefore, in his very earliest philosophical writing rejected the dualism of matter and spirit in favor of a purely mechanical view of the world.

Hobbes's philosophical work was pushed in a different direction at the end of the 1630s, as political events unfolded in England. As the country moved towards civil war, during the final years of the so-called personal rule of King Charles I,§ there was an intense public debate about the degree of absoluteness of the power of the sovereign. The main issue was whether there were any limits to the power of the king at all. It was recognized that the monarch could exceed his normal powers during exceptional circumstances—but the king, himself, claimed to be the judge of which circumstances were exceptional, and this essentially allowed him to exceed his "normal" powers whenever he chose. In 1640, after the Scots invaded and occupied northern England, the King recalled Parliament to grant him extra taxes to raise an army. They refused, and what became known as the "Short Parliament" was abruptly dissolved. In the same year, Hobbes wrote and circulated an unabashedly pro-royalist work called *The Elements of Law*, which attempted to justify the nature and extent of sovereign power from philosophical first principles. By the end of that year, facing a backlash from anti-royalist parliamen-

---

* John Aubrey, *Brief Lives, Chiefly of Contemporaries, Set Down by John Aubrey, Between the Years 1669 & 1696*, Vol. 1, ed. A. Clark (Oxford University Press, 1898), 387.

† Thomas Hobbes, Letter 21 in Vol. 4 of *The Clarendon Edition of the Works of Thomas Hobbes*, ed. H. Warender, et al. (Oxford University Press, 1983).

‡ "Since vision is formally and really nothing but motion, it follows that that which sees is also formally and strictly speaking nothing other than that which is moved; for nothing other than a body ... can be moved." (Thomas Hobbes, "Tractatus opticus: prima edizione integrale," ed. F. Alessio, *Revista Critica di Storia dela Filosofia* 18 (1963): 147–88. This translation is by Noel Malcolm, p. 207.)

§ In 1629, after a series of clashes with Parliament, Charles dissolved the legislative body permanently and began an 11-year period of ruling alone, as an absolute monarch.

tarians as tensions grew, Hobbes called in all his investments and left England for Paris.

In Paris, Hobbes was quickly reabsorbed into the intellectual life of the great city, and his reputation was established by the 1642 publication of *De Cive*, a remodeled version of *The Elements of Law*. After this, Hobbes returned to the study of scientific philosophy and theology, and spent several years working on a substantial book on logic, metaphysics, and physics, which was eventually published in 1655 as *De Corpore*. However, his work was frequently interrupted, once by a serious illness from which he nearly died (in 1647), and repeatedly by visitors from England, including royalist exiles from the English Civil War (which had erupted in 1642 and dragged on until 1648). In 1646, Hobbes was made mathematical tutor to the young Prince Charles, now in exile in Paris. This turned Hobbes's thoughts back to politics, and—secretively and rapidly—he completed the major work *Leviathan* between the autumn of 1649 and the spring of 1651.

By this time, Hobbes was keen to return to England. The war had been won by the Parliamentarians (Charles I was beheaded in 1649, the monarchy and House of Lords abolished, and a Commonwealth, led by Oliver Cromwell, set up) and *Leviathan*—which Hobbes took care to ensure was published in London—was partly intended to ease his passage back home. Hobbes did not abandon, or even substantially modify, the central arguments of his earlier, royalist writings, but in *Leviathan* he does emphasize that his project is to justify *political authority* generally (and not necessarily just that of a monarch). He also discusses extensively the question—which at that time was of vital interest to the former aristocratic supporters of the old king—of when it is legitimate to shift allegiance from one ruler to another. Hobbes later said he had written *Leviathan* on behalf of "those many and faithful servants and subjects of His Majesty," who had fought on the royalist side and lost, and who were now in the position of negotiating with the new Parliamentary rulers for their old lands and titles. "They that had done their utmost endeavor to perform their obligation to the King, had done all that they could be obliged unto; and were consequently at liberty to seek the safety of their lives and livelihood wheresover, and without treachery."

Hobbes probably did not expect his work to cause offense among the court-in-exile of the young Charles II in Paris,* and he presented a hand-written copy to the king in 1651. However, because he denied that kings ruled by a divine right handed down directly from God, Hobbes was perceived as turning against the monarchy. Furthermore, the attack on organized religion, and especially Catholicism, that *Leviathan* contained provoked fury among Charles's courtiers. Hobbes was banned from the court, and shortly afterwards the French clergy attempted to have him arrested; Hobbes quickly fled back to England.

There he settled back into the employ of the Earl of Devonshire, and resumed a quiet bachelor life of light secretarial work and intellectual discussion. However, the notoriety of *Leviathan* slowly grew, and—because of its bitter attacks on religion and the universities—Hobbes made enemies of many influential groups. For example, when the Royal Society was formed in 1660, Hobbes was pointedly *not* invited to become a member, partly because his fellow exponents of the new "mechanical philosophy" were highly wary of being associated with atheism and reacted by violently attacking Hobbes's supposedly "atheistic" new world-view. Throughout the 1660s and 1670s, Hobbes and his works were denounced from pulpits all over England for what was said to be his godlessness and denial of objective moral values. There were even rumors that Hobbes—also sometimes known as the "Beast of Malmesbury"—was to be charged for heresy (which could, even then, have resulted in his being burned at the stake, though the last people to be executed for heresy in England died in 1612). In contrast with the general public vilification Hobbes faced in his own country, in France and Holland his reputation was soaring and (after the death of acclaimed scientist Pierre Gassendi in 1655) he was widely regarded by French scientists and men of letters as the greatest living philosopher.

Hobbes, though now well into old age (and suffering severely from Parkinson's disease), continued to write prolifically, including several public defenses of *Leviathan*, several treatises on mathematics, a debate with Robert Boyle about the experimental evidence for vacuums, a short book on six problems in physics, a controversial critical church history in Latin verse, translations

---

* Charles II was eventually restored to the throne, by a vote of Parliament, in 1660.

of Homer's *Iliad* and *Odyssey* into English verse, and a history of the English civil war entitled *Behemoth*. When Hobbes died, shortly after suffering a severe stroke in December 1679, he was 91 years old.

What Was Hobbes's Overall Philosophical Project?

Hobbes thought of himself as primarily a scientist. Not only was he interested in what we would, today, think of as science (optics, physics, geometry), he was also concerned to place the study of human beings—especially psychology, ethics, and politics—on what he considered a *scientific* footing. Hobbes was deeply conscious that he was living during a period of intellectual revolution—a time when the old Aristotelian assumptions were being stripped away by the new mechanical and mathematical science which Hobbes enthusiastically endorsed—as well as during an era of political and religious revolution. He wanted to play a significant role in both these movements.

Since Hobbes considered himself a scientist, his view of what *constitutes* science is particularly significant. Hobbes's scheme of the sciences changes somewhat throughout his writings, but its most stable core looks something like this. The most fundamental science is what Hobbes (like Aristotle) called "first philosophy," and it consists in "universal definitions"—of *body, motion, time, place, cause*, and so on—and their logical consequences. Thus the most basic kind of science, for Hobbes, is more purely rational than it is experimental. After first philosophy, comes geometry, which (for Hobbes) was the science of the simple motions of bodies. For example, Hobbes rejected the view that geometry is the study of abstract objects and their relations, but instead insisted that it concerns itself with the movements of concrete objects in real space. The next step in the ladder of the sciences is mechanics, which investigates the more complex motions due to whole bodies working together, and this is followed by physics, the study of the invisible motions of the parts of bodies (including the effects on the human senses of the motions of external bodies). Then comes moral philosophy, which Hobbes thought of as primarily the investigation of passion and volition, which he considered the internal effects of sensation on the human mind. Finally, civil philosophy—the science of politics—formulates the laws of conduct that

will ensure peace and self-preservation for communities of creatures with our particular internal psychological constitution.

A central—and at the time infamous—plank of Hobbes's scientific world-view was his unrelenting *materialism*. According to the new "mechanical" philosophy which had caught Hobbes up in its sweep across the thinkers of Europe, all physical phenomena are ultimately to be explained in terms of the motions and interactions of large numbers of tiny, material bodies. Hobbes enthusiastically accepted this view, and was one of the earliest thinkers to extend it to phenomena his peers generally did not think of as "physical." In particular, Hobbes declared that *mental* phenomena ought to be just as susceptible to mechanical explanation as anything else in nature. For Hobbes, then, the natural world did not contain both matter and spirit (minds): it was entirely made up of material bodies, and human beings were to be viewed as nothing more than very complex material objects, like sophisticated robots or automata.

Along similar lines, Hobbes was very skeptical of claims to religious knowledge, and this was one among several reasons why he devoted so much energy to attacks on the authority of the church. According to Hobbes's theory of language, words have meaning only if they express thoughts, and thoughts are nothing more than the residue in our minds of sensations produced by the action of external objects upon our bodies. Since God is supposed to be an infinite, transcendent being, beyond our powers to perceive, Hobbes—although it is not at all clear that he was actually an atheist—was led to assert we can have no meaningful thoughts about God, and thus can say nothing positive about him. Furthermore, according to Hobbes's materialism, the notion of an "incorporeal substance" is simply incoherent, and so, if God exists at all, he must exist as a *material* body (which Hobbes claimed, in fact, to believe).

Like Descartes, Hobbes saw himself as developing the foundations for a completely new and radical philosophy which was to decisively change the way his contemporaries saw the world. Furthermore, Hobbes did not see moral and political philosophy as a purely intellectual exercise. He firmly believed the great and tragic upheaval of the English Civil War was directly caused by the promulgation of false and dangerous moral ideas, and could have been avoided by proper appreciation of the moral truth. In *Leviathan*, then, Hobbes's project was to place social and political philosophy on a *scientific* foundation for the first time (and he thought doing so would be of immense service to humanity). His model for this was geometry: he begins with a sequence of axiomatic definitions—such as "justice," "obligation," "right of nature," and "law of nature"—and then tries to show that his philosophical results are rationally derivable from these basic assumptions. His goal was to derive and prove universal political laws—rather like the laws of physics—from which infallible judgments about particular cases can be made.*

What Is the Structure of This Reading?

Leviathan is divided into four parts: "Of Man," which deals primarily with human psychology and the state of nature; "Of Commonwealth," which discusses the formation of political states and the powers of their sovereigns; "Of a Christian Commonwealth," which examines the relationship between secular and religious law; and "Of the Kingdom of Darkness," which is a vitriolic attack on certain kinds of organized religion, and especially Catholicism. The excerpts given here come from Parts I and II.

First, there is a sequence of three chapters which come nearly at the end of Part I. In these Hobbes describes the unhappy "state of nature" for human beings and argues that several (nineteen, of which the first five are included in this excerpt) moral "laws of nature" or "theorems" arise as "convenient articles of peace upon which men may be drawn to agreement." Then we jump to the first two chapters of "Of Commonwealth," in which Hobbes discusses how political states arise and argues that state sovereigns are entitled to almost absolute power over their subjects.

Some Useful Background Information

1. *Leviathan* was published just 40 years after the first "King James" English translation of the Bible; hence Hobbes's writing style, dating from the same period, is what we might think of today as "biblical."

This makes Hobbes all the more interesting to read, but can impose something of a barrier for modern audiences. Some words in the reading might be unfamiliar or used in an unfamiliar or archaic way (footnotes are provided throughout to assist the modern reader).

2. The fundamental political problem for Hobbes, and the issue *Leviathan* primarily sets out to address, was the following: How can any political system unambiguously and indisputably determine the answer to the question What is the law? How can universally, uncontroversially acceptable rules of conduct by which the citizens of a state must lead their public lives be determined? A precondition, Hobbes thought, was for there to be only a single source of law, and for that source to be absolute in the sense that whatever the legislator declared as law was law. Any other kind of political system, Hobbes believed, would descend inevitably into factionalism, insecurity, and civil war.

3. Hobbes was quite explicit in rejecting the Aristotelian view of human nature which had been passed down to his day. For Aristotle, human beings are naturally social animals, our natural situation is as active members of a political community, and our highest good is the sort of happiness, or flourishing, for which our biological species is best suited. Furthermore, according to Aristotle, there is a natural hierarchy among human beings, with some people being inherently more noble than others. These inequalities are not created by society, on the Aristotelian picture, but ideally should be mirrored in the social order.

For Hobbes, by contrast, human beings are *not* naturally social animals, and furthermore there is no single conception of happiness tied to the human 'essence.' Instead, according to Hobbes, human happiness is a matter of the continual satisfaction of desires or appetites, and since individual human beings differ in their particular desires, so too will what makes people happy. Because people's desires often come into conflict—especially when several people compete for the same scarce

---

* On the other hand, it is important to note that, unlike physics, politics is a *normative* science. It does not simply describe what people do do, but in some sense prescribes what they *ought* to do. In this respect, Hobbes's political science resembles modern economics more than mathematics or experimental science.

resource, such as land, money, or honor—human beings are naturally *anti*-social. Furthermore, even when civil society has been established, according to Hobbes, most of its citizens will not, and should not, be active participants in political life, but will simply lead private lives, out of the public sphere, within the constraints of their obedience to the commands of the sovereign. Finally, it was Hobbes's view that human beings, in the state of nature, are in a state of radical equality, where no one is substantially any better (or worse) than anyone else; similarly, in civil society, although there will be gradations of honor among men, everyone is fundamentally equal under the sovereign.

4. Like Aristotle, however, Hobbes sees justice, and morality generally, as applying to character traits—what Hobbes calls "manners"—rather than primarily to states of affairs or types of action. For Hobbes, moral virtues are those habits which it is rational for all people to praise; that is, they are those dispositions which contribute to the preservation, not merely of the individual, but of everyone in the community by contributing to peace and stable society.

Some Common Misconceptions

1. When Hobbes talks about "the state of nature" he is referring *neither* to a particular historical period in human history (such as the age of hunter-gatherers) *nor* to a mere theoretical possibility (a time that never actually occurred). What Hobbes has in mind is any situation, at any time or place, where there is no effective government capable of imposing order on the local population. Thus primitive or prehistoric societies may (or may not) be in the state of nature; but so may modern societies locked in a civil war, destroyed by conflict with other countries, or simply experiencing a constitutional crisis. Likewise, the international community of nations (then, as now) is in a state of nature, lacking any overarching world government capable of determining and enforcing international law. (Hence, as he points out in the text, when Hobbes describes the state of nature as being "a condition of war" he does not mean it will necessarily involve constant fighting and bloodshed, but rather that no one can feel *secure* against the threat of force.)

2. Hobbes is not the "immoralist" he is sometimes taken to be. Far from arguing *against* the existence of universal moral principles, Hobbes is concerned to *combat* the kind of moral relativism which holds that all laws, including moral laws, are mere matters of arbitrary human convention. Hobbes adopts the assumption of the moral skeptic that the only fundamental, universal moral principle is self-interest, but he then argues that, from the skeptic's *own assumption*, certain "natural" laws of justice follow deductively. In this way, he tries to show there can be laws without a lawgiver: moral principles based, not in divine or human command, but in human nature itself. (On the other hand, Hobbes does stress, we are bound by these laws only if we can be sure others will obey them too—that is, on the whole, only once we have agreed to form a civil society. To that extent, at least, the principles of justice remain, for Hobbes, a matter of convention, that is, a societal arrangement for the purpose of mutual advantage.)

3. A mainspring of Hobbes's political philosophy is the claim that human beings seek their own self-preservation. There is textual evidence that Hobbes saw this desire for self-preservation not as merely a non-rational desire, even one which all human beings naturally share, but as actually being a *primary goal of reason*. That is, one of the dictates *of rationality*, for Hobbes, is that we should take all measures necessary for our self-preservation, and so the ethical laws Hobbes generates out of this principle are not merely *hypothetical* commands ("Do this if you care more about your self-preservation than anything else") but are dictates that all rational creatures should recognize as binding.

4. Though Hobbes is, legitimately, often said to be rather pessimistic about human nature, this can be overstated. His view, essentially, is not that *everyone* is selfish, but that *enough* people are fundamentally selfish that it would be unwise to construct a civil society on the assumption that people are generally benevolent. According to Hobbes, children are born concerned only with themselves and, though they can learn to care for others, this can be brought about only with proper moral education. Unfortunately, he believed, not very many children are actually brought up in this

way, and so most of the citizens of a commonwealth will, in fact, care primarily for themselves
and their families and not be much moved by the
interests of strangers.

5. Hobbes did not think that people *in fact* always
act to preserve themselves: his claim is not that
people always behave in a way which is optimal in
avoiding hardship or death for themselves—on the
contrary, Hobbes was convinced that people are
often rash and vainglorious and prone to irrational quarrels—but that it is always *reasonable*
or *rational* for people to seek self-preservation,
and furthermore that this fact is so universally
recognized by human beings that it is capable of
serving as a solid basis for civil society. (Contrary
to popular belief, then, Hobbes is not quite what
is technically called a "psychological egoist":
someone who believes that all people, as a matter
of psychological necessity, always act only in their
own self-interest.)

6. Although Hobbes is frequently thought of as a
social contract theorist, he actually does not see
the foundation of the state as involving a contract
or covenant between *all* members of that society,
but instead as a kind of *free gift* by the citizens
to their sovereign. That is, people in the state of
nature (covenant together to) freely turn over their
right of nature to a sovereign power, in the hope
that this sovereign will protect them and allow
them to live in greater security. (Importantly, this
means the sovereign cannot *break a covenant* if
they fail to protect their subjects, though they do
come to be bound by the law of nature prohibiting

ingratitude, and so must "endeavour that he which
giveth [a gift] have no reasonable cause to repent
him of his good will.")

7. Hobbes thought that his new political science
could conclusively demonstrate that all states
need a sovereign (an absolute dispenser of law).
He did not, however, insist that this sovereign must
be a *monarch*; he was quite ready to recognize
that a republic, led by an assembly of senators
for example, could be an equally effective form of
government.

How Important and Influential Is This Passage?

Hobbes's *Leviathan* is arguably the most important work
of political philosophy in English before the twentieth
century, even though the work's *conclusions* have been
widely rejected from Hobbes's day to this. The project of
justifying and delimiting the extent of the state's power
over its subjects, without appeal to such supernatural
mechanisms as the divine right of kings, is an immensely
important one, and it can be said that Hobbes gave this
question its first great answer in modern times. The selections reprinted here include several themes for which
Hobbes is most notorious: the doctrine that life in a state
of nature is "solitary, poor, nasty, brutish, and short"; the
attempt to ground universal principles of justice in the
essential selfishness of human nature; the notion that
the institution of a political state consists in a kind of
"contract" between its members; and the claim that the
power of a sovereign is absolute.

FROM *Leviathan**

PART I: OF MAN

Chapter XIII: Of the Natural Condition of Mankind as Concerning Their Felicity and Misery

Nature hath made men so equal in the faculties of body and mind as that, though there be found one man sometimes manifestly stronger in body or of quicker mind than another, yet when all is reckoned together the difference between man and man is not so considerable as that one man can thereupon claim to himself any benefit to which another may not pretend† as well as he. For as to the strength of body, the weakest has strength enough to kill the strongest, either by secret machination‡ or by confederacy§ with others that are in the same danger with himself.

And as to the faculties of the mind—setting aside the arts grounded upon words, and especially that skill of proceeding upon general and infallible rules, called science, which very few have and but in few things, as being not a native faculty born with us, nor attained, as prudence, while we look after somewhat else—I find yet a greater equality amongst men than that of strength. For prudence is but experience, which equal time equally bestows on all men in those things they equally apply themselves unto. That which may perhaps make such equality incredible is but a vain conceit of one's own wisdom, which almost all men think they have in a greater degree than the vulgar;¶

that is, than all men but themselves, and a few others, whom by fame, or for concurring with themselves, they approve. For such is the nature of men that howsoever they may acknowledge many others to be more witty, or more eloquent, or more learned, yet they will hardly believe there be many so wise as themselves; for they see their own wit** at hand, and other men's at a distance. But this proveth rather that men are in that point equal, than unequal. For there is not ordinarily a greater sign of the equal distribution of anything than that every man is contented with his share.

From this equality of ability ariseth equality of hope in the attaining of our ends. And therefore if any two men desire the same thing, which nevertheless they cannot both enjoy, they become enemies; and in the way to their end†† (which is principally their own conservation, and sometimes their delectation‡‡ only) endeavour to destroy or subdue one another. And from hence it comes to pass that where an invader hath no more to fear than another man's single power, if one plant, sow, build, or possess a convenient seat,§§ others may probably be expected to come prepared with forces united to dispossess and deprive him, not only of the fruit of his labour, but also of his life or liberty. And the invader again is in the like danger of another.

And from this diffidence¶¶ of one another, there is no way for any man to secure himself so*** reasonable

---

*   *Leviathan* was first published, in London, in 1651; the excerpts reprinted here are from that edition (with modernized spelling, and partly modernized punctuation). As well as his English version, Hobbes also prepared an edition in Latin (much of which was probably written before the English version), first published in Amsterdam in 1681.

†   Lay claim to or profess (not necessarily deceitfully).

‡   Plotting or scheming.

§   An alliance or league for joint action or mutual support.

¶   Ordinary people.

**   Intelligence.

††   Goal, desire.

‡‡   Delight, pleasure.

§§   An attractive dwelling place.

¶¶   Distrust (as opposed to the more modern sense, timidity).

***   As.

as anticipation;* that is, by force, or wiles, to master the persons of all men he can so long till he see no other power great enough to endanger him: and this is no more than his own conservation requireth, and is generally allowed. Also, because there be some that, taking pleasure in contemplating their own power in the acts of conquest, which they pursue farther than their security requires, if others (that otherwise would be glad to be at ease within modest bounds) should not by invasion increase their power, they would not be able, long time, by standing only on their defence, to subsist. And by consequence, such augmentation of dominion over men being necessary to a man's conservation, it ought to be allowed him.

Again, men have no pleasure (but on the contrary a great deal of grief) in keeping company† where there is no power able to overawe‡ them all. For every man looketh that his companion should value him at the same rate he sets upon himself, and upon all signs of contempt or undervaluing naturally endeavours, as far as he dares (which amongst them that have no common power to keep them in quiet is far enough to make them destroy each other), to extort a greater value from his contemners,§ by damage; and from others, by the example.

So that in the nature of man, we find three principal causes of quarrel. First, competition; secondly, diffidence; thirdly, glory.

The first maketh men invade for gain; the second, for safety; and the third, for reputation. The first use violence, to make themselves masters of other men's persons, wives, children, and cattle; the second, to defend them; the third, for trifles, as a word, a smile, a different opinion, and any other sign of undervalue, either direct in their persons or by reflection in their kindred, their friends, their nation, their profession, or their name.

Hereby it is manifest that during the time men live without a common power to keep them all in awe,¶ they are in that condition which is called war; and such a war as is of every man against every man. For war consisteth not in battle only, or the act of fighting, but in a tract of time, wherein the will to contend by battle is sufficiently known: and therefore the notion of *time* is to be considered in the nature of war, as it is in the nature of weather. For as the nature of foul weather lieth not in a shower or two of rain, but in an inclination thereto of many days together: so the nature of war consisteth not in actual fighting, but in the known disposition thereto during all the time there is no assurance to the contrary. All other time is peace.

Whatsoever therefore is consequent to** a time of war, where every man is enemy to every man, the same consequent to the time wherein men live without other security than what their own strength and their own invention shall furnish them withal. In such condition there is no place for industry,†† because the fruit thereof is uncertain: and consequently no culture of the earth;‡‡ no navigation, nor use of the commodities that may be imported by sea; no commodious§§ building; no instruments of moving and removing such things as require much force; no knowledge of the face of the earth; no account of time; no arts; no letters; no society; and which is worst of all, continual fear, and danger of violent death; and the life of man, solitary, poor, nasty, brutish, and short.

… To this war of every man against every man, this also is consequent; that nothing can be unjust. The notions of right and wrong, justice and injustice, have there no place. Where there is no common power, there is no law; where no law, no injustice. Force and fraud are in war the two cardinal virtues. Justice and injustice are none of the faculties neither of the body nor mind. If they were, they might be in a man that were alone in

---

* To prevent someone's action by acting first.
† Spending time with other people.
‡ To restrain by fear.
§ People who treat others with contempt or scorn.
¶ Fear
** The result of, caused by.
†† Diligent, energetic work.
‡‡ Farming.
§§ Comfortable, pleasant.

the world, as well as* his senses and passions. They are qualities that relate to men in society, not in solitude. It is consequent also to the same condition that there be no propriety,† no dominion, no *mine* and *thine* distinct; but only that to be every man's that he can get, and for so long as he can keep it. And thus much for the ill condition which man by mere nature is actually placed in; though with a possibility to come out of it, consisting partly in the passions, partly in his reason.

The passions that incline men to peace are: fear of death; desire of such things as are necessary to commodious living; and a hope by their industry to obtain them. And reason suggesteth convenient articles of peace‡ upon which men may be drawn to agreement. These articles are they which otherwise are called the laws of nature, whereof I shall speak more particularly in the two following chapters.

Chapter XIV: Of the First and Second Natural Laws, and of Contracts

The *right of nature*, which writers commonly call *jus naturale*, is the liberty each man hath to use his own power as he will himself for the preservation of his own nature; that is to say, of his own life; and consequently, of doing anything which, in his own judgement and reason, he shall conceive to be the aptest means thereunto.

By *liberty* is understood, according to the proper signification of the word, the absence of external impediments; which impediments may oft take away part of a man's power to do what he would, but cannot hinder him from using the power left him according as his judgement and reason shall dictate to him.

A *law of nature*, *lex naturalis*, is a precept, or general rule, found out by reason, by which a man is forbidden to do that which is destructive of his life, or taketh away the means of preserving the same, and to omit that by which he thinketh it may be best preserved. For though they that speak of this subject use to confound§ *jus* and *lex*, *right* and *law*, yet they ought

to be distinguished, because *right* consisteth in liberty to do, or to forbear; whereas *law* determineth and bindeth to one of them: so that law and right differ as much as obligation and liberty, which in one and the same matter are inconsistent.

And because the condition of man (as hath been declared in the precedent chapter) is a condition of war of every one against every one, in which case every one is governed by his own reason, and there is nothing he can make use of that may not be a help unto him in preserving his life against his enemies; it followeth that in such a condition every man has a right to every thing, even to one another's body. And therefore, as long as this natural right of every man to every thing endureth, there can be no security to any man, how strong or wise soever he be, of living out the time which nature ordinarily alloweth men to live.¶ And consequently it is a precept, or general rule of reason: *that every man ought to endeavour peace, as far as he has hope of obtaining it; and when he cannot obtain it, that he may seek and use all helps and advantages of war.* The first branch of which rule containeth the first and fundamental law of nature, which is: *to seek peace and follow it.* The second, the sum of the right of nature, which is: *by all means we can to defend ourselves.*

From this fundamental law of nature, by which men are commanded to endeavour peace, is derived this second law: *that a man be willing, when others are so too, as far forth as for peace and defence of himself he shall think it necessary, to lay down** this right to all things; and be contented with so much liberty against other men as he would allow other men against himself.* For as long as every man holdeth this right, of doing anything he liketh; so long are all men in the condition of war. But if other men will not lay down their right, as well as he, then there is no reason for anyone to divest himself of his: for that were to expose himself to prey, which no man is bound to, rather than to dispose himself to peace. This is that law of the Gospel: Whatsoever you require that others should do to you, that do ye to them. And that law of all men, *quod tibi fieri non vis, alteri ne feceris.*††

---

* Just as much as.
† Property, ownership (as opposed to the more modern sense, suitableness).
‡ A peace treaty.
§ Have in the past mixed up or confused (one thing for the other).
¶ That is, people will die young—nobody will be able to live a full natural lifespan.
** To give up.
†† "Do not do to others what you would not want done to yourself."

To *lay down* a man's *right* to anything is to divest himself of the *liberty* of hindering another of the benefit of his own right to the same.* For he that renounceth or passeth away his right giveth not to any other man a right which he had not before, because there is nothing to which every man had not right by nature, but only standeth out of his way that he may enjoy his own original right without hindrance from him, not without hindrance from another. So that the effect which redoundeth to one man by another man's defect of right is but so much diminution of impediments to the use of his own right original.†

Right is laid aside, either by simply renouncing it, or by transferring it to another....

Whensoever a man transferreth his right, or renounceth it, it is either in consideration of some right reciprocally transferred to himself, or for some other good he hopeth for thereby. For it is a voluntary act: and of the voluntary acts of every man, the object is some *good to himself*. And therefore there be some rights which no man can be understood by any words, or other signs, to have abandoned or transferred. As, first, a man cannot lay down the right of resisting them that assault him by force to take away his life, because he cannot be understood to aim thereby at any good to himself. The same may be said of wounds, and chains, and imprisonment, both because there is no benefit consequent to such patience, as there is to the patience of suffering another to be wounded or imprisoned, as also because a man cannot tell when he seeth men proceed against him by violence whether they intend his death or not. And lastly the motive and end for which this renouncing and transferring of right is introduced is nothing else but the security of a man's person, in his life, and in the means of so preserving life as not to be weary of it. And therefore if a man by words, or other signs, seem to despoil‡ himself of the end for which those signs were intended, he is not

to be understood as if he meant it, or that it was his will, but that he was ignorant of how such words and actions were to be interpreted.

The mutual transferring of right is that which men call *contract*....

Chapter XV: Of Other Laws of Nature

From that law of nature by which we are obliged to transfer to another such rights as, being retained, hinder the peace of mankind, there followeth a third; which is this: *that men perform their covenants§ made*; without which covenants are in vain, and but empty words; and the right of all men to all things remaining, we are still in the condition of war.

And in this law of nature consisteth the fountain and original of¶ *justice*. For where no covenant hath preceded, there hath no right been transferred, and every man has right to everything and consequently, no action can be unjust. But when a covenant is made, then to break it is *unjust* and the definition of *injustice* is no other than *the not performance of covenant*. And whatsoever is not unjust is *just*.

But because covenants of mutual trust, where there is a fear of not performance on either part (as hath been said in the former chapter), are invalid, though the original of justice be the making of covenants, yet injustice actually there can be none till the cause of such fear be taken away; which, while men are in the natural condition of war, cannot be done. Therefore before the names of just and unjust can have place, there must be some coercive power to compel men equally** to the performance of their covenants, by the terror of some punishment greater than the benefit they expect by the breach of their covenant, and to make good that propriety which by mutual contract men acquire in recompense of the universal right they abandon: and such power there is none before the

---

* To deprive himself of the liberty of blocking someone else from getting the benefit of his right to the same thing.
† "So that the effect on person A from person B's giving up their right to something is only a reduction in a barrier to the use of person A's already-existing (original) right to that thing."
‡ Rob.
§ Promises, solemn agreements.
¶ The origin of.
** To force all people.

erection of a commonwealth.* And this is also to be gathered out of the ordinary definition of justice in the Schools,† for they say that *justice is the constant will of giving to every man his own*. And therefore where there is no *own*, that is, no propriety, there is no injustice; and where there is no coercive power erected, that is, where there is no commonwealth, there is no propriety, all men having right to all things: therefore where there is no commonwealth, there nothing is unjust. So that the nature of justice consisteth in keeping of valid covenants, but the validity of covenants begins not but with‡ the constitution of a civil power sufficient to compel men to keep them: and then it is also that propriety begins.

The fool hath said in his heart, there is no such thing as justice,§ and sometimes also with his tongue, seriously alleging that: every man's conservation and contentment being committed to his own care, there could be no reason why every man might not do what he thought conduced thereunto: and therefore also to make, or not make, keep, or not keep, covenants was not against reason when it conduced to one's benefit.... This specious reasoning is ... false.

For the question is not of promises mutual, where there is no security of performance on either side, as when there is no civil power erected over the parties promising; for such promises are no covenants: but either where one of the parties has performed already, or where there is a power to make him perform, there is the question whether it be against reason; that is, against the benefit of the other to perform, or not. And I say it is not against reason. For the manifestation whereof we are to consider: first, that when a man doth a thing which, notwithstanding anything can be foreseen and reckoned on, tendeth to his own destruction (howsoever some accident, which he could not expect, arriving may turn it to his benefit); yet such events do not make it reasonably or wisely done. Secondly, that in a condition of war, wherein every man to every man, for want of a common power to keep them all in awe, is an enemy, there is no man can hope by his own strength, or wit, to defend himself from destruction without the help of confederates (where every one expects the same defence by the confederation that any one else does); and therefore he which declares he thinks it reason to deceive those that help him can in reason expect no other means of safety than what can be had from his own single power. He, therefore, that breaketh his covenant, and consequently declareth that he thinks he may with reason do so, cannot be received into any society that unite themselves for peace and defence but by the error of them that receive him; nor when he is received be retained in it without seeing the danger of their error; which errors a man cannot reasonably reckon upon as the means of his security: and therefore if he be left or cast out of society, he perisheth; and if he live in society, it is by the errors of other men, which he could not foresee nor reckon upon, and consequently against the reason of his preservation; and so, as all men that contribute not to his destruction forbear him only out of ignorance of what is good for themselves.

...

Whatsoever is done to a man, conformable to¶ his own will signified to the doer, is not injury to him. For if he that doeth it hath not passed away his original right to do what he please by some antecedent covenant, there is no breach of covenant, and therefore no injury done him. And if he have, then his will to have it done, being signified, is a release of that covenant, and so again there is no injury done him.

Justice of actions is by writers** divided into *commutative* and *distributive*: and the former they say consisteth in proportion arithmetical; the latter in proportion geometrical. Commutative, therefore, they place in the equality of value of the things contracted for; and distributive, in the distribution of equal benefit to men of equal merit. As if it were injustice to sell

---

*   A political unit (such as a state) founded on law and united by explicit or tacit agreement of the people for the common good.

†   The universities or their teachings, the traditional "scholastic" syllabus handed down from the Middle Ages.

‡   Doesn't begin without.

§   A paraphrase from Psalm 14 (and Psalm 53) of the Bible: "The Fool has said in his heart, there is no God."

¶   Consistent with.

** See the selection from Aristotle in this section. A similar distinction would also have been known to Hobbes from Thomas Aquinas's *Summa Theologiae* (the second part of Part II, question 61).

dearer than we buy, or to give more to a man than he merits. The value of all things contracted for is measured by the appetite of the contractors, and therefore the just value is that which they be contented to give. And merit (besides that which is by covenant, where the performance on one part meriteth the performance of the other part, and falls under justice commutative, not distributive) is not due by justice, but is rewarded of grace* only. And therefore this distinction, in the sense wherein it useth to be expounded, is not right. To speak properly, commutative justice is the justice of a contractor; that is, a performance of covenant in buying and selling, hiring and letting to hire, lending and borrowing, exchanging, bartering, and other acts of contract.

And distributive justice, the justice of an arbitrator; that is to say, the act of defining what is just. Wherein, being trusted by them that make him arbitrator, if he perform his trust, he is said to distribute to every man his own: and this is indeed just distribution, and may be called, though improperly, distributive justice, but more properly equity, which also is a law of nature, as shall be shown in due place.

As justice dependeth on antecedent covenant;† so does *gratitude* depend on antecedent grace; that is to say, antecedent free-gift; and is the fourth law of nature, which may be conceived in this form: *that a man which receiveth benefit from another of mere grace endeavour that he which giveth it have no reasonable cause to repent him of his good will.* For no man giveth but with intention of good to himself, because gift is voluntary; and of all voluntary acts, the object is to every man his own good; of which if men see they shall be frustrated, there will be no beginning of benevolence or trust, nor consequently of mutual help, nor of reconciliation of one man to another; and therefore they are to remain still in the condition of war, which is contrary to the first and fundamental law of nature which commandeth men to *seek peace.* The breach of this law is called *ingratitude,* and hath the same relation to grace that injustice hath to obligation by covenant.

A fifth law of nature is *complaisance*;‡ that is to say, *that every man strive to accommodate himself to the rest.* For the understanding whereof we may consider that there is in men's aptness to society a diversity of nature, rising from their diversity of affections, not unlike to that we see in stones brought together for building of an edifice. For as that stone which by the asperity§ and irregularity of figure takes more room from others than itself fills, and for hardness cannot be easily made plain,¶ and thereby hindereth the building, is by the builders cast away as unprofitable and troublesome: so also, a man that by asperity of nature will strive to retain those things which to himself are superfluous, and to others necessary, and for the stubbornness of his passions cannot be corrected, is to be left or cast out of society as cumbersome thereunto. For seeing every man, not only by right, but also by necessity of nature, is supposed to endeavour all he can to obtain that which is necessary for his conservation, he that shall oppose himself against it for things superfluous is guilty of the war that thereupon is to follow, and therefore doth that which is contrary to the fundamental law of nature, which commandeth to *seek peace.* The observers of this law may be called *sociable* (the Latins call them *commodi*); the contrary, *stubborn, insociable, froward,*** intractable.

...

These are the laws of nature, dictating peace, for a means of the conservation of men in multitudes; and which only concern the doctrine of civil society. There be other things tending to the destruction of particular men; as drunkenness, and all other parts of intemperance, which may therefore also be reckoned amongst those things which the law of nature hath forbidden, but are not necessary to be mentioned, nor are pertinent enough to this place.

And though this may seem too subtle a deduction of the laws of nature to be taken notice of by all men, whereof the most part are too busy in getting food, and the rest too negligent to understand; yet to

---

* Something freely given (even though it may not be deserved—that is, something the giver is entitled to either give or withhold, as they choose).
† A prior (already existing) contract.
‡ A desire to please others, affability.
§ Roughness.
¶ Smooth.
** Difficult to deal with, hard to please.

leave all men inexcusable, they have been contracted into one easy sum, intelligible even to the meanest capacity; and that is: *Do not that to another which thou wouldest not have done to thyself*, which showeth him that he has no more to do in learning the laws of nature but, when weighing the actions of other men with his own they seem too heavy, to put them into the other part of the balance, and his own into their place, that his own passions and self-love may add nothing to the weight; and then there is none of these laws of nature that will not appear unto him very reasonable.

The laws of nature oblige *in foro interno*;* that is to say, they bind to a desire they should take place: but *in foro externo*;† that is, to the putting them in act, not always. For he that should be modest and tractable, and perform all he promises in such time and place where no man else should do so, should but make himself a prey to others, and procure his own certain ruin, contrary to the ground of all laws of nature which tend to nature's preservation. And again, he that having sufficient security that others shall observe the same laws towards him, observes them not himself, seeketh not peace, but war, and consequently the destruction of his nature by violence.

And whatsoever laws bind *in foro interno* may be broken, not only by a fact contrary to the law, but also by a fact according to it, in case a man think it contrary. For though his action in this case be according to the law, yet his purpose was against the law; which, where the obligation is *in foro interno*, is a breach.

The laws of nature are immutable and eternal; for injustice, ingratitude, arrogance, pride, iniquity, acception‡ of persons, and the rest can never be made lawful. For it can never be that war shall preserve life, and peace destroy it.

The same laws, because they oblige§ only to a desire and endeavour (I mean an unfeigned and constant endeavour) are easy to be observed. For in that they require nothing but endeavour, he that endeavoureth their performance fulfilleth them; and he that fulfilleth the law is just.

And the science of them is the true and only moral philosophy. For moral philosophy is nothing else but the science of what is *good* and *evil* in the conversation and society of mankind. *Good* and *evil* are names that signify our appetites and aversions, which in different tempers, customs, and doctrines of men are different: and diverse men differ not only in their judgement on the senses of what is pleasant and unpleasant to the taste, smell, hearing, touch, and sight; but also of what is conformable or disagreeable to reason in the actions of common life. Nay, the same man, in diverse times, differs from himself; and one time praiseth, that is, calleth good, what another time he dispraiseth, and calleth evil: from whence arise disputes, controversies, and at last war. And therefore so long as a man is in the condition of mere nature, which is a condition of war, private appetite is the measure of good and evil: and consequently all men agree on this, that peace is good, and therefore also the way or means of peace, which (as I have shown before) are *justice, gratitude, modesty, equity, mercy*, and the rest of the laws of nature, are good; that is to say, *moral virtues*; and their contrary vices, evil. Now the science of virtue and vice is moral philosophy; and therefore the true doctrine of the laws of nature is the true moral philosophy. But the writers of moral philosophy, though they acknowledge the same virtues and vices; yet, not seeing wherein consisted their goodness, nor that they come to be praised as the means of peaceable, sociable, and comfortable living, place them in a mediocrity¶ of passions: as if not the cause, but the degree of daring, made fortitude; or not the cause, but the quantity of a gift, made liberality.

...

---

* In the internal domain (literally, the "inner marketplace")—that is, psychologically or with respect to an individual's conscience or judgment.

† In the external domain—that is, with respect to the social context.

‡ Favoritism, corrupt preference for one person over another.

§ Require (of one)

¶ A moderate amount, a mean (as in Aristotle's moral philosophy).

PART II: OF COMMONWEALTH

Chapter XVII: Of the Causes, Generation, and Definition of a Commonwealth

The final cause, end, or design of men (who naturally love liberty, and dominion over others) in the introduction of that restraint upon themselves, in which we see them live in commonwealths, is the foresight of their own preservation, and of a more contented life thereby; that is to say, of getting themselves out from that miserable condition of war which is necessarily consequent, as hath been shown, to the natural passions of men when there is no visible power to keep them in awe, and tie them by fear of punishment to the performance of their covenants, and observation of those laws of nature set down in the fourteenth and fifteenth chapters.

For the laws of nature—as *justice, equity, modesty, mercy*, and, in sum, *doing to others as we would be done to*—of themselves, without the terror of some power to cause them to be observed, are contrary to our natural passions, that carry us to partiality,* pride, revenge, and the like. And covenants, without the sword, are but words and of no strength to secure a man at all. Therefore, notwithstanding the laws of nature (which every one hath then kept, when he has the will to keep them, when he can do it safely), if there be no power erected, or not great enough for our security, every man will and may lawfully rely on his own strength and art for caution† against all other men. And in all places, where men have lived by small families,‡ to rob and spoil one another has been a trade, and so far from being reputed against the law of nature that the greater spoils they gained, the greater was their honour; and men observed no other laws therein but the laws of honour; that is, to abstain from cruelty, leaving to men their lives and instruments of husbandry. And as small families did then; so now do cities and kingdoms, which are but greater families (for their own security), enlarge their dominions upon all pretences of danger, and fear of invasion, or assistance that may be given to invaders; endeavour as much as they can to subdue or weaken their neighbours by open force, and secret arts, for want of other caution, justly; and are remembered for it in after ages with honour.

Nor is it the joining together of a small number of men that gives them this security; because in small numbers, small additions on the one side or the other make the advantage of strength so great as is sufficient to carry the victory, and therefore gives encouragement to an invasion. The multitude sufficient to confide in for our security is not determined by any certain number, but by comparison with the enemy we fear; and is then sufficient when the odds of the enemy§ is not of so visible and conspicuous moment to determine the event of war, as to move him to attempt.

And be there never so great a multitude; yet if their actions be directed according to their particular judgements, and particular appetites, they can expect thereby no defence, nor protection, neither against a common enemy, nor against the injuries of one another. For being distracted in opinions concerning the best use and application of their strength, they do not help, but hinder one another, and reduce their strength by mutual opposition to nothing: whereby they are easily, not only subdued by a very few that agree together, but also, when there is no common enemy, they make war upon each other for their particular interests. For if we could suppose a great multitude of men to consent in the observation of justice, and other laws of nature, without a common power to keep them all in awe, we might as well suppose all mankind to do the same; and then there neither would be, nor need to be, any civil government or commonwealth at all, because there would be peace without subjection.

Nor is it enough for the security, which men desire should last all the time of their life, that they be governed and directed by one judgement for a limited time; as in one battle, or one war. For though they obtain a victory by their unanimous endeavour against a foreign

---

* Prejudice, bias (probably in favor of oneself).
† Security, confident lack of anxiety.
‡ That is, in no larger organized groups.
§ The ratio of the enemy's strength to that of the defenders'.

enemy, yet afterwards, when either they have no common enemy, or he that by one part is held for an enemy is by another part held for a friend, they must needs by the difference of their interests dissolve, and fall again into a war amongst themselves....

The only way to erect such a common power, as may be able to defend them from the invasion of foreigners, and the injuries of one another, and thereby to secure them in such sort as that by their own industry and by the fruits of the earth they may nourish themselves and live contentedly, is to confer all their power and strength upon one man, or upon one assembly of men, that may reduce all their wills, by plurality of voices, unto one will: which is as much as to say, to appoint one man, or assembly of men, to bear their person;* and every one to own† and acknowledge himself to be author of whatsoever he that so beareth their person shall act, or cause to be acted, in those things which concern the common peace and safety; and therein to submit their wills, every one to his will, and their judgements to his judgement. This is more than consent, or concord; it is a real unity of them all in one and the same person, made by covenant of every man with every man, in such manner as if every man should say to every man: *I authorise and give up my right of governing myself to this man, or to this assembly of men, on this condition; that thou give up, thy right to him, and authorise all his actions in like manner.* This done, the multitude so united in one person is called a *commonwealth*; in Latin, *civitas*. This is the generation of that great *Leviathan*,‡ or rather, to speak more reverently, of that *Mortal God* to which we owe, under the *Immortal God*, our peace and defence. For by this authority, given him by every particular man in the commonwealth, he hath the use of so much power and strength conferred

on him that, by terror thereof, he is enabled to form the wills of them all, to peace at home, and mutual aid against their enemies abroad. And in him consisteth the essence of the commonwealth; which, to define it, is: *one person, of whose acts a great multitude, by mutual covenants one with another, have made themselves every one the author, to the end he may use the strength and means of them all as he shall think expedient for their peace and common defence.*

And he that carryeth this person is called sovereign, and said to have *sovereign power*; and every one besides,§ his subject.

The attaining to this sovereign power is by two ways. One, by natural force: as when a man maketh his children to submit themselves, and their children, to his government, as being able to destroy them if they refuse; or by war subdueth his enemies to his will, giving them their lives on that condition. The other, is when men agree amongst themselves to submit to some man, or assembly of men, voluntarily, on confidence to be protected by him against all others. This latter may be called a political commonwealth, or commonwealth by *institution*; and the former, a commonwealth by *acquisition*. And first, I shall speak of a commonwealth by institution.

Chapter XVIII: Of the Rights of Sovereigns by Institution

A *commonwealth* is said to be *instituted* when a *multitude* of men do agree, and *covenant, every one with every one*, that to whatsoever *man*, or *assembly of men*, shall be given by the major part the *right* to *present* the person of them all, that is to say, to be their *representative*; every

---

*   Act as their representative.

†   Admit, agree.

‡   This is an allusion to the Old Testament book of Job, where Leviathan is described as a fearsome, fire-breathing, many-headed sea monster. Leviathan's symbolic meaning in the Bible is obscure, but it was sometimes associated with the devil by biblical commentators (such as Aquinas). In the book of Revelation, it is written that God's final victory over Leviathan will herald the end of the world. Why Hobbes chose this controversy-inducing label for the state, and even made it the title of his work, is obscure. However, in a later passage (at the end of Chapter XXVIII) Hobbes quotes from Job: "There is nothing on earth to be compared with him. He is made so as not to be afraid. He seeth every high thing below him, and is king of all the children of pride" (Job 41:33–34). Yet, Hobbes points out, Leviathan "is mortal and subject to decay, as all other earthly creatures are, and ... there is that in heaven (though not on earth) that he should stand in fear of, and whose laws he ought to obey."

§   Everyone else.

one, as well* he that *voted for it* as he that *voted against it*, shall *authorize* all the actions and judgements of that man, or assembly of men, in the same manner as if they were his own, to the end to live peaceably amongst themselves, and be protected against other men.

From this institution of a commonwealth are derived all the *rights* and *faculties* of him, or them, on whom the sovereign power is conferred by the consent of the people assembled.

First, because they covenant, it is to be understood they are not obliged by former covenant to anything repugnant hereunto.† And consequently they that have already instituted a commonwealth, being thereby bound by covenant to own the actions and judgements of one, cannot lawfully make a new covenant amongst themselves to be obedient to any other, in anything whatsoever, without his permission. And therefore, they that are subjects to a monarch cannot without his leave cast off monarchy and return to the confusion of a disunited multitude; nor transfer their person from him that beareth it to another man, or other assembly of men: for they are bound, every man to every man, to own and be reputed author of all that he that already is their sovereign shall do and judge fit to be done; so that any one man dissenting, all the rest should break their covenant made to that man, which is injustice: and they have also every man given the sovereignty to him that beareth their person; and therefore if they depose him, they take from him that which is his own, and so again it is injustice....

Secondly, because the right of bearing the person of them all is given to him they make sovereign, by covenant only of one to another, and not of him to any of them, there can happen no breach of covenant on the part of the sovereign; and consequently none of his subjects, by any pretence of forfeiture,‡ can be freed from his subjection. That he which is made sovereign maketh no covenant with his subjects beforehand is manifest; because either he must make it with the whole multitude, as one party to the covenant, or he must make a several§ covenant with every man. With the whole, as one party, it is impossible, because as yet they are not

one person: and if he make so many several covenants as there be men, those covenants after he hath the sovereignty are void; because what act soever can be pretended by any one of them for breach thereof is the act both of himself, and of all the rest, because done in the person and by the right of every one of them in particular. Besides, if any one or more of them pretend a breach of the covenant made by the sovereign at his institution, and others or one other of his subjects, or himself alone, pretend there was no such breach, there is in this case no judge to decide the controversy: it returns therefore to the sword again; and every man recovereth the right of protecting himself by his own strength, contrary to the design they had in the institution. It is therefore in vain to grant sovereignty by way of precedent covenant. The opinion that any monarch receiveth his power by covenant, that is to say, on condition, proceedeth from want of understanding this easy truth: that covenants being but words, and breath, have no force to oblige, contain, constrain, or protect any man, but what it has from the public sword; that is, from the untied hands of that man, or assembly of men, that hath the sovereignty, and whose actions are avouched by them all, and performed by the strength of them all, in him united....

Thirdly, because the major part¶ hath by consenting voices declared a sovereign, he that dissented must now consent with the rest; that is, be contented to avow all the actions he shall do, or else justly be destroyed by the rest. For if he voluntarily entered into the congregation of them that were assembled, he sufficiently declared thereby his will, and therefore tacitly covenanted, to stand to what the major part should ordain: and therefore if he refuse to stand thereto, or make protestation against any of their decrees, he does contrary to his covenant, and therefore unjustly. And whether he be of the congregation or not, and whether his consent be asked or not, he must either submit to their decrees or be left in the condition of war he was in before; wherein he might without injustice be destroyed by any man whatsoever.

Fourthly, because every subject is by this institution author of all the actions and judgements of the

---

* Just as much.
† In conflict with (the present covenant).
‡ Breaking of an agreement.
§ Separate, individual.
¶ The majority.

sovereign instituted, it follows that whatsoever he doth, can be no injury to any of his subjects; nor ought he to be by any of them accused of injustice....

Fifthly, and consequently to that which was said last, no man that hath sovereign power can justly be put to death, or otherwise in any manner by his subjects punished. For seeing every subject is author of the actions of his sovereign, he punisheth another for the actions committed by himself.

And because the end of this institution is the peace and defence of them all, and whosoever has right to the end has right to the means, it belongeth of right to whatsoever man or assembly that hath the sovereignty to be judge both of the means of peace and defence, and also of the hindrances and disturbances of the same; and to do whatsoever he shall think necessary to be done, both beforehand (for the preserving of peace and security, by prevention of discord at home, and hostility from abroad) and when peace and security are lost, for the recovery of the same. And therefore,

Sixthly, it is annexed to the sovereignty to be judge of what opinions and doctrines are averse, and what conducing, to peace; and consequently, on what occasions, how far, and what men are to be trusted withal in speaking to multitudes of people; and who shall examine the doctrines of all books before they be published. For the actions of men proceed from their opinions, and in the well-governing of opinions consisteth the well-governing of men's actions in order to their peace and concord....

Seventhly, is annexed to the sovereignty the whole power of prescribing the rules whereby every man may know what goods he may enjoy, and what actions he may do, without being molested by any of his fellow subjects: and this is it men call *propriety*. For before constitution of sovereign power, as hath already been shown, all men had right to all things, which necessarily causeth war: and therefore this propriety, being necessary to peace, and depending on sovereign power, is the act of that power, in order to the public peace....

Eighthly, is annexed to the sovereignty the right of *judicature*; that is to say, of hearing and deciding all controversies which may arise concerning law, either civil or natural, or concerning fact....

Ninthly, is annexed to the sovereignty the right of making war and peace with other nations and commonwealths; that is to say, of judging when it is for the public good, and how great forces are to be assembled, armed, and paid for that end, and to levy money upon the subjects to defray the expenses thereof....

Tenthly, is annexed to the sovereignty the choosing of all counsellors, ministers, magistrates, and officers, both in peace and war. For seeing the sovereign is charged with the end, which is the common peace and defence, he is understood to have power to use such means as he shall think most fit for his discharge.

Eleventhly, to the sovereign is committed the power of rewarding with riches or honour; and of punishing with corporal or pecuniary punishment,* or with ignominy,† every subject according to the law he hath formerly made; or if there be no law made, according as he shall judge most to conduce to the encouraging of men to serve the commonwealth, or deterring of them from doing disservice to the same.

Lastly, considering what values men are naturally apt to set upon themselves, what respect they look for from others, and how little they value other men; from whence continually arise amongst them, emulation,‡ quarrels, factions, and at last war, to the destroying of one another, and diminution of their strength against a common enemy; it is necessary that there be laws of honour, and a public rate of the worth of such men as have deserved or are able to deserve well of the commonwealth, and that there be force in the hands of some or other to put those laws in execution. But it hath already been shown that not only the whole *militia*, or forces of the commonwealth, but also the judicature of all controversies, is annexed to the sovereignty. To the sovereign therefore it belongeth also to give titles of honour, and to appoint what order of place and dignity each man shall hold, and what signs of respect in public or private meetings they shall give to one another.

These are the rights which make the essence of sovereignty, and which are the marks whereby a man may discern in what man, or assembly of men, the sovereign power is placed and resideth.... ■

---

* Monetary punishment, that is, a fine.
† Shame, public disgrace.
‡ Ambitious or envious rivalry for power or honor.

Suggestions for Critical Reflection

1. Hobbes appears to argue that, in the state of nature, everybody is fundamentally equal in ability and in rights. Is that what he means? If so, is he right about this? If he is, does this mean all *social* inequalities are based on nothing more than convention?

2. Hobbes argues that human beings, in the state of nature, are in a continual state of "war of every one against every one." How good are his arguments for this claim? Are there any real-world examples of groups of people who are in the state of nature (as Hobbes defines it) but *not* at war with each other? If Hobbes incorrectly equates the state of nature with a condition of warfare, how seriously does this affect his subsequent arguments?

3. "By *liberty* is understood, according to the proper signification of the word, the absence of external impediments." Is this a fully adequate definition? Is Hobbes's view of liberty significant for the political theory that he develops? (For example, would someone who took a different view of freedom be happy with Hobbes's view of sovereign power?)

4. At one point, Hobbes suggests injustice is a kind of absurdity or inconsistency, and thus to be unjust is simply to be irrational. Is Hobbes right (in the terms of his own theory)? If so, does this show something about Hobbes's *definition* of injustice? Is injustice really nothing more or less than "*the not performance of covenant*"?

5. "Of the voluntary acts of every man, the object is some *good to himself.*" Is this true? Is it a realistic assumption, or is Hobbes being excessively pessimistic about human nature? (Taken in the wider context of this reading, does it seem that Hobbes means to describe how human beings invariably *do* behave, or to state how people *should* behave if they are being rational? Does the way his claim is understood make a difference to Hobbes's argument?)

6. Hobbes argues that, in the state of nature, there is no justice. If Hobbes is right about this, does it follow that all human beings are *immoral* by nature?

7. Does Hobbes reconcile morality and self-interest? That is, does he successfully show that they are *the same thing*? (Is this, in fact, what he is trying to do?)

8. Hobbes formulates his principles of justice, in part, as a reaction to Aristotle's moral theory. If you have read the previous selection, you might want to think about the differences and similarities between, and the relative merits of, Hobbes and Aristotle.

9. "Whatsoever is done to a man, conformable to his own will signified to the doer, is not injury to him." Does this follow logically from Hobbes's assumptions? If it does, is this a problem for those assumptions?

10. Does Hobbes count the exit from the state of nature into a commonwealth as a contract? Is this (or would this be) contrary to his own views? Since there is no mechanism for enforcing agreements in the state of nature, how can people in that state first contract together to form a commonwealth? How could this first crucial covenant be made *before* there exists a power to enforce covenants?

11. Hobbes argues that, once a commonwealth has been set up, every member of the commonwealth must treat the sovereign's actions as being *their own* actions—must "*authorize* all the actions and judgments of that man, or assembly of men, in the same manner as if they were his own"—even if those actions cause them personal hardship. (So, for example, if the state puts you in prison it is no different than if you had voluntarily locked yourself up.) Does this seem reasonable? Is it a crucial part of Hobbes's political theory, or could he have adopted a weaker position on this point?

12. What view do you think Hobbes would take of the notion of *democratically elected* government? What would be his view of civil disobedience or protest movements?

JOHN STUART MILL

FROM *On Liberty*

For some information on Mill's life and his overall philosophical project, please see the introduction to Mill earlier in this volume.

What Is the Structure of This Reading?

On Liberty is a short five-chapter book, parts of the first, second, and fourth chapters of which are reprinted here. Mill's topic is the extent to which the state, and society in general, ought to have authority over the lives of individuals: the problem of setting limits to society's claims upon the individual, Mill asserts, is "the principal question in human affairs" but, he laments, its solution has not yet been put on a properly rational footing. Mill seeks to address this by formulating "one very simple principle"—sometimes today known as the "harm principle"—that should "govern absolutely the dealings of society with the individual in the way of compulsion and control." After some clarificatory remarks about this principle, Mill argues in defense of it beginning, in Chapter II, with the particular case of liberty of thought and discussion.

Mill's argument for the freedom of thought has three parts. He considers, first, the possibility that the received opinions might be false and the heretical ones true; second, the possibility that the received views are completely true and the heresy false; and lastly, a situation where dogma and heresy both contain only a part of the truth. In each case, Mill argues, allowing complete freedom of thought and discussion provides much greater value than harm to society.

In Chapter III (not included here) Mill discusses the importance of individuality to human well-being, describing it as a valuable component of personal happiness and an essential motor of social progress. In Chapter IV, therefore, he goes on to consider the question of the proper borderline between personal individuality and social authority, and uses his "harm principle" to show how this border should be drawn. The final chapter (not included) describes some illustrative applications of the principle to detailed sample cases, such as trade regulation, liquor taxation, and marriage laws.

Some Common Misconceptions

1. In arguing for the freedom of thought and discussion, Mill asserts we can never be *completely sure* that views which oppose our own, and which we might want to suppress, are not true (and thus we can never be completely sure that our own views are not false). However, he stresses that he does not mean that we should never feel certain of our own views, or that we should never act on them, or even that we should not attempt to persuade others of their truth. Mill is by no means a skeptic about the possibility of human knowledge and certainty. Rather, Mill argues that we should not *force* others to adopt our views—even if we are completely satisfied with their truth—by preventing them from hearing or thinking about alternative positions.

2. In arguing for firm limits on the authority of society over the individual, Mill is not arguing for the kind of a *laissez-faire* system in which everyone is assumed to be fundamentally self-interested, and where individuals are thought to have no moral duties towards their fellow-citizens except those arising from their own self-interest. On the contrary, he claims "[h]uman beings owe to each other help to distinguish the better from the worse, and encouragement to choose the former and avoid the latter," and he thought it was very much society's role to provide opportunities and incentives for self-improvement to its citizens.

   Similarly, Mill is not simply claiming that society should interfere with individuals as little as possible—that, for example, the coercion of individuals by the state is always a bad thing and should be resorted to only when necessary. By contrast, he thinks there is a sphere in which society should not interfere with its members but also a sphere in which it *ought* to do so: individuals do have duties to the other members of the societies of which they are a part, and society has the right to force people to perform those duties.

3. Mill's style of argument in this essay includes (appropriately enough) raising objections to his own position and making them as forcefully as he can, and then responding to them. As you read, take care that you distinguish between Mill's own views and those he presents and then argues against.

How Important and Influential Is This Passage?

Mill's *On Liberty* has been a 'classic' since it was first published. To his great satisfaction, it immediately inspired intense debate between fervent supporters of the views expressed in the book and sharp critics of them, and—though many of the ideas it contains have now become quite familiar—the work is still the focus of substantial controversy today. *On Liberty* is generally considered to be one of the central statements of classical liberalism, and one of the finest defenses of individualism and freedom of thought ever written.

FROM *On Liberty**

Chapter I: Introductory

... A time ... came in the progress of human affairs, when men ceased to think it a necessity of nature that their governors should be an independent power, opposed in interest to themselves. It appeared to them much better that the various magistrates of the State should be their tenants or delegates, revocable at their pleasure. In that way alone, it seemed, could they have complete security that the powers of government would never be abused to their disadvantage. By degrees, this new demand for elective and temporary rulers became the prominent object of the exertions of the popular party, wherever any such party existed; and superseded, to a considerable extent, the previous efforts to limit the power of rulers. As the struggle proceeded for making the ruling power emanate from the periodical choice of the ruled, some persons began to think that too much importance had been attached to the limitation of the power itself. That (it might seem) was a resource against rulers whose interests were habitually opposed to those of the people. What

was now wanted was, that the rulers should be identified with the people; that their interest and will should be the interest and will of the nation. The nation did not need to be protected against its own will. There was no fear of its tyrannizing over itself. Let the rulers be effectually responsible to it, promptly removable by it, and it could afford to trust them with power of which it could itself dictate the use to be made. Their power was but the nation's own power, concentrated, and in a form convenient for exercise....

But, in political and philosophical theories, as well as in persons, success discloses faults and infirmities which failure might have concealed from observation. The notion, that the people have no need to limit their power over themselves, might seem axiomatic, when popular government was a thing only dreamed about, or read of as having existed at some distant period of the past. Neither was that notion necessarily disturbed by such temporary aberrations as those of the French Revolution,† the worst of which were the work of an usurping few, and which, in any case, belonged, not to the permanent working of popular institutions, but to

---

*   *On Liberty* was first published in London in 1859.

†   The French Revolution, which began with the storming of the Bastille prison in 1789, toppled the Bourbon monarchy—King Louis XVI was executed in 1793—but failed to produce a stable form of republican government and, after a period of ruthless extremism known as the Reign of Terror (1793–94), was eventually replaced by Napoleon Bonaparte's imperial reign in 1799.

a sudden and convulsive outbreak against monarchical and aristocratic despotism. In time, however, a democratic republic* came to occupy a large portion of the earth's surface, and made itself felt as one of the most powerful members of the community of nations; and elective and responsible government became subject to the observations and criticisms which wait upon a great existing fact. It was now perceived that such phrases as "self-government," and "the power of the people over themselves," do not express the true state of the case. The "people" who exercise the power, are not always the same people with those over whom it is exercised, and the "self-government" spoken of, is not the government of each by himself, but of each by all the rest. The will of the people, moreover, practically means, the will of the most numerous or the most active *part* of the people; the majority, or those who succeed in making themselves accepted as the majority; the people, consequently, *may* desire to oppress a part of their number; and precautions are as much needed against this, as against any other abuse of power. The limitation, therefore, of the power of government over individuals, loses none of its importance when the holders of power are regularly accountable to the community, that is, to the strongest party therein. This view of things, recommending itself equally to the intelligence of thinkers and to the inclination of those important classes in European society to whose real or supposed interests democracy is adverse, has had no difficulty in establishing itself; and in political speculations "the tyranny of the majority" is now generally included among the evils against which society requires to be on its guard.

Like other tyrannies, the tyranny of the majority was at first, and is still vulgarly,[†] held in dread, chiefly as operating through the acts of the public authorities. But reflecting persons perceived that when society is itself the tyrant—society collectively, over the separate individuals who compose it—its means of tyrannizing are not restricted to the acts which it may do by the hands of its political functionaries. Society can and does execute its own mandates: and if it issues wrong mandates instead of right, or any mandates at all in things with which it ought not to meddle, it practises

a social tyranny more formidable than many kinds of political oppression, since, though not usually upheld by such extreme penalties, it leaves fewer means of escape, penetrating much more deeply into the details of life, and enslaving the soul itself. Protection, therefore, against the tyranny of the magistrate is not enough; there needs protection also against the tyranny of the prevailing opinion and feeling; against the tendency of society to impose, by other means than civil penalties, its own ideas and practices as rules of conduct on those who dissent from them; to fetter the development, and, if possible, prevent the formation, of any individuality not in harmony with its ways, and compel all characters to fashion themselves upon the model of its own. There is a limit to the legitimate interference of collective opinion with individual independence; and to find that limit, and maintain it against encroachment, is as indispensable to a good condition of human affairs, as protection against political despotism.

But though this proposition is not likely to be contested in general terms, the practical question, where to place the limit—how to make the fitting adjustment between individual independence and social control—is a subject on which nearly everything remains to be done. All that makes existence valuable to any one, depends on the enforcement of restraints upon the actions of other people. Some rules of conduct, therefore, must be imposed, by law in the first place, and by opinion on many things which are not fit subjects for the operation of law. What these rules should be, is the principal question in human affairs; but if we except a few of the most obvious cases, it is one of those which least progress has been made in resolving. No two ages, and scarcely any two countries, have decided it alike; and the decision of one age or country is a wonder to another. Yet the people of any given age and country no more suspect any difficulty in it, than if it were a subject on which mankind had always been agreed. The rules which obtain among themselves appear to them self-evident and self-justifying. This all but universal illusion is one of the examples of the magical influence of custom, which is not only, as the proverb says a second nature, but is continually mistaken for the first. The

---

*   The United States of America.

†   Commonly, popularly.

effect of custom, in preventing any misgiving respecting the rules of conduct which mankind impose on one another, is all the more complete because the subject is one on which it is not generally considered necessary that reasons should be given, either by one person to others, or by each to himself. People are accustomed to believe and have been encouraged in the belief by some who aspire to the character of philosophers, that their feelings, on subjects of this nature, are better than reasons, and render reasons unnecessary. The practical principle which guides them to their opinions on the regulation of human conduct, is the feeling in each person's mind that everybody should be required to act as he, and those with whom he sympathizes, would like them to act....

The likings and dislikings of society, or of some powerful portion of it, are thus the main thing which has practically determined the rules laid down for general observance, under the penalties of law or opinion. And in general, those who have been in advance of society in thought and feeling, have left this condition of things unassailed in principle, however they may have come into conflict with it in some of its details. They have occupied themselves rather in inquiring what things society ought to like or dislike, than in questioning whether its likings or dislikings should be a law to individuals. They preferred endeavouring to alter the feelings of mankind on the particular points on which they were themselves heretical, rather than make common cause in defence of freedom, with heretics generally....

The object of this Essay is to assert one very simple principle, as entitled to govern absolutely the dealings of society with the individual in the way of compulsion and control, whether the means used be physical force in the form of legal penalties, or the moral coercion of public opinion. That principle is, that the sole end for which mankind are warranted, individually or collectively in interfering with the liberty of action of any of their number, is self-protection. That the only purpose for which power can be rightfully exercised over any

member of a civilized community, against his will, is to prevent harm to others. His own good, either physical or moral, is not a sufficient warrant. He cannot rightfully be compelled to do or forbear because it will be better for him to do so, because it will make him happier, because, in the opinions of others, to do so would be wise, or even right. These are good reasons for remonstrating* with him, or reasoning with him, or persuading him, or entreating him, but not for compelling him, or visiting him with any evil, in case† he do otherwise. To justify that, the conduct from which it is desired to deter him must be calculated to produce evil to some one else. The only part of the conduct of any one, for which he is amenable to society, is that which concerns others. In the part which merely concerns himself, his independence is, of right, absolute. Over himself, over his own body and mind, the individual is sovereign.

It is, perhaps, hardly necessary to say that this doctrine is meant to apply only to human beings in the maturity of their faculties. We are not speaking of children, or of young persons below the age which the law may fix as that of manhood or womanhood. Those who are still in a state to require being taken care of by others, must be protected against their own actions as well as against external injury. For the same reason, we may leave out of consideration those backward states of society in which the race itself may be considered as in its nonage.‡ The early difficulties in the way of spontaneous progress are so great, that there is seldom any choice of means for overcoming them; and a ruler full of the spirit of improvement is warranted in the use of any expedients that will attain an end, perhaps otherwise unattainable. Despotism is a legitimate mode of government in dealing with barbarians, provided the end be their improvement, and the means justified by actually effecting that end. Liberty, as a principle, has no application to any state of things anterior to the time when mankind have become capable of being improved by free and equal discussion. Until then, there is nothing for them but implicit obedience to an Akbar or a

---

* Forcefully arguing.

† If.

‡ A period of immaturity, being underage.

Charlemagne,* if they are so fortunate as to find one. But as soon as mankind have attained the capacity of being guided to their own improvement by conviction or persuasion (a period long since reached in all nations with whom we need here concern ourselves), compulsion, either in the direct form or in that of pains and penalties for non-compliance, is no longer admissible as a means to their own good, and justifiable only for the security of others.

It is proper to state that I forego any advantage which could be derived to my argument from the idea of abstract right as a thing independent of utility. I regard utility as the ultimate appeal on all ethical questions; but it must be utility in the largest sense, grounded on the permanent interests of man as a progressive being. Those interests, I contend, authorize the subjection of individual spontaneity to external control, only in respect to those actions of each, which concern the interest of other people. If any one does an act hurtful to others, there is a *prima facie*† case for punishing him, by law, or, where legal penalties are not safely applicable, by general disapprobation.‡ There are also many positive acts for the benefit of others, which he may rightfully be compelled to perform; such as, to give evidence in a court of justice; to bear his fair share in the common defence, or in any other joint work necessary to the interest of the society of which he enjoys the protection; and to perform certain acts of individual beneficence, such as saving a fellow-creature's life, or interposing to protect the defenceless against ill-usage, things which whenever it is obviously a man's duty to do, he may rightfully be made responsible to society for not doing. A person may cause evil to others not only by his actions but by his inaction, and in either case he is justly accountable to them for the injury....

But there is a sphere of action in which society, as distinguished from the individual, has, if any, only an indirect interest; comprehending§ all that portion of a person's life and conduct which affects only himself, or, if it also affects others, only with their free, voluntary, and undeceived consent and participation. When I say only himself, I mean directly, and in the first instance: for whatever affects himself, may affect others through himself; and the objection which may be grounded on this contingency, will receive consideration in the sequel. This, then, is the appropriate region of human liberty. It comprises, first, the inward domain of consciousness; demanding liberty of conscience, in the most comprehensive sense; liberty of thought and feeling; absolute freedom of opinion and sentiment on all subjects, practical or speculative, scientific, moral, or theological. The liberty of expressing and publishing opinions may seem to fall under a different principle, since it belongs to that part of the conduct of an individual which concerns other people; but, being almost of as much importance as the liberty of thought itself, and resting in great part on the same reasons, is practically inseparable from it. Secondly, the principle requires liberty of tastes and pursuits; of framing the plan of our life to suit our own character; of doing as we like, subject to such consequences as may follow; without impediment from our fellow-creatures, so long as what we do does not harm them even though they should think our conduct foolish, perverse, or wrong. Thirdly, from this liberty of each individual, follows the liberty, within the same limits, of combination among individuals; freedom to unite, for any purpose not involving harm to others: the persons combining being supposed to be of full age, and not forced or deceived.

No society in which these liberties are not, on the whole, respected, is free, whatever may be its form of government; and none is completely free in which they do not exist absolute and unqualified. The only

---

* Akbar the Great was Mogul emperor of northern India from 1556 to 1605. He is generally considered the founder of the Mogul empire, and was famous for implementing an effective administrative system, imposing religious tolerance, and making his court a center for art and literature. Charlemagne ("Charles the Great") was king of the Franks from 768 to 814. His armies conquered much of central and western Europe—including parts of Spain, Italy, Saxony, Bavaria, Austria, and Hungary—and, in 800, he was anointed the first Holy Roman Emperor by Pope Leo III. Like Akbar, Charlemagne is known for making his court a great center of culture and scholarship, and for imposing an effective legal and administrative structure on his dominions.

† At first sight, on first impression.

‡ Strong (moral) disapproval.

§ Including, covering.

freedom which deserves the name, is that of pursuing our own good in our own way, so long as we do not attempt to deprive others of theirs, or impede their efforts to obtain it. Each is the proper guardian of his own health, whether bodily, or mental or spiritual. Mankind are greater gainers by suffering each other to live as seems good to themselves, than by compelling each to live as seems good to the rest....

Chapter II: Of the Liberty of Thought and Discussion

The time, it is to be hoped, is gone by when any defence would be necessary of the "liberty of the press" as one of the securities against corrupt or tyrannical government. No argument, we may suppose, can now be needed, against permitting a legislature or an executive, not identified in interest with the people, to prescribe opinions to them, and determine what doctrines or what arguments they shall be allowed to hear. This aspect of the question, besides, has been so often and so triumphantly enforced by preceding writers, that it needs not be specially insisted on in this place. Though the law of England, on the subject of the press, is as servile to this day as it was in the time of the Tudors,* there is little danger of its being actually put in force against political discussion, except during some temporary panic, when fear of insurrection drives ministers and judges from their propriety; ... and, speaking generally, it is not, in constitutional countries, to be apprehended that the government, whether completely responsible to the people or not, will often attempt to control the expression of opinion, except when in doing so it makes itself the organ of the general intolerance of the public. Let us suppose, therefore, that the government is entirely at one with the people, and never thinks of exerting any power of coercion unless in agreement with what it conceives to be their voice. But I deny the right of the people to exercise such coercion, either by themselves or by their government. The power itself is illegitimate. The best government has no more title to it than the worst. It is as noxious, or more noxious, when exerted in accordance with public opinion, than when in opposition to it. If all mankind minus one, were of one opinion, and only one person were of the contrary opinion, mankind would be no more justified in silencing that one person, than he, if he had the power, would be justified in silencing mankind. Were an opinion a personal possession of no value except to the owner; if to be obstructed in the enjoyment of it were simply a private injury, it would make some difference whether the injury was inflicted only on a few persons or on many. But the peculiar evil of silencing the expression of an opinion is, that it is robbing the human race; posterity† as well as the existing generation; those who dissent from the opinion, still more than those who hold it. If the opinion is right, they are deprived of the opportunity of exchanging error for truth: if wrong, they lose, what is almost as great a benefit, the clearer perception and livelier impression of truth, produced by its collision with error.

It is necessary to consider separately these two hypotheses, each of which has a distinct branch of the argument corresponding to it. We can never be sure that the opinion we are endeavouring to stifle is a false opinion; and if we were sure, stifling it would be an evil still.

First: the opinion which it is attempted to suppress by authority may possibly be true. Those who desire to suppress it, of course deny its truth; but they are not infallible. They have no authority to decide the question for all mankind, and exclude every other person from the means of judging. To refuse a hearing to an opinion, because they are sure that it is false, is to assume that *their* certainty is the same thing as *absolute* certainty. All silencing of discussion is an assumption of infallibility. Its condemnation may be allowed to rest on this common argument, not the worse for being common.

Unfortunately for the good sense of mankind, the fact of their fallibility is far from carrying the weight in their practical judgment, which is always allowed to it in theory; for while every one well knows himself to be fallible, few think it necessary to take any precautions against their own fallibility, or admit the supposition that any opinion of which they feel very certain, may be one of the examples of the error to which they

---

*   The royal dynasty ruling England from 1485 to 1603 (Henry VII–Elizabeth I).

†   Future generations of people.

acknowledge themselves to be liable. Absolute princes, or others who are accustomed to unlimited deference, usually feel this complete confidence in their own opinions on nearly all subjects. People more happily situated, who sometimes hear their opinions disputed, and are not wholly unused to be set right when they are wrong, place the same unbounded reliance only on such of their opinions as are shared by all who surround them, or to whom they habitually defer: for in proportion to a man's want of confidence in his own solitary judgment, does he usually repose, with implicit trust, on the infallibility of "the world" in general. And the world, to each individual, means the part of it with which he comes in contact; his party, his sect, his church, his class of society: the man may be called, by comparison, almost liberal and large-minded to whom it means anything so comprehensive as his own country or his own age. Nor is his faith in this collective authority at all shaken by his being aware that other ages, countries, sects, churches, classes, and parties have thought, and even now think, the exact reverse. He devolves upon* his own world the responsibility of being in the right against the dissentient worlds of other people; and it never troubles him that mere accident has decided which of these numerous worlds is the object of his reliance, and that the same causes which make him a Churchman in London, would have made him a Buddhist or a Confucian in Pekin.† Yet it is as evident in itself as any amount of argument can make it, that ages are no more infallible than individuals; every age having held many opinions which subsequent ages have deemed not only false but absurd; and it is as certain that many opinions, now general, will be rejected by future ages, as it is that many, once general, are rejected by the present.

The objection likely to be made to this argument, would probably take some such form as the following. There is no greater assumption of infallibility in forbidding the propagation of error, than in any other thing which is done by public authority on its own judgment and responsibility. Judgment is given to men that they may use it. Because it may be used erroneously, are men to be told that they ought not to use it at all? To prohibit what they think pernicious, is not

claiming exemption from error, but fulfilling the duty incumbent on them, although fallible, of acting on their conscientious conviction. If we were never to act on our opinions, because those opinions may be wrong, we should leave all our interests uncared for, and all our duties unperformed. An objection which applies to all conduct can be no valid objection to any conduct in particular. It is the duty of governments, and of individuals, to form the truest opinions they can; to form them carefully, and never impose them upon others unless they are quite sure of being right. But when they are sure (such reasoners may say), it is not conscientiousness but cowardice to shrink from acting on their opinions, and allow doctrines which they honestly think dangerous to the welfare of mankind, either in this life or in another, to be scattered abroad without restraint, because other people, in less enlightened times, have persecuted opinions now believed to be true. Let us take care, it may be said, not to make the same mistake: but governments and nations have made mistakes in other things, which are not denied to be fit subjects for the exercise of authority: they have laid on bad taxes, made unjust wars. Ought we therefore to lay on no taxes, and, under whatever provocation, make no wars? Men, and governments, must act to the best of their ability. There is no such thing as absolute certainty, but there is assurance sufficient for the purposes of human life. We may, and must, assume our opinion to be true for the guidance of our own conduct: and it is assuming no more when we forbid bad men to pervert society by the propagation of opinions which we regard as false and pernicious.

I answer, that it is assuming very much more. There is the greatest difference between presuming an opinion to be true, because, with every opportunity for contesting it, it has not been refuted, and assuming its truth for the purpose of not permitting its refutation. Complete liberty of contradicting and disproving our opinion, is the very condition which justifies us in assuming its truth for purposes of action; and on no other terms can a being with human faculties have any rational assurance of being right.

When we consider either the history of opinion, or the ordinary conduct of human life, to what is it to

---

*   Delegates, transfers to.

†   Today called Beijing, the capital of China.

be ascribed that the one and the other are no worse than they are? Not certainly to the inherent force of the human understanding; for, on any matter not self-evident, there are ninety-nine persons totally incapable of judging of it, for one who is capable; and the capacity of the hundredth person is only comparative; for the majority of the eminent men of every past generation held many opinions now known to be erroneous, and did or approved numerous things which no one will now justify. Why is it, then, that there is on the whole a preponderance* among mankind of rational opinions and rational conduct? If there really is this preponderance—which there must be, unless human affairs are, and have always been, in an almost desperate state—it is owing to a quality of the human mind, the source of everything respectable in man, either as an intellectual or as a moral being, namely, that his errors are corrigible.† He is capable of rectifying his mistakes by discussion and experience. Not by experience alone. There must be discussion, to show how experience is to be interpreted. Wrong opinions and practices gradually yield to fact and argument: but facts and arguments, to produce any effect on the mind, must be brought before it. Very few facts are able to tell their own story, without comments to bring out their meaning. The whole strength and value, then, of human judgment, depending on the one property, that it can be set right when it is wrong, reliance can be placed on it only when the means of setting it right are kept constantly at hand. In the case of any person whose judgment is really deserving of confidence, how has it become so? Because he has kept his mind open to criticism of his opinions and conduct. Because it has been his practice to listen to all that could be said against him; to profit by as much of it as was just, and expound to himself, and upon occasion to others, the fallacy of what was fallacious. Because he has felt, that the only way in which a human being can make some approach to knowing the whole of a subject, is by hearing what can be said about it by persons of every variety of opinion, and studying all modes in

which it can be looked at by every character of mind. No wise man ever acquired his wisdom in any mode but this; nor is it in the nature of human intellect to become wise in any other manner. The steady habit of correcting and completing his own opinion by collating it with those of others, so far from causing doubt and hesitation in carrying it into practice, is the only stable foundation for a just reliance on it: for, being cognizant of all that can, at least obviously, be said against him, and having taken up his position against all gainsayers knowing that he has sought for objections and difficulties, instead of avoiding them, and has shut out no light which can be thrown upon the subject from any quarter—he has a right to think his judgment better than that of any person, or any multitude, who have not gone through a similar process.

... In order more fully to illustrate the mischief of denying a hearing to opinions because we, in our own judgment, have condemned them, it will be desirable to fix down the discussion to a concrete case; and I choose, by preference, the cases which are least favourable to me—in which the argument against freedom of opinion, both on the score of truth and on that of utility, is considered the strongest. Let the opinions impugned be the belief in a God and in a future state,‡ or any of the commonly received doctrines of morality. To fight the battle on such ground, gives a great advantage to an unfair antagonist; since he will be sure to say (and many who have no desire to be unfair will say it internally), Are these the doctrines which you do not deem sufficiently certain to be taken under the protection of law? Is the belief in a God one of the opinions, to feel sure of which, you hold to be assuming infallibility? But I must be permitted to observe, that it is not the feeling sure of a doctrine (be it what it may) which I call an assumption of infallibility. It is the undertaking to decide that question *for others*, without allowing them to hear what can be said on the contrary side. And I denounce and reprobate this pretension§ not the less, if put forth on the side of my most solemn convictions. However positive any one's

---

* Superiority in weight or number.
† Correctable.
‡ An afterlife.
§ Reject this claim (that is, to infallibility).

persuasion may be, not only of the falsity, but of the pernicious* consequences—not only of the pernicious consequences, but (to adopt expressions which I altogether condemn) the immorality and impiety of an opinion; yet if, in pursuance of that private judgment, though backed by the public judgment of his country or his contemporaries, he prevents the opinion from being heard in its defence, he assumes infallibility. And so far from the assumption being less objectionable or less dangerous because the opinion is called immoral or impious, this is the case of all others in which it is most fatal. These are exactly the occasions on which the men of one generation commit those dreadful mistakes which excite the astonishment and horror of posterity. It is among such that we find the instances memorable in history, when the arm of the law has been employed to root out the best men and the noblest doctrines; with deplorable success as to the men, though some of the doctrines have survived to be (as if in mockery) invoked, in defence of similar conduct towards those who dissent from *them*, or from their received interpretation.

... A theory which maintains that truth may justifiably be persecuted because persecution cannot possibly do it any harm, cannot be charged with being intentionally hostile to the reception of new truths; but we cannot commend the generosity of its dealing with the persons to whom mankind are indebted for them. To discover to† the world something which deeply concerns it, and of which it was previously ignorant; to prove to it that it had been mistaken on some vital point of temporal or spiritual interest, is as important a service as a human being can render to his fellow-creatures, and in certain cases, as in those of the early Christians and of the Reformers,‡ those who think with Dr. Johnson§ believe it to have been the most precious gift which could be bestowed on mankind. That the authors of such splendid benefits should be requited by martyrdom; that their reward should be to be dealt with as the vilest of criminals, is not, upon this theory, a deplorable error and misfortune, for which humanity should mourn in sackcloth and ashes, but the normal and justifiable state of things. The propounder of a new truth, according to this doctrine, should stand, as stood, in the legislation of the Locrians,¶ the proposer of a new law, with a halter round his neck, to be instantly tightened if the public assembly did not, on hearing his reasons, then and there adopt his proposition.

People who defend this mode of treating benefactors, can not be supposed to set much value on the benefit; and I believe this view of the subject is mostly confined to the sort of persons who think that new truths may have been desirable once, but that we have had enough of them now.

But, indeed, the dictum that truth always triumphs over persecution, is one of those pleasant falsehoods which men repeat after one another till they pass into commonplaces, but which all experience refutes. History teems with instances of truth put down by persecution. If not suppressed forever, it may be thrown back for centuries. To speak only of religious opinions: the Reformation broke out at least twenty times before Luther,** and was put down. Arnold of Brescia was put down. Fra Dolcino was put down. Savonarola was put down. The Albigeois were put down. The Vaudois were put down. The Lollards were put down. The Hussites were put down.†† Even after the era of

---

* Harmful.

† Expose, reveal to.

‡ Protestant Reformers, such as Martin Luther and John Calvin, who challenged the doctrines and authority of the Catholic Church in the sixteenth century.

§ Mill has earlier mentioned that Johnson—a well-known eighteenth-century writer and lexicographer—said "that the persecutors of Christianity were in the right; that persecution is an ordeal through which truth ought to pass, and always passes successfully" (recorded in James Boswell's *Life of Johnson* [1791], Volume II, entry for May 7, 1773).

¶ Locris was a minor state in ancient Greece, and among the first to adopt a written code of law (in about 660 BCE). Its regulations were severe: in addition to the principle mentioned in the text, it also enshrined the *lex talionis*, the law of retaliation (of taking an eye for an eye, a tooth for a tooth).

** Martin Luther (1483–1546) was a German theologian who initiated the Protestant Reformation in 1517.

†† Arnold of Brescia was executed as a heretic in 1155; Fra Dolcino of Novara was tortured to death in 1307; Savonarola Girolamo was burned to death in 1498. The Albigeois, or Albigenses, tried to establish a church independent of

Luther, wherever persecution was persisted in, it was successful. In Spain, Italy, Flanders, the Austrian empire, Protestantism was rooted out; and, most likely, would have been so in England, had Queen Mary lived, or Queen Elizabeth died. Persecution has always succeeded, save where the heretics were too strong a party to be effectually persecuted. No reasonable person can doubt that Christianity might have been extirpated* in the Roman empire. It spread, and became predominant, because the persecutions were only occasional, lasting but a short time, and separated by long intervals of almost undisturbed propagandism. It is a piece of idle sentimentality that truth, merely as truth, has any inherent power denied to error, of prevailing against the dungeon and the stake. Men are not more zealous for truth than they often are for error, and a sufficient application of legal or even of social penalties will generally succeed in stopping the propagation of either. The real advantage which truth has, consists in this, that when an opinion is true, it may be extinguished once, twice, or many times, but in the course of ages there will generally be found persons to rediscover it, until some one of its reappearances falls on a time when from favourable circumstances it escapes persecution until it has made such head as to withstand all subsequent attempts to suppress it.

It will be said, that we do not now put to death the introducers of new opinions: we are not like our fathers who slew the prophets, we even build sepulchres† to them. It is true we no longer put heretics to death; and the amount of penal infliction which modern feeling would probably tolerate, even against the most obnoxious opinions, is not sufficient to extirpate them. But let us not flatter ourselves that we are yet free from the stain even of legal persecution. Penalties for opinion, or at least for its expression, still exist by law; and their enforcement is not, even in these times, so unexampled as to make it at all incredible that they may some day be revived in full force....

But though we do not now inflict so much evil on those who think differently from us, as it was formerly our custom to do, it may be that we do ourselves as much evil as ever by our treatment of them. Socrates‡ was put to death, but the Socratic philosophy rose like the sun in heaven, and spread its illumination over the whole intellectual firmament. Christians were cast to the lions, but the Christian Church grew up a stately and spreading tree, overtopping the older and less vigorous growths, and stifling them by its shade. Our merely social intolerance, kills no one, roots out no opinions, but induces men to disguise them, or to abstain from any active effort for their diffusion. With us, heretical opinions do not perceptibly gain or even lose, ground in each decade or generation; they never blaze out far and wide, but continue to smoulder in the narrow circles of thinking and studious persons among whom they originate, without ever lighting up the general affairs of mankind with either a true or a deceptive light. And thus is kept up a state of things very satisfactory to some minds, because, without the unpleasant process of fining or imprisoning anybody, it maintains all prevailing opinions outwardly undisturbed, while it does not absolutely interdict§ the exercise of reason by dissentients afflicted with the malady of thought. A convenient plan for having peace in the intellectual world, and keeping all things going on therein very much as they do already. But the price paid for this sort of intellectual pacification, is the sacrifice of the entire moral courage of the human mind. A state of things in which a large portion of the most active and inquiring intellects find it advisable to keep the genuine principles and grounds of their convictions within their own breasts, and attempt, in what they address to the public, to fit as much as

---

Roman Catholicism and were exterminated by the Inquisition in the thirteenth century. The Vaudois, or Waldenses, also attempted to break free of Catholicism in the late twelfth century and, though greatly weakened by the oppression of the Inquisition, survived to join the Calvinist movement in the sixteenth century. The Lollards were followers of John Wycliffe (1320–84) and the Hussites of John Huss (1369–1415). Both movements revolted against the authority of the Church, and both were vigorously suppressed.

* Pulled out by the roots—i.e., thoroughly eliminated.

† Tombs; so churches or structures inside them erected in memory of Jesus' tomb; so, figuratively, to build a sepulcher to someone to demonstrate reverential respect to them.

‡ Fifth-century BCE Athenian philosopher and teacher of Plato.

§ Forbid.

they can of their own conclusions to premises which they have internally renounced, cannot send forth the open, fearless characters, and logical, consistent intellects who once adorned the thinking world. The sort of men who can be looked for under it, are either mere conformers to commonplace, or time-servers* for truth whose arguments on all great subjects are meant for their hearers, and are not those which have convinced themselves. Those who avoid this alternative, do so by narrowing their thoughts and interests to things which can be spoken of without venturing within the region of principles, that is, to small practical matters, which would come right of themselves, if but the minds of mankind were strengthened and enlarged, and which will never be made effectually right until then; while that which would strengthen and enlarge men's minds, free and daring speculation on the highest subjects, is abandoned.

Those in whose eyes this reticence on the part of heretics is no evil, should consider in the first place, that in consequence of it there is never any fair and thorough discussion of heretical opinions; and that such of them as could not stand such a discussion, though they may be prevented from spreading, do not disappear. But it is not the minds of heretics that are deteriorated most, by the ban placed on all inquiry which does not end in the orthodox conclusions. The greatest harm done is to those who are not heretics, and whose whole mental development is cramped, and their reason cowed, by the fear of heresy. Who can compute what the world loses in the multitude of promising intellects combined with timid characters, who dare not follow out any bold, vigorous, independent train of thought, lest it should land them in something which would admit of being considered irreligious or immoral?...

Let us now pass to the second division of the argument, and dismissing the supposition that any of the received opinions may be false, let us assume them to be true, and examine into the worth of the manner in which they are likely to be held, when their truth is not freely and openly canvassed. However unwillingly a person who has a strong opinion may admit the possibility that his opinion may be false, he ought to be moved by the consideration that however true it may be, if it is not fully, frequently, and fearlessly discussed, it will be held as a dead dogma, not a living truth.

There is a class of persons (happily not quite so numerous as formerly) who think it enough if a person assents undoubtingly to what they think true, though he has no knowledge whatever of the grounds of the opinion, and could not make a tenable defence of it against the most superficial objections. Such persons, if they can once get their creed taught from authority, naturally think that no good, and some harm, comes of its being allowed to be questioned. Where their influence prevails, they make it nearly impossible for the received opinion to be rejected wisely and considerately, though it may still be rejected rashly and ignorantly; for to shut out discussion entirely is seldom possible, and when it once gets in, beliefs not grounded on conviction are apt to give way before the slightest semblance of an argument. Waiving, however, this possibility—assuming that the true opinion abides in the mind, but abides as a prejudice, a belief independent of, and proof against, argument—this is not the way in which truth ought to be held by a rational being. This is not knowing the truth. Truth, thus held, is but one superstition the more, accidentally clinging to the words which enunciate a truth.

If the intellect and judgment of mankind ought to be cultivated, a thing which Protestants at least do not deny, on what can these faculties be more appropriately exercised by any one, than on the things which concern him so much that it is considered necessary for him to hold opinions on them? If the cultivation of the understanding consists in one thing more than in another, it is surely in learning the grounds of one's own opinions. Whatever people believe, on subjects on which it is of the first importance to believe rightly, they ought to be able to defend against at least the common objections. But, some one may say, "Let them be *taught* the grounds of their opinions. It does not follow that opinions must be merely parroted because they are never heard controverted.† Persons who learn geometry do not simply commit the theorems to memory, but understand and learn likewise the demonstrations; and it would be absurd to say that

---

* People who, for convenience or self-interest, adopt their views to suit circumstances.

† Opposed, disputed.

they remain ignorant of the grounds of geometrical truths, because they never hear any one deny, and attempt to disprove them." Undoubtedly: and such teaching suffices on a subject like mathematics, where there is nothing at all to be said on the wrong side of the question. The peculiarity of the evidence of mathematical truths is, that all the argument is on one side. There are no objections, and no answers to objections. But on every subject on which difference of opinion is possible, the truth depends on a balance to be struck between two sets of conflicting reasons. Even in natural philosophy,* there is always some other explanation possible of the same facts; some geocentric theory instead of heliocentric,† some phlogiston‡ instead of oxygen; and it has to be shown why that other theory cannot be the true one: and until this is shown and until we know how it is shown, we do not understand the grounds of our opinion. But when we turn to subjects infinitely more complicated, to morals, religion, politics, social relations, and the business of life, three-fourths of the arguments for every disputed opinion consist in dispelling the appearances which favour some opinion different from it. The greatest orator, save one, of antiquity,§ has left it on record that he always studied his adversary's case with as great, if not with still greater, intensity than even his own. What Cicero practised as the means of forensic¶ success, requires to be imitated by all who study any subject in order to arrive at the truth. He who knows only his own side of the case, knows little of that. His reasons may be good, and no one may have been able to refute them. But if he is equally unable to refute the reasons on the opposite side; if he does not so much as know what they are, he has no ground for preferring either opinion. The rational position for him would be suspension of judgment, and unless he contents himself with that, he is either led by authority, or adopts, like the generality of the world, the side to which he feels most inclination. Nor is it enough that he should hear the arguments of adversaries from his own teachers, presented as they state them, and accompanied by what they offer as refutations. This is not the way to do justice to the arguments, or bring them into real contact with his own mind. He must be able to hear them from persons who actually believe them; who defend them in earnest, and do their very utmost for them. He must know them in their most plausible and persuasive form; he must feel the whole force of the difficulty which the true view of the subject has to encounter and dispose of, else he will never really possess himself of the portion of truth which meets and removes that difficulty. Ninety-nine in a hundred of what are called educated men are in this condition, even of those who can argue fluently for their opinions. Their conclusion may be true, but it might be false for anything they know: they have never thrown themselves into the mental position of those who think differently from them, and considered what such persons may have to say; and consequently they do not, in any proper sense of the word, know the doctrine which they themselves profess. They do not know those parts of it which explain and justify the remainder; the considerations which show that a fact which seemingly conflicts with another is reconcilable with it, or that, of two apparently strong reasons, one and not the other ought to be preferred. All that part of the truth which turns the scale, and decides the judgment of a completely informed mind, they are strangers to; nor is it ever really known, but to those who have attended equally and impartially to both sides, and endeavoured to see the reasons of both in the strongest light. So essential is this discipline to a real understanding of moral and human subjects, that if opponents of all important truths do not exist, it is indispensable to imagine them

---

* Science.
† On the geocentric theory, the sun, planets, and other heavenly bodies circle the Earth. According to heliocentric accounts, the planets orbit the Sun.
‡ Phlogiston is a theoretical substance, which turned out not to exist, once thought to be a volatile constituent of all combustible substances, released as flame in combustion. It is now known that combustion is, in general, a chemical interaction with oxygen.
§ The greatest orator of antiquity was said to be Demosthenes, and the second greatest was Cicero.
¶ Relating to debate or argument, especially in a court of law or public discussion.

and supply them with the strongest arguments which the most skilful devil's advocate* can conjure up.

To abate the force of these considerations, an enemy of free discussion may be supposed to say, that there is no necessity for mankind in general to know and understand all that can be said against or for their opinions by philosophers and theologians. That it is not needful for common men to be able to expose all the misstatements or fallacies of an ingenious opponent. That it is enough if there is always somebody capable of answering them, so that nothing likely to mislead uninstructed persons remains unrefuted. That simple minds, having been taught the obvious grounds of the truths inculcated on them, may trust to authority for the rest, and being aware that they have neither knowledge nor talent to resolve every difficulty which can be raised, may repose in the assurance that all those which have been raised have been or can be answered, by those who are specially trained to the task.

Conceding to this view of the subject the utmost that can be claimed for it by those most easily satisfied with the amount of understanding of truth which ought to accompany the belief of it; even so, the argument for free discussion is no way weakened. For even this doctrine acknowledges that mankind ought to have a rational assurance that all objections have been satisfactorily answered; and how are they to be answered if that which requires to be answered is not spoken? or how can the answer be known to be satisfactory, if the objectors have no opportunity of showing that it is unsatisfactory? If not the public, at least the philosophers and theologians who are to resolve the difficulties, must make themselves familiar with those difficulties in their most puzzling form; and this cannot be accomplished unless they are freely stated, and placed in the most advantageous light which they admit of....

If, however, the mischievous† operation of the absence of free discussion, when the received opinions are true, were confined to leaving men ignorant of the grounds of those opinions, it might be thought that this, if an intellectual, is no moral evil, and does not affect the worth of the opinions, regarded in their influence on the character. The fact, however, is, that not only the grounds of the opinion are forgotten in the absence of discussion, but too often the meaning of the opinion itself. The words which convey it, cease to suggest ideas, or suggest only a small portion of those they were originally employed to communicate. Instead of a vivid conception and a living belief, there remain only a few phrases retained by rote; or, if any part, the shell and husk only of the meaning is retained, the finer essence being lost. The great chapter in human history which this fact occupies and fills, cannot be too earnestly studied and meditated on.

It is illustrated in the experience of almost all ethical doctrines and religious creeds. They are all full of meaning and vitality to those who originate them, and to the direct disciples of the originators. Their meaning continues to be felt in undiminished strength, and is perhaps brought out into even fuller consciousness, so long as the struggle lasts to give the doctrine or creed an ascendancy over other creeds. At last it either prevails, and becomes the general opinion, or its progress stops; it keeps possession of the ground it has gained, but ceases to spread further. When either of these results has become apparent, controversy on the subject flags, and gradually dies away. The doctrine has taken its place, if not as a received opinion, as one of the admitted sects or divisions of opinion: those who hold it have generally inherited, not adopted it; and conversion from one of these doctrines to another, being now an exceptional fact, occupies little place in the thoughts of their professors.‡ Instead of being, as at first, constantly on the alert either to defend themselves against the world, or to bring the world over to them, they have subsided into acquiescence, and neither listen, when they can help it, to arguments against their creed, nor trouble dissentients (if there be such) with arguments in its favour. From this time may usually be dated the decline in the living power of the doctrine....

But what! (it may be asked) Is the absence of unanimity an indispensable condition of true knowledge?

---

* Formerly, one who argued in favor of an evil conclusion; later (and here) one who takes a position in order to test the strength of reasons for and against it.

† Causing harm or injury.

‡ I.e., of those who profess—assert—them.

Is it necessary that some part of mankind should persist in error, to enable any to realize the truth? Does a belief cease to be real and vital as soon as it is generally received—and is a proposition never thoroughly understood and felt unless some doubt of it remains? As soon as mankind have unanimously accepted a truth, does the truth perish within them? The highest aim and best result of improved intelligence, it has hitherto been thought, is to unite mankind more and more in the acknowledgment of all important truths: and does the intelligence only last as long as it has not achieved its object? Do the fruits of conquest perish by the very completeness of the victory?

I affirm no such thing. As mankind improve, the number of doctrines which are no longer disputed or doubted will be constantly on the increase: and the well-being of mankind may almost be measured by the number and gravity of the truths which have reached the point of being uncontested. The cessation, on one question after another, of serious controversy, is one of the necessary incidents of the consolidation of opinion; a consolidation as salutary in the case of true opinions, as it is dangerous and noxious when the opinions are erroneous. But though this gradual narrowing of the bounds of diversity of opinion is necessary in both senses of the term, being at once inevitable and indispensable, we are not therefore obliged to conclude that all its consequences must be beneficial. The loss of so important an aid to the intelligent and living apprehension of a truth, as is afforded by the necessity of explaining it to, or defending it against, opponents, though not sufficient to outweigh, is no trifling drawback from, the benefit of its universal recognition. Where this advantage can no longer be had, I confess I should like to see the teachers of mankind endeavouring to provide a substitute for it; some contrivance for making the difficulties of the question as present to the learner's consciousness, as if they were pressed upon him by a dissentient champion, eager for his conversion.

But instead of seeking contrivances for this purpose, they have lost those they formerly had. The Socratic dialectics, so magnificently exemplified in the dialogues of Plato, were a contrivance of this description. They were essentially a negative discussion of the great questions of philosophy and life, directed with consummate skill to the purpose of convincing any one who had merely adopted the commonplaces of received opinion, that he did not understand the subject—that he as yet attached no definite meaning to the doctrines he professed; in order that, becoming aware of his ignorance, he might be put in the way to attain a stable belief, resting on a clear apprehension both of the meaning of doctrines and of their evidence. The school disputations of the Middle Ages had a somewhat similar object. They were intended to make sure that the pupil understood his own opinion, and (by necessary correlation) the opinion opposed to it, and could enforce the grounds of the one and confute those of the other....

It still remains to speak of one of the principal causes which make diversity of opinion advantageous, and will continue to do so until mankind shall have entered a stage of intellectual advancement which at present seems at an incalculable distance. We have hitherto considered only two possibilities: that the received opinion may be false, and some other opinion, consequently, true; or that, the received opinion being true, a conflict with the opposite error is essential to a clear apprehension and deep feeling of its truth. But there is a commoner case than either of these; when the conflicting doctrines, instead of being one true and the other false, share the truth between them; and the nonconforming opinion is needed to supply the remainder of the truth, of which the received doctrine embodies only a part. Popular opinions, on subjects not palpable to sense,* are often true, but seldom or never the whole truth. They are a part of the truth; sometimes a greater, sometimes a smaller part, but exaggerated, distorted, and disjoined from the truths by which they ought to be accompanied and limited. Heretical opinions, on the other hand, are generally some of these suppressed and neglected truths, bursting the bonds which kept them down, and either seeking reconciliation with the truth contained in the common opinion, or fronting† it as enemies, and setting themselves up, with similar exclusiveness, as the whole truth. The latter case is hitherto the most

---

* Not obvious or easily grasped.
† Confronting.

frequent, as, in the human mind, one-sidedness has always been the rule, and many-sidedness the exception. Hence, even in revolutions of opinion, one part of the truth usually sets while another rises. Even progress, which ought to superadd, for the most part only substitutes one partial and incomplete truth for another; improvement consisting chiefly in this, that the new fragment of truth is more wanted, more adapted to the needs of the time, than that which it displaces. Such being the partial character of prevailing opinions, even when resting on a true foundation; every opinion which embodies somewhat of the portion of truth which the common opinion omits, ought to be considered precious, with whatever amount of error and confusion that truth may be blended. No sober judge of human affairs will feel bound to be indignant because those who force on our notice truths which we should otherwise have overlooked, overlook some of those which we see. Rather, he will think that so long as popular truth is one-sided, it is more desirable than otherwise that unpopular truth should have one-sided asserters too; such being usually the most energetic, and the most likely to compel reluctant attention to the fragment of wisdom which they proclaim as if it were the whole....

We have now recognized the necessity to the mental well-being of mankind (on which all their other well-being depends) of freedom of opinion, and freedom of the expression of opinion, on four distinct grounds; which we will now briefly recapitulate.

First, if any opinion is compelled to silence, that opinion may, for aught we can certainly know, be true. To deny this is to assume our own infallibility.

Secondly, though the silenced opinion be an error, it may, and very commonly does, contain a portion of truth; and since the general or prevailing opinion on any object is rarely or never the whole truth, it is only by the collision of adverse opinions that the remainder of the truth has any chance of being supplied.

Thirdly, even if the received opinion be not only true, but the whole truth; unless it is suffered to be, and actually is, vigorously and earnestly contested, it will, by most of those who receive it, be held in the manner of a prejudice, with little comprehension or feeling of its rational grounds. And not only this, but,

fourthly, the meaning of the doctrine itself will be in danger of being lost, or enfeebled, and deprived of its vital effect on the character and conduct: the dogma becoming a mere formal profession, inefficacious for good, but cumbering* the ground, and preventing the growth of any real and heartfelt conviction, from reason or personal experience....

Chapter IV: Of the Limits to the Authority of Society over the Individual

What, then, is the rightful limit to the sovereignty of the individual over himself? Where does the authority of society begin? How much of human life should be assigned to individuality, and how much to society?

Each will receive its proper share, if each has that which more particularly concerns it. To individuality should belong the part of life in which it is chiefly the individual that is interested; to society, the part which chiefly interests society.

Though society is not founded on a contract, and though no good purpose is answered by inventing a contract in order to deduce social obligations from it, every one who receives the protection of society owes a return for the benefit, and the fact of living in society renders it indispensable that each should be bound to observe a certain line of conduct towards the rest. This conduct consists, first, in not injuring the interests of one another; or rather certain interests, which, either by express legal provision or by tacit understanding, ought to be considered as rights; and secondly, in each person's bearing his share (to be fixed on some equitable principle) of the labours and sacrifices incurred for defending the society or its members from injury and molestation. These conditions society is justified in enforcing, at all costs to those who endeavour to withhold fulfilment. Nor is this all that society may do. The acts of an individual may be hurtful to others, or wanting in due consideration for their welfare, without going the length of violating any of their constituted rights. The offender may then be justly punished by opinion, though not by law. As soon as any part of a person's conduct affects prejudicially the interests of others, society has jurisdiction over it, and the question whether the general welfare will or will

---

* Encumbering.

not be promoted by interfering with it, becomes open to discussion. But there is no room for entertaining any such question when a person's conduct affects the interests of no persons besides himself, or needs not affect them unless they like (all the persons concerned being of full age, and the ordinary amount of understanding). In all such cases there should be perfect freedom, legal and social, to do the action and stand the consequences.

It would be a great misunderstanding of this doctrine, to suppose that it is one of selfish indifference, which pretends that human beings have no business with each other's conduct in life, and that they should not concern themselves about the well-doing or well-being of one another, unless their own interest is involved. Instead of any diminution, there is need of a great increase of disinterested exertion to promote the good of others. But disinterested benevolence can find other instruments to persuade people to their good, than whips and scourges, either of the literal or the metaphorical sort. I am the last person to undervalue the self-regarding virtues; they are only second in importance, if even second, to the social. It is equally the business of education to cultivate both. But even education works by conviction and persuasion as well as by compulsion, and it is by the former only that, when the period of education is past, the self-regarding virtues should be inculcated. Human beings owe to each other help to distinguish the better from the worse, and encouragement to choose the former and avoid the latter. They should be forever stimulating each other to increased exercise of their higher faculties, and increased direction of their feelings and aims towards wise instead of foolish, elevating instead of degrading, objects and contemplations. But neither one person, nor any number of persons, is warranted in saying to another human creature of ripe years, that he shall not do with his life for his own benefit what he chooses to do with it. He is the person most interested in his own well-being, the interest which any other person, except in cases of strong personal attachment, can have in it, is trifling, compared with that which he himself has; the interest which society has in him individually (except as to his conduct to others) is fractional, and altogether indirect: while, with respect to

his own feelings and circumstances, the most ordinary man or woman has means of knowledge immeasurably surpassing those that can be possessed by any one else. The interference of society to overrule his judgment and purposes in what only regards himself, must be grounded on general presumptions; which may be altogether wrong, and even if right, are as likely as not to be misapplied to individual cases, by persons no better acquainted with the circumstances of such cases than those are who look at them merely from without. In this department, therefore, of human affairs, Individuality has its proper field of action. In the conduct of human beings towards one another, it is necessary that general rules should for the most part be observed, in order that people may know what they have to expect; but in each person's own concerns, his individual spontaneity is entitled to free exercise. Considerations to aid his judgment, exhortations to strengthen his will, may be offered to him, even obtruded on* him, by others; but he, himself, is the final judge. All errors which he is likely to commit against advice and warning, are far outweighed by the evil of allowing others to constrain him to what they deem his good.

I do not mean that the feelings with which a person is regarded by others, ought not to be in any way affected by his self-regarding qualities or deficiencies. This is neither possible nor desirable. If he is eminent in any of the qualities which conduce to his own good, he is, so far, a proper object of admiration. He is so much the nearer to the ideal perfection of human nature. If he is grossly deficient in those qualities, a sentiment the opposite of admiration will follow. There is a degree of folly, and a degree of what may be called (though the phrase is not unobjectionable) lowness or depravation of taste, which, though it cannot justify doing harm to the person who manifests it, renders him necessarily and properly a subject of distaste, or, in extreme cases, even of contempt: a person could not have the opposite qualities in due strength without entertaining these feelings. Though doing no wrong to any one, a person may so act as to compel us to judge him, and feel to him, as a fool, or as a being of an inferior order: and since this judgment and feeling are a fact which he would prefer to avoid, it is doing him

---

* Forced upon, even without that person's permission.

a service to warn him of it beforehand, as of any other disagreeable consequence to which he exposes himself. It would be well, indeed, if this good office* were much more freely rendered than the common notions of politeness at present permit, and if one person could honestly point out to another that he thinks him in fault, without being considered unmannerly or presuming. We have a right, also, in various ways, to act upon our unfavourable opinion of any one, not to the oppression of his individuality, but in the exercise of ours. We are not bound, for example, to seek his society; we have a right to avoid it (though not to parade the avoidance), for we have a right to choose the society most acceptable to us. We have a right, and it may be our duty, to caution others against him, if we think his example or conversation likely to have a pernicious effect on those with whom he associates. We may give others a preference over him in optional good offices, except those which tend to his improvement. In these various modes a person may suffer very severe penalties at the hands of others, for faults which directly concern only himself; but he suffers these penalties only in so far as they are the natural, and, as it were, the spontaneous consequences of the faults themselves, not because they are purposely inflicted on him for the sake of punishment. A person who shows rashness, obstinacy, self-conceit—who cannot live within moderate means—who cannot restrain himself from hurtful indulgences—who pursues animal pleasures at the expense of those of feeling and intellect—must expect to be lowered in the opinion of others, and to have a less share of their favourable sentiments, but of this he has no right to complain, unless he has merited their favour by special excellence in his social relations, and has thus established a title to their good offices, which is not affected by his demerits towards himself.

What I contend for is, that the inconveniences which are strictly inseparable from the unfavourable judgment of others, are the only ones to which a person should ever be subjected for that portion of his conduct and character which concerns his own good, but which does not affect the interests of others in their relations with him. Acts injurious to others require a totally different treatment. Encroachment on their rights; infliction on them of any loss or damage not justified by his own rights; falsehood or duplicity in dealing with them; unfair or ungenerous use of advantages over them; even selfish abstinence from defending them against injury—these are fit objects of moral reprobation, and, in grave cases, of moral retribution and punishment. And not only these acts, but the dispositions which lead to them, are properly immoral, and fit subjects of disapprobation which may rise to abhorrence. Cruelty of disposition; malice and ill-nature; that most anti-social and odious of all passions, envy; dissimulation and insincerity, irascibility on insufficient cause, and resentment disproportioned to the provocation; the love of domineering over others; the desire to engross more than one's share of advantages (the πλεονεξία† of the Greeks); the pride which derives gratification from the abasement of others; the egotism which thinks self and its concerns more important than everything else, and decides all doubtful questions in his own favour;—these are moral vices, and constitute a bad and odious moral character: unlike the self-regarding faults previously mentioned, which are not properly immoralities, and to whatever pitch they may be carried, do not constitute wickedness. They may be proofs of any amount of folly, or want of personal dignity and self-respect; but they are only a subject of moral reprobation when they involve a breach of duty to others, for whose sake the individual is bound to have care for himself. What are called duties to ourselves are not socially obligatory, unless circumstances render them at the same time duties to others. The term duty to oneself, when it means anything more than prudence, means self-respect or self-development; and for none of these is any one accountable to his fellow-creatures, because for none of them is it for the good of mankind that he be held accountable to them.

The distinction between the loss of consideration which a person may rightly incur by defect of prudence or of personal dignity, and the reprobation which is due to him for an offence against the rights of others, is not a merely nominal distinction. It makes a vast difference both in our feelings and in our conduct towards him, whether he displeases us in things

---

* Helpful service, favor.

† πλεονεξία or "pleonexia" is an ancient Greek word meaning greediness or graspingness.

in which we think we have a right to control him, or in things in which we know that we have not. If he displeases us, we may express our distaste, and we may stand aloof from a person as well as from a thing that displeases us; but we shall not therefore feel called on to make his life uncomfortable. We shall reflect that he already bears, or will bear, the whole penalty of his error; if he spoils his life by mismanagement, we shall not, for that reason, desire to spoil it still further: instead of wishing to punish him, we shall rather endeavour to alleviate his punishment, by showing him how he may avoid or cure the evils his conduct tends to bring upon him. He may be to us an object of pity, perhaps of dislike, but not of anger or resentment; we shall not treat him like an enemy of society: the worst we shall think ourselves justified in doing is leaving him to himself, if we do not interfere benevolently by showing interest or concern for him. It is far otherwise if he has infringed the rules necessary for the protection of his fellow-creatures, individually or collectively. The evil consequences of his acts do not then fall on himself, but on others; and society, as the protector of all its members, must retaliate on him; must inflict pain on him for the express purpose of punishment, and must take care that it be sufficiently severe. In the one case, he is an offender at our bar,* and we are called on not only to sit in judgment on him, but, in one shape or another, to execute our own sentence: in the other case, it is not our part to inflict any suffering on him, except what may incidentally follow from our using the same liberty in the regulation of our own affairs, which we allow to him in his.

The distinction here pointed out between the part of a person's life which concerns only himself, and that which concerns others, many persons will refuse to admit. How (it may be asked) can any part of the conduct of a member of society be a matter of indifference to the other members? No person is an entirely isolated being; it is impossible for a person to do anything seriously or permanently hurtful to himself, without mischief reaching at least to his near connections, and often far beyond them. If he injures his property, he does harm to those who directly or indirectly derived support from it, and usually diminishes, by a greater or less amount, the general resources of the community. If he deteriorates his bodily or mental faculties, he not only brings evil upon all who depended on him for any portion of their happiness, but disqualifies himself for rendering the services which he owes to his fellow-creatures generally; perhaps becomes a burthen† on their affection or benevolence; and if such conduct were very frequent, hardly any offence that is committed would detract more from the general sum of good. Finally, if by his vices or follies a person does no direct harm to others, he is nevertheless (it may be said) injurious by his example; and ought to be compelled to control himself, for the sake of those whom the sight or knowledge of his conduct might corrupt or mislead.

And even (it will be added) if the consequences of misconduct could be confined to the vicious or thoughtless individual, ought society to abandon to their own guidance those who are manifestly unfit for it? If protection against themselves is confessedly due to children and persons under age, is not society equally bound to afford it to persons of mature years who are equally incapable of self-government? If gambling, or drunkenness, or incontinence,‡ or idleness, or uncleanliness, are as injurious to happiness, and as great a hindrance to improvement, as many or most of the acts prohibited by law, why (it may be asked) should not law, so far as is consistent with practicability and social convenience, endeavour to repress these also? And as a supplement to the unavoidable imperfections of law, ought not opinion at least to organize a powerful police against these vices, and visit rigidly with social penalties those who are known to practise them? There is no question here (it may be said) about restricting individuality, or impeding the trial of new and original experiments in living. The only things it is sought to prevent are things which have been tried and condemned from the beginning of the world until now; things which experience has shown not to be useful or suitable to any person's individuality. There must be some length of time and amount of experience, after which a moral or prudential truth may

---

* Tribunal, place of judgment.
† Burden.
‡ Lack of self-control.

be regarded as established, and it is merely desired to prevent generation after generation from falling over the same precipice which has been fatal to their predecessors.

I fully admit that the mischief which a person does to himself, may seriously affect, both through their sympathies and their interests, those nearly connected with him, and in a minor degree, society at large. When, by conduct of this sort, a person is led to violate a distinct and assignable obligation to any other person or persons, the case is taken out of the self-regarding class, and becomes amenable to moral disapprobation in the proper sense of the term. If, for example, a man, through intemperance or extravagance, becomes unable to pay his debts, or, having undertaken the moral responsibility of a family, becomes from the same cause incapable of supporting or educating them, he is deservedly reprobated, and might be justly punished; but it is for the breach of duty to his family or creditors, not for the extravagance. If the resources which ought to have been devoted to them, had been diverted from them for the most prudent investment, the moral culpability would have been the same. George Barnwell murdered his uncle to get money for his mistress, but if he had done it to set himself up in business, he would equally have been hanged.* Again, in the frequent case of a man who causes grief to his family by addiction to bad habits, he deserves reproach for his unkindness or ingratitude; but so he may for cultivating habits not in themselves vicious, if they are painful to those with whom he passes his life, or who from personal ties are dependent on him for their comfort. Whoever fails in the consideration generally due to the interests and feelings of others, not being compelled by some more imperative duty, or justified by allowable self-preference, is a subject of moral disapprobation for that failure, but not for the cause of it, nor for the errors, merely personal to himself, which may have remotely led to it. In like manner, when a person disables himself, by conduct purely self-regarding, from the performance of some definite duty incumbent on him to the public, he is guilty of a social offence. No person ought to be punished simply for being drunk; but a soldier or a policeman should be punished for being drunk on duty. Whenever, in short, there is a definite damage, or a definite risk of damage, either to an individual or to the public, the case is taken out of the province of liberty, and placed in that of morality or law.

But with regard to the merely contingent or, as it may be called, constructive injury which a person causes to society, by conduct which neither violates any specific duty to the public, nor occasions perceptible hurt to any assignable individual except himself; the inconvenience is one which society can afford to bear, for the sake of the greater good of human freedom. If grown persons are to be punished for not taking proper care of themselves, I would rather it were for their own sake, than under pretence of preventing them from impairing their capacity of rendering to society benefits which society does not pretend it has a right to exact. But I cannot consent to argue the point as if society had no means of bringing its weaker members up to its ordinary standard of rational conduct, except waiting till they do something irrational, and then punishing them, legally or morally, for it. Society has had absolute power over them during all the early portion of their existence: it has had the whole period of childhood and nonage in which to try whether it could make them capable of rational conduct in life. The existing generation is master both of the training and the entire circumstances of the generation to come; it cannot indeed make them perfectly wise and good, because it is itself so lamentably deficient in goodness and wisdom; and its best efforts are not always, in individual cases, its most successful ones; but it is perfectly well able to make the rising generation, as a whole, as good as, and a little better than, itself. If society lets any considerable number of its members grow up mere children, incapable of being acted on by rational consideration of distant motives, society has itself to blame for the consequences. Armed not only with all the powers of education, but with the ascendancy

---

* This tale was featured in the popular seventeenth-century ballad "George Barnwell," and later formed the subject matter of a play by George Lillo, *The London Merchant, or, the History of George Barnwell* (1731), which was one of the first prose works of domestic tragedy in English. It is the story of a young apprentice's downfall caused by his love for a beautiful, but unfeeling, prostitute.

which the authority of a received opinion always exercises over the minds who are least fitted to judge for themselves; and aided by the *natural* penalties which cannot be prevented from falling on those who incur the distaste or the contempt of those who know them; let not society pretend that it needs, besides all this, the power to issue commands and enforce obedience in the personal concerns of individuals, in which, on all principles of justice and policy, the decision ought to rest with those who are to abide the consequences....

But the strongest of all the arguments against the interference of the public with purely personal conduct, is that when it does interfere, the odds are that it interferes wrongly, and in the wrong place. On questions of social morality, of duty to others, the opinion of the public, that is, of an overruling majority, though often wrong, is likely to be still oftener right; because on such questions they are only required to judge of their own interests; of the manner in which some mode of conduct, if allowed to be practised, would affect themselves. But the opinion of a similar majority, imposed as a law on the minority, on questions of self-regarding conduct, is quite as likely to be wrong as right; for in these cases public opinion means, at the best, some people's opinion of what is good or bad for other people; while very often it does not even mean that; the public, with the most perfect indifference, passing over the pleasure or convenience of those whose conduct they censure, and considering only their own preference. There are many who consider as an injury to themselves any conduct which they have a distaste for, and resent it as an outrage to their feelings; as a religious bigot, when charged with disregarding the religious feelings of others, has been known to retort that they disregard his feelings, by persisting in their abominable worship or creed. But there is no parity between the feeling of a person for his own opinion, and the feeling of another who is offended at his holding it; no more than between the desire of a thief to take a purse, and the desire of the right owner to keep it. And a person's taste is as much his own peculiar concern as his opinion or his purse. It is easy for any one to imagine an ideal public, which leaves the freedom and choice of individuals in all uncertain matters undisturbed, and only requires them to abstain from modes of conduct which universal experience has condemned. But where has there been seen a public which set any such limit to its censorship? or when does the public trouble itself about universal experience? In its interferences with personal conduct it is seldom thinking of anything but the enormity* of acting or feeling differently from itself; and this standard of judgment, thinly disguised, is held up to mankind as the dictate of religion and philosophy, by nine tenths of all moralists and speculative writers. These teach that things are right because they are right; because we feel them to be so. They tell us to search in our own minds and hearts for laws of conduct binding on ourselves and on all others. What can the poor public do but apply these instructions, and make their own personal feelings of good and evil, if they are tolerably unanimous in them, obligatory on all the world? ... ∎

Suggestions for Critical Reflection

1. Mill suggests that, in modern democratic societies, the question of individual liberty requires "a different and more fundamental treatment" than it has historically been given, since in the past people were governed by an independent ruler while in a democracy it is "the people" themselves who exercise power. What exactly is the difference that democracy makes to the question of individual liberty, according to Mill? Do you think Mill might say—or should have said—that the rise of democracy, ironically, makes it *harder* for individuals to be free of illegitimate social interference?

2. Mill asserts (famously) that "the only purpose for which power can be rightfully exercised over any member of a civilized community, against his will, is to prevent harm to others." Given this principle, it is obviously crucial to specify what constitutes "harm." Does Mill ever do so adequately? What is

---

* Outrageousness.

the best way of cashing out this crucial concept? Will it require drawing a distinction between *real* harms and what people merely *perceive* to be a harm to them (such as, say, witnessing a homosexual couple kissing)? If so, how can these 'real' harms be distinguished from the merely apparent ones? *Is* there a way of doing so that supports all the conclusions Mill wants to draw?

3. Before he begins his defense of his "harm principle," Mill notes that "I regard utility as the ultimate appeal on all ethical questions." If you have read the selection from Mill's *Utilitarianism* in the Ethical Theory section of this book, you might want to consider how much of his subsequent reasoning is rooted in utilitarianism ... or indeed, whether the principle he defends in *On Liberty* is even *consistent* with Mill's utilitarian theory. What do you think Mill means by "utility in the largest sense, grounded on the permanent interests of man as a progressive being"?

4. "The only freedom which deserves the name, is that of pursuing our own good in our own way...." Is this true, or might there be a deeper, more valuable kind of freedom? What if someone's conception of their own good is importantly limited in some way, or is fallacious (even though it causes no harm to other people)? For example, what if I choose to spend my entire life in a basement watching TV, eating pizza, and growing and smoking (but not buying or selling) marijuana—could this really be an example of "the only freedom which deserves the name"? Further, what if I live this way, not through deliberate choice, but simply because it is how I grew up and is all I have ever experienced, and suppose I would, in fact, be much happier if some social authority were empowered to force me to get out more and make some friends. Must Mill still say I am free *only* if society leaves me alone? If so, is he right about that?

5. Part of Mill's argument in Chapter II involves the claim that "[c]omplete liberty of contradicting and disproving our opinion, is the very condition which justifies us in assuming its truth for purposes of action; and on no other terms can a being with human faculties have any rational assurance of being right." Does Mill really mean that we can have *no* "rational assurance" of being right about anything unless there is *complete* freedom of thought on the issue? If so, does he show that this is a plausible claim? Is there a less black-and-white version of this claim which seems more plausible (and which Mill might really have meant)? If so, does this less extreme version adequately support Mill's conclusions about the value of complete freedom of thought?

6. Mill argues that believing something merely on the basis of authority, even if it is true, "is not the way in which truth ought to be held by a rational being." That is, he seems to suggest, believing some claim to be true without first having considered all the available arguments for and against that claim is mere vacant "superstition" and not genuine knowledge. Do Mill's arguments make this claim seem plausible, or does it strike you as too extreme? If he is right, how much of what most people believe could count as genuine knowledge? Is there a less contentious intermediate position? If so, would this weaker claim still support Mill's conclusions about the value of complete freedom of thought?

7. Should people be free to express *any* opinion, whatsoever? Imagine the most morally offensive view you can (involving, for example, the horrible torture of innocent toddlers or the most bizarre and uncomfortable kind of sexual act): should society allow people to, for example, make and distribute movies advocating this view? What if, to your horror, these movies prove highly popular and lots of people start watching them: should they still be allowed? Where, if anywhere, should the line be drawn, and does Mill get this line right?

8. Mill begins Chapter IV by stating "every one who receives the protection of society owes a return for the benefit, and the fact of living in society renders it indispensable that each should be bound to observe a certain line of conduct towards the rest." This, according to Mill, is what justifies society in placing at least *some* limits on the freedom of the individual. Does Mill have an argument for this principle, or is it just an assumption he makes? How philosophically significant is this assumption? For example, do you agree (and does Mill mean) that you have duties to your fellow citizens—such as (according to Mill) the duty to serve in the army in times of war, or to perform jury duty when called upon, or to rescue someone who has fallen into an icy river—*merely* by virtue of your living in a society?

9. Mill tries to distinguish between the "natural" social penalties of having a poor and foolish character, and penalties that might be deliberately inflicted on stupid people to punish them for their stupidity. According to Mill, the former kind of harm is an inevitable and acceptable consequence of one's own choices, while the latter constitutes morally unacceptable social interference. Is the crucial distinction between "natural" and punitive social harms an entirely clear one? (For example, what about repeatedly passing someone over for promotion or preventing them from attending a social organization such as a club or educational institution? Would these be "natural" consequences of someone's unpopularity, or a way of punishing them for being unpopular?) If this distinction is unclear, how serious a problem is this for Mill's position?

10. Mill also distinguishes between "self-regarding" and "social" virtues and vices, and claims only the latter are, properly speaking, *moral* virtues and vices, and that only these are properly within the ambit of social control. Again, is this an entirely clear distinction? For example, is it clear which of your character traits affect only you, personally, and which affect other people as well? If this kind of distinction is unclear or unworkable, how serious a blow is this for Mill's account of individual liberty?

KARL MARX AND FRIEDRICH ENGELS

FROM *The Communist Manifesto*

The philosophers have only *interpreted* the world in different ways; the point is to *change* it—Karl Marx (*Theses on Feuerbach*, Thesis 11)

Who Were Karl Marx and Friedrich Engels?

Karl Heinrich Marx was born in 1818 in the town of Trier in the Rhineland, formerly a region of Prussia lying next to the French border that is today part of Germany. Both his parents were Jewish, descended from a long line of rabbis and Jewish intellectuals. They were part of the first generation of German Jews to enjoy equal legal status with Christians and to be granted free choice of residence and profession. The Rhineland had been ruled by the French during the Napoleonic period, from 1792 until 1815, and Marx's father Heinrich had benefited from the relatively enlightened French regime, using the opportunity to forge a successful career as a respected lawyer. However, after Prussian power was restored in Trier in 1815, Marx's father felt obliged to convert himself and his family to Lutheranism in order to protect his career, and so Karl was not brought up as a Jew.

Karl's father wanted him to become a lawyer, but Karl was a rowdy, rebellious child and, as a young man, chose to spend his time studying philosophy and history, dueling, and writing romantic verses to his childhood sweetheart, the daughter of his neighbor, Jenny von Westphalen (whom he married in 1843). From 1835 to 1841 Marx studied at the universities of Bonn (where he spent a year studying law) and Berlin, where he was exposed to, and heavily influenced by, the idealist philosophy of G.W.F. Hegel.* Marx's early writings show his preoccupation with the notion of human self-realization through the struggle for freedom and a view of the nature of reality as turbulently changing, themes which find resonance in Hegel. However, like many contemporary "Young Hegelians," Marx found the Hegelian system, as it was then taught in the Prussian universities, to be politically and religiously much too conservative.

In 1841 Marx successfully submitted a doctoral dissertation (on Greek philosophy) to the university of Jena, but—because his political radicalism made him effectively unhireable in the contemporary political climate—he quickly gave up any prospect of an academic career. Instead, he wrote for a liberal newspaper in Cologne, the *Rheinische Zeitung*, and in short order became its editor. Under Marx, the paper went from cautious criticism of the government to a more radical critique of prevailing conditions, especially issues of economic justice. Inevitably, the paper was first heavily censored and then, in 1843, shut down by the Prussian authorities. At this point Marx and his new wife left for the more bohemian city of Paris, where Marx worked as a journalist for another radical publication, the *Deutsch-Französische Jahrbücher* [German-French Annals]. Realizing that he knew little about the economic issues which he saw as so politically significant, Marx threw himself into the study of political economy. Even before these studies began, however, Marx was already—like many of his compatriots—politically left-wing in a way that could loosely be called "communist." He was convinced of the need for "cooperative" rather than individual control of economic resources, and was ferociously concerned about the need to alleviate the living conditions of the swelling numbers of urban poor.

In 1845, pressure from the Prussian government caused Marx to be expelled from France and he and his family moved to Brussels. There he developed a close friendship, begun in France, with Friedrich Engels, the man who was to be Marx's most important intellectual collaborator, supporter, and friend (indeed, the only lasting friend Marx ever had).

---

*   Hegel argued that the whole universe ('being')—including thinking subjects such as human beings—is ultimately comprehensible as an all-inclusive rational whole ('the Absolute') governed by dynamic logical principles.

Engels was born in 1820 in Barmen, near Düsseldorf. His family were wealthy mill owners in the rapidly industrializing northwest German Ruhr valley, and although Engels had hoped for a career in literature, his father insisted that he leave school at 17 to work for the family firm. He worked first in a local factory, then in an export office in the port city of Bremen, and finally as an accountant for the English branch of the firm Ermen and Engels. Thus, from the time he was a young man, Engels saw first-hand the profound social changes brought about by the introduction of new methods of production in the textile industry. Although he never formally attended university, he did sit in on lectures at Berlin University during his spell of compulsory military service and, through his exposure to the radical democratic movement, acquired a working knowledge of Hegelian philosophy. He worked for the *Rheinische Zeitung* while Marx was its editor, writing articles from Manchester, England, where, employed by the family firm, he was appalled to witness the living conditions of the English working class. In 1844 he wrote the impassioned *Condition of the Working Classes in England*. He also wrote a critical study of the standard positions in political economy—a work that greatly impressed Marx, and directly intersected with his interests at the time. After Engels's return to Germany in 1844, the two began collaborating on writings, speeches, and debates intended to spread their radical ideas among workers and intellectuals. Their most important publication of this period was the *Communist Manifesto*.

1848, the year *The Communist Manifesto* was published, was a year of revolution in Europe. Most of the countries of Europe, except Britain, Belgium, and Russia, underwent a spasm of social upheaval in which old, aristocratic regimes fell and were replaced (briefly) by bold, new republican governments. Marx and Engels, in their different ways, attempted to play a role in this revolutionary process. Marx, now expelled from Belgium for his activism, returned to Cologne and started up a new radical newspaper, the *Neue Rheinische Zeitung*, his goal being to inspire and educate the revolutionary leaders (along the lines of *The Communist Manifesto*). Meanwhile, Engels was an officer in a short-lived military uprising in the German region of Baden. Within a

matter of months, however, the European upheaval was over and, everywhere except France, the new democratic, republican regimes began to collapse and the old order reasserted itself. Marx and his associates were tried in a Cologne court for charges of inciting revolt and, although Marx successfully defended himself in court, he was nevertheless exiled from Prussian territory in 1849. As a result, Marx and Engels emigrated permanently to England: Marx, to live and write in London, and Engels to work for his family firm in Manchester.

Conditions were extremely hard for the Marx family, especially for the first decade of their lives in London. Marx was unwilling to take work that would interfere with his writing, and when he did seek stable employment he was unable to get it. (At one point he applied for a job as a railway clerk, but was unsuccessful because of the—now notorious—illegibility of his handwriting.) He and his family—his wife, her servant, and six children—subsisted on financial gifts from family and friends and on the income from Marx's occasional freelance journalism (mostly as a European correspondent for the *New York Tribune*, which paid £1 per article). Their main financial benefactor was Engels, who sent them grants and allowances taken from his own income and the money from his investments. Nevertheless, the Marx household lived in relative poverty for many years, enduring poor housing and bad food. Three of Marx's children died young, in part because of these hard conditions, and his own health suffered a collapse from which it never fully recovered.*

Meanwhile, Marx single-mindedly devoted his life to the cause of ending what he saw as the serious, and increasing, inequalities and exploitation inherent in capitalist society. His role, he thought, was to formulate the theoretical framework that would reveal the true state of things to the masses of workers and, by doing so, would both incite and guide the impending revolutionary replacement of capitalism by communism. He saw himself mainly as an 'ideas man' and a publicist for the communist movement, rather than an organizer or leader (and indeed, during his lifetime, his personal political influence was quite small). He spent 10 hours a day, most days, in the Reading Room of the British Museum, conducting research and writing; after returning home, he

---

* Despite these hardships, however, Marx's marriage was apparently a very happy one, and he was a devoted husband and father.

would often continue to write late into the night. His main work during these years, a massive, wide-ranging, detailed analysis of capitalist society and what Marx saw as the tensions intrinsic to it, was eventually published in three substantial volumes as *Das Kapital* (in English, *Capital*).*

Engels, meanwhile, ran his family's cotton mills in Lancashire and became a respected figure in Manchester society. He rode horses two days a week with the aristocratic Cheshire Hunt (valuable training, he claimed, for a future leader of the armies of the revolution), but at heart, Engels was unquestionably a devoted revolutionary, sincerely committed to the cause of communism, and he did his best to support Marx's work. He lived with an Irish factory girl called Mary Burns, and when she died he took in, and eventually married, her sister Lizzie.

In 1864 the International Working Men's Association (otherwise known as the First International) was formed. This was a watershed in the history of the working class movement, and for the next eight years the organization was highly influential in European left-wing politics. Marx was one of its main leaders, and was heavily engaged with its internal politics. By the 1870s he had become the leading theoretician for the radical movement in Europe, especially in Germany, and had become notorious across the continent as the "Red Doctor Marx."

Marx died, of chronic respiratory disease, in London in 1883. (Despite Engels's best efforts: he took him on a tour of France, Switzerland, and Algiers in the hope that a change of climate might help his condition.) He is buried next to his wife in Highgate Cemetery.

After 1870, Engels—who retired at 50, an independently wealthy man—had devoted all of his time to helping Marx with his research, and after Marx's death he continued the writing of *Capital* from Marx's notes, completing it in 1894, a year before his own death.

In a speech given at Marx's graveside, Engels said

> ... Marx was above all else a revolutionist. His real mission in life was to contribute, in one way or another, to the overthrow of capitalist society and of the state institutions which it had brought into being, to contribute to the liberation of the modern

proletariat, which *he* was the first to make conscious of its own position and needs, conscious of the conditions of its emancipation. Fighting was his element. And he fought with a passion, a tenacity and a success such as few could rival.[†]

What Was Marx's Overall Philosophical Project?

In 1852, Marx summarized his three most important political ideas in the following way:

1. That social classes are not permanent features of society, but instead are phases in the historical development of the relations of economic production.
2. That the struggle between these classes will necessarily lead to the "dictatorship of the proletariat," in which the working people will forcibly take over political power from the property-owners.
3. That the dictatorship of the proletariat is not an end in itself, but a transition period before the advent of a classless communist society devoted to the free development and flourishing of individuals.

What does Marx mean by these three claims? The first is best approached through Marx's analysis of capitalism. A large proportion of his writing was devoted to this analysis, and it provides the clearest example of how he thought social class divisions were produced and perpetuated by a particular type of economic system.

A society is capitalist, according to Marx, if the production of goods is dominated by the use of wage-labor: that is, by the use of labor power sold, as their only way to make a living, by people who have no significant control over means of production (the proletariat), and bought by other people who do have control over means of production such as raw materials, capital, and machinery (the bourgeoisie). The bourgeoisie make their money mostly by combining the purchased labor power with the means of production they own, and selling the commodities thus produced. Marx held that the relationship between these

---

* Marx's mother is said to have commented that it was a shame that her boy merely wrote about capital and never acquired any.

† Friedrich Engels, from Marx and Engels, *Collected Works*, Vol. 24 (International Publishers, 1989), 468–69.

two classes, bourgeoisie and proletariat, was intrinsically and inescapably *antagonistic*, and he attempted to explain all the main institutional features of capitalist society in terms of this relation. Since, in Marx's view, the main institutions of a capitalist society have the function of preserving the interests of the bourgeoisie, and since these interests are opposed to those of the proletarians, capitalist society is therefore a kind of class rule, or oppression, of the majority by the minority.

Furthermore, for Marx, social structures, such as capitalism, that are based on the oppression of one class by another, give rise to what he called *ideologies*. An ideology is a (socially influential) system of beliefs or assumptions that reflects a false perception of reality—a perception of reality distorted by the social forces involved in class oppression. Central examples, for Marx, were systems of religious belief and the capitalist doctrine of the "free market." The dominance of a ruling class, whose members usually make up only a tiny minority of society, cannot be preserved through physical coercion alone: it can only survive as long as most people believe (falsely) that the social status quo is in their own interests, or that there is no realistic alternative to the current system, or in a situation where the oppressed classes are divided against each other (e.g., by nationalism, racism, or sexism) and fail to see their own common interest.

Considerations like these give rise to one of the best-known components of Marx's philosophical system, *historical materialism*: "[t]he mode of production of material life conditions the social, political, and intellectual life-process in general."* This is the view that the foundation or "base" of society is its economic structure, which is defined by historical facts about the means of production (for example, facts about the level of agricultural sophistication, industrial technology, trade and transportation networks, and so on). As productive forces change, economic adjustments—changes to the relations of production—give rise to revolutions in society's "superstructure": the political, legal, moral, religious, and philosophical components of culture. In other words, political and social changes do not cause economic change,

but the other way around: political and social systems are determined by their economic basis.

Marx's second main political-philosophical idea, in his 1852 summary, was the view that capitalism contains internal tensions which, in time, will inevitably produce the revolutionary overthrow of the bourgeoisie by the workers and usher in a "dictatorship of the proletariat." This view is, in part, the heritage of Marx's early influence by, and reaction to, the philosophical system of Hegel. For Hegel, history is a "dialectical" movement in which a thesis—a principle or idea—is challenged by its antithesis, and from this conflict there emerges a synthesis of the two, a new principle. In time this new principle meets *its* antithesis, and so on (until the ideal, final synthesis is achieved). Thus Hegel was an *idealist*, in the sense that for him the engine of world change was the clash of *Ideas*.† In Engels's words, Marx "turned the Hegelian system on its head": instead of conflicts between ideas (in the shape of political structures) driving change, Marx held that the world contains its own internal conflicts and that political ideas actually spring up *from* this conflict rather than causing it. These built-in conflicts, the mainspring of historical change, are *economic* in nature, generated by people's attempts to satisfy their material needs—for food, clothing, shelter, and so on—and their subsequent pursuit of personal wealth, within the context of their society's particular level of economic development. (Thus, Marx's system is often called *dialectical materialism*, though Marx himself never used this label.)

Marx's diagnosis of the economic conflicts driving capitalism towards revolution is complex and many-faceted. One of its central notions is that of *alienation*, which in turn arises from two other fundamental ideas in Marx's system: his theory of human nature and his "labor theory of value." According to Marx, human beings are essentially *active* and *creative* beings. Human flourishing consists in the continual transformation of one's inherent creative power into objective products, the constant *realization* of one's "subjectivity." Thus, productive activity—that is, work—is an essential component of human well-being. Marx's concern for the poor was never merely concern for their basic "material

---

* From the preface to *A Contribution to the Critique of Political Economy* in Karl Marx, *Early Writings*, trans. Livingstone and Benton (Penguin Books and New Left Review, 1975), 425.

† This is, of necessity, rather a caricature of Hegel's philosophical system. A good first introduction to Hegel's work is Charles Taylor's *Hegel* (Cambridge University Press, 1977).

needs," such as food and housing, but was part of his view of human flourishing as being a matter of "free self-activity," of true self-expression in a social context.

The institution of private property, in Marx's view, stifles the flourishing of the human spirit. Since private property represents the products of labor as if they were mere *things*, it alienates labor—and thus, human nature—from itself. Workers in a modern economy typically do not experience the economic goods they spend their lives producing as expressions of *themselves*, but merely as things to be sold. Furthermore, capitalism intensifies this process of alienation by treating *labor itself* as a commodity, to be bought and sold. Not only is the product of your creative activity alienated from you, but that very activity, work itself, is alienated—it is no longer *yours*, once you have sold it to an employer.

Furthermore, on Marx's analysis, the capitalist sale of goods for profit is inherently exploitative. According to the labor theory of value, which Marx took over from British economists Adam Smith (1723–90) and David Ricardo (1772–1823) and developed into his own economic theory, the fair value of anything in a free market is determined by the amount of labor required to produce it. This has two major implications. First it means, according to Marx, that *capital* adds no value to goods over and above the labor taken to produce them, and thus the capitalist, after recompensing his workers for the value of the labor they have expended in his factories, simply appropriates the "surplus value" which is generated as profits. Although not economically "unfair," in Marx's view, this is nevertheless a form of exploitation. Second, when the labor theory of value is applied to a free market for *labor itself*, it has the implication that the working classes will necessarily (and not "unjustly," by the lights of capitalism) be forced into permanent poverty. This is because the labor-value of labor itself is simply the amount necessary to keep the worker healthy and ready to work each day—that is, the minimum amount of food and shelter necessary to sustain the worker. This therefore, no more and no less, is the labor wage in a free capitalist market, and this produces a huge class of workers with no security, no prospects, no savings, no interest in preserving the current social conditions—in short, "nothing to lose but their chains."

Finally, there is the third part of Marx's 1852 summary: communism. Marx actually had relatively little to say about the nature of a future communist society, but it is clear that he saw it as a society in which the tensions inherent in capitalism have annihilated themselves and produced an economic system that—because there is no private property or capital—does not generate alienation and exploitation but instead allows for genuine human flourishing as active, creative individuals, self-determined and self-sufficient within a community of other self-determined human beings.

What Is the Structure of This Reading?

The Communist Manifesto was written to be a statement of the ideals and aims of the Communist League. The Communist League, an umbrella organization linking the main centers of communist activity in London, Paris, Brussels, and Cologne, was formed in June 1847, largely at the instigation of Marx and Engels, and was descended from a shadowy Parisian 'secret society' called the League of the Just. Most of its (few) members were German émigrés, and included several tailors, a few students, a typesetter, a cobbler, a watchmaker, a painter of miniatures, a disgraced Prussian officer, and Marx's aristocratic brother-in-law. A Congress of the League was held in London in November of 1847. To quote the eminent British historian A.J.P. Taylor:

> Marx attended in person. He listened impatiently while the worthy tailors lamented the wickedness of capitalism and preached universal brotherhood. He rose and denounced brotherhood in the name of class war. The tailors were entranced. Where they relied on sentiment, a learned man explained to them how society worked and placed the key to the future in their hands. They invited Marx to write a declaration of principles for them. He agreed.*

Engels wrote a first draft—a question-and-answer brief on the main principles of communism—which was then completely rewritten by Marx (who was less than 30 years old at the time) in the space of less than six weeks.

---

* A.J.P. Taylor, "Introduction" to Marx and Engels, *The Communist Manifesto* (Penguin Books, 1967), 22.

The *Manifesto* has four sections. The first part is a history of society from the Middle Ages to the present day, presented as a succession of class struggles, and predicting the imminent victory of the proletariat over the present ruling class, the bourgeoisie. Part II describes the position of communists with respect to the proletarian class and then goes on to reject a sequence of bourgeois objections to communism. This is followed by a brief characterization of the nature of the forthcoming communist revolution. The third part, not included here, contains an extended criticism of other forms of socialism: reactionary, bourgeois, and utopian. The final section provides a short description of communist tactics toward opposition parties and culminates with a call for proletarian unity.

Some Useful Background Information

For Marx, no external force or random accident is required to topple capitalism. He believed the overthrow of capitalism by socialism was inescapable, that it would come about because of the very nature of capitalism itself. An accurate grasp of the forces that sustain almost all social systems throughout history, Marx thought, would show that they must inevitably, as a result of internal processes, decline and be replaced by a radically different social system. However, *inevitably* does not mean *spontaneously*: the actual overthrow of existing society must be performed by a band of determined revolutionaries, joining the already existing, day-to-day class struggles and introducing revolutionary ideas to combat the ruling ideology, emphasizing the need for unity among the oppressed, and, when the time is ripe, boldly leading the revolution. The key is to follow the course of history *knowingly* by controlling the circumstances that generate it.

Some Common Misconceptions

1. Although Marx believed all the main institutions of society function to preserve the interests of the ruling class, he was not a conspiracy theorist. He did not believe, for example, that leading political figures receive covert orders from the business community. Instead, he held that institutional mechanisms press the actions of successful political figures into reflecting the long-term interests of the bourgeoisie (including the need for social and economic stability and the suppression of revolution). One especially important mechanism for this, according to Marx, is national debt: governments depend on capitalists to renew huge but routine loans, and these financiers could throw national finances into chaos if their interests are too directly threatened. Another major influence is the pace of investment: if capitalists are displeased, the rate of investment slows and this has serious repercussions for employment rates and income levels. A third major factor is bourgeois ownership of the media (in Marx's time, mass-circulation newspapers—today, television or social media networks), and their consequent ability to manipulate and mould public opinion.

2. Marx's philosophy, as it is found in his writings, is not exactly the same thing as the ideological system often called "Marxism" today. His thought has been built on and interpreted by many other writers, starting with Engels and including several prominent Russian thinkers such as Georgy Plekhanov (1856–1918) and Vladimir Ilich Lenin (1870–1924) who formulated an 'orthodox,' systematic Soviet version of Marxism, and the so-called Western Marxists such as Georg Lukács (1885–1971), Theodor Adorno (1903–69), and Louis Althusser (1918–90). Nor is it quite the same thing as communism. The notion of the abolition of private property dates back at least to the early Christians, and was proposed during the French Revolution by a few fringe groups whom even the revolutionaries considered beyond the pale. And of course, the modern association of Communism with the political and economic structures of China and the Soviet Union is a development which occurred after Marx's death (and it is highly unlikely that Marx would have unconditionally approved of those regimes).

How Important and Influential Is This Passage?

The Communist Manifesto is the most successful political pamphlet of all time: for a substantial period of the twentieth century, roughly a third of the human race was ruled by governments that claimed allegiance to the ideas expressed in it. Practically, Marx's thought is the chief inspiration for all modern forms of social radicalism. Intellectually, according to the *Blackwell Encyclopedia of Political Thought*, "[o]ver the whole range of the social sciences, Marx has proved probably the most influential figure of the twentieth century."* Marx's central ideas—"historical materialism," the labor theory of value, the notion of class struggle—have had an inestimable influence on the development of contemporary economics, history, and sociology, even though they are not widely accepted by most Western intellectuals today.

FROM *The Communist Manifesto*†

A spectre is haunting Europe—the spectre of Communism. All the Powers of old Europe have entered into a holy alliance to exorcise this spectre: Pope and Tsar, Metternich and Guizot,‡ French Radicals and German police-spies.

Where is the party in opposition that has not been decried as Communistic by its opponents in power? Where the Opposition that has not hurled back the branding reproach of Communism, against the more advanced opposition parties, as well as against its reactionary adversaries?

Two things result from this fact:

1. Communism is already acknowledged by all European Powers to be itself a Power.
2. It is high time that Communists should openly, in the face of the whole world, publish their views, their aims, their tendencies, and meet this nursery tale of the Spectre of Communism with a Manifesto of the party itself.

To this end, Communists of various nationalities have assembled in London and sketched the following Manifesto, to be published in the English, French, German, Italian, Flemish and Danish languages.§

I. Bourgeois and Proletarians[1]

The history of all hitherto existing society[2] is the history of class struggles.

Freeman and slave, patrician and plebeian, lord and serf, guild-master¶[3] and journeyman,** in a word, oppressor and oppressed, stood in constant opposition to one another, carried on an uninterrupted, now

---

* David McLellan in *The Blackwell Encyclopedia of Political Thought*, ed. Miller et al. (Blackwell, 1987), 322.

† *Manifest der Kommunistischen Partei* was first published, in German, in London in 1848. The text reprinted here is the English translation made in 1888 by Samuel Moore, which was edited and authorized by Friedrich Engels. The author's notes in the text are those made by Engels in 1888.

‡ Prince Klemens Metternich (1773–1859) was the conservative chancellor of the Austrian empire; he was the dominant figure in European politics at this time, but was soon to be driven from power by the Revolutions of 1848. François Guizot (1787–1874) was the liberal moderate premier of France until he also was overthrown in the political turbulence of 1848.

§ Only one translation—into Swedish—was published in 1848–49, and widespread translation and reprinting of the *Manifesto* did not begin until after 1870.

¶ 'Master' here means master-craftsman, a medieval independent skilled craftsman, who (as Marx's footnote mentions) was a full member of a guild, a mutual-aid association of similar workers.

** A patrician was a member of one of the noble families of the ancient Roman republic, while plebeians were the common people of Rome. The terminology was also used in later ages (e.g., in the medieval free cities of Italy and Germany) to mark a similar distinction. A serf was a member of a particular feudal class of people in Europe, those bound by law to a particular piece of land and, like the land, owned by a lord. A journeyman is a craftsman who has completed his apprenticeship and is employed at a fixed wage by a master artisan, but who is not yet allowed (by his guild) to work for himself.

hidden, now open fight, a fight that each time ended, either in a revolutionary re-constitution of society at large, or in the common ruin of the contending classes.

In the earlier epochs of history, we find almost everywhere a complicated arrangement of society into various orders, a manifold gradation of social rank. In ancient Rome we have patricians, knights, plebeians, slaves; in the Middle Ages, feudal lords, vassals,* guild-masters, journeymen, apprentices, serfs; in almost all of these classes, again, subordinate gradations.

The modern bourgeois society that has sprouted from the ruins of feudal society has not done away with class antagonisms. It has but established new classes, new conditions of oppression, new forms of struggle in place of the old ones.

Our epoch, the epoch of the bourgeoisie, possesses, however, this distinctive feature: it has simplified class antagonisms. Society as a whole is more and more splitting up into two great hostile camps, into two great classes directly facing each other: Bourgeoisie and Proletariat.

From the serfs of the Middle Ages sprang the chartered burghers† of the earliest towns. From these burgesses the first elements of the bourgeoisie were developed.

The discovery of America, the rounding of the Cape,‡ opened up fresh ground for the rising bourgeoisie. The East-Indian and Chinese markets, the colonisation of America, trade with the colonies, the increase in the means of exchange and in commodities generally, gave to commerce, to navigation, to industry, an impulse never before known, and thereby, to the revolutionary element in the tottering feudal society, a rapid development.

The feudal system of industry, under which industrial production was monopolized by closed guilds, now no longer sufficed for the growing wants of the new markets. The manufacturing system took its place. The guild-masters were pushed on one side by the manufacturing middle class; division of labour between the different corporate guilds vanished in the face of division of labour in each single workshop.

Meantime the markets kept ever growing, the demand ever rising. Even manufacture no longer sufficed. Thereupon, steam and machinery revolutionized industrial production. The place of manufacture was taken by the giant, Modern Industry, the place of the industrial middle class, by industrial millionaires, the leaders of whole industrial armies, the modern bourgeois.

Modern Industry has established the world market, for which the discovery of America paved the way. This market has given an immense development to commerce, to navigation, to communication by land. This development has, in its turn, reacted on the extension of industry; and in proportion as industry, commerce, navigation, railways extended, in the same proportion the bourgeoisie developed, increased its capital, and pushed into the background every class handed down from the Middle Ages.

We see, therefore, how the modern bourgeoisie is itself the product of a long course of development, of a series of revolutions in the modes of production and of exchange.

Each step in the development of the bourgeoisie was accompanied by a corresponding political advance in that class. An oppressed class under the sway of the feudal nobility, an armed and self-governing association in the medieval commune;§ here independent urban republic (as in Italy and Germany), there taxable "third estate"¶ of the monarchy (as in France), afterwards, in the period of manufacture proper, serving either the semi-feudal or the absolute monarchy as a counterpoise against the nobility, and, in fact, cornerstone of the great monarchies in general, the bourgeoisie has at last, since the establishment of Modern Industry and of the world market, conquered for itself, in the modern representative State,** exclusive

---

* A vassal received land and protection from a feudal lord, in return for homage and allegiance.
† Someone who is a citizen of a town in virtue of being a full member of a legally chartered trade association or guild.
‡ The Cape of Good Hope, at the southern tip of Africa.
§ An association of medieval townspeople for mutual defense, often a self-governing "community."
¶ The three divisions of society in pre-Revolutionary France were the first estate (clergy), the second estate (nobility), and the third estate (commoners).
** A modern, rather than a feudal, state: one whose institutions are based on the political representation of *individuals*, rather than of social corporations (such as towns or guilds) or estates (such as the nobility or the clergy).

political sway. The executive of the modern State is but a committee for managing the common affairs of the whole bourgeoisie.

The bourgeoisie, historically, has played a most revolutionary part.

The bourgeoisie, wherever it has got the upper hand, has put an end to all feudal, patriarchal, idyllic relations. It has pitilessly torn asunder the motley feudal ties that bound man to his "natural superiors," and has left no other nexus between man and man than naked self-interest, than callous "cash payment." It has drowned out the most heavenly ecstasies of religious fervour, of chivalrous enthusiasm, of philistine sentimentalism, in the icy water of egotistical calculation. It has resolved personal worth into exchange value, and in place of the numberless indefeasible chartered freedoms,* has set up that single, unconscionable freedom—Free Trade. In one word, for exploitation, veiled by religious and political illusions, it has substituted naked, shameless, direct, brutal exploitation.

The bourgeoisie has stripped of its halo every occupation hitherto honoured and looked up to with reverent awe. It has converted the physician, the lawyer, the priest, the poet, the man of science, into its paid wage-labourers.

The bourgeoisie has torn away from the family its sentimental veil, and has reduced the family relation to a mere money relation.

The bourgeoisie has disclosed how it came to pass that the brutal display of vigour in the Middle Ages, which Reactionists† so much admire, found its fitting complement in the most slothful indolence. It has been the first to show what man's activity can bring about. It has accomplished wonders far surpassing Egyptian pyramids, Roman aqueducts, and Gothic cathedrals; it has conducted expeditions that put in the shade all former Exoduses of nations and crusades.

The bourgeoisie cannot exist without constantly revolutionizing the instruments of production, and thereby the relations of production, and with them the whole relations of society. Conservation of the old modes of production in unaltered form, was, on the contrary, the first condition of existence for all earlier industrial classes. Constant revolutionizing of production, uninterrupted disturbance of all social conditions, everlasting uncertainty and agitation distinguish the bourgeois epoch from all earlier ones. All fixed, fast-frozen relations, with their train of ancient and venerable prejudices and opinions, are swept away, all new-formed ones become antiquated before they can ossify.‡ All that is solid melts into air, all that is holy is profaned, and man is at last compelled to face with sober senses, his real condition of life and his relations with his kind.

The need of a constantly expanding market for its products chases the bourgeoisie over the entire surface of the globe. It must nestle everywhere, settle everywhere, establish connections everywhere.

The bourgeoisie has, through its exploitation of the world market, given a cosmopolitan character to production and consumption in every country. To the great chagrin of Reactionists, it has drawn from under the feet of industry the national ground on which it stood. All old-established national industries have been destroyed or are daily being destroyed. They are dislodged by new industries, whose introduction becomes a life and death question for all civilized nations, by industries that no longer work up indigenous raw material, but raw material drawn from the remotest zones; industries whose products are consumed, not only at home, but in every quarter of the globe. In place of the old wants, satisfied by the production of the country, we find new wants, requiring for their satisfaction the products of distant lands and climes. In place of the old local and national seclusion and self-sufficiency, we have intercourse§ in every direction, universal interdependence of nations. And as in material, so also in intellectual production. The intellectual creations of individual nations become common property. National one-sidedness and narrow-mindedness become more and more impossible, and from the numerous national and local literatures, there arises a world literature.

---

* The charters were granted (or sold) by royalty to associations of townspeople, guaranteeing them protection and certain freedoms.
† Those who resist change and seek to return to an older social and political order.
‡ Turn into stone.
§ Communication and trade between different localities.

The bourgeoisie, by the rapid improvement of all instruments of production, by the immensely facilitated means of communication, draws all, even the most barbarian, nations into civilization. The cheap prices of its commodities are the heavy artillery with which it batters down all Chinese walls, with which it forces the barbarians' intensely obstinate hatred of foreigners to capitulate.* It compels all nations, on pain of extinction, to adopt the bourgeois mode of production; it compels them to introduce what it calls civilization into their midst, *i.e.*, to become bourgeois themselves. In one word, it creates a world after its own image.

The bourgeoisie has subjected the country to the rule of the towns. It has created enormous cities, has greatly increased the urban population as compared with the rural, and has thus rescued a considerable part of the population from the idiocy of rural life. Just as it has made the country dependent on the towns, so it has made barbarian and semi-barbarian countries dependent on the civilized ones, nations of peasants on nations of bourgeois, the East on the West.

The bourgeoisie keeps more and more doing away with the scattered state of the population, of the means of production, and of property. It has agglomerated† population, centralized means of production, and has concentrated property in a few hands. The necessary consequence of this was political centralization. Independent, or but loosely connected provinces with separate interests, laws, governments and systems of taxation, became lumped together into one nation, with one government, one code of laws, one national class-interest, one frontier,‡ and one customs-tariff.

The bourgeoisie, during its rule of scarce one hundred years, has created more massive and more colossal productive forces than have all preceding generations together. Subjection of Nature's forces to man, machinery, application of chemistry to industry and agriculture, steam-navigation, railways, electric telegraphs, clearing of whole continents for cultivation, canalization of rivers, whole populations conjured out of the ground—what earlier century had even a presentiment that such productive forces slumbered in the lap of social labour?

We see then: the means of production and of exchange, on whose foundation the bourgeoisie built itself up, were generated in feudal society. At a certain stage in the development of these means of production and of exchange, the conditions under which feudal society produced and exchanged, the feudal organization of agriculture and manufacturing industry, in one word, the feudal relations of property became no longer compatible with the already developed productive forces; they became so many fetters.§ They had to be burst asunder; they were burst asunder.

Into their place stepped free competition, accompanied by a social and political constitution adapted in it, and the economical and political sway of the bourgeois class.

A similar movement is going on before our own eyes. Modern bourgeois society, with its relations of production, of exchange and of property, a society that has conjured up such gigantic means of production and of exchange, is like the sorcerer who is no longer able to control the powers of the nether world whom he has called up by his spells. For many a decade past the history of industry and commerce is but the history of the revolt of modern productive forces against modern conditions of production, against the property relations that are the conditions for the existence of the bourgeois and of its rule. It is enough to mention the commercial crises that by their periodical return put on its trial, each time more threateningly, the existence of the entire bourgeois society. In these crises a great part not only of the existing products, but also of the previously created productive forces, are periodically destroyed. In these crises there breaks out an epidemic that, in all earlier epochs, would have seemed an absurdity—the epidemic of overproduction.¶ Society suddenly finds itself put back

---

* A reference to the first Opium War in China (1839–43), which forced the Chinese to cede Hong Kong to the British and to open five of their ports to foreign trade.

† Combined together.

‡ External border.

§ Leg chains or shackles.

¶ Such crises occurred regularly in advanced capitalist economies from 1825 until 1939. Periodically, as more and more companies joined a particular industry, firms found themselves facing a glut of their products on the market. This

into a state of momentary barbarism; it appears as if a famine, a universal war of devastation had cut off the supply of every means of subsistence; industry and commerce seem to be destroyed; and why? Because there is too much civilization, too much means of subsistence, too much industry, too much commerce. The productive forces at the disposal of society no longer tend to further the development of the conditions of bourgeois property; on the contrary, they have become too powerful for these conditions, by which they are fettered, and so soon as they overcome these fetters, they bring disorder into the whole of bourgeois society, endanger the existence of bourgeois property. The conditions of bourgeois society are too narrow to comprise the wealth created by them. And how does the bourgeoisie get over these crises? On the one hand by enforced destruction of a mass of productive forces; on the other, by the conquest of new markets, and by the more thorough exploitation of the old ones. That is to say, by paving the way for more extensive and more destructive crises, and by diminishing the means whereby crises are prevented.

The weapons with which the bourgeoisie felled feudalism to the ground are now turned against the bourgeoisie itself.

But not only has the bourgeoisie forged the weapons that bring death to itself; it has also called into existence the men who are to wield those weapons— the modern working class—the proletarians.

In proportion as the bourgeoisie, *i.e.*, capital, is developed, in the same proportion is the proletariat, the modern working class, developed—a class of labourers, who live only so long as they find work, and who find work only so long as their labour increases capital. These labourers, who must sell themselves piecemeal, are a commodity, like every other article of commerce, and are consequently exposed to all the vicissitudes of competition, to all the fluctuations of the market.

Owing to the extensive use of machinery and to division of labour, the work of the proletarians has lost all individual character, and, consequently, all charm for the workman. He becomes an appendage of the machine, and it is only the most simple, most monotonous, and most easily acquired knack, that is required of him. Hence, the cost of production of a workman is restricted, almost entirely, to the means of subsistence that he requires for maintenance, and for the propagation of his race. But the price of a commodity, and therefore also of labour, is equal to its cost of production. In proportion, therefore, as the repulsiveness of the work increases, the wage decreases. Nay more, in proportion as the use of machinery and division of labour increases, in the same proportion the burden of toil also increases, whether by prolongation of the working hours, by the increase of the work exacted in a given time, or by increased speed of the machinery, etc.

Modern industry has converted the little workshop of the patriarchal master into the great factory of the industrial capitalist. Masses of labourers, crowded into the factory, are organized like soldiers. As privates of the industrial army they are placed under the command of a perfect hierarchy of officers and sergeants. Not only are they slaves of the bourgeois class, and of the bourgeois State; they are daily and hourly enslaved by the machine, by the overlooker, and, above all, by the individual bourgeois manufacturer himself. The more openly this despotism proclaims gain to be its end and aim, the more petty, the more hateful and the more embittering it is.

The less the skill and exertion of strength implied in manual labour, in other words, the more modern industry becomes developed, the more is the labour of men superseded by that of women. Differences of age and sex have no longer any distinctive social validity for the working class. All are instruments of labour, more or less expensive to use, according to their age and sex.

No sooner is the exploitation of the labourer by the manufacturer, so far, at an end, and he receives his wages in cash, than he is set upon by the other

---

over-supply depressed prices below expected profit levels, and so companies suddenly began to cut back production. Each time, these cutbacks started a vicious chain reaction, as suppliers were also forced to make cutbacks, which increased the unemployment rate, which reduced consumer spending and so increased over-supply, which depressed prices still further, and so on. At the height of the Great Depression of the 1930s, the worst such crisis, unemployment reached 25 per cent in the United States. Marx provided a sophisticated analysis of this sort of crisis in *Capital*.

portions of the bourgeoisie, the landlord, the shop-keeper, the pawnbroker, etc.

The lower strata of the middle class—the small tradespeople, shopkeepers, and retired tradesmen generally, the handicraftsmen and peasants—all these sink gradually into the proletariat, partly because their diminutive capital does not suffice for the scale on which Modern Industry is carried on, and is swamped in the competition with the large capitalists, partly because their specialized skill is rendered worthless by new methods of production. Thus, the proletariat is recruited from all classes of the population.

The proletariat goes through various stages of development. With its birth begins its struggle with the bourgeoisie. At first, the contest is carried on by individual labourers, then by the workpeople of a factory, then by the operatives of one trade, in one locality, against the individual bourgeois who directly exploits them. They direct their attacks not against the bourgeois condition of production, but against the instruments of production themselves; they destroy imported wares that compete with their labour, they smash to pieces machinery, they set factories ablaze, they seek to restore by force the vanished status of the workman of the Middle Ages.

At this stage the labourers still form an incoherent mass scattered over the whole country, and broken up by their mutual competition. If anywhere they unite to form more compact bodies, this is not yet the consequence of their own active union, but of the union of the bourgeoisie, which class, in order to attain its own political ends, is compelled to set the whole proletariat in motion, and is moreover yet, for a time, able to do so. At this stage, therefore, the proletarians do not fight their enemies, but the enemies of their enemies, the remnants of absolute monarchy, the landowners, the non-industrial bourgeois, the petty bourgeoisie.* Thus, the whole historical movement is concentrated in the hands of the bourgeoisie; every victory so obtained is a victory for the bourgeoisie.

But with the development of industry, the proletariat not only increases in number; it becomes concentrated in greater masses, its strength grows, and it feels that strength more. The various interests and conditions of life within the ranks of the proletariat are more and more equalized, in proportion as machinery obliterates all distinctions of labour, and nearly everywhere reduces wages to the same low level. The growing competition among the bourgeois, and the resulting commercial crises, make the wages of the workers ever more fluctuating. The increasing improvement of machinery, ever more rapidly developing, makes their livelihood more and more precarious; the collisions between individual workmen and individual bourgeois take more and more the character of collisions between two classes. Thereupon, the workers begin to form combinations (Trades' Unions) against the bourgeois; they club together in order to keep up the rate of wages; they found permanent associations in order to make provision beforehand for these occasional revolts. Here and there the contest breaks out into riots.

Now and then the workers are victorious, but only for a time. The real fruit of their battles lies, not in the immediate result, but in the ever expanding union of the workers. This union is helped on by the improved means of communication that are created by modern industry and that place the workers of different localities in contact with one another. It was just this contact that was needed to centralize the numerous local struggles, all of the same character, into one national struggle between classes. But every class struggle is a political struggle. And that union, to attain which the burghers of the Middle Ages, with their miserable highways, required centuries, the modern proletarian, thanks to railways, achieve in a few years.

This organization of the proletarians into a class, and consequently into a political party, is continually being upset again by the competition between the workers themselves. But it ever rises up again, stronger, firmer, mightier. It compels legislative recognition of particular interests of the workers, by taking advantage of the divisions among the bourgeoisie itself. Thus, the ten-hours' bill in England was carried.†

---

* The petty (i.e., lesser) bourgeoisie, for Marx, are those who control means of production (like the bourgeoisie) but work them with their own labor (like the proletariat): for example, independent shopkeepers or small farmers.

† This law—part of the 1847 Factory Act—limited the daily working hours of women and children to 58 hours a week. It was highly controversial, and was passed by Parliament only because conservative "Old England" landowners opposed

Altogether collisions between the classes of the old society further, in many ways, the course of development of the proletariat. The bourgeoisie finds itself involved in a constant battle. At first with the aristocracy; later on, with those portions of the bourgeoisie itself, whose interests have become antagonistic to the progress of industry; at all times, with the bourgeoisie of foreign countries. In all these battles it sees itself compelled to appeal to the proletariat, to ask for its help, and thus, to drag it into the political arena. The bourgeoisie itself, therefore, supplies the proletariat with its own elements of political and general education, in other words, it furnishes the proletariat with weapons for fighting the bourgeoisie.

Further, as we have already seen, entire sections of the ruling class are, by the advance of industry, precipitated into the proletariat, or are at least threatened in their conditions of existence. These also supply the proletariat with fresh elements of enlightenment and progress.

Finally, in times when the class struggle nears the decisive hour, the progress of dissolution going on within the ruling class, in fact within the whole range of old society, assumes such a violent, glaring character, that a small section of the ruling class cuts itself adrift, and joins the revolutionary class, the class that holds the future in its hands. Just as, therefore, at an earlier period, a section of the nobility went over to the bourgeoisie, so now a portion of the bourgeoisie goes over to the proletariat, and in particular, a portion of the bourgeois ideologists, who have raised themselves to the level of comprehending theoretically the historical movement as a whole.

Of all the classes that stand face to face with the bourgeoisie today, the proletariat alone is a genuinely revolutionary class. The other classes decay and finally disappear in the face of Modern Industry; the proletariat is its special and essential product.

The lower middle class, the small manufacturer, the shopkeeper, the artisan, the peasant, all these fight against the bourgeoisie, to save from extinction their existence as fractions of the middle class. They are therefore not revolutionary, but conservative. Nay more, they are reactionary, for they try to roll back the wheel of history. If by chance they are revolutionary, they are only so in view of their impending transfer into the proletariat, they thus defend not their present, but their future interests, they desert their own standpoint to place themselves at that of the proletariat.

The "dangerous class," the social scum,* that passively rotting mass thrown off by the lowest layers of the old society may, here and there, be swept into the movement by a proletarian revolution; its conditions of life, however, prepare it far more for the part of a bribed tool of reactionary intrigue.

In the condition of the proletariat, those of old society at large are already virtually swamped. The proletarian is without property; his relation to his wife and children has no longer anything in common with the bourgeois family relations; modern industrial labour, modern subjection to capital, the same in England as in France, in America as in Germany, has stripped him of every trace of national character. Law, morality, religion, are to him so many bourgeois prejudices, behind which lurk in ambush just as many bourgeois interests.

All the preceding classes that got the upper hand sought to fortify their already acquired status by subjecting society at large to their conditions of appropriation. The proletarians cannot become masters of the productive forces of society, except by abolishing their own previous mode of appropriation, and thereby also every other previous mode of appropriation. They have nothing of their own to secure and to fortify; their mission is to destroy all previous securities for, and insurances of, individual property.

All previous historical movements were movements of minorities, or in the interest of minorities. The proletarian movement is the self-conscious, independent movement of the immense majority, in the interest of the immense majority. The proletariat, the lowest stratum of our present society, cannot stir, cannot raise itself up, without the whole super-incumbent strata of official society being sprung into the air.

Though not in substance, yet in form, the struggle of the proletariat with the bourgeoisie is at first

---

the interests of the ever-more-powerful industrialists and mill owners.

* The original German word here—one that has found its way into English—is *Lumpenproletariat*, literally, "proletariat in rags."

a national struggle. The proletariat of each country must, of course, first of all settle matters with its own bourgeoisie.

In depicting the most general phases of the development of the proletariat, we traced the more or less veiled civil war, raging within existing society, up to the point where that war breaks out into open revolution, and where the violent overthrow of the bourgeoisie lays the foundation for the sway of the proletariat.

Hitherto, every form of society has been based, as we have already seen, on the antagonism of oppressing and oppressed classes. But in order to oppress a class, certain conditions must be assured to it under which it can, at least, continue its slavish existence. The serf, in the period of serfdom, raised himself to membership in the commune, just as the petty bourgeois, under the yoke of the feudal absolutism, managed to develop into a bourgeois. The modern labourer, on the contrary, instead of rising with the progress of industry, sinks deeper and deeper below the conditions of existence of his own class. He becomes a pauper, and pauperism develops more rapidly than population and wealth. And here it becomes evident that the bourgeoisie is unfit any longer to be the ruling class in society, and to impose its conditions of existence upon society as an over-riding law. It is unfit to rule because it is incompetent to assure an existence to its slave within his slavery, because it cannot help letting him sink into such a state, that it has to feed him, instead of being fed by him. Society can no longer live under this bourgeoisie, in other words, its existence is no longer compatible with society.

The essential condition for the existence, and for the sway of the bourgeois class, is the formation and augmentation of capital; the condition for capital is wage-labour. Wage-labour rests exclusively on competition between the labourers. The advance of industry, whose involuntary promoter is the bourgeoisie, replaces the isolation of the labourers, due to competition, by their revolutionary combination, due to association. The development of Modern Industry, therefore, cuts from under its feet the very foundation on which the bourgeoisie produces and appropriates products. What the bourgeoisie, therefore, produces, above all, is its own grave-diggers. Its fall and the victory of the proletariat are equally inevitable.

II. Proletarians and Communists

In what relation do the Communists stand to the proletarians as a whole?

The Communists do not form a separate party opposed to the other working-class parties.

They have no interests separate and apart from those of the proletariat as a whole.

They do not set up any sectarian principles of their own, by which to shape and mold the proletarian movement.

The Communists are distinguished from the other working-class parties by this only: (1) In the national struggles of the proletarians of the different countries, they point out and bring to the front the common interests of the entire proletariat, independently of all nationality. (2) In the various stages of development which the struggle of the working class against the bourgeoisie has to pass through, they always and everywhere represent the interests of the movement as a whole.

The Communists, therefore, are on the one hand, practically, the most advanced and resolute section of the working-class parties of every country, that section which pushes forward all others; on the other hand, theoretically, they have over the great mass of the proletariat the advantage of clearly understanding the line of march, the conditions, and the ultimate general results of the proletarian movement.

The immediate aim of the Communists is the same as that of all other proletarian parties: formation of the proletariat into a class, overthrow of the bourgeois supremacy, conquest of political power by the proletariat.

The theoretical conclusions of the Communists are in no way based on ideas or principles that have been invented, or discovered, by this or that would-be universal reformer.

They merely express, in general terms, actual relations springing from an existing class struggle, from a historical movement going on under our very eyes. The abolition of existing property relations is not at all a distinctive feature of Communism.

All property relations in the past have continually been subject to historical change consequent upon the change in historical conditions.

The French Revolution, for example, abolished feudal property in favour of bourgeois property.

The distinguishing feature of Communism is not the abolition of property generally, but the abolition of bourgeois property. But modern bourgeois private property is the final and most complete expression of the system of producing and appropriating products, that is based on class antagonisms, on the exploitation of the many by the few.

In this sense, the theory of the Communists may be summed up in the single sentence: Abolition of private property.

We Communists have been reproached with the desire of abolishing the right of personally acquiring property as the fruit of a man's own labour, which property is alleged to be the groundwork of all personal freedom, activity and independence.

Hard-won, self-acquired, self-earned property! Do you mean the property of the petty artisan and of the small peasant, a form of property that preceded the bourgeois form? There is no need to abolish that; the development of industry has to a great extent already destroyed it, and is still destroying it daily.

Or do you mean the modern bourgeois private property?

But does wage-labour create any property for the labourer? Not a bit. It creates capital, *i.e.*, that kind of property which exploits wage-labour, and which cannot increase except upon conditions of begetting a new supply of wage-labour for fresh exploitation. Property, in its present form, is based on the antagonism of capital and wage-labour. Let us examine both sides of this antagonism.

To be a capitalist, is to have not only a purely personal, but a social *status* in production. Capital is a collective product, and only by the united action of many members, nay, in the last resort, only by the united action of all members of society, can it be set in motion.

Capital is, therefore, not a personal, it is a social power.

When, therefore, capital is converted into common property, into the property of all members of society, personal property is not thereby transformed into social property. It is only the social character of the property that is changed. It loses its class character.

Let us now take wage-labour.

The average price of wage-labour is the minimum wage, *i.e.*, that quantum of the means of subsistence, which is absolutely requisite to keep the labourer in bare existence as a labourer. What, therefore, the wage-labourer appropriates by means of his labour, merely suffices to prolong and reproduce a bare existence. We by no means intend to abolish this personal appropriation of the products of labour, an appropriation that is made for the maintenance and reproduction of human life, and that leaves no surplus wherewith to command the labour of others. All that we want to do away with is the miserable character of this appropriation, under which the labourer lives merely to increase capital, and is allowed to live only in so far as the interest of the ruling class requires it.

In bourgeois society, living labour is but a means to increase accumulated labour. In Communist society, accumulated labour is but a means to widen, to enrich, to promote the existence of the labourer.

In bourgeois society, therefore, the past dominates the present; in Communist society, the present dominates the past. In bourgeois society capital is independent and has individuality, while the living person is dependent and has no individuality.

And the abolition of this state of things is called by the bourgeois abolition of individuality and freedom! And rightly so. The abolition of bourgeois individuality, bourgeois independence, and bourgeois freedom is undoubtedly aimed at.

By freedom is meant, under the present bourgeois conditions of production, free trade, free selling and buying.

But if selling and buying disappears, free selling and buying disappears also. This talk about free selling and buying, and all the other "brave words" of our bourgeoisie about freedom in general, have a meaning, if any, only in contrast with restricted selling and buying, with the fettered traders of the Middle Ages, but have no meaning when opposed to the Communistic abolition of buying and selling, or the bourgeois conditions of production, and of the bourgeoisie itself.

You are horrified at our intending to do away with private property. But in your existing society, private property is already done away with for nine-tenths of the population; its existence for the few is solely due to its non-existence in the hands of those nine-tenths. You reproach us, therefore, with intending to do away with a form of property, the necessary condition for whose existence is the non-existence of any property for the immense majority of society.

In one word, you reproach us with intending to do away with your property. Precisely so; that is just what we intend.

From the moment when labour can no longer be converted into capital, money, or rent, into a social power capable of being monopolized, *i.e.*, from the moment when individual property can no longer be transformed into bourgeois property, into capital, from that moment, you say, individuality vanishes.

You must, therefore, confess that by "individual" you mean no other person than the bourgeois, than the middle-class owner of property. This person must, indeed, be swept out of the way, and made impossible.

Communism deprives no man of the power to appropriate the products of society; all that it does is to deprive him of the power to subjugate the labour of others by means of such appropriation.

It has been objected that upon the abolition of private property all work will cease, and universal laziness will overtake us.

According to this, bourgeois society ought long ago to have gone to the dogs through sheer idleness; for those who work, acquire nothing, and those who acquire anything, do not work. The whole of this objection is but another expression of the tautology: that there can no longer be any wage-labour when there is no longer any capital.

All objections urged against the Communistic mode of producing and appropriating material products, have, in the same way, been urged against the Communistic mode of producing and appropriating intellectual products. Just as, to the bourgeois, the disappearance of class property is the disappearance of production itself, so the disappearance of class culture is to him identical with the disappearance of all culture.

That culture, the loss of which he laments, is, for the enormous majority, a mere training to act as a machine.

But don't wrangle with us so long as you apply, to our intended abolition of bourgeois property, the standard of your bourgeois notions of freedom, culture, law, etc. Your very ideas are but the outgrowth of the conditions of your bourgeois production and bourgeois property, just as your jurisprudence is but the will of your class made into a law for all, a will, whose essential character and direction are determined by the economical conditions of existence of your class.

The selfish misconception that induces you to transform into eternal laws of nature and of reason, the social forms springing from your present mode of production and form of property—historical relations that rise and disappear in the progress of production—this misconception you share with every ruling class that has preceded you. What you see clearly in the case of ancient property, what you admit in the case of feudal property, you are of course forbidden to admit in the case of your own bourgeois form of property.

Abolition of the family! Even the most radical flare up at this infamous proposal of the Communists.

On what foundation is the present family, the bourgeois family, based? On capital, on private gain. In its completely developed form this family exists only among the bourgeoisie. But this state of things finds its complement in the practical absence of the family among proletarians, and in public prostitution.

The bourgeois family will vanish as a matter of course when its complement vanishes, and both will vanish with the vanishing of capital.

Do you charge us with wanting to stop the exploitation of children by their parents? To this crime we plead guilty.

But, you will say, we destroy the most hallowed of relations, when we replace home education by social.

And your education! Is not that also social, and determined by the social conditions under which you educate, by the intervention, direct or indirect, of society, by means of schools, etc.? The Communists have not invented the intervention of society in education; they do but seek to alter the character of that intervention, and to rescue education from the influence of the ruling class.

The bourgeois clap-trap about the family and education, about the hallowed co-relation of parent and child, becomes all the more disgusting, the more, by the action of Modern Industry, all family ties among the proletarians are torn asunder, and their children transformed into simple articles of commerce and instruments of labour.

But you Communists would introduce community of women, screams the bourgeoisie in chorus.

The bourgeois sees his wife a mere instrument of production. He hears that the instruments of production are to be exploited in common, and, naturally, can come to no other conclusion that the lot of being common to all will likewise fall to the women.

He has not even a suspicion that the real point aimed at is to do away with the status of women as mere instruments of production.

For the rest, nothing is more ridiculous than the virtuous indignation of our bourgeois at the community of women* which, they pretend, is to be openly and officially established by the Communists. The Communists have no need to introduce community of women; it has existed almost from time immemorial.

Our bourgeois, not content with having the wives and daughters of their proletarians at their disposal, not to speak of common prostitutes, take the greatest pleasure in seducing each other's wives.

Bourgeois marriage is in reality a system of wives in common and thus, at the most, what the Communists might possibly be reproached with is that they desire to introduce, in substitution for a hypocritically concealed, an openly legalized community of women. For the rest, it is self-evident that the abolition of the present system of production must bring with it the abolition of the community of women springing from that system, *i.e.*, of prostitution both public and private.

The Communists are further reproached with desiring to abolish countries and nationality.

The workers have no country. We cannot take from them what they have not got. Since the proletariat must first of all acquire political supremacy, must rise to be the leading class of the nation, must constitute itself *the* nation, it is so far, itself national, though not in the bourgeois sense of the word.

National differences and antagonism between peoples are daily more and more vanishing, owing to the development of the bourgeoisie, to freedom of commerce, to the world market, to uniformity in the mode of production and in the conditions of life corresponding thereto.

The supremacy of the proletariat will cause them to vanish still faster. United action, of the leading civilized countries at least, is one of the first conditions for the emancipation of the proletariat.

In proportion as the exploitation of one individual by another is put an end to, the exploitation of one nation by another will also be put an end to. In proportion as the antagonism between classes within the nation vanishes, the hostility of one nation to another will come to an end.

The charges against Communism made from a religious, a philosophical, and, generally, from an ideological standpoint, are not deserving of serious examination.

Does it require deep intuition to comprehend that man's ideas, views, and conception, in one word, man's consciousness, changes with every change in the conditions of his material existence, in his social relations and in his social life?

What else does the history of ideas prove, than that intellectual production changes its character in proportion as material production is changed? The ruling ideas of each age have ever been the ideas of its ruling class.

When people speak of ideas that revolutionize society, they do but express that fact, that within the old society, the elements of a new one have been created, and that the dissolution of the old ideas keeps even pace with the dissolution of the old conditions of existence.

When the ancient world was in its last throes, the ancient religions were overcome by Christianity. When Christian ideas succumbed in the eighteenth century to rationalist ideas, feudal society fought its death battle with the then revolutionary bourgeoisie. The ideas of religious liberty and freedom of conscience merely gave expression to the sway of free competition within the domain of knowledge.

"Undoubtedly," it will be said, "religious, moral, philosophical, and juridical ideas have been modified in the course of historical development. But religion, morality, philosophy, political science, and law, constantly survived this change.

"There are, besides, eternal truths, such as Freedom, Justice, etc., that are common to all states of society. But Communism abolishes eternal truths, it abolishes all religion and all morality, instead of

---

*   Women no longer legally bound in couples by marriage.

constituting them on a new basis; it therefore acts in contradiction to all past historical experience."

What does this accusation reduce itself to? The history of all past society has consisted in the development of class antagonisms, antagonisms that assumed different forms at different epochs.

But whatever form they may have taken, one fact is common to all past ages, *viz.*, the exploitation of one part of society by the other. No wonder, then, that the social consciousness of past ages, despite all the multiplicity and variety it displays, moves within certain common forms, or general ideas, which cannot completely vanish except with the total disappearance of class antagonisms.

The Communist revolution is the most radical rupture with traditional relations; no wonder that its development involved the most radical rupture with traditional ideas.

But let us have done with the bourgeois objections to Communism.

We have seen above, that the first step in the revolution by the working class is to raise the proletariat to the position of ruling class, to win the battle of democracy.

The proletariat will use its political supremacy to wrest, by degrees, all capital from the bourgeoisie, to centralize all instruments of production in the hands of the State, *i.e.*, of the proletariat organized as the ruling class; and to increase the total productive forces as rapidly as possible.

Of course, in the beginning, this cannot be effected except by means of despotic inroads on the rights of property, and on the conditions of bourgeois production; by means of measures, therefore, which appear economically insufficient and untenable, but which, in the course of the movement, outstrip themselves, necessitate further inroads upon the old social order, and are unavoidable as a means of entirely revolutionizing the mode of production.

These measures will, of course, be different in different countries.

Nevertheless in most advanced countries, the following will be pretty generally applicable:

1. Abolition of property in land and application of all rents of land to public purposes.
2. A heavy progressive or graduated income tax.
3. Abolition of all right of inheritance.
4. Confiscation of the property of all emigrants and rebels.
5. Centralization of credit in the banks of the State, by means of a national bank with State capital and an exclusive monopoly.
6. Centralization of the means of communication and transport in the hands of the State.
7. Extension of factories and instruments of production owned by the State; the bringing into cultivation of waste-lands, and the improvement of the soil generally in accordance with a common plan.
8. Equal liability of all to labour. Establishment of industrial armies, especially for agriculture.
9. Combination of agriculture with manufacturing industries; gradual abolition of all the distinction between town and country by a more equable distribution of the population over the country.
10. Free education for all children in public schools. Abolition of children's factory labour in its present form. Combination of education with industrial production, etc., etc.

When, in the course of development, class distinctions have disappeared, and all production has been concentrated in the hands of a vast association of the whole nation, the public power will lose its political character. Political power, properly so called, is merely the organized power of one class for oppressing another. If the proletariat during its contest with the bourgeoisie is compelled, by the force of circumstances, to organize itself as a class, if, by means of a revolution, it makes itself the ruling class, and, as such, sweeps away by force the old conditions of production, then it will, along with these conditions, have swept away the conditions for the existence of class antagonisms and of classes generally, and will thereby have abolished its own supremacy as a class.

In place of the old bourgeois society, with its classes and class antagonisms, we shall have an association, in which the free development of each is the condition for the free development of all.

...

IV. Position of the Communists in Relation to the Various Existing Opposition Parties

Section II has made clear the relations of the Communists to the existing working-class parties, such as the Chartists in England and the Agrarian Reformers in America.*

The Communists fight for the attainment of the immediate aims, for the enforcement of the momentary interests of the working class; but in the movement of the present, they also represent and take care of the future of that movement. In France the Communists ally with the Social Democrats, against the conservative and radical bourgeoisie, reserving, however, the right to take up a critical position in regard to phases and illusions traditionally handed down from the great Revolution.

In Switzerland, they support the Radicals, without losing sight of the fact that this party consists of antagonistic elements, partly of Democratic Socialists, in the French sense, partly of radical bourgeois.

In Poland, they support the party that insists on an agrarian revolution as the prime condition for national emancipation, that party which fomented the insurrection of Kraków in 1846.†

In Germany, they fight with the bourgeoisie whenever it acts in a revolutionary way, against the absolute monarchy, the feudal squirearchy,‡ and the petty bourgeoisie.

But they never cease, for a single instant, to instil into the working class the clearest possible recognition of the hostile antagonism between bourgeoisie and proletariat, in order that the German workers may straightway use, as so many weapons against the bourgeoisie, the social and political conditions that the bourgeoisie must necessarily introduce along with its supremacy, and in order that, after the fall of the reactionary classes in Germany, the fight against the bourgeoisie itself may immediately begin.

The Communists turn their attention chiefly to Germany, because that country is on the eve of a bourgeois revolution that is bound to be carried out under more advanced conditions of European civilization, and with a much more developed proletariat, than that of England was in the seventeenth, and France in the eighteenth century, and because the bourgeois revolution in Germany will be but the prelude to an immediately following proletarian revolution.

In short, the Communists everywhere support every revolutionary movement against the existing social and political order of things.

In all these movements they bring to the front, as the leading question in each, the property question, no matter what its degree of development at the time.

Finally, they labour everywhere for the union and agreement of the democratic parties of all countries.

The Communists disdain to conceal their views and aims. They openly declare that their ends can be attained only by the forcible overthrow of all existing social conditions. Let the ruling classes tremble at a Communist revolution. The proletarians have nothing to lose but their chains. They have a world to win.

WORKING MEN OF ALL COUNTRIES, UNITE! ■

---

* Chartism was a popular reformist movement that lasted from 1837 to 1848. Among its demands (outlined in an 1837 "People's Charter") were universal male voting rights, equal electoral districts, abolition of the property qualification for running for Parliament, and annual parliaments. The National Reform Association was founded in 1844 to campaign for free settlement of the landless on public lands, a moratorium on seizure of family farms for non-payment of debt, and establishment of a 160-acre ceiling on land ownership to ensure there would be enough small-holdings to go around.

† A nationalist, republican uprising in southern Poland against the Russians, Prussians, and Austrians who had jointly occupied it since the collapse of Napoleon's empire in 1815. The rebellion was crushed, and Kraków incorporated into the Austrian empire.

‡ Landed gentry.

Suggestions for Critical Reflection

1. "The history of all hitherto existing society is the history of class struggles." What role does this resounding phrase have in Marx's argument? Is it a *true* claim? (How easy would it be for professional historians to show it to be either true or false?) If its historical truth is open to question, how serious a problem is this for Marx's views?

2. Marx's critique of the bourgeoisie has both positive and negative elements. For example, he notes that they have "accomplished wonders far surpassing ... Gothic cathedrals," but also claims the bourgeois have reduced the family to "a mere money relation." What is Marx's overall judgment of the bourgeoisie? How far do you agree with it?

3. "The executive of the modern State is but a committee for managing the common affairs of the whole bourgeoisie." How does Marx support this claim? What, exactly, do you think he means by it? What implications does it have, if true?

4. Marx suggests modern bourgeois society contains within it the seeds of its own self-destruction (as did feudal society before it). How compelling are his arguments for this claim?

5. Marx says that, for the proletariat, "[l]aw, morality, religion, are to him so many bourgeois prejudices, behind which lurk in ambush just as many bourgeois interests." What are the implications of this statement? Why do you think Marx says it, and do you think he is justified in doing so?

6. Marx addresses the criticism of communism which says that, if private property and personal wealth are abolished, people will have no incentive to be productive at all "and universal laziness will overtake us." How adequately do you think Marx handles this objection?

7. What do you make of Marx's list of 10 components for the dictatorship of the proletariat? How radical or unreasonable do they seem today? How likely would they be to result in the elimination of private property and the emancipation of the proletariat?

8. What, if anything, do historical developments since Marx's death—in particular, the rise and fall of the Soviet Union, and the failure of capitalism to end in revolution in the democratic West—show about the validity of his philosophical thought?

Notes

1 By bourgeoisie is meant the class of modern Capitalists, owners of the means of social production and employers of wage-labour. By proletariat, the class of modern wage-labourers who, having no means of production of their own, are reduced to selling their labour-power in order to live.

2 That is, all *written* history. In 1847, the pre-history of society, the social organization existing previous to recorded history, was all but unknown. Since then, [August von] Haxthausen discovered common ownership of land in Russia, [Georg Ludwig von] Maurer proved it to be the social foundation from which all Teutonic races started in history, and by and by village communities were found to be, or to have been the primitive form of society everywhere from India to Ireland. The inner organization of this primitive Communistic society was laid bare, in its typical form, by [Lewis Henry] Morgan's crowning discovery of the true nature of the *gens* and its relation to the *tribe*. With the dissolution of these primaeval communities society begins to be differentiated into separate and finally antagonistic classes. I have attempted to retrace this dissolution in *Der Ursprung der Familie, des Privateigenthums und des Staats* [*The Origins of the Family, Private Property and the State*], second edition, Stuttgart, 1886.

3 Guild-master, that is, a full member of a guild, a master within, not a head of a guild.

4 "Commune" was the name taken, in France, by the nascent towns even before they had conquered from their feudal lords and masters local self-government and political rights as the "Third Estate." Generally speaking, for the economical development of the bourgeoisie, England is here taken as the typical country; for its political development, France.

JOHN RAWLS

FROM *Justice as Fairness: A Restatement*

Who Was John Rawls?

John Borden Rawls was, until his death in 2002, perhaps the world's most important contemporary political philosopher, and his 1971 book *A Theory of Justice* is generally regarded as the most significant work of political theory published in the twentieth century. Born in 1921 in Baltimore to an upper-class southern family, Rawls's father was a successful tax lawyer and constitutional expert while his mother was the feminist president of the local League of Women Voters. As a boy, the intensely religious Rawls was sent to Kent, a renowned Episcopalian preparatory school in Connecticut, and then went on to Princeton for his undergraduate degree. In 1943, he joined the US infantry and served in New Guinea, the Philippines, and Japan (where he witnessed first-hand the aftermath of the atomic bombing of Hiroshima). The horrors he experienced during the war caused Rawls to lose his Christian faith. Rawls was awarded a Bronze Star for valor in New Guinea, and later promoted to sergeant. However he was demoted back to private for refusing to discipline a soldier because he believed the punishment was unjust, and he left the army as a private in 1946, returning to Princeton to pursue his PhD in philosophy.

After completing the doctorate, he taught at Princeton for two years, visited Oxford University for a year on a Fulbright Fellowship, and was then employed as a professor at Cornell. In 1964 Rawls moved to Harvard University, where he was appointed James Bryant Conant Professor of Philosophy in 1979. During the 1960s, despite his "bat-like horror of the limelight,"[*] Rawls spoke out publicly against American involvement in the Vietnam War, and he was influenced by this to develop a theoretical underpinning for citizen resistance against a government's unjust policies.

Throughout the 1980s and early 1990s Rawls was an omnipresent figure in political philosophy, and exerted a great influence on the discipline through his teaching and mentoring of younger academics as well as his writings. Former US President Bill Clinton said of him that Rawls "almost singlehandedly ... revived the disciplines of political and ethical philosophy with his argument that a society in which the most fortunate helped the least fortunate is not only a moral society, but a logical one."[†] Unfortunately, in 1995, Rawls suffered the first of several strokes that seriously impeded his ability to continue working, though he was able to complete his final book, *The Law of Peoples* (1999), which laid out his views on international justice.

What Was Rawls's Overall Philosophical Project?

Though Rawls was always much more the reclusive academic than a campaigning public figure, his work was nevertheless guided by a deep personal commitment to combating injustice. Because of his family's origins in the American south, one of Rawls's earliest moral concerns was the injustice of black slavery. He was interested in formulating a moral theory that not only showed slavery to be unjust, but described its injustice *in the right way*. For Rawls, the immorality of slavery does not lie merely in the fact that benefits for slaveowners were outweighed by harms done to slaves—rather, slavery is the kind of thing that should *never* be imposed on any human being, no matter what overall benefits or efficiencies it might bring about. Thus, Rawls found himself opposed to the then-dominant political morality of utilitarianism, and seeking a new foundation for social justice in the work

---

[*]   Ben Rogers, obituary for John Rawls, *The Guardian*, 27 November 2002.
[†]   Speech at the occasion of awarding Rawls the National Humanities Medal in 1999.

of Immanuel Kant and social contract theorists such as John Locke and Jean-Jacques Rousseau.*

Two guiding assumptions behind Rawls's neo-Kantian project (which he called "Kantian constructivism") were, first, that there is such a thing as moral truth—that at least some fundamental moral questions have objectively correct answers, even if it is difficult to discover them—and second, that "the right" is separate from and prior to "the good." This latter claim is the idea (which is found in Kant) that the morally right thing to do cannot be defined as, and will not always be the same thing as, the maximization of some moral good, such as happiness or equality. There are certain constraints on how people can be treated which always take precedence over the general welfare.

The central doctrine which has informed the resulting political morality is what Rawls calls "justice as fairness." This is the view that social institutions should not confer morally arbitrary long-term advantages on some persons at the expense of others. According to Rawls, one's prospects and opportunities in life are strongly influenced by the circumstances of one's birth—one's place in the social, political, and economic structure defined by the basic institutions of one's society. For example, one might have been born to slaveowners or to slaves, to a wealthy political dynasty in New England or to a poor family in a Philadelphia ghetto, to an Anglophone or to a Francophone family in 1950s Montréal. These important differences are morally arbitrary—a mere matter of luck—not something for which people deserve to be either rewarded or punished. According to Rawls, therefore, the fundamental problem of social justice is to ensure that the basic institutions of our society are set up in such a way that they do not generate and perpetuate morally arbitrary inequalities.

The upshot of this, in Rawls's view, includes the radical result that inequalities in wealth, income, and other "primary social goods" are justified *only* if they are to the advantage of the least well off in society. Rawls's work has thus been widely seen (and criticized) as the philosophical foundation for a particularly egalitarian and left-wing version of the modern welfare state, and also—because of his emphasis on a set of universal, indefeasible basic rights and liberties—as an important successor to the rich tradition of liberal political thought.

What Is the Structure of This Reading?

The selection reprinted here comes from Rawls's 2001 book *Justice as Fairness*. In it he sets out to represent, in their final form, the ideas first laid out in his seminal 1971 work *A Theory of Justice*. The heart of his substantive theory is the so-called two principles of justice, and his description of these (though not his extended argument for their adequacy) is included here.

In Part I of *Justice as Fairness* Rawls lays out the fundamental ideas underlying his political theory, including the important notion of society as a fair system of cooperation, and the main concepts involved in arguing for his theory of justice as being justified by a "contract" made in the "original position." Some of these basic notions are briefly described in "Some Useful Background Information," below. Part II of the book presents his two principles of justice, and the first two sections of it are reprinted here. In the first section, Rawls summarizes three basic points which inform and constrain his reasoning, and in the second he describes the two principles themselves. In the rest of Part II (not included) he provides more details about the two principles, and in Part III he lays out the argument from the original position. In Part IV he describes some of the institutions of a just basic structure, and finally in Part V he addresses questions about the political stability of such a society.

Some Useful Background Information

1. Rawls believes democratic societies are always characterized by what he calls "the fact of reasonable pluralism." By this he means "the fact of profound and irreconcilable differences in citizens' reasonable comprehensive religious and philosophical conceptions of the world, and in their views of the moral and aesthetic values to be sought in human life."† A consequence of

---

* See the Ethical Theory section for readings on utilitarianism and Kant's moral theory. Social contract theory is represented by the Hobbes reading earlier in this section.

† John Rawls, *Justice as Fairness: A Restatement* (Harvard University Press, 2001), 3.

this reasonable pluralism, Rawls believes, is that a democratic society can never genuinely be a *community*—a collection of persons united in affirming and pursuing the same conception of the good life. Rawls therefore proposes that we adopt—in fact, tacitly already have adopted—a different view of contemporary society: one that sees it as *a fair system of co-operation between free and equal citizens*. The task of a theory of justice then becomes one of specifying the fair terms of co-operation (and doing so in a way that is acceptable—that seems fair—even to citizens who have widely divergent conceptions of the good).

2. Rawls assumes the primary subject of this kind of theory of justice will be what he calls the *basic structure* of society. "[T]he basic structure of society is the way in which the main political and social institutions of society fit together into one system of social co-operation, and the way they assign basic rights and duties and regulate the division of advantages that arises from social co-operation over time.... The basic structure is the background social framework within which the activities of associations and individuals take place."* Examples of components of the basic structure include the political constitution, the relationship between the judiciary and the government, the structure of the economic system, and the social institution of the family. The kinds of things *not* included in the basic structure—and thus affected only indirectly by Rawls's theory of justice—are the internal arrangements of associations such as churches and universities, particular pieces of non-constitutional legislation or legal decisions, and social relationships between individual citizens.

3. If justice consists in the fair terms of co-operation for society viewed as a system of cooperation, then the question becomes: how are these fair terms of cooperation arrived at? Since the fact of reasonable pluralism precludes appeal to any kind of shared moral authority or outlook, Rawls concludes that the free terms of cooperation must be "settled by an agreement reached by free and equal citizens engaged in cooperation, and made in view of what they regard as their reciprocal advantage."†

Furthermore, this contract, like any agreement, must be made under conditions which are fair to all the parties involved. Rawls's attempt to specify the circumstances in which agreement on the basic structure of society would be fair is a thought-experiment called the *original position*.

In the original position, the parties to the contract are imagined placed behind what Rawls calls a *veil of ignorance*: they are not allowed to know their social positions; their particular comprehensive doctrines of the good; their race, sex, or ethnic group; or their genetic endowments of such things as strength and intelligence. In other words, knowledge of all the contingent or arbitrary aspects of one's place in actual society are removed. On the other hand, the parties in the original position are assumed to be well-informed about such things as economic and political theory and human psychology, and to be rational. In this way, all information which would—in Rawls's view—introduce unfair distortions into the social contract is excluded from the original position and only the data needed to make a fair decision are allowed in: thus, for example, there could be no question of rich people trying to establish a basic social structure which protects their wealth by disadvantaging the poor, since nobody in the original position knows whether they are rich or poor.

Rawls's idea is that whatever contract would be agreed to by representatives in the original position must be a fair one, one that any reasonable citizen could accept no matter what their place in society or their conception of the good. This contract is, of course, merely hypothetical (there was never actually any original position). Rawls's point is not that citizens are actually bound by a historical social contract, but that the thought-experiment of making a contract in the original position is a device for showing what principles of justice *we should accept if we are reasonable*. And, Rawls argues, the principles that would be rationally arrived at in the original position will not be, say, utilitarian, or non-egalitarian, but will be something very much like his two principles of justice.

---

* Ibid., 10.
† Ibid., 15.

FROM *Justice as Fairness: A Restatement**

PART II: PRINCIPLES OF JUSTICE, §§ 12–13

§12. *Three Basic Points*

12.1. In Part II we discuss the content of the two principles of justice that apply to the basic structure, as well as various grounds in favor of them and replies to a number of objections. A more formal and organized argument for these principles is presented in Part III, where we discuss the reasoning that moves the parties in the original position. In that argument the original position serves to keep track of all our assumptions and to bring out their combined force by uniting them into one framework so that we can more easily see their implications.

I begin with three basic points which review some matters discussed in Part I and introduce others we are about to examine. Recall first that justice as fairness is framed for a democratic society. Its principles are meant to answer the question: once we view a democratic society as a fair system of social cooperation between citizens regarded as free and equal, what principles are most appropriate to it? Alternatively: which principles are most appropriate for a democratic society that not only professes but wants to take seriously the idea that citizens are free and equal, and tries to realize that idea in its main institutions? The question of whether a constitutional regime is to be preferred to majoritarian democracy, we postpone until later (Part IV, §44).†

12.2. The second point is that justice as fairness takes the primary subject of political justice to be the basic structure of society, that is, its main political and social institutions and how they fit together into one unified system of cooperation (§4). We suppose that citizens are born into society and will normally spend their whole lives within its basic institutions. The nature and role of the basic structure importantly influence social and economic inequalities and enter into determining the appropriate principles of justice.

In particular, let us suppose that the fundamental social and economic inequalities are the differences in citizens' life-prospects (their prospects over a complete life) as these are affected by such things as their social class of origin, their native endowments, their opportunities for education, and their good or ill fortune over the course of life (§16). We ask: by what principles are differences of that kind—differences in life-prospects—made legitimate and consistent with the idea of free and equal citizenship in society seen as a fair system of cooperation?

12.3. The third point is that justice as fairness is a form of political liberalism: it tries to articulate a family of highly significant (moral) values that characteristically apply to the political and social institutions of the basic structure. It gives an account of these values in the light of certain special features of the political relationship as distinct from other relationships, associational, familial, and personal.

1. It is a relationship of persons within the basic structure of society, a structure we enter only by birth and exit only by death (or so we may assume for the moment). Political society is closed, as it were; and we do not, and indeed cannot, enter or leave it voluntarily.

2. Political power is always coercive power applied by the state and its apparatus of enforcement; but

* Reprinted with permission of the publisher from "Three Basic Points" and "Two Principles of Justice" in *Justice as Fairness: A Restatement* by John Rawls, edited by Erin Kelly (Cambridge: MA: The Belknap Press of Harvard University Press), 39–50. Copyright © 2001 by the President and Fellows of Harvard College.

† In that section, Rawls explains that "[a] constitutional regime is one in which laws and statutes must be consistent with certain fundamental rights and liberties.... There is in effect a constitution (not necessarily written) with a bill of rights specifying those freedoms and interpreted by the courts as constitutional limits on legislation." By contrast, there are no constitutional limits on legislation in a majoritarian democracy, and whatever the majority decides (according to the proper procedures) is law.

in a constitutional regime political power is at the same time the power of free and equal citizens as a collective body. Thus political power is citizens' power, which they impose on themselves and one another as free and equal.

The idea of political liberalism arises as follows. We start from two facts: first, from the fact of reasonable pluralism, the fact that a diversity of reasonable comprehensive doctrines is a permanent feature of a democratic society; and second, from the fact that in a democratic regime political power is regarded as the power of free and equal citizens as a collective body. These two points give rise to a problem of political legitimacy. For if the fact of reasonable pluralism always characterizes democratic societies and if political power is indeed the power of free and equal citizens, in the light of what reasons and values—of what kind of a conception of justice—can citizens legitimately exercise that coercive power over one another?

Political liberalism answers that the conception of justice must be a political conception, as defined in §9.1.* Such a conception when satisfied allows us to say: political power is legitimate only when it is exercised in accordance with a constitution (written or unwritten) the essentials of which all citizens, as reasonable and rational, can endorse in the light of their common human reason. This is the liberal principle of legitimacy. It is a further desideratum† that all legislative questions that concern or border on these essentials, or are highly divisive, should also be settled, so far as possible, by guidelines and values that can be similarly endorsed.

In matters of constitutional essentials, as well as on questions of basic justice, we try to appeal only to principles and values each citizen can endorse. A political conception of justice hopes to formulate these values: its shared principles and values make reason public, while freedom of speech and thought in a constitutional regime make it free. In providing a public basis of justification, a political conception of justice provides the framework for the liberal idea of political legitimacy. As noted in §9.4, however, and discussed further in §26, we do not say that a political conception formulates political values that can settle all legislative questions. This is neither possible nor desirable. There are many questions legislatures must consider that can only be settled by voting that is properly influenced by nonpolitical values. Yet at least on constitutional essentials and matters of basic justice we do try for an agreed basis; so long as there is at least rough agreement here, fair social cooperation among citizens can, we hope, be maintained.[1]

12.4. Given these three points, our question is: viewing society as a fair system of cooperation between citizens regarded as free and equal, what principles of justice are most appropriate to specify basic rights and liberties, and to regulate social and economic inequalities in citizens' prospects over a complete life? These inequalities are our primary concern.

To find a principle to regulate these inequalities, we look to our firmest considered convictions about equal basic rights and liberties, the fair value of the political liberties as well as fair equality of opportunity. We look outside the sphere of distributive justice more narrowly construed to see whether an appropriate distributive principle is singled out by those firmest convictions once their essential elements are represented in the original position as a device of representation (§6). This device is to assist us in working out which principle, or principles, the representatives of free and equal citizens would select to regulate social and economic inequalities in these prospects over a complete life when they assume that the equal basic liberties and fair opportunities are already secured.

The idea here is to use our firmest considered convictions about the nature of a democratic society as a fair system of cooperation between free and equal citizens—as modeled in the original position—to see whether the combined assertion of those convictions so expressed will help us to identify an appropriate distributive principle for the basic structure with

---

*   According to Rawls, a conception of justice is *political* if, (a) it applies only to the basic structure of society (and not directly to particular groups of people within those societies); (b) it does not presuppose any particular comprehensive conception of the good life; and (c) it is formulated, as far as possible, from ideas already implicit in the public political culture of a democratic society.

†   Something which is needed or considered highly desirable.

its economic and social inequalities in citizens' life-prospects. Our convictions about principles regulating those inequalities are much less firm and assured; so we look to our firmest convictions for guidance where assurance is lacking and guidance is needed (*Theory*, §§4, 20*).

§13. Two Principles of Justice

13.1. To try to answer our question, let us turn to a revised statement of the two principles of justice discussed in *Theory*, §§11–14. They should now read:[2]

1. Each person has the same indefeasible[†] claim to a fully adequate scheme of equal basic liberties, which scheme is compatible with the same scheme of liberties for all; and
2. Social and economic inequalities are to satisfy two conditions: first, they are to be attached to offices and positions open to all under conditions of fair equality of opportunity; and second, they are to be to the greatest benefit of the least-advantaged members of society (the difference principle).[3]

As I explain below, the first principle is prior to the second; also, in the second principle fair equality of opportunity is prior to the difference principle. This priority means that in applying a principle (or checking it against test cases) we assume that the prior principles are fully satisfied. We seek a principle of distribution (in the narrower sense) that holds within the setting of background institutions that secure the basic equal liberties (including the fair value of the political liberties)[4] as well as fair equality of opportunity. How far that principle holds outside that setting is a separate question we shall not consider.[5]

13.2. The revisions in the second principle are merely stylistic. But before noting the revisions in the first principle, which are significant,[‡] we should attend to the meaning of fair equality of opportunity. This is a difficult and not altogether clear idea; its role is perhaps best gathered from why it is introduced: namely, to correct the defects of formal equality of opportunity—careers open to talents—in the system of natural liberty, so-called (*Theory*, §12: 62ff.; §14).[§] To this end, fair equality of opportunity is said to require not merely that public offices and social positions be open in the formal sense, but that all should have a fair chance to attain them. To specify the idea of a fair chance we say: supposing that there is a distribution of native endowments, those who have the same level of talent and ability and the same willingness to use these gifts should have the same prospects of success regardless of their social class of origin, the class into which they are born and develop until the age of reason. In all parts of society there are to be roughly the same prospects of culture and achievement for those similarly motivated and endowed.

Fair equality of opportunity here means liberal equality. To accomplish its aims, certain requirements must be imposed on the basic structure beyond those of the system of natural liberty. A free market system must be set within a framework of political and legal institutions that adjust the long-run trend of economic forces so as to prevent excessive concentrations of property and wealth, especially those likely to lead to political domination. Society must also establish, among other things, equal opportunities of education for all regardless of family income (§15).[6]

13.3. Consider now the reasons for revising the first principle.[7] One is that the equal basic liberties in this principle are specified by a list as follows: freedom of thought and liberty of conscience; political liberties (for example, the right to vote and to participate in politics) and freedom of association, as well as the rights and liberties specified by the liberty and integrity (physical and psychological) of the person; and finally, the rights and liberties covered by the rule of

---

* *Theory: A Theory of Justice* (Harvard University Press, 1971).

† Cannot, under any circumstances, be annulled.

‡ Rawls's original, 1971 formulation was: "Each person is to have an equal right to the most extensive total system of equal basic liberties compatible with a similar system of liberty for all."

§ The "system of natural liberty," in Rawls's terminology, is one which assumes that, in an economically efficient free market economy, a basic structure "in which positions are open to those able and willing to strive for them will lead to a just distribution" (*A Theory of Justice*, §12), but which makes no effort to correct for arbitrary inequalities in the initial social conditions of the competitors.

law. That the basic liberties are specified by a list is quite clear from *Theory*, §11: 61 (1st ed.); but the use of the singular term "basic liberty" in the statement of the principle in *Theory*, §11: 60 (1st ed.), obscures this important feature of these liberties.

This revision brings out that no priority is assigned to liberty as such, as if the exercise of something called "liberty" had a preeminent value and were the main, if not the sole, end of political and social justice. While there is a general presumption against imposing legal and other restrictions on conduct without a sufficient reason, this presumption creates no special priority for any particular liberty. Throughout the history of democratic thought the focus has been on achieving certain specific rights and liberties as well as specific constitutional guarantees, as found, for example, in various bills of rights and declarations of the rights of man. Justice as fairness follows this traditional view.

13.4. A list of basic liberties can be drawn up in two ways. One is historical: we survey various democratic regimes and assemble a list of rights and liberties that seem basic and are securely protected in what seem to be historically the more successful regimes. Of course, the veil of ignorance means that this kind of particular information is not available to the parties in the original position, but it is available to you and me in setting up justice as fairness.[8] We are perfectly free to use it to specify the principles of justice we make available to the parties.

A second way of drawing up a list of basic rights and liberties is analytical: we consider what liberties provide the political and social conditions essential for the adequate development and full exercise of the two moral powers of free and equal persons (§7.1).[*] Following this we say: first, that the equal political liberties and freedom of thought enable citizens to develop and to exercise these powers in judging the justice of the basic structure of society and its social policies; and second, that liberty of conscience and freedom of association enable citizens to develop and exercise their moral powers in forming and revising and in rationally pursuing (individually or, more

often, in association with others) their conceptions of the good.

Those basic rights and liberties protect and secure the scope required for the exercise of the two moral powers in the two fundamental cases just mentioned: that is to say, the first fundamental case is the exercise of those powers in judging the justice of basic institutions and social policies; while the second fundamental case is the exercise of those powers in pursuing our conception of the good. To exercise our powers in these ways is essential to us as free and equal citizens.

13.5. Observe that the first principle of justice applies not only to the basic structure (both principles do this) but more specifically to what we think of as the constitution, whether written or unwritten. Observe also that some of these liberties, especially the equal political liberties and freedom of thought and association, are to be guaranteed by a constitution (*Theory*, chap. IV). What we may call "constituent power," as opposed to "ordinary power,"[9] is to be suitably institutionalized in the form of a regime: in the right to vote and to hold office, and in so-called bills of rights, as well as in the procedures for amending the constitution, for example.

These matters belong to the so-called constitutional essentials, these essentials being those crucial matters about which, given the fact of pluralism, working political agreement is most urgent (§9.4). In view of the fundamental nature of the basic rights and liberties, explained in part by the fundamental interests they protect, and given that the power of the people to constitute the form of government is a superior power (distinct from the ordinary power exercised routinely by officers of a regime), the first principle is assigned priority.

This priority means (as we have said) that the second principle (which includes the difference principle as one part) is always to be applied within a setting of background institutions that satisfy the requirements of the first principle (including the requirement of securing the fair value of the political liberties), as by definition they will in a well-ordered society.[†10] The

---

* These moral powers are a) the capacity to understand, apply, and act from the principles of political justice, and b) the capacity to have, revise, and rationally pursue a conception of the good (i.e., what is of value in human life).

† By "well-ordered society," Rawls means a society in which the following are true: (a) all citizens accept the same political conception of justice, (b) its basic structure is publicly known to satisfy those shared principles of justice, and

fair value of the political liberties ensures that citizens similarly gifted and motivated have roughly an equal chance of influencing the government's policy and of attaining positions of authority irrespective of their economic and social class.[11] To explain the priority of the first principle over the second: this priority rules out exchanges ("trade-offs," as economists say) between the basic rights and liberties covered by the first principle and the social and economic advantages regulated by the difference principle. For example, the equal political liberties cannot be denied to certain groups on the grounds that their having these liberties may enable them to block policies needed for economic growth and efficiency.

Nor can we justify a selective service act that grants educational deferments or exemptions to some on the grounds that doing this is a socially efficient way both to maintain the armed forces and to provide incentives to those otherwise subject to conscription to acquire valuable skills by continuing their education. Since conscription is a drastic interference with the basic liberties of equal citizenship, it cannot be justified by any needs less compelling than those of the defense of these equal liberties themselves (*Theory*, §58: 333f.).

A further point about priority: in asserting the priority of the basic rights and liberties, we suppose reasonably favorable conditions to obtain. That is, we suppose historical, economic and social conditions to be such that, provided the political will exists, effective political institutions can be established to give adequate scope for the exercise of those freedoms. These conditions mean that the barriers to constitutional government (if such there are) spring largely from the political culture and existing effective interests, and not from, for instance, a lack of economic means, or education, or the many skills needed to run a democratic regime.[12]

13.6. It is important to note a distinction between the first and second principles of justice. The first principle, as explained by its interpretation, covers the constitutional essentials. The second principle requires fair equality of opportunity and that social and economic inequalities be governed by the difference principle, which we discuss in §§17–19. While some principle of opportunity is a constitutional essential—for example, a principle requiring an open society, one with careers open to talents (to use the eighteenth-century phrase)—fair equality of opportunity requires more than that, and is not counted a constitutional essential. Similarly, although a social minimum providing for the basic needs of all citizens is also a constitutional essential (§38.3–4; §49.5), the difference principle is more demanding and is not so regarded.

The basis for the distinction between the two principles is not that the first expresses political values while the second does not. Both principles express political values. Rather, we see the basic structure of society as having two coordinate roles, the first principle applying to one, the second principle to the other (*Theory*, §11: 53). In one role the basic structure specifies and secures citizens' equal basic liberties (including the fair value of the political liberties (§45)) and establishes a just constitutional regime. In the other role it provides the background institutions of social and economic justice in the form most appropriate to citizens seen as free and equal. The questions involved in the first role concern the acquisition and the exercise of political power. To fulfill the liberal principle of legitimacy (§12.3), we hope to settle at least these questions by appeal to the political values that constitute the basis of free public reason (§26).*

The principles of justice are adopted and applied in a four-stage sequence.[13] In the first stage, the parties adopt the principles of justice behind a veil of ignorance. Limitations on knowledge available to the parties are progressively relaxed in the next three stages: the stage of the constitutional convention, the legislative stage in which laws are enacted as the constitution allows and as the principles of justice require and permit, and the final stage in which the rules are applied by administrators and followed by citizens generally and the constitution and laws are

---

(c) citizens have an "effective sense of justice," i.e., they understand and act in accordance with those principles of justice.

* By "free public reason," Rawls means the principles of reasoning and the rules of evidence which are accepted by all the citizens of a well-ordered society (irrespective of their differing conceptions of the good).

interpreted by members of the judiciary. At this last stage, everyone has complete access to all the facts. The first principle applies at the stage of the constitutional convention, and whether the constitutional essentials are assured is more or less visible on the face of the constitution and in its political arrangements and the way these work in practice. By contrast the second principle applies at the legislative stage and it bears on all kinds of social and economic legislation, and on the many kinds of issues arising at this point (*Theory*, §31: 172–176). Whether the aims of the second principle are realized is far more difficult to ascertain. To some degree these matters are always open to reasonable differences of opinion; they depend on inference and judgment in assessing complex social and economic information. Also, we can expect more agreement on constitutional essentials than on issues of distributive justice in the narrower sense.

Thus the grounds for distinguishing the constitutional essentials covered by the first principle and the institutions of distributive justice covered by the second are not that the first principle expresses political values and the second does not. Rather, the grounds of the distinction are four:

1. The two principles apply to different stages in the application of principles and identify two distinct roles of the basic structure;
2. It is more urgent to settle the constitutional essentials;

3. It is far easier to tell whether those essentials are realized; and
4. It seems possible to gain agreement on what those essentials should be, not in every detail, of course, but in the main outlines.

13.7. One way to see the point of the idea of constitutional essentials is to connect it with the idea of loyal opposition, itself an essential idea of a constitutional regime. The government and its loyal opposition agree on these constitutional essentials. Their so agreeing makes the government legitimate in intention and the opposition loyal in its opposition. Where the loyalty of both is firm and their agreement mutually recognized, a constitutional regime is secure. Differences about the most appropriate principles of distributive justice in the narrower sense, and the ideals that underlie them, can be adjudicated, though not always properly, within the existing political framework.

While the difference principle does not fall under the constitutional essentials, it is nevertheless important to try to identify the idea of equality most appropriate to citizens viewed as free and equal, and as normally and fully cooperating members of society over a complete life. I believe this idea involves reciprocity[14] at the deepest level and thus democratic equality properly understood requires something like the difference principle. (I say "something like," for there may be various nearby possibilities.) The remaining sections of this part (§§14–22) try to clarify the content of this principle and to clear up a number of difficulties. ■

Suggestions for Critical Reflection

1. Rawls restricts the application of his theory of justice to democratic societies. Why do you think he makes this restriction? Is it appropriate to stipulate such preconditions for a philosophical theory of social justice? Could his theory of justice as fairness be recast to apply to *all* kinds of societies, and not just democracies?

2. Rawls argues "the fact of reasonable pluralism" in democratic societies gives rise to a problem of political legitimacy, and offers what he calls a "liberal" solution to that problem via a "political" conception of justice. How plausible is it that

democracies really do face the deep problem of political legitimacy which Rawls describes? How adequate and attractive do you find his proposed solution? Is the kind of political conception of justice Rawls describes even *available* in contemporary liberal democratic societies?

3. Rawls appeals several times to "our firmest considered convictions" to help us decide what the basic structure of a just society should look like. Is this kind of appeal to intuition legitimate—or avoidable—in political philosophy?

4. Rawls's theory of justice as fairness is encapsulated in his two principles. How plausible and attractive are they? How radical are they? Might they have any controversial implications? What changes would we have to make to bring our society into accord with these principles (in particular with the second principle, which deals with distributive justice)?

5. The "difference principle" makes a crucial reference to the "least-advantaged members of society." Who exactly is Rawls thinking of here? What difference does it make?

6. The first part of the second principle stipulates "fair equality of opportunity." What does Rawls seem to have in mind? How different is Rawls's idea of fair equality of opportunity from what one might think of as the "free market" view of equal opportunity?

7. Rawls emphasizes that the question of the justice of social inequalities arises, for his theory, only *after* basic equal liberties and fair equality of opportunity have been secured. Why does he prioritize his principles in this way? Is he right to do so? Does this "lexical ordering" of the principles mean substantial social inequalities could, in fact, be justified in a Rawlsian society?

8. Why does Rawls not consider the second principle of justice a "constitutional essential"? What is the significance of this?

9. Rawls suggests the notion of democratic equality "involves reciprocity at the deepest level," and that this in turn requires "something like the difference principle." Is he right? What kind of argument might he have in mind?

Notes

1 It is not always clear whether a question involves a constitutional essential, as will be mentioned in due course. If there is doubt about this and the question is highly divisive, then citizens have a duty of civility to try to articulate their claims on one another by reference to political values, if that is possible.

2 This section summarizes some points from "The Basic Liberties and Their Priority," *Tanner Lectures on Human Values*, vol. 3, ed. Sterling McMurrin (Salt Lake City: University of Utah Press, 1982), §I, reprinted in *Political Liberalism* [New York City: Columbia University Press, 1993]. In that essay I try to reply to what I believe are two of the more serious objections to my account of liberty in *Theory* raised by H.L.A. Hart in his splendid critical review essay, "Rawls on Liberty and Its Priority," *University of Chicago Law Review* 40 (Spring 1975): 551–555, reprinted in his *Essays in Jurisprudence and Philosophy* (Oxford: Oxford University Press, 1983). No changes made in justice as fairness in this restatement are more significant than those forced by Hart's review.

3 Instead of "the difference principle," many writers prefer the term "the maximin principle," or simply "maximin justice," or some such locution. See, for example, Joshua Cohen's very full and accurate account of the difference principle in "Democratic Equality," *Ethics* 99 (July 1989): 727–751. But I still use the term "difference principle" to emphasize first, that this principle and the maximin rule for decision under uncertainty

(§28.1) are two very distinct things; and second, that in arguing for the difference principle over other distributive principles (say a restricted principle of (average) utility, which includes a social minimum), there is no appeal at all to the maximin rule for decision under uncertainty. The widespread idea that the argument for the difference principle depends on extreme aversion to uncertainty is a mistake, although a mistake unhappily encouraged by the faults of exposition in *Theory*, faults to be corrected in Part III of this restatement.

4 See *Theory*, §36: 197–199.

5 Some have found this kind of restriction objectionable; they think a political conception should be framed to cover all logically possible cases, or all conceivable cases, and not restricted to cases that can arise only within a specified institutional context. See for example Brian Barry, *The Liberal Theory of Justice* (Oxford: Oxford University Press, 1973), p. 112. In contrast, we seek a principle to govern social and economic inequalities in democratic regimes as we know them, and so we are concerned with inequalities in citizens' life-prospects that may actually arise, given our understanding of how certain institutions work.

6 These remarks are the merest sketch of a difficult idea. We come back to it from time to time.

7 This principle may be preceded by a lexically prior principle requiring that basic needs be met, as least insofar as their being met is a necessary condition

for citizens to understand and to be able fruitfully to exercise the basic rights and liberties. For a statement of such a principle with further discussion, see R.G. Peffer, *Marxism, Morality, and Social Justice* (Princeton: Princeton University Press, 1990), p.14.

8 Here I should mention that there are three points of view in justice as fairness that it is essential to distinguish: the point of view of the parties in the original position, the point of view of citizens in a well-ordered society, and the point of view of you and me who are setting up justice as fairness as a political conception and trying to use it to organize into one coherent view our considered judgments at all levels of generality. Keep in mind that the parties are, as it were, artificial persons who are part of a procedure of construction that we frame for our philosophical purposes. We may know many things that we keep from them. For these three points of view, see *Political Liberalism*, p. 28.

9 This distinction is derived from Locke, who speaks of the people's power to constitute the legislative as the first and fundamental law of all commonwealths. John Locke, *Second Treatise of Government*, §§134, 141, 149.

10 It is sometimes objected to the difference principle as a principle of distributive justice that it contains no restrictions on the overall nature of permissible distributions. It is concerned, the objection runs, solely with the least advantaged. But this objection is incorrect: it overlooks the fact that the parts of the two principles of justice are designed to work in tandem and apply as a unit. The requirements of the prior principles have important distributive effects. Consider the effects of fair equality of opportunity as applied to education, say, or the distributive effects

of the fair value of the political liberties. We cannot possibly take the difference principle seriously so long as we think of it by itself, apart from its setting within prior principles.

11 See *Political Liberalism*, p. 358.

12 The priority (or the primacy) of the basic equal liberties does not, contrary to much opinion, presuppose a high level of wealth and income. See Amartya Sen and Jean Dreze, *Hunger and Public Action* (Oxford: Oxford University Press, 1989), chap. 13; and Partha Dasgupta, *An Inquiry into Well-Being and Destitution* (Oxford: Oxford University Press, 1999), chaps. 1–2, 5 and passim.

13 See *Theory*, §31: 172–176, and *Political Liberalism*, pp. 397–398.

14 As understood in justice as fairness, reciprocity is a relation between citizens expressed by principles of justice that regulate a social world in which all who are engaged in cooperation and do their part as the rules and procedures require are to benefit in an appropriate way as assessed by a suitable benchmark of comparison. The two principles of justice, including the difference principle with its implicit reference to equal division as a benchmark, formulate an idea of reciprocity between citizens. For a fuller discussion of the idea of reciprocity, see *Political Liberalism*, pp. 16–17, and the introduction to the paperback edition, pp. xliv, xlvi, li. The idea of reciprocity also plays an important part in "The Idea of Public Reason Revisited," *University of Chicago Law Review*, 64 (Summer 1997): 765–807, reprinted in *The Law of Peoples* (Cambridge, Mass.: Harvard University Press, 1999) and *Collected Papers* [Cambridge, Mass.: Harvard University Press, 1999].

ROBERT NOZICK

FROM *Anarchy, State, and Utopia*

Who Was Robert Nozick?

Robert Nozick was born in 1938, to Russian Jewish immigrants, and grew up in Brooklyn, New York. He took his undergraduate degree at Columbia College and his PhD, on theories of rational decision-making, at Princeton. He taught at Princeton from 1962 to 1965, Harvard from 1965 to 1967, Rockefeller University from 1967 to 1969, and then returned to Harvard, a full professor of philosophy, at the tender age of 30. Nozick was already well-known in philosophical circles, but his first book, *Anarchy, State, and Utopia* (1974) propelled him into the public eye with its controversial but intellectually dazzling defense of political libertarianism. This book—which was widely perceived as an energetic response to his Harvard colleague John Rawls's liberal *Theory of Justice*—won the National Book Award and was named by *The Times Literary Supplement* as one of "The Hundred Most Influential Books Since the War." In 1998, Nozick was made Joseph Pellegrino University Professor at Harvard. Sadly he died of stomach cancer in 2002, at the relatively young age of 63.

What Was Nozick's Overall Philosophical Project?

As a young man, Nozick was a radical left-winger; he was converted to libertarianism—the view that individual rights should be maximized and the role of the state minimized—as a graduate student, largely through reading *laissez-faire* economists like F.A. Hayek and Milton Friedman. However, he was never fully comfortable with his public reputation as a right-wing ideologue. In a 1978 article in *The New York Times Magazine*,* he said, "right-wing people like the pro-free-market argument, but don't like the arguments for individual liberty in cases like gay rights—although I view them as an interconnecting whole."[†]

In the same article, Nozick also described his fresh and lively approach to philosophical writing, noting, "[i]t is as though what philosophers want is a way of saying something that will leave the person they're talking to no escape. Well, why should they be bludgeoning people like that? It's not a nice way to behave."

Nozick's philosophical interests were notably broad. Best known for his work in political philosophy, he also made important contributions to epistemology (especially his notion of knowledge as a kind of "truth tracking"), metaphysics (with his "closest continuer" theory of personal identity), and decision theory (particularly through his introduction of "Newcomb's problem" to the philosophical literature).

What Is the Structure of This Reading?

In Part I of *Anarchy, State, and Utopia*, Nozick argues that a minimal state is justified; then, in Part II, that no state more powerful or extensive than a minimal state is morally justified. In Part III he argues this is not an unfortunate result; rather, the minimal state is "a framework for utopia" and "inspiring as well as right." The material reprinted here is from the first section of the first chapter of Part II, where Nozick argues that considerations of distributive justice do not require going beyond the minimal state, and, in fact, on the contrary, a proper account of distributive justice shows that state

---

* "Harvard's Nozick: Philosopher of the New Right," by Jonathan Lieberson, 17 December 1978.

† As Alan Ryan wrote in his obituary for Nozick in *The Independent* (30 January 2002), "*Anarchy, State and Utopia* is a book that is more misunderstood by its admirers than its critics. It is often thought to have provided philosophical support for the policies of Ronald Reagan and Margaret Thatcher, but its criticism of social conservatism is at least as devastating as its criticism of the redistributive welfare state."

interference in distributive patterns must violate the rights of individuals.

Nozick first outlines what he considers the correct theory of distributive justice. He calls this the *entitlement theory of justice in holdings*, and presents it as made up of exactly three principles of justice. Nozick goes on to contrast what he calls *historical* theories of justice with *end-state* principles, and explains that the entitlement theory belongs to the former—in his view more plausible—type. He then distinguishes between two possible varieties of historical principles of justice—*patterned* or *non-patterned*—and claims that his entitlement theory belongs to the latter class. In the next section, Nozick argues that all end-state or patterned theories of distributive justice are inconsistent with liberty—i.e., they are committed to the repeated violation of the rights of individuals.

Some Useful Background Information

Nozick argues in *Anarchy, State, and Utopia* that only a minimal "night-watchman" state is consistent with individual liberty. A minimal state has a monopoly on the use of force within its boundaries (except for force used in immediate self-defense), and it uses this monopoly to guard its citizens against violence, theft, and fraud, and to enforce compliance with legally-made contracts. Beyond this, however, the minimal state has no legitimate function. For example, in the minimal state there can be no central bank or other form of economic regulation, no department of public works, no public education system, no welfare provisions or state pensions, no social healthcare system, no environmental protection regulations or agencies, and so on.

A Common Misconception

Nozick does not believe it is actually *immoral* to help the poor (or preserve the environment, or provide universal healthcare, or foster the arts ...). He argues that it is immoral to *force* people to do these things—in other words, that we have no legally enforceable *duty* to do them—but it is perfectly consistent to believe that it would be *morally good* if we were (voluntarily) to contribute to these ends.

FROM *Anarchy, State, and Utopia**

The minimal state is the most extensive state that can be justified. Any state more extensive violates people's rights. Yet many persons have put forth reasons purporting to justify a more extensive state. It is impossible within the compass of this book to examine all the reasons that have been put forth. Therefore, I shall focus upon those generally acknowledged to be most weighty and influential, to see precisely wherein they fail. In this chapter we consider the claim that a more extensive state is justified, because necessary (or the best instrument) to achieve distributive justice....

The term "distributive justice" is not a neutral one. Hearing the term "distribution," most people presume that some thing or mechanism uses some principle or criterion to give out a supply of things. Into this process of distributing shares some error may have crept. So it is an open question, at least, whether *re*distribution should take place; whether we should do again what has already been done once, though poorly. However, we are not in the position of children who have been given portions of pie by someone who now makes last minute adjustments to rectify careless cutting. There is no *central* distribution, no person or group entitled to control all the resources, jointly deciding how they are to be doled out. What each person gets, he gets from others who give to him in exchange for something, or as a gift. In a free society, diverse persons control different resources, and new holdings arise out of the voluntary exchanges and actions of persons. There is no more a distributing or distribution of shares than there is a distributing of mates in a society in which persons choose whom they shall marry. The total result is

* From Robert Nozick, "Distributive Justice," in *Anarchy, State, and Utopia* by (Basic Books, 1974), 149–64, 174–82.

the product of many individual decisions which the different individuals involved are entitled to make. Some uses of the term "distribution," it is true, do not imply a previous distributing appropriately judged by some criterion (for example, "probability distribution"); nevertheless, despite the title of this chapter, it would be best to use a terminology that clearly is neutral. We shall speak of people's holdings; a principle of justice in holdings describes (part of) what justice tells us (requires) about holdings....

The Entitlement Theory

The subject of justice in holdings consists of three major topics. The first is the *original acquisition of holdings*, the appropriation of unheld things. This includes the issues of how unheld things may come to be held, the process, or processes, by which unheld things may come to be held, the things that may come to be held by these processes, the extent of what comes to be held by a particular process, and so on. We shall refer to the complicated truth about this topic, which we shall not formulate here, as the principle of justice in acquisition. The second topic concerns the *transfer of holdings* from one person to another. By what processes may a person transfer holdings to another? How may a person acquire a holding from another who holds it? Under this topic come general descriptions of voluntary exchange, and gift and (on the other hand) fraud, as well as reference to particular conventional details fixed upon in a given society. The complicated truth about this subject (with placeholders for conventional details) we shall call the principle of justice in transfer. (And we shall suppose it also includes principles governing how a person may divest himself of a holding, passing it into an unheld state.)

If the world were wholly just, the following inductive definition* would exhaustively cover the subject of justice in holdings.

1. A person who acquires a holding in accordance with the principle of justice in acquisition is entitled to that holding.

2. A person who acquires a holding in accordance with the principle of justice in transfer, from someone else entitled to the holding, is entitled to the holding.

3. No one is entitled to a holding except by (repeated) applications of 1 and 2.

The complete principle of distributive justice would say simply that a distribution is just if everyone is entitled to the holdings they possess under the distribution.

A distribution is just if it arises from another just distribution by legitimate means. The legitimate means of moving from one distribution to another are specified by the principle of justice in transfer. The legitimate first "moves" are specified by the principle of justice in acquisition.[1] Whatever arises from a just situation by just steps is itself just. The means of change specified by the principle of justice in transfer preserve justice. As correct rules of inference are truth-preserving, and any conclusion deduced via repeated application of such rules from only true premises is itself true, so the means of transition from one situation to another specified by the principle of justice in transfer are justice-preserving, and any situation actually arising from repeated transitions in accordance with the principle from a just situation is itself just. The parallel between justice-preserving transformations and truth-preserving transformations illuminates where it fails as well as where it holds. That a conclusion could have been deduced by truth-preserving means from premises that are true suffices to show its truth. That from a just situation a situation *could* have arisen via justice-preserving means does *not* suffice to show its justice. The fact that a thief's victims voluntarily *could* have presented him with gifts does not entitle the thief to his ill-gotten gains. Justice in holdings is historical; it depends upon what actually has happened. We shall return to this point later.

Not all actual situations are generated in accordance with the two principles of justice in holdings: the principle of justice in acquisition and the principle of justice in transfer. Some people steal from others, or defraud them, or enslave them, seizing their product and preventing them from living as they choose, or

---

* An inductive definition works by defining a base case and then giving a rule for generalizing from that case which covers everything else in the domain to be defined.

forcibly exclude others from competing in exchanges. None of these are permissible modes of transition from one situation to another. And some persons acquire holdings by means not sanctioned by the principle of justice in acquisition. The existence of past injustice (previous violations of the first two principles of justice in holdings) raises the third major topic under justice in holdings: the rectification of injustice in holdings. If past injustice has shaped present holdings in various ways, some identifiable and some not, what now, if anything, ought to be done to rectify these injustices? What obligations do the performers of injustice have toward those whose position is worse than it would have been had the injustice not been done? Or, than it would have been had compensation been paid promptly? How, if at all, do things change if the beneficiaries and those made worse off are not the direct parties in the act of injustice, but, for example, their descendants? Is an injustice done to someone whose holding was itself based upon an unrectified injustice? How far back must one go in wiping clean the historical slate of injustices? What may victims of injustice permissibly do in order to rectify the injustices being done to them, including the many injustices done by persons acting through their government? I do not know of a thorough or theoretically sophisticated treatment of such issues.[2] Idealizing greatly, let us suppose theoretical investigation will produce a principle of rectification. This principle uses historical information about previous situations and injustices done in them (as defined by the first two principles of justice and rights against interference), and information about the actual course of events that flowed from these injustices, until the present, and it yields a description (or descriptions) of holdings in the society. The principle of rectification presumably will make use of its best estimate of subjunctive information* about what would have occurred (or a probability distribution† over what might have occurred, using the expected value) if the injustice had not taken place. If the actual description of holdings turns out not to be one of the descriptions yielded by the principle, then one of the descriptions yielded must be realized.[3]

The general outlines of the theory of justice in holdings are that the holdings of a person are just if he is entitled to them by the principles of justice in acquisition and transfer, or by the principle of rectification of injustice (as specified by the first two principles). If each person's holdings are just, then the total set (distribution) of holdings is just. To turn these general outlines into a specific theory we would have to specify the details of each of the three principles of justice in holdings: the principle of acquisition of holdings, the principle of transfer of holdings, and the principle of rectification of violations of the first two principles. I shall not attempt that task here....

Historical Principles and the End-Result Principle

The general outlines of the entitlement theory illuminate the nature and defects of other conceptions of distributive justice. The entitlement theory of justice in distribution is *historical*; whether a distribution is just depends upon how it came about. In contrast, *current time-slice principles* of justice hold that the justice of a distribution is determined by how things are distributed (who has what) as judged by some *structural* principle(s) of just distribution. A utilitarian‡ who judges between any two distributions by seeing which has the greater sum of utility and, if the sums tie, applies some fixed equality criterion to choose the more equal distribution, would hold a current time-slice principle of justice. As would someone who had a fixed schedule of trade-offs between the sum of happiness and equality. According to a current time-slice principle, all that needs to be looked at, in judging the justice of a distribution, is who ends up with what; in comparing any two distributions one need look only at the matrix presenting the distributions. No further information need be fed into a principle of justice. It is a consequence of such principles of justice that any two structurally identical distributions are equally just. (Two distributions are structurally identical if they present the same profile, but perhaps have different persons occupying the particular slots. My having

---

* Information about a hypothetical, non-actual situation.
† A specification of all possible values of a variable along with the probability that each will occur.
‡ See the selection by Mill in the Ethical Theory section of this volume.

ten and your having five, and my having five and your having ten are structurally identical distributions.) Welfare economics is the theory of current time-slice principles of justice. The subject is conceived as operating on matrices representing only current information about distribution. This, as well as some of the usual conditions (for example, the choice of distribution is invariant under relabeling of columns), guarantees that welfare economics will be a current time-slice theory, with all of its inadequacies.

Most persons do not accept current time-slice principles as constituting the whole story about distributive shares. They think it relevant in assessing the justice of a situation to consider not only the distribution it embodies, but also how that distribution came about. If some persons are in prison for murder or war crimes, we do not say that to assess the justice of the distribution in the society we must look only at what this person has, and that person has, and that person has, ... at the current time. We think it relevant to ask whether someone did something so that he *deserved* to be punished, deserved to have a lower share. Most will agree to the relevance of further information with regard to punishments and penalties. Consider also desired things. One traditional socialist view is that workers are entitled to the product and full fruits of their labor; they have earned it; a distribution is unjust if it does not give the workers what they are entitled to. Such entitlements are based upon some past history. No socialist holding this view would find it comforting to be told that because the actual distribution *A* happens to coincide structurally with the one he desires *D*, *A* therefore is no less just than *D*; it differs only in that the "parasitic" owners of capital receive under *A* what the workers are entitled to under *D*, and the workers receive under *A* what the owners are entitled to under *D*, namely very little. This socialist rightly, in my view, holds onto the notions of earning, producing, entitlement, desert, and so forth, and he rejects current time-slice principles that look only to the structure of the resulting set of holdings. (The set of holdings resulting from what? Isn't it implausible that how holdings are produced and come to exist has no effect at all on who should hold what?) His mistake lies in his view of what entitlements arise out of what sorts of productive processes.

We construe the position we discuss too narrowly by speaking of *current* time-slice principles. Nothing is changed if structural principles operate upon a time sequence of current time-slice profiles and, for example, give someone more now to counterbalance the less he has had earlier. A utilitarian or an egalitarian or any mixture of the two over time will inherit the difficulties of his more myopic comrades. He is not helped by the fact that *some* of the information others consider relevant in assessing a distribution is reflected, unrecoverably, in past matrices. Henceforth, we shall refer to such unhistorical principles of distributive justice, including the current time-slice principles, as *end-result principles* or *end-state principles*.

In contrast to end-result principles of justice, *historical principles* of justice hold that past circumstances or actions of people can create differential entitlements or differential deserts to things. An injustice can be worked by moving from one distribution to another structurally identical one, for the second, in profile the same, may violate people's entitlements or deserts; it may not fit the actual history.

Patterning

The entitlement principles of justice in holdings that we have sketched are historical principles of justice. To better understand their precise character, we shall distinguish them from another subclass of the historical principles. Consider, as an example, the principle of distribution according to moral merit. This principle requires that total distributive shares vary directly with moral merit; no person should have a greater share than anyone whose moral merit is greater. (If moral merit could be not merely ordered but measured on an interval or ratio scale, stronger principles could be formulated.) Or consider the principle that results by substituting "usefulness to society" for "moral merit" in the previous principle. Or instead of "distribute according to moral merit," or "distribute according to usefulness to society," we might consider "distribute according to the weighted sum* of

---

*   A weighted sum is obtained by adding terms, each of which is given a certain value (weight) by using a multiplier which reflects their relative importance.

moral merit, usefulness to society, and need," with the weights of the different dimensions equal. Let us call a principle of distribution *patterned* if it specifies that a distribution is to vary along with some natural dimension, weighted sum of natural dimensions, or lexicographic ordering* of natural dimensions. And let us say a distribution is patterned if it accords with some patterned principle. (I speak of natural dimensions, admittedly without a general criterion for them, because for any set of holdings some artificial dimensions can be gimmicked up to vary along with the distribution of the set.) The principle of distribution in accordance with moral merit is a patterned historical principle, which specifies a patterned distribution. "Distribute according to I.Q." is a patterned principle that looks to information not contained in distributional matrices. It is not historical, however, in that it does not look to any past actions creating differential entitlements to evaluate a distribution; it requires only distributional matrices whose columns are labeled by I.Q. scores. The distribution in a society, however, may be composed of such simple patterned distributions, without itself being simply patterned. Different sectors may operate different patterns, or some combination of patterns may operate in different proportions across a society. A distribution composed in this manner, from a small number of patterned distributions, we also shall term "patterned." And we extend the use of "pattern" to include the overall designs put forth by combinations of end-state principles.

Almost every suggested principle of distributive justice is patterned: to each according to his moral merit, or needs, or marginal product,[†] or how hard he tries, or the weighted sum of the foregoing, and so on. The principle of entitlement we have sketched is not patterned.[4] There is no one natural dimension or weighted sum or combination of a small number of natural dimensions that yields the distributions generated in accordance with the principle of entitlement. The set of holdings that results when some persons receive their marginal products, others win at gambling, others receive a share of their mate's income, others receive gifts from foundations, others receive interest on loans, others receive gifts from admirers, others receive returns on investment, others make for themselves much of what they have, others find things, and so on, will not be patterned. Heavy strands of patterns will run through it; significant portions of the variance in holdings will be accounted for by pattern-variables. If most people most of the time choose to transfer some of their entitlements to others only in exchange for something from them, then a large part of what many people hold will vary with what they held that others wanted. More details are provided by the theory of marginal productivity. But gifts to relatives, charitable donations, bequests to children, and the like, are not best conceived, in the first instance, in this manner. Ignoring the strands of pattern, let us suppose for the moment that a distribution actually arrived at by the operation of the principle of entitlement is random with respect to any pattern. Though the resulting set of holdings will be unpatterned, it will not be incomprehensible, for it can be seen as arising from the operation of a small number of principles. These principles specify how an initial distribution may arise (the principle of acquisition of holdings) and how distributions may be transformed into others (the principle of transfer of holdings). The process whereby the set of holdings is generated will be intelligible, though the set of holdings itself that results from this process will be unpatterned.

...Will people tolerate for long a system yielding distributions that they believe are unpatterned? ... No doubt people will not long accept a distribution they believe is *unjust*. People want their society to be and to look just. But must the look of justice reside in a

---

* Strictly speaking, this means sorting a group of items in the order they would appear if they were listed in a dictionary (i.e., roughly, alphabetically), but listing first all the words made up of only one letter, then all the words made up of two letters, then all those with three letters, and so on. (The main idea here is to impose a useful order on an infinite sequence of formulae.) In the philosophical literature on justice, however, the phrase is generally used to mean a strict *prioritizing* of principles: first principle A must be satisfied, and only then should we worry about principle B; only when both A and B are satisfied can we apply principle C; and so on.

† The contribution that each additional worker makes to total output. Thus, to be rewarded according to one's marginal product is to be paid in proportion to the amount that your contribution has increased output over what it would have been if you hadn't been employed.

resulting pattern rather than in the underlying generating principles? We are in no position to conclude that the inhabitants of a society embodying an entitlement conception of justice in holdings will find it unacceptable. Still, it must be granted that were people's reasons for transferring some of their holdings to others always irrational or arbitrary, we would find this disturbing. (Suppose people always determined what holdings they would transfer, and to whom, by using a random device.) We feel more comfortable upholding the justice of an entitlement system if most of the transfers under it are done for reasons. This does not mean necessarily that all deserve what holdings they receive. It means only that there is a purpose or point to someone's transferring a holding to one person rather than to another; that usually we can see what the transferrer thinks he's gaining, what cause he thinks he's serving, what goals he thinks he's helping to achieve, and so forth. Since in a capitalist society people often transfer holdings to others in accordance with how much they perceive these others benefiting them, the fabric constituted by the individual transactions and transfers is largely reasonable and intelligible.[5] (Gifts to loved ones, bequests to children, charity to the needy also are nonarbitrary components of the fabric.) ... The system of entitlements is defensible when constituted by the individual aims of individual transactions. No overarching aim is needed, no distributional pattern is required.

To think that the task of a theory of distributive justice is to fill in the blank in "to each according to his _____" is to be predisposed to search for a pattern; and the separate treatment of "from each according to his _____" treats production and distribution as two separate and independent issues. On an entitlement view these are *not* two separate questions. Whoever makes something, having bought or contracted for all other held resources used in the process (transferring some of his holdings for these cooperating factors), is entitled to it. The situation is *not* one of something's getting made, and there being an open question of who is to get it. Things come into the world already attached to people having entitlements

over them. From the point of view of the historical entitlement conception of justice in holdings, those who start afresh to complete "to each according to his _____" treat objects as if they appeared from nowhere, out of nothing. A complete theory of justice might cover this limit case as well; perhaps here is a use for the usual conceptions of distributive justice.[6]

So entrenched are maxims of the usual form that perhaps we should present the entitlement conception as a competitor. Ignoring acquisition and rectification, we might say:

From each according to what he chooses to do, to each according to what he makes for himself (perhaps with the contracted aid of others) and what others choose to do for him and choose to give him of what they've been given previously (under this maxim) and haven't yet expended or transferred.

This, the discerning reader will have noticed, has its defects as a slogan. So as a summary and great simplification (and not as a maxim with any independent meaning) we have:

From each as they choose, to each as they are chosen.

How Liberty Upsets Patterns

It is not clear how those holding alternative conceptions of distributive justice can reject the entitlement conception of justice in holdings. For suppose a distribution favored by one of these non-entitlement conceptions is realized. Let us suppose it is your favorite one and let us call this distribution D_1; perhaps everyone has an equal share, perhaps shares vary in accordance with some dimension you treasure. Now suppose that Wilt Chamberlain* is greatly in demand by basketball teams, being a great gate attraction. (Also suppose contracts run only for a year, with players being free agents.) He signs the following sort of contract with a team: In each home game, twenty-five cents from the price of each ticket of admission goes to him. (We ignore the question of whether he is "gouging" the owners, letting them look out for

---

* Wilt Chamberlain was a well-known American basketball player during the 1960s. He was seven-time consecutive winner of the National Basketball Association scoring title from 1960 to 1966, and in 1962 he scored a record 100 points in a single game.

themselves.) The season starts, and people cheerfully attend his team's games; they buy their tickets, each time dropping a separate twenty-five cents of their admission price into a special box with Chamberlain's name on it. They are excited about seeing him play; it is worth the total admission price to them. Let us suppose that in one season one million persons attend his home games, and Wilt Chamberlain winds up with $250,000, a much larger sum than the average income and larger even than anyone else has.* Is he entitled to this income? Is this new distribution D_2, unjust? If so, why? There is *no* question about whether each of the people was entitled to the control over the resources they held in D_1; because that was the distribution (your favorite) that (for the purposes of argument) we assumed was acceptable. Each of these persons *chose* to give twenty-five cents of their money to Chamberlain. They could have spent it on going to the movies, or on candy bars, or on copies of *Dissent* magazine, or of *Monthly Review*.† But they all, at least one million of them, converged on giving it to Wilt Chamberlain in exchange for watching him play basketball. If D_1 was a just distribution, and people voluntarily moved from it to D_2, transferring parts of their shares they were given under D_1 (what was it for if not to do something with?), isn't D_2 also just? If the people were entitled to dispose of the resources to which they were entitled (under D_1), didn't this include their being entitled to give it to, or exchange it with, Wilt Chamberlain? Can anyone else complain on grounds of justice? Each other person already has his legitimate share under D_1. Under D_1, there is nothing that anyone has that anyone else has a claim of justice against. After someone transfers something to Wilt Chamberlain, third parties *still* have their legitimate shares; *their* shares are not changed. By what process could such a transfer among two persons give rise to a legitimate claim of distributive justice on a portion of what was transferred, by a third party who had no claim of justice on any holding of the others *before* the transfer?[7] To cut off objections irrelevant here, we might imagine the exchanges occurring in a socialist society, after hours. After playing whatever basketball he does in

his daily work, or doing whatever other daily work he does, Wilt Chamberlain decides to put in *overtime* to earn additional money. (First his work quota is set; he works time over that.) Or imagine it is a skilled juggler people like to see, who puts on shows after hours.

Why might someone work overtime in a society in which it is assumed their needs are satisfied? Perhaps because they care about things other than needs. I like to write in books that I read, and to have easy access to books for browsing at odd hours. It would be very pleasant and convenient to have the resources of Widener Library‡ in my back yard. No society, I assume, will provide such resources close to each person who would like them as part of his regular allotment (under D_1). Thus, persons either must do without some extra things that they want, or be allowed to do something extra to get some of these things. On what basis could the inequalities that would eventuate be forbidden? Notice also that small factories would spring up in a socialist society, unless forbidden. I melt down some of my personal possessions (under D_1) and build a machine out of the material. I offer you, and others, a philosophy lecture once a week in exchange for your cranking the handle on my machine, whose products I exchange for yet other things, and so on. (The raw materials used by the machine are given to me by others who possess them under D_1, in exchange for hearing lectures.) Each person might participate to gain things over and above their allotment under D_1. Some persons even might want to leave their job in socialist industry and work full time in this private sector. I shall say something more about these issues in the next chapter. Here I wish merely to note how private property even in means of production would occur in a socialist society that did not forbid people to use as they wished some of the resources they are given under the socialist distribution D_1.[8] The socialist society would have to forbid capitalist acts between consenting adults.

The general point illustrated by the Wilt Chamberlain example and the example of the entrepreneur in a socialist society is that no end-state principle or distributional patterned principle of justice can

---

*   In 1974, the US average (mean) household income was around $13,000.
†   *Dissent* and *Monthly Review* are left-wing/socialist periodicals.
‡   Harvard University's library.

be continuously realized without continuous interference with people's lives. Any favored pattern would be transformed into one unfavored by the principle, by people choosing to act in various ways; for example, by people exchanging goods and services with other people, or giving things to other people, things the transferrers are entitled to under the favored distributional pattern. To maintain a pattern one must either continually interfere to stop people from transferring resources as they wish to, or continually (or periodically) interfere to take from some persons resources that others for some reason chose to transfer to them. (But if some time limit is to be set on how long people may keep resources others voluntarily transfer to them, why let them keep these resources for *any*

period of time? Why not have immediate confiscation?) It might be objected that all persons voluntarily will choose to refrain from actions which would upset the pattern. This presupposes unrealistically (1) that all will most want to maintain the pattern (are those who don't, to be "reeducated" or forced to undergo "self-criticism"?), (2) that each can gather enough information about his own actions and the ongoing activities of others to discover which of his actions will upset the pattern, and (3) that diverse and far-flung persons can coordinate their actions to dovetail into the pattern. Compare the manner in which the market is neutral among persons' desires, as it reflects and transmits widely scattered information via prices, and coordinates persons' activities.... ■

Suggestions for Critical Reflection

1. What does Nozick mean when he claims that "[t]he term 'distributive justice' is not a neutral one"? Is the terminology he introduces instead any more "neutral"? What is the significance of this issue (if any) for the arguments that follow?

2. "Whatever arises from a just situation by just steps is itself just." Is this apparently straightforward claim *really* true? Can you think of any reasons to doubt it—for example, can you come up with any plausible counter-examples to this general claim? How significant a part of Nozick's general argument is this assertion? If we accept it, might we then be forced to accept a version of libertarianism, or is there a way of making it consistent with a more extensive state?

3. How plausible do you find Nozick's sketch of a principle of rectification of injustice? Is the goal of such rectifications to return injured parties (such as former slaves or their present-day children) to the position they would have been in had the injustice not occurred, or do we normally think there is more (or less) to it than that?

4. Is the distinction between historical and end-state principles of justice as clear-cut as Nozick presents it? Are most—or even many—theories of justice pure forms of one or the other? How comfortably, if at all, can historical and end-state

views of justice be combined in a single theory (for example, an egalitarian theory)?

5. "People want their society to be and to look just. But must the look of justice reside in a resulting pattern rather than in the underlying generating principles?" This is a crucial question for Nozick, and the plausibility of his theory depends upon our willingness to answer "No." But what if the entitlement theory generates distributive patterns which many people intuitively find *unjust*, such as very wide inequalities in wealth, educational opportunities, access to health care, and so on? Would we then want to say that distributive justice *does* place constraints on appropriate patterns of distribution for social goods? If so, what implications would this have for Nozick's theory of justice?

6. What do you think of Nozick's Wilt Chamberlain argument? If it is sound, what are its implications? If you think it is not sound, what, exactly, is wrong with it (bearing in mind that it's not enough to simply disagree with its conclusion)?

7. Nozick argues that distributional patterns "cannot be continuously realized without continuous interference with people's lives." Does this, in itself, show that no adequate principles of justice can be patterned? What ethical assumptions might Nozick be making here? Are these assumptions justified?

Notes

1 Applications of the principle of justice in acquisition may also occur as part of the move from one distribution to another. You may find an unheld thing now and appropriate it. Acquisitions also are to be understood as included when, to simplify, I speak only of transitions by transfers.

2 See, however, the useful book by Boris Bittker, *The Case for Black Reparations* (New York: Random House, 1973).

3 If the principle of rectification of violations of the first two principles yields more than one description of holdings, then some choice must be made as to which of these is to be realized. Perhaps the sort of considerations about distributive justice and equality that I argue against play a legitimate role in *this* subsidiary choice. Similarly, there may be room for such considerations in deciding which otherwise arbitrary features a statute will embody, when such features are unavoidable because other considerations do not specify a precise line; yet a line must be drawn.

4 One might try to squeeze a patterned conception of distributive justice into the framework of the entitlement conception, by formulating a gimmicky obligatory "principle of transfer" that would lead to the pattern. For example, the principle that if one has more than the mean income one must transfer everything one holds above the mean to persons below the mean so as to bring them up to (but not over) the mean. We can formulate a criterion for a "principle of transfer" to rule out such obligatory transfers, or we can say that no correct principle of transfer, no principle of transfer in a free society will be like this. The former is probably the better course, though the latter also is true.

Alternatively, one might think to make the entitlement conception instantiate a pattern, by using matrix entries that express the relative strength of a person's entitlements as measured by some real-valued function. But even if the limitation to natural dimensions failed to exclude this function, the resulting edifice would *not* capture our system of entitlements to *particular* things.

5 We certainly benefit because great economic incentives operate to get others to spend much time and energy to figure out how to serve us by providing things we will want to pay for. It is not mere paradox mongering to wonder whether capitalism should be criticized for most rewarding and hence encouraging, not individualists like Thoreau who go about their own lives, but people who are occupied with serving others and winning them as customers. But to defend capitalism one need not think businessmen are the finest human types. (I do not mean to join here the general maligning of businessmen, either.) Those who think the finest should

acquire the most can try to convince their fellows to transfer resources in accordance with *that* principle.

6 Varying situations continuously from that limit situation to our own would force us to make explicit the underlying rationale of entitlements and to consider whether entitlement considerations lexicographically precede the considerations of the usual theories of distributive justice, so that the *slightest* strand of entitlement outweighs the considerations of the usual theories of distributive justice.

7 Might not a transfer have instrumental effects on a third party, changing his feasible options? (But what if the two parties to the transfer independently had used their holdings in this fashion?) I discuss this question below, but note here that this question concedes the point for distributions of ultimate intrinsic noninstrumental goods (pure utility experiences, so to speak) that are transferrable. It also might be objected that the transfer might make a third party more envious because it worsens his position relative to someone else. I find it incomprehensible how this can be thought to involve a claim of justice. On envy, see Chapter 8 [of *Anarchy, State and Utopia*].

Here and elsewhere in this chapter, a theory which incorporates elements of pure procedural justice might find what I say acceptable, *if* kept in its proper place; that is, if background institutions exist to ensure the satisfaction of certain conditions on distributive shares. But if these institutions are not themselves the sum or invisible-hand result of people's voluntary (nonaggressive) actions, the constraints they impose require justification. At no point does *our* argument assume any background institutions more extensive than those of the minimal night-watchman state, a state limited to protecting persons against murder, assault, theft, fraud, and so forth.

8 See the selection from John Henry MacKay's novel, *The Anarchists*, reprinted in Leonard Krimmerman and Lewis Perry, eds., *Patterns of Anarchy* (New York: Doubleday Anchor Books, 1966), in which an individualist anarchist presses upon a communist anarchist the following question: "Would you, in the system of society which you call 'free Communism' prevent individuals from exchanging their labour among themselves by means of their own medium of exchange? And further: Would you prevent them from occupying land for the purpose of personal use?" The novel continues: "[the] question was not to be escaped. If he answered 'Yes!' he admitted that society had the right of control over the individual and threw overboard the autonomy of the

individual which he had always zealously defended; if on the other hand, he answered 'No!' he admitted the right of private property which he had just denied so emphatically.... Then he answered 'In Anarchy any number of men must have the right of forming a voluntary association, and so realizing their ideas in practice. Nor can I understand how any one could justly be driven from the land and house which he uses and occupies ... every serious man must declare himself:

for Socialism, and thereby for force and against liberty, or for Anarchism, and thereby for liberty and against force.'" In contrast, we find Noam Chomsky writing, "Any consistent anarchist must oppose private ownership of the means of production," "the consistent anarchist then ... will be a socialist ... of a particular sort." Introduction to Daniel Guerin, *Anarchism: From Theory to Practice* (New York: Monthly Review Press, 1970), pages xiii, xv.

SUSAN MOLLER OKIN

Justice and Gender

Who Was Susan Moller Okin?

Susan Moller Okin, who was once described as "perhaps the best feminist political philosopher in the world,"* was born in 1946 in Auckland, New Zealand, and died suddenly in 2004 at the age of only 57. At the time of her death she was a professor of political science at Stanford University, and she had previously taught at Auckland, Vassar, Brandeis, and Harvard. Her doctorate, which she received in 1975, was from Harvard.

Okin's main importance as a political philosopher lay in her insistence that gender—the status and position of women—is an issue that lies at the heart of political theory, and is not merely a fringe topic that can be addressed after the main principles of justice have been laid down. As the article reprinted here makes clear, at the time that Okin began writing—in the 1970s—this was a radical view: one which, it seems fair to say, had not even occurred to the (male) writers who were mainly responsible for carrying on the liberal political tradition. Okin formulated careful and forceful arguments that, in particular, the role and structure of the family—the so-called domestic sphere, that shaped, and still shapes, the opportunities available to women in society—were crucial to any adequate account of social justice. These arguments brought about a sea change in political philosophy, carrying issues surrounding gender roles and the family to the center of the discipline.

Near the end of her career, Okin's interests shifted towards the situation of women in less developed countries, and she worked on the complex tangle of issues raised by the interaction between gender issues, poverty, and multiculturalism. Once again, she was among the first to identify an issue that at the time was barely on the radar and has since become a main theme in political thought: the potential for conflict between the aim of gender equality, and sensitivity to the customs of other cultures and religions. Okin's own view was a provocative defense of the liberal egalitarian position that all citizens in a state should have equal rights and privileges and that this trumps certain oppressive cultural practices, such as forced marriage, polygamy, or female genital mutilation. She became a highly visible supporter of the Global Fund for Women, an international foundation devoted to the support of women's human rights.

Probably Okin's best-known work is the book *Justice, Gender and the Family*, published in 1989, and her article "Reason and Feeling in Thinking about Justice." She also wrote two other very influential books—*Women in Western Political Thought* (1979), and *Is Multiculturalism Bad for Women?* (1999)—and many more widely read articles, including the one excerpted here.

What Is the Structure of This Reading?

After introducing the topic "how just is gender?," Okin begins by outlining the role of gender in justifying inequality in the western tradition of political thought, including that of Aristotle, Rousseau, Kant, Hegel, and Bentham. She then asks whether modern political theory fares any better on this front—whether modern theorists are more sensitive to the problem of gender-based inequalities in society—and examines two representative leading writers: John Rawls, the most prominent liberal ideologist, and Michael Walzer, a leading communitarian. In this selection, the discussion of Walzer has been omitted, leaving the focus on Rawls. Okin concludes that insufficient attention is still being devoted to gender. She argues that, although Walzer appears on the surface to be more sympathetic to feminist concerns, in fact it is the Rawlsian tradition that is best able to accommodate feminism. However, she concludes by suggesting that full consideration of the problem of gender in a theory of social justice will require not only modifying contemporary liberal theory but also, potentially, a radical alteration of gender itself.

---

* Debra Satz, a Stanford philosopher, quoted in Okin's obituary in the *Stanford Report*, March 9, 2004.

A Common Misconception

Although Okin, in this article and elsewhere in her work, attacks liberalism for its historical bias against women, she nevertheless does not reject liberal political theory. On the contrary, her view is that liberalism is an emancipatory doctrine that simply has not been taken far enough. The basic idea of freedom and equality for all citizens is the right one—but in order to apply fully to women (and, indeed, to men), these liberal principles must be applied to the family as well as to the public spheres of government and economics.

Justice and Gender [1*]

Theories of justice are centrally concerned with whether, how, and why persons should be treated differently from each other. Which initial or acquired characteristics or positions in society, they ask, legitimize differential treatment of persons by social institutions, laws, and customs? In particular, how should beginnings affect outcomes? The division of humanity into two sexes would seem to provide an obvious subject for such inquiries. We live in a society in whose past the innate characteristic of sex has been regarded as one of the clearest legitimizers of different rights and restrictions, both formal and informal. While the legal sanctions that uphold male dominance have been to some extent eroded within the past century, and more rapidly in the last twenty years, the heavy weight of tradition, combined with the effects of socialization broadly defined, still work powerfully to reinforce roles for the two sexes that are commonly regarded as of unequal prestige and worth.[2] The sexual division of labor within the family, in particular, is not only a fundamental part of the marriage contract, but so deeply influences us in our most formative years that feminists of both sexes who try to reject it find themselves struggling against it with varying degrees of ambivalence. Based on this linchpin, the deeply entrenched social institutionalization of sex difference, which I will refer to as "the gender system" or simply "gender," still permeates our society.

This gender system has rarely been subjected to the tests of justice. When we turn to the great tradition of Western political thought with questions about the justice of gender in mind, it is to little avail. Bold feminists like Mary Astell, Mary Wollstonecraft, Harriet Taylor, and George Bernard Shaw have occasionally challenged the tradition,[†] often using its own premises and arguments to overturn its justification of the unequal treatment of women. But John Stuart Mill is a rare exception to the rule that those who hold central positions in the tradition almost never questioned the justice of the subordination and oppression of women. This phenomenon is undoubtedly due in part to the fact that Aristotle, whose theory of justice has been so influential, relegated women and slaves to a realm of "household justice," whose participants are not fundamentally equal to the free men who participate in political justice, but inferiors whose natural function is to serve those who are more fully human. The liberal tradition, despite its supposed foundation of individual rights and human equality, is more Aristotelian in this respect than is generally acknowledged.[3] In one way or another, liberals have assumed that the "individual" who is the basic subject of their theories is the male head of a patriarchal household.[4] Thus the application of principles of justice to relations between the sexes, or within the household, has frequently been ruled out from the start.

---

*   From *Philosophy and Public Affairs*, 16, 1 (Winter 1987): 42–72.

†   Mary Astell (1666–1731) wrote *A Serious Proposal to the Ladies, for the Advancement of Their True and Greatest Interest* (1694) and fought for more equal educational opportunities for women; Mary Wollstonecraft (1759–97) was the author of *A Vindication of the Rights of Woman* (1792); Harriet Taylor (1807–58) worked with John Stuart Mill (her second husband) as a key contributor to *On Liberty* (1859); George Bernard Shaw (1856–1950), the playwright, was a prominent socialist and author of *The Intelligent Woman's Guide to Socialism and Capitalism* (1928).

Other assumptions, too, contribute to the widespread belief that neither women nor the family are appropriate subjects for discussions of justice. One is that women, whether because of their essential disorderliness, their enslavement to nature, their private and particularist inclinations, or their oedipal development,* are incapable of developing a sense of justice. This notion can be found—sometimes briefly suggested, sometimes developed at greater length—in the works of theorists from Plato to Freud, including Bodin, John Knox,† Rousseau, Kant, Hegel and Bentham.[5] The frequent implication is that those who do not possess the qualifications for fully ethical reasoning or action need not have principles of justice applied to them. Finally, in Rousseau (as so often, original) we find the unique claim that woman, being "made to submit to man and even to put up with his injustice," is imbued innately with a capacity to tolerate the unjust treatment with which she is likely to meet.[6]

For those who are not satisfied with these reasons for excluding women and gender from the subject matter of justice, the great tradition has little to offer, directly at least, to our inquiry. When we turn to contemporary theories of justice, however, we can expect to find more illuminating and positive contributions to the subject of gender and justice. I turn to ... John Rawls's *A Theory of Justice* ... to [it says or implies] ... in response to the question "How just is gender?"[7]

Justice as Fairness

An ambiguity runs throughout John Rawls's *A Theory of Justice*, continually noticeable to anyone reading it from a feminist perspective. On the one hand, as I shall argue below, a consistent and wholehearted application of Rawls's liberal principles can lead us to challenge fundamentally the gender system of our

society. On the other hand, in his own account of his theory, this challenge is barely hinted at, much less developed. The major reason is that throughout most of the argument, it is assumed (as throughout almost the entire liberal tradition) that the appropriate subjects of political theories are heads of families. As a result, although Rawls indicates on several occasions that a person's sex is a morally arbitrary and contingent characteristic, and although he states explicitly that the family itself is one of those basic social institutions to which the principles of justice must apply, his theory of justice fails to develop either of these convictions.

Rawls, like almost all political theorists until very recent years, employs supposedly generic male terms of reference. "Men," "mankind," "he" and "his" are interspersed with nonsexist terms of reference such as "individual" and "moral person." Examples of intergenerational concern are worded in terms of "fathers" and "sons," and the difference principle‡ is said to correspond to "the principle of fraternity."[8] This linguistic usage would perhaps be less significant if it were not for the fact that Rawls is self-consciously a member of a long tradition of moral and political philosophy that has used in its arguments either such supposedly generic masculine terms, or even more inclusive terms of reference ("human beings," "persons," "all rational beings as such"), only to exclude women from the scope of the conclusions reached. Kant is a clear example.[9] But when Rawls refers to the generality and universality of Kant's ethics, and when he compares the principles chosen in his own original position to those regulative of Kant's kingdom of ends,§ "acting from [which] expresses our nature as free and equal rational persons,"[10] he does not mention the fact that women were not included in that category of "free and equal rational persons," to which Kant meant his moral theory to apply. Again, in a brief discussion of

---

*   That is, according to Freudian psychoanalytic theory, the psychosexual development of children, passing through a period during which they develop the unconscious desire to possess the parent of the opposite sex and eliminate the parent of the same sex. This has become known as the Oedipus complex.

†   Jean Bodin (1530–96) was a French legal theorist who argued for the absolute authority of the sovereign; John Knox (c. 1510–72) was the leading Protestant reformer in Scotland, and author of *The First Blast of the Trumpet against the Monstrous Regiment of Women* (1558).

‡   The principle, developed by Rawls, that inequalities in the distribution of goods are justified only if those inequalities benefit the worst-off members of society. See the selection by Rawls earlier in this section.

§   See the selection by Kant in the Moral Theory section of this volume.

Freud's account of moral development, Rawls presents Freud's theory of the formation of the male super-ego in largely gender-neutral terms, without mentioning that Freud considered women's moral development to be sadly deficient, on account of their incomplete resolution of the Oedipus complex.[11] Thus there is a certain blindness to the sexism of the tradition in which Rawls is a participant, which tends to render his terms of reference even more ambiguous than they might otherwise be. A feminist reader finds it difficult not to keep asking: "Does this theory of justice apply to women, or not?"

This question is not answered in the important passages that list the characteristics that persons in the original position* are not to know about themselves, in order to formulate impartial principles of justice. In a subsequent article, Rawls has made it clear that sex is one of those morally irrelevant contingencies that is to be hidden by the veil of ignorance.[12] But throughout *A Theory of Justice*, while the list of things unknown by a person in the original position includes

> his place in society, his class position or social status, ... his fortune in the distribution of natural assets and abilities, his intelligence and strength, and the like, ... his conception of the good, the particulars of his rational plan of life, [and] even the special features of his psychology ...[13]

"his" sex is not mentioned. Since the parties also "know the general facts about human society,"[14] presumably including the fact that it is structured along the lines of gender both by custom and by law, one might think that whether or not they knew their sex might matter enough to be mentioned. Perhaps Rawls means to cover it by his phrase "and the like," but it is also possible that he did not consider it significant.

The ambiguity is exacerbated by Rawls's statement that those free and equal moral persons in the original position who formulate the principles of justice are to be thought of not as "single individuals" but as "heads of families" or "representatives of families."[15] He says that it is not necessary to think of the parties as heads of families, but that he will generally do so. The reason he does this, he explains, is to ensure that each person in the original position cares about the well-being of some persons in the next generation. These "ties of sentiment" between generations, which Rawls regards as important in the establishment of his just savings principle,† would otherwise constitute a problem, because of the general assumption that the parties in the original position are mutually disinterested. In spite of the ties of sentiment *within* families, then, "as representatives of families their interests are opposed as the circumstances of justice imply."[16]

The head of a family need not necessarily, of course, be a man. The very fact, however, that in common usage the term "female-headed households" is used *only* in reference to households without resident adult males, tends to suggest that it is assumed that any present male adult takes precedence over a female as the household or family head. Rawls does nothing to dispel this impression when he says of those in the original position that "imagining themselves to be fathers, say, they are to ascertain how much they should set aside for their sons by noting what they would believe themselves entitled to claim of their fathers."[17] He makes the "heads of families" assumption only in order to address the problem of savings between generations, and presumably does not intend it to be a sexist assumption. Nevertheless, Rawls is effectively trapped by this assumption into the traditional mode of thinking that life within the family and relations between the sexes are not properly to be regarded as part of the subject matter of a theory of social justice.

Before I go on to argue this, I must first point out that Rawls states at the outset of his theory that the family *is* part of the subject matter of social justice. "For us" he says,

---

* A hypothetical situation in which people are deprived of all knowledge of their personal and historical circumstances that are irrelevant to justice—they are behind "the veil of ignorance"—in order to ensure that any judgments they make about the proper structure of society will be appropriately impartial.

† Rawls—who is often credited with providing the first thorough discussion of what the current generation owes to future people—argues that the main duty owed to our successors is the saving of sufficient material capital to maintain just institutions over time.

the primary subject of justice is the basic structure of society, or more exactly, the way in which the major social institutions distribute fundamental rights and duties and determine the division of advantages from social cooperation.[18]

He goes on to specify "the monogamous family" as an example of such major social institutions, together with the political constitution, the legal protection of essential freedoms, competitive markets, and private property. The reason that Rawls makes such institutions the primary subject of his theory of social justice is that they have such profound effects on people's lives from the start, depending on where they find themselves placed in relation to them. He explicitly distinguishes between these major institutions and other "private associations," "less comprehensive social groups," and "various informal conventions and customs of everyday life,"[19] for which the principles of justice satisfactory for the basic structure might be less appropriate or relevant. There is no doubt, then, that in his initial definition of the sphere of social justice, the family is included.[20] The two principles of justice that Rawls defends in Part I, the principle of equal basic liberty, and the difference principle combined with the requirement of fair equality of opportunity, are intended to apply to the basic structure of society. They are "to govern the assignment of rights and duties and to regulate the distribution of social and economic advantages."[21] Whenever in these basic institutions there are differences in authority, in responsibility, in the distribution of resources such as wealth or leisure, these differences must be both to the greatest benefit of the least advantaged, and attached to positions accessible to all under conditions of fair equality of opportunity.

In Part II, Rawls discusses at some length the application of his principles of justice to almost all of the major social institutions listed at the beginning of the book. The legal protection of freedom of thought and liberty of conscience is defended, as are just democratic constitutional institutions and procedures; competitive markets feature prominently in the discussion of the just distribution of income; the issue of the private or public ownership of the means of production is explicitly left open, since Rawls argues that justice as fairness might be compatible with certain versions of either. But throughout these discussions, the question

of whether the monogamous family, in either its traditional or any other form, is a just social institution, is never raised. When Rawls announces that "the sketch of the system of institutions that satisfy the two principles of justice is now complete,"[22] he has still paid no attention at all to the internal justice of the family. The family, in fact, apart from passing references, appears in *A Theory of Justice* in only three contexts: as the link between generations necessary for the savings principle, as a possible obstacle to fair equality of opportunity—on account of inequalities amongst families—and as the first school of moral development. It is in the third of these contexts that Rawls first specifically mentions the family as a just institution. He mentions it, however, not to *consider* whether or not the family "in some form" is a just institution, but to *assume* it. Clearly regarding it as important, Rawls states as part of his first psychological law of moral development: "given that family institutions are just...."[23]

Clearly, however, by Rawls's own reasoning about the social justice of major institutions, this assumption is unwarranted. For the central tenet of the theory is that justice characterizes institutions whose members could hypothetically have agreed to their structure and rules from a position in which they did not know which place in the structure they were to occupy. The argument of the book is designed to show that the two principles of justice as fairness are those that individuals in such a hypothetical situation would indeed agree upon. But since those in the original position are the heads or representatives of families, they are *not in a position to determine questions of justice within families.*[24] As far as children are concerned, Rawls makes a convincing argument from paternalism for their temporary inequality. But wives (or whichever adult member[s] of a family are *not* its "head") go completely unrepresented in the original position. If families are just, as Rawls assumes, then they must *get* to be just in some different way (unspecified by Rawls) than other institutions, for it is impossible to see how the viewpoint of their less advantaged members ever gets to be heard.

There are two occasions where Rawls seems either to depart from his assumption that those in the original position are "family heads" or to assume that a "head of a family" is equally likely to be a woman as a man. In the assumption of the basic rights of citizenship, Rawls argues, favoring men over women is "justified by the difference principle ... only if it is to the advantage of women and acceptable from their standpoint."[25] Later, he seems to imply that the injustice and irrationality of racist doctrines are also characteristic of sexist ones.[26] But in spite of these passages, which appear to challenge formal sex discrimination, the discussions of institutions in Part II implicitly rely, in a number of respects, on the assumption that the parties formulating just institutions are (male) heads of (fairly traditional) families, and are therefore not concerned with issues of just distribution within the family. Thus the "head of family" assumption, far from being neutral or innocent, has the effect of banishing a large sphere of human life—and a particularly large sphere of most women's lives—from the scope of the theory.

First, Rawls's discussion of the distribution of wealth seems to assume that all the parties in the original position expect to be, once the veil of ignorance is removed, participants in the paid labor market. Distributive shares are discussed in terms of household income, but reference to "individuals" is interspersed into this discussion as if there were no difference between the advantage or welfare of a household and that of an individual.[27] This confusion obscures the fact that wages are paid to those in the labor force but that in societies characterized by a gender system (all current societies) a much larger proportion of women's than men's labor is unpaid, and is often not even acknowledged to be labor. It obscures the fact that such resulting disparities and the economic dependence of women on men are likely to affect power relations within the household, as well as access to leisure, prestige, political office, and so on amongst its adult members. Any discussion of justice *within* the family would have to address these issues.

Later, too, in his discussion of the obligations of citizens, Rawls's assumption that justice is the result of agreement amongst heads of families in the original position seems to prevent him from considering an issue of crucial importance to women as citizens—their exemption from the draft. He concludes that military conscription is justifiable in the case of defense against an unjust attack on liberty, so long as institutions "try to make sure that the risks of suffering from these imposed misfortunes are more or less evenly shared by all members of society over the course of their life, and that there is no avoidable *class* bias in selecting those who are called for duty."[28] However, the issue of the exemption of women from this major interference with the basic liberties of equal citizenship is not even mentioned.

In spite of two explicit rejections of the justice of formal sex discrimination in Part I, then, Rawls seems in Part II to be so heavily influenced by his "family heads" assumption that he fails to consider as part of the basic structure of society the greater economic dependence of women and the sexual division of labor within the typical family, or any of the broader social repercussions of this basic gender structure. Moreover, in Part III, where Rawls *assumes* the justice of the family "in some form" as a given, although he has not discussed any alternative forms, he sounds very much as though he is thinking in terms of traditional, gendered family structure. The family, he says, is "a small association, normally characterized by a definite hierarchy, in which each member has certain rights and duties."[29] The family's role as moral teacher is achieved partly through parental expectations of "the virtues of a good son or a good daughter."[30] In the family and in other associations such as schools, neighborhoods, and peer groups, Rawls continues, one learns various moral virtues and ideals, leading to those adopted in the various statuses, occupations, and family positions of later life. "The content of these ideals is given by the various conceptions of a good wife and husband, a good friend and citizen, and so on."[31] It seems likely, given these unusual departures from the supposedly generic male terms of reference used throughout the rest of the book, that Rawls means to imply that the goodness of daughters is distinct from the goodness of sons, and that of wives from that of husbands. A fairly traditional gender system seems to be assumed.

However, despite this, not only does Rawls, as noted above, "assume that the basic structure of a well-ordered society includes the family *in some form*." He adds to this the comment that "in a broader inquiry the institution of the family might be questioned, and other arrangements might indeed prove to be preferable."[32] But why should it require a broader inquiry than that engaged in *A Theory of Justice*, to ask questions about the institution of the family? Surely Rawls is right at the outset when he names it as one of those basic social institutions that most affects the life chances of individuals. The family is not a private association like a church or a university, which vary considerably in type, and which one can join and leave voluntarily. For although one has some choice (albeit highly constrained) about marrying into a gender-structured family, one has no choice at all about being born into one. Given this, Rawls's failure to subject the structure of the family to his principles of justice is particularly serious in the light of his belief that a theory of justice must take account of "how [individuals] get to be what they are" and "cannot take their final aims and interests, their attitudes to themselves and their life, as given."[33] For the family with its gender structure, female parenting in particular, is clearly a crucial determinant in the different socialization of the two sexes—in how men and women "get to be what they are."

If Rawls were to assume throughout the construction of his theory that all human adults are to be participants in what goes on behind the veil of ignorance, he would have no option but to require that the family, as a major social institution affecting the life chances of individuals, be constructed in accordance with the two principles of justice....

Women and Justice in Theory and Practice

... As I have shown above, while Rawls briefly rules out formal, legal discrimination on the grounds of sex (as on other grounds that he regards as "morally irrelevant"), he fails entirely to address the justice of the gender system, which—with its roots in the sex roles of the family and with its branches extending into virtually every corner of our lives—is one of the fundamental structures of our society. If, however, we read Rawls taking seriously both the notion that those behind the veil of ignorance are sexless persons, and the requirement that the family and the gender system—as basic social institutions—are to be subject to scrutiny, constructive feminist criticism of these contemporary institutions follows. So, also, do hidden difficulties for a Rawlsian theory of justice in a gendered society.

I will explain each of these points in turn. But first, both the critical perspective and the incipient problems of a feminist reading of Rawls can perhaps be illuminated by a description of a cartoon I saw a few years ago. Three elderly, robed male justices are depicted, looking down with astonishment at their very pregnant bellies. One says to the others, without

further elaboration: "Perhaps we'd better reconsider that decision." This illustration points to several things. First, it graphically demonstrates the importance, in thinking about justice, of a concept like Rawls's original position, which makes us put ourselves into the positions of others—especially positions that we ourselves can never be in. Second, it suggests that those thinking in such a way might well conclude that more than formal legal equality of the sexes is required if justice is to be done. As we have seen in recent years, it is quite possible to institutionalize the formal legal equality of the sexes and at the same time to enact laws concerning pregnancy, abortion, maternity leave, and so on, that in effect discriminate against women, not as women *per se*, but as "pregnant persons." The U.S. Supreme Court decided in 1976, for example, that "an exclusion of pregnancy from a disability benefits plan ... providing general coverage is not a gender-based discrimination at all."[34] One of the virtues of the cartoon is its suggestion that one's thinking on such matters is likely to be affected by the knowledge that one might become a "pregnant person." Finally, however, the illustration suggests the limits of what is possible, in terms of thinking ourselves into the original position, as long as we live in a gender-structured society. While the elderly male justices can, in a sense, imagine *themselves* pregnant, what is much more doubtful is whether, in constructing principles of justice, they can imagine themselves *women*. This raises the question whether, in fact, sex *is* a morally irrelevant and contingent human characteristic, in a society structured by gender.

Let us first assume that sex is contingent in this way, though I will later question this assumption. Let us suppose that it is possible, as Rawls clearly considers that it is, to hypothesize the moral thinking of representative human beings, ignorant of their sex and of all the other things that are hidden by the veil of ignorance. It seems clear that, while Rawls does not do this, we must consistently take the relevant positions of both sexes into account in formulating principles of justice. In particular, those in the original position must take special account of the perspective of women, since their knowledge of "the general facts about human society"[35] must include the knowledge that women have been and continue to be the less advantaged sex in a number of respects. In considering the basic institutions of society, they are more likely to pay special attention to the family than virtually to ignore it, since its unequal assigning of responsibilities and privileges to the two sexes and its socialization of children into sex roles make it, in its current form, a crucial institution for the preservation of sex inequality.

It is impossible to discuss here all the ways in which the principles of justice that Rawls arrives at are inconsistent with a gender-structured society. A general explanation of this point and three examples to illustrate it will have to suffice. The critical impact of a feminist reading of Rawls comes chiefly from his second principle, which requires that inequalities be "to the greatest benefit of the least advantaged" and "attached to offices and positions open to all."[36] This means that if any roles or positions analogous to our current sex roles, including those of husband and wife, mother and father, were to survive the demands of the first requirement, the second requirement would disallow any linkage between these roles and sex. Gender, as I have defined it in this article, with its ascriptive designation of positions and expectations of behavior in accordance with the inborn characteristic of sex, could no longer form a legitimate part of the social structure, whether inside or outside the family. Three illustrations will help to link this conclusion with specific major requirements that Rawls makes of a just or well-ordered society.

First, after the basic political liberties, one of the most essential liberties is "the important liberty of free choice of occupation."[37] It is not difficult to see that this liberty is compromised by the assumption and customary expectation, central to our gender system, that women take far greater responsibility than men for housework and child care, whether or not they also work for wages outside the home. In fact, both the assigning of these responsibilities to women—resulting in their asymmetrical economic dependency on men—and also the related responsibility of husbands to support their wives, compromise the liberty of choice of occupation of both sexes. While Rawls has no objection to some aspects of the division of labor, he asserts that, in a well-ordered society, "no one need be servilely dependent on others and made to choose between monotonous and routine occupations which are deadening to human thought and sensibility" but that work can be "meaningful for all."[38] These conditions are far more likely to be met in a society which

does not assign family responsibilities in a way that makes women into a marginal sector of the paid work force and renders likely their economic dependence upon men.

Second, the abolition of gender seems essential for the fulfillment of Rawls's criteria for political justice. For he argues that not only would equal formal political liberties be espoused by those in the original position, but that any inequalities in the *worth* of these liberties (for example, the effects on them of factors like poverty and ignorance) must be justified by the difference principle. Indeed, "the constitutional process should preserve the equal representation of the original position to the degree that this is practicable."[39] While Rawls discusses this requirement in the context of *class* differences, stating that those who devote themselves to politics should be "drawn more or less equally from all sectors of society,"[40] it is just as clearly applicable to sex differences. And the equal political representation of women and men, especially if they are parents, is clearly inconsistent with our gender system.

Finally, Rawls argues that the rational moral persons in the original position would place a great deal of emphasis on the securing of self-respect or self-esteem. They "would wish to avoid at almost any cost the social conditions that undermine self-respect," which is "perhaps the most important" of all the primary goods.[41] In the interests of this primary value, if those in the original position did not know whether they were to be men or women, they would surely be concerned to establish a thoroughgoing social and economic equality between the sexes that would preserve either from the need to pander to or servilely provide for the pleasures of the other. They would be highly motivated, for example, to find a means of regulating pornography that did not seriously compromise freedom of speech. In general, they would be unlikely to tolerate basic social institutions that asymmetrically either forced or gave strong incentives to members of one sex to become sex objects for the other.

There is, then, implicit in Rawls's theory of justice a potential critique of gender-structured social institutions, which can be made explicit by taking seriously the fact that those formulating the principles of justice do not know their sex. At the beginning of my brief discussion of this feminist critique, however, I made an assumption that I said would later be questioned—that a person's sex is, as Rawls at times indicates, a contingent and morally irrelevant characteristic, such that human beings can hypothesize ignorance of this fact about them, imagining themselves as *sexless*, free and equal, rational, moral persons. First, I will explain why, unless this assumption is a reasonable one, there are likely to be further feminist ramifications for a Rawlsian theory of justice, as well as those I have just sketched out. I will then argue that the assumption is very probably not plausible in any society that is structured along the lines of gender. The conclusion I reach is that not only is the disappearance of gender necessary if social justice is to be enjoyed in practice by members of both sexes, but that the disappearance of gender is a prerequisite for the *complete* development of a nonsexist, fully human *theory* of justice.

Although Rawls is clearly aware of the effects on individuals of their different places in the social system, he regards it as possible to hypothesize free and rational moral persons in the original position who, freed from the contingencies of actual characteristics and social circumstances, will adopt the viewpoint of the "representative human being." He is under no illusions about the difficulty of this task, which requires "a great shift in perspective" from the way we think about fairness in everyday life. But with the help of the veil of ignorance, he believes that we can "take up a point of view that everyone can adopt on an equal footing," so that "we share a common standpoint along with others and do not make our judgments from a personal slant."[42] The result of this rational impartiality or objectivity, Rawls argues, is that, all being convinced by the same arguments, agreement about the basic principles of justice will be unanimous.[43] He does not mean that those in the original position will agree about *all* moral or social issues, but that complete agreement will be reached on all basic principles, or "essential understandings."[44] It is a crucial assumption of this argument for unanimity, however, that all the parties have similar motivations and psychologies (he assumes mutually disinterested rationality and an absence of envy), and that they have experienced similar patterns of moral development (they are presumed capable of a sense of justice).

Rawls regards these assumptions as the kind of "weak stipulations" on which a general theory can safely be founded.[45]

The coherence of Rawls's hypothetical original position, with its unanimity of representative human beings, however, is placed in doubt if the kinds of human beings we actually become in society not only differ in respect of interests, superficial opinions, prejudices, and points of view that we can discard for the purpose of formulating principles of justice, but also differ in their basic psychologies, conceptions of self in relation to others, and experiences of moral development. A number of feminist scholars have argued in recent years that, in a gender-structured society, women's and men's different life experiences in fact affect their respective psychologies, modes of thinking, and patterns of moral development in significant ways.[46] Special attention has been paid to the effects on the psychological and moral development of both sexes of the fact, fundamental to our gendered society, that children of both sexes are primarily reared by women. It has been argued that the experience of individuation—of separating oneself from the nurturer with whom one is originally psychologically fused—is a very different experience for girls than for boys, leaving the members of each sex with a different perception of themselves and of their relations with others. In addition, it has been argued that the experience of *being* primary nurturers (and of growing up with this expectation) also affects the psychological and moral perspective of women, as does the experience of growing up in a society in which members of one's sex are in many respects subordinate to the other. Feminist theorists' scrutiny and analysis of the different experiences that we encounter as we develop, from our actual lived lives to our absorption of their ideological underpinnings, have in valuable ways filled out Beauvoir's claim that "one is not born, but rather becomes, a woman."*[47]

What is already clearly indicated by these studies, despite their incompleteness so far, is that in a gender-structured society there is such a thing as the distinct standpoint of women, and that this standpoint cannot be adequately taken into account by male philosophers doing the theoretical equivalent

---

*   See the selection by Simone de Beauvoir in the Equality and Fairness section of this volume.

of the elderly male justices in the cartoon. The formative influence on small children of female parenting, especially, seems to suggest that sex difference is more likely to affect one's moral psychology, and therefore one's thinking about justice, in a gendered society than, for example, racial difference in a society in which race has social significance or class difference in a class society. The notion of the standpoint of women, while not without its own problems, suggests that a fully human moral theory can be developed only when there is full participation by both sexes in the dialogue that is moral and political philosophy. This will not come to pass until women take their place with men in the enterprise in approximately equal numbers and in positions of comparable influence. In a society structured along the lines of gender, this is most unlikely to happen.

In itself, moreover, it is insufficient for the complete development of a fully human theory of justice. For if principles of justice are to be adopted unanimously by representative human beings ignorant of their particular characteristics and positions in society, they must be persons whose psychological and moral development is in all essentials identical. This means that the social factors influencing the differences presently found between the sexes—from female parenting to all the manifestations of female subordination and dependence—would have to be replaced by genderless institutions and customs. Only when men participate equally in what has been principally women's realm of meeting the daily material and psychological needs of those close to them, and when women participate equally in what have been principally men's realms of larger scale production, government, and intellectual and creative life, will members of both sexes develop a more complete *human* personality than has hitherto been possible. Whereas Rawls and most other philosophers have assumed that human psychology, rationality, moral

development and so on are completely represented by the males of the species, this assumption itself is revealed as a part of the male-dominated ideology of our gendered society.

It is not feasible to indicate here at any length what effect the consideration of women's standpoint might have on a theory of justice. I would suggest, however, that in the case of Rawls's theory, it might place in doubt some assumptions and conclusions, while reinforcing others. For example, Rawls's discussion of rational plans of life and primary goods might be focused more on relationships and less exclusively on the complex activities that his "Aristotelian principle"* values most highly, if it were to encompass the traditionally more female parts of life.[48] On the other hand, those aspects of Rawls's theory, such as the difference principle, that seem to require a greater capacity to identify with others than is normally characteristic of liberalism, might be strengthened by reference to conceptions of relations between self and others that seem in a gendered society to be more predominantly female.

In the earlier stages of working on this article, I thought mainly in terms of what justice has to say about gender, rather than about the effects of gender on justice.... But, given the reliance of [Rawls'] ... theory on the agreement of representative human beings about the basic moral principles that are to govern their lives, I conclude that, while we can use it along the way to critique existing inequalities, we cannot complete such a theory of justice until the life experiences of the two sexes become as similar as their biological differences permit. Such a theory, and the society that puts it into practice, will be fundamentally influenced by the participation of both women and men in all spheres of human life. Not only is gender incompatible with a just society but the disappearance of gender is likely to lead in turn to important changes in the theory and practices of justice. ■

---

* This, Rawls says, is the "deep psychological fact" that, other things being equal, people find complex activities that require the exercise of more developed skills or capacities to be more interesting, enjoyable, and preferable to simpler or more rote tasks.

Suggestions for Critical Reflection

1. Okin writes that, "[i]n one way or another, liberals have assumed that the 'individual' who is the basic subject of their theories is the male head of a patriarchal household." Consider the works from this tradition that you might have read: is Okin right in her judgment? What implications should we draw from this?

2. Is there a difference between the way we should understand justice and equity within families as opposed to in society at large? Does Okin think there should be? Do you?

3. "For the family with its gender structure, female parenting in particular, is clearly a crucial determinant in the different socialization of the two sexes—in how men and women 'get to be what they are.'" Is Okin right about this? What implications does it have?

4. Okin quotes Rawls as assuming "that family institutions are just," and then proceeds to argue that, by Rawls's own lights, the institution of the family cannot be considered just. Does Okin mean by this that it must be considered *unjust*? How effective are Okin's arguments on this point? Do they apply only to Rawls, or do they have wider application?

5. Okin asserts that "a much larger proportion of women's than men's labor is unpaid, and is often not even acknowledged to be labor." What are the implications of this claim for social justice?

6. In the final section of her paper, Okin "raises the question whether, in fact, sex *is* a morally irrelevant and contingent human characteristic, in a society structured by gender." What is the significance of this question? How does Okin answer it?

7. Okin points out Rawls's use of male pronouns and other non-inclusive language. What role does this play in her argument? If Rawls had made the same claims using gender-inclusive language, would this have bearing on the strength of Okin's criticisms?

8. "[I]n a gender-structured society there is such a thing as the distinct standpoint of women, and ... this standpoint cannot be adequately taken into account by male philosophers." Okin makes this claim only cautiously, but it is a striking one. What are its consequences?

9. Okin concludes that "gender [is] incompatible with a just society." What does she mean by this? How radical a claim is this? Do you think it is warranted?

10. Okin's points largely concern issues that Rawls neglected to discuss. Do you think that what's left out could be added consistently to what Rawls said, or is Okin's position incompatible with Rawls's?

11. This article was published in 1987. In your view, have there been any significant changes to the attitudes that Okin describes concerning the relevance of gender to justice, or the place of principles of justice within the family?

Notes

1 An earlier version of this article was presented at the 80th Annual Meeting of the American Political Science Association, August 30–September 2, 1984 in Washington, D.C. I gratefully acknowledge the helpful comments of the following people: Robert Amdur, Peter Euben, Robert Goodin, Anne Harper, Robert Keohane, Carole Pateman, John Rawls, Nancy Rosenblum, Robert Simon, Quentin Skinner, Michael Walzer, Iris Young and the Editors of *Philosophy & Public Affairs*. Thanks also to Lisa Carisella and Elaine Herrmann for typing the manuscript.

2 On the history of the legal enforcement of traditional sex roles and recent changes therein, see Leo Kanowitz, *Sex Roles in Law and Society* (Albuquerque: University of New Mexico Press, 1973, and 1974

Supplement), esp. pts. 2, 4, 5; also Kenneth M. Davidson, Ruth Bader Ginsburg and Henna Hill Kay, *Sex-Based Discrimination* (St. Paul: West Publishing Co., 1974, and 1978 Supplement by Wendy Williams), esp. chap. 2.

3 See Judith Hicks Stiehm, "The Unit of Political Analysis: Our Aristotelian Hangover," in Sandra Harding and Merrill B. Hintikka, eds., *Discovering Reality: Feminist Perspectives on Epistemology, Metaphysics, Methodology, and Philosophy of Science* (Dordrecht: Reidel, 1983), pp. 31–43.

4 See Carole Pateman and Theresa Brennan, "'Mere Auxiliaries to the Commonwealth': Women and the Origins of Liberalism," *Political Studies* 27, no. 2 (June 1979): 183–200; also Susan Moller Okin, "Women and

the Making of the Sentimental Family," *Philosophy & Public Affairs* 11, no. 1 (Winter 1982): 65–88.

5 See Nannerl O. Keohane, "Female Citizenship: The Monstrous Regiment of Women," presented at the Annual Meeting of the Conference for the Study of Political Thought, April 6–8, 1979, on Bodin, John Knox and Rousseau; Carole Pateman, "'The Disorder of Women'; Women, Love, and The Sense of Justice," *Ethics* 81, no. 1 (October 1980): 20–34, on Rousseau and Freud; Susan Moller Okin, "Thinking like a Woman," unpublished ms., 1984, on Plato and Hegel; Terence Ball, "Utilitarianism, Feminism and the Franchise: James Mill and His Critics," *History of Political Thought* 1, no. 1 (Spring 1980): 91–115, on Bentham.

6 Jean-Jacques Rousseau, *Émile*, in *Oeuvres Complètes* 4 (Paris: Pléiade, 1969), pp. 734–35, 750.

7 John Rawls, *A Theory of Justice* (Cambridge, MA: Harvard University Press, 1971), hereafter referred to as *Theory*....

8 *Theory*, pp. 105–106, 208–209, 288–289.

9 See Okin, "Women and the Making of the Sentimental Family," pp. 78–82.

10 *Theory*, pp. 251, 256.

11 Ibid., p. 459.

12 "Fairness to Goodness," *Philosophical Review* 84 (1975): 537. He says: "That we have one conception of the good rather than another is not relevant from a moral standpoint. In acquiring it we are influenced by the same sort of contingencies that lead us to rule out a knowledge of our sex and class."

13 *Theory*, p. 137; see also p. 12.

14 Ibid., p. 137.

15 Ibid., pp. 128, 146.

16 Ibid., p. 128; see also p. 292.

17 Ibid., p. 289.

18 Ibid., p. 8.

19 Ibid., p. 7.

20 It is interesting to note that in a subsequent paper on the question why the basic structure of society is the primary subject of justice, Rawls does not mention the family as part of the basic structure. "The Basic Structure as Subject," *American Philosophical Quarterly* 14, no. 2 (April 1977): 159.

21 *Theory*, p. 61.

22 Ibid., p. 303.

23 *Theory*, p. 490. See Deborah Kearns, "A Theory of Justice—and Love; Rawls on the Family," *Politics* (Australasian Political Studies Association Journal) 18, no. 2 (November 1983): 30–40 for an interesting discussion of the significance of Rawls's failure to address the justice of the family for his theory of moral development.

24 As Jane English says, in a paper that is more centrally concerned with the problems of establishing Rawls's savings principle than with justice within the family *per se*: "By making the parties in the original position heads of families rather than individuals, Rawls makes the family opaque to claims of justice." "Justice between Generations," *Philosophical Studies* 31 (1977): 95.

25 *Theory*, p. 99.

26 Ibid., p. 149.

27 Ibid., pp. 270–274, 304–309.

28 Ibid., pp. 380–381 (emphasis added).

29 Ibid., p. 467.

30 Ibid., p. 468.

31 Ibid.

32 Ibid., pp. 462–63 (emphasis added).

33 "The Basic Structure as Subject," p. 160.

34 *General Electric vs. Gilbert*, 429, U.S. 125 (1976).

35 *Theory*, p. 137.

36 Ibid., p. 302.

37 Ibid., p. 274.

38 Ibid., p. 529.

39 Ibid., p. 222; see also pp. 202–205, 221–228.

40 Ibid., p. 228.

41 Ibid., pp. 440, 396; see also pp. 178–179.

42 Ibid., pp. 516–517.

43 Ibid., pp. 139–141.

44 Ibid., pp. 516–517.

45 Ibid., p. 149.

46 Major works contributing to this thesis are Jean Baker Miller, *Toward a New Psychology of Women* (Boston: Beacon Press, 1976); Dorothy Dinnerstein, *The Mermaid and the Minotaur* (New York: Harper and Row, 1977); Nancy Chodorow, *The Reproduction of Mothering* (Berkeley: University of California Press, 1978); Carol Gilligan, *In a Different Voice* (Cambridge, MA: Harvard University Press, 1982); Nancy Hartsock, *Money, Sex, and Power* (New York: Longmans, 1983). Two of the more important individual papers are Jane Flax, "The Conflict between Nurturance and Autonomy in Mother-Daughter Relationships and within Feminism," *Feminist Studies* 4, no. 2 (Summer 1978); Sara Ruddick, "Maternal Thinking," *Feminist Studies* 6, no. 2 (Summer 1980). A good summary and discussion of "women's standpoint" is presented in Alison Jaggar, *Feminist Politics and Human Nature* (Totowa, NJ: Rowman and Allanheld, 1983), chap. 11.

47 Simone de Beauvoir, *The Second Sex* (1949; reprinted., London: New English Library, 1969), p. 9.

48 Brian Barry has made a similar, though more general, criticism of the Aristotelian principle in *The Liberal Theory of Justice* (Oxford: Oxford University Press, 1973), pp. 27–30.

Equality and Fairness

The previous chapter introduced some main theories of justice: Aristotle's distinction between distributive and rectificatory justice, and his emphasis on the virtue of desiring only your fair share of social goods; Hobbes's justification for the almost absolute power of the sovereign; Mill's classic statement of liberalism; Marx's communism; Rawls's modern formulation of welfarist liberalism; and Nozick's libertarian and Okin's feminist responses to Rawls. In this chapter we turn to some pressing real-world examples of injustice.

The first two readings address sexism and the oppression of women. In the first reading Mary Wollstonecraft argues, against prevailing assumptions in the late eighteenth century, that women are just as capable of rational thought and moral virtue as men, and not only deserve equal rights to freedom and independence but would benefit society if they had those rights. In the next reading Simone de Beauvoir, a mid-twentieth-century precursor of what is sometimes called "second-wave feminism," goes beyond the demand for equal rights for women within existing legal structures, and argues that, since there is no pre-existing, inborn "female nature," women's whole consciousness is shaped by the patriarchal society into which they are born, and so social change needs to go much deeper than mere equality of opportunity.

The following reading, by Talia Mae Bettcher, is a philosophical examination of the concept of gender and its application to people in the trans community. She argues that, because trans people cannot be adequately understood in terms of the gender definitions already established by dominant culture, these definitions are morally inadequate and should be revised. "Five Faces of Oppression," by Iris Marion Young, lays out an "enabling conception of justice" that, Young argues, provides a more accurate model than the theories we encountered in the last chapter for understanding the varieties of injustice affecting a variety of marginalized groups in liberal democracies: exploitation, marginalization, powerlessness, cultural imperialism, and violence.

The final two selections in this chapter deal with issues of race. Kwame Anthony Appiah critically examines racial categories and argues that, at best, they are socially constructed identities and have no basis in biology. Finally, a moving selection from Ta-Nehisi Coates's

semi-autobiographical book *Between the World and Me* describes how his personal and educational experience led him to his current ideological position regarding black oppression.

There is a rich and growing philosophical literature on sexism, racism, homophobia, the treatment of LGBTQ+ groups, economic exploitation, and other forms of injustice. To give just a few illustrative examples: Zack, Shrage, and Sartwell, eds., *Race, Class, Gender, and Sexuality: The Big Questions* (Blackwell, 1998); Susan Ferguson, ed., *Race, Gender, Sexuality and Social Class: Dimensions of Inequality and Identity* (Sage, 2015); Alison Stone, *An Introduction to Feminist Philosophy* (Polity Press, 2007); Cudd and Andreasen, eds., *Feminist Theory: A Philosophical Anthology* (Blackwell, 2005); Georgia Warnke, *Debating Sex and Gender* (Oxford University Press, 2010); Linda Martín Alcoff, *Visible Identities: Race, Gender, and the Self* (Oxford University Press, 2006); Stryker and Whittle, eds., *The Transgender Studies Reader* (Routledge, 2006); Naomi Zack, *Philosophy of Race: An Introduction* (Palgrave, 2018); Taylor, Alcoff, and Anderson, eds., *The Routledge Companion to the Philosophy of Race* (Routledge, 2017); and Andrew Valls, ed., *Race and Racism in Modern Philosophy* (Cornell University Press, 2005).

MARY WOLLSTONECRAFT

FROM *A Vindication of the Rights of Woman*

Who Was Mary Wollstonecraft?

Mary Wollstonecraft, an eighteenth-century British writer, has come to be considered one of the most influential feminist philosophers of the Western tradition. She is also well-known for her turbulent and difficult personal life.

Wollstonecraft was born in 1759 into a comfortably well-off London family. Her father, however, was a drunken, violent spendthrift who squandered the family's modest fortune during Mary's childhood years (including money that Mary was to have inherited from another relative at 21). The family moved frequently as her father tried, and repeatedly failed, to make a go of farming in Epping, Whalebone (East London), Essex, Yorkshire, and Wales before they finally moved back to London when Mary was eighteen.

During these years Mary came to adopt a protective role toward her mother and two younger sisters. She sometimes slept outside the door of her mother's bedroom as a teenager in order to protect her from her father's alcohol-fueled rages. Later she nursed her sister, Eliza, after the difficult birth of her daughter. Eliza was probably suffering from post-partum depression, and Mary also suspected that her husband abused her; Mary convinced her sister to leave her husband, and helped her to do so. Unfortunately she was forced to leave behind her baby, who died within the year; this left Eliza disgraced in society, unable to remarry, and she spent the rest of her life struggling against poverty.

Wollstonecraft was also a passionate friend. A key friendship in her early life was with Fanny Blood, with whom she dreamed of setting up a female utopia. Together with Wollstonecraft's sisters they set up a school in Newington Green, London (a center for non-conformist religious communities*). However it was not long before Blood became engaged and left the school. Blood's husband, Hugh Skeys, took her to Europe to try and improve her delicate health, but when she became pregnant she fell seriously ill. Wollstonecraft visited her in Lisbon to try and nurse her to health, but Blood died of complications from premature childbirth in 1785. This was a severe emotional blow for Wollstonecraft, and part of the inspiration for her first novel *Mary, a Fiction* (1788).

On Wollstonecraft's return to England† she closed the school—which had declined in her absence—and took a position as governess to the daughters of Lord Viscount Kingsborough in Ireland. She stayed with the Kingsboroughs for a year, and then made a decision which, for that time, was almost unprecedented: she decided to attempt to support herself as an author. Some of the reasons for this can be seen in her first work, *Thoughts on the Education of Daughters* (1877), subtitled "Unfortunate Situation of Females, Fashionably Educated, and Left without a Fortune," in which she expressed her frustration at the very limited opportunities available for 'respectable' women who nevertheless needed to work.

Wollstonecraft moved to London where, encouraged and assisted by the radical liberal publisher and bookseller Joseph Johnson, she settled down to make her living by writing. She learned French and German so that she could work as a translator of continental texts, and wrote reviews, some of which were published in Johnson's liberal *Analytical Review*. She also published two books. *A Vindication of the Rights of Men* (1790) was a response to Edmund Burke's conservative critique of the French Revolution in *Reflections on the Revolution in France*. Its even more famous and influential partner was *A Vindication of the Rights of Woman* (1792). Wollstonecraft began to move in radical intellectual circles that included Thomas Paine, Joseph Priestley, Samuel Taylor Coleridge, William Blake, William Wordsworth, and William Godwin.

---

* Religious groups that dissented from the Anglican Church.
† One anecdote that shows Wollstonecraft's character is that, on the voyage home from Portugal, she browbeat the captain of the ship into rescuing a wrecked French vessel that he wanted to pass by.

During this period she became enraptured with the painter Henry Fuseli and pursued a relationship with him even though he was married. In a typically forthright fashion, Wollstonecraft proposed that she come to live with Fuseli and his wife in order to carry on a platonic (i.e., non-sexual) relationship with the artist; Fuseli's wife was appalled and he broke off his relationship with Mary.

Humiliated, Wollstonecraft left for Paris late in 1792 in order to escape London and to witness first-hand the revolutionary events in France. She arrived alone in a country in turmoil, only a few weeks before the execution of the deposed King Louis XVI. Wollstonecraft plunged into the excitement, and quickly fell passionately in love with an American adventurer named Gilbert Imlay (formerly an officer in the American Revolutionary War, he was acting as a diplomatic representative of the US while simultaneously lining his pockets by running the British blockade of French ports). Although Imlay had no interest in marrying her—and Wollstonecraft herself had strong reservations about marriage—Mary became pregnant with her first daughter, Fanny. After Britain declared war on France in 1793, Imlay registered Wollstonecraft as his wife in order to protect her from being arrested as a British citizen; however he did not marry her, and after leaving her at Le Havre, where she was to give birth, he never returned. Despite all this Wollstonecraft continued her writing, publishing *An Historical and Moral View of the French Revolution* in 1794. The violent excesses she had witnessed caused her to temper her radical zeal somewhat, but she felt that appropriate changes to education, concurrent with gradual political change, would prevent too much upheaval accompanying social change.

Wollstonecraft finally returned to London in 1795, seeking Imlay who had since left France for England. Imlay, who had begun an affair with a young actress, rejected her,* but when she attempted to commit suicide with an overdose of tincture of opium he saved her life. In a last desperate attempt to win back his affections Wollstonecraft undertook to travel to Scandinavia—taking only her maid and young daughter—to attempt to track down a ship's captain who had absconded with a small fortune in Imlay's money intended to buy Swedish goods to import into France. But when she got back to England and found him living with another woman, it became clear to her that Imlay would never return her love. Once again, she attempted suicide—by jumping in the Thames—and once again she was saved, this time by a passing stranger.

Gradually Wollstonecraft's depression began to lift and—throwing off any financial support from Imlay—she returned to the literary life she had previously developed in London. Cautiously, she entered once more into a love affair, this time with the journalist, novelist, and utilitarian philosopher William Godwin. The relationship was a happy and reciprocated one, and when Wollstonecraft became pregnant they decided to marry. This forced Wollstonecraft to reveal publicly that her 'marriage' to Imlay had been a fake one, and once again she was the subject of social scandal. Godwin, too, was attacked, this time for hypocrisy by some of his radical friends, because he had argued in his *Enquiry Concerning Political Justice* (1793) that marriage should be abolished as a social institution.

Nevertheless Wollstonecraft and Godwin were wed in March 1797, and, so that they could retain their independence, moved into adjoining houses in London. Wollstonecraft was full of plans for the future, and had embarked on a new novel, to be called *Maria, or The Wrongs of Woman*. In August, Wollstonecraft gave birth to her second daughter, Mary; but although at first the delivery seemed to go well, Wollstonecraft developed septicemia and died several days later. She was 38.

Godwin was grief-stricken. In 1798 he published his *Memoirs of the Author of a Vindication of the Rights of Woman* which, though deeply felt and sincere, caused yet more scandal for revealing in print the history of his dead wife's love affairs, illegitimate child, and suicide attempts. Their daughter, Mary Godwin, went on to elope outrageously with the Romantic poet Percy Bysshe Shelley, and wrote *Frankenstein* (1818).

---

* Virginia Woolf's diagnosis of Imlay's feelings about Wollstonecraft is delightful (though no doubt too charitable to him): "Tickling minnows he had hooked a dolphin, and the creature rushed him through the waters till he was dizzy and only wanted to escape" (from "Four Figures").

What Was Wollstonecraft's Overall Philosophical Project?

Wollstonecraft is best known for her argument, presented in *A Vindication of the Rights of Woman*, that women and men are inherently equal—equally rational, equally intelligent, equally moral—and that any appearances of intellectual or moral inequality are an artifact of differing education and social upbringing. She argued that men had enslaved women by educating them to care only for romantic love, and by fetishizing weak and passive ideals of femininity. Instead of rational, active, strong, and independent women, society rewarded women who remained childlike, passive, weak, and dependent. Wollstonecraft argued that real social change had to occur at the level of the family, with women educated to rationally fulfill their duties as mothers, wives, and daughters. She proposed a new social order, which would better serve the natural capacities of human beings, in which men and women are both treated as rational, autonomous beings. She argued that social changes of this sort would produce citizens—especially female citizens—that were better able to serve social justice, which would in turn produce a better, more robust and healthy society, that would then raise even more virtuous citizens, and so on in an upward spiral of social progress. Thus, equality for women would benefit all members of society, and not just the female sex.

A key concern for Wollstonecraft was the importance of personal independence. For her, self-government was a key aspect of individual human development. In particular, moral virtue essentially involves acting autonomously on the basis of moral principles. These principles, according to Wollstonecraft, do not arise merely out of sympathy for others or other moral passions, or in accordance with merely social strictures, but are grasped by rational reflection on the attributes of God and God's design manifested through human nature. It was on this basis that she felt the rights of women could be asserted and found indisputable, if people would consider the subject impartially. Arbitrary power structures and entrenched ideologies were under attack in revolutionary France, and Wollstonecraft pointed out that such structures also kept women from being accorded the rights that were demanded for men. "Who," she asked, "made man the exclusive judge, if woman partake with him the gift of reason?"

The principles that shaped Wollstonecraft's political philosophy also shaped her moral philosophy. Reason, because it cultivates virtue, should guide an individual's moral life. Education for girls and young women should focus on nurturing their reason, so they can achieve both economic and psychological independence. (Wollstonecraft even wrote a children's book, *Original Stories from Real Life* [1788], which encourages a balance between reason and emotion.) Not only the mind, but also the body, should be made strong and resilient, in order to meet the changes and difficulties of life with fortitude. Such an education would prevent women from being "blown about by every momentary gust of feeling." Rather, reason and feeling should balance each other, with reason taking the upper hand. A woman so guided, according to Wollstonecraft, would not be entirely subject to the whims of fathers, husbands, and brothers for her well-being and happiness.

What Is the Structure of This Reading?

A Vindication of the Rights of Woman focuses on the condition of women in society, as well as on the social construction of gender. It is a more abstract work of political theory than the preceding *Vindication of the Rights of Men*, expanding to address metaphysical and psychological aspects of the question of universal rights. Wollstonecraft originally planned on writing a second volume, but she completed only the first, which comprises a dedication, an introduction, and 13 chapters.

The dedication to Talleyrand-Périgord, French statesman and former bishop of Autun,* is the first excerpt included here. Talleyrand was one of the writers of the new French Constitution of 1791, as well as the author of a new program for French public education, one that excluded women at the higher levels and sought only to prepare them for domestic life. Wollstonecraft's dedi-

---

* Charles-Maurice de Talleyrand-Périgord (1754–1838) became Bishop of Autun in 1788. A year later he supported anti-clerical revolutionaries and helped in the seizure of Church properties across France. Serving under Louis XVI, the Revolution, Napoleon, and beyond, Talleyrand was considered a crafty and adaptable diplomat and politician. Wollstonecraft met him on one of his diplomatic journeys to England.

cation asks Talleyrand to reconsider the reasoning that prompted the leaders of the Revolution to leave women out of their new Constitution and exclude them from their program for national education. In this Dedication, she outlines her chief argument, that if women are not given social rights and equal educational opportunities, they will resort to power tactics of dubious morality, thereby undermining the family, and by extension, society. She argues that women possess reason, and as such have the right to unfold their talents in society. She calls for the legislators of France to revise their Constitution and to grant equality to women under the law.

The second excerpt is from the Introduction, in which Wollstonecraft considers the situation of women in society and outlines her arguments for changing it. Here she addresses the "false system of education" that trains upper and middle-class women to be ornamental and weak. Conceding that women are physically weaker than men, she asserts that their capacity for reason is equal. An education that undermines reason, she argues, nurtures immorality, and if society is to improve, women must be given opportunity to escape from their "slavish dependence" and to develop themselves as strong and independent human beings.

The last section is from Chapter Two, entitled "The Prevailing Opinion of a Sexual Character Discussed." Here, Wollstonecraft considers the dominant opinions of her society regarding the character of women and the kind of education best suited to them. She outlines the consensus among educational theorists of her day, who thought that women and men had essentially different virtues and should be educated accordingly. Women, it was thought, should be educated for obedience and passivity, to be ruled over by men. Wollstonecraft argues against these ideas, insisting instead that virtue is not relative, and that women should be educated in the same way as men: to strengthen the body, develop reason, and nurture the heart. Give women freedom and independence, she states, and virtue will result, not only in the individual but also in society.

Some Useful Background Information

1. Wollstonecraft argues against women cultivating an excess of what in the eighteenth and nineteenth centuries was called "sensibility." This term referred to a particular kind of refined aesthetic and moral responsiveness and sympathy, particularly to beauty and the sorrows of others. This kind of sentiment became a central motif in literature from the 1740s to the 1770s, particularly in the novels of Laurence Sterne, Jean-Jacques Rousseau, and Johann Wolfgang von Goethe. Wollstonecraft was concerned that women who over-cultivated sensibility were at risk of valuing feeling over common sense and reason. She was, however, herself influenced by this movement, and her political action was in many ways spurred by her sympathetic engagement with the sorrows of others.

2. Two of Wollstonecraft's first publications, *Thoughts on the Education of Daughters* (1787) and *Original Stories from Real Life* (1788), were focused on pedagogy, particularly the education of girls. Education continued to be an abiding interest, and in the *Vindication* Wollstonecraft argues that only by changing educational practices can social and political changes be fostered in society. Wollstonecraft believed that children should be taught at co-educational day schools, while living at home. While this does not seem controversial to us, it was quite radical at a time when children were taught separately, boys at boarding schools to be educated for public life, and girls at home to attend to domestic duties. Many eighteenth-century moralists and philosophers, including Rousseau in his well-known novel *Émile, or On Education* (1762), argued that women and men had different moral natures, and that a woman's education should be limited to what is necessary to form a pleasing companion for man. These opinions of female character were prevalent in society, and Wollstonecraft takes pains to show that they were the opinions of custom and prejudice, not of reason.

A Common Misconception

Wollstonecraft is considered by many to be the "founding mother" of feminism, but 'feminism' was not a term that became current until the late nineteenth century, and Wollstonecraft would not have used it. Her work certainly contains ideas that became foundational to feminism; she was far ahead of her time, for example, in her insistence that women and men were equal in terms of possessing reason, and that a just society must recognize a woman's right to a life that fulfills her utmost potential. Unlike modern feminists, however, Wollstonecraft thought that superior physical strength in men reflected a higher capacity for virtue. She also believed that women's duties were bound first and foremost to the domestic sphere.

How Important and Influential Is This Reading?

Mary Wollstonecraft's reputation—never very secure during her own lifetime—was heavily affected by her husband's memoir of her 'scandalous' and emotionally turbulent life. She was, more than anything else, a figure of derision and pity (see, e.g., Richard Polwhele's 1798 poem "The Unsex'd Females") until the late nineteenth century, when figures within the nascent feminist movement rediscovered the power of her ideas—and, for some, the inspirational example of her own unconventional life story. (For example, Virginia Woolf praised Wollstonecraft for her "experiments in living.") By the 1970s Wollstonecraft was recognized as a key originator of modern feminism, though even then perhaps as much attention was focused on her unconventional life as on her philosophical writings. A further re-evaluation of Wollstonecraft occurred in the 1990s, with more focus on her ideas and the source of those ideas in the intellectual currents of the eighteenth century. Today, *A Vindication of the Rights of Woman* is considered a classic of feminist thought, and an important bridge between Enlightenment and Romantic thought.

FROM *A Vindication of the Rights of Woman**

To M. Talleyrand-Périgord, Late Bishop of Autun

Sir,

Having read with great pleasure a pamphlet which you have lately published,[†] I dedicate this volume to you; to induce you to reconsider the subject, and maturely weigh what I have advanced respecting the rights of woman and national education: and I call with the firm tone of humanity; for my arguments, Sir, are dictated by a disinterested spirit—I plead for my sex—not for myself. Independence I have long considered as the grand blessing of life, the basis of every virtue—and independence I will ever secure by contracting my wants, though I were to live on a barren heath....

Contending for the rights of woman, my main argument is built on this simple principle, that if she be not prepared by education to become the companion of man, she will stop the progress of knowledge and virtue; for truth must be common to all, or it will be inefficacious with respect to its influence on general practice. And how can woman be expected to co-operate unless she know why she ought to be virtuous? unless freedom strengthen her reason till she comprehend her duty, and see in what manner it is connected with her real good? If children are to be educated to understand the true principle of patriotism, their mother must be a patriot; and the love of mankind, from which an orderly train of virtues spring, can only be produced by considering the moral and civil interest of mankind; but the education and situation of woman, at present, shuts her out from such investigations.

In this work I have produced many arguments, which to me were conclusive, to prove that the prevailing notion respecting a sexual[‡] character was subversive of morality, and I have contended, that to render the human body and mind more perfect, chastity[§] must more universally prevail, and that chastity will

---

* The full title of this work is *A Vindication of The Rights of Woman: with Strictures on Political and Moral Subjects*, and it was first published in 1792.

† Talleyrand published his *Report on Public Instruction* in 1791. This long treatise was inspired by Enlightenment ideals and argued for national public education from primary to higher levels of education—for men. Talleyrand argued that women should receive no higher education but only instruction that would aid in their domestic duties.

‡ Gender-specific.

§ Modesty, restraint (not necessarily sexual abstinence).

never be respected in the male world till the person of a woman is not, as it were, idolized, when little virtue or sense embellish it with the grand traces of mental beauty, or the interesting simplicity of affection.

Consider, Sir, dispassionately, these observations—for a glimpse of the truth seemed to open before you when you observed, "that to see one half of the human race excluded by the other from all participation of government, was a political phenomenon that, according to abstract principles, it was impossible to explain."* If so, on what does your constitution rest? If the abstract rights of man will bear discussion and explanation, those of woman, by a parity of reasoning, will not shrink from the same test: though a different opinion prevails in this country, built on the very arguments which you use to justify the oppression of woman—prescription.†

Consider, I address you as a legislator, whether, when men contend for their freedom, and to be allowed to judge for themselves respecting their own happiness, it be not inconsistent and unjust to subjugate women, even though you firmly believe that you are acting in the manner best calculated to promote their happiness? Who made man the exclusive judge, if woman partake with him the gift of reason?

In this style, argue tyrants of every denomination, from the weak king to the weak father of a family; they are all eager to crush reason; yet always assert that they usurp its throne only to be useful. Do you not act a similar part, when you *force* all women, by denying them civil and political rights, to remain immured in their families groping in the dark? For surely, Sir, you will not assert, that a duty can be binding which is not founded on reason? If indeed this be their destination, arguments may be drawn from reason: and thus augustly supported, the more understanding women acquire, the more they will be attached to their duty—comprehending it—for unless they comprehend it,

unless their morals be fixed on the same immutable principle as those of man, no authority can make them discharge it in a virtuous manner. They may be convenient slaves, but slavery will have its constant effect, degrading the master and the abject dependent.

But, if women are to be excluded, without having a voice, from a participation of the natural rights of mankind, prove first, to ward off the charge of injustice and inconsistency, that they want reason‡—else this flaw in your NEW CONSTITUTION will ever show that man must, in some shape, act like a tyrant, and tyranny, in whatever part of society it rears its brazen front, will ever undermine morality.

I have repeatedly asserted, and produced what appeared to me irrefragable§ arguments drawn from matters of fact, to prove my assertion, that women cannot, by force, be confined to domestic concerns; for they will, however ignorant, intermeddle with more weighty affairs, neglecting private duties only to disturb, by cunning tricks, the orderly plans of reason which rise above their comprehension.

Besides, whilst they are only made to acquire personal accomplishments, men will seek for pleasure in variety, and faithless husbands will make faithless wives; such ignorant beings, indeed, will be very excusable when, not taught to respect public good, nor allowed any civil rights, they attempt to do themselves justice by retaliation.

The box of mischief thus opened¶ in society, what is to preserve private virtue, the only security of public freedom and universal happiness?

Let there be then no coercion *established* in society, and the common law of gravity prevailing, the sexes will fall into their proper places. And, now that more equitable laws are forming your citizens, marriage may become more sacred: your young men may choose wives from motives of affection, and your maidens allow love to root out vanity.

---

* From *Report on Public Instruction*, Appendix B.I.ii. Only men over 25 were recognized as citizens in the French constitution of 1791. French women did not receive the vote until 1944.

† Authority of long-held custom and tradition.

‡ Lack reason.

§ Irrefutable.

¶ This is a reference to the Greek story of Pandora's box. In Hesiod's *Works and Days* (c. 700 BCE), Pandora—the first human woman—is given a receptacle containing all the evils of the world, including death; not knowing what was inside, her curiosity led her to open the box, unleashing its contents on the world. 'Mischief' here means harmful action.

The father of a family will not then weaken his constitution and debase his sentiments, by visiting the harlot, nor forget, in obeying the call of appetite, the purpose for which it was implanted. And, the mother will not neglect her children to practice the arts of coquetry,* when sense and modesty secure her the friendship of her husband.

But, till men become attentive to the duty of a father, it is vain to expect women to spend that time in their nursery which they, "wise in their generation,"† choose to spend at their glass;‡ for this exertion of cunning is only an instinct of nature to enable them to obtain indirectly a little of that power of which they are unjustly denied a share: for, if women are not permitted to enjoy legitimate rights, they will render both men and themselves vicious, to obtain illicit privileges.

I wish, Sir, to set some investigations of this kind afloat in France; and should they lead to a confirmation of my principles, when your constitution is revised the Rights of Woman may be respected, if it be fully proved that reason calls for this respect, and loudly demands JUSTICE for one half of the human race.

I am, SIR,
Yours respectfully,
M.W.

Introduction

After considering the historic page,§ and viewing the living world with anxious solicitude, the most melancholy emotions of sorrowful indignation have depressed my spirits, and I have sighed when obliged to confess, that either nature has made a great difference between man and man, or that the civilization which has hitherto taken place in the world has been very partial. I have turned over various books written on the subject of education, and patiently observed the conduct of parents and the management of schools; but what has been the result?—a profound conviction that the neglected education of my fellow-creatures is the grand source of the misery I deplore; and that women, in particular, are rendered weak and wretched by a variety of concurring causes, originating from one hasty conclusion. The conduct and manners of women, in fact, evidently prove that their minds are not in a healthy state; for, like the flowers which are planted in too rich a soil, strength and usefulness are sacrificed to beauty; and the flaunting leaves, after having pleased a fastidious eye, fade, disregarded on the stalk, long before the season when they ought to have arrived at maturity.—One cause of this barren blooming I attribute to a false system of education, gathered from the books written on this subject by men who, considering females rather as women than human creatures, have been more anxious to make them alluring mistresses than affectionate wives and rational mothers; and the understanding of the sex has been so bubbled by this specious homage, that the civilized women of the present century, with a few exceptions, are only anxious to inspire love, when they ought to cherish a nobler ambition, and by their abilities and virtues exact respect.

In a treatise, therefore, on female rights and manners, the works which have been particularly written for their improvement must not be overlooked; especially when it is asserted, in direct terms, that the minds of women are enfeebled by false refinement; that the books of instruction, written by men of genius, have had the same tendency as more frivolous productions; and that, in the true style of Mahometanism,¶ they are treated as a kind of subordinate beings, and not as a part of the human species, when improveable reason is allowed to be the dignified distinction which raises men above the brute creation, and puts a natural scepter in a feeble hand.

Yet, because I am a woman, I would not lead my readers to suppose that I mean violently to agitate the contested question respecting the equality or inferiority of the sex; but as the subject lies in my way, and I cannot pass it over without subjecting the main tendency of my reasoning to misconstruction, I shall stop

---

* Flirting and other arts used to gain the affection of men, usually for the sense of power it confers and with no intent of reciprocation.

† See Luke 16:8.

‡ Mirror.

§ Written histories.

¶ Islam.

a moment to deliver, in a few words, my opinion.—In the government of the physical world it is observable that the female in point of strength is, in general, inferior to the male. This is the law of nature; and it does not appear to be suspended or abrogated in favor of woman. A degree of physical superiority cannot, therefore, be denied—and it is a noble prerogative! But not content with this natural pre-eminence, men endeavor to sink us still lower, merely to render us alluring objects for a moment; and women, intoxicated by the adoration which men, under the influence of their senses, pay them, do not seek to obtain a durable interest in their hearts, or to become the friends of the fellow creatures who find amusement in their society.

I am aware of an obvious inference:—from every quarter have I heard exclamations against masculine women; but where are they to be found? If by this appellation men mean to inveigh against their ardor in hunting, shooting, and gaming, I shall most cordially join in the cry; but if it be against the imitation of manly virtues, or, more properly speaking, the attainment of those talents and virtues, the exercise of which ennobles the human character, and which raise females in the scale of animal being, when they are comprehensively termed mankind;—all those who view them with a philosophic eye must, I should think, wish with me, that they may every day grow more and more masculine.

This discussion naturally divides the subject. I shall first consider women in the grand light of human creatures, who, in common with men, are placed on this earth to unfold their faculties; and afterwards I shall more particularly point out their peculiar designation.

I wish also to steer clear of an error which many respectable writers have fallen into; for the instruction which has hitherto been addressed to women, has rather been applicable to *ladies*, if the little indirect advice, that is scattered through Sandford and Merton,* be excepted; but, addressing my sex in a firmer tone, I pay particular attention to those in the middle class, because they appear to be in the most natural state. Perhaps the seeds of false-refinement, immorality, and vanity, have ever been shed by the great. Weak, artificial beings, raised above the common wants and affections of their race, in a premature unnatural manner, undermine the very foundation of virtue, and spread corruption through the whole mass of society! As a class of mankind they have the strongest claim to pity; the education of the rich tends to render them vain and helpless, and the unfolding mind is not strengthened by the practice of those duties which dignify the human character.—They only live to amuse themselves, and by the same law which in nature invariably produces certain effects, they soon only afford barren amusement.

But as I purpose taking a separate view of the different ranks of society, and of the moral character of women, in each, this hint is, for the present, sufficient; and I have only alluded to the subject, because it appears to me to be the very essence of an introduction to give a cursory account of the contents of the work it introduces.

My own sex, I hope, will excuse me, if I treat them like rational creatures, instead of flattering their fascinating graces, and viewing them as if they were in a state of perpetual childhood, unable to stand alone. I earnestly wish to point out in what true dignity and human happiness consists—I wish to persuade women to endeavor to acquire strength, both of mind and body, and to convince them that the soft phrases, susceptibility of heart, delicacy of sentiment, and refinement of taste, are almost synonymous with epithets of weakness, and that those beings who are only the objects of pity and that kind of love, which has been termed its sister, will soon become objects of contempt.

Dismissing then those pretty feminine phrases, which the men condescendingly use to soften our slavish dependence, and despising that weak elegancy of mind, exquisite sensibility, and sweet docility of manners, supposed to be the sexual characteristics of the weaker vessel, I wish to show that elegance is inferior to virtue, that the first object of laudable ambition is to obtain a character as a human being, regardless of the distinction of sex; and that secondary views should be brought to this simple touchstone.† ...

---

*   Children's novel by Thomas Day (1748–89) featuring two male child protagonists, a farm boy and a rich boy. The novel includes lessons in manners, masculinity, and class politics; Wollstonecraft reviewed the third volume for the *Analytical Review*.

†   Test.

Chapter 2: The Prevailing Opinion of a Sexual Character Discussed

To account for, and excuse the tyranny of man, many ingenious arguments have been brought forward to prove, that the two sexes, in the acquirement of virtue, ought to aim at attaining a very different character: or, to speak explicitly, women are not allowed to have sufficient strength of mind to acquire what really deserves the name of virtue. Yet it should seem, allowing them to have souls, that there is but one way appointed by Providence to lead *mankind* to either virtue or happiness....

It is, however, sufficient for my present purpose to assert, that, whatever effect circumstances have on the abilities, every being may become virtuous by the exercise of its own reason; for if but one being was created with vicious inclinations, that is positively bad, what can save us from atheism? or if we worship a God, is not that God a devil?

Consequently, the most perfect education, in my opinion, is such an exercise of the understanding as is best calculated to strengthen the body and form the heart. Or, in other words, to enable the individual to attain such habits of virtue as will render it independent. In fact, it is a farce to call any being virtuous whose virtues do not result from the exercise of its own reason. This was Rousseau's opinion respecting men:* I extend it to women, and confidently assert that they have been drawn out of their sphere by false refinement and not by an endeavor to acquire masculine qualities. Still the regal homage which they receive is so intoxicating that until the manners of the times are changed and formed on more reasonable principles, it may be impossible to convince them that the illegitimate power, which they obtain by degrading themselves, is a curse, and that they must return to nature and equality if they wish to secure the placid satisfaction that unsophisticated affections impart. But for this epoch we must wait—wait, perhaps, till kings and nobles, enlightened by reason, and preferring the real dignity of man to childish state, throw off their gaudy hereditary trappings: and if then women do not resign the arbitrary power of beauty, they will prove that they have *less* mind than man.

I may be accused of arrogance; still I must declare what I firmly believe, that all the writers who have written on the subject of female education and manners from Rousseau to Dr. Gregory,† have contributed to render women more artificial, weak characters than they would otherwise have been; and, consequently, more useless members of society. I might have expressed this conviction in a lower key; but I am afraid it would have been the whine of affectation, and not the faithful expression of my feelings, of the clear result, which experience and reflection have led me to draw....

Strengthen the female mind by enlarging it, and there will be an end to blind obedience; but, as blind obedience is ever sought for by power, tyrants and sensualists are in the right when they endeavor to keep women in the dark, because the former only want slaves, and the latter a play-thing. The sensualist, indeed, has been the most dangerous of tyrants, and women have been duped by their lovers, as princes by their ministers, whilst dreaming that they reigned over them....

Rousseau declares that a woman should never, for a moment, feel herself independent, that she should be governed by fear to exercise her *natural* cunning, and made a coquettish slave in order to render her a more alluring object of desire, a *sweeter* companion to man, whenever he chooses to relax himself. He carries the arguments, which he pretends to draw from the indications of nature, still further, and insinuates that truth and fortitude, the corner stones of all human virtue, should be cultivated with certain restrictions, because, with respect to the female character, obedience is the grand lesson which ought to be impressed with unrelenting rigor.

What nonsense! When will a great man arise with sufficient strength of mind to puff away the fumes which pride and sensuality have thus spread over the subject! If women are by nature inferior to men, their

---

* In his novel *Émile, or On Education* (1762), French philosopher Jean-Jacques Rousseau (1712–78) asserts that a man's virtues must follow from reason, but he does not assert the same for women. Wollstonecraft frequently argues against the narrow ideas of femininity and female education outlined in *Émile*.

† Scottish moralist John Gregory (1724–73) wrote the best-selling tract *A Father's Legacy to His Daughters* (1774). In it, women and parents are given advice on morality and conduct, and he advises women to hide any learning they might have, in case it scares off suitors.

virtues must be the same in quality, if not in degree, or virtue is a relative idea; consequently, their conduct should be founded on the same principles, and have the same aim.*

Connected with man as daughters, wives, and mothers, their moral character may be estimated by their manner of fulfilling those simple duties; but the end, the grand end of their exertions should be to unfold their own faculties and acquire the dignity of conscious virtue. They may try to render their road pleasant; but ought never to forget, in common with man, that life yields not the felicity which can satisfy an immortal soul. I do not mean to insinuate, that either sex should be so lost in abstract reflections or distant views, as to forget the affections and duties that lie before them, and are, in truth, the means appointed to produce the fruit of life; on the contrary, I would warmly recommend them, even while I assert, that they afford most satisfaction when they are considered in their true, sober light.

Probably the prevailing opinion, that woman was created for man, may have taken its rise from Moses's poetical story;† yet, as very few, it is presumed, who have bestowed any serious thought on the subject, ever supposed that Eve was, literally speaking, one of Adam's ribs, the deduction must be allowed to fall to the ground; or, only be so far admitted as it proves that man, from the remotest antiquity, found it convenient to exert his strength to subjugate his companion, and his invention to show that she ought to have her neck bent under the yoke, because the whole creation was only created for his convenience or pleasure.

Let it not be concluded that I wish to invert the order of things; I have already granted, that, from the constitution of their bodies, men seem to be designed by Providence to attain a greater degree of virtue. I speak collectively of the whole sex; but I see not the shadow of a reason to conclude that their virtues should differ in respect to their nature. In fact, how can they, if virtue has only one eternal standard? I must therefore, if I reason consequentially, as strenuously maintain that they have the same simple direction, as that there is a God....

Women ought to endeavour to purify their heart;‡ but can they do so when their uncultivated understandings make them entirely dependent on their senses for employment and amusement, when no noble pursuit sets them above the little vanities of the day, or enables them to curb the wild emotions that agitate a reed over which every passing breeze§ has power? To gain the affections of a virtuous man is affectation necessary? Nature has given woman a weaker frame than man; but, to ensure her husband's affections, must a wife, who by the exercise of her mind and body whilst she was discharging the duties of a daughter, wife, and mother, has allowed her constitution to retain its natural strength, and her nerves a healthy tone, is she, I say, to condescend to use art and feign a sickly delicacy in order to secure her husband's affection? Weakness may excite tenderness, and gratify the arrogant pride of man; but the lordly caresses of a protector will not gratify a noble mind that pants for, and deserves to be respected. Fondness is a poor substitute for friendship!

In a seraglio,¶ I grant, that all these arts are necessary; the epicure must have his palate tickled, or he will sink into apathy; but have women so little ambition as to be satisfied with such a condition? Can they supinely dream life away in the lap of pleasure, or the languor of weariness, rather than assert their claim to pursue reasonable pleasures and render themselves conspicuous by practicing the virtues which dignify mankind? Surely she has not an immortal soul who can loiter life away merely employed to adorn her person, that she may amuse the languid hours, and soften the cares of a fellow-creature who is willing to be enlivened by her smiles and tricks, when the serious business of life is over.

Besides, the woman who strengthens her body and exercises her mind will, by managing her family and practicing various virtues, become the friend, and not the humble dependent of her husband; and

---

* In *Émile*, Rousseau argues that men's and women's virtues are essentially different.
† Genesis 2:18–25. Moses was at this time thought to be the author of Genesis.
‡ See Matthew 5:8.
§ See Matthew 11:7.
¶ Harem.

if she, by possessing such substantial qualities, merit his regard, she will not find it necessary to conceal her affection, nor to pretend to an unnatural coldness of constitution to excite her husband's passions. In fact, if we revert to history, we shall find that the women who have distinguished themselves have neither been the most beautiful nor the most gentle of their sex....

It appears to me necessary to dwell on these obvious truths, because females have been insulated, as it were; and, while they have been stripped of the virtues that should clothe humanity, they have been decked with artificial graces that enable them to exercise a short-lived tyranny. Love, in their bosoms, taking place of every nobler passion, their sole ambition is to be fair, to raise emotion instead of inspiring respect; and this ignoble desire, like the servility in absolute monarchies, destroys all strength of character. Liberty is the mother of virtue, and if women be, by their very constitution, slaves, and not allowed to breathe the sharp invigorating air of freedom, they must ever languish like exotics, and be reckoned beautiful flaws in nature.

As to the argument respecting the subjection in which the sex has ever been held, it retorts on man. The many have always been enthralled by the few; and monsters, who scarcely have shown any discernment of human excellence, have tyrannized over thousands of their fellow-creatures. Why have men of superior endowments submitted to such degradation? For, is it not universally acknowledged that kings, viewed collectively, have ever been inferior, in abilities and virtue, to the same number of men taken from the common mass of mankind—yet, have they not, and are they not still treated with a degree of reverence that is an insult to reason? China is not the only country where a living man has been made a God.* Men have submitted to superior strength to enjoy with impunity the pleasure of the moment—women have only done the same, and therefore till it is proved that the courtier, who servilely resigns the birthright of a man, is not a moral agent, it cannot be demonstrated that woman is essentially inferior to man because she has always been subjugated.

Brutal force has hitherto governed the world, and that the science of politics is in its infancy, is evident from philosophers scrupling to give the knowledge most useful to man that determinate distinction.

I shall not pursue this argument any further than to establish an obvious inference, that as sound politics diffuse liberty, mankind, including woman, will become more wise and virtuous. ■

Suggestions for Critical Reflection

1. How, according to Wollstonecraft, did men justify excluding women from the "abstract rights of man"?

2. Does Wollstonecraft think women, once liberated and educated, could take on roles traditionally filled by men in society? Why or why not?

3. On what class of society does Wollstonecraft focus? Why? How does this choice affect her argument?

4. What are the characteristics that most people thought defined women in Wollstonecraft's day? Does this perception of women still exist in our society? If so, by whom is it held?

5. For Wollstonecraft, what is the relationship between reason and virtue?

6. "Let it not be concluded that I wish to invert the order of things," writes Wollstonecraft—why does she say this? What does she mean?

---

* Wollstonecraft is alluding here to the doctrine of the divine right of kings, which states that a monarch receives his or her authority from God and is not subject to earthly election or oversight. In some cases, notably in Egypt and Rome, some rulers went a step further and claimed divinity for themselves. Chinese Emperors ruled according to what was called the "Mandate of Heaven," and they were considered the "Heavenly Sons" of the universe. Similar beliefs about the divinity of kings existed in most monarchical societies, including England. Wollstonecraft believed that the people should appoint their legislators, and that the so-called divine right of kings was an illegitimate means of usurping that elective power.

7. In the "Dedication" to Talleyrand, Wollstonecraft describes the *Vindication* as a treatise about "the rights of woman and national education." Why, for Wollstonecraft, is educational reform crucial to enacting the social changes she envisions? What, for her, was wrong with the theories of female education that were current in her day?

8. The French Revolution and associated civil rights struggles in the late eighteenth century were concerned with overthrowing "arbitrary" hierarchies based on birth, custom, and the institutions that upheld them. What was that power based in? What, according to Wollstonecraft, is the moral consequence of such power?

SIMONE DE BEAUVOIR

FROM *The Second Sex*

Who Was Simone de Beauvoir?

Born in Paris in 1908, Simone de Beauvoir had become such an important figure in France by the time of her death in 1986 that her funeral was attended by 5,000 people, including four former ministers of the Mitterrand government. A headline announcing her death read "Women, you owe her everything!"

Beauvoir was the eldest of two daughters in a respectable, conservative bourgeois family, and she spent her formative years heatedly reacting against her parents and their values. She became an atheist while still a teenager, and decided early on to devote her life to writing and studying 'rather than' becoming a wife and mother. She studied philosophy at the ancient Sorbonne University in Paris and was the youngest person ever to obtain the *agrégation* (a high-level competitive examination for recruiting teachers in France) in philosophy, in 1929. She was 21. In that same year she met the famous existentialist philosopher Jean-Paul Sartre and began an intense relationship with him—the most important of her life—that lasted until his death in 1980.*

Beauvoir and Sartre became notorious throughout France as a couple who were lovers and soul-mates but who maintained an open relationship; both considered themselves highly sexually "liberated," and Beauvoir was openly bisexual. Sartre made what he called a "pact" with her—they could have affairs with other people, but they were required to tell each other everything—and he proceeded to match his actions to this rule. As he put it to Beauvoir: "What *we* have is an *essential* love; but it is a good idea for us also to experience *contingent* love affairs."

Despite the rotating cast of lovers, Beauvoir remained devoted to Sartre all her life and always maintained that he was the most brilliant man she had ever known. Indeed, she once declared that, her many books, literary prizes, and social influence notwithstanding, her greatest achievement in life was her relationship with Sartre.

Between 1932 and 1943, Beauvoir was a high school teacher of philosophy in Rouen, in north-western France. There, she was subject to official reprimands for her protests about male chauvinism and for her pacifism; finally, a parental complaint made against her for 'corrupting' one of her female students caused her dismissal. For the rest of her life, Beauvoir lived in Paris and made her living from her writing. At the end of World War II, she became an editor at *Les Temps Modernes*, a new political journal founded by Sartre and other French intellectuals. She used this journal to disseminate her own work, and several excerpts from *The Second Sex* were first published in it.

Interestingly, part of the impetus to write *The Second Sex* came to her as she gradually realized that, unlike some of her female friends, she did *not* at first feel any sense that she was disadvantaged as a woman, but that this feeling of personal satisfaction and of independence resulted primarily from her relationship with a well-known, influential man—Sartre. When she reflected on this relationship, she realized with astonishment that she was fundamentally different from Sartre "because he was a man and I was only a woman."† As she put it, "In writing *The Second Sex* I became aware, for the first time, that I myself was leading a false life, or rather, that I was profiting from this male-oriented society without even knowing it."‡

---

* When the university *agrégation* results came out, Sartre and Beauvoir tied for first place, although Sartre was subsequently awarded first place with Beauvoir second. Also, incidentally, 1929 was the year Beauvoir acquired her lifelong nickname, le Castor (French for 'beaver,' because of the resemblance of her surname to "beaver").

† As cited by Deirdre Bair in her introduction to the 1989 Vintage edition of *The Second Sex*, from interviews Bair conducted with Beauvoir in the 1980s.

‡ From an interview with Beauvoir published in *Society*, February 1976.

She was also influenced by what she saw in America, during a visit in 1947, of the experience of blacks in a segregated society. For example, she was friends with the African American short story writer and novelist Richard Wright, who, with his white wife Ellen, was a tireless advocate for black equality. For Beauvoir, feminism was part of a larger project of social justice and human rights. From the late 1940s until the 1960s she was a very public left-wing political activist and a vocal supporter of communism (and critic of American-style capitalism).

The Second Sex is an extended examination of the problems women have encountered throughout history and of the possibilities left open to them. After the Introduction (reprinted here), the book is divided into two halves: Book One is a historical overview of "Facts and Myths" about women, and Book Two deals with "Women's Life Today." Book One is divided into sections describing the "Destiny" of women according to theories of biology, psychoanalysis, and Marxist historical materialism; the "History" of women from prehistoric times to the granting of the vote to women in France in 1944; and "Myths" about women in literature. Book Two is more personal, and discusses women in childhood, adolescence, sexual initiation, various forms of mature loving and sexual relationships, and old age. The conclusion of the book is positive and optimistic, as Beauvoir tries to set out a model of life and action for future generations of women.

Some Useful Background Information

1. The first words of Book Two of *The Second Sex* are "One is not born, but rather becomes, a woman. No biological, psychological or economic fate determines the figure that the human female presents in society; it is civilization as a whole that determines this creature." This is how Beauvoir most famously expresses an influential central thesis of the book: that "woman," as a biological category, is separable from "feminine," as a social construction—or more generally, that sex is not the same thing as gender. Thus, woman's status under the patriarchy as the Other is a contingent, socially constructed fact rather than an essential truth about the female gender.

    It is important to appreciate that Beauvoir is not denying that there are biological differences between men and women, nor does she insist that these biological differences must be simply ignored in a properly constituted society. Rather, she is arguing that our *biological* constitutions do not determine our *gender* characteristics: such things as "femininity" or "masculinity," being "nurturing" or "modest" or "emotional" or "delicate"—these things are constructed and constrained purely by *social* influences. Under different social conditions women and men might naturally and freely behave in ways radically different from contemporary social norms.

    Thus, according to Beauvoir, gender is more something we *do*—a way we live—than something we *are*. Gender is constrained by social pressures in large part because social pressures constrain how we can legitimately behave. A woman in, say, Canada in the 1950s could not just decide as an individual to behave like a man—or like someone who is neither masculine nor feminine—and in this way change her gender unilaterally. Even if she were brave enough to attempt the experiment, according to Beauvoir—and the other existentialists—one cannot possess a certain trait, such as being masculine, unless others recognize one as doing so.

2. This emphasis on the social construction of gender, race, and other aspects of the reality we experience in our day-to-day lives is related to Beauvoir's commitment to existentialism. Central to existentialism is the doctrine that *existence precedes essence*: humans have no pre-given purpose or essence determined for them by God or by biology. According to existentialism, each consciousness faces the world as an isolated individual, and inevitably creates itself—gives itself determinate form—by making choices. We are forced to make these choices by the need to respond to the things around us, including both passive natural objects and other consciousnesses; but what we choose is not forced.

    Beauvoir and Sartre see the meeting of one consciousness with another as profoundly disturbing: faced with the gaze of an Other, we recognize a point of view which is necessarily different from our own and so we are required to concede our own incompleteness; furthermore, the opposing consciousness must treat *us* as an Other, which we feel as a threat to destroy us by turning us into an object.

Beauvoir's feminism can be seen as a development of this idea: in response to the threat posed by other consciousnesses, according to existentialism, one might retaliate by objectifying and dominating the Other, to be able to control it without destroying it and thus be able to withstand its gaze. Thus, according to Beauvoir, men have objectified and dominated women as the Other, and by succumbing to all-pervasive social pressures women have allowed themselves to be dominated.

3.   Towards the end of this essay, Beauvoir mentions the contrast between being *en-soi* (in-itself) and being *pour-soi* (for-itself). Being for-itself is a mode of existence that is purposive and, as it were, constituted by its own activity; being in-itself, by contrast, is a less fully human kind of existence that is more like being a 'thing'—self-sufficient, non-purposive, and driven by merely contingent current conditions.

How Important and Influential Is This Passage?

The Second Sex is often considered the founding work of twentieth-century feminism. It has been called "one of the most important and far-reaching books on women ever published"[*] and "the best book about women ever written."[†] From the day it was published it was both popular and controversial: 22,000 copies of the first volume were sold in France in the first week, and Beauvoir received large quantities of hate mail, including some from "very active members of the First Sex," and from other women: "How courageous you are.... You're going to lose a lot of friends!" one of her friends wrote to her.[‡] She was accused of writing a pornographic book (because of *The Second Sex*'s discussion of female sexuality), and the Vatican put it on the index of prohibited

books. "Once," Beauvoir reported in her autobiography, "during an entire dinner at Nos Provinces on the Boulevard Montparnasse, a table of people nearby stared at me and giggled; I didn't like dragging [her lover, Nelson] Algren into a scene, but as I left I gave them a piece of my mind."[§] On the other hand, some of the contemporary reviews were glowing: *The New Yorker* called it "more than a work of scholarship; it is a work of art, with the salt of recklessness that makes art sting."[¶]

After the initial furor died down, the book was criticized by scholars and critics as having too much of a middle-class, distorted viewpoint—as having been written by someone who had no cause to actually feel the pressures that give life to feminism. The poet Stevie Smith wrote, in 1953: "She has written an enormous book about women and it is soon clear that she does not like them, nor does she like being a woman."[**] This debate continues today, and arguably it is only recently that *The Second Sex* has come to be appreciated seriously as a work of philosophy that stands on its own merits, rather than read solely in terms of Beauvoir's "biography, relationship with ... Sartre, psyche, or feminist credentials."[††]

Simone de Beauvoir is a pivotal figure in the history of feminist thought from the Renaissance to the twenty-first century. In the Renaissance and early modern period, writers that we would today think of as feminist (such as Christine de Pizan [1365–c. 1430] and Mary Astell [1666–1731]) tended to focus on the social asymmetries between women and men. They argued that women have similar innate abilities to men and should be granted opportunities equivalent to those their male counterparts enjoyed in certain key areas, especially education, the family, and sometimes work and politics. The eighteenth and nineteenth centuries (in work by writers such as Olympe de Gouges [1745–93], Mary Wollstonecraft [1759–97], Sojourner Truth [1797–1883], John Stuart Mill [1806–73], and Harriet Taylor [1807–58]) saw a greater accumulation of forceful writings against the oppression of women, combined with more explicit (but only grad-

*   Terry Keefe, *Simone de Beauvoir: A Study of Her Writings* (Barnes & Noble Books, 1983), 111.

†   Maureen Freely, *The Guardian*, June 6, 1999.

‡   From a letter by Claudine Chonez and mentioned by Beauvoir in her autobiography *Force of Circumstances* (1963, translated by Richard Howard and published by Penguin in 1968).

§   Also from Beauvoir's *Force of Circumstances*.

¶   From a review by Brendan Gill, February 28, 1953.

** From Smith's review of the book published in *The Spectator*, November 20, 1953.

†† Allison Fell, *Times Literary Supplement*, December 9, 2005.

ually successful) political campaigns to have women's equal status with men enshrined in law. It was at the end of the nineteenth century—in France, during the 1890s—that the term "feminism" first appeared.

Up to this point, feminism can be usefully—albeit simplistically—understood as characterized by a demand for equal rights with men. Once women are educated as extensively as men, are given the opportunity to vote, are not forbidden from joining certain professions, and so on, then it was assumed that their innate capacities—in many (though perhaps not all) respects equal to, or even superior to, those of the male sex—would flourish free from oppression. That is, pre-twentieth-century feminism tended to focus on the suppression and distortion of woman's nature by contingent social structures such as laws and institutions. Beauvoir's writings marked a significant shift and deepening in the nature of feminist thought. She denied that there is an inborn "female nature" that just awaits the opportunity to break free from male oppression, and insisted that women are dominated by men in *all* aspects of their lives—that their very consciousness, the very shape of their minds, is formed by the patriarchal society of which they are a part. Feminism cannot aspire simply to change the laws and institutions of a country; this will leave the subordinate position of women essentially untouched. Feminists must fight for much more thoroughgoing change to the basic practices and assumptions of the whole society.

Later twentieth-century feminism, often known as *second-wave feminism*—representatives of which include Susan Moller Okin (1946–2004), Catharine MacKinnon (b. 1946), Martha Nussbaum (b. 1947), and Iris Young (b. 1949)—took up this emphasis on the deep and subtle nature of patriarchal dominance (though often without a very self-conscious sense of the debt to Beauvoir). The distinction between sex and gender—the notion of gender as a social construct—proved especially significant in making this case. For many feminists, this has evolved into a critique of standards that are taken to have an objective and universal status—such as "rational," "true," and "right"—but which, feminists argue, in fact reflect particular gender interests. Thus, for example, to argue—as Wollstonecraft did—that women are "equally rational" as men is to succumb to, rather than combat, one of the hidden patriarchal structures that oppress women.

The so-called *third-wave* (or sometimes, *postmodern*) feminism that began in the 1980s can also be seen as having roots in the work of Beauvoir. Third-wave feminism emphasizes the claim that gender is a social, contingent, rather than a natural category, and adopts an "anti-essentialist" stance about women: that is, there is nothing that can be usefully said about woman 'as such,' and instead we must focus in an explicitly un-unified way on different conceptions of femininity in particular ethnic, religious, and social groups.

FROM *The Second Sex**

INTRODUCTION

I hesitated a long time before writing a book on woman. The subject is irritating, especially for women; and it is not new. Enough ink has flowed over the quarrel about feminism; it is now almost over: let's not talk about it anymore. Yet it is still being talked about. And the volumes of idiocies churned out over this past century do not seem to have clarified the problem. Besides, is there

a problem? And what is it? Are there even women? True, the theory of the eternal feminine still has its followers; they whisper, "Even in Russia,[†] *women* are still very much women"; but other well-informed people—and also at times those same ones—lament, "Woman is losing herself, woman is lost." It is hard to know any longer if women still exist, if they will always exist, if

---

* *The Second Sex* was first published in French in 1949. This translation, by Constance Borde and Sheila Malovany-Chevallier, is from 2009.

† That is, even after the reorganization of society in Russia after the Communist Revolution of 1917 (and the upheaval of World War II).

there should be women at all, what place they hold in this world, what place they should hold. "Where are the women?" asked a short-lived magazine recently.[1] But first, what is a woman? "*Tota mulier in utero*: she is a womb,"* some say. Yet speaking of certain women, the experts proclaim, "They are not women," even though they have a uterus like the others. Everyone agrees there are females in the human species; today, as in the past, they make up about half of humanity; and yet we are told that "femininity is in jeopardy"; we are urged, "Be women, stay women, become women." So not every female human being is necessarily a woman; she must take part in this mysterious and endangered reality known as femininity. Is femininity secreted by the ovaries? Is it enshrined in a Platonic heaven? Is a frilly petticoat enough to bring it down to earth? Although some women zealously strive to embody it, the model has never been patented. It is typically described in vague and shimmering terms borrowed from a clairvoyant's vocabulary. In Saint Thomas's[†] time it was an essence defined with as much certainty as the sedative quality of a poppy. But conceptualism has lost ground: biological and social sciences no longer believe there are immutably determined entities that define given characteristics like those of the woman, the Jew, or the black; science considers characteristics as secondary reactions to a *situation*. If there is no such thing today as femininity, it is because there never was. Does the word "woman," then, have no content? It is what advocates of Enlightenment philosophy, rationalism, or nominalism[‡] vigorously assert: women are, among human beings, merely those who are arbitrarily designated by the word "woman"; American women in particular are inclined to think that woman as such no longer exists. If some backward individual still takes herself for a woman, her friends advise her to undergo

psychoanalysis to get rid of this obsession. Referring to a book—a very irritating one at that—*Modern Woman: The Lost Sex*,[§] Dorothy Parker[¶] wrote: "I cannot be fair about books that treat women as women. My idea is that all of us, men as well as women, whoever we are, should be considered as human beings." But nominalism is a doctrine that falls a bit short; and it is easy for antifeminists to show that women *are* not men. Certainly woman like man is a human being; but such an assertion is abstract; the fact is that every concrete human being is always uniquely situated. To reject the notions of the eternal feminine, the black soul, or the Jewish character is not to deny that there are today Jews, blacks, or women: this denial is not a liberation for those concerned but an inauthentic flight. Clearly, no woman can claim without bad faith to be situated beyond her sex. A few years ago, a well-known woman writer refused to have her portrait appear in a series of photographs devoted specifically to women writers. She wanted to be included in the men's category; but to get this privilege, she used her husband's influence. Women who assert they are men still claim masculine consideration and respect. I also remember a young Trotskyite[**] standing on a platform during a stormy meeting, about to come to blows in spite of her obvious fragility. She was denying her feminine frailty; but it was for the love of a militant man she wanted to be equal to. The defiant position that American women occupy proves they are haunted by the feeling of their own femininity. And the truth is that anyone can clearly see that humanity is split into two categories of individuals with manifestly different clothes, faces, bodies, smiles, movements, interests, and occupations; these differences are perhaps superficial; perhaps they are destined to disappear. What is certain is that for the moment they exist in a strikingly obvious way.

---

*　Latin for "The whole woman is in her uterus," or, more snappily, "Woman is a womb." This aphorism dates back to medieval scholastic theology.

†　St. Thomas Aquinas (1225–74).

‡　Nominalism is the view that only particular things exist, and 'abstract' things—universals—such as beauty, redness, or species-membership, are not real. Conceptualism (mentioned above) is the view that abstractions do exist as mental concepts.

§　By Ferdinand Lundberg and Marynia F. Farnham, published in 1947. Among other things, this book proposed that laws be adopted prohibiting single women from working, thus forcing them into marriage.

¶　Parker (1893–1967) was an American critic, satirical poet, and short-story writer, famous for her acerbic wit.

**　A follower of the brand of Marxism advocated by Leon Trotsky (1879–1940), who advocated permanent global revolution on behalf of the world's workers, and was critical of Joseph Stalin's theory of socialism in one country (Russia).

If the female function is not enough to define woman, and if we also reject the explanation of the "eternal feminine," but if we accept, even temporarily, that there are women on the earth, we then have to ask: What is a woman?

Merely stating the problem suggests an immediate answer to me. It is significant that I pose it. It would never occur to a man to write a book on the singular situation of males in humanity.[2] If I want to define myself, I first have to say, "I am a woman"; all other assertions will arise from this basic truth. A man never begins by positing himself as an individual of a certain sex: that he is a man is obvious. The categories masculine and feminine appear as symmetrical in a formal way on town hall records or identification papers. The relation of the two sexes is not that of two electrical poles: the man represents both the positive and the neuter to such an extent that in French *hommes* designates human beings, the particular meaning of the word *vir* being assimilated into the general meaning of the word "homo." Woman is the negative, to such a point that any determination is imputed to her as a limitation, without reciprocity. I used to get annoyed in abstract discussions to hear men tell me: "You think such and such a thing because you're a woman." But I know my only defense is to answer, "I think it because it is true," thereby eliminating my subjectivity; it was out of the question to answer, "And you think the contrary because you are a man," because it is understood that being a man is not a particularity; a man is in his right by virtue of being man; it is the woman who is in the wrong. In fact, just as for the ancients there was an absolute vertical that defined the oblique, there is an absolute human type that is masculine. Woman has ovaries and a uterus; such are the particular conditions that lock her in her subjectivity; some even say she thinks with her hormones. Man vainly forgets that his anatomy also includes hormones and testicles. He grasps his body as a direct and normal link with the world that he believes he apprehends in all objectivity, whereas he considers woman's body an obstacle, a prison, burdened by everything that particularizes it. "The female is female by virtue of a certain *lack of* qualities," Aristotle said. "We should regard women's nature as suffering from natural defectiveness."[*] And Saint Thomas in his turn decreed that woman was an "incomplete man," an "incidental" being. This is what the Genesis story symbolizes, where Eve appears as if drawn from Adam's "supernumerary" bone, in Bossuet's words.[†] Humanity is male, and man defines woman, not in herself, but in relation to himself; she is not considered an autonomous being. "Woman, the relative being," writes Michelet. Thus Monsieur Benda declares in *Le rapport d'Uriel* (Uriel's Report): "A man's body has meaning by itself, disregarding the body of the woman, whereas the woman's body seems devoid of meaning without reference to the male. Man thinks himself without woman. Woman does not think herself without man."[‡] And she is nothing other than what man decides; she is thus called "the sex," meaning that the male sees her essentially as a sexed being; for him she is sex, so she is it in the absolute. She is determined and differentiated in relation to man, while he is not in relation to her; she is the inessential in front of the essential. He is the Subject; he is the Absolute. She is the Other.[3]

The category of *Other* is as original[§] as consciousness itself. The duality between Self and Other can be found in the most primitive societies, in the most ancient mythologies; this division did not always fall into the category of the division of the sexes, it was not based on any empirical given: this comes out in works like Granet's on Chinese thought, and Dumézil's on India and Rome.[¶] In couples such as Varuna–Mitra,

---

*   *   *On the Generation of Animals*, Book IV.
†   Jacques-Bénigne Bossuet (1627–1704) was a French bishop famous for his brilliant sermons. Supernumerary means "superfluous," "exceeding the required number."
‡   Jules Michelet (1798–1874) was a French historian. Julien Benda (1867–1956) was a French novelist and critic; *Le rapport d'Uriel* was published in 1946.
§   Dating back to origins.
¶   Marcel Granet (1884–1940) was a French sociologist, and Georges Dumézil (1898–1986) was a philologist and historian of religions.

Uranus–Zeus,* Sun–Moon, Day–Night, no feminine element is involved at the outset; neither in Good–Evil, auspicious and inauspicious, left and right, God and Lucifer; alterity† is the fundamental category of human thought. No group ever defines itself as One without immediately setting up the Other opposite itself. It only takes three travelers brought together by chance in the same train compartment for the rest of the travelers to become vaguely hostile "others." Village people view anyone not belonging to the village as suspicious "others." For the native of a country inhabitants of other countries are viewed as "foreigners"; Jews are the "others" for anti-Semites, blacks for racist Americans, indigenous people for colonists, proletarians for the propertied classes. After studying the diverse forms of primitive society in depth, Lévi-Strauss‡ could conclude: "The passage from the state of Nature to the state of Culture is defined by man's ability to think biological relations as systems of oppositions; duality, alternation, opposition, and symmetry, whether occurring in defined or less clear form, are not so much phenomena to explain as fundamental and immediate givens of social reality."[4] These phenomena could not be understood if human reality were solely a *Mitsein*§ based on solidarity and friendship. On the contrary, they become clear if, following Hegel, a fundamental hostility to any other consciousness is found in consciousness itself; the subject posits itself only in opposition; it asserts itself as the essential and sets up the other as inessential, as the object.

But the other consciousness has an opposing reciprocal claim: traveling, a local is shocked to realize that in neighboring countries locals view him as a foreigner; between villages, clans, nations, and classes there are wars, potlatches, agreements, treaties, and struggles that remove the absolute meaning from the idea of the *Other* and bring out its relativity; whether one likes it or not, individuals and groups have no choice but to recognize the reciprocity of their relation. How is it, then, that between the sexes this reciprocity has not been put forward, that one of the terms has been asserted as the only essential one, denying any relativity in regard to its correlative, defining the latter as pure alterity? Why do women not contest male sovereignty? No subject posits itself spontaneously and at once as the inessential from the outset; it is not the Other who, defining itself as Other, defines the One; the Other is posited as Other by the One positing itself as One. But in order for the Other not to turn into the One, the Other has to submit to this foreign point of view. Where does this submission in woman come from?

There are other cases where, for a shorter or longer time, one category has managed to dominate another absolutely. It is often numerical inequality that confers this privilege: the majority imposes its law on or persecutes the minority. But women are not a minority like American blacks, or like Jews: there are as many women as men on the earth. Often, the two opposing groups concerned were once independent of each other; either they were not aware of each other in the past, or they accepted each other's autonomy; and some historical event subordinated the weaker to the stronger: the Jewish Diaspora, slavery in America, and the colonial conquests are facts with dates. In these cases, for the oppressed there was a *before*: they share a past, a tradition, sometimes a religion, or a culture. In this sense, the parallel Bebel¶ draws between

---

* Varuna and Mitra are Hindu gods (both concerned with upholding law and order), and Uranus and Zeus were Greek gods. One of Dumézil's classic books is *Mitra-Varuna: An Essay on Two Indo-European Representations of Sovereignty* (1948).

† Alterity is the state of being different, especially lack of identification with some part of one's personality or community. It has come to be a technical, philosophical term for the principle of exchanging one's own perspective for that of the Other.

‡ Claude Lévi-Strauss (1908–2009) was a French anthropologist, famous for developing structuralism as a method of understanding human society and culture (e.g., the structures of kinship systems).

§ A Hegelian term, literally meaning "being with."

¶ August Bebel (1840–1913) was a German Marxist revolutionary. In *Woman and Socialism*, first published in 1879, he argued that the social emancipation of women was a crucial precursor to the overthrow of capitalism. In Marxist theory the proletariat is the lower class of society that does not have ownership of the means of production and must instead work for wages.

women and the proletariat would be the best founded: proletarians are not a numerical minority either, and yet they have never formed a separate group. However, not *one* event but a whole historical development explains their existence as a class and accounts for the distribution of *these* individuals in this class. There have not always been proletarians: there have always been women; they are women by their physiological structure; as far back as history can be traced, they have always been subordinate to men; their dependence is not the consequence of an event or a becoming, it did not *happen*. Alterity here appears to be an absolute, partly because it falls outside the accidental nature of historical fact. A situation created over time can come undone at another time—blacks in Haiti for one are a good example; on the contrary, a natural condition seems to defy change. In truth, nature is no more an immutable given than is historical reality. If woman discovers herself as the inessential and never turns into the essential, it is because she does not bring about this transformation herself. Proletarians say "we." So do blacks. Positing themselves as subjects, they thus transform the bourgeois or whites into "others." Women—except in certain abstract gatherings such as conferences—do not use "we"; men say "women," and women adopt this word to refer to themselves; but they do not posit themselves authentically as Subjects. The proletarians made the revolution in Russia, the blacks in Haiti, the Indo-Chinese are fighting in Indochina.* Women's actions have never been more than symbolic agitation; they have won only what men have been willing to concede to them; they have taken nothing; they have received.[5] It is that they lack the concrete means to organize themselves into a unit that could posit itself in opposition. They have no past, no history, no religion of their own; and unlike the proletariat, they have no solidarity of labor or interests; they even lack their own space that makes communities of American blacks, the Jews in ghettos, or the workers in Saint-Denis[†] or Renault[‡] factories. They live dispersed among men, tied by homes, work, economic interests, and social conditions to certain men—fathers or husbands—more closely than to other women. As bourgeois women, they are in solidarity with bourgeois men and not with women proletarians; as white women, they are in solidarity with white men and not with black women. The proletariat could plan to massacre the whole ruling class; a fanatic Jew or black could dream of seizing the secret of the atomic bomb and turning all of humanity entirely Jewish or entirely black: but a woman could not even dream of exterminating males. The tie that binds her to her oppressors is unlike any other. The division of the sexes is a biological given, not a moment in human history. Their opposition took shape within an original *Mitsein*, and she has not broken it. The couple is a fundamental unit with the two halves riveted to each other: cleavage of society by sex is not possible. This is the fundamental characteristic of woman: she is the Other at the heart of a whole whose two components are necessary to each other.

One might think that this reciprocity would have facilitated her liberation; when Hercules spins wool at Omphale's[§] feet, his desire enchains him. Why was Omphale unable to acquire long-lasting power? Medea, in revenge against Jason, kills her children:[¶]

---

* The Communist Revolution took place in Russia in 1917. The Haitian Revolution was a slave revolt which broke out in 1791 and ended in 1804 with the former French colony's independence. The First Indochina War lasted from 1945 until 1954 and pushed the French out of their colonies in what are now Vietnam, Laos, and Cambodia. (The Second Indochina War began in 1955 and lasted until 1975, and was known in the West as the Vietnam War.)

† Saint-Denis is a region including the northern suburbs of Paris and has been the scene of several significant worker uprisings and strikes, including the revolt of 1848 (and others as recently as 2003). Saint-Ouen, in Saint-Denis, was one of the first cities where a factory worker was elected mayor.

‡ A French automobile manufacturer.

§ A queen of Lydia, an ancient kingdom in the region that is today Turkey, who is said to have owned Hercules as her slave for three years. (Hercules was being punished for the murder of his friend Iphitus. The story goes that during his time as a slave he became so weak that he wore women's clothes and did 'women's work,' while the queen wore his lion skin and carried his club.)

¶ Medea was a powerful sorceress, the daughter of King Aeëtes of Colchis (at the eastern end of the Black Sea), and the granddaughter of Helios, the sun god. When Jason and the crew of the Argo arrived at Colchis seeking the Golden

this brutal legend suggests that the bond attaching the woman to her child could have given her a formidable upper hand. In *Lysistrata*,* Aristophanes light-heartedly imagined a group of women who, uniting together for the social good, tried to take advantage of men's need for them: but it is only a comedy. The legend that claims that the ravished Sabine women resisted their ravishers with obstinate sterility also recounts that by whipping them with leather straps, the men magically won them over into submission.† Biological need—sexual desire and desire for posterity—which makes the male dependent on the female, has not liberated women socially. Master and slave are also linked by a reciprocal economic need that does not free the slave. That is, in the master-slave relation, the master does not *posit* the need he has for the other; he holds the power to satisfy this need and does not mediate it; the slave, on the other hand, out of dependence, hope, or fear, internalizes his need for the master; however equally compelling the need may be to them both, it always plays in favor of the oppressor over the oppressed: this explains the slow pace of working-class liberation, for example. Now, woman has always been, if not man's slave, at least his vassal; the two sexes have never divided the world up equally; and still today, even though her condition is changing, woman is heavily handicapped. In no country is her legal status identical to man's, and often it puts her at a considerable disadvantage. Even when her rights are recognized abstractly, long-standing habit keeps them from being concretely manifested in customs. Economically, men and women almost form two castes; all things being equal, the former

have better jobs, higher wages, and greater chances to succeed than their new female competitors; they occupy many more places in industry, in politics, and so forth, and they hold the most important positions. In addition to their concrete power, they are invested with a prestige whose tradition is reinforced by the child's whole education: the present incorporates the past, and in the past all history was made by males. At the moment that women are beginning to share in the making of the world, this world still belongs to men: men have no doubt about this, and women barely doubt it. Refusing to be the Other, refusing complicity with man, would mean renouncing all the advantages an alliance with the superior caste confers on them. Lord-man will materially protect liege-woman and will be in charge of justifying her existence: along with the economic risk, she eludes the metaphysical risk of a freedom that must invent its goals without help. Indeed, beside every individual's claim to assert himself as subject—an ethical claim—lies the temptation to flee freedom and to make himself into a thing: it is a pernicious path because the individual, passive, alienated, and lost, is prey to a foreign will, cut off from his transcendence, robbed of all worth. But it is an easy path: the anguish and stress of authentically assumed existence are thus avoided. The man who sets the woman up as an *Other* will thus find in her a deep complicity. Hence woman makes no claim for herself as subject because she lacks the concrete means, because she senses the necessary link connecting her to man without positing its reciprocity, and because she often derives satisfaction from her role as *Other*.

Fleece, Medea fell in love with Jason and used her magic to help him, in return for Jason's promise to marry her. When Jason later deserted her and married the daughter of Creon, the king of Corinth, Medea took her revenge by killing the new bride with a poisoned robe and crown which burned the flesh from her body (and killed King Creon as well when he tried to embrace his dying daughter), and also by murdering the two children she had with Jason.

* A play, written in about 411 BCE, in which the women of Hellas (ancient Greece) agree to withhold sex from their men folk until they agree to end the long-running war between Athens and Sparta.

† At the beginning of Roman history, according to myth, the newly founded city of Rome needed to increase its population quickly in order to defend itself against its neighbors, but it did not have enough women to sustain its numbers. The Romans therefore invited the neighboring community of the Sabines to a religious celebration in honor of Neptune, and during the party the younger Roman men kidnapped the Sabine women and raped them. The Sabines—some months later!—returned with an army to bring back their women by force, but discovered (according to legend) that their erstwhile wives and daughters had reconciled with their new Roman husbands, and borne their children. The women stopped the battle before it started by placing themselves between the two armies; the Romans and the Sabines made peace, and Rome continued to grow.

But a question immediately arises: How did this whole story begin? It is understandable that the duality of the sexes, like all duality, be expressed in conflict. It is understandable that if one of the two succeeded in imposing its superiority, it had to establish itself as absolute. It remains to be explained how it was that man won at the outset. It seems possible that women might have carried off the victory, or that the battle might never be resolved. Why is it that this world has always belonged to men and that only today things are beginning to change? Is this change a good thing? Will it bring about an equal sharing of the world between men and women or not?

These questions are far from new; they have already had many answers; but the very fact that woman is *Other* challenges all the justifications that men have ever given: these were only too clearly dictated by their own interest. "Everything that men have written about women should be viewed with suspicion, because they are both judge and party," wrote Poulain de la Barre,* a little-known seventeenth-century feminist. Males have always and everywhere paraded their satisfaction of feeling they are kings of creation. "Blessed be the Lord our God, and the Lord of all worlds that has not made me a woman," Jews say in their morning prayers; meanwhile, their wives resignedly murmur: "Blessed be the Lord for creating me according to his will." Among the blessings Plato thanked the gods for was, first, being born free and not a slave and, second, a man and not a woman. But males could not have enjoyed this privilege so fully had they not considered it as founded in the absolute and in eternity: they sought to make the fact of their supremacy a right. "Those who made and compiled the laws, being men, favored their own sex, and the jurisconsults† have turned the laws into principles," Poulain de la Barre continues. Lawmakers, priests, philosophers, writers, and scholars have gone to great lengths to prove that women's subordinate condition was willed in heaven and profitable on earth. Religions forged by men reflect this will for domination: they found ammunition in the legends of Eve and Pandora. They have put philosophy and theology in their service, as seen in the previously cited words of Aristotle and Saint Thomas. Since ancient times, satirists and moralists have delighted in depicting women's weaknesses. The violent indictments brought against them all through French literature are well-known: Montherlant, with less verve, picks up the tradition from Jean de Meung.‡ This hostility seems sometimes founded but is often gratuitous; in truth, it covers up a more or less skillfully camouflaged will to self-justification. "It is much easier to accuse one sex than to excuse the other," says Montaigne.§ In certain cases, the process is transparent. It is striking, for example, that the Roman code limiting a wife's rights invokes "the imbecility and fragility of the sex" just when a weakening family structure makes her a threat to male heirs. It is striking that in the sixteenth century, to keep a married woman under wardship, the authority of Saint Augustine¶ affirming "the wife is an animal neither reliable nor stable" is called on, whereas the unmarried woman is recognized as capable of managing her own affairs. Montaigne well understood the arbitrariness and injustice of the lot assigned to women: "Women are not wrong at all when they reject

---

*   François Poulain de la Barre, a French Catholic village priest, published three pamphlets urging the equality of the sexes, including "De l'égalité des deux sexes" (1671) from which this quote is taken.

†   One learned in law.

‡   Henri de Montherlant (1896–1972) was a French writer, soldier, athlete, and bullfighter whose novels glorify force and masculinity. Jean de Meung (c. 1240–c. 1305) was a French poet and alchemist known for his continuation of the *Roman de la rose* (*Romance of the Rose*), an allegorical poem in the courtly love tradition begun by Guillaume de Lorris in about 1230. His section of the poem is particularly noted for its controversial digressions on a variety of topics, including a quatrain vilifying womankind. (For this offense, it is said, he was cornered by the ladies of the court of Charles VI who tried to have him stripped naked and whipped; only his impish eloquence allowed him to escape.)

§   Michel de Montaigne (1533–92) was a French courtier and the author of *Essais*, which established, as a new literary form, the essay (a short piece dealing with the author's personal thoughts about a particular subject).

¶   St. Augustine of Hippo (354–430), a "church father" whose writings (and political victories) were extremely influential on the future doctrine of the Church. (Not St. Augustine of Canterbury (d. 604), considered the originator of the Christian Church in Britain.)

the rules of life that have been introduced into the world, inasmuch as it is the men who have made these without them. There is a natural plotting and scheming between them and us." But he does not go so far as to champion their cause. It is only in the eighteenth century that deeply democratic men begin to consider the issue objectively. Diderot,* for one, tries to prove that, like man, woman is a human being. A bit later, John Stuart Mill ardently defends women. But these philosophers are exceptional in their impartiality. In the nineteenth century the feminist quarrel once again becomes a partisan quarrel; one of the consequences of the Industrial Revolution is that women enter the labor force: at that point, women's demands leave the realm of the theoretical and find economic grounds; their adversaries become all the more aggressive; even though landed property is partially discredited, the bourgeoisie clings to the old values where family solidity guarantees private property: it insists all the more fiercely that woman's place be in the home as her emancipation becomes a real threat; even within the working class, men tried to thwart women's liberation because women were becoming dangerous competitors—especially as women were used to working for low salaries.[6] To prove women's inferiority, antifeminists began to draw not only, as before, on religion, philosophy, and theology but also on science: biology, experimental psychology, and so forth. At most they were willing to grant "separate but equal status" to the *other* sex.[7] That winning formula is most significant: it is exactly that formula the Jim Crow laws[†] put into practice with regard to black Americans; this so-called egalitarian segregation served only to introduce the most extreme forms of discrimination. This convergence is in no way pure chance: whether it is race, caste, class, or sex reduced to an inferior condition, the justification process is the same. "The

eternal feminine" corresponds to "the black soul" or "the Jewish character." However, the Jewish problem on the whole is very different from the two others: for the anti-Semite, the Jew is more an enemy than an inferior, and no place on this earth is recognized as his own; it would be preferable to see him annihilated. But there are deep analogies between the situations of women and blacks: both are liberated today from the same paternalism, and the former master caste wants to keep them "in their place," that is, the place chosen for them; in both cases, they praise, more or less sincerely, the virtues of the "good black," the carefree, childlike, merry soul of the resigned black, and the woman who is a "true woman"—frivolous, infantile, irresponsible, the woman subjugated to man. In both cases, the ruling caste bases its argument on the state of affairs it created itself. The familiar line from George Bernard Shaw[‡] sums it up: The white American relegates the black to the rank of shoe-shine boy, and then concludes that blacks are only good for shining shoes. The same vicious circle can be found in all analogous circumstances: when an individual or a group of individuals is kept in a situation of inferiority, the fact is that he or they *are* inferior. But the scope of the verb *to be* must be understood; bad faith means giving it a substantive value, when in fact it has the sense of the Hegelian dynamic: *to be* is to have become, to have been made as one manifests oneself. Yes, women in general *are* today inferior to men; that is, their situation provides them with fewer possibilities: the question is whether this state of affairs must be perpetuated.

Many men wish it would be: not all men have yet laid down their arms. The conservative bourgeoisie continues to view women's liberation as a danger threatening their morality and their interests. Some men feel threatened by women's competition. In

---

* Denis Diderot (1713–84) was a French philosopher best known as the chief editor of *Encyclopédie*. Arguably the supreme literary creation of the Age of Enlightenment, *Encyclopédie* attempted to present all the achievements of human learning in a single (28-volume) work.

† From the 1880s until, in many cases, the 1960s, more than half of the US states passed "Jim Crow" laws (so-called after a black character in minstrel shows) to enforce segregation, imposing legal punishments on people for consorting with members of another race. For example, business owners and public institutions were often ordered to keep their black and white clientele separated.

‡ Shaw (1856–1950) was an Irish playwright and critic, awarded the Nobel Prize in Literature in 1925. In addition to his plays, he is also the author of *The Intelligent Woman's Guide to Socialism and Capitalism* (1928).

*Hebdo-Latin** the other day, a student declared: "Every woman student who takes a position as a doctor or lawyer is *stealing* a place from us." That student never questioned his rights over this world. Economic interests are not the only ones in play. One of the benefits that oppression secures for the oppressor is that the humblest among them *feels superior*: in the United States a "poor white" from the South can console himself for not being a "dirty nigger"; and more prosperous whites cleverly exploit this pride. Likewise, the most mediocre of males believes himself a demigod next to women. It was easier for M. de Montherlant to think himself a hero in front of women (handpicked, by the way) than to act the man among men, a role that many women assumed better than he did. Thus, in one of his articles in *Le Figaro Littéraire* in September 1948, M. Claude Mauriac[†]—whom everyone admires for his powerful originality—could[8] write about women: "*We* listen in a tone [*sic*] of polite indifference ... to the most brilliant one among them, knowing that her intelligence, in a more or less dazzling way, reflects ideas that come from *us*." Clearly his female interlocutor does not reflect M. Mauriac's own ideas, since he is known not to have any; that she reflects ideas originating with men is possible: among males themselves, more than one of them takes as his own opinions he did not invent; one might wonder if it would not be in M. Claude Mauriac's interest to converse with a good reflection of Descartes, Marx, or Gide[‡] rather than with himself; what is remarkable is that with the ambiguous "*we*," he identifies with Saint Paul, Hegel, Lenin, and Nietzsche, and from their heights he looks down on the herd of women who dare to speak to him on an equal footing; frankly, I know of more than one woman who would not put up with M. Mauriac's "tone of polite indifference."

I have stressed this example because of its disarming masculine naïveté. Men profit in many other more subtle ways from woman's alterity. For all those suffering from an inferiority complex, this is a miraculous liniment; no one is more arrogant toward women, more aggressive or more disdainful, than a man anxious about his own virility. Those who are not threatened by their fellow men are far more likely to recognize woman as a counterpart; but even for them the myth of the Woman, of the Other, remains precious for many reasons;[9] they can hardly be blamed for not wanting to lightheartedly sacrifice all the benefits they derive from the myth: they know what they lose by relinquishing the woman of their dreams, but they do not know what the woman of tomorrow will bring them. It takes great abnegation to refuse to posit oneself as unique and absolute Subject. Besides, the vast majority of men do not explicitly make this position their own. They do not *posit* woman as inferior: they are too imbued today with the democratic ideal not to recognize all human beings as equals. Within the family, the male child and then the young man sees the woman as having the same social dignity as the adult male; afterward, he experiences in desire and love the resistance and independence of the desired and loved woman; married, he respects in his wife the spouse and the mother, and in the concrete experience of married life she affirms herself opposite him as a freedom. He can thus convince himself that there is no longer a social hierarchy between the sexes and that on the whole, in spite of their differences, woman is an equal. As he nevertheless recognizes some points of inferiority—professional incapacity being the predominant one—he attributes them to nature. When he has an attitude of benevolence and partnership toward a woman, he applies the principle of abstract equality; and he does not *posit* the concrete inequality he recognizes. But as soon as he clashes with her, the situation is reversed. He will apply the concrete inequality theme and will even allow himself to disavow abstract equality.[10] This is how many men affirm, with quasi good faith, that women *are* equal to men and have no demands to make, and *at the same time* that women will never be equal to men and that their demands are in vain. It is difficult for men to measure the enormous extent of social discrimination that seems insignificant from the outside and whose moral and intellectual

---

* Like *Franchise*, another ephemeral magazine of the era.
† Claude Mauriac (1914–96) was a French journalist, critic, and avant-garde novelist. Several of his experimental novels (published in the late 1950s and early 1960s) focus on the exploits of a cold-hearted, womanizing egoist named Bertrand Carnéjoux. *Figaro littéraire* is the literary supplement of the French daily newspaper *Le Figaro* (founded 1826).
‡ André Gide (1869–1951), a French novelist, intellectual, literary critic, and social crusader (for, especially, homosexual rights). He received the Nobel Prize for Literature in 1947.

repercussions are so deep in woman that they appear to spring from an original nature.[11] The man most sympathetic to women never knows her concrete situation fully. So there is no good reason to believe men when they try to defend privileges whose scope they cannot even fathom. We will not let ourselves be intimidated by the number and violence of attacks against women; nor be fooled by the self-serving praise showered on the "real woman"; nor be won over by men's enthusiasm for her destiny, a destiny they would not for the world want to share.

We must not, however, be any less mistrustful of feminists' arguments: very often their attempt to polemicize robs them of all value. If the "question of women" is so trivial, it is because masculine arrogance turned it into a "quarrel"; when people quarrel, they no longer reason well. What people have endlessly sought to prove is that woman is superior, inferior, or equal to man: created after Adam, she is obviously a secondary being, some say; on the contrary, say others, Adam was only a rough draft, and God perfected the human being when he created Eve; her brain is smaller, but relatively bigger; Christ was made man, but perhaps out of humility. Every argument has its opposite, and both are often misleading. To see clearly, one needs to get out of these ruts; these vague notions of superiority, inferiority, and equality that have distorted all discussions must be discarded in order to start anew.

But how, then, will we ask the question? And in the first place, who are we to ask it? Men are judge and party: so are women. Can an angel be found? In fact, an angel would be ill qualified to speak, would not understand all the givens of the problem; as for the hermaphrodite, it is a case of its own: it is not both a man and a woman, but neither man nor woman. I think certain women are still best suited to elucidate the situation of women. It is a sophism to claim that Epimenides should be enclosed within the concept of Cretan and all Cretans within the concept of liar:* it is not a mysterious essence that dictates good or bad faith to men and women; it is their situation that disposes them to seek the truth to a greater or lesser extent. Many women today, fortunate to have had all the privileges of the

human being restored to them, can afford the luxury of impartiality: we even feel the necessity of it. We are no longer like our militant predecessors; we have more or less won the game; in the latest discussions on women's status, the UN has not ceased to imperiously demand equality of the sexes, and indeed many of us have never felt our femaleness to be a difficulty or an obstacle; many other problems seem more essential than those that concern us uniquely: this very detachment makes it possible to hope our attitude will be objective. Yet we know the feminine world more intimately than men do because our roots are in it; we grasp more immediately what the fact of being female means for a human being, and we care more about knowing it. I said that there are more essential problems; but this one still has a certain importance from our point of view: How will the fact of being women have affected our lives? What precise opportunities have been given us, and which ones have been denied? What destiny awaits our younger sisters, and in which direction should we point them? It is striking that most feminine literature is driven today by an attempt at lucidity more than by a will to make demands; coming out of an era of muddled controversy, this book is one attempt among others to take stock of the current state.

But it is no doubt impossible to approach any human problem without partiality: even the way of asking the questions, of adopting perspectives, presupposes hierarchies of interests; all characteristics comprise values; every so-called objective description is set against an ethical background. Instead of trying to conceal those principles that are more or less explicitly implied, we would be better off stating them from the start; then it would not be necessary to specify on each page the meaning given to the words "superior," "inferior," "better," "worse," "progress," "regression," and so on. If we examine some of the books on women, we see that one of the most frequently held points of view is that of public good or general interest: in reality, this is taken to mean the interest of society as each one wishes to maintain or establish it. In our opinion, there is no public good other than one that assures the citizens' private good; we judge institutions from the point of view

---

* The Cretan philosopher Epimenides of Knossos (who lived around 600 BCE) invented a famous logical paradox by asserting, "Cretans, always liars." That is, since Epimenides himself was a Cretan, if this sentence is true then it must be false; a bit less obviously, if it is false then (arguably) it is true since it says of itself that it is false, which is true.

of the concrete opportunities they give to individuals. But neither do we confuse the idea of private interest with happiness: that is another frequently encountered point of view; are women in a harem* not happier than a woman voter? Is a housewife not happier than a woman worker? We cannot really know what the word "happiness" means, and still less what authentic values it covers; there is no way to measure the happiness of others, and it is always easy to call a situation that one would like to impose on others happy: in particular, we declare happy those condemned to stagnation, under the pretext that happiness is immobility. This is a notion, then, we will not refer to. The perspective we have adopted is one of existentialist morality. Every subject posits itself as a transcendence concretely, through projects; it accomplishes its freedom only by perpetual surpassing toward other freedoms; there is no other justification for present existence than its expansion toward an indefinitely open future. Every time transcendence lapses into immanence, there is degradation of existence into "in-itself," of freedom into facticity; this fall is a moral fault if the subject consents to it; if this fall is inflicted on the subject, it takes the form of frustration and oppression; in both cases it is an absolute evil. Every individual concerned with justifying his existence experiences his existence as an indefinite need to transcend himself. But what singularly defines the situation of woman is that being, like all humans, an autonomous freedom, she discovers and chooses herself in a world where men force her to assume herself as Other: an attempt is made to freeze her as an object and doom her to immanence, since her transcendence will be forever transcended by another essential and sovereign consciousness. Woman's drama lies in this conflict between the fundamental claim of every subject, which always posits itself as essential, and the demands of a situation that constitutes her as inessential. How, in the feminine condition, can a human being accomplish herself? What paths are open to her? Which ones lead to dead ends? How can she find independence within dependence? What circumstances limit women's freedom and can she overcome them? These are the fundamental questions we would like to elucidate. This means that in focusing on the individual's possibilities, we will define these possibilities not in terms of happiness but in terms of freedom.

Clearly this problem would have no meaning if we thought that a physiological, psychological, or economic destiny weighed on woman. So we will begin by discussing woman from a biological, psychoanalytical, and historical materialist point of view. We will then attempt to positively demonstrate how "feminine reality" has been constituted, why woman has been defined as Other, and what the consequences have been from men's point of view. Then we will describe the world from the woman's point of view such as it is offered to her,[12] and we will see the difficulties women are up against just when, trying to escape the sphere they have been assigned until now, they seek to be part of the human *Mitsein*. ■

Suggestions for Critical Reflection

1. Beauvoir begins her book by asking "what is a woman?" How do you think she answers this question?

2. Beauvoir claims that the terms *masculine* and *feminine* are not symmetrical opposites. What do you make of this claim? How does Beauvoir develop it? What is its importance?

3. "[A]s far back as history can be traced, [women] have always been subordinate to men; their dependence is not a consequence of an event or a becoming, it did not *happen*." Does this claim seem plausible? How important is it to Beauvoir's argument?

4. Beauvoir suggests that for women to renounce their status as an Other would be to abandon "all the advantages an alliance with the superior caste confers on them." What does she mean by this? Is she right? How serious a difficulty is this for feminism?

---

* The private part of an Arab household, traditionally forbidden to male strangers.

5. Beauvoir writes that "there are deep analogies between the situations of women and blacks," and goes on to explain this claim. What do you think of this analogy?

6. "[T]he ruling caste bases its argument on the state of affairs it created itself." Does this ring true? How important is it for the social activist, including the feminist, to notice this? How much does this explain the behavior towards women by even well-intentioned men?

7. "We are no longer like our militant predecessors; we have more or less won the game." Is Beauvoir right about this? Is this claim consistent with her general theory of the oppression of women in society?

8. "One is not born, but rather becomes, a woman." Some commentators have argued that, in making this central claim, Beauvoir herself falls victim to the patriarchal mindset she is criticizing—that she is tacitly assuming that "femaleness is indeed optional and subhuman, and maleness the slipped-from standard."* Does this criticism strike you as plausible? Does it suggest a fundamental problem with Beauvoir's project, or with the way she carries it out?

Notes

1 Out of print today, titled *Franchise*.

2 The Kinsey Report [Alfred C. Kinsey and others: *Sexual Behavior in the Human Male*. (W.B. Saunders Co., 1948)], for example, confines itself to defining the sexual characteristics of the American man, which is completely different.

3 This idea has been expressed in its most explicit form by E. Levinas in his essay *Le temps et l'autre* (*Time and the Other*). He expresses it like this: "Is there not a situation where alterity would be borne by a being in a positive sense, as essence? What is the alterity that does not purely and simply enter into the opposition of two species of the same genus? I think that the absolutely contrary contrary, whose contrariety is in no way affected by the relationship that can be established between it and its correlative, the contrariety that permits its terms to remain absolutely other, is the feminine. Sex is not some specific difference ... Neither is the difference between the sexes a contradiction ... Neither is the difference between the sexes the duality of two complementary terms, for two complementary terms presuppose a preexisting whole ... [A]lterity is accomplished in the feminine. The term is on the same level as, but in meaning opposed to, consciousness." I suppose Mr. Levinas is not forgetting that woman also is consciousness for herself. But it is striking that he deliberately adopts a man's point of view, disregarding the reciprocity of the subject and the object. When he writes that woman is mystery, he assumes that she is mystery for man. So this apparently objective description is in fact an affirmation of masculine privilege.

4 See Claude Lévi-Strauss, *Les structures élémentaires de la parenté* (*The Elementary Structures of Kinship*). I thank Claude Lévi-Strauss for sharing the proofs of his thesis, which I drew on heavily, particularly in the second part, pp. 76–89.

5 See second part, page 126.

6 See Part Two, pp. 135–136.

7 "*L'égalité dans la différence*" in the French text. Literal translation: "different but equal."—TRANS.

8 At least he thought he could.

9 The article by Michel Carrouges on this theme in *Cahiers du Sud*, no. 292, is significant. He writes with indignation: "If only there were no feminine myth but only bands of cooks, matrons, prostitutes, and bluestockings with functions of pleasure or utility!" So, according to him, woman has no existence for herself; he only takes into account her *function* in the male world. Her finality is in man; in fact, it is possible to prefer her poetic "function" to all others. The exact question is why she should be defined in relation to the man.

10 For example, man declares that he does not find his wife in any way diminished just because she does not have a profession: work in the home is just as noble and so on. Yet at the first argument he remonstrates, "You wouldn't be able to earn a living without me."

11 Describing this very process will be the object of Volume II of this study.

12 This will be the subject of a second volume.

---

* From Jane O'Grady, writing in the *Oxford Companion to Philosophy* (1995), 179; O'Grady is not making this claim herself, but only describing it.

TALIA MAE BETTCHER

Trans Women and the Meaning of "Woman"

Who Is Talia Mae Bettcher?

Born in Canada in 1966, Talia Mae Bettcher holds a PhD from UCLA and is Professor and Chair of Philosophy at California State University, Los Angeles, where for several years she served as Director of the Center for the Study of Genders and Sexualities. In recent decades, Bettcher's philosophical work has focused primarily on transgender and gender issues; much of this work, she says, is informed by her own experience as a trans woman and her involvement in trans subculture in Los Angeles. In addition to publishing numerous articles that combine philosophy and trans studies, she explores similar questions in works of performance art. Bettcher was a founding editor of the ground-breaking interdisciplinary journal *Transgender Studies Quarterly* and she co-edited a special issue of the feminist philosophy journal *Hypatia* titled *Transgender Studies and Feminism: Theory, Politics, and Gender Realities* (2009). She has also written two books on the eighteenth-century philosopher George Berkeley: *Berkeley's Philosophy of Spirit: Consciousness, Ontology and the Elusive Subject* (2007) and *Berkeley: A Guide for the Perplexed* (2009).

What Is the Structure of This Reading?

Bettcher opens this article by summarizing the two dominant views that are often used to make sense of trans people's lives: the "Wrong Body Model" and the "Transgender Model." In the course of the article, she argues that both of these models are flawed in multiple ways, and she proposes a new model intended to avoid the pitfalls she has identified.

The first major flaw Bettcher describes is that proponents of both the Wrong Body Model and the Transgender Model adopt what she refers to as a "single-meaning position": they presume, for example, that "woman" has a single definition and argue that this definition should include trans women. Bettcher outlines several variations on the single-meaning position, including definitions that describe womanhood according to specific biological markers—an approach that falls apart in practice, given the biological variety of human beings. She also discusses definitions that use a "family resemblance" approach in which a person fits into the category of "woman" by possessing a critical number of features of that category. Bettcher argues that even the family resemblance approach is inadequate, since at best it allows that a trans woman is merely "a marginal instance" of womanhood—and at worst it leaves the gender status of trans women more open to questioning if they possess fewer physical features of paradigmatic womanhood.

Bettcher goes on to introduce "semantic contextualism," an alternative to the single-meaning position. According to this approach, the meaning of "woman" changes according to context—which can mean that, in some contexts at least, self-identification is enough to determine that an individual is a woman. But semantic contextualism also has a serious flaw: if it allows for the possibility that trans women are women in some contexts, it also allows for the possibility that trans women are men in other contexts. Which definitions apply in which situations becomes a question of political debate, so that once again trans women must defend their womanhood while the womanhood of non-trans women is taken for granted.

The alternative Bettcher offers is what she calls a "multiple-meaning position." According to this view, the term "trans woman" has a different meaning in dominant culture from the meaning it has in trans subculture—and in trans subculture, if one is a trans woman, one is necessarily a woman. Acknowledging that the terms "woman" and "trans woman" have multiple meanings allows us to assert that trans subculture's understanding of womanhood should be accepted while also leaving room to observe that a dominant definition of womanhood exists, and to critique it.

This leads Bettcher to identify a major problem with both the "Wrong Body Model" and the "Transgender Model": both attempt to describe trans lives in terms of the gender definitions that have already been established by dominant culture. We must start from the ways trans people define gender, she argues, if we are to reach a model that will better help us to understand and resist the oppression of trans people.

Some Useful Background Information

1. Because the question Bettcher discusses underlies the relationship between transfeminism and other forms of feminism, it is worth noting that, while many feminists seek intersections between feminist and trans theory, strongly anti-trans views have also been articulated within feminist thought. Some feminists have argued that trans men are misogynist in their rejection of femininity* or that trans women should not be recognized as women in contexts where doing so would interfere with the achievement of feminist objectives.† Others have made such overtly transphobic claims as the assertion that trans women appropriate and objectify the female body in a way that is tantamount to rape.‡ Controversy regarding the relationship between trans and feminist politics was particularly intense in the 1970s, and it continues in the twenty-first century. Is it also worth noting

that trans studies as an independent discipline is relatively new; it emerged in the 1990s.

2. A major line of philosophical exploration in trans studies concerns the nature of gender (generally understood as role or identity) and its relationship to sex (generally understood as physical or biological—though the definition of the terms is also part of the inquiry). Bettcher's argument alludes to the idea that gender is socially constructed—an idea that is very important in some feminist theory and is also held by some trans theorists. The nuances of this position are different for different thinkers, but, broadly speaking, advocates of this position hold that gender is produced by culture (rather than gendered characteristics being something we innately possess by virtue of our biology), and that rather than inherently *being* or *possessing* a gender, we *enact* a gender by performing its role over time according to social norms. Some go so far as to say that even physical sex is culturally constructed in the sense that we can only represent or talk about the body in the gendered language offered by our culture; sex is thus really a part of gender. On the other hand, some thinkers—both in feminist and in trans theory—reject the constructionist view entirely.

Trans Women and the Meaning of "Woman"§

There is a familiar view of transsexuality that speaks of women trapped inside male bodies and men trapped inside female bodies. On this view—let's call it the "Wrong Body Model"—transsexuality is a misalignment between gender identity and sexed body. At its most extreme, the idea is that one's real sex, given by internal identity, is innate. It is on the basis of this identity that one affirms that one has always really belonged to a particular sex and has a claim to the surgical procedures that bring one's body into alignment with one's identity.[1] However, one of the problems with this account is that it naturalizes sex and gender differences in a troubling way. Christine Overall remarks, for example, "On this theory, gender is

---

* Jack (publishing as Judith) Halberstam discusses examples of this in "Transgender Butch: Butch/FTM Border Wars and the Masculine Continuum," *GLQ: A Journal of Lesbian and Gay Studies* 4, 2 (1998): 287–310.

† See, for example, Kathleen Stock, "Academic Philosophy and the UK Gender Recognition Act," *Medium* (7 May 2018).

‡ See, for example, Janice Raymond's influential work *The Transsexual Empire: The Making of the She-Male* (Boston: Beacon Press, 1979).

§ Talia Mae Bettcher, "Trans Women and the Meaning of 'Woman,'" in *Philosophy of Sex: Contemporary Readings*, 6th ed., ed. A. Soble, N. Power, and R. Halwani (Rowan & Littlefield, 2013), 233–50.

reified,* at least for some individuals. As a member of the social group 'women,' I find this idea frightening."[2] As a (trans) woman and as a feminist, I find this idea frightening, too.

There is another view, explicitly political, that has developed over the past twenty years, which says that trans people challenge the traditional binary† between man and woman. Because, on this view, trans people do not fit neatly into the two categories "man" and "woman," mainstream society attempts to force trans people into this system in order to make it appear that there is a sharp dichotomy between men and women (when trans people show that there is not). The medical establishment is but one way in which society makes trans people disappear. The forces of oppression aim at invisibility, and the strategy of resistance is to come out and make oneself visible.[3] On this view— let's call it the "Transgender Model"—it is not trans people who are the problem but society itself. One of the difficulties with this account is that many trans people don't view themselves as "beyond the binary" at all but as either men or women. Thus, the Transgender Model seems to invalidate the self-identities of some transsexual people.[4]

Due to problems with both models, I am interested in providing an alternative account that relies on a multiple-meaning view (it is not quite yet a model rivaling the above two, but the beginnings of one). Specifically, my aim is to develop an account that accommodates trans people who see themselves as situated in a binary category while avoiding the pathologization and naturalization of gender identity.[5] I aim to probe deeper into the Wrong Body Model and the Transgender Model and to use the results of this investigation to eventually develop a model both more plausible and more accommodating to the experiences of trans people. In this essay, I make a few preliminary moves in that direction.

My claim is that we can understand the gender identities of (at least some) trans people who situate themselves in a binary category to stand in a "meaning conflict" with more mainstream conceptions of what and who they are. Both the Wrong Body Model and the Transgender Model err in adopting what I call a "single-meaning position"; that is, they assume that a gender term has one meaning only. This leads them to presuppose the dominant meaning of gender terms while erasing resistant ones. Moreover, by presupposing the dominant meanings, both accounts end up accepting the marginal status of trans people. This leads them to try to justify the view that trans people are who they say they are. This is a bad place to start trans theory and politics, I argue, since non-trans people do not need to justify who they say they are in the same way: to accept this asymmetry is to effectively yield political ground from the very beginning. On the contrary, once we accept resistant, subcultural meanings, there is no need to defend the self-identifying claims of trans people. Instead, the power relations by which trans identities are institutionally enforced from without become fully visible.

My work is informed by my own experience as a (white) trans woman living in the trans activist subcultures of Los Angeles. There we've developed different gender practices (including the use of gender terms such as "woman" and "man") that do not always accord with more mainstream ones. It is my methodological starting point to take such practices seriously. As philosophers, we often rely on our intuitions about language use. This case is no different. It is just that my knowledge concerns a subculture that may seem foreign to some. My starting point is that in analyzing the meaning of terms such as "woman," it is inappropriate to dismiss alternative ways in which those terms are actually used in trans subcultures; such usage needs to be taken into consideration as part of the analysis. This is certainly the case when the question precisely concerns whether a trans person *counts* as a woman or a man.

The Single-Meaning Position

Consider a form of transphobia I call "the basic denial of authenticity." A central feature of it is "identity

---

* To reify something is to make that thing (or at least treat it as being) real and definite—for example, to turn something abstract into something concrete.

† A binary is a set of two terms that are deemed to be comprehensive and mutually exclusive; according to a binary conception of gender, one must be either a man or a woman, and one cannot be both or neither.

enforcement," whereby trans women are identified as "really men" and trans men are identified as "really women" (regardless of how we ourselves self-identify). Often this kind of identity enforcement (particularly through pronoun use) occurs repeatedly and runs against the trans person's own frequent requests to be treated otherwise. It can appear in mundane inter-actions between a trans person and a store clerk (e.g., repeated references to a trans woman as "sir") to cases in which a trans person is "exposed" as "really a man/woman, disguised as a woman/man" and subjected to extreme forms of violence and murder.[6]

Now consider the self-identifying claim "I am a trans woman." Frequently, in dominant cultural con-texts, the expression "trans woman" is understood to mean "a man who lives as a woman." Is this a case in which an individual merely misunderstands the meaning of the expression? No, because that mean-ing is accepted by many people and, indeed, often by the media, law enforcement agencies, domestic vio-lence and homeless shelters, and so forth. Yet when I use that expression ("I am a trans woman") in trans subcultures, it simply does not mean that. So it is fair to say that identity enforcement does not merely con-cern whether a gender category expression applies to a person but also what an expression even means. The enforcer thinks (in the case of the trans woman) that the category "man" applies while the category "woman" doesn't. So the enforcer thinks that if "trans woman" is truthfully said, it can't possibly mean that the per-son is a woman (and isn't actually a man). Instead, it must mean that the person is merely pretending to be a woman. "Trans" would flag something involving pretense and would perhaps have the force of "fake" (as in "fake woman").

There are two ways one might respond to the enforcer. The first involves accepting the single-meaning position; the second involves accepting the multiple-meaning position. In the single-meaning position, "woman" is taken to have a fixed meaning; it is taken for granted that there is one concept. The dis-pute between the enforcer and the trans woman hinges on whether the concept "woman" applies or doesn't apply to her. On this view, "trans" would qualify the term "woman" (taken in the standard meaning) as a particular kind (one who had been assigned male sex at birth, perhaps, who became a woman later). The disagreement concerning the meaning of "transgen-der" ("fake" versus "transitional") would then hinge on the correct applicability of the term "woman" (or "female"). So to the enforcer, "trans woman" means "man living as a woman" while to the trans woman, "trans woman" means "woman assigned to the male sex at birth." This obviously raises difficult questions about how we ought to analyze terms such as "woman" and "man."

Most people would define "woman" as "adult female human being" and "man" as "adult male human being," thereby considering the differences as biolog-ical. Yet many feminists have argued that "woman" picks out a *social* kind, role, or status.[7] If so, that would require an alternative analysis of "woman." Of course, even if we accept a biological definition, we would still have the difficulty of defining "female" and "male" because there are multiple features involved in sex determination (including chromosomal karyotype,[*] gonadal structure, genital structure, reproductive capacity, and hormone levels), not to mention cases in which these features come apart. For example, a per-son with complete androgen insensitivity syndrome will have XY chromosomes and internal male gonads but a female phenotype.[†] In such cases it may be very difficult to tell whether the person is male, female, or neither. Indeed, it seems plausible that there is no fact of the matter in such cases.

One way to accommodate this multiplicity of fea-tures in the single-meaning position is to take gender terms as expressing family resemblance concepts. An analysis of such concepts would not involve specifying their necessary and sufficient conditions but listing their various overlapping features (or family resem-blances). This list would include the multiple features above. And one could easily add more cultural fea-tures to the list as well, thereby addressing the femi-nist insight that there is a significant social component to gender categories like "woman."

With this type of account in hand, one could show that at least *some* trans women meet enough of

---

[*]   The observable characteristics (number and appearance) of an individual's chromosomes.

[†]   The observable characteristics of an individual organism, as shaped by genetic and environmental factors.

the conditions required for the application of the category "woman." One might point to hormone levels, surgically altered genitalia, and so forth to defend a claim to womanhood. The enforcer, by contrast, might point to karyotype and birth genitalia in order to defend a verdict of manhood. In such a conflict, the stakes concern which criteria are to weigh more in applying "woman." Notably, however, this strategy does not yield the kind of certainty one wants to validate a trans person's identity claims; at bottom we probably have a factually undecidable question. A trans woman in this case is, far from being a paradigm of womanhood, merely a marginal instance.[8] Whether she counts as a woman would depend on pragmatic and political considerations (concerns about *how best* to draw the line or about which criteria to use and how much weight they have). One might argue that in such hard cases it is best to consider self-identification (rather than karyotype) as decisive.[9] But that decision is not determined by a simple analysis of the concept "woman" but by the view that, in difficult cases, it is better to let people self-identify rather than pick a gender term for them. Despite the fact that the Transgender Model seems to ignore the self-identities of some transsexual people, it actually seems *to get it right* in positioning a postoperative trans woman problematically with respect to the binary. If a postoperative trans woman counts as a woman at all, it is not because she is a paradigmatic woman but because, while problematically positioned with regard to the binary categories, she is, owing to political considerations, *best viewed* as a woman.

The case is grimmer when we consider trans women who have not undergone genital reconstruction surgery and, particularly, those who have not undergone any bodily changes at all (hormone therapy, "top surgery,"* and the like). In terms of governmentally issued IDs, a trans woman who has not undergone any medical intervention is likely to not be allowed any changes (so her documentation will consistently say "male"). In cases of public sex segregation, including public changerooms, domestic violence shelters, homeless shelters, shared hospital rooms, jail and prison housing, and same-sex searches by police officers and other security officials, she is likely viewed

as "really male." To be sure, gender presentation may help secure that claim to womanhood. But that might not be enough. Certainly, it seems very hard to see how a trans woman could claim to be a veritable woman on the basis of gender identity alone (without such presentation). It even seems unclear how she can be recognized as "in-between" or "problematically positioned" with regard to the categories as the transgender model says. On the contrary, she would probably count as a "man" (just as the enforcer claims). The problem with the single-meaning position, then, is that it does not appear to do justice to trans people's self-identifying claims about their gender.

Semantic Contextualism

We can understand this disagreement differently if we understand it in terms of a more robust conflict over the very meaning of the term "woman." Already we have had to allow that the term "trans" means something different to the enforcer and to the trans woman: to the former it means "fake" and to the trans woman it might mean "transitional."[10] In the multiple-meaning account I propose, the same is true in the case of the term "woman." In order to bring out the details of my account, I contrast it with a view that is superficially similar to it, namely semantic contextualism. According to semantic contextualism, the extension of "woman" changes depending on the context. Jennifer Mather Saul considers a definition according to which "*X is a woman* is true in a context C [if and only if] X is human and relevantly similar (according to the standards at work in C) to most of those possessing all of the biological markers of female sex."[11]

On this definition, the term "woman" operates as an indexical: its content is determined by the specific context in which it is used since the standards for correct application of the concept contextually vary. However, despite this variability of content, the meaning of "woman" is still fixed in the sense that there is a single rule-governed way in which the content is determined. By analogy, while the indexical "I" changes its referent when different people utter it, the indexical still has a fixed "meaning" insofar as the referent is determined by the rule: "'I' refers to the person

---

* Surgical procedures on the breasts of transgender patients.

who utters it."[12] Because of this, I consider contextualism to endorse a single-meaning position.

In the account Saul considers, there can be a context C_1 in which the relevant similarity (for correct application of the term "woman") involves "sincerely self-identifying as a woman" and another context C_2 in which the relevant similarity involves "having XX chromosomes."[13] Thus, whether a trans woman counts as a woman depends on which standards are relevant in a given context. One of the benefits of this view is that it makes it possible for any trans woman (regardless of whether she has undergone medical procedures) to count as woman. It does this by allowing for contexts in which the standard of self-identification is salient in determining correct applicability. It also has the advantage that when trans women count as women in context C_1, they do so for metaphysical reasons, that is, for reasons owing to the semantics of the term "woman" and the facts that obtain in the world of that context rather than for political reasons or decisions.

Despite these advantages, however, the account has problems. One major worry Saul raises with this account is that while it allows a trans woman to assert something true when she says, "I am a woman," it trivializes her assertion. For the enforcer is also correct. Explaining the worry, Saul says:

> The reason the trans woman's claims are true, on the contextualist view, is simply that there are a huge range of acceptable ways to use the term "woman" and the trans woman's way of using "woman" isn't ruled out.... What the trans woman needs to do justice to her claim is surely not just the acknowledgement that her claim is true but also the acknowledgement that her opponent's claim is false.[14]

A second, related worry is that in questions concerning whether a trans woman is a woman, there does not seem to be room for metaphysical disagreement. First, note that this question is going to have to be context sensitive. That is, the question whether a trans woman is a woman must be relative to a given context. So the question comes down to which standards are applicable in a given context (say, for example, the context of restroom use). But the only way to make sense of the dispute is to see it as a political

one. That is, the only way to arbitrate the dispute is by appealing to political and moral facts. Meditating on the word "woman" is probably not going to yield an answer. As Saul explains, "On my view of woman, I cannot argue that the lawmakers are making a mistake about how the word 'woman' works. But what I can do is argue that they are morally and politically wrong to apply the standards that they do."[15] While trans women can claim womanhood as a metaphysical fact (relative to a context), in cases of controversy over which standards apply in a particular context, their status as women is once again decided by the political rather than the metaphysical.

Consider two additional concerns. First, there are no similar consequences for most non-trans women because most non-trans women are going to count as women *on almost any reasonable standard* (e.g., self-identification, karyotype, and reproductive capacity). Because of this, there is far less room for somebody to truthfully deny her womanhood (relative to some context). And in cases of dispute over which standards are relevant, most non-trans women count as women regardless of which standards are selected. That is, the question whether non-trans women count as women need not be decided by political decision (largely because the need for a decision would not arise). Most non-trans women would count as women across all or most contexts ("transcontextually"). In this sense, most non-trans women would count as paradigms of "woman." By contrast, trans women would not count as women transcontextually since there are obvious contexts when they do not count (e.g., when karyotype is salient), and so there are cases in which it is controversial whether trans women are women (it is controversial, that is, which standards to apply).

The second, related worry is that there will be certain contexts in which some trans women do count as men due to the fact that they have an XY karyotype, or a penis, or testes. A variation of an example Saul considers is the use of "woman" and "man" by the American Cancer Society when testing for prostate cancer. If it is decided that men of a certain age should be tested, then all trans women who are of that age would count as men in that specific context. The difficulty is that the trans women might not count themselves as men at all in *any* context, or they might not consider their prostates to undermine their claims to (trans) womanhood. Indeed, I know many trans women, for example, who are content with their "male genitalia." However, many do not consider them *male* genitalia in the first place, but the sort of genitalia congruent with transgender femaleness. Similarly, I know many trans men who have no interest in phalloplasty* and who consider their genitalia (transgender) *male* genitalia. Often, what happens is that the social meaning commonly associated with a body part is, in a subcultural context, completely changed. In light of this, a trans woman might reasonably complain that testing for prostate cancer cannot be viewed in terms of testing only men (or males). Such a claim, she might argue, is transphobic in that it erases the existence of trans women by treating them as nothing but (non-trans) men. Instead, once trans women are taken seriously, the testing ought to be framed in terms of testing both non-trans men and trans women of a certain age. More simply, the testing could be done on *people* with prostates. That testicles, penises, XY karyotype, and prostates count as *male* in the first place is precisely what trans subcultures are *contesting*.

The Multiple-Meaning Position

As there are different gendered practices in different cultural contexts, the conflict over meaning exhibits itself in the contrast between dominant or mainstream culture and trans subcultures. This includes the practice of gender attribution. So a trans person can count as "really a man" according to dominant cultural practices while counting as a woman in friendlier trans subcultures.[16]

It is a fact that in some trans community contexts, the meanings of gender terms (such as "woman") are altered and their extensions broadened. This is a two-step process. First, "trans woman" is taken as a basic expression, not as a qualification of the dominant meaning of "woman." This means that whether someone is a trans woman does not depend primarily on questions about the applicability of the terms "man" and "woman." Recall that on the enforcer's view,

"trans woman" means "fake woman" because "woman" does not apply to the individual (despite her "trying to pass herself off" as one). By contrast, on the family resemblance view, being a "trans woman" depends on one's counting as a woman *simpliciter*.† On that view, it seems that only some trans women would count (and marginally so); as we saw above, trans women would have at best a mixture of family resemblance features and so would at best count as difficult cases. As to contextualism, there are at least two possibilities. The first is that when a trans woman does not count as a woman she also does not count as a "trans woman" (i.e., transitional woman). The second is that "trans woman" means "fake woman" in some contexts and "transitional woman" in others.

When I say that "trans woman" is basic I mean that it does not route through the question whether "woman" applies or not; that is, the criteria for the correct application of "trans woman" do not depend on the criteria governing the application of "woman." The criteria are roughly equivalent to the criteria governing "male-to-female trans person." Crudely, a person counts as a trans woman if she was assigned to the male sex at birth, currently lives as a woman, and self-identifies as a trans woman (or as a woman).[17] This means that "trans woman" applies *unproblematically* and *without qualification* to all self-identified trans women. For example, even if a trans woman has no surgical or hormonal changes in her body (while "living as a woman"), she can still count as a paradigm instance of "trans woman."

The second step is that being a trans woman is a sufficient condition for being a woman. "Woman" is then taken to apply to *both* trans and non-trans women (where "non-trans woman" is a person who counts as a woman but who does not count as a trans woman). We thereby end up with entirely new criteria for who is a woman (specified in the criteria for counting a person as a trans woman). And we end up with an extension‡ of "woman" different from the one that refers to only non-trans women (and to trans women who have just enough features to be argued into the category).

---

* Surgical construction of a penis.

† Latin: "in the most complete sense, without qualification."

‡ The extension of a term is the set of things to which that term correctly applies (e.g., the extension of "green" is the set of all and only green things).

Indeed, we end up with a notion of "woman" on which a trans woman is a paradigmatic (rather than a borderline) case. Thus, the expression "non-trans woman" operates in the way that "woman" used to operate. "Woman," by contrast, now operates in such a way that it applies to trans women unproblematically. The same shift can occur with terms such as "female" and "male." Subculturally, what counts as male and female is broadened. So we can have trans women/females with penises and trans men/males with vaginas (although it is not clear even that terms such as "penis" and "vagina" would always be used in such cases). In such a context, a vagina would not necessarily be female and a penis would not necessarily be male.

The worry with this account is that it also (like the semantic contextualist approach but in a different way) trivializes the claims of trans women (and men). One might say, "*Of course* you're a teapot, if by 'teapot' we mean 'human being.' And *of course* you're a woman if by 'woman' we mean 'man who lives as a woman.'" The account, however, is no verbal trick but tracks a difference between cultural practices of gender and the relation of these practices to the interpretation of the body and self-presentation. Whether one is viewed as a "gender rebel" depends on interpretation. If one were viewed as a man, then one's gender presentation would be read as a form of "gender bending" if one wears a skirt. But if the same person were viewed as a woman, then her gender presentation would not be construed as misaligned with her status. The key is whether genitalia are viewed as necessary to one's normative* gender status. Since in trans subcultural practices they are not, then in trans subculture a normative social status is reassigned in a very real way: what would count as gender non-normative (in the mainstream) is entirely normative (in the subculture).

This affects the way sex is segregated. To be sure, in trans subcultural formations there is no control over institutions (such as jail housing and strip-search requirements). But there can certainly be control over the way bodies may be subject to different privacy and decency boundaries. For example, "normally" a man's chest is not subject to taboos against nudity, but in trans subcultures, it might be read as a woman's chest or at least a chest that is subject to such taboos.

So this conflict of meaning is undergirded by a conflict in gender practice. And this gendered practice informs (and is informed by) a basic conception (or narrative) of how the world is composed of various different types of gendered people. There is a genuine dispute concerning two competing visions of gender. And the taken-for-granted assumption that the dominant cultural view is the only valid one can be seen as a kind of cultural arrogance bolstered by institutional power.

Consider someone who lives as a woman, sees herself as a woman, and has been sustained in a subculture that respects her intimacy boundaries, only to find that she is subject to violence because she is "really male." She goes through mainstream institutions (hospitals, jails) where she is housed as male, searched as male, and turned away from a shelter as male. This invalidation is not only of an individual's self-identity but also of an entire life that has been lived with dignity in a competing cultural world.[18] My point is that this conflict over meaning is deeply bound up with the distribution of power and the capacity to enforce a way of life, regardless of the emotional and physical damage done to the individual.

The multiple-meaning view allows us to avoid the difficulties that plague the family resemblance account, for according to my view, all trans women count as women and do so paradigmatically, not marginally. And trans women count as women not owing to a political decision that arises as a consequence of their status as "difficult cases" but owing to the metaphysical facts that accord with the very meaning of the word "man" and "woman" *as deployed in trans subcultures*. That is, from the perspective of trans subculture, the enforcer who denies that a trans woman is a woman would be *making an error* every bit as much as if he were to call a non-trans woman a man.

My view also avoids some of the difficulties that plague semantic contextualism. This might not be obvious since the multiple-meaning account might seem to be merely a version of it, given that it seems I have only added a new context-relative standard. In particular, one might worry that this account is open to the following objections that suggest its similarity to semantic contextualism. First, while it is true that from the perspective of trans subculture the enforcer

---

*   Having to do with prevailing social values or norms.

is incorrect in denying that a trans woman is a woman, it is also true that from the perspective of dominant culture he is correct. Since the trans woman cannot claim that the enforcer's view is false, her self-identity claim is trivialized. In this way, the account is similar to semantic contextualism. Second, the decision regarding which perspective to take (the dominant or the resistant one) is a political one. So whether a trans woman counts as a woman is again a political decision. By contrast, a non-trans woman will count as a woman regardless of such political decisions; there is an asymmetry. Again, this is a problem that also plagued semantic contextualism. Replying to these objections helps show how my account differs from contextualism. I start with the first objection.

First, a trans woman can reject the entire dominant gender system as based on false beliefs about gender and gender practices that are harmful and even oppressive.[19] That is, while she might agree that she is not a woman in dominant culture, she can reject, on philosophical grounds, the entire system of gender that dominant cultures circulate. To see this, consider the following analogy. According to an evangelical account of "sinner," I would count as one. But it does not follow that I am one even though I might meet all the criteria of the evangelical account. In rejecting the claim that I'm a sinner, I'm rejecting the entire picture of the world in which that term has its definition fixed. Similarly, a trans woman can reject as false the claim that she is "really a man" by rejecting the entire system of gender in which that claim is true (on the grounds discussed above). This move does not work in the case of semantic contextualism, of course, since a trans woman who fails to accept that there are some contexts (e.g., karyotype-salient contexts) in which she is not a woman is simply wrong. On the multiple-meaning view, a trans woman can say that she is a woman in all legitimate contexts because those contexts in which she is not a woman occur in a dominant culture that has been rejected for the reasons mentioned above. She can argue that the very belief in contexts in which she counts as a man (for example, a context in which genital structure is relevant) rests on the assumption that penises are male and is therefore grounded in a vision that marginalizes trans women from the start.

Once we accept this response, we obviously also need to recognize that the shift in usage is *far more radical* than the mere introduction of a new contextually relative standard. It makes more sense to speak of a transformation in meaning or concept than to speak of a new contextually relative standard. Put another way, there are actually two concepts and two meanings of "womanhood." The two concepts (and the two meanings) are related in that the latter is the result of changes performed on the former. One starts with a particular concept and then expands it, for example, to include something that wasn't included in it before. This makes sense if we think of gender concepts as determined, in part, by underlying gender practices and conceptions of what a gendered world is. Once practice and conception seriously change, one can plausibly argue that the concepts change as well.

This allows us to reply to the second objection: we need not think that trans women only count as women on the basis of a political decision while non-trans women do not. Given that we can now speak of two concepts of "womanhood" (a dominant one and a resistant one), the question, "Are trans women really women?" does not get off the ground. Instead, we need to disambiguate the two concepts. A preoperative trans woman might be a woman-R ("woman" in the resistant sense) but not as a woman-D ("woman" in the dominant sense). She would be a woman-R and fail to be a woman-D not as a matter of political decision but metaphysically speaking. The political question, instead, concerns which concept we should take seriously, and this is connected to the larger question regarding which gendered vision of the world (if any) we commit to. Notably, these questions do not arise because of trans women counting as "difficult cases." And these questions also confront non-trans women. A non-trans woman who self-identifies as a woman-D can be seen as taking up a political stance that marginalizes trans women by endorsing a transphobic gendered view of the world. Or a feminist project that proceeds with the concept women-D could be viewed as anti-trans. In my account, the worry is not that non-trans women alone count as paradigmatic women. The worry, rather, is that a non-trans woman can avail herself of a concept (that is part of a larger gendered vision of the world) that marginalizes trans women. When a non-trans woman accepts this concept about what counts as a woman-D, this is the effect of privilege, not of it being the case that she is a paradigmatic woman while trans women are not.

So the multiple-meaning account I have outlined is not a variant of semantic contextualism, for it can solve the problems that confronted that account. Insofar as it squares with the reality of trans subcultural usage while addressing these problems, it seems to be the best account for our purposes. And by taking the multiple-meaning account seriously, we can now see some basic problems with both the Wrong Body Model and the Transgender Model.

Starting Points for Trans Stories

This distinction between the single-meaning and multiple-meaning positions reveals something important about starting points in trans politics. Consider the question (among some non-trans feminists) whether trans women do or do not count as women. In raising such a question, trans women are viewed as difficult cases with respect to the category "woman." In this way, the inclusion of trans women in the category of "woman" is something in need of defense (unlike the taken-for-granted inclusion of non-trans women). Notably, this asymmetry, which places the womanhood of trans women in jeopardy, arises only if we assume the dominant understanding of "woman." If we assume a resistant understanding of "woman," no question arises since trans women are exemplars of womanhood. While it might sometimes be a useful strategy to assume a dominant understanding of "woman" in order to defend the inclusion of trans women (as difficult cases), an unquestioned assumption of the dominant understanding is a bad starting point in trans politics and theory. It ignores resistant meanings produced in trans subcultures, thereby leaving us scrambling to find a home in the dominant meanings, those meanings that marginalize us from the get-go.

Consider an analogy. When I teach an undergraduate course in the philosophy of gender, I examine arguments that purport to show the immorality of "homosexuality."[20] I try to show students why these arguments are unsound because it is important to debunk the (bad) arguments that harm lesbian, gay, bisexual, and transsexual (LGBT) people. However, in a graduate seminar in LGBT studies, I would not engage this issue because this would play into the hands of a heterosexist cultural asymmetry that places homosexuality in moral jeopardy while leaving the moral status of heterosexuality unquestioned—a questionable political starting point.

Similarly, it is a questionable political starting point to accept as valid the dominant understanding of gender categories that situate trans people as, at best, problematic cases. To be sure, it might be a useful strategy to adopt the dominant understanding in particular situations. But I worry about any theory designed to illuminate trans oppression or resistance that unreflectively accepts a dominant understanding of categories.

In the Wrong Body Model, one counts as a woman-D (at best) to some degree and with qualification, so long as an appropriate authority recognizes one as possessing the right gender identity and one undergoes, as much as possible, a transformative process to conform to the dominant concept of woman. A dominant understanding of the category is presupposed and an asymmetry is tacitly accepted whereby trans membership in the category requires justification. As a consequence, trans people who do not value genital reconstruction surgery are taken not to have the right gender identity, and they are delegitimated as "mere" crossdressers. A result of the Wrong Body Model's affiliation with dominant meanings is that trans people who live their lives with dignity in different subcultural worlds of meaning are simply kicked to the curb.

The Transgender Model also marginalizes trans people. It presupposes a dominant understanding of the categories "man" and "woman" under which trans people fit only marginally or as difficult cases not easily categorized. Here, a trans person would be—at most—legitimized as a (marginal) woman through somehow arguing that she meets enough of the dominant criteria of membership. Similarly, a trans person could be legitimized as "in-between" by showing under which dominant categories the person falls and does not fall. In both cases, the dominant understanding is presupposed and the position of trans people vis-à-vis the categories is justified by pointing to the criteria of membership in *these categories* (unlike non-trans people who are accepted as paradigmatic of the dominant categories and therefore in no need of justification). Once we take resistant meanings seriously, however, it is no longer clear why a trans person who sees herself as a woman is only marginally so at best. And it is far from clear why certain bodies count as in-between. Once trans men and trans women are taken as paradigms of concepts like "man" and "woman," it becomes doubtful that their bodies are problematic or in-between. Perversely, then, the Transgender Model, like the Wrong Body Model, ends up dismissing the lived lives of trans people.

Final Remarks

As I have framed it, there is a different and expanded notion of womanhood in trans subcultures. Although I have spoken as if there is only one understanding, this is misleading because trans subculture is generally replete with multiple and sometimes conflicting accounts of gender. After all, it is hard to be trans and avoid thinking a little bit about what a woman is, what a man is, what gender is, and the like. Gender terms ("trans," "transgender," "transsexual," "woman," etc.) simply won't stay put. Instead of understanding "trans woman" as a subcategory of an expanded category of womanhood, trans women may also be conceptualized as in-between with respect to the traditional categories where they do not count as women *simpliciter* (i.e., as non-trans women) who *are* seen as part of the binary. It is just not obvious how trans people are going to understand the term "woman" when they self-identify (or do not self-identify) with that term.

Such variability is not an "anything goes" approach. In trans subcultures, the use of these gender terms is subject to some constraint. Moreover, there is a fairly common linguistic practice. Claims about self-identity in (some) trans subcultures have the form of first-person, present-tense avowals of mental attitudes (e.g. "I am angry at you").[21] This means that the shift in meaning involves not only an expansion of the category but also a change in use, reflected in the grammar of first- and thirdperson assertions. It is no longer merely a question whether the category is truthfully predicated of the object in question. Instead, there is a firstperson, present-tense avowal of gender. For example, the claim "I am a trans woman" may be an avowal of a deep sense of "who one is" (that is, of one's deepest values and commitments). And as such, this is the prerogative of the first person alone where

defensible avowals of gender are presumptively taken as authoritative. Fundamental to this practice is the idea that gender categories do not merely apply (or fail to apply) on the basis of objective criteria but are adopted for personal and political reasons. For example, the category "trans woman" might be avowed or disavowed because the category does not speak to "who they are," because it does not fit or feel right. Alternatively, it might be avowed or disavowed on solely political grounds. Insofar as such considerations are fundamental to the very practice of gender attribution in these contexts it is easy to see why this is such a shift from the dominant practice of gender attribution, which operates independently of such considerations. The shift makes room for the multiplicity of meaning by allowing first-person authority over both gender avowal and the very meaning of the avowal.

The point I have defended in this essay is that accounts that take for granted singular, fixed meanings of gender terms cannot plausibly provide a liberatory theory. Not only do such accounts go wrong by failing to square with the actual reality of the situation, namely the fact that central terms are used in trans contexts in multiple and contested ways; they actually undermine trans self-identifications by foreclosing the possibility of multiplicity. These accounts do so, in part, because they aim to justify the categorization of trans people by appealing to the dominant meanings. This, I have argued, implies an acceptance of a marginalizing asymmetry between trans and non-trans people from the beginning. To provide a satisfying account of trans phenomena, gender marginalization cannot be accepted as a starting point. The demand for justification and the demand for illumination are not the same. We need new accounts, I believe, that don't begin with a *justification* for trans self-identity claims but that follow subcultural practice in taking the presumptive legitimacy of such claims for granted. This requires recognizing the multiplicity of resistant meanings rather than acquiescing to the dominant culture's erasure of them. In my view, it is the only way to yield illuminating accounts of trans phenomena that do not proceed from transphobic starting points.[22] ■

Suggestions for Critical Reflection

1. Why does Bettcher object to the "family resemblance" approach to defining "woman"? Evaluate her objections.

2. Why does Bettcher object to the "semantic contextualist" approach to defining "woman"? Evaluate her objections.

3. Bettcher acknowledges that "one might worry" that the multiple-meaning approach "is open to ... objections that suggest its similarity to semantic contextualism." In your view, is the multiple-meaning approach sufficiently different from semantic contextualism to avoid its pitfalls? How clear is the distinction between a "context" and a "world"?

4. Bettcher criticizes definitions of "woman" that proceed from the assumption that non-trans women are women but that the womanhood of trans women requires demonstration. In your view, are there valid reasons to require demonstration of the womanhood of one group but not the other? Why or why not? If there are reasons, are they purely metaphysical or are they also to do with values?

5. Bettcher engages in this article with both metaphysical and political ideas. How are the metaphysical and the political related here? Is one given primacy over the other? Should it be?

6. Regarding the discussion of trans people in philosophy, Bettcher has said the following:

> I'm afraid there's a tendency among some philosophers to suppose that philosophical investigations into race, gender, disability, trans issues, and so forth are no different methodologically from investigations into the question whether tables really exist. One difference, however, is that while tables aren't part of the philosophical conversation, trans people, disabled people, people of color, are part of the conversation.*

How (if at all) is this view reflected in the methodology Bettcher uses in "Trans Women and the Meaning of 'Woman'"? To the extent that it is reflected, does it strengthen—or weaken—the persuasiveness of the article?

Notes

1 For some examples, see Henry Rubin, *Self-Made Men: Identity and Embodiment among Transsexual Men* (Nashville, Tenn.: Vanderbilt University Press, 2003), 150–51. Not all transsexuals have endorsed this view.

2 Christine Overall, "Sex/Gender Transitions and Life-Changing Aspirations," in *"You've Changed": Sex Reassignment and Personal Identity*, edited by Laurie Shrage (Oxford, U.K.: Oxford University Press, 2009), 11–27, at 14. The worry is that culturally determined gender behavior, beliefs, and attitudes are often very harmful to women. So it is troublesome to treat them as natural or as essential because it makes them seem unchangeable and even suggests that this "is how it is meant to be."

3 This account glosses over significant differences among thinkers such as Kate Bornstein, Leslie Feinberg, and Sandy Stone. See Kate Bornstein, *Gender Outlaw: On Men, Women, and the Rest of Us* (New York: Routledge, 1994); Leslie Feinberg, *Stone Butch Blues: A Novel* (Los Angeles: Alyson Books, 1993); Sandy Stone, "The Empire Strikes Back: A Posttransexual Manifesto," in *Body Guards: The Cultural Politics of Gender Ambiguity*, edited by Julia Epstein and Kristina Straub (New York: Routledge, 1991), 280–304. However, this account captures the general idea frequently assumed in discussions of trans issues. For a more in-depth discussion of the transgender paradigm, see Talia Mae Bettcher, "Feminist Perspectives on Trans Issues," http://plato.stanford.edu/entries/feminism-trans, *Stanford Encyclopedia of Philosophy*, edited by Edward N. Zalta (accessed March 10, 2012).

4 It is possible for variants of the Transgender Model to appeal to the notion of an innate gender identity. However, social constructionism about gender has definitely figured very prominently in this model.

5 By "naturalization" I mean that something cultural is treated as "natural" (that is, as independent of culture). In this case, I mean that gender identity is treated as

---

* Talia Mae Bettcher, "'When Tables Speak': On the Existence of Trans Philosophy," *Daily Nous*, May 30, 2018.

innate. By "pathologization" I mean that something nonpathological is treated as though it is pathological.

6 For a more detailed account of the basic denial of authenticity, see Talia Mae Bettcher, "Appearance, Reality, and Gender Deception: Reflections on Transphobic Violence and the Politics of Pretence," in *Violence, Victims, and Justifications*, edited by Felix Ó Murchadha (Bern: Peter Lang, 2006), 175–200.

7 For a detailed discussion of the sex/gender distinction in feminist theory, see Mari Mikkola, "Feminist Perspectives on Sex and Gender," plato.stanford.edu/entries/feminism-gender, *Stanford Encyclopedia of Philosophy*, edited by Edward N. Zalta (accessed March 10, 2012).

8 For this style of approach, see C. Jacob Hale, "Are Lesbians Women?" *Hypatia* 11:2 (Spring 1996): 94–121; John Corvino, "Analyzing Gender," *Southwest Philosophy Review* 17:1 (2000): 173–80; Cressida Heyes, *Line Drawings: Defining Women through Feminist Practice* (Ithaca, N.Y.: Cornell University Press, 2000); and Jennifer McKitrick "Gender Identity Disorder," in *Establishing Medical Reality: Essays in the Metaphysics and Epistemology of Biomedical Science*, edited by Harold Kincaid and Jennifer McKitrick (Dordrecht: Springer, 2007), 137–48.

9 See Corvino, "Analyzing Gender," 179, for this type of view.

10 I say "might" because I argue below that different trans women can mean different things by the expression "trans woman."

11 Jennifer Mather Saul, "Politically Significant Terms and the Philosophy of Language: Methodological Issues," in *Out from the Shadows: Analytical Feminist Contributions to Traditional Philosophy*, edited by Sharon L. Crasnow and Anita M. Superson (Oxford, U.K.: Oxford University Press, 2012), 195–216, at 201. Saul does not accept this account but uses it to develop the methodological point that very different considerations can inform analysis when the term is politically significant. For example, in analyzing "woman," Saul thinks that it is important to do justice to a trans woman's self-identity claims. Such intuitions are not easily explained away as they might be when we are not thinking of politically fraught cases precisely because so much more seems to hinge on them. She then suggests that this is relevant to philosophers of language more generally. My point is less methodological, although I'm obviously concerned to take the claims of trans women seriously. My proposed account does justice to trans women's self-identity claims in a way that a semantic contextualist account does not. Besides, I do draw on trans subcultures' use of gendered language as crucial data in my analysis of gender terms.

Taking seriously how trans people use the terms is often overlooked in analyses of these types.

12 My formulation of the rule is obviously too simple. But that doesn't matter for my purposes.

13 Saul, "Politically Significant Terms," 201, 203.

14 Saul, "Politically Significant Terms," 209–10.

15 Saul, "Politically Significant Terms," 204.

16 I am largely indebted to C. Jacob Hale for this type of view. See his "Leather Dyke Boys and Their Daddies: How to Have Sex without Men and Women," *Social Text* 52/53, 16:3–4 (1997): 223–36.

17 It is also possible to recognize somebody as a trans woman despite the fact that she has not yet "transitioned" and does not yet self-identify as a woman (or a trans woman) in case this person eventually transitions. Explaining this is actually quite tricky, however, so I won't worry about it in this paper. I am grateful to Jennifer Saul for pressing me to think about this more.

18 The notion of "world" originates in the work of Maria Lugones. My understanding of cultural conflicts over meaning is informed by her view. See her "Playfulness, 'World'-Travelling, and Loving Perception," *Hypatia: A Journal of Feminist Philosophy* 2:2 (Summer 1987): 3–19.

19 Here are some examples. One false belief is that gender terms only have single (dominant) meanings. Another is that all people are either "naturally" male or female. And, of course, there are many others that involve treating cultural phenomena as "natural" manifestations of gender. By "harmful gender practices" I mean to include those practices that involve treating trans people with violence and those that are sexist and sexually violent. For a discussion of these practices see Talia Mae Bettcher, "Evil Deceivers and Make-Believers: Transphobic Violence and the Politics of Illusion," *Hypatia: A Journal of Feminist Philosophy* 22:3 (Summer 2007): 43–65.

20 I have worries about the term "homosexuality" as it derives from a sexological framework in which same-sex sexuality is viewed as pathological.

21 For development of this view, see my "Trans Identities and First Person Authority," in *"You've Changed": Sex Reassignment and Personal Identity*, edited by Laurie Shrage (Oxford, U.K.: Oxford University Press, 2009): 98–120.

22 Parts of this essay were published as "Without a Net: Starting Points for Trans Stories," *American Philosophical Association LGBT Newsletter* 10:2 (Spring 2011): 2–5. I am grateful to the editor, William Wilkerson, for his comments. I am also grateful for the extremely helpful feedback by Raja Halwani and Nicholas Power in finalizing this version of the essay. I would also like to thank Jennifer Saul for her (always) insightful and constructive comments.

IRIS MARION YOUNG

Five Faces of Oppression

Who Was Iris Marion Young?

Iris Marion Young (1949–2006) was an American political theorist, philosopher, and activist, who is widely considered to be one of the most important political philosophers of the last quarter of the twentieth century. Her work focused on gender and race theory, global justice, continental political theory, and ethics. She was Professor of Political Science at the University of Chicago and was affiliated with the Center for Gender Studies there. One of her colleagues, Patchen Markell, said of her that "she was one of those scholars who practiced ... what she preached; in her case, a systematic egalitarianism and opposition to hierarchy."*

Young published a great deal of influential work but is best known for *Justice and the Politics of Difference* (1990), a landmark text in moral and political philosophy. In it, she critiques prevalent theories of justice and argues that liberal democracies have not only failed to address the structural oppressions that afflict social groups in capitalist states, but that they may in fact be involved in maintaining those oppressions. The book had an important influence in shaping identity politics and in offering an alternative set of criteria for analyzing the engrained power structures that continue to oppress groups in liberal democracies.

What Is the Structure of This Reading?

The following reading is excerpted from Chapter Two of *Justice and the Politics of Difference* (1990). In it, Young proposes a new conception of justice, which she terms an "enabling conception of justice," that includes but moves beyond distributive patterns to include other social phenomena: decision-making procedures, division of labor, and culture. Injustice, under this model, takes the forms of oppression and domination.

For Young, oppression describes structural phenomena that "immobilize or diminish a group in society." Oppression is a central category for contemporary political discourse, particularly for social movements that seek to free groups from injustice: socialists, feminists, Native American activists, Black activists, and LGBTQ activists (among others). Young focuses her analysis on structural oppression, which, in modern democracies, is embedded in social norms, habits, and symbols, and in the unconscious assumptions that shape institutions, the media, and all the other processes of daily life.

Young argues that social justice can best be achieved not by doing away with group distinctions, but by shaping institutions that respect differences among groups. She argues that groups should be understood in terms of a shared sense of identity. From this perspective, the self does not stand outside and prior to its group membership, but is instead shaped by social processes. Social groups, she states, should be fluid, and one must recognize that they are intersectional: they overlap, cut across one another, and are differentiated by many factors (such as age, nationality, sexuality, region, and class).

According to Young, we cannot use the concepts and language of liberalism effectively to analyze the oppression that is manifested in our social structures, because these concepts focus on the rights and freedoms of individuals rather than the welfare of social groups. With the "five faces of oppression," she offers instead a language and conceptual framework for identifying and analyzing group oppression.

She begins by explaining what she means by treating oppression as a *structural* concept, and then goes on to justify and defend her focus on social groups—rather than individuals—as the subject of oppression. In the

* Danielle Allen, Robert Gooding-Williams, Patchen Markell, John P. McCormick, Martha Nussbaum, Cass R. Sunstein, and Nathan Tarcov, "Iris Marion Young: Tributes from Her Colleagues in Political Theory at the University of Chicago," *PS: Political Science and Politics* 40, 1 (January 2007): 168–70.

next, main section of this chapter she introduces each of the "five faces" of oppression in turn: exploitation, marginalization, powerlessness, cultural imperialism, and violence. Her claim is that none of these forms of oppression can be reduced to—analyzed away in terms of—the others, and that together these five forms are adequate for understanding the important ways in which groups are oppressed in contemporary democratic societies, as well as the complex similarities and differences that exist among different groups' experience of oppression.

Some Useful Background Information

Young makes reference to models of distributive justice, such as those developed by John Rawls and Robert Nozick (see the chapter on Justice in this volume), which analyze justice primarily in terms of how society distributes goods—money, jobs, benefits, resources—among individuals in society. Young finds this approach problematic, because it focuses the discussion on possession: how much do individuals have, what don't they have, and how does what one individual has compare with what another has? Young prefers to focus on human behaviors and social processes that take place within institutions, to discover whether or not society is enabling people to flourish. She is also interested in seeking justice not only for the individual, but for groups. For example, even in societies where every individual is given the right to vote, that does not ensure that some oppressed minorities are not prevented by various means from exercising that right. Young is interested in developing a conception of justice that pays attention to oppressive processes and seeks for means to redress them.

Five Faces of Oppression*

Someone who does not see a pane of glass does not know that he does not see it. Someone who, being placed differently, does see it, does not know the other does not see it.

When our will finds expression outside ourselves in actions performed by others, we do not waste our time and our power of attention in examining whether they have consented to this. This is true for all of us. Our attention, given entirely to the success of the undertaking, is not claimed by them as long as they are docile....

Rape is a terrible caricature of love from which consent is absent. After rape, oppression is the second horror of human existence. It is a terrible caricature of obedience.

—Simone Weil[†]

I have proposed an enabling conception of justice. Justice should refer not only to distribution, but also to the institutional conditions necessary for the development and exercise of individual capacities and collective communication and cooperation. Under this conception of justice, injustice refers primarily to two forms of disabling constraints, oppression and domination. While these constraints include distributive patterns,[‡] they also involve matters which cannot easily be assimilated to the logic of distribution: decision-making procedures, division of labor, and culture....

In this chapter I offer some explication of the concept of oppression as I understand its use by new social movements in the United States since the 1960s. My starting point is reflection on the conditions of the groups said by these movements to be oppressed: among others women, Blacks, Chicanos,[§] Puerto Ricans and other Spanish-speaking Americans,

---

* "Five Faces of Oppression" is Chapter 2 of Young's *Justice and the Politics of Difference* (Princeton University Press, 1990).

† French philosopher and mystic (1909–43). This quotation is taken from her 1943 essay, "Are We Struggling for Justice?"

‡ Patterns in how goods are distributed—the subject of distributive justice.

§ Chicano or Chicana is a chosen identity of some Mexican Americans in the United States.

American Indians, Jews, lesbians, gay men, Arabs, Asians, old people, working-class people, and the physically and mentally disabled. I aim to systematize the meaning of the concept of oppression as used by these diverse political movements, and to provide normative argument to clarify the wrongs the term names.

Obviously the above-named groups are not oppressed to the same extent or in the same ways. In the most general sense, all oppressed people suffer some inhibition of their ability to develop and exercise their capacities and express their needs, thoughts, and feelings. In that abstract sense all oppressed people face a common condition. Beyond that, in any more specific sense, it is not possible to define a single set of criteria that describe the condition of oppression of the above groups. Consequently, attempts by theorists and activists to discover a common description or the essential causes of the oppression of all these groups have frequently led to fruitless disputes about whose oppression is more fundamental or more grave. The contexts in which members of these groups use the term oppression to describe the injustices of their situation suggest that oppression names in fact a family of concepts and conditions, which I divide into five categories: exploitation, marginalization, powerlessness, cultural imperialism, and violence.

In this chapter I explicate each of these forms of oppression. Each may entail or cause distributive injustices, but all involve issues of justice beyond distribution. In accordance with ordinary political usage, I suggest that oppression is a condition of groups....

Oppression as a Structural Concept

New left social movements of the 1960s and 1970s ... shifted the meaning of the concept of oppression. In its new usage, oppression designates the disadvantage and injustice some people suffer not because a tyrannical power coerces them, but because of the everyday practices of a well-intentioned liberal* society. In this new left usage, the tyranny of a ruling group over

another, as in South Africa, must certainly be called oppressive. But oppression also refers to systemic constraints on groups that are not necessarily the result of the intentions of a tyrant. Oppression in this sense is structural, rather than the result of a few people's choices or policies. Its causes are embedded in unquestioned norms, habits, and symbols, in the assumptions underlying institutional rules and the collective consequences of following those rules. It names, as Marilyn Frye puts it, "an enclosing structure of forces and barriers which tends to the immobilization and reduction of a group or category of people" (Frye, 1983, p. 11). In this extended structural sense oppression refers to the vast and deep injustices some groups suffer as a consequence of often unconscious assumptions and reactions of well-meaning people in ordinary interactions, media and cultural stereotypes, and structural features of bureaucratic hierarchies and market mechanisms—in short, the normal processes of everyday life. We cannot eliminate this structural oppression by getting rid of the rulers or making some new laws, because oppressions are systematically reproduced in major economic, political, and cultural institutions.

The systemic character of oppression implies that an oppressed group need not have a correlate oppressing group. While structural oppression involves relations among groups, these relations do not always fit the paradigm of conscious and intentional oppression of one group by another. Foucault† (1977) suggests that to understand the meaning and operation of power in modern society we must look beyond the model of power as "sovereignty," a dyadic relation‡ of ruler and subject, and instead analyze the exercise of power as the effect of often liberal and "humane" practices of education, bureaucratic administration, production and distribution of consumer goods, medicine, and so on. The conscious actions of many individuals daily contribute to maintaining and reproducing oppression, but those people are usually simply doing their jobs or living their lives, and do not understand themselves as agents of oppression.

---

*   The term "liberal" or "liberalism" has been applied to a family of historical and contemporary political views. In this context, liberalism can be broadly characterized as the view that individual freedoms and rights are central to the functioning of society.
†   Michel Foucault (1926–84), French philosopher and historian.
‡   A relationship between two individuals.

I do not mean to suggest that within a system of oppression individual persons do not intentionally harm others in oppressed groups. The raped woman, the beaten Black youth, the locked-out worker, the gay man harassed on the street, are victims of intentional actions by identifiable agents. I also do not mean to deny that specific groups are beneficiaries of the oppression of other groups, and thus have an interest in their continued oppression. Indeed, for every oppressed group there is a group that is *privileged* in relation to that group....

I offer below an explication of five faces of oppression as a useful set of categories and distinctions which I believe is comprehensive, in the sense that it covers all the groups said by new left social movements to be oppressed and all the ways they are oppressed. I derive the five faces of oppression from reflection on the condition of these groups. Because different factors, or combinations of factors, constitute the oppression of different groups, making their oppression irreducible, I believe it is not possible to give one essential definition of oppression. The five categories articulated in this chapter, however, are adequate to describe the oppression of any group, as well as its similarities with and differences from the oppression of other groups. But first we must ask what a group is.

The Concept of a Social Group

Oppression refers to structural phenomena that immobilize or diminish a group. But what is a group? Our ordinary discourse differentiates people according to social groups such as women and men, age groups, racial and ethnic groups, religious groups, and so on. Social groups of this sort are not simply collections of people, for they are more fundamentally intertwined with the identities of the people described as belonging to them. They are a specific kind of collectivity, with specific consequences for how people understand one another and themselves. Yet neither social theory nor philosophy has a clear and developed concept of the social group (see Turner et al., 1987).

A social group is a collective of persons differentiated from at least one other group by cultural forms, practices, or way of life. Members of a group have a specific affinity with one another because of their similar experience or way of life, which prompts them to associate with one another more than with those not identified with the group, or in a different way. Groups are an expression of social relations; a group exists only in relation to at least one other group. Group identification arises, that is, in the encounter and interaction between social collectivities that experience some differences in their way of life and forms of association, even if they regard themselves as belonging to the same society....

[Groups] constitute individuals. A person's particular sense of history, affinity, and separateness, even the person's mode of reasoning, evaluating, and expressing feeling, are constituted partly by her or his group affinities. This does not mean that persons have no individual styles, or are unable to transcend or reject a group identity. Nor does it preclude persons from having many aspects that are independent of these group identities.

The social ontology underlying many contemporary theories of justice is methodologically individualist or atomist.* It presumes that the individual is ontologically prior to the social. This individualist social ontology usually goes together with a normative conception of the self as independent. The authentic self is autonomous, unified, free, and self-made, standing apart from history and affiliations, choosing its life plan entirely for itself.

One of the main contributions of poststructuralist† philosophy has been to expose as illusory this metaphysic of a unified self-making subjectivity, which posits the subject as an autonomous origin or

---

* In social and political philosophy, atomist theories are those that view individual action as the basis for understanding the whole—that is, group behaviors can be understood wholly through describing the behaviors of separate individuals, and furthermore that those individual actions can each be fully understood without making reference to the whole. An 'ontology' is a view about what sorts of individual things and groups of things are the basic constituents of some domain.

† Poststructuralism is a mid-twentieth-century European philosophical movement defined by its opposition to the prior theory of structuralism. *Structuralism* is a view of human culture which sees it as a meaningful structure, rather like a conceptual scheme, that is distinct from 'raw' concrete reality and is our way of interpreting that reality—all the

an underlying substance to which attributes of gender, nationality, family role, intellectual disposition, and so on might attach. Conceiving the subject in this fashion implies conceiving consciousness as outside of and prior to language and the context of social interaction, which the subject enters. Several currents of recent philosophy challenge this deeply held Cartesian assumption.* Lacanian psychoanalysis,[†] for example, and the social and philosophical theory influenced by it, conceive the self as an achievement of linguistic positioning that is always contextualized in concrete relations with other persons, with their mixed identities (Coward and Ellis, 1977). The self is a product of social processes, not their origin.

From a rather different perspective, Habermas[‡] indicates that theory of communicative action also must challenge the "philosophy of consciousness" which locates intentional egos as the ontological origins of social relations. A theory of communicative action conceives individual identity not as an origin but as a product of linguistic and practical interaction (Habermas, 1987; pp. 3–40). As Stephen Epstein describes it, identity is a "socialized sense of individuality, an internal organization of self-perception concerning one's relationship to social categories, that also incorporates views of the self perceived to be held by others. Identity is constituted relationally, through involvement with—and incorporation of—significant others and integration into communities" (Epstein, 1987, p. 29). Group categorization and norms are major constituents of individual identity (see Turner et al., 1987).

A person joins an association, and even if membership in it fundamentally affects one's life, one does not take that membership to define one's very identity, in the way, for example, being Navaho might. Group affinity, on the other hand, has the character of what Martin Heidegger[§] (1962) calls "thrownness": one *finds oneself* as a member of a group, which one experiences as always already having been. For our identities are defined in relation to how others identify us, and they do so in terms of groups which are always already associated with specific attributes, stereotypes, and norms.

From the thrownness of group affinity it does not follow that one cannot leave groups and enter new ones. Many women become lesbian after first identifying as heterosexual. Anyone who lives long enough becomes old. These cases exemplify thrownness precisely because such changes in group affinity are experienced as transformations in one's identity. Nor does it follow from the thrownness of group affinity that one cannot define the meaning of group identity for oneself; those who identify with a group can redefine the meaning and norms of group identity. The present point is only that one first finds a group identity as given, and then takes it up in a certain way. While groups may come into being, they are never founded....

[S]ome people think that social groups are invidious fictions, essentializing arbitrary attributes. From this point of view problems of prejudice, stereotyping, discrimination, and exclusion exist because some people mistakenly believe that group identification makes a difference to the capacities, temperament, or virtues of group members. This individualist conception of persons and their relation to one another tends to identify oppression with group identification. Oppression, on this view, is something that happens to people when they are classified in groups. Because others identify them as a group, they are excluded and despised. Eliminating oppression thus requires eliminating groups. People should be treated as individuals, not as members of groups, and allowed to form their lives freely without stereotypes or group norms.

---

phenomena of human life can be made intelligible by revealing their place in this overall, interconnecting structure. There are several varieties of *poststructuralism*, but what they have in common is their rejection of the notion of a unified, universal, ahistorical conceptual structure. Leading poststructuralist figures include Jacques Derrida, Michel Foucault, Gilles Deleuze, Judith Butler, Jean Baudrillard, and Julia Kristeva.

*   In this context, the view that a person can be understood as—and begins as—an isolated individual, separate from and prior to any particular social context (e.g., any particular language or set of cultural assumptions). This view is associated with René Descartes (1596–1650), who understood persons as metaphysically self-sufficient non-physical souls that can exist even without a physical body, never mind a social setting.

†   Theories of psychoanalysis put forward by French theorist and psychiatrist Jacques Lacan (1901–81).

‡   German philosopher and social theorist Jürgen Habermas (b. 1929).

§   Martin Heidegger (1889–1976) was an influential German philosopher.

[I take] issue with that position. While I agree that individuals should be free to pursue life plans in their own way, it is foolish to deny the reality of groups. Despite the modern myth of a decline of parochial attachments and ascribed identities, in modern society group differentiation remains endemic. As both markets and social administration increase the web of social interdependency on a world scale, and as more people encounter one another as strangers in cities and states, people retain and renew ethnic, locale, age, sex, and occupational group identifications, and form new ones in the processes of encounter (cf. Ross, 1980, p. 19; Rothschild, 1981, p. 130). Even when they belong to oppressed groups, people's group identifications are often important to them, and they often feel a special affinity for others in their group. I believe that group differentiation is both an inevitable and a desirable aspect of modern social processes. Social justice ... requires not the melting away of differences, but institutions that promote reproduction of and respect for group differences without oppression.

Though some groups have come to be formed out of oppression, and relations of privilege and oppression structure the interactions between many groups, group differentiation is not in itself oppressive. Not all groups are oppressed. In the United States Roman Catholics are a specific social group, with distinct practices and affinities with one another, but they are no longer an oppressed group. Whether a group is oppressed depends on whether it is subject to one or more of the five conditions I shall discuss below.

The view that groups are fictions does carry an important antideterminist or antiessentialist intuition. Oppression has often been perpetrated by a conceptualization of group difference in terms of unalterable essential natures that determine what group members deserve or are capable of, and that exclude groups so entirely from one another that they have no similarities or overlapping attributes. To assert that it is possible to have social group difference without oppression, it is necessary to conceptualize groups in a much more relational and fluid fashion....

Arising from social relations and processes, finally, group differences usually cut across one another.

Especially in a large, complex, and highly differentiated society, social groups are not themselves homogeneous, but mirror in their own differentiations many of the other groups in the wider society. In American society today, for example, Blacks are not a simple, unified group with a common life. Like other racial and ethnic groups, they are differentiated by age, gender, class, sexuality, region, and nationality, any of which in a given context may become a salient group identity.

This view of group differentiation as multiple, cross-cutting, fluid, and shifting implies another critique of the model of the autonomous, unified self. In complex, highly differentiated societies like our own, all persons have multiple group identifications. The culture, perspective, and relations of privilege and oppression of these various groups, moreover, may not cohere. Thus individual persons, as constituted partly by their group affinities and relations, cannot be unified, themselves are heterogeneous and not necessarily coherent.

The Faces of Oppression

EXPLOITATION

The central function of Marx's* theory of exploitation is to explain how class structure can exist in the absence of legally and normatively sanctioned class distinctions. In precapitalist societies domination is overt and accomplished through directly political means. In both slave society and feudal society the right to appropriate the product of the labor of others partly defines class privilege, and these societies legitimate class distinctions with ideologies of natural superiority and inferiority.

Capitalist society, on the other hand, removes traditional juridically enforced class distinctions and promotes a belief in the legal freedom of persons. Workers freely contract with employers and receive a wage; no formal mechanisms of law or custom force them to work for that employer or any employer. Thus the mystery of capitalism arises: when everyone is formally free, how can there be class domination? Why do class distinctions persist between the wealthy, who

---

* German political theorist and philosopher Karl Marx (1818–83): see the reading by Marx and Engels in the Justice chapter of this volume.

own the means of production, and the mass of people, who work for them? The theory of exploitation answers this question....

The injustice of capitalist society consists in the fact that some people exercise their capacities under the control, according to the purposes, and for the benefit of other people. Through private ownership of the means of production, and through markets that allocate labor and the ability to buy goods, capitalism systematically transfers the powers of some persons to others, thereby augmenting the power of the latter. In this process of the transfer of powers, according to Macpherson (1973), the capitalist class acquires and maintains an ability to extract benefits from workers. Not only are powers transferred from workers to capitalists, but also the powers of workers diminish by more than the amount of transfer, because workers suffer material deprivation and a loss of control, and hence are deprived of important elements of self-respect. Justice, then, requires eliminating the institutional forms that enable and enforce this process of transference and replacing them with institutional forms that enable all to develop and use their capacities in a way that does not inhibit, but rather can enhance, similar development and use in others.

The central insight expressed in the concept of exploitation, then, is that this oppression occurs through a steady process of the transfer of the results of this labor of one social group to benefit another. The injustice of class division does not consist only in the distributive fact that some people have great wealth while most people have little (cf. Buchanan, 1982, pp. 44–49; Holmstrom 1977). Exploitation enacts a structural relation between social groups. Social rules about what work is, who does what for whom, how work is compensated, and the social process by which the results of work are appropriated operate to enact relations of power and inequality. These relations are produced and reproduced through a systematic process in which the energies of the have-nots are continuously expended to maintain and augment the power, status, and wealth of the haves.

Many writers have cogently argued that the Marxist concept of exploitation is too narrow to encompass all forms of domination and oppression (Giddens, 1981, p. 242; Brittan and Maynard, 1984, p. 93; Murphy, 1985; Bowles and Giotis, 1986, pp. 20–24). In particular, the Marxist concept of class leaves important phenomena of sexual and racial oppression unexplained. Does this mean that sexual and racial oppression are nonexploitative, and that we should reserve wholly distinct categories for these oppressions? Or can the concept of exploitation be broadened to include other ways in which the labor and energy expenditure of one group benefits another, and reproduces a relation of domination between them?

Feminists have had little difficulty showing that women's oppression consists partly in a systematic and unreciprocated transfer of powers from women to men. Women's oppression consists not merely in an inequality of status, power, and wealth resulting from men's excluding them from privileged activities. The freedom, power, status, and self-realization of men is possible precisely because women work for them. Gender exploitation has two aspects, transfer of the fruits of material labor to men and transfer of nurturing and sexual energies to men....

Race is a structure of oppression at least as basic as class or gender. Are there, then, racially specific forms of exploitation? There is no doubt that racialized groups in the United States, especially Blacks and Latinos, are oppressed through capitalist superexploitation* resulting from a segmented labor market that tends to reserve skilled, high-paying, unionized jobs for whites. There is wide disagreement about whether such superexploitation benefits whites as a group or only benefits the capitalist class (see Reich, 1981), and I do not intend to enter into that dispute here.

However one answers the question about capitalist superexploitation of racialized groups, is it possible to conceptualize a form of exploitation that is racially specific on analogy with the gender-specific forms just discussed? I suggest that the category of *menial* labor might supply a means for such conceptualization. In

---

* A Marxist term to describe the exploitation inflicted on laborers who work in systems creating "superprofits," or above-average profit margins; for example, colonial superexploitation resulted in superprofits for imperial nations. Young is stating here that modern capitalist societies, in this case the United States, have been built and maintained by superprofits harnessed by a white ruling class through the superexploitation of other racial groups.

its derivation "menial" designates the labor of servants. Wherever there is racism, there is the assumption, more or less enforced, that members of the oppressed racial groups are or ought to be servants of those, or some of those, in the privileged group. In most white racist societies this means that many white people have dark- or yellow-skinned domestic servants, and in the United States today there remains significant racial structuring of private household service....

Menial labor usually refers not only to service, however, but also to any servile, unskilled, low-paying work lacking in autonomy, in which a person is subject to taking orders from many people. Menial work tends to be auxiliary work, instrumental to the work of others, where those others receive primary recognition for doing the job. Laborers on a construction site for example are at the beck and call of welders, electricians, carpenters, and other skilled workers, who receive recognition for the job done. In the United States explicit racial discrimination once reserved menial work for Blacks, Chicanos, American Indians, and Chinese, and menial work still tends to be linked to Black and Latino workers (Symanski, 1985). I offer this category of menial labor as a form of racially specific exploitation, as a provisional category in need of exploration....

The injustice of exploitation consists in social processes that bring about a transfer of energies from one group to another to produce unequal distributions, and in the way in which social institutions enable a few to accumulate while they constrain many more. The injustices of exploitation cannot be eliminated by redistribution of goods, for as long as institutionalized practices and structural relations remain unaltered, the process of transfer will re-create an unequal distribution of benefits. Bringing about justice where there is exploitation requires reorganization of institutions and practices of decision-making; alteration of the division of labor, and similar measure of institutional, structural, and cultural change.

MARGINALIZATION

Increasingly in the United States racial oppression occurs in the form of marginalization rather than exploitation. Marginals are people the system of labor cannot or will not use. Not only in Third World capitalist countries, but also in most Western capitalist societies, there is a growing underclass of people permanently confined to lives of social marginality, most of whom are racially marked—Blacks or Indians in Latin America, and Blacks, East Indians, Eastern Europeans, or North Africans in Europe.

Marginalization is by no means the fate only of racially marked groups, however. In the United States a shamefully large proportion of the population is marginal: old people, and increasingly people who are not very old but get laid off from their jobs and cannot find new work: young people, especially Black or Latino, who cannot find first or second jobs; many single mothers and their children; other people involuntarily unemployed; many mentally and physically disabled people; American Indians, especially those on reservations.

Marginalization is perhaps the most dangerous form of oppression. A whole category of people is expelled from useful participation in social life and thus potentially subjected to severe material deprivation and even extermination. The material deprivation marginalization often causes is certainly unjust, especially in a society where others have plenty. Contemporary advanced capitalist societies have in principle acknowledged the injustice of material deprivation caused by marginalization, and have taken some steps to address it by providing welfare payments and services. The continuance of this welfare state is by no means assured, and in most welfare state societies, especially the United States, welfare redistributions do not eliminate large-scale suffering and deprivation.

Material deprivation, which can be addressed by redistributive social policies, is not, however, the extent of the harm caused by marginalization. Two categories of injustice beyond distribution are associated with marginality in advanced capitalist societies. First, the provision of welfare itself produces new injustice by depriving those dependent on it of rights and freedoms that others have. Second, even when material deprivation is somewhat mitigated by the welfare state, marginalization is unjust because it blocks the opportunity to exercise capacities in socially defined and recognized ways. I shall explicate each of these in turn.

Liberalism has traditionally asserted the right of all rational autonomous agents to equal citizenship. Early bourgeois liberalism explicitly excluded from citizenship all those whose reason was questionable or not fully developed, and all those not independent (Pateman, 1988, chap. 3; cf. Bowles and Gintis, 1986, chap. 2). Thus poor people, women, the mad and the feeble-minded, and children were explicitly excluded from citizenship, and many of these were housed in institutions modeled on the modern prison: poorhouses, insane asylums, schools.

Today the exclusion of dependent persons from equal citizenship rights is only barely hidden beneath the surface. Because they depend on bureaucratic institutions for support or services, the old, the poor, and the mentally or physically disabled are subject to patronizing, punitive, demeaning, and arbitrary treatment by the policies and people associated with welfare bureaucracies. Being a dependent in our society implies being legitimately subject to the often arbitrary and invasive authority of social service providers and other public and private administrators, who enforce rules with which the marginal must comply, and otherwise exercise power over the conditions of their lives. In meeting needs of the marginalized, often with aid of social scientific disciplines, welfare agencies also construct the needs themselves. Medical and social service professionals know what is good for those they serve, and the marginals and dependents themselves do not have the right to claim to know what is good for them (Fraser, 1987a; K. Ferguson, 1984, chap. 4). Dependency in our society thus implies, as it has in all liberal societies, a sufficient warrant to suspend basic rights to privacy, respect, and individual choice.

Although dependency produces conditions of injustice in our society, dependency in itself need not be oppressive. One cannot imagine a society in which some people would not need to be dependent on others at least some of the time: children, sick people, women recovering from childbirth, old people who have become frail, depressed or otherwise emotionally needy persons, have the moral right to depend on others for subsistence and support.

An important contribution of feminist moral theory has been to question the deeply held assumption that moral agency and full citizenship require that a person be autonomous and independent. Feminists have exposed this assumption as inappropriately individualistic and derived from a specifically male experience of social relations, which values competition and

solitary achievement (see Gilligan, 1982; Friedman, 1985). Female experience of social relations, arising both from women's typical domestic care responsibilities and from the kinds of paid work that many women do, tends to recognize dependence as a basic human condition (cf. Hartsock, 1983, chap. 10). Whereas on the autonomy model a just society would as much as possible give people the opportunity to be independent, the feminist model envisions justice as according respect and participation in decisionmaking to those who are dependent as well as to those who are independent (Held, 1987). Dependency should not be a reason to be deprived of choice and respect, and much of the oppression many marginals experience would be lessened if a less individualistic model of rights prevailed.

Marginalization does not cease to be oppressive when one has shelter and food. Many old people, for example, have sufficient means to live comfortably but remain oppressed in their marginal status. Even if marginals were provided a comfortable material life within institutions that respected their freedom and dignity, injustices of marginality would remain in the form of uselessness, boredom, and lack of self-respect. Most of our society's productive and recognized activities take place in contexts of organized social cooperation, and social structures and processes that close persons out of participation in such social cooperation are unjust. Thus while marginalization definitely entails serious issues of distributive justice, it also involves the deprivation of cultural, practical, and institutionalized conditions for exercising capacities in a context of recognition and interaction....

POWERLESSNESS

While it is false to claim that a division between capitalist and working classes no longer describes our society, it is also false to say that class relations have remained unaltered since the nineteenth century. An adequate conception of oppression cannot ignore the experience of social division reflected in the colloquial distinction between the "middle class" and the "working class," a division structured by the social division of labor between professionals and nonprofessionals. Professionals are privileged in relation to nonprofessionals, by virtue of their position in the division of labor and the status it carries. Nonprofessionals suffer a form of oppression in addition to exploitation, which I call powerlessness.

In the United States, as in other advanced capitalist countries, most workplaces are not organized democratically, direct participation in public policy decisions is rare, and policy implementation is for the most part hierarchical, imposing rules on bureaucrats and citizens. Thus most people in these societies do not regularly participate in making decisions that affect the conditions of their lives and actions, and in this sense most people lack significant power. At the same time, domination in modern society is enacted through the widely dispersed powers of many agents mediating the decisions of others. To that extent many people have some power in relation to others, even though they lack the power to decide policies or results. The powerless are those who lack authority or power even in this mediated sense, those over whom power is exercised without their exercising it; the powerless are situated so that they must take orders and rarely have the right to give them. Powerlessness also designates a position in the division of labor and the concomitant social position that allow persons little opportunity to develop and exercise skills. The powerless have little or no work autonomy, exercise little creativity or judgment in their work, have no technical expertise or authority, express themselves awkwardly, especially in public or bureaucratic settings, and do not command respect....

This powerless status is perhaps best described negatively: the powerless lack the authority, status, and sense of self that professionals tend to have. The status privilege of professionals has three aspects, the lack of which produces oppression for nonprofessionals.

First, acquiring and practicing a profession has an expansive, progressive character. Being professional usually requires a college education and the acquisition of a specialized knowledge that entails working with symbols and concepts. Professionals experience progress first in acquiring the expertise, and then in the course of professional advancement and the rise in status. The life of the nonprofessional by comparison is powerless in the sense that it lacks this orientation toward the progressive development of capacities and avenues for recognition.

Second, while many professionals have supervisors and cannot directly influence many decisions or the actions of many people, most nevertheless have considerable day-to-day work autonomy. Professionals usually have some authority over others, moreover—either over workers they supervise, or over auxiliaries, or over clients. Nonprofessionals, on the other hand, lack autonomy, and in both their working and their consumer-client lives often stand under the authority of professionals.

Though based on a division of labor between "mental" and "manual" work, the distinction between "middle class" and "working class" designates a division not only in working life, but also in nearly all aspects of social life. Professionals and nonprofessionals belong to different cultures in the United States. The two groups tend to live in segregated neighborhoods or even different towns, a process itself mediated by planners, zoning officials, and real estate people. The groups tend to have different tastes in food, decor, clothes, music, and vacations, and often different health and educational needs. Members of each group socialize for the most part with others in the same status group. While there is some intergroup mobility between generations, for the most part the children of professionals become professionals and the children of nonprofessionals do not.

Thus, third, the privileges of the professional extend beyond the workplace to a whole way of life. I call this way of life "respectability." To treat people with respect is to be prepared to listen to what they have to say or to do what they request because they have some authority, expertise, or influence. The norms of respectability in our society are associated specifically with professional culture. Professional dress, speech, tastes, demeanor, all connote respectability. Generally professionals expect and receive respect from others. In restaurants, banks, hotels, real estate offices, and many other such public places, as well as in the media, professionals typically receive more respectful treatment than nonprofessionals. For this reason nonprofessionals seeking a loan or a job, or to buy a house or a car, will often try to look "professional" and "respectable" in those settings.

The privilege of this professional respectability appears starkly in the dynamics of racism and sexism. In daily interchange women and men of color must prove their respectability. At first they are often not treated by strangers with respectful distance or deference. Once people discover that this woman or that Puerto Rican man is a college teacher or a business executive, however, they often behave more respectfully toward her or him. Working-class white men, on the other hand, are often treated with respect until their working-class status is revealed....

CULTURAL IMPERIALISM

To experience cultural imperialism means to experience how the dominant meanings of a society render the particular perspective of one's own group invisible at the same time as they stereotype one's group and mark it out as the Other.

Cultural imperialism involves the universalization of a dominant group's experience and culture, and its establishment as the norm. Some groups have exclusive or primary access to what Nancy Fraser (1987b) calls the means of interpretation and communication in a society. As a consequence, the dominant cultural products of the society, that is, those most widely disseminated, express the experience, values, goals, and achievements of these groups. Often without noticing they do so, the dominant groups project their own experience as a representative of humanity as such. Cultural products also express the dominant group's perspective on and interpretation of events and elements in the society, including other groups in the society, insofar as they attain cultural status at all.

An encounter with other groups, however, can challenge the dominant group's claim to universality. The dominant group reinforces its position by bringing the other groups under the measure of its dominant norms. Consequently, the difference of women from men, American Indians or Africans from Europeans, Jews from Christians, homosexuals from heterosexuals, workers from professionals, becomes reconstructed largely as deviance and inferiority. Since only the dominant group's cultural expressions receive wide dissemination, their cultural expressions become the normal, or the universal, and thereby the unremarkable. Given the normality of its own cultural expressions and identity, the dominant group constructs the differences which some groups exhibit as lack and negation. These groups become marked as Other.

The culturally dominated undergo a paradoxical oppression, in that they are both marked by stereotypes and at the same time rendered invisible. As remarkable, deviant beings, the culturally imperialized are stamped with an essence. The stereotypes confine them to a nature which is often attached in some way to their bodies, and which thus cannot easily be denied. These stereotypes so permeate the society that they are not noticed as contestable. Just as everyone knows that the earth goes around the sun, so everyone knows that gay people are promiscuous, that Indians are alcoholics, and that women are good with children. White males, on the other hand, insofar as they escape group marking, can be individuals....

The group defined by the dominant culture as deviant, as a stereotyped Other, *is* culturally different from the dominant group, because the status of Otherness creates specific experiences not shared by the dominant group, and because culturally oppressed groups also are often socially segregated and occupy specific positions in the social division of labor. Members of such groups express their specific group experiences and interpretations of the world to one another, developing and perpetuating their own culture. Double consciousness, then, occurs because one finds one's being defined by two cultures: a dominant and a subordinate culture. Because they can affirm and recognize one another as sharing similar experiences and perspectives on social life, people in culturally imperialized groups can often maintain a sense of positive subjectivity.

Cultural imperialism involves the paradox of experiencing oneself as invisible at the same time that one is marked out as different. The invisibility comes about when dominant groups fail to recognize the perspective embodied in their cultural expressions as a perspective. These dominant cultural expressions often simply have little place for the experience of other groups, at most only mentioning or referring to them in stereotyped or marginalized ways. This, then is the injustice of cultural imperialism: that the oppressed group's own experience and interpretation of social life finds little expression that touches the dominant culture, while that same culture imposes on the oppressed group its experience and interpretation of social life.

VIOLENCE

Finally, many groups suffer the oppression of systematic violence. Members of some groups live with the knowledge that they must fear random, unprovoked attacks on their persons or property, which have no motive but to damage, humiliate, or destroy the person. In American society women, Blacks, Asians, Arabs, gay men, and lesbians live under such threats of violence, and in at least some regions Jews, Puerto Ricans, Chicanos, and other Spanish-speaking Americans must fear such violence as well. Physical violence against these groups is shockingly frequent.... While the frequency of physical attack on members of these and other racially or sexually marked groups is very disturbing, I also include in this category less severe incidents of harassment, intimidation, or ridicule simply for the purpose of degrading, humiliating, or stigmatizing group members.

Given the frequency of such violence in our society, why are theories of justice usually silent about it? I think the reason is that theorists do not typically take such incidents of violence and harassment as matters of social injustice. No moral theorist would deny that such acts are very wrong. But unless all immoralities are injustices, they might wonder, why should such acts be interpreted as symptoms of social injustice? Acts of violence or petty harassment are committed by particular individuals, often extremists, deviants, or the mentally unsound. How then can they be said to involve the sorts of institutional issues I have said are properly the subject of justice?

What makes violence a face of oppression is less the particular acts themselves, though these are often utterly horrible, than the social context surrounding them, which makes them possible and even acceptable. What makes violence a phenomenon of social injustice, and not merely an individual moral wrong, is its systemic character, its existence as a social practice.

Violence is systemic because it is directed at members of a group simply because they are members of that group. Any woman, for example, has a reason to fear rape. Regardless of what a Black man has done to escape the oppressions of marginality of powerlessness, he lives knowing he is subject to attack or harassment. The oppression of violence consists not only in direct victimization, but in the daily knowledge shared by all members of oppressed groups that they are *liable* to violation, solely on account of their group identity. Just living under such a threat of attack on oneself or family or friends deprives the oppressed of freedom and dignity, and needlessly expends their energy.

Violence is a social practice. It is a social given that everyone knows happens and will happen again. It is always at the horizon of social imagination, even for those who do not perpetrate it. According to the prevailing social logic, some circumstances make such violence more "called for" than others. The idea of rape will occur to many men who pick up a hitch-hiking woman; the idea of hounding or teasing a gay man on their dorm floor will occur to many straight male college students. Often several persons inflict the violence together, especially in all-male groupings. Sometimes violators set out looking for people to beat up, rape, or taunt. This rule-bound, social, and often premeditated character makes violence against groups a social practice.

Group violence approaches legitimacy, moreover, in the sense that it is tolerated. Often third parties find it unsurprising because it happens frequently and lies as a constant possibility at the horizon of the social imagination. Even when they are caught, those who perpetrate acts of group-directed violence or harassment often receive light or no punishment. To that extent society renders their acts acceptable.

An important aspect of random, systematic violence is its irrationality. Xenophobic* violence differs from the violence of states or ruling-class repression. Repressive violence has a rational, albeit evil, motive: rulers use it as a coercive tool to maintain their power. Many accounts of racist, sexist, or homophobic violence attempt to explain its motivation as a desire to maintain group privilege or domination. I do not doubt that fear of violence often functions to keep oppressed groups subordinate, but do not think xenophobic violence is rationally motivated in the way that, for example, violence against strikers is.

On the contrary, the violation of rape, beating, killing, and harassment of women, people of color, gays, and other marked groups is motivated by fear or hatred of those groups. Sometimes the motive may be a simple will to power, to victimize those marked as vulnerable by the very social fact that they are subject to violence. If so, this motive is secondary in the sense that it depends on a social practice of group violence. Violence-causing fear or hatred of the other at least partly involves insecurities on the part of the violators: its irrationality suggests that unconscious processes are at work.

Cultural imperialism, moreover, itself intersects with violence. The culturally imperialized may reject the dominant meanings and attempt to assert their own subjectivity, or the fact of their cultural difference may

---

* Irrationally fearful or mistrustful of what is foreign or strange.

put the lie to the dominant culture's implicit claim to universality. The dissonance generated by such a challenge to the hegemonic* cultural meanings can also be a source of irrational violence.

Violence is a form of injustice that a distributive understanding of justice seems ill equipped to capture. This may be why contemporary discussions of justice rarely mention it. I have argued that group-directed violence is institutionalized and systemic. To the degree that institutions and social practices encourage, tolerate, or enable the perpetration of violence against members of specific groups, those institutions and practices are unjust and should be reformed. Such reform may require the redistribution of resources or positions, but in large part can come only through a change in cultural images, stereotypes, and the mundane reproduction of relations of dominance and aversion in the gestures of everyday life.

Applying the Criteria

Social theories that construct oppression as a unified phenomenon usually either leave out groups that even the theorists think are oppressed, or leave out important ways in which groups are oppressed. Black liberation theorists and feminist theorists have argued persuasively, for example, that Marxism's reduction of all oppressions to class oppression leaves out much about the specific oppression of Blacks and women. By pluralizing the category of oppression in the way explained in this chapter, social theory can avoid the exclusive and oversimplifying effects of such reductionism.

I have avoided pluralizing the category in the way some others have done, by constructing an account of separate systems of oppression for each oppressed group: racism, sexism, classism, heterosexism, ageism, and so on. There is a double problem with considering each group's oppression a unified and distinct structure or system. On the one hand, this way of conceiving oppression fails to accommodate the similarities and overlaps in the oppressions of different groups. On the other hand, it falsely represents the situation of all group members as the same.

I have arrived at the five faces of oppression—exploitation, marginalization, powerlessness, cultural imperialism, and violence—as the best way to avoid such exclusions and reductions. They function as criteria for determining whether individuals and groups are oppressed, rather than as a full theory of oppression. I believe that these criteria are objective. They provide a means of refuting some people's belief that their group is oppressed when it is not, as well as a means of persuading others that a group is oppressed when they doubt it. Each criterion can be operationalized; each can be applied through the assessment of observable behavior, status relationships, distributions, texts and other cultural artifacts. I have no illusions that such assessments can be value-neutral. But these criteria can nevertheless serve as means of evaluating claims that a group is oppressed, or adjudicating disputes about whether or how a group is oppressed.

The presence of any of these five conditions is sufficient for calling a group oppressed. But different group oppressions exhibit different combinations of these forms, as do different individuals in the groups. Nearly all, if not all, groups said by contemporary social movements to be oppressed suffer cultural imperialism. The other oppressions they experience vary. Working-class people are exploited and powerless, for example, but if employed and white do not experience marginalization and violence. Gay men, on the other hand, are not qua gay exploited or powerless, but they experience severe cultural imperialism and violence. Similarly, Jews and Arabs as groups are victims of cultural imperialism and violence, though many members of these groups also suffer exploitation or powerlessness. Old people are oppressed by marginalization and cultural imperialism, and this is also true of physically and mentally disabled people. As a group women are subject to gender-based exploitation, powerlessness, cultural imperialism, and violence. Racism in the United States condemns many Blacks and Latinos to marginalization, and puts many more at risk, even though many members of these groups escape that condition; members of these groups often suffer all five forms of oppression.

---

* Ruling, dominant.

Applying these five criteria to the situation of groups makes it possible to compare oppressions without reducing them to a common essence or claiming that one is more fundamental than another. One can compare the ways in which a particular form of oppression appears in different groups. For example, while the operations of cultural imperialism are often experienced in similar fashion by different groups, there are also important differences. One can compare the combinations of oppressions groups experience, or the intensity of those oppressions. Thus with these criteria one can plausibly claim that one group is more oppressed than another without reducing all oppressions to a single scale.

Why are particular groups oppressed in the way they are? Are there any causal connections among the five forms of oppression? Causal or explanatory questions such as these are beyond the scope of this discussion. While I think general social theory has a place, causal explanation must always be particular and historical. Thus an explanatory account of why a particular group is oppressed in the ways that it is must trace the history and current structure of particular social relations. Such concrete historical and structural explanations will often show causal connections among the different forms of oppression experienced by a group. The cultural imperialism in which white men make stereotypical assumptions about and refuse to recognize the values of Blacks or women, for example, contributes to the marginalization and powerlessness many Blacks and women suffer. But cultural imperialism does not always have these effects. ■

Suggestions for Critical Reflection

1. Consider the quotation by Simone Weil used as an epigraph to this reading. Why do you think Young chose it to open her argument?

2. Young states that she has "proposed an enabling conception of justice." How, if at all, could the framework of the five faces of oppression be enabling for oppressed groups working to improve their lives? If you have read the selections in this volume by Rawls and Nozick, how do you think it differs from a distributive account of justice?

3. "The systemic character of oppression implies that an oppressed group need not have a correlate oppressing group." What does Young mean by this—what do you think are its implications if she is right?

4. Young claims that the five faces of oppression can serve as criteria for determining whether a group is oppressed. Consider a particular category of people who may be oppressed, such as a specific ethnic or gender group. Do Young's criteria help in assessing the oppression of this group? Does applying the criteria help you to better understand the group's concerns?

5. Philosophers disagree about the role of social groups in society, with some viewing them as positive, a means to create a society in which many interconnecting but distinct groups live together supportively, whereas others believe the best way forward would be to move beyond group membership and into a post-racial, post-gender society. What do you think? Is group membership positive, or is it a source of prejudice and determinism that stands in the way of a just society?

6. Consider Young's discussion of marginalization. What are the two categories of injustice caused by marginalization that she says are beyond the scope of distributive remedy? How do societies try to address these types of structural oppressions?

7. Young writes that "acquiring and practicing a profession has an expansive, progressive character." Why does she say this? Is she right? Could non-professional careers be "expansive" in a similar way, and if so does this have implications for her argument?

8. Are Young's five categories of oppression comprehensive? Are there any forms of oppression which they do not cover? (Does Young mean them to be totally comprehensive?)

9. If you have read the Beauvoir selection in this chapter, consider whether she is one of the people whom Young criticizes as thinking that "social groups are invidious fictions, essentializing arbitrary attributes." If so, how might Beauvoir reply?

References

Bowles, Samuel and Herbert Gintis. 1986. *Democracy and Capitalism*. New York: Basic.

Brittan, Arthur and Mary Maynard. 1984. *Sexism, Racism and Oppression*. Oxford: Blackwell.

Buchanan, Allen. 1982. *Marx and Justice*. Totowa, N.J.: Roman and Allanheld.

Coward, Rosalind and John Ellis. 1977. *Language and Materialism*. London: Routledge and Kegan Paul.

Epstein, Steven. 1987. "Gay Politics, Ethnic Identity: The Limits of Social Constructionism." *Socialist Review* 17 (May–August): 9–54.

Ferguson, Kathy. 1984. *The Feminist Case against Bureaucracy*. Philadelphia: Temple University Press.

Foucault, Michel. 1977. *Discipline and Punish*. New York: Pantheon.

Fraser, Nancy. 1987a "Women, Welfare, and the Politics of Need Interpretation." *Hypatia: A Journal of Feminist Philosophy* 2 (Winter): 103–22.

——. 1987b. "Social Movements vs. Disciplinary Bureaucracies: The Discourse of Social Needs." CHS Occasional Paper No. 8. Center for Humanistic Studies, University of Minnesota.

Friedman, Marilyn. 1985. "Care and Context in Moral Reasoning." In Carol Harding, ed., *Moral Dilemmas: Philosophical and Psychological Issues in the Development of Moral Reasoning*. Chicago: Precedent.

Friedman, Marilyn and Larry May. 1985. "Harming Women as a Group." *Social Theory and Practice* 11 (Summer): 297–34.

Frye, Marilyn. 1983. "Oppression." In *The Politics of Reality*. Trumansburg, N.Y.: Crossing Press.

Giddens, Anthony. 1981. *A Contemporary Critique of Historical Materialism*. Berkeley and Los Angeles: University of California Press.

Gilligan, Carol. 1982. *In a Different Voice*. Cambridge: Harvard University Press.

Habermas, Jürgen. 1987. *The Theory of Communicative Competence*. Vol. 2: *Lifeworld and System*. Boston: Beacon.

Hartsock, Nancy. 1983. *Money, Sex and Power*. New York: Longman.

Heidegger, Martin. 1962. *Being and Time*. New York: Harper and Row.

Held, Virginia. 1987. "A Non-Contractual Society." In Marsha Hanen and Kai Nielsen, eds., *Science, Morality and Feminist Theory*. Calgary: University of Calgary Press.

Holmstrom, Nancy. 1977. "Exploitation." *Canadian Journal of Philosophy* 7 (June): 353–69.

Macpherson, C.B. 1973. *Democratic Theory: Essays in Retrieval*. Oxford: Oxford University Press.

Murphy, Raymond. 1985. "Exploitation or Exclusion?" *Sociology* 19 (May): 225–43.

Pateman, Carole. 1988. *The Sexual Contract*. Stanford: Stanford University Press.

Reich, Michael. 1981. *Racial Inequality*. Princeton: Princeton University Press.

Ross, Jeffrey. 1980. Introduction to Jeffrey Ross and Ann Baker Cottrell, eds., *The Mobilization of Collective Identity*. Lanham, Md.: University Press of America.

Rothschild, Joseph. 1981. *Ethnopolitics*. New York: Columbia University Press.

Symanski, Al. 1985. "The Structure of Race." *Review of Radical Political Economy* 17 (Winter): 106–20.

Turner, John C., Michael A. Hogg, Penelope V. Oakes, Stephen D. Rucher, and Margaret S. Wethrell. 1987. *Rediscovering the Social Group: A Self-Categorization Theory*. Oxford: Blackwell.

KWAME ANTHONY APPIAH

How to Decide If Races Exist

Who Is Kwame Anthony Appiah?

British-Ghanaian philosopher Kwame Anthony Appiah was born in London in 1954. His father, Joseph Appiah, was a well-known Ghanaian politician and lawyer, and his mother, born Peggy Cripps, was a British writer and art historian. Appiah grew up in Kumasi, Ghana, and attended high school in Britain. He received his BA from Clare College, Cambridge in 1975, and his PhD in philosophy from Cambridge in 1982. His research interests include the philosophy of language, African and African American history and literature, race theory, and moral and political philosophy.

Appiah's work is focused on questions of race, culture, and identity: "The challenge," he writes in *Cosmopolitanism: Ethics in a World of Strangers* (2006), "is to take minds and hearts formed over the long millennia of living in local troops and equip them with ideas and institutions that will allow us to live together as the global tribe we have become." As a proponent of cosmopolitanism, Appiah has argued for moving beyond ethno-racial identities into a "post-racial" world, though he recognizes that this dream is unlikely to be fulfilled any time soon.

Appiah's doctoral thesis and early work focused on the philosophy of language, but he soon began working in African and African-American cultural studies. His first major publication, *In My Father's House: Africa in the Philosophy of Culture* (1992), considers African identity in relation to the West and an increasingly globalized world. Though criticized by some scholars as Eurocentric, the book was generally well received, and it garnered several awards. In *Color Conscious: The Political Morality of Race* (1996) (co-authored with Amy Gutmann), Appiah discusses the falsity of biological concepts of race, and, on the basis of this, criticizes the role that group identities can sometimes play in determining individual identity. This skepticism towards group identities is further explored in *The Ethics of Identity* (2005), in which Appiah considers how group membership can both foster and limit individual freedom. He questions

how the ways we categorize ourselves and others determine who we are.

Appiah has taught at Yale, Cornell, Duke, and Harvard Universities, and he is currently Professor of Philosophy and Law at New York University.

What Is the Structure of This Reading?

"How to Decide If Races Exist" analyzes how we think about race, the role racial categories play in identity formation, and whether our categorizations have any basis in biological science.

Appiah opens his argument by considering what he calls "folk races," the racial categories that are commonly used and accepted in society (applications and forms that ask you to identify your race, for example, would list these categories). These "folk races" are the categories we absorb as children that shape our social world. Appiah emphasizes that these categories are essentialized, meaning that they aren't based simply on appearance: people assigned to these categories are also thought to share inherited intrinsic qualities that explain their aptitudes and behaviors.

Appiah notes that racial categories exert a shaping influence on individuals and societies, particularly in the formation of social identities, despite the fact that these categories are not well-grounded in biology. He analyzes our social identities by parsing the labels we give them: What does it mean when we say someone is "Asian," for example, and what does it mean to call oneself "Asian"? Appiah suggests that three things are necessary for a label to function as a social identity: it needs to be applied to a group of people ("ascription"), people need to identify themselves by the label ("identification"), and the group needs to be treated differently from others on account of its label, whether positively, negatively, or both ("treatment"). Most social identities will also have norms attached to them, which are traits that a group is widely held to share. Appiah argues that these elements are present for all social identities—not only ethno-racial, but also sexual, national, professional, and political (among others).

Appiah next considers the possibility that genetic science might reveal a biological grounding for racial identities. As an example, he discusses a trend among African Americans to use genetic testing in order to trace their roots to a particular region and people in Africa, and thereby establish their ethno-racial identity. This testing then connects people across the globe who share African ancestry. While not hostile to this emerging aspect of the Pan-African movement, Appiah is skeptical of the existence of a genetic basis for racial identity, given that almost all people have multiple ancestors from a variety of regions across the globe. Genetics, while it can reveal important information about diseases that are more common in certain places in the world, does not, according to Appiah, lend support for our commonly held essentialized racial categories.

While Appiah does not argue here, as he does elsewhere, that racial categories should be abandoned entirely, he does lay the foundation for this argument. If we want to continue to say there are races, he argues, we should understand them as constructed social identities rather than as biologically based subspecies.

Some Useful Background Information

1. Appiah refers to racial essentialism several times in this piece, which he defines as "the idea that human groups have core properties in common that explain not just their shared superficial appearances but also the deep tendencies of their moral and cultural lives."* Nineteenth-century theorists combined essentialism with a belief in the biological reality of race, and eventually this theory merged with nationalism to produce some of the most hateful and destructive racism the world has yet known. Though we now recognize the horrors caused by racial genocide in past centuries, Appiah notes that belief in essential differences among people persists widely across the world, and that this is unlikely to change drastically very soon.

2. In contemporary philosophical debates about race, Appiah is considered a "racial skeptic." He argues that since essentialist race categories aren't supported by biological evidence, we should stop classifying people according to these categories. Appiah believes that the concept of race hinders us from creating healthier societies. In his 2015 article "Race in the Modern World," he suggests that "the price of trying to move beyond ethno-racial identities is worth paying, not only for moral reasons but also for the sake of intellectual hygiene. It would allow us to live and work together more harmoniously and productively, in offices, neighborhoods, towns, states, and nations. Why, after all, should we tie our fates to groups whose existence seems always to involve misunderstandings about the facts of human difference? Why rely on imaginary natural commonalities rather than build cohesion through intentional communities?" The article printed here, "How to Decide If Races Exist," provides a foundation for this position of racial skepticism.

    It is important to note that Appiah's skepticism regarding racial categories does not extend to "race-like social identities," which he says can be positive forces in the struggle against racism. He does, however, approach identity politics with some ambivalence, too, lest our racial (and sexual, gender, national, etc.) identities subject us to "new tyrannies."

---

*   See Appiah, "Race in the Modern World: The Problem with the Color Line," *Foreign Affairs*, March/April 2015.

*How to Decide If Races Exist**

I

From a very early age, people across cultures classify others on the basis of appearance without any particular encouragement. As Susan Gelman has argued in her fascinating book *The Essential Child*, evidence from developmental psychology shows that by the age of six children treat races as "possessing inborn features, inherent in the ... person, and passed down from parent to child."[1] Young children, she argues, also *essentialize* these groups: they believe that the "outer" characteristics by which they assign people to groups reflect shared "inner" properties that explain both appearance and behavior.[2] So there is a large set of ways of classifying people all around the world and throughout history that reflect this cognitive predisposition.

By talk of "folk races"—and this is just a stipulation—I mean to pick out those folk categories that are based on the idea that membership in the relevant group is determined by intrinsic properties inherited from one's parents, properties that are shared by all normal members of the group. Using this terminology, the hypothesis that there are human folk races is the hypothesis that there are human groups of common ancestry that are (roughly) definable by shared inherited intrinsic properties.

It's a consequence of this stipulation that biological subspecies, at least as many evolutionary biologists have conceived of them, are not likely to be folk races.[3] That's because membership in a subspecies is not an intrinsic property, but a relational one. A subspecies is a kind of biological population. In a sexually reproducing species like ours, a population is a collection of organisms whose members have a significantly higher propensity to reproduce with opposite-sex members of the group than they have to reproduce with organisms outside it. As a result, two organisms that are quite alike in intrinsic biological properties can belong to different populations, and two organisms that are quite dissimilar in properties can belong to the same population. Indeed, you can have two organisms, *A* and *B*, in the same population where *A* is far more different in intrinsic properties from *B* than from *C*, which is not in the population at all. (Imagine a population split in two by the sudden appearance of a new river formed after an earthquake. Consider *A*, *B* and *C*, who were members of the original population before the split. Suppose *A* and *C* are close kin, but *A* and *B* have no recent common ancestor; suppose that *A* and *B* are now on one side of the river and *C* is on the other. Organisms that can't meet can't mate. So *A* and *C* belong to different populations now.)

I advertise this fact—that what I call folk races aren't likely to behave like modern biological classifications—since it *is* the pretty direct result of a stipulation and some well-known biology. For clarity's sake, I'll use the word "subspecies" for this biological kind. I want to insist that my stipulation isn't arbitrary, though: it is motivated by the fact that folk practices of ethno-racial classification are generally essentialist (in Gelman's sense) because we have the cognitive tendency that Gelman has described so well.

Folk classifications in the modern West are quite typical. We assign people to races in a way that is governed by this rule: if your parents are of the same race, you're of the same race as your parents. Since you get your genetic endowment from your parents, racial identities governed by this rule will sometimes be statistically correlated with genetic characteristics, provided there are genes in the local members of a folk race that are commoner than in the general population. Since people are also often assigned to racial groups in part on the basis of phenotypic characteristics[†] that have a genetic basis, there will often, in fact, be such correlations. But Westerners are inclined to suppose

---

*   Kwame Anthony Appiah, "How to Decide If Races Exist," *Proceedings of the Aristotelian Society* 106 (2006): 365–82. Paper delivered at a meeting of the Aristotelian Society, held in Senate House, University of London, on Monday 19 June 2006.
†   Observable features of the bodies and behaviors of organisms.

not just that there are biologically-based features of people that are statistically characteristic of their race, but also that those features extend far beyond the superficial characteristics on the basis of which racial categorization is usually based. So we *essentialize* race, in Gelman's sense of that term. And a great deal of what people believe about the biological basis of these deeper differences is false.

Because the central beliefs of many people about folk races are mistaken in these ways, we cannot explain how people are assigned to races by discovering some folk theory and supposing it to be roughly true. So—since folk races are, like it or not, an important feature of our social landscape—we need an account of the racial categories actually in place that is consistent with the pervasiveness of erroneous beliefs.

II

Here is such an account.[4] It begins by supposing that folk race is an important kind of social identity. That's because I think that folk races are of interest to us largely because they *are* forms of social identity. They continue to be interesting in that way whether or not they are interesting for biological purposes.

My explication of social identities is nominalist:* it explains how the identities work by talking about the labels for them. The main motivation for the nominalism is that it allows us to leave open the question of whether the empirical presuppositions of a labelling practice are correct. Since many social identities are like folk races in being shot through with false belief, this is a decided advantage. So, take a representative label, *X*, for some identity.

> IDENTITY: There will be criteria of ascription[†] for the term "*X*"; some people will identify as *X*s; some people will treat others as *X*s; and there will be norms of identification.

Each of these notions—ascription, identification, treatment and norms of identification—requires brief commentary.

III

A person's criteria of ascription for "*X*" are properties on the basis of which she sorts people into those to whom she does and those to whom she doesn't apply the label "*X*." The criteria of ascription need not be the same for every user of the term; indeed, there will rarely be a socially agreed set of properties individually necessary and jointly sufficient for being an *X*.[5]

Here is what characterizes competence with the term "*X*." There will be certain kinds of people—we can call them "prototypical *X*s"—such that your criteria of ascription must pick them out as *X*s. There will be other kinds—"antitypes," let us call them—that your criteria of ascription must exclude. A prototype is not an actual person: it is a specification of conditions sufficient for being an *X*; just so, an antitype specifies conditions sufficient for not-being one. But something may be neither a prototype nor an antitype of an *X*. A Cuban-American, most of whose ancestors came to Cuba before the eighteenth century, and who arrived in Florida in 1950 is a prototype of a Latino. A normal European or African who does not speak Spanish or Portuguese and does not come from the Iberian peninsula is an antitype. List all the prototypes and antitypes and you may find that they do not divide logical space into two classes.

Because prototypes and antitypes don't always divide logical space in two, criteria of ascription need not divide actual people into *X*s and not-*X*s, either. Rather, they must divide all actual people roughly into three classes, which we can call (modeling our classification on Max Black's account of metaphor[‡]) the positive, negative and neutral classes. That is, they must make some people, in the positive class, *X*s;

---

* In this context, nominalism is the view that the names or labels for things may not correspond to any actually existing abstract object or property.

† To ascribe a characteristic to someone or something is to say that the characteristic is true of them.

‡ Philosopher Max Black (1909–88) put forward in 1954 what is known as a "semantic twist" account of metaphor. His theory divides a metaphoric utterance into two halves: the focal words (the ones used metaphorically) and the framing words (which are not being used metaphorically). By having the two yoked together by metaphoric utterance, new meaning is imposed on the focal word by the frame—for instance (one of Black's own central examples) "the chairman ploughed through the discussion."

some people, in the negative class, not-*X*s; and they may leave some people, in the neutral class, as neither determinately *X*s nor determinately not-*X*s.[6] Let me underline that, whereas prototypes are abstract, these classes are classes of actual people. I am not trying to get at the way the predicate works across possibilia.*

This is what competence consists in; but people do not need to know that their criteria of ascription have these features to be competent. And, in general, they won't know what the relationship is between their criteria of ascription and the total human population. So they may well think, for example, that they can divide the world precisely into *X*s and not-*X*s, even though there do in fact exist people (people they have not met) who would be in the neutral class for them, if they did know about them. I shall say that someone who has criteria of ascription for an identity-term "*X*" that meet the conditions for competence has a *conception* of an *X*.

This is, no doubt, too abstract; so let me just exemplify. Take the term "Asian" as used by Johnny from Cornwall, who has met very few people from anywhere in Asia and very few British Asians either. Johnny says "Asians are a race" and ascribes the term "Asian" to everyone who looks a certain way, in fact the sort of way most movie stars in Bollywood movies would look to him. (I'll call this "looking Asian to" Johnny.) He also thinks that the label is properly applied to anyone whose ancestors for many generations have come from India, because he supposes that everybody in those countries would look Asian to him. Now Johnny will get all the prototypes and antitypes right. Give him a Bangladeshi? "Asian." Give him most Finns or Congolese? "Not Asian." So he's competent. But presented with a Kirghiz or a Kazakh† (people, let us suppose, of whose existence he is currently unaware) he might not know what to say. So his conception has a neutral class, even though he doesn't know this. He may also have false beliefs—such as that almost everyone in Asia looks roughly the way Indian people look—even though most people in Asia

do not: a couple of billion people in China and South-East Asia, for example.

IV

By itself a way of classifying people that works in this way by ascription would not produce a social identity. What makes it a social identity of the relevant kind is not just that people suppose themselves or others to be *X*s but that being-an-*X* figures in a certain typical way in their thoughts, feelings and acts. When a person thinks of herself as an *X* in the relevant way, she *identifies as an X*. What this means is that she sometimes *feels like an X* or *acts as an X*.

An agent *acts as an X* when the thought "because I am an *X*" figures in her reasons for acting or abstaining. Perhaps you never act as a British person (hereafter "Brit"). But feelings can constitute identification too. You discover that hundreds of thousands of Brits responded to the Asian tsunami‡ by sending money. You feel proud to be British. To *feel like an X* is for your being an *X* to figure in the intentional content§ of your feeling. The intentional content doesn't have to be *that you're an X*, though: you may feel proud of Mary, a fellow Brit, say. Here your being British figures in the intentional content of the feeling, because part of the intentional structure of the feeling is that Mary is *British like me*, even though you're not proud *that you're British*.

Similarly, our treatment of and feelings about other people reflect identity. You treat *A* as an *X* when "because *A* is an *X*" figures in your reason for doing something to *A*. Supererogatory¶ kindness is a common form of treatment-as directed towards fellow in-group members. Morally opprobrious unkindness is, alas, a horribly frequent form of treatment—as directed towards out-group members. It takes ascription, identification and treatment for a label to be functioning as the label for a social identity of the sort that I am explicating.

---

* Merely possible (non-actual) things.
† People from the former (central Asian) Soviet republics of Kyrgyzstan and Kazakhstan, respectively, whose citizens belong primarily to the Turkic ethnic group.
‡ The 2004 Indian Ocean earthquake and tsunami that killed more than 250,000 people, mainly in Indonesia, Sri Lanka, India, and Thailand.
§ Intentional content is what a mental state (or other meaningful thing, such as a sentence) is about.
¶ A supererogatory action is one that is morally good but goes beyond what is morally required.

One reason identities are useful is that they allow us to predict how people will behave. This is not just because the existence of criteria of ascription entails that members of the group have or tend to have certain properties. It is also because social identities are associated with *norms for Xs*. That is the final element of my explication of the notion.

There are things that, *qua Xs*,* people ought and ought not to do. The "ought" here is the general practical ought, not some special moral one. Here are some examples. Negatively: men ought not to wear dresses; gay men ought not to fall in love with women; blacks ought not to embarrass the race. Positively: men ought to open doors for women; gay people ought to come out; blacks ought to support affirmative action.† To say that these norms exist is evidently not to endorse them. I don't myself endorse any of the norms I just listed. The existence of a norm that *X*s ought to *A* amounts only to its being widely thought—and widely known to be thought—that many people believe that *X*s ought to *A*.[7]

V

I should underline how many and various are the predicates‡ of persons that fit this general rubric. I started with racial and ethnic terms; and I mentioned a nationality, British. But I could also have mentioned professional identities, vocations, affiliations, formal and informal (like Man U§ fan or Conservative), and other more airy labels ... dandy, say, or cosmopolitan.

I am pointing to this range not just because, like a well-bred philosopher, I am interested in generality, but also because this range invites an obvious question. *Why* do we have such a diverse range of social identities

and relations? One answer, an aetiological¶ one, will talk about our evolution as a social species and the fact that we are designed evolutionarily for the social game of coalition-building in search of food, mates and protection. This is, I think, a good explanation for our having the sort of psychology of in-group and out-group solidarities and antagonisms that social and developmental psychologists, like Susan Gelman, have been exploring for the last half-century.

But the psychologies that evolution has given us mean that there is a way the world looks from the inside, from the point of view of a creature with that psychology. And from that point of view I think there is another, equally persuasive answer. Each of us has to make a life and to try to make it go well, and we need identities to make our human lives.

We make our lives, that is, *as* men and *as* women; *as* Americans and *as* Brits; *as* philosophers and *as* novelists. Morality—by which I mean what we owe to one another—is part of the scaffolding on which we make that construction. So are various projects that we voluntarily undertake: Voltaire's garden—the one, perhaps, to whose cultivation he consigned his *picaro* Candide—shaped the last part of his life.** But identities are another central resource for making our lives. Identities are diverse and extensive, I think, because people need an enormous diversity of tools for making their lives. Each person needs many options. And, because people are various, the range of options that would be sufficient for each of us won't be sufficient for us all.

VI

There are positive, negative and neutral classes for each competent speaker: that is, there is a way she would

---

* In the capacity of being an *X*.

† Policies specifically promoting the employment and education of disadvantaged groups who have suffered and continue to suffer discrimination.

‡ Describing terms.

§ The English football club Manchester United.

¶ An explanation in terms of causes.

** French philosopher Voltaire (1694–1778) grew extensive gardens in the estates he rented while exiled to Switzerland in the later years of his life. In his novel *Candide* (1759), the protagonist reflects on the life of a Turkish landowner, who cultivated his land with his own labor and the labor of his children. Working in the garden keeps off "three great evils—idleness, vice, and want." Candide reflects that such a quietly productive life is far preferable to the violent and stressful life of kings. The last words of the novel, spoken by Candide, are: "let us cultivate our garden." The word *picaro* is a Spanish term meaning "rascal." It is also used to refer to the protagonist of picaresque novels.

assign everybody on the planet roughly to one of these three classes, if that person showed up in her environment and answered truthfully questions about herself. The prototypes and antitypes define the socially permissible limits of individual positive and negative classes. So we might ask whether there is an interesting property—intrinsic or relational, simple or logically compound—shared by (most) prototypes that is not shared by (most) antitypes. Can we tell a story about racial identity, for example, that shows it to correspond roughly, in this way, to a biological property of genuine interest? If so, folk races are, in a sense, biologically real.

It's in answering this question that new work on the human genome* strikes some people as helpful. Genomics teaches us not only what genes are, but also how they tend to be associated with each other. This offers the prospect of associating certain social groups statistically with genomic features. And where those statistical correlations are distinctive enough of the group and the genomic feature is of importance—for example, for medical reasons—there can be an obvious sense in which biological claims about the group can turn out to be statistical truths. This has been part of folk wisdom for quite a while for a few cases: sickle-cell disease, glucose-6-phosphate dehydrogenase deficiency, and Tay-Sachs disease,[†] for example, are both rare in human beings generally and much more frequent in some groups of common ancestry than in others.

Sometimes the groups in question are quite small: there are alleles[‡] that have been found in certain families and nowhere else. Sometimes the groups are large: Yoruba people, of whom there are more than thirty million in south-west Nigeria, have a 6% frequency of the gene for haemoglobin C (which produces a relatively mild blood disease even in heterozygotes,[§]

who carry two copies of it); and 25% of the population of Nigeria as a whole carries the gene for haemoglobin S, which produces the classic and serious form of sickle-cell disease in heterozygotes.[8] A normal haemoglobin[¶] molecule is made up of four subunits, two α and two β chains; each chain is produced by a distinct gene, and there are many variants of both the α and the β chains. Since the α and β chains are required in equal numbers to form normal haemoglobin, there is also a range of genetic diseases associated with non-standard haemoglobins—the thalassaemias—in which one or other chain is produced in too small a quantity. 39% of Nigerians have some form of α-thalassaemia, the diseases produced when you have an under-production of α chains. These disorders—sickle-cell and thalassaemia—can be inherited both separately and together, producing a dazzling array of blood diseases, and so there is a very wide range of clinical contexts in which it is relevant to know if someone has Nigerian ancestry.

Of course, it's the differences in frequency between populations that make these correlations significant. As a standard discussion of blood diseases points out:

> α-Thalassemia is perhaps the most common single-gene disorder in the world. The frequency of α-thalassemia alleles is 5–10% in persons from the Mediterranean basin, 20–30% in portions of West Africa, and as high as 68% in the southwest Pacific. The frequency of heterozygote carrier status among the Chinese population has been reported to vary from 5–15%. The frequency of α-thalassemia is less than 0.01% in Great Britain, Iceland, and Japan.[9]

---

*   An organism's complete set of genes.

†   This is an inherited group of diseases, the most common being sickle-cell anemia, which causes anemia, infections, long-term pain, and possible stroke. About 80 per cent of sickle cell disease cases are believed to occur in Sub-Saharan Africa. G6PDD is a genetic disease that affects the metabolism and predisposes the patient to red blood cell breakdown—patients are often unsymptomatic, and the condition confers an evolutionary advantage, as it gives some protection against malaria. It is particularly common among males from certain parts of Africa, Asia, the Mediterranean, and the Middle East. Tay-Sachs disease is a serious genetic disorder that destroys nerve cells in the brain and spinal cord, and is particularly associated with Ashkenazi Jews.

‡   Variant forms of a gene that have been altered by mutation and are located on the same site on a homologous chromosome (i.e., a chromosome which contains the same genes in the same order).

§   An organism having different alleles at a given genetic locus.

¶   The protein found in red blood cells that carries oxygen.

What is most obviously distinctive of reproductively isolated biological populations is the frequency with which variant alleles occur in that population. As we saw earlier, an *individual* in one biological population could, in principle, have almost the same genotype as an individual in another. That is, in essence, why attempts to define biological populations by biological properties shared by their members won't work. A population is a collection of organisms defined, as I said earlier, by the fact that they have a significantly higher probability of reproducing with oppositesex members of the group than they have of reproducing with organisms outside it. This is a relational property—though it is one that is sometimes explained by an intrinsic property: some sub-populations of *Drosophila** have male genitalia that don't work with the genitalia of females in others. Sometimes the explanation is not an intrinsic property of the organism: populations may just be separated by a mountain range. And sometimes, in humans at least, the explanation could be cultural. If two human populations had ever lived side by side for a long time with no exchange of genes, indeed that would be the most likely explanation. History does not, so far as I know, afford examples of total reproductive isolation of this kind.

So, for example, a majority of members of the folk race of African-Americans have relatively dark skin for genetic reasons. Biological remains that contain some of the genes that characteristically account for this darker skin colour can therefore reasonably be identified for forensic purposes as (socially) African-American. Here there is a genuine biological trait that can be used to identify a genuine social trait, even though the social trait is not identical with any intrinsic biological property. So the utility of genomic properties in identifying a social group doesn't entail that the social group is a subspecies.

This is all consistent with recognizing that many African-Americans do not bear the genes that produce darker skin; that there are other genomic characteristics statistically distinctive of African populations that a person of African ancestry may share without having the skin-colour genes; and that you can be an African-American while having many fewer of the genomic characteristics statistically distinctive of an African population than many people who are identified as white.

Perhaps all this is obvious. But I find in discussion that people seem not to grasp these points intuitively, so perhaps they are worth making. And if they are worth making, perhaps it is also worth filling in some of the conceptual background.

VII

As we all now know, genes consist of sequences of bases,[†] and each sequence of three such bases (a *triplet* or DNA *codon*) has a functional significance in determining what protein is produced. Mutations in genes occur when one base is replaced with another. Because the relationship between codons and amino acids is many–one, some such substitutions make little functional difference, since the same polypeptide[‡] sequences result and the same proteins are formed. Other substitutions change the polypeptide sequence, by substituting one amino acid for another, but make little difference to the biological functioning of the resulting protein: enzymes, for example, characteristically have certain active regions that are important to their functioning, while other sequences are structural supports for the active regions.

Where a mutation has a functional significance, it is most likely to have a negative effect on the organisms that carry it: we are complex wholes with interdependent parts adapted to one another over a relatively long period in a relatively stable environment, and in general a change in the functioning of one element of this complex stable whole will reduce, not increase, our overall fitness. But where a mutation has little or no functional significance it can survive. There will be no selection pressure against it. And so there will be single nucleotide polymorphisms—DNA sequences that differ in just one base from each other—that produce different forms of a gene that are nevertheless

---

* Commonly known as fruit flies, drosophila are often used in genetics research.
† Nitrogen-containing biological compounds including adenine, cytosine, guanine, and thymine, which are the basic building blocks of DNA.
‡ A chain of amino acids, which can be the building block for a protein.

functionally equivalent. ("Single nucleotide polymorphism" is a long expression for a short change. Usually it's abbreviated to SNP, pronounced "snip.") A SNP refers both to a site on a chromosome which is occupied in different people by different bases and to the various bases that can be there.[10] Most loci on most genes are the same in everybody: many of the base sequences it takes to be a functioning organism are identical, because changes in most base sequences don't produce a functioning individual. But it's usually estimated that 0.1% of the DNA consists of sites where SNPs can occur in living people. By October 2005, about 3.6 million SNPs had been "validated."[11]

The *genotype* of a person is a specification of every pair of alleles that she carries for every locus* on the genome. Consider two people, each of whom carries the same two alleles at the same two sites: say, *Aa* and *Bb*. But suppose in John *A* and *B* are on one chromosome and *a* and *b* are on another, while in James *A* and *b* are on the same chromosome and *a* and *B* are on another. Suppose that these sites are close together on the same chromosome: as a result the alleles that they carry are extremely unlikely to be separated in cell division.

Now consider the results of sex with a partner whose genotype is *AABB*. With John, she will have offspring *AABB* or *AaBb*. With James, the options are *AABb* or *AaBB*. While John's and James's genotypes are the same, the genotypes of their offspring with the same partner will be different. We will be able to tell, in particular, if we come across one of these offspring, which of the two males was their father simply by looking at two loci, *even though, for those loci, the two potential fathers have the same genotype.* What determines your propensity to produce offspring of a certain genotype, simply put, isn't just your genotype, it's the way in which that genotype is placed on your chromosomes.

That's why the notion of a haplotype—or haploid genotype—is useful in tracing ancestry. It's the specification not of your genotype, but of the sequence of genes on just one of each pair of your chromosomes.

Each individual can be thought of genetically, then, as having two haplotypes. Of course, because there are twenty-three chromosome pairs, you could specify the haplotype in 2^{23} ways: but once you had picked one such way—by selecting one from each pair of chromosomes—you would also have fixed which other haplotype you needed to specify.

One non-arbitrary way to pick a way of specifying the haplotype would be to specify the sequence of alleles on the chromosomes derived from the mother's egg and then specify the sequence on the chromosomes derived from the father's sperm. In the process of meiosis—the type of cell division that produces sex cells—material can be swapped between the two versions of a chromosome carried in a normal somatic cell,† in the process called "crossing over." But if crossing over did not occur, you could think of a person as the combination of a maternal and a paternal haplotype, since without crossing over each person would get exactly one chromosome of each homologous pair of chromosomes from each parent. (Bear in mind, though, that there are 2^{23}—or 8,388,608—possible haplotypes derivable from each parent without crossing over; that's one reason why children of the same parents would be different from one another even if there were no recombination of genes in meiosis.)[12]

The word "haplotype" is also used to refer to classes of haplotypes in the sense I have just defined: namely, a class of haplotypes that are identical in some sequence of alleles close to each other on a single chromosome, often, more particularly, a set of genes for proteins that carry out related activities. More precisely, a haplotype in this second sense is fixed by the sequence of alleles on a relatively short continuous stretch of a chromosome (modulo‡ a few SNPs that have little functional significance). From now on I'll use "haplotypes" in this second sense. So to say two people have the same haplotype is to say, roughly, that they share an interesting collection of genes on a single chromosome.

Since the genes in short regions of a chromosome seldom get separated in cell division, your haplotype

---

* Fixed position (plural loci).

† A cell making up the body of an organism, and thus (roughly) any cell except a gamete—a sperm or an egg—or stem cell.

‡ Except for differences with respect to x (usually, that make no relevant difference to the case under discussion).

in this sense is almost always derived from a single parent. As a result, when a SNP arises by mutation in an ancestral chromosome, it provides a marker for descendants of that ancestor, so long as that SNP does not undergo further mutation and the sequence of genes that includes it does not get broken by crossing over. And this is the basis on which African-Americans are now seeking to identify ancestral ties to particular places in Africa.

VIII

Many contemporary African-Americans have come to take an interest in Yoruba religion, especially in the forms mediated by Haitian *vodou* and the Afro-Brazilian traditions of Bahia.* To discover that you have SNPs associated with a haplotype distinctive of contemporary Yorubaland† would be, for many African-Americans, therefore, an exciting discovery. But Yoruba identity provides a good paradigm of the difficulties faced by those seeking an African identity through the human genome project.

The HapMap Project‡ has a site in Ibadan in Nigeria, a city that is predominantly Yoruba, and the ninety or so individuals in thirty families whose genes were sampled there identified themselves as having four Yoruba grandparents. The theory is simple enough. Find SNPs (or sets of them) in haplotypes that are common in Ibadan today, and that have not been found elsewhere. While there will be contemporary Yoruba people who don't have this polymorphism, it is extremely unlikely that anyone that does carry it does not share ancestry with those that do.

For someone not descended from the ancestor to have both the haplotype and the SNP, they would both have to have both the same sequence of alleles and have an ancestor who had the same SNP produced by a mutation at exactly the same locus. With 3.6 million SNPs already validated, that is extremely unlikely.

The empirical conditions under which this sort of thing can be reliably done are quite constraining, however. You must first be sure that you have identified SNPs that are in fact distinctive of a certain population. To do that, you have, of course, not only to have detailed knowledge of the genome in Yorubaland, but also knowledge of the genome in other (especially nearby) places. That is the knowledge that the HapMap aims to provide.

Notice that if a SNP originated with a mutation, say a thousand or even five hundred years ago, it may in fact be quite widely dispersed. So, for example, some significant number of the contemporary descendants of that common ancestor might have been living hundreds of miles west of their distant cousins for several centuries. Suppose that the reason you share the Yoruba haplotype is that you are descended from someone who was born in what is now the country of Benin in the early eighteenth century. Then, while your ancestor had cousins in what is now Yorubaland, he never identified as Yoruba. For despite the antiquity of many Yoruba traditions, Yoruba identity itself was developed largely in the last hundred years.

Of course, the city of Ife,§ now regarded as the origin and heartland of the Yoruba people, was founded at least a millennium ago. But the city-state that was there in the eleventh century was superseded in the

---

* Faith practiced by the Yoruba, a West African people. Central to the faith are interactions between people and spirits called "Orishas," each of them associated with various ideas and phenomena. Ancestral reincarnation is also a central belief. Many of the enslaved people taken from Africa were Yoruba, and they brought their faith with them to the various places they were taken, where they would continue to practice it within the Christian context forced upon them by slave owners. Haitian *vodou* is a syncretic faith first practiced by West African slaves in the French Empire during the seventeenth and eighteenth centuries, which blends Roman Catholic practices with those of West African Vodun, as practiced by the Fon and Ewe peoples, as well as by the Yoruba. Bahia is a northeastern state of Brazil: the area was the slaving center of Brazil, and its culture was defined in many ways by the West African slaves who were brought there, and their Yoruba-based religious system, Candomblé.

† The cultural region of the Yoruba people in West Africa, spanning southwest and western Nigeria, south and central Benin, and central Togo, and comprising about 55 million people.

‡ An international project that sought to create a haplotype map of the human genome, in an attempt to find the causes of common genetic diseases. The project concluded in 2009.

§ A city in south-western Nigeria.

fourteenth century by the kingdoms of Oyo and Benin (each of which traced the ancestry of its royal lineage to Ife). As Benin declined, Oyo became the dominant state in the region; by the eighteenth century the kings of Oyo were being paid tribute by the kings of Dahomey, a practice that continued well into the nineteenth century. As a result of warfare and trade in the region—including the trade in slaves—some men travelled widely and took wives from, or had children in, political communities other than their own. Dahomey, a major slave-trading state, sold people from Oyo or Benin into the slave trade. But it was only in the twentieth century that people in south-western Nigeria who spoke related dialects of the Yoruba language, began to think of themselves as a single Yoruba nation. Suppose that your haplotype with some of its distinctive SNPs is very likely derived from someone who has many descendants in Ibadan today. Even if your ancestor had been taken from near Ibadan in the eighteenth century, he would not have thought of himself as Yoruba.

Simply put, the interpretation of haplotype data requires that you know some non-biological history. A couple of thousand years ago, iron-smelting people moved south from somewhere north of the Bight of Biafra,* started migrating south and east into equatorial Africa. We call this the Bantu migration because in many of the languages spoken by their descendants from Congo south to the Cape, the word for people is "Bantu." Haplotypes distinctive of that ancestral population could be spread across half the continent. The Ndebele of southern Zimbabwe are largely descendants of migrants from Zululand who escaped from Shaka† in the early nineteenth century. Haplotypes distinctive of Zululand might be found in a person whose ancestor was taken into slavery from Zimbabwe and exported through Angola to Brazil.

Because pre-existing ethnic solidarities were strongly discouraged among slaves in the New World, they were deliberately introduced into groups of multiple origins and discouraged from holding on to their mother tongues. As a result, by the nineteenth century many slaves in the western Atlantic would have had ancestors from a variety of African societies. Finding that one has ancestry in one place is interesting, I suppose. But, given those facts, it seems odd to insist that this is where one is really from. More than this, the population that we call African-American is likely to have eighteenth-century ancestors from many parts of Europe and from Native American Indian populations as well. The converse is also true. It has been estimated that there are as many US citizens who identify as white descended from American slaves as there are who identify as African-American. This is a consequence of two things: the fact that you may claim African-American ancestry if just one of your parents is African-American, and the fact that many people who could have claimed that ancestry chose, beginning in the nineteenth century, to identify as white, because their skins were light enough for them to be able to "pass." As a result, while not many white Americans are going to go hunting for Yoruba haplotypes in their genomes, perhaps thirty or forty million of them in fact have haplotypes derived from ancestors born in Africa in the last four hundred years.

If you grasp these points you are likely to notice that racial identities in social life tend to be configured in a way that takes account of these sorts of complexities, even while people announce commitments to folk biological theories that are inconsistent with them. In practice, for example, race-like social identities in local contexts are important to patterns of solidarity: in these contexts, people whose (partially genetically determined) physical appearance doesn't fit the physical stereotype of the group are counted in or out in part on the basis of whether they identify with the interests of the group, in part by their utility to the group. As claims to be able to settle issues of ancestry by genomic analysis become more common, it will be interesting to see whether the appeal of the determinateness and objectivity of scientific claims will come to override more flexible and interest-relative folk understandings; or whether, on the other hand, people will become increasingly clear about the gap between folk races and the interests of biology.[13]

---

* A large bay on the West African coast.

† A warrior ruler of the Zulu who, during his short lifetime (c. 1787–1828), combined more than a hundred chiefdoms into a powerful Zulu kingdom in southern Africa. Zulu expansion was a significant factor of the *Mfecane* ("Crushing") that depopulated large areas of southern Africa between 1815 and about 1840.

IX

We live in a scientistic civilization.* That is one reason, I suspect, that people want the categories they care about to be "scientific." There are, as I have suggested, ways in which folk race might be connected with biological facts. But current biology, even after the genome project, is very unlikely to endorse race-like categories that are essentialized (in the psychologist's sense); or to find much interest in human subspecies, given the

rather low barriers to gene flow between human groups over the evolutionary timescale. If you want to say there are races, understand race as a social identity, I suggest. But know that as biological and historical knowledge about them is diffused, the criteria of ascription associated with them are likely to change. Know also that as long as they are essentialized they won't correspond to classifications that are likely to be central to theoretical biology, though the statistical distribution of their haplotypes may, from time to time, be of medical interest. ■

Suggestions for Critical Reflection

1. In a 2016 interview with *The Guardian* magazine, Appiah said, "I do think that in the long run if everybody grasped the facts about the relevant biology and the social facts, they'd have to treat race in a different way and stop using it to define each [other]."† Would widespread belief that race is a social construct make a difference in how we treat each other? Why or why not?

2. What, according to Appiah, is a social identity?

3. Evaluate Appiah's claims about the insight offered by the human genome project into the biological basis of races. What does biology have to teach us about the nature of race? What are the implications?

4. How does Appiah's argument challenge ideas of racial essentialism? To what extent does his

argument apply to issues of essentialism in other contexts (in feminist and gender studies, for example)?

5. Why, according to Appiah, might it be useful to know if one had Nigerian ancestry?

6. Think of three group categories with which you self-identify or to which you think others would ascribe you. Examine them using Appiah's various criteria (ascription, identification, treatment, norms). What are the effects of these categories on your life? Would you do better without them, or do they contribute to your life?

7. To what degree would it be difficult to eliminate folk racial categories and move toward a "post-racial" society? To what degree do you think it would be desirable?

Notes

1 Susan Gelman, *The Essential Child*, New York: Oxford University Press, 2003, p. 105.

2 See Gelman 2003, Chapter 11, "Why Do We Essentialize?"

3 See Philip Kitcher, "Race, Ethnicity, Biology, Culture," in Leonard Harris (ed.), *Racism*, Amherst, NY: Humanity, 1999, pp. 87–120.

4 See K.A. Appiah and Amy Gutmann, *Color Conscious: The Political Morality of Race*, Princeton, NJ: Princeton University Press, 1998, and K.A. Appiah, *The Ethics*

of Identity, Princeton, NJ: Princeton University Press, 2005.

5 For those who want to go this way, I suggest the best chance you have is to suppose that someone is competent if their conception picks out most of the Xs in their social environment; where what it is to be an X is explicated in terms of the best scientific account of what it is most users are talking about. One reason I don't favour this approach is that I think that for some social identities the best scientific account is that they're not

---

* Culture that places an exaggerated amount of trust in scientific knowledge over other kinds of knowledge.

† Hannah Ellis-Peterson, "Racial Identity Is a Biological Nonsense, Says Reith Lecturer," October 18, 2016.

referring to anything; but then that would make no users competent, if they thought there were any *X*s at all.

6 I say "roughly" to acknowledge a complication that I will ignore from now on: these classes will usually each be fuzzy.

7 I put it this way because I think it sometimes turns out that hardly anybody really believes in the norm; still, it exists if people mostly think most people endorse it.

8 See O.O. Akinyanju, "A Profile of Sickle Cell Disease in Nigeria," *Annals of the New York Academy of Sciences*, 565.1, 1989, pp. 126–36; and Kenneth R. Bridges, *Information Center for Sickle Cell and Thalassemic Disorders*, http://sickle.bwh.harvard.edu/index.html.

9 Alexandra C. Cherva, Afshin Ameri and Ashok Raj, "Hemoglobin H Disease," *eMedicine*, http://www.emedicine.com/ped/topic955.htm. Last updated: April 2, 2002.

10 This is like the word "gene," which is used to refer both to a locus on the chromosome and to the various alleles that can occur at that locus.

11 The International HapMap Consortium, "A Haplotype Map of the Human Genome," *Nature*, 437, 27 October 2005, p. 1316.

12 This is the reason haplotypes are called haplotypes: the spermatozoa and the oocytes are haploid—they have only one member of each type of chromosome—unlike most somatic cells, which are diploid, having two of each.

13 In thinking about their ancestral roots, the descendants of my English grandparents will have to bear in mind that most of Granny and Grandpa's haplotypes had descendant tokens in at least England, Ghana, Kenya, Namibia, Nigeria, Thailand and the United States, in the bodies of people with haplotypes recently derived from England, Ghana, India, Kenya, Nigeria and Norway, less than fifty years after they died.

References

Akinyanju, O.O. 1989: "A Profile of Sickle Cell Disease in Nigeria." *Annals of the New York Academy of Sciences*, 565.1, pp. 126–36.

Appiah, K.A. 2005: *The Ethics of Identity*. Princeton, NJ: Princeton University Press.

Appiah, K.A. and Amy Gutmann 1998: *Color Conscious: The Political Morality of Race*. Princeton, NJ: Princeton University Press.

Bridges, Kenneth R.: *Information Center for Sickle Cell and Thalassemic Disorders*. http://sickle.bwh.harvard.edu/index.html.

Cherva, Alexandra C., Afshin Ameri and Ashok Raj 2002: "Hemoglobin H Disease." *eMedicine*. http://www.emedicine.com/ped/topic955.htm

Gelman, Susan 2003: *The Essential Child*. New York: Oxford University Press.

International HapMap Consortium 2005: "A Haplotype Map of the Human Genome." *Nature*, 437, 27 October 2005.

Kitcher, Philip 1999: "Race, Ethnicity, Biology, Culture." In Leonard Harris (ed.), *Racism*, Amherst, NY: Humanity, 1999.

TA-NEHISI COATES

FROM *Between the World and Me*

Who Is Ta-Nehisi Coates?

One of North America's most prominent public intellectuals, Ta-Nehisi Coates is best known for his writing on black oppression in the United States. Born in 1975, Coates grew up in inner-city Baltimore, where, as he recounts in his autobiographical writings, he attended a substandard school but received an informal education from his parents; his mother was a teacher and his father was an activist who operated an independent press focused on classic works by black writers. Coates attended Howard University for five years before becoming a journalist. He rose to prominence as a regular blogger for the political magazine *The Atlantic*; his career accelerated around the same time as Barack Obama achieved the presidency, and Coates became known especially as a commentator on race and the Obama administration. His position as a journalist was cemented with "The Case for Reparations" (2014), an extensive feature article in *The Atlantic* that provoked a national conversation with its meticulous account of black oppression as fundamental to American economic, social, and political life. "The Case for Reparations" would later be reprinted in *We Were Eight Years in Power: An American Tragedy* (2017), a collection featuring one of Coates's essays for each year of Obama's presidency.

In 2015, Coates published *Between the World and Me*, a book-length essay in the form of a letter combining memoir, political commentary, and philosophical reflection. With this work, Coates came to be seen as the latest star in an intellectual genealogy of celebrated black American writers and thinkers; Toni Morrison, for example, famously praised him for "fill[ing] the intellectual void" left by the iconic mid-twentieth-century essayist and novelist James Baldwin. Coates received a National Book Award for *Between the World and Me*, and in the same year he was awarded a prestigious MacArthur "Genius Grant." He also broadened his audience considerably by becoming a writer for Marvel comics, first as the author of a *Black Panther* series beginning in 2016, and then as a writer of *Captain America*.

What Is the Structure of This Reading?

Between the World and Me takes the form of an extended letter to Coates's teenage son Samori—an approach many have seen as referencing the opening of Baldwin's important work *The Fire Next Time* (1963), which the author addressed to his nephew. The structure of Coates's book is thus more discursive and less systematic than is typical of academic philosophy; Coates's presentation of his ideas is intermingled with analysis of American politics and history, as well as his own autobiography.

The book as a whole is divided into three sections, and the portion excerpted below is drawn from the first. In this section, Coates traces his own development from childhood to university, outlining how his personal and educational experience led him to his current ideological position regarding black oppression. The rest of the book, not excerpted here, addresses aspects of his life after graduation, including the killing of his friend Prince Jones by police, as well as Coates's travels to France, where he experiences life beyond the shadow of American racism.

Some Useful Background Information

1. Coates's book addresses the full sweep of the history of black oppression in America; thus, it may be helpful to keep the following dates and events in mind:
    *   The first black slaves taken to America arrived in 1619, and, though slavery was outlawed earlier in some states, it was not declared illegal in all states until 1865. Over the course of this period, millions of black people were enslaved (there were almost

four million black slaves in America in 1860 alone),* and they performed an estimated quarter billion hours of forced unpaid labor.†

- The era of slavery was quickly followed by the era of Jim Crow, a name given to a system of laws in various American states between the 1870s and 1960s that required racial segregation in public places and in organizations such as schools and the military. These laws thus effectively ensured that amenities and opportunities for black Americans were far inferior to those available to white Americans. Black-led protest movements led to the removal of many of these laws, but structural inequality and racism persist in the twenty-first century.

- The early 2010s saw the rise of Black Lives Matter, a protest movement combating contemporary black oppression, including the unjustified killing and brutal treatment of black people by police and the mass incarceration of black people (in America in the year Coates wrote *Between the World and Me*, a black man was six times more likely to be in jail than a white man).‡ *Between the World and Me* was published in the year following the 2014 death of Michael Brown, a black teenager who was killed, while unarmed, by a police officer who shot him six times. In Ferguson, Missouri, where the shooting occurred, weeks of protest followed his death, and protest resumed when the officer responsible was not indicted.

FROM *Between the World and Me*§

Son,

Last Sunday the host of a popular news show asked me what it meant to lose my body. The host was broadcasting from Washington, D.C., and I was seated in a remote studio on the far west side of Manhattan. A satellite closed the miles between us, but no machinery could close the gap between her world and the world for which I had been summoned to speak. When the host asked me about my body, her face faded from the screen, and was replaced by a scroll of words, written by me earlier that week.

The host read these words for the audience, and when she finished she turned to the subject of my body, although she did not mention it specifically. But by now I am accustomed to intelligent people asking about the condition of my body without realizing the nature of their request. Specifically, the host wished to know why I felt that white America's progress, or rather the

progress of those Americans who believe that they are white,¶ was built on looting and violence. Hearing this, I felt an old and indistinct sadness well up in me. The answer to this question is the record of the believers themselves. The answer is American history.

There is nothing extreme in this statement. Americans deify democracy in a way that allows for a dim awareness that they have, from time to time, stood in defiance of their God. But democracy is a forgiving God and America's heresies—torture, theft, enslavement—are so common among individuals and nations that none can declare themselves immune. In fact, Americans, in a real sense, have never betrayed their God. When Abraham Lincoln declared, in 1863, that the battle of Gettysburg must ensure "that government of the people, by the people, for the people, shall not perish from the earth," he was not merely being aspirational; at the onset of the Civil War, the

---

* Ta-Nehisi Coates, "Slavery Made America," *The Atlantic*, June 24, 2014.

† Clarence J. Mumford, *Race and Reparations: A Black Perspective for the 21st Century* (Africa World Press, 1996), 428.

‡ "Fact Sheet: Trends in U.S. Corrections," The Sentencing Project, 2015.

§ Ta-Nehisi Coates, *Between the World and Me* (Spiegel & Grau, 2015).

¶ This phrasing echoes James Baldwin's 1987 essay "On Being 'White' ... and Other Lies": "[white Americans] have brought humanity to the edge of oblivion: because they think they are white. Because they think they are white, they do not dare confront the ravage and the lie of their history...."

United States of America had one of the highest rates of suffrage* in the world. The question is not whether Lincoln truly meant "government of the people" but what our country has, throughout its history, taken the political term "people" to actually mean. In 1863 it did not mean your mother or your grandmother, and it did not mean you and me. Thus America's problem is not its betrayal of "government of the people," but the means by which "the people" acquired their names.

This leads us to another equally important ideal, one that Americans implicitly accept but to which they make no conscious claim. Americans believe in the reality of "race" as a defined, indubitable feature of the natural world. Racism—the need to ascribe bone-deep features to people and then humiliate, reduce, and destroy them—inevitably follows from this inalterable condition. In this way, racism is rendered as the innocent daughter of Mother Nature, and one is left to deplore the Middle Passage or the Trail of Tears† the way one deplores an earthquake, a tornado, or any other phenomenon that can be cast as beyond the handiwork of men.

But race is the child of racism, not the father. And the process of naming "the people" has never been a matter of genealogy and physiognomy so much as one of hierarchy. Difference in hue and hair is old. But the belief in the pre-eminence of hue and hair, the notion that these factors can correctly organize a society and that they signify deeper attributes, which are indelible—this is the new idea at the heart of these new people who have been brought up hopelessly, tragically, deceitfully, to believe that they are white.

These new people are, like us, a modern invention. But unlike us, their new name has no real meaning divorced from the machinery of criminal power. The new people were something else before they were white—Catholic, Corsican, Welsh, Mennonite, Jewish—and if all our national hopes have any fulfillment, then they will have to be something else again.

Perhaps they will truly become American and create a nobler basis for their myths. I cannot call it. As for now, it must be said that the process of washing the disparate tribes white, the elevation of the belief in being white, was not achieved through wine tastings and ice cream socials, but rather through the pillaging of life, liberty, labor, and land; through the flaying of backs; the chaining of limbs; the strangling of dissidents; the destruction of families; the rape of mothers; the sale of children; and various other acts meant, first and foremost, to deny you and me the right to secure and govern our own bodies.

The new people are not original in this. Perhaps there has been, at some point in history, some great power whose elevation was exempt from the violent exploitation of other human bodies. If there has been, I have yet to discover it. But this banality of violence can never excuse America, because America makes no claim to the banal. America believes itself exceptional, the greatest and noblest nation ever to exist, a lone champion standing between the white city of democracy and the terrorists, despots, barbarians, and other enemies of civilization. One cannot, at once, claim to be superhuman and then plead mortal error. I propose to take our countrymen's claims of American exceptionalism seriously, which is to say I propose subjecting our country to an exceptional moral standard. This is difficult because there exists, all around us, an apparatus urging us to accept American innocence at face value and not to inquire too much. And it is so easy to look away, to live with the fruits of our history and to ignore the great evil done in all of our names. But you and I have never truly had that luxury. I think you know.

I write you in your fifteenth year. I am writing you because this was the year you saw Eric Garner choked to death for selling cigarettes; because you know now that Renisha McBride was shot for seeking help, that John Crawford was shot down for browsing in a department store. And you have seen men in

---

* The right to vote.

† The Middle Passage refers to the forced sea transportation of slaves from Africa to the Americas. It was the second leg of a profitable eighteenth-century triangular trading route that went from Europe to West Africa (carrying manufactured trade goods), from Africa to America (carrying slaves), and then from the Americas back to Europe (carrying raw materials such as sugar, cotton, or tobacco). Travel conditions were deplorable and about 15 per cent of the slaves transported died before arrival. The Trail of Tears is the name given to the 1848 forced displacement of Cherokee people from their homes in Georgia to an area in what is now Oklahoma. The American government compelled the displaced people to march in large groups with inadequate provisions, and thousands died on the way.

uniform drive by and murder Tamir Rice, a twelve-year-old child whom they were oath-bound to protect.[*] And you have seen men in the same uniforms pummel Marlene Pinnock,[†] someone's grandmother, on the side of a road. And you know now, if you did not before, that the police departments of your country have been endowed with the authority to destroy your body. It does not matter if the destruction is the result of an unfortunate overreaction. It does not matter if it originates in a misunderstanding. It does not matter if the destruction springs from a foolish policy. Sell cigarettes without the proper authority and your body can be destroyed. Resent the people trying to entrap your body and it can be destroyed. Turn into a dark stairwell and your body can be destroyed. The destroyers will rarely be held accountable. Mostly they will receive pensions. And destruction is merely the superlative form of a dominion whose prerogatives include friskings, detainings, beatings, and humiliations. All of this is common to black people. And all of this is old for black people. No one is held responsible.

There is nothing uniquely evil in these destroyers or even in this moment. The destroyers are merely men enforcing the whims of our country, correctly interpreting its heritage and legacy. It is hard to face this. But all our phrasing—race relations, racial chasm, racial justice, racial profiling, white privilege, even white supremacy—serves to obscure that racism is a visceral experience, that it dislodges brains, blocks airways, rips muscle, extracts organs, cracks bones, breaks teeth. You must never look away from this. You must always remember that the sociology, the history, the economics, the graphs, the charts, the regressions all land, with great violence, upon the body.

That Sunday, with that host, on that news show, I tried to explain this as best I could within the time allotted. But at the end of the segment, the host flashed a widely shared picture of an eleven-year-old black boy tearfully hugging a white police officer. Then she asked me about "hope." And I knew then that I had failed. And I remembered that I had expected to fail. And I wondered again at the indistinct sadness welling up in me. Why exactly was I sad? I came out of the studio and walked for a while. It was a calm December day. Families, believing themselves white, were out on the streets. Infants, raised to be white, were bundled in strollers. And I was sad for these people, much as I was sad for the host and sad for all the people out there watching and reveling in a specious hope. I realized then why I was sad. When the journalist asked me about my body, it was like she was asking me to awaken her from the most gorgeous dream. I have seen that dream all my life. It is perfect houses with nice lawns. It is Memorial Day cookouts, block associations, and driveways. The Dream is treehouses and the Cub Scouts. The Dream smells like peppermint but tastes like strawberry shortcake. And for so long I have wanted to escape into the Dream, to fold my country over my head like a blanket. But this has never been an option because the Dream rests on our backs, the bedding made from our bodies. And knowing this, knowing that the Dream persists by warring with the known world, I was sad for the host, I was sad for all those families, I was sad for my country, but above all, in that moment, I was sad for you.

That was the week you learned that the killers of Michael Brown would go free.[‡] The men who had left his body in the street like some awesome declaration of their inviolable power would never be punished. It was not my expectation that anyone would ever be punished. But you were young and still believed. You stayed up till 11 P.M. that night, waiting for the announcement of an indictment, and when instead it was announced that there was none you said, "I've got to go," and you went into your room, and I heard you crying. I came in five minutes after, and I didn't hug you, and I didn't comfort you, because I thought it would be wrong to comfort you. I did not tell you

---

[*] This passage lists black people whose killing provoked public outcry: Eric Garner, killed by New York police in 2014 when he was arrested under suspicion of illegally selling individual cigarettes; Renisha McBride, a teenager who died in 2013 when, after having been in a traffic accident, she walked up to a house and was shot by its occupant; John Crawford III, who was shot by police in 2015 because he was carrying a BB gun that was for sale in the Walmart where he was shopping; and Tamir Rice, a child who was shot and killed by Cleveland police in 2014.

[†] A black woman who in 2014 was punched forcefully and repeatedly by a police officer, Pinnock has a mental health condition, and the officer claimed that he was attempting to prevent her from walking into traffic.

[‡] See the Introduction section of this reading.

that it would be okay, because I have never believed it would be okay. What I told you is what your grandparents tried to tell me: that this is your country, that this is your world, that this is your body, and you must find some way to live within the all of it. I tell you now that the question of how one should live within a black body, within a country lost in the Dream, is the question of my life, and the pursuit of this question, I have found, ultimately answers itself.

This must seem strange to you. We live in a "goal-oriented" era. Our media vocabulary is full of hot takes, big ideas, and grand theories of everything. But some time ago I rejected magic in all its forms. This rejection was a gift from your grandparents, who never tried to console me with ideas of an afterlife and were skeptical of preordained American glory. In accepting both the chaos of history and the fact of my total end, I was freed to truly consider how I wished to live—specifically, how do I live free in this black body? It is a profound question because America understands itself as God's handiwork, but the black body is the clearest evidence that America is the work of men. I have asked the question through my reading and writings, through the music of my youth, through arguments with your grandfather, with your mother, your aunt Janai, your uncle Ben. I have searched for answers in nationalist myth, in classrooms, out on the streets, and on other continents. The question is unanswerable, which is not to say futile. The greatest reward of this constant interrogation, of confrontation with the brutality of my country, is that it has freed me from ghosts and girded me against the sheer terror of disembodiment....

[As a child] I could not retreat, as did so many, into the church and its mysteries. My parents rejected all dogmas. We spurned the holidays marketed by the people who wanted to be white. We would not stand for their anthems. We would not kneel before their God. And so I had no sense that any just God was on my side. "The meek shall inherit the earth" meant nothing to me. The meek were battered in West Baltimore, stomped out at Walbrook Junction, bashed up on Park Heights,* and raped in the showers of the city jail. My understanding of the universe was physical, and its moral arc bent toward chaos then concluded in a box....

Every February my classmates and I were herded into assemblies for a ritual review of the Civil Rights Movement. Our teachers urged us toward the example of freedom marchers, Freedom Riders, and Freedom Summers,† and it seemed that the month could not pass without a series of films dedicated to the glories of being beaten on camera. The black people in these films seemed to love the worst things in life—love the dogs that rent their children apart, the tear gas that clawed at their lungs, the fire-hoses that tore off their clothes and tumbled them into the streets. They seemed to love the men who raped them, the women who cursed them, love the children who spat on them, the terrorists that bombed them. *Why are they showing this to us?* Why were only our heroes nonviolent? I speak not of the morality of nonviolence, but of the sense that blacks are in especial need of this morality. Back then all I could do was measure these freedom-lovers by what I knew. Which is to say, I measured them against children pulling out in the 7-Eleven parking lot, against parents wielding extension cords, and "Yeah, nigger, what's up now?"‡ I judged them against the country I knew, which had acquired the land through murder and tamed it under slavery, against the country whose armies fanned out across the world to extend their dominion. The world, the real one, was civilization secured and ruled by savage means. How could the schools valorize men and women whose values society actively scorned? How could they send us out into the streets of Baltimore, knowing all that they were, and then speak of nonviolence?

I came to see the streets and the schools as arms of the same beast. One enjoyed the official power of the

---

* These areas of Baltimore have a predominantly black population and high rates of poverty and crime.

† The Freedom Rides of 1961 protested the segregation of public buses, while the Freedom Summer was an intensive campaign to register black voters in Mississippi in 1964. The nonviolent civil rights activists engaged in these projects, like those who participated in the freedom marches, often experienced brutal violence from both police and civilians.

‡ In a portion of this book not reprinted here, Coates discusses an incident in which, at the age of 11, he witnessed an older boy pull out a gun in a 7-Eleven parking lot. He also recounts that safety concerns forced him to belong to a "crew" that controlled a portion of the city; he mentions the phrase "Yeah, nigger, what's up now?" in the context of one crew returning aggression expressed by another.

state while the other enjoyed its implicit sanction. But fear and violence were the weaponry of both. Fail in the streets and the crews would catch you slipping and take your body. Fail in the schools and you would be suspended and sent back to those same streets, where they would take your body. And I began to see these two arms in relation—those who failed in the schools justified their destruction in the streets. The society could say, "He should have stayed in school," and then wash its hands of him.

It does not matter that the "intentions" of individual educators were noble. Forget about intentions. What any institution, or its agents, "intend" for you is secondary. Our world is physical. Learn to play defense—ignore the head and keep your eyes on the body. Very few Americans will directly proclaim that they are in favor of black people being left to the streets. But a very large number of Americans will do all they can to preserve the Dream. No one directly proclaimed that schools were designed to sanctify failure and destruction. But a great number of educators spoke of "personal responsibility" in a country authored and sustained by a criminal irresponsibility. The point of this language of "intention" and "personal responsibility" is broad exoneration. Mistakes were made. Bodies were broken. People were enslaved. We meant well. We tried our best. "Good intention" is a hall pass through history, a sleeping pill that ensures the Dream....

My only Mecca was, is, and shall always be Howard University.* ... I was admitted to Howard University, but formed and shaped by The Mecca. These institutions are related but not the same. Howard University is an institution of higher education, concerned with the LSAT, magna cum laude, and Phi Beta Kappa. The Mecca is a machine, crafted to capture and concentrate the dark energy of all African peoples and inject it directly into the student body. The Mecca derives its power from the heritage of Howard University, which in Jim Crow days enjoyed a near-monopoly on black talent.... The history, the location, the alumni combined to create The Mecca—the crossroads of the black diaspora....

[During my time at university the] black world was expanding before me, and I could see now that that world was more than a photonegative of that of the people who believe they are white. "White America" is a syndicate arrayed to protect its exclusive power to dominate and control our bodies. Sometimes this power is direct (lynching), and sometimes it is insidious (redlining†). But however it appears, the power of domination and exclusion is central to the belief in being white, and without it, "white people" would cease to exist for want of reasons. There will surely always be people with straight hair and blue eyes, as there have been for all history. But some of these straight-haired people with blue eyes have been "black," and this points to the great difference between their world and ours. We did not choose our fences. They were imposed on us by Virginia planters obsessed with enslaving as many Americans as possible. They are the ones who came up with a one-drop rule that separated the "white" from the "black," even if it meant that their own blue-eyed sons would live under the lash.‡ The result is a people, black people, who embody all physical varieties and whose life stories mirror this physical range. Through The Mecca I saw that we were, in our own segregated body politic, cosmopolitans. The black diaspora was not just our own world but, in so many ways, the Western world itself.

Now, the heirs of those Virginia planters could never directly acknowledge this legacy or reckon with

---

* A prestigious historically black university in Washington, DC.

† The practice of withholding services to people because of the racial or ethnic makeup of the neighborhoods they live in.

‡ The one-drop rule is a principle of racial classification that holds that any person with even one ancestor of sub-Saharan African ancestry ("one drop" of black blood) is considered black rather than white. By the 1930s this was explicitly the law in Tennessee, Louisiana, Texas, Arkansas, Mississippi, North Carolina, Virginia, Alabama, Georgia, and Oklahoma, and similarly restrictive statutes were on the books in Florida, Indiana, Kentucky, Maryland, Missouri, Nebraska, North Dakota, and Utah. It wasn't until 1967 that the US Supreme Court found such laws to be unconstitutional.

its power. And so that beauty that Malcolm* pledged us to protect, black beauty, was never celebrated in movies, in television, or in the textbooks I'd seen as a child. Everyone of any import,† from Jesus to George Washington, was white. This was why your grandparents banned Tarzan and the Lone Ranger and toys with white faces from the house. They were rebelling against the history books that spoke of black people only as sentimental "firsts"—first black five-star general, first black congressman, first black mayor—always presented in the bemused manner of a category of Trivial Pursuit. Serious history was the West, and the West was white. This was all distilled for me in a quote I once read from the novelist Saul Bellow.‡ I can't remember where I read it, or when—only that I was already at Howard. "Who is the Tolstoy§ of the Zulus?" Bellow quipped. Tolstoy was "white," and so Tolstoy "mattered," like everything else that was white "mattered." And this view of things was connected to the fear that passed through the generations, to the sense of dispossession. We were black, beyond the visible spectrum, beyond civilization. Our history was inferior because we were inferior, which is to say our bodies were inferior. And our inferior bodies could not possibly be accorded the same respect as those that built the West. Would it not be better, then, if our bodies were civilized, improved, and put to some legitimate Christian use?

Contrary to this theory, I had Malcolm. I had my mother and father. I had my readings of every issue of *The Source* and *Vibe*.¶ I read them not merely because I loved black music—I did—but because of the writing itself. Writers Greg Tate, Chairman Mao, dream hampton—barely older than me—were out there creating a new language, one that I intuitively understood, to analyze our art, our world. This was, in and of itself, an argument for the weight and beauty of our culture and thus of our bodies. And now each day, out on the Yard,** I felt this weight and saw this beauty, not just as a matter of theory but also as demonstrable fact. And I wanted desperately to communicate this evidence to the world, because I felt—even if I did not completely know—that the larger culture's erasure of black beauty was intimately connected to the destruction of black bodies.

What was required was a new story, a new history told through the lens of our struggle. I had always known this, had heard the need for a new history in Malcolm, had seen the need addressed in my father's books. It was in the promise behind their grand titles—*Children of the Sun*, *Wonderful Ethiopians of the Ancient Cushite Empire*, *The African Origin of Civilization*. Here was not just our history but the history of the world, weaponized to our noble ends. Here was the primordial stuff of our own Dream—the Dream of a "black race"—of our own Tolstoys who lived deep in the African past, where we authored operas, pioneered secret algebra, erected ornate walls, pyramids, colossi, bridges, roads, and all the inventions that I then thought must qualify one's lineage for the ranks of civilization. They had their champions, and somewhere we must have ours. By then I'd read Chancellor Williams, J.A. Rogers, and John Jackson††—writers central to the canon of our new noble history. From them I knew that Mansa Musa of Mali was black, and Shabaka of Egypt was black, and Yaa Asantewaa of Ashanti was black‡‡—and "the black

---

* Malcolm X (1925–65) was an important mid-century black activist and intellectual; elsewhere in the book, Coates recounts the important role Malcolm's ideas played in the formation of Coates's own worldview.

† Importance.

‡ Bellow (1915–2005) was a Canadian-American writer, recipient of the Nobel Prize for Literature in 1976.

§ Leo Tolstoy (1828–1910) was an important Russian novelist of the nineteenth century.

¶ *The Source* and *Vibe* are both magazines with a focus on hip hop music and culture.

** An open space on the Howard University campus.

†† The three writers mentioned are associated with twentieth-century Afrocentrism, a movement focused on the celebration and study of African history, especially as a means of empowering people of African ancestry.

‡‡ Musa I (c. 1280–c. 1337), Mansa (emperor) of the Mali Empire in West Africa, presided over a period of rapid expansion and remarkable economic prosperity. Shabaka, an Egyptian pharaoh of the eighth century BCE, encouraged a revival of Egyptian culture and reconsolidated power after a period of division in Egypt. Yaa Asantewaa (1840–1921) led the Ashanti Empire in a war against British colonization; the Ashanti were ultimately unsuccessful, but her courage and strategic brilliance made her an inspirational figure.

race" was a thing I supposed existed from time immemorial, a thing that was real and mattered.

When I came to Howard, Chancellor Williams's *Destruction of Black Civilization* was my Bible. Williams himself had taught at Howard. I read him when I was sixteen, and his work offered a grand theory of multi-millennial European plunder. The theory relieved me of certain troubling questions—this is the point of nationalism—and it gave me my Tolstoy. I read about Queen Nzinga, who ruled in Central Africa in the sixteenth century, resisting the Portuguese. I read about her negotiating with the Dutch. When the Dutch ambassador tried to humiliate her by refusing her a seat, Nzinga had shown her power by ordering one of her advisers to all fours to make a human chair of her body. That was the kind of power I sought, and the story of our own royalty became for me a weapon. My working theory then held all black people as kings in exile, a nation of original men severed from our original names and our majestic Nubian culture. Surely this was the message I took from gazing out on the Yard. Had any people, anywhere, ever been as sprawling and beautiful as us? ...

I would walk out into the city and find other searchers at lectures, book signings, and poetry readings. I was still writing bad poetry. I read this bad poetry at open mics in local cafés populated mostly by other poets who also felt the insecurity of their bodies. All of these poets were older and wiser than me, and many of them were well read, and they brought this wisdom to bear on me and my work. What did I mean, *specifically*, by the loss of my body? And if every black body was precious, a one of one, if Malcolm was correct and you must preserve your life, how could I see these precious lives as simply a collective mass, as the amorphous residue of plunder? How could I privilege the spectrum of dark energy over each particular ray of light? These were notes on how to write, and thus notes on how to think. The Dream thrives on generalization, on limiting the number of possible questions, on privileging immediate answers. The Dream is the enemy of all art, courageous thinking, and honest writing. And it became clear that this was

not just for the dreams concocted by Americans to justify themselves but also for the dreams that I had conjured to replace them. I had thought that I must mirror the outside world, create a carbon copy of white claims to civilization. It was beginning to occur to me to question the logic of the claim itself. I had forgotten my own self-interrogations pushed upon me by my mother, or rather I had not yet apprehended their deeper, lifelong meaning. I was only beginning to learn to be wary of my own humanity, of my own hurt and anger—I didn't yet realize that the boot on your neck is just as likely to make you delusional as it is to ennoble....

I began to see discord, argument, chaos, perhaps even fear, as a kind of power. I was learning to live in the disquiet I felt in Moorland-Spingarn,* in the mess of my mind. The gnawing discomfort, the chaos, the intellectual vertigo was not an alarm. It was a beacon.

It began to strike me that the point of my education was a kind of discomfort, was the process that would not award me my own especial Dream but would break all the dreams, all the comforting myths of Africa, of America, and everywhere, and would leave me only with humanity in all its terribleness. And there was so much terrible out there, even among us. You must understand this.

Back then, I knew, for instance, that just outside of Washington, D.C., there was a great enclave of black people who seemed, as much as anyone, to have seized control of their bodies. This enclave was Prince George's County—"PG County" to the locals—and it was, to my eyes, very rich. Its residents had the same homes, with the same backyards, with the same bathrooms, I'd seen in those televised dispatches. They were black people who elected their own politicians, but these politicians, I learned, superintended a police force as vicious as any in America. I had heard stories about PG County from the same poets who opened my world. These poets assured me that the PG County police were not police at all but privateers, gangsters, gunmen, plunderers operating under the color of law. They told me this because they wanted to protect my body. But there was another lesson here: To be black

---

* The Moorland-Spingarn Research Center (MSRC), founded in 1973 on the campus of Howard University, is one of the world's largest and most comprehensive repositories documenting the history and culture of people of African descent.

and beautiful was not a matter for gloating. Being black did not immunize us from history's logic or the lure of the Dream. The writer, and that was what I was becoming, must be wary of every Dream and every nation, even his own nation. Perhaps his own nation more than any other, precisely because it was his own.

I began to feel that something more than a national trophy case was needed if I was to be truly free, and for that I have the history department of Howard University to thank. My history professors thought nothing of telling me that my search for myth was doomed, that the stories I wanted to tell myself could not be matched to truths. Indeed, they felt it their duty to disabuse me of my weaponized history. They had seen so many Malcolmites before and were ready. Their method was rough and direct. Did black skin really convey nobility? Always? *Yes.* What about the blacks who'd practiced slavery for millennia and sold slaves across the Sahara and then across the sea? *Victims of a trick.* Would those be the same black kings who birthed all of civilization? Were they then both deposed masters of the galaxy and gullible puppets all at once? And what did I mean by "black"? *You know, black.* Did I think this a timeless category stretching into the deep past? *Yes?* Could it be supposed that simply because color was important to me, it had always been so?

I remember taking a survey class focusing on Central Africa. My professor, Linda Heywood, was slight and bespectacled, spoke with a high Trinidadian lilt that she employed like a hammer against young students like me who confused agitprop* with hard study. There was nothing romantic about her Africa, or rather, there was nothing romantic in the sense that I conceived of it. And she took it back to the legacy of Queen Nzinga—my Tolstoy—the very same Nzinga whose life I wished to put in my trophy case. But when she told the story of Nzinga conducting negotiations upon the woman's back, she told it without any fantastic gloss, and it hit me hard as a sucker punch: Among the people in that room, all those centuries ago, my body, breakable at will, endangered in the streets, fearful in the schools, was not closest to the queen's but to her adviser's, who'd been broken down into a chair so that a queen, heir to everything she'd ever seen, could sit.

I took a survey of Europe post-1800. I saw black people, rendered through "white" eyes, unlike any I'd seen before—the black people looked regal and human. I remember the soft face of Alessandro de' Medici, the royal bearing of Bosch's black magi.† These images, cast in the sixteenth and seventeenth centuries, were contrasted with those created after enslavement, the Sambo‡ caricatures I had always known. What was the difference? In my survey course of America, I'd seen portraits of the Irish drawn in the same ravenous, lustful, and simian way. Perhaps there had been other bodies, mocked, terrorized, and insecure. Perhaps the Irish too had once lost their bodies. Perhaps being named "black" had nothing to do with any of this; perhaps being named "black" was just someone's name for being at the bottom, a human turned to object, object turned to pariah.

This heap of realizations was a weight. I found them physically painful and exhausting. True, I was coming to enjoy the dizziness, the vertigo that must come with any odyssey. But in those early moments, the unceasing contradictions sent me into a gloom. There was nothing holy or particular in my skin; I was black because of history and heritage. There was no nobility in falling, in being bound, in living oppressed, and there was no inherent meaning in black blood. Black blood wasn't black; black *skin* wasn't even black. And now I looked back on my need for a trophy case, on the desire to live by the standards of Saul Bellow, and I felt that this need was not an escape but fear again—fear that "they," the alleged authors and heirs of the universe, were right. And this fear ran so deep that we accepted their standards of civilization and humanity.

But not all of us. It must have been around that time that I discovered an essay by Ralph Wiley in

---

*   Political propaganda.

†   Alessandro de' Medici (1511–37), Duke of Florence, was of mixed Italian and African heritage; he is depicted in several portraits. A particularly striking figure in Hieronymus Bosch's *The Adoration of the Magi* (late fifteenth century) is the African king depicted as one of the three magi.

‡   "Sambo" was a common slave name that became a derogatory term for any black person.

which he responded to Bellow's quip. "Tolstoy is the Tolstoy of the Zulus," wrote Wiley. "Unless you find a profit in fencing off universal properties of mankind into exclusive tribal ownership."* And there it was. I had accepted Bellow's premise. In fact, Bellow was no closer to Tolstoy than I was to Nzinga. And if I were closer it would be because I chose to be, not because of destiny written in DNA. My great error was not that I had accepted someone else's dream but that I had accepted the fact of dreams, the need for escape, and the invention of racecraft.

And still and all I knew that *we were* something, that we were a tribe—on one hand, invented, and on the other, no less real....

I think now of the old rule that held that should a boy be set upon in someone else's chancy hood, his friends must stand with him, and they must all take their beating together. I now know that within this edict lay the key to all living. None of us were promised to end the fight on our feet, fists raised to the sky. We could not control our enemies' number, strength, nor weaponry. Sometimes you just caught a bad one. But whether you fought or ran, you did it together, because that is the part that was in our control. What we must never do is willingly hand over our own bodies or the bodies of our friends. That was the wisdom: We knew we did not lay down the direction of the street, but despite that, we could—and must—fashion the way of our walk. And that is the deeper meaning of your name†—that the struggle, in and of itself, has meaning.

That wisdom is not unique to our people, but I think it has special meaning to those of us born out of mass rape, whose ancestors were carried off and divided up into policies and stocks. I have raised you to respect every human being as singular, and you must extend that same respect into the past. Slavery is not an indefinable mass of flesh. It is a particular, specific enslaved woman, whose mind is as active as your own, whose range of feeling is as vast as your own; who prefers the way the light falls in one particular spot in the woods, who enjoys fishing where the water eddies in a nearby stream, who loves her mother in her own complicated way, thinks her sister talks too loud, has a favorite cousin, a favorite season, who excels at dress-making and knows, inside herself, that she is as intelligent and capable as anyone. "Slavery" is this same woman born in a world that loudly proclaims its love of freedom and inscribes this love in its essential texts, a world in which these same professors‡ hold this woman a slave, hold her mother a slave, her father a slave, her daughter a slave, and when this woman peers back into the generations all she sees is the enslaved. She can hope for more. She can imagine some future for her grandchildren. But when she dies, the world—which is really the only world she can ever know—ends. For this woman, enslavement is not a parable. It is damnation. It is the never-ending night. And the length of that night is most of our history. Never forget that we were enslaved in this country longer than we have been free. Never forget that for 250 years black people were born into chains—whole generations followed by more generations who knew nothing but chains.

You must struggle to truly remember this past in all its nuance, error, and humanity. You must resist the common urge toward the comforting narrative of divine law, toward fairy tales that imply some irrepressible justice. The enslaved were not bricks in your road, and their lives were not chapters in your redemptive history. They were people turned to fuel for the American machine. Enslavement was not destined to end, and it is wrong to claim our present circumstance—no matter how improved—as the redemption for the lives of people who never asked for the posthumous, untouchable glory of dying for their children. Our triumphs can never compensate for this. Perhaps our triumphs are not even the point. Perhaps struggle is all we have because the god of history is an atheist, and nothing about his world is meant to be. So you must wake up every morning knowing that no promise is unbreakable, least of all the promise of waking up at all. This is not despair. These are the preferences

---

* Ralph Wiley (1952–2004), a leading sports journalist, was also a well-regarded essayist on race in America. This quotation is from "Why Black People Are So Stupid," in *Dark Witness: When Black People Should Be Sacrificed* (Again) (Ballantine Books, 1996).

† Coates's son is named after Samori Ture (c. 1830–1900), a West African emperor who achieved several victories against French colonial forces, although his resistance ultimately failed.

‡ Those who profess (love of freedom).

of the universe itself: verbs over nouns, actions over states, struggle over hope.

The birth of a better world is not ultimately up to you, though I know, each day, there are grown men and women who tell you otherwise. The world needs saving precisely because of the actions of these same men and women. I am not a cynic. I love you, and I love the world, and I love it more with every new inch I discover. But you are a black boy, and you must be responsible for your body in a way that other boys cannot know. Indeed, you must be responsible for the worst actions of other black bodies, which, somehow, will always be assigned to you. And you must be responsible for the bodies of the powerful—the policeman who cracks you with a nightstick will quickly find his excuse in your furtive movements. And this is not reducible to just you—the women around you must be responsible for their bodies in a way that you never will know. You have to make your peace with the chaos, but you cannot lie. You cannot forget how much they took from us and how they transfigured our very bodies into sugar, tobacco, cotton, and gold. ■

Suggestions for Critical Reflection

1. Coates asks himself this question: "How do I live free in this black body?" How does he respond to this question? Is his response satisfactory?

2. What, according to Coates, is race? In what way—if at all—should it be considered real? If you have read the article by Kwame Anthony Appiah in this chapter, you might want to consider how Coates's and Appiah's views on race fit together (if they do).

3. Coates's argument is focused on experiences of blackness in the United States. What portion (if any) of his key claims are applicable only to the United States, and what portion (if any) are applicable elsewhere? (If you live outside the United States, consider what claims are applicable to your own country; if you live within the United States, consider what claims are applicable globally.)

4. How does atheism shape the view of history put forward in *Between the World and Me*? How is this view of history reflected in the vision of personal ethics offered in the book?

5. What is "the Dream"? How is the Dream for people who are considered white different from the Dream for those who are considered black—and how is it similar?

6. What does Coates suggest about the relationship between the body and the self? How does this inform his interpretation of the harm done to individuals by racial injustice?

7. While *Between the World and Me* has been widely acclaimed, the book has also been criticized as advocating hopelessness in the face of black oppression rather than encouraging political resistance. Michelle Alexander, for example argues the following in her review of the book:

> [W]e must not ask whether it is possible for a human being or society to become just or moral; we must believe it is possible. Believing in this possibility—no matter how slim—and dedicating oneself to playing a meaningful role in the struggle to make it a reality focuses one's energy and attention in a useful way.*

Is this a legitimate objection to the ideas Coates puts forward? Why or why not?

---

* Michelle Alexander, "Ta-Nehisi Coates's 'Between the World and Me,'" *The New York Times*, 17 August 2015.

What Is the Meaning of Life?

What makes life meaningful? Does life have a purpose, and if so, what is it? Is this purpose—if there is one—something that comes from outside of ourselves, and that we need to discover, or are we responsible for creating our own purpose? In general, what is it to lead a good life? For example, if part of leading a good life is being happy, then how do we do that—how can we construct a happy life?

Many philosophers throughout history have sought to clarify and to answer these important questions, and if you have worked your way through the readings in the other chapters of this book—especially the chapter on Ethical Theory—you will have already encountered some important efforts to address these issues. For example, Plato examined the connection between being good and being happy, and argued that true psychologi-

cal health comes from moral virtue; Aristotle influentially asserted that human beings have a *telos*—an intrinsic function or nature—and that human flourishing consists in living in accordance with this function; Kant argued carefully that the highest good for human beings is the good will; while Mill focused on sensations of pleasure and developed a nuanced view of the best way to cultivate and preserve human happiness.

What most pre-twentieth-century responses to the problem of the meaning of life have in common is that they depend upon some substantive metaphysical framework or other: a commitment to the position that the universe has meaning *built in to it*, either into human nature itself, or some super-natural organizing principle for the world (such as God's design, or pure rationality), or both. From this perspective, the task of the philosopher is to find out what the actual meaning of life really is, so that we can do a better job of living our lives in accordance with it; and this is a question that has a particular answer that we can either get right or get wrong. (Furthermore, since there is only one right answer and multiple competing theories, most people presumably get it at least partially wrong.)

Suppose, however, that the universe does not come with meaning baked in. Suppose that we, as human beings, are not responsible for finding and matching the predetermined pattern by which we (really, objectively) should live our lives—because there simply is no such pattern—but instead we have the awful responsibility of *creating* meaning—of bringing meaning into a universe that, prior to our decision, had no such meaning. What should we do then? Is this a counsel of despair, pure nihilism, or could there still be a satisfying story to be told about the meaning of life under such conditions? Could we still be happy? This, roughly, is the starting point for the readings in this chapter.

Epictetus represents the ancient Greek and Roman school of thought called stoicism. A guiding principle of stoicism is that the universe is driven by deterministic natural principles that are beyond our control, and the secret of happiness is to bring our will into line with what is going to happen anyway—to accept each moment as it presents itself, rather than struggling against it and wishing it were otherwise than it is.* Epictetus lays out some concrete advice for how to achieve this kind of serenity.

We then jump to the twentieth century and a selection from A.J. Ayer who argues briskly, as a logical positivist, that the question "What is the meaning of life?" makes no sense—is nonsensical—and therefore has no coherent answer. We should not regret being unable to answer this impossible question, therefore, but instead, Ayer advises, should decide as individuals how we want to live, based on our own personal interests and projects.

Jean-Paul Sartre, in the next reading, explains the philosophical stance called Existentialism, which similarly (though for different reasons) asserts that the universe is meaningless, that God does not exist and hence that it is up to us to create meaning for ourselves from our position of anguish, abandonment and despair. Albert Camus is often considered an existentialist also, though he disavowed the label, and in "The Myth of Sisyphus" he introduces the notion of the Absurd: the idea that the human condition is that we live in a world that offers neither meaning nor clear understanding and yet—absurdly—we yearn for both. Camus argues that our response to this fact of life should be heroic defiance. Thomas Nagel, in the next reading, also discusses the absurdity of life in a universe without built-in meaning, but offers a different diagnosis and response than Camus, arguing that "we can approach our absurd lives with irony instead of heroism or despair."

Finally, Kathy Behrendt addresses the question of whether "any reason for living is a reason for not dying." She runs through a series of theories about what makes for a good life, and argues that it is less clear than it might first seem what our response to this question should be.

Want to know more about what philosophers have said about the meaning of life? Some good starting points are: Julian Baggini, *What's It All About?: Philosophy and the Meaning of Life* (Granta, 2004); Christopher Belshaw, *10 Good Questions about Life and Death* (Blackwell, 2005); David Benatar, ed., *Life, Death & Meaning* (Rowman & Littlefield, 2016); Jon Cottingham, *On the Meaning of Life* (Routledge, 2002); Terry Eagleton, *The Meaning of Life: A Very Short Introduction* (Oxford University Press, 2008); Dennis Ford, *The Search for Meaning: A Short History* (University of California Press, 2007); Daniel Klein, *Every Time I Find the Meaning of Life, They Change It: Wisdom of the Great Philosophers on How to Live* (Penguin, 2015); Klemke and Cahn, eds., *The Meaning of Life: A Reader* (Oxford University Press, 2017); Runzo and Martin, eds., 2000, *The Meaning of Life in the World Religions* (Oneworld Publications, 2000); Joshua W. Seachris, ed., *Exploring the Meaning of Life: An Anthology and Guide* (Wiley-Blackwell, 2012); and Julian Young, *The Death of God and the Meaning of Life* (Routledge, 2014).

---

* Stoicism is not a perfect fit with the rough classification described above, between metaphysical and nihilistic approaches to the meaning of life, since the stoics in fact did believe that the deterministic principles guiding the universe are rational principles that we might be able to understand and endorse, and so we might come to understand that what looks like misfortune is really nothing of the sort.

EPICTETUS

FROM *Enchiridion*

Who Was Epictetus?

Epictetus was born a slave in about 55 CE in Phrygia, a region of what is now south-western Turkey. The name his parents gave him is unknown: Epictetus is the Greek word (*epíktetos*) for a thing that is acquired as property. He was brought up in Rome as a slave in the household of a wealthy master who was himself a former slave but had been freed and had risen to become a secretary to the notorious Roman emperor Nero. Because of this, Epictetus would have been familiar with life at the imperial court and would have had some exposure to the shifting world of Roman politics. He also seems to have been given unusual privileges by his master, Epaphroditus, and was given permission to attend lectures by one of the foremost Stoic philosophers of the time, Musonius Rufus.

At some point—we don't know exactly when—Epictetus was granted his freedom, and from that point until his old age he devoted his life entirely to the study and teaching of philosophy. In 95 CE Nero's successor Domitian expelled all the philosophers in Italy, suspecting them of stirring up republican sympathies, and Epictetus moved to Greece, where he founded a school at Nicopolis. His boarding school was successful and became a destination for the sons of upper-class Roman families who admired and wanted to learn from Greek culture and philosophy. Epictetus focused on teaching practical philosophical lessons, based on rational arguments, aimed at inspiring his students to make a break with received moral and social notions and to learn to live better lives. Over time his reputation grew, and his school may even have been visited by the emperor Hadrian.

Epictetus did not write down any of his lectures, but they were recorded by some of his students, in particular one named Arrian. The written lectures (only half of which survived) are now known as the *Discourses*, and Arrian also prepared a practical guide to Epictetus's thought called the *Manual* or, in Greek, *Enchiridion*. Although not written by Epictetus himself, these works were thought at the time and since to be essentially his words.

In accordance with his philosophy, Epictetus lived very simply and had few attachments or possessions. It was only late in his life that he retired from teaching and the responsibilities of being a philosopher and allowed himself to take on a family, adopting an abandoned child and taking in a female servant to act as a mother and domestic helper. Though Epictetus suffered from ill health and walked with a limp throughout his life,* he lived to the age of about 80 and died in 135 CE.

What Is the Structure of This Reading?

The *Enchiridion* is not intended to be a summary of Epictetus's overall thought but instead is a compilation of practical pieces of advice for daily life based on his philosophy. These are the kinds of things Epictetus would have taught his students, though presented here without the rhetorical flourish that can be found in his *Discourses*, and separated from much of the argumentation he would have used to support them.

Some Useful Background Information

1. Epictetus is known as a Stoic philosopher. Stoicism was a school of thought founded in the third century BCE by Zeno of Citium in Athens, and largely developed by his successor Chrysippus between about 230 and 210 BCE. It was the dominant philosophy

---

* There is an apocryphal story which goes that, while he was a slave, he was tortured by his master who twisted his leg. Enduring the pain with apparent indifference, Epictetus warned Epaphroditus that his leg would break; when it did break, he said, "There, did I not tell you that it would break?" From then on Epictetus was lame.

of the Roman world until the rise of Christianity as a state religion in the fourth century CE. At its core Stoicism combines a belief in a deterministic natural world, governed by natural laws or *logos*, with an emphasis on the human capacity to make free choices and to use our reason to see the world as it really is rather than merely as it appears to be. It is thus up to us how to act, and wise persons will bring their actions into line with the natural course of things—which, according to Stoicism, is itself part of the larger rationality of the universe and not merely arbitrary—rather than try to change things that cannot be changed. For Epictetus, as for the other Stoics, philosophy is not merely an intellectual discipline but a way of life, involving constant training and practice. We should seek to free ourselves from the undue influence of our passions and instead follow the path of reason, in order to achieve peace of mind and clear judgment. Following Socrates, the Stoics believed that unhappiness and (apparent) misfortune are the results of human ignorance of the reason inherent in nature.

Some Common Misconceptions

1. Today the word "stoic" has come to mean unemotional and able to endure hardship without complaint. This meaning is not completely disconnected from its origins in this philosophical movement, but it can be misleading: the Stoics did not seek to eliminate or ignore emotion, but to train themselves to use careful, clear judgment to assess the appropriateness of these passions or sensations rather than passively reacting to them.

2. Epictetus advises, in part, that we can find peace of mind by adapting our will to how the world is, rather than by vainly seeking to impose our will on something that cannot be changed. This is more than the simple fatalism it might seem, however. According to Stoic philosophy the world of things that are beyond our power, understood properly, is a universe that contains an inherent rational order—in fact, is sometimes described as God becoming immanent—and so it is not just prudent but also right to make ourselves in tune with it.

How Important and Influential Is This Passage?

Epictetus's writings had enormous influence for hundreds of years after his death. Marcus Aurelius, Roman Emperor from 161 to 180 CE and the author of the very influential *Meditations*, describes reading Epictetus's *Discourses* as a crucial event in his intellectual development. Epictetus's work was one of only a handful of pagan writings that were respected and protected by the early Christian Church, and the *Enchiridion* was used almost verbatim as a rulebook for Eastern Orthodox monasteries. With the advent of the printing press, the *Discourses* and *Enchiridion* were some of the first works to be mechanically printed and they have remained continuously in print since 1535. Epictetus's views are often a touchstone of modern self-help psychology, especially in holding that our emotional responses to events are what create anxiety and depression, rather than the events themselves, and that with proper counseling these responses can be understood as irrational and unnecessary.

FROM *Enchiridion**

I

There are things which are within our power, and there are things which are beyond our power. Within our power are opinion, aim, desire, aversion—in a word, whatever affairs are our own. Beyond our power are body, property, reputation, status, and, in a word, anything we don't have the power to control.

Now the things within our power are by nature free, unrestricted, unhindered; but those beyond our power are weak, dependent, restricted, alien. Remember, then, that if you attribute freedom to things by nature dependent and take what belongs to others for your own, you will be hindered, you will lament, you will be disturbed, you will find fault both with gods and men. But if you take for your own only that which is your own and view what belongs to others just as it really is, then no one will ever compel you, no one will restrict you; you will find fault with no one, you will accuse no one, you will do nothing against your will; no one will hurt you, you will not have an enemy, nor will you suffer any harm.

Aiming, therefore, at such great things, remember that you must not allow yourself any inclination, however slight, toward the attainment of the others;† but that you must entirely give up on some of them, and for the present postpone the rest. But if you would have these, and possess power and wealth likewise, you may miss the latter in seeking the former; and you will certainly fail to get the only thing which can bring happiness and freedom.

Seek at once, therefore, to be able to say to every unpleasing appearance, "You are but an appearance and by no means the real thing." And then examine it by those rules which you have; and first and chiefly by this: whether it concerns the things which are within our own power or those which are not; and if it concerns anything beyond our power, be prepared to say that it is nothing to you.

II

Remember that desire demands the attainment of that of which you are desirous; and aversion demands the avoidance of that to which you are averse; that he who fails of the object of his desires is disappointed; and he who incurs the object of his aversion is wretched. If, then, you shun only those undesirable things which you can control, you will never incur anything which you shun; but if you shun sickness, or death, or poverty, you will run the risk of wretchedness. Remove the habit of aversion, then, from all things that are not within our power, and apply it to things undesirable which are within our power. But for now, suspend desire completely; for if you desire any of the things not within our own power, you must necessarily be disappointed; and you are not yet secure of those which are within our power, and so are legitimate objects of desire. Where it is practically necessary for you to pursue or avoid anything, do even this with discretion and gentleness and moderation.

III

With regard to whatever objects either delight the mind or are useful or are tenderly beloved, remind yourself of what nature they are, beginning with the merest trifles: if you have a favorite cup, that it is but a cup of which you are fond—for thus, if it is broken, you can bear it; if you embrace your child or your wife, that you embrace a mortal—and thus, if either of them dies, you can bear it.

...

V

Men are disturbed not by things, but by the views which they take of things. Thus death is nothing terrible, or otherwise it would have appeared so to Socrates. But the terror consists in our notion of death, that it is terrible. When, therefore, we are hindered or

---

* Translated by Thomas Wentworth Higginson, with modifications by the editor.
† Things you cannot control, such as riches or reputation.

disturbed, or grieved, let us never impute it to others, but to ourselves—that is, to our own views. It is the action of an uninstructed person to reproach others for his own misfortunes; of one entering upon instruction, to reproach himself; and one perfectly instructed, to reproach neither others nor himself.

VI

Be not elated at any excellence not your own. If a horse should be elated, and say, "I am handsome," it might be endurable. But when you are elated and say, "I have a handsome horse," know that you are elated only on the merit of the horse. What then is your own? The use of the phenomena of existence.* So that when you are in harmony with nature in this respect, you will be elated with some reason; for you will be elated at some good of your own.

...

VIII

Don't demand that events should happen as you wish; but wish them to happen as they do happen, and you will find peace.

IX

Sickness is an impediment to the body, but not to the mind unless the mind decides that it is. Lameness is an impediment to the leg, but not to the mind. Say this to yourself with regard to everything that happens. For you will find it to be an impediment to something else, but not truly to yourself.

...

XII

If you would improve, lay aside such reasonings as these: "If I neglect my affairs, I shall not have enough to live on; if I do not punish my servant, he will be good for nothing." For it is better to die of hunger, free from grief and fear, than to be wealthy but uneasy;

and it is better that your servant should be bad than you unhappy.

Begin therefore with little things. Is a little oil spilled or a little wine stolen? Say to yourself, "This is the price paid for peace and tranquillity; and nothing is to be had for nothing." And when you call your servant, consider that it is possible he may not come at your call; or, if he does, that he may not do what you wish. But it is not at all desirable for him, and very undesirable for you, that it should be in his power to disrupt your peace of mind.

XIII

If you would improve, be content to be thought foolish and dull with regard to externals.† Do not desire to be thought to know anything; and though you should appear to others to be somebody, distrust yourself. For be assured, it is not easy simultaneously to keep your will in harmony with nature and to secure externals; while you are absorbed in the one, you must necessarily neglect the other.

XIV

If you wish your children and your wife and your friends to live forever, you are foolish, for you wish things to be in your power which are not so, and what belongs to others to be your own. Similarly, if you wish your servant to be without fault, you are foolish, for you wish vice not to be vice but something else. But if you wish not to be disappointed in your desires, that is in your own power. Exercise, therefore, what is in your power. A man's master is he who is able to provide or remove whatever that man seeks or shuns. Whoever then would be free, let him wish nothing, let him decline nothing, which depends on others; otherwise he must necessarily be a slave.

XV

Remember that you must behave as at a banquet. Is anything brought round to you? Put out your hand and take a moderate share. Does it pass by you? Do

---

* "The phenomena of existence": the appearances of things, impressions.
† Merely external or conventional signs (e.g., status symbols), as opposed to the genuinely important things.

not stop it. Is it not yet come? Do not yearn in desire toward it, but wait till it reaches you. Behave like this with regard to children, wife, status, riches, and you will in time be worthy to feast with the gods. And if you do not so much as take the things which are set before you, but are able even to forego them, then you will not only be worthy to feast with the gods, but to rule with them also. For, by thus doing, Diogenes and Heraclitus,* and others like them, deservedly became divine, and were so recognized.

XVI

When you see anyone weeping for grief, either that his son has gone abroad or that he has lost some money or property, take care not to be overcome by the apparent evil, but discriminate and be ready to say, "What hurts this man is not this occurrence itself—for another man might not be hurt by it—but the view he chooses to take of it." As far as conversation goes, however, do not disdain to sympathize with him and, if need be, to groan with him. Take heed, however, not to groan inwardly, too.

...

XX

Remember that it is not he who gives abuse or blows, who affronts, but the view we take of these things as insulting. When, therefore, anyone provokes you, be assured that it is your own opinion which provokes you. Try, therefore, in the first place, not to be bewildered by appearances. For if you take some time before reacting, you will more easily command yourself.

...

XXII

If you have an earnest desire toward philosophy, prepare yourself from the very first to have the multitude laugh and sneer, and say, "Suddenly we have a philosopher among us"; and, "What makes him so pretentious now?" Now, for your part, don't be pretentious, but keep steadily to those things which appear best to you, as one appointed by God to the role of philosopher. For remember that, if you are persistent, those very people who at first ridiculed you will afterwards admire you. But if you let them persuade you not to be a philosopher, you will incur a double ridicule.

XXIII

If you ever happen to turn your attention to externals, for the pleasure of anyone, be assured that you have ruined your scheme of life. Be content, then, in everything, with being a philosopher; and if you wish to seem so likewise to anyone, appear so to yourself, and it will be enough for you.

...

XXV

Is anyone given preferential treatment over you at a formal party, or in being honoured, or in being asked to join a confidential conversation? If these things are good, you ought to rejoice that he has them; and if they are evil, do not be grieved that you have them not. And remember that you cannot be permitted to rival others in externals without using the same means to obtain them. For how can he who will not haunt the door of any man, will not attend him, will not praise him, have an equal share with him who does these things? You are unjust, then, and unreasonable if you are unwilling to pay the price for which these things are sold, and would have them for nothing. For how much are lettuces sold? An obol,† for instance. If another, then, paying an obol, takes the lettuces, and you, not paying it, go without them, do not imagine that he has gained any advantage over you. For as he has the lettuces, so you have the obol which you did not give. So, in the present case, you have not been invited to such a person's formal dinner because you have not paid him the price for which a supper is sold. It is sold for praise; it is sold for paying court. Give him, then, the value if it be for your advantage. But if you would at the same time not pay the one, and

---

* Diogenes of Apollonia (fifth century BCE) and Heraclitus of Ephesus (c. 535–c. 475 BCE) were Greek philosophers and precursors of Socrates.

† A small Greek coin.

yet receive the other, you are unreasonable and foolish. Have you nothing, then, in place of the dinner? Yes, indeed, you have—not to praise him whom you do not like to praise; not to bear the insolence of his lackeys.

XXVI

The will of nature may be learned from things upon which we are all agreed. As when our neighbor's boy has broken a cup, or the like, we are ready at once to say, "These are casualties that will happen"; be assured, then, that when your own cup is likewise broken, you ought to be affected just as when another's cup was broken. Now apply this to greater things. Is the child or wife of another dead? There is no one who would not say, "This is an accident of mortality." But if anyone's own child happens to die, it is immediately, "Alas! how wretched am I!" It should be always remembered how we are affected on hearing the same thing concerning others.

...

XXIX

In every affair consider what precedes and what follows, and then undertake it. Otherwise you will begin enthusiastically, indeed, careless of the consequences, and when these are developed, you will shamefully give up. "I would conquer at the Olympic Games." But consider what precedes and what follows, and then, if it be for your advantage, engage in the affair. You must conform to rules, submit to a diet, refrain from rich food; exercise your body, whether you choose it or not, at a stated hour, in heat and cold; you must drink no cold water, and sometimes no wine—in a word, you must give yourself up to your trainer as to a physician. Then, in the combat, you may be thrown into a ditch, dislocate your arm, turn your ankle, swallow an abundance of dust, be whipped, and, after all, lose the victory. When you have reckoned up all this, if your inclination still holds, set about the combat. Otherwise, take notice, you will behave like children who sometimes play at being wrestlers, sometimes gladiators, sometimes blow a trumpet, and sometimes act a tragedy, when they happen to have seen and admired these shows. Thus you too will be at one time a wrestler, and another a gladiator; now a philosopher, now an orator; but nothing in earnest. Like an ape you mimic all you see, and one thing after another is sure to please you, but is out of favor as soon as it becomes familiar. For you have never entered upon anything thoughtfully; nor after having surveyed and tested the whole matter, but carelessly, and with a halfway zeal. Thus some, when they have seen a philosopher and heard a man speaking like Euphrates*—though, indeed, who can speak like him?—have a mind to be philosophers, too. Consider first, friend, what the matter is, and what your own nature is able to bear. If you would be a wrestler, consider your shoulders, your back, your thighs; for different persons are made for different things. Do you think that you can act as you do and be a philosopher, that you can eat, drink, be angry, be discontented, as you are now? You must watch, you must labor, you must get the better of certain appetites, must break off with your friends and family, be despised by your servant, be laughed at by those you meet; come off worse than others in everything—in positions, in honors, before tribunals. When you have fully considered all these things, approach, if you please—that is, if, by parting with them, you have a mind to purchase serenity, freedom, and tranquility. If not, do not come hither; do not, like children, be now a philosopher, then a tax collector, then an orator, and then one of Caesar's officers. These things are not consistent. You must be one man, either good or bad. You must cultivate either your own reason or else externals; apply yourself either to things within or without you—that is, be either a philosopher or one of the mob.†

XXX

Duties are universally defined by social relations. Is a certain man your father? In this are implied taking care of him, submitting to him in all things, patiently receiving his reproaches, his correction. But he is a bad

---

* Euphrates was a well-known Stoic philosopher from the generation before Epictetus, who lived in the southern area of what is today Syria between 35 and 118 CE. Several contemporaries praise his great talent as an orator.

† Common people, masses.

father. Is your natural tie, then, to a *good* father? No, but to a father. Is a brother unjust? Well, preserve your own just relation toward him. Consider not what *he* does, but what *you* are to do to keep your own mind in a state conforming to nature, for another cannot hurt you unless you allow it. You will then be hurt when you consent to be hurt. In this manner, therefore, if you accustom yourself to contemplate the relations of neighbor, citizen, commander, you can deduce from each the corresponding duties.

...

XXXIII

Begin by prescribing to yourself some character and demeanor, which you are able to stick to whether alone or in company.

Be mostly silent, or speak only what is necessary, and in few words. We may, however, enter sparingly into discourse sometimes, when occasion calls for it; but let it not run on any of the common subjects, as gladiators, or horse races, or athletic champions, or food, or drink—the vulgar* topics of conversation— and especially not on men, so as either to blame, or praise, or make comparisons. If you are able, then, by your own conversation, bring over that of your company to proper subjects; but if you happen to find yourself among strangers, be silent.

Let not your laughter be loud, frequent, or abundant.

Avoid taking oaths, if possible, altogether; at any rate, so far as you are able.

Avoid public and vulgar entertainments; but if ever an occasion calls you to them, pay attention not to imperceptibly slide into vulgarity. For be assured that if a person be ever so pure himself, yet, if his companion be corrupted, he who converses with him will be corrupted likewise.

Provide things relating to the body no further than absolute need requires, as meat, drink, clothing, house, servants. But cut off everything that looks toward show and luxury.

Before marriage guard yourself with all your ability from unlawful sexual intercourse with women; yet be not uncharitable or severe to those who are led into this, nor boast frequently that you yourself do otherwise.

If anyone tells you that a certain person speaks ill of you, do not make excuses about what is said of you, but answer: "He was ignorant of my other faults, otherwise he would have mentioned these as well."

It is not necessary for you to appear often at public spectacles;† but if ever there is a proper occasion for you to be there, do not appear more solicitous for any other than for yourself—that is, wish things to be only just as they are, and only the best man to win; for thus nothing will go against you. But abstain entirely from acclamations and derision and violent emotions. And when you come away, do not discourse a great deal on what has passed, or no more than is necessary to get it out of your system. For it would appear by such discourse that you were dazzled by the show.

Be not eager or ready to attend private recitations;‡ but if you do attend, preserve your gravity and dignity, and yet avoid making yourself disagreeable.

When you are going to confer with anyone, and especially with one who seems your superior, think about how Socrates or Zeno§ would behave in such a case, and you will not be at a loss to meet properly whatever may occur.

When you are going to meet someone powerful, imagine to yourself that you may not find him at home, that you may be shut out, that the doors may not be opened to you, that he may not notice you. If, with all this, it be your duty to go, bear what happens and never say to yourself, "It was not worth so much"; for this is vulgar, and like a man bewildered by externals.

In company, avoid a frequent and excessive mention of your own actions and adventures. For however agreeable it may be to yourself to allude to the risks you have run, it is not equally agreeable to others to hear about your exploits. Avoid likewise an endeavor to excite laughter, for this may readily slide you into

---

* Characteristic of ordinary, unsophisticated people (from the Latin *vulgaris* meaning "of the common people").
† Public games, such as sporting events.
‡ Private lectures or poetry recitals.
§ Socrates and Zeno were famous Greek philosophers. Zeno of Cyprus (335–263 BCE) was the founder of Stoicism.

vulgarity, and, besides, may be apt to lower you in the esteem of your acquaintance. Approaches to indecent conversation are likewise dangerous. Therefore, when anything of this sort happens, use the first fit opportunity to rebuke him who makes advances that way, or, at least, by silence and blushing and a serious look show yourself to be displeased by such talk.

...

XLI

It is a sign of lack of intellect to spend much time in things relating to the body, as to be immoderate in exercises, in eating and drinking, and in the discharge of other animal functions. These things should be done incidentally and our main strength be applied to our reason.

XLII

When any person does ill by you, or speaks ill of you, remember that he acts or speaks from an impression that it is right for him to do so. Now it is not possible that he should follow what appears right to you, but only what appears so to himself. Therefore, if he judges from false appearances, he is the person hurt, since he, too, is the person deceived. For if anyone takes a true proposition to be false, the proposition is not hurt, but only the man is deceived. Setting out, then, from these principles, you will meekly bear with a person who reviles you, for you will say upon every occasion, "It seemed so to him."

...

XLVIII

The condition and characteristic of a vulgar person is that he never looks for either help or harm from himself, but only from externals. The condition and characteristic of a philosopher is that he looks to himself for all help or harm. The marks of a proficient are that he censures no one, praises no one, blames no one, accuses no one; says nothing concerning himself as being anybody or knowing anything. When he is in any instance hindered or restrained, he accuses himself; and if he is praised, he smiles to himself at the person who praises him; and if he is censured, he makes no defense. But he goes about with the caution of a convalescent, careful of interference with anything that is doing well but not yet quite secure. He restrains desire; he transfers his aversion to only those things which thwart the proper use of our own will; he employs his energies moderately in all directions; if he appears stupid or ignorant, he does not care; and, in a word, he keeps watch over himself as if he were an enemy waiting in ambush. ∎

Suggestions for Critical Reflection

1. Does Epictetus say that you can avoid being disappointed by disciplining yourself not to want the things that you can't—or might not—get? How practical, or healthy, is this advice?

2. "Sickness is an impediment to the body, but not to the mind unless the mind decides that it is." What do you make of this?

3. Why do you think Epictetus says that "it is not easy simultaneously to keep your will in harmony with nature and to secure externals"?

4. How attractive do you find Epictetus's stoicism? Is it a good guide for everyday life? Does it seem to you a good way to be happy?

A.J. AYER

The Claims of Philosophy

Who Was A.J. Ayer?

Sir Alfred Jules Ayer (1910–89), known to all his friends as Freddie, was born into a wealthy European-origin family in London. He attended the pre-eminent English private school Eton, then went on scholarship to Oxford. He served as an officer in a British espionage and sabotage unit during World War II, then taught at University College London and at Oxford.

When only 24, Ayer wrote *Language, Truth, and Logic*, the book that made his name. In it, he briefly, simply, and persuasively to many, argued for logical positivism, a form of radical empiricism that had been developed largely by the group of philosophers called the Vienna Circle, whose ideas Ayer had picked up while studying with them in Austria. Logical positivism dominated Anglophone philosophy for decades; while objections (especially to Ayer's rather simplified version) came thick and fast, everyone was at least aware of it as a philosophical force to be reckoned with.

While *Language, Truth, and Logic* was by far his best-seller, Ayer wrote a good deal of other important work, especially in epistemology. Though his work is not now generally included in lists of all-time philosophical landmarks, he was considered, in terms of influence if not of originality, second only to Bertrand Russell among the English philosophers of his day. He was also known for his advocacy of humanism and was the first executive director of the British Humanist Association, a charitable organization working towards "a tolerant world where rational thinking and kindness prevail."*

Ayer was extraordinarily well-known by the British public. He wrote and spoke on all sorts of popular issues, all over the media. In those days, TV networks programmed witty intellectual chatter, and Ayer was a master at this. He loved his celebrity, and hobnobbed with the famous and influential. He was knighted in 1970.

What Is the Structure of This Reading?

Ayer begins by distinguishing between two types of philosophy; he raises criticisms of both types, and argues that neither can help with the question "what is the meaning of life?" This is because, he argues, the question makes no sense and has no possible coherent answer. In Part III he argues that appealing to God's purpose for the universe will not provide an answer, and in Part IV he similarly argues that appeals to human nature or to evolution cannot tell us how we should behave. All we are left with are our own individual goals and values.

Some Useful Background Information

The background to this article is Ayer's philosophy of logical positivism. The core principle of logical positivism is a view of meaning called *verificationism*. On this view, what a statement means can be wholly captured by understanding what difference it makes whether it is true or not—by understanding its 'truth conditions.' For example, if I say that my dog has three legs then this is true just so long as, if you were to meet my dog and count its legs, there were three of them; if it had any other number of legs, my claim would be false. For logical positivists, the only way that we can make sense of a statement having truth conditions is by thinking about the possible ways in which our sensory experiences might differ depending on whether the statement is true or false—ultimately, we can verify that a dog has three legs only by looking at it (or perhaps feeling it in a dark room) and counting the appendages. In the end, even very complicated scientific propositions boil down to some set of claims about what we would experience under such and such conditions; they are true just in case we do (or would) have those experiences, and false if we do (or would) not.

---

* https://humanism.org.uk/about/

This may seem a fairly straightforward and sensible account of how language works, but it has quite far-reaching consequences. One of these is that certain pieces of language may masquerade as meaningful statements but, if the truth or falsity of those claims would make no difference to our possible sensory experiences, then they in fact are not meaningful at all. They are not false (which would have to be discovered by experience)—they are simply not the kind of thing that could be true or false. Despite surface grammatical appearances, they tell us nothing about how the world might be. Notorious examples include "There exists a transcendent God" or "Stealing is morally wrong."

If these sorts of non-empirical sentences—sentences about metaphysics or values, for example—have no literal meaning, then what is their function? According to some logical positivists, including Ayer, they are rather like exclamations or expressive actions. Saying "ouch" when you stub your toe, or giving someone a heart-felt hug, are not things that have literal meaning—they are not things that can be true or false—but they nevertheless are a kind of expression. In a similar way, perhaps, saying "stealing is deeply immoral" might have the function of expressing strong disapproval of stealing—metaphorically, punching stealing in the face—even if it is not a claim that could be either true or false.

The Claims of Philosophy[*]

I

Contemporary philosophers may be divided into two classes: the pontiffs and the journeymen.[†] As the names that I have chosen indicate, the basis of this division is not so much a difference of opinion as a difference of attitude. It is not merely that the journeyman denies certain propositions which the pontiff asserts, or that he asserts certain propositions which the pontiff denies. It is rather that he has a radically different conception of the method of philosophy and of the ends that it is fitted to achieve. Thus, it is characteristic of those whom I describe as pontiffs that they think it within the province of philosophy to compete with natural science. They may, indeed, be willing to admit that the scientist achieves valuable results in his own domain, but they insist that he does not, and cannot, attain to the complete and final truth about reality; and they think that it is open to the philosopher to make this deficiency good. In support of this view, they may, for example, argue that every scientific theory is based upon presuppositions

which cannot themselves be scientifically proved; and from this they may infer, in the interests of their own 'philosophical' brand of irrationality, that science itself is fundamentally irrational; or else they may have recourse to metaphysics to supply the missing proof. Alternatively, they may hold that the scientist deals only with the appearances of things, whereas the philosopher by the use of his special methods penetrates to the reality beyond. In general, the ideal of the pontiff is to construct a metaphysical system. Such a system may actually include some scientific hypotheses, either as premises or, more frequently, as deductions from metaphysical first principles. It may, on the other hand, be uncompromisingly metaphysical. In either case, the aim is to give a complete and definitive account of 'ultimate' reality.

Unfortunately, as the journeymen on their side have been at pains to show, this 'ultimate' reality is a fiction, and the ideal of a metaphysical system that is anything other than a scientific encyclopaedia is devoid of any basis in reason. To some extent, indeed, this fact has been borne in upon the pontiffs, and the result is

---

[*] Published in *Polemic* 7 (March 1947).

[†] A pontiff is a high priest, and a journeyman is a skilled worker who has completed an apprenticeship in a particular trade.

that they now tend to desert reason and even to decry it. This separates them sharply from their philosophical ancestors, who at least professed to reason, even if they did not always reason well. Few men, indeed, can ever have reasoned worse than Hegel, the arch-pontiff of the nineteenth century,* but at least he claimed the support of reason for his fantasies. His ground for thinking that a mobile logic is needed to describe a mobile world may have been no better than the principle that 'who drives fat oxen must himself be fat'; but at least, if he rejected the 'static' Aristotelian logic, he did so in favour of what he, no doubt mistakenly, believed to be a superior logic of his own. Though he misused logic abominably, he did not affect to be above it. But now if we turn to Heidegger, the high priest of the modern school of existentialists, and the leading pontiff of our times,† we find ourselves in a country from which the ordinary processes of logic, or indeed reasoning of any kind, appear to have been banished. For what we learn from him is that it is only in the clear light of Nothing that Being has being, and consequently that it is the supreme privilege of the philosopher to concern himself with Nothing.[1] For this he requires no special intellectual discipline. It is sufficient that he experiences anguish, provided always that it is an anguish without any special object. For it is thus, according to Heidegger, that the Nothing reveals itself. This strange thesis is indeed backed by a pretence of argument, but since the argument depends upon the elementary fallacy of treating 'nothing' as a name, it is hardly to be taken seriously. Nor does Heidegger himself appear to attach very much weight to it. For it is not by logic that he seeks to convince: nor is his the Socratic method of following an argument wherever it may lead. Like the sermons of Dr. Dodd,[2] his work is addressed to the passions; and it is no doubt for this reason that it has succeeded in becoming fashionable.

Now just as William James thought that all prigs must sooner or later end by becoming Hegelians, so it seems to me that the fate of the contemporary pontiff must be to go the way of Heidegger. I do not mean by this that he will have to subscribe to Heidegger's doctrines. There are other types of 'deeply significant nonsense' available. But inasmuch as his quest for ultimate reality cannot be made to prosper by any rational means, he is likely, if he adheres to it, to seek some non-rational source of enlightenment. At this point he devolves into a mystic or a poet. As such he may express an attitude to life which is interesting in itself and even a source of inspiration to others; and perhaps it would be churlish to refuse him the title of philosopher. But it is to be remarked that when philosophy has been brought to this stage then, whatever its emotional value, it has ceased to be, in any ordinary sense, a vehicle of knowledge.

II

The history of philosophy, as it is taught in the textbooks, is largely a parade of pontiffs; and it might be thought that the only course open to the budding philosopher was either to enrol himself under one of their banners, or else to try to become a pontiff in his own right. But in this, as in so many other cases, the textbooks are behind the times. For, at least in England and America, the philosophical scene has been dominated for the last fifty years, not by the pontiffs, but by those whom I describe as journeymen. Unlike the pontiffs, the journeymen do not set out in quest of ultimate reality. Nor do they try to bring philosophy into competition with the natural sciences. Believing, as they do, that the only way to discover what the world is like is to form hypotheses and test them by observation, which is in fact the method of science, they are content to leave the scientist in full possession of the field of speculative knowledge. Consequently they do not try to build systems. The task of the philosopher, as they see it, is rather to deal piecemeal with a special set of problems. Some of these problems are historical, in the sense that they involve the criticism and interpretation of the work of previous philosophers; others are primarily mathematical, as belonging to the specialized

---

* Georg Wilhelm Friedrich Hegel (1770–1831) was a German philosopher who expounded a very influential form of "absolute idealism." He developed the dialectical method of logic, whereby a thesis and its antithesis are resolved into their synthesis.

† Martin Heidegger (1889–1976) is another German philosopher who made important and original contributions to phenomenology and existentialism.

field of formal logic; others again are set by the sciences: they involve the analysis of scientific method, the evaluation of scientific theories, the clarification of scientific terms. It is, for example, a philosophical problem to decide what is meant by 'probability': and the journeymen have already contributed much towards its solution. Finally, there are a number of problems, such as the problem of perception, the problem of our knowledge of other minds, the question of the significance of moral judgments, that arise out of the common usages and assumptions of everyday life. In a broad sense, all these problems are semantic: that is to say, they can all be represented as concerned with the use of language. But since the term 'semantics' is technically applied to a particular formal discipline which does not, even for the journeymen, comprehend the whole of philosophy, I think it better to resume their philosophical activities under the general heading of logical analysis.

Essentially, the journeymen are technicians; and from this point of view the comparison with the pontiffs is very much to their advantage. They suffer, however, from a certain thinness of material. Consider, for example, the so-called philosophers of common-sense, who follow the distinguished leadership of Professor G.E. Moore.* In the opinion of this school, it is not sensible for a philosopher to question the truth of such common-sense statements as that this is a sheet of paper or that I am wearing shoes on my feet. And if anyone were to question it, they would reply simply that, on the relevant occasions, they knew for certain that statements of this sort were true. Thus, Professor Moore himself has proved, to his own satisfaction, the existence of external objects, a question much canvassed by philosophers, by the simple method of holding up his hands and saying that he knows for certain that they exist;[3] and indeed there is no denying that in its way this a valid proof. At the same time these philosophers confess to being very doubtful of the correct analysis of the common-sense propositions which they know to be true. The question whether or not this really

is a sheet of paper does not puzzle them at all; but the question of what precisely is implied by saying that it is puzzles them a great deal. In technical language, it is a matter of discovering the relationship between the sense-data[†] which are immediately experienced and the physical objects which it is their function to present; and this is a problem which, in the opinion of our common-sense philosophers, has not yet been satisfactorily solved. Now I do not wish to suggest that this is not a difficult problem, or to belittle the ingenuity with which the journeymen have tackled it. But I am afraid that a layman who was told that a question of this sort was of sufficient interest to a modern philosopher to occupy him for a lifetime would be inclined to think that modern philosophy was degenerating into scholasticism.[‡] If he were told, as he might be by a pontiff, that there was serious doubt of the existence of this piece of paper he would be very properly incredulous, but he might also be impressed: he might even be brought to think that he himself had been excessively naïve in taking such a thing for granted. But once he had been assured that the truth of his common-sense assumption that the paper existed was not after all in doubt, I think it would be difficult to interest him in a meticulous analysis of its implications. He would remark that he understood very well what he meant by saying that this was a piece of paper, and that he did not see what was to be gained by a laborious attempt at further clarification. To this it could, indeed, be objected that he might think very differently if he had been properly educated in philosophy; and that in any case there is no reason why the layman's judgments of value should be binding upon the philosopher. But even so it is difficult not to feel some sympathy for our layman. It is difficult not to suspect that the philosopher of common-sense must sometimes be inclined to say to himself what the poet Clough said when he found himself exclusively engaged in doing up parcels for Florence Nightingale: 'This that I see is not all, and this that I do is but little. It is good but there is better than it.'[§] ...

---

* G.E. Moore (1873–1958) was an English philosopher and one of the founders of twentieth-century analytic philosophy.

† The, presumably mental, sensations of which we are non-inferentially conscious, such as a red, round visual image of a tomato (as opposed to the tomato itself).

‡ The method of teaching and learning that dominated medieval universities in Europe. Ayer is using the term in a pejorative way to mean nit-picking attention to little details within a closed system of thought.

§ Arthur Hugh Clough (1819–61) was an English poet; in the 1850s he devoted himself to working as a secretarial assistant to his wife's cousin Florence Nightingale and wrote virtually no poetry for six years during this period. Florence

III

On the side of the pontiffs, imaginative literature. On the side of the journeymen, the reintegration of philosophy with science or the piece-meal solution of logical or linguistic puzzles. Surely, it will be said, this is not what the public expects of its philosophers. Surely, the business of the philosopher is to make clear the meaning of life, to show people how they ought to live. Call him a pontiff or a journeyman, according to his method of approach; the distinction is not of any great importance. What is important is the message that he has to give. It is wisdom that is needed, not merely scientific knowledge. Of what use to us is the understanding of nature if we do not know the purpose of our existence or how we ought to live? And who is to answer these supremely important questions if not the philosopher?

The reply to this is that there is no true answer to these questions; and since this is so it is no use expecting even the philosopher to provide one. What can be done, however, is to make clear why, and in what sense, these questions are unanswerable; and once this is achieved it will be seen that there is also a sense in which they can be answered. It will be found that the form of answer is not a proposition, which must be either true or false, but the adoption of a rule, which cannot properly be characterized as either true or false, but can nevertheless be judged as more or less acceptable. And with this the problem is solved, so far as reasoning can solve it. The rest is a matter of personal decision, and ultimately of action.

Let us begin then by considering the purpose of our existence. How is it possible for existence to have a purpose? We know very well what it is for a man to have a purpose. It is a matter of his intending, on the basis of a given situation, to bring about some further situation which for some reason or other he conceives to be desirable. And in that case it may be said that events have a meaning for him according as they conduce, or fail to conduce, towards the end* that he desires. But how can life in general be said to have

any meaning? A simple answer is that all events are tending towards a certain specifiable end: so that to understand the meaning of life it is necessary only to discover this end. But, in the first place, there is no good reason whatever for supposing this assumption to be true, and secondly, even if it were true, it would not do the work that is required of it. For what is being sought by those who demand to know the meaning of life is not an explanation of the facts of their existence, but a justification. Consequently a theory which informs them merely that the course of events is so arranged as to lead inevitably to a certain end does nothing to meet their need. For the end in question will not be one that they themselves have chosen. As far as they are concerned it will be entirely arbitrary; and it will be a no less arbitrary fact that their existence is such as necessarily to lead to its fulfilment. In short, from the point of view of justifying one's existence, there is no essential difference between a teleological explanation of events and a mechanical explanation.† In either case, it is a matter of brute fact that events succeed one another in the ways that they do and are explicable in the ways that they are. And indeed what is called an explanation is nothing other than a more general description. Thus, an attempt to answer the question why events are as they are must always resolve itself into saying only how they are. But what is required by those who seek the meaning of life is precisely an answer to their question 'Why?' that is something other than an answer to any question 'How?' And just because this is so they can never legitimately be satisfied.

But now, it may be objected, suppose that the world is designed by a superior being. In that case the purpose of our existence will be the purpose that it realizes for him; and the meaning of life will be found in our conscious adaptation to his purpose. But here again, the answer is, first, that there is no good reason whatsoever for believing that there is any such superior being; and, secondly, that even if there were, he could not accomplish what is here required of him. For let us

---

Nightingale (1820–1910) was a pioneer of modern nursing, coming to prominence as a manager and trainer of nurses during the Crimean War (1853–56); she was also a social reformer, and an innovator in the graphical presentation of statistical data.

*   Goal, outcome.

†   A teleological explanation explains in terms of purposes, while a mechanical explanation explains by appealing to causes.

assume, for the sake of argument, that everything happens as it does because a superior being has intended that it should. As far as we are concerned, the course of events still remains entirely arbitrary. True, it can now be said to fulfil a purpose; but the purpose is not ours. And just as, on the previous assumption, it merely happened to be the case that the course of events conduced to the end that it did, so, on this assumption, it merely happens to be the case that the deity has the purpose that he has, and not some other purpose, or no purpose at all. Nor does this unwarrantable assumption provide us even with a rule of life. For even those who believe most firmly that the world was designed by a superior being are not in a position to tell us what his purpose can have been. They may indeed claim that it has been mysteriously revealed to them, but how can it be proved that the revelation is genuine? And even if we waive this objection, even if we assume not only the world as we find it is working out the purpose of a superior being, but also that we are capable of discovering what this purpose is, we are still not provided with a rule of life. For either his purpose is sovereign or it is not. If it is sovereign, that is, if everything that happens is necessarily in accordance with it, then this is true also of our behaviour. Consequently, there is no point in our deciding to conform to it, for the simple reason that we cannot do otherwise. However we behave, we shall fulfil the purpose of this deity; and if we were to behave differently, we should still be fulfilling it; for if it were possible for us not to fulfil it it would not be sovereign in the requisite sense. But suppose that it is not sovereign, or, in other words, that not all events must necessarily bear it out. In that case, there is no reason why we should try to conform to it, unless we independently judge it to be good. But that means that the significance of our behaviour depends finally upon our own judgments of value; and the concurrence of a deity then becomes superfluous.

The point is, in short, that even the invocation of a deity does not enable us to answer the question why things are as they are. At the most it complicates the answer to the question how they are by pushing the level of explanation to a further stage. For even if the ways of the deity were clear to those who believed in him, which they apparently are not, it would still be, even to them, a matter of brute fact that he behaved as he did, just as to those who do not believe in him it is a matter of brute fact that the world is what it

is. In either case the question 'Why?' remains unanswered, for the very good reason that it is unanswerable. That is to say, it may be answerable at any given level but the answer is always a matter of describing at a higher level not why things are as they are, but simply how they are. And so, to whatever level our explanations may be carried, the final statement is never an answer to the question 'Why?' but necessarily only an answer to the question 'How?'

It follows, if my argument is correct, that there is no sense in asking what is the ultimate purpose of our existence, or what is the real meaning of life. For to ask this is to assume that there can be a reason for our living as we do which is somehow more profound than any mere explanation of the facts; and we have seen that this assumption is untenable. Moreover it is untenable in logic and not merely in fact. The position is not that our existence unfortunately lacks a purpose which, if the fates had been kinder, it might conceivably have had. It is rather that those who inquire, in this way, after the meaning of life are raising a question to which it is not logically possible that there should be an answer. Consequently, the fact that they are disappointed is not, as some romanticists would make it, an occasion for cynicism or despair. It is not an occasion for any emotional attitude at all. And the reason why it is not is just that it could not conceivably have been otherwise. If it were logically possible for our existence to have a purpose, in the sense required, then it might be sensible to lament the fact that it had none. But it is not sensible to cry for what is logically impossible. If a question is so framed as to be unanswerable, then it is not a matter for regret that it remains unanswered. It is, therefore, misleading to say that life has no meaning; for that suggests that the statement that life has a meaning is factually significant, but false; whereas the truth is that, in the sense in which it is taken in this context, it is not factually significant.

There is, however, a sense in which it can be said that life does have a meaning. It has for each of us whatever meaning we severally choose to give it. The purpose of a man's existence is constituted by the ends to which he, consciously or unconsciously, devotes himself. Some men have a single overriding purpose to which all their activities are subordinated. If they are at all successful in achieving it, they are probably the happiest, but they are the exceptions. Most men pass from one object to another; and at any one time they may pursue a number of different ends, which may or may not be capable of being harmonized. Philosophers, with a preference for tidiness, have sometimes tried to show that all these apparently diverse objects can really be reduced to one: but the fact is that there is no end that is common to all men, not even happiness. For setting aside the question whether men ought always to pursue happiness, it is not true even that they always do pursue it, unless the word 'happiness' is used merely as a description of any end that is in fact pursued. Thus the question what is the meaning of life proves, when it is taken empirically, to be incomplete. For there is no single thing of which it can truly be said that this is the meaning of life. All that can be said is that life has at various times a different meaning for different people, according as they pursue their several ends.

That different people have different purposes is an empirical matter of fact. But what is required by those who seek to know the purpose of their existence is not a factual description of the way that people actually do conduct themselves, but rather a decision as to how they should conduct themselves. Having been taught to believe that not all purposes are of equal value, they require to be guided in their choice. And thus the inquiry into the purpose of our existence dissolves into the question 'How ought men to live?'

IV

The question how ought men to live is one that would seem to fall within the province of moral philosophy; but it cannot be said of every moral philosopher that he makes a serious attempt to answer it. Moreover, those who do make a serious attempt to answer it are mostly pontiffs, who approach it wrongly. For having decided, on metaphysical grounds, that reality is of such and such a character they try to deduce from this the superiority of a certain mode of life. But, quite apart from the merits or demerits of their metaphysics, it is a mistake on their part to suppose that a mere description of reality is sufficient to establish any rule of life at all. A familiar instance of this mistake is the claim that men ought to live in such and such a way because such and such is their real nature. But if what is meant by their having such and such a real nature is that they really are of the nature in question, then all that can possibly be established is that they really do

behave in the manner indicated. For if they behaved differently, they thereby show that they had a different nature. Thus in telling men that they ought to live in accordance with their real nature you are telling them to do what they do; and your pretended rule of life dissolves into nothing, since it is equally consistent with any course of conduct whatsoever. If, on the other hand, what is meant by a man's real nature is not the nature that he actually displays but the nature that he ought to display, then the moral rule that the argument is supposed to justify is assumed at the outset, and assumed without proof. As a moral rule, it may be acceptable in itself; but the supposed deduction of it from a non-moral premiss turns out inevitably to be a fraud.

It is not only metaphysicians who commit this fallacy. There is, for example, a brand of 'scientific ethics' according to which the right rule of life is that which harmonizes with the course of human evolution. But here again the same ambiguity arises. For if 'the course of human evolution' is understood as an actually existent process, then there is no sense in telling people that they ought to adapt themselves to it, for the very good reason that they cannot possibly do otherwise. However they may behave they will be acting rightly, since it is just their behaving as they do that makes the course of evolution what it is. In short, if progress is defined in terms of merely historical development, all conduct is progressive; for every human action necessarily furthers the course of evolution, in the straightforward sense of adding to its history. If on the other hand, it is only some among the many possible developments of human history that are considered to be progressive, then there is some sense in saying that we ought to strive to bring them about; but here again the moral rule which we are invited to adopt is not deduced but simply posited. It is neither itself a scientific statement of fact, nor a logical consequence of any such statement. By scientific methods we can indeed discover that certain events are more or less likely to occur; but the transition from this to deciding that some of these possible developments are more valuable than others carries us outside the domain of science altogether. In saying this, I do not wish to repudiate the humanistic values of those who put forward the claims of scientific ethics, or even to suggest that any other system of values is more securely founded. My objection to these moralists is simply that they fall into the logical error of confusing normative* judgments of value with scientific statements of fact. They may have the advantage of the metaphysicians, in that their factual premises are more deserving of belief, but the fundamental mistake of trying to extract normative rules from supposedly factual descriptions is common to them both.

In moral, as in natural, philosophy it is characteristic of the journeyman to have detected the flaw in the method of the pontiffs, but here also they have purchased their freedom from error at the price of a certain aridity. For not only do they not attempt to prove their judgments of value; for the most part they refrain from expressing them at all. What they do instead, apart from criticizing other moral philosophers, is to subject the terminology of ethics to logical analysis. Thus the questions that they discuss are whether the term 'good' or the term 'right' is to be taken as fundamental, and whether either is definable; whether it is a man's duty to do an action or merely to set himself to do it; whether his duty is to do what is objectively right or merely what he thinks to be right; whether the rightness of an action depends upon its actual consequences, or upon its probable consequences, or upon its consequences as foreseen by the agent, or not upon its consequences at all; whether it is possible to fulfil an obligation unintentionally; whether the moral goodness of an action depends upon its motive; and many other questions of a similar sort. Such questions can be interesting, though they are not always made so, and I do not wish to say that they are not important; but to the practical man they must appear somewhat academic. By taking a course in this kind of moral philosophy a man may learn how to make the expression of his moral judgments secure from formal criticism. What he will not learn is what, in any concrete situation, he actually ought to do.

I think, then, that it can fairly be made a reproach to the journeymen that they have overlooked the Aristotelian principle that the end of moral philosophy is 'not knowledge but action'.[4] But their excuse is that once the philosopher who wishes to be practical has said this, there is very little more that he can say. Like anyone else, he can make moral recommendations, but he cannot legitimately claim for them the sanction of philosophy. He cannot prove that his judgments

of value are correct, for the sufficient reason that no judgment of value is capable of proof. Or rather, if it is capable of proof, it is only by reference to some other judgment of value, which must itself be left unproved. The moral philosopher can sometimes affect men's conduct by drawing their attention to certain matters of fact; he may show, for example, that certain sorts of action have unsuspected consequences, or that the motives for which they are done are different from what they appear to be; and he may then hope that when his audience is fully aware of the circumstances it will assess the situation in the same way as he does himself. Nevertheless there may be some who differ from him, not on any question of fact, but on a question of value, and in that case he has no way of demonstrating that his judgment is superior. He lays down one rule, and they lay down another; and the decision between them is a subject for persuasion and finally a matter of individual choice.

Since judgments of value are not reducible to statements of fact, they are strictly speaking neither true nor false; and it is tempting to infer from this that no course of conduct is better or worse than any other. But this would be a mistake. For the judgment that no course of conduct is better or worse than any other is itself a judgment of value and consequently neither true nor false. And while an attitude of moral indifference is legitimate in itself, it is not easily maintained. For since we are constantly faced with the practical necessity of action, it is natural for most of us to act in accordance with certain principles; and the choice of principles implies the adoption of a positive set of values. That these values should be consistent is a necessary condition of their being fully realized; for it is logically impossible to achieve the complete fulfilment of an inconsistent set of ends. But, once their consistency is established, they can be criticized only on practical grounds, and from the standpoint of the critic's own moral system, which his adversary may or may not accept. No doubt, in practice, many people are content to follow the model rules that are prescribed to them by others; but the decision to submit oneself to authority on such a point is itself a judgment of value. In the last resort, therefore, each individual has the responsibility of choice; and it is a responsibility that is not to be escaped.

---

*   Having to do with values.

V

... No more than the scientist is the philosopher specially privileged to lay down the rules of conduct, or to prescribe an ideal form of life. If he has strong opinions on these points, and wishes to convert others to them, his philosophical training may give him a certain advantage in putting them persuasively: but, whether or not the values that he recommends are found to be acceptable, it is not from his philosophy that they can derive their title to acceptance. His professional task is done when he has made the issues clear. For in morals and in politics, at the stage where politics become a matter of morals, there is no repository of truth to which only the learned few have access. The question how men ought to live is one to which there is no authoritative answer. It has to be decided by each man for himself. ■

Suggestions for Critical Reflection

1. Ayer distinguishes between two kinds of philosopher, the "pontiffs" and the "journeymen," but he is critical of both kinds. What do you make of this distinction? Is there a third option for philosophy? How fair are Ayer's complaints?

2. "Surely, the business of the philosopher is to make clear the meaning of life, to show people how they ought to live." Ayer denies that this is a coherent task—for philosophers or anyone else—but then admits that there is "a sense" in which philosophy can be useful here. How effectively do you think Ayer argues for his main claim: that the question "what is the meaning of life?" makes no sense because it has no possible answer? What is left over, on Ayer's account, for philosophers to say about the meaning of life?

3. Ayer raises the possibility (which he doubts) that there exists a God who has designed the universe to serve a certain purpose, and that we could come to understand this cosmic purpose and consciously choose to endorse it. *Even then*, Ayer, says this would not answer, for us, the question "what is the meaning of life?" How does Ayer argue for this conclusion? Is he right?

4. Ayer insists that it is misleading to say that life has no meaning. Why does he say this?

5. Ayer makes a sharp distinction between *describing* how things are and judging how they *ought* to be; his arguments in section III often depend on this contrast—sometimes called the fact-value distinction—being clear. But is it really? Are all facts value-free and are all values completely independent of facts? If this distinction can be blurred, what does this do to Ayer's argument?

6. "In the last resort, therefore, each individual has the responsibility of choice; and it is a responsibility that is not to be escaped." How does this proclamation by Ayer compare to similar sentiments expressed by existentialist philosophers such as, say, Camus (in a later selection in this chapter)? In the end, is Ayer's stance on the meaning of life empowering or deflating, do you think?

Notes

1 *Vide* [see] *Was ist Metaphysik*. Published by Friedrich Cohen in Bonn, 1929.

2 *Vide* Boswell's *Life of Johnson*. 'A clergyman (whose name I do not recollect): "Were not Dodd's sermons addressed to the passions?" Johnson: "They were nothing, sir, be they addressed to what they may."'

3 *Vide* his 'Proof of an External World'. Proceedings of the British Academy, vol. XXV.

4 *Vide* 'Nicomachean Ethics' Book I, Section 3.

JEAN-PAUL SARTRE

FROM *Existentialism Is a Humanism*

Who Was Jean-Paul Sartre?

Jean-Paul Sartre, a leading figure in twentieth-century French philosophy as well as a prominent playwright, novelist, and political activist, was born in 1905 in Paris. His father was a naval officer, who died when Jean-Paul was one, and his mother was the first cousin of Nobel Prize laureate Albert Schweitzer. When he was 12 his mother remarried and they moved to La Rochelle, a coastal city in western France, where Jean-Paul was subjected to frequent bullying from other boys. Sartre fell in love with philosophy as a teenager, and was educated at a private school in Paris and then at the elite Parisian university, the École Normale Supérieure. While there, he was a notorious practical joker, and eventually (inadvertently) caused the forced resignation of the director of the university after Sartre invited the press to a staged event awarding Charles Lindbergh—or rather, a Lindbergh lookalike—an honorary degree for completing the first New York City to Paris non-stop flight. It was also at university that Sartre met Simone de Beauvoir, who would go on to become a famous and influential philosopher and feminist. Sartre and Beauvoir had a lifelong romantic relationship, though both also had other relationships and partners throughout their lives. The first time Sartre took the *agrégation*—the competitive examination to teach at French high schools and universities—he failed; when he took it a second time, he and Beauvoir tied for first place, although Sartre was subsequently awarded first place, with Beauvoir second.

Sartre was drafted into the French army between 1929 and 1931 and served as a meteorologist. After that he taught at various high schools until the outbreak of World War II, when he was again drafted as a meteorologist into the French army. He was captured by German troops in 1940 and spent nine months as a prisoner of war. In 1941 he was released due to his failing eyesight (though a more exciting story has him escaping after a visit to the ophthalmologist) and given civilian status. He returned to teaching at a high school in Paris, replacing a Jewish teacher who had been forbidden to teach by Vichy law. Nevertheless Sartre, with Beauvoir and other writers, founded an underground group called "Socialism and Liberty" and contemplated assassinating prominent French collaborators, though in the end they took no such action. Instead Sartre wrote, publishing some of his most famous works, including *Being and Nothingness* (1943), *The Flies* (1943), and *No Exit* (1944).* He was also an active contributor to *Combat*, the resistance newspaper edited by Albert Camus.

After the war, Sartre mostly stopped teaching and devoted his time to writing and political activism. He became very active in glorifying the French Resistance and attacking anyone who had either collaborated or been passive during the occupation. He defended Marxism, socialism, and the Soviet Union, though not wholly uncritically (for example he condemned the 1956 invasion of Hungary, and he didn't become a member of the Communist party). He often took the opportunity to criticize the United States, and was a prominent anti-colonialist. He supported the National Liberation Front of Algeria in its armed struggle against French rule,† and

---

* None of these works were censored by the Germans. However, they contained some sly digs at the Occupation. For example, *mouche* (fly) was slang for an informer, and the French often called the Germans *les autres* (the others) so that the most famous line from *No Exit*—"Hell is other people" ("l'enfer, c'est les autres")—had a double meaning at the time.

† In his preface to Frantz Fanon's *The Wretched of the Earth* (1961) Sartre wrote, "To shoot down a European is to kill two birds with one stone, to destroy an oppressor and the man he oppresses at the same time: there remains a dead man and a free man."

as a result was the target of two assassination attempts by the paramilitary Organisation Armée Secrète (OAS) in the early 1960s.* Along with Bertrand Russell and others, he organized a tribunal in 1967 intended to expose US war crimes in the Vietnam War, but he became increasingly disillusioned by what he thought of as the 'Americanization' of the French working class who would rather watch American TV shows than agitate for a revolution. Even literature, he argued in a scorched-earth autobiography called *Les Mots* (1964), functioned ultimately as a middle-class substitute for real commitment or engagement. In the same year he was awarded the Nobel Prize for Literature but turned it down (the first person ever to do so). Towards the end of his life he became an anarchist.

Despite his thorny political views, Sartre was a household name in France and highly valued as a public intellectual. When he was arrested for civil disobedience during the uprisings of the summer of 1968, President Charles de Gaulle had him released, reputedly commenting that "you don't arrest Voltaire." In his final decade Sartre—a lifelong chain smoker, and frequent taker of amphetamines in order to keep up the pace of his work—suffered from serious ill health. He was almost blind by 1973, and died in 1980 from fluid on the lung. Fifty thousand Parisians attended his funeral.

What Is the Structure of This Reading?

Sartre starts by summarizing several complaints made against existentialism: that it is sordid; that it leads to despair and passivity; that it is selfish, subjective or anti-social. He proceeds to defend his philosophy by first offering an account of the basic commitment of existentialism held in common by both Christian and atheistic existentialists, and arguing that this is a commitment to a kind of "subjectivity," but not the bad kind of subjectivity of which existentialism has been accused. Sartre discusses the freedom to which existentialism leads, and then explains this further by defining three key terms: anguish, abandonment, and despair. The final section of his essay, which is not reprinted here, addresses some further possible misunderstandings of the kind of subjectivity to which existentialism is committed.

Some Useful Background Information

1. This essay is based on a public lecture Sartre gave in 1945, to a large mixed audience of academics and laypeople, at a venue called *Le Club Maintenant* (the 'Now' club) which was founded shortly after the liberation of Paris from German occupation after World War II. The context for this talk, therefore, was a time of great turmoil in French society: one in which 'ordinary' people living under the occupation had been faced with momentous personal decisions and difficult choices about loyalty and integrity; in which stern reprisals against collaborators were still being meted out; and in which the atomic bombs had recently been dropped and the scope of the Holocaust was becoming widely known. Unsettling moral questions would have been of more than merely theoretical interest to this audience. Similarly, the theme of freedom would have been especially resonant at that moment, although Sartre certainly thinks that what he has to say applies generally and not just for that particular historical juncture.

2. A core commitment for the existentialist, including Sartre, is that, in a famous dictum, "existence precedes essence." This is a consequential idea which takes a lot of unpacking, and Sartre discusses it in this essay (from which, in fact, this phrase originates). The basic idea though is that, for a human being, that person's identity—the thing that makes them the particular person they are—arises only *after* they have come into existence as a concrete, physical thing. This essence is *created*, by the individual, through that person's conscious choices and deliberate adoption of certain values rather than others. This doctrine is (arguably) a radical departure from pretty much the entire tradition of western thought, which generally asserts that human beings—like everything else in the world—have an essential nature, laid down by God or nature, and that to be a good or flourishing human being is to be in harmony with this nature: Aristotle, for example, defined human beings as rational animals, Christianity describes humans as created

---

* He had an Algerian mistress, Arlette Elkaïm, who became his adopted daughter in 1965.

in the image of God, Descartes thought we were a metaphysical union of mind and body, Darwin gave rise to an evolutionary conception of human nature, and so on. On all these views, we are born with an essential nature that, at least, constrains what kind of person we can be or ought to be. Existentialism denies that any such constraint exists.

A Common Misconception

Although Sartre focuses on abandonment, anguish, and despair in this essay, in fact Sartre does not intend these terms wholly negatively: one of his core concerns is to show that, though inescapable, they also have a positive, optimistic aspect.

FROM *Existentialism Is a Humanism**

My purpose here is to defend existentialism against some charges that have been brought against it.

First, it has been blamed for encouraging people to remain in a state of quietism[†] and despair. For if all solutions are barred, we have to regard any action in this world as futile, and so at last we arrive at a contemplative philosophy. And inasmuch as contemplation is a luxury, we are only espousing yet another kind of bourgeois[‡] philosophy. These are the main reproaches made by the Communists.

Others have condemned us for emphasizing what is despicable about humanity, for exposing all that is sordid, suspicious, or base, while ignoring beauty and the brighter side of human nature. For example, according to Miss Mercier,[§] a Catholic critic, we have forgotten the innocence of a child's smile.

One group after another censures us for overlooking humanity's solidarity, and for considering man as an isolated being. This, contend the Communists, is primarily because we base our doctrine on pure subjectivity—that is, on the Cartesian *I think*—on the very moment in which man fully comprehends his isolation, rendering us incapable of re-establishing solidarity with those who exist outside of the self, and who are inaccessible to us through the *cogito*.[¶]

Christians, on the other hand, reproach us for denying the reality and validity of human enterprise, for inasmuch as we choose to ignore God's commandments and all values thought to be eternal, all that remains is the strictly gratuitous; everyone can do whatever he pleases and is incapable, from his own small vantage point, of finding fault with the points of view or actions of others.

It is these various charges that I want to address today, which is why I have entitled this brief discourse "Existentialism Is a Humanism." Many will be surprised by what I have to say here about humanism. We shall attempt to discover in what sense we understand it. In any case, let us begin by saying that what we mean by "existentialism" is a doctrine that makes human life possible and also affirms that every truth and every action imply an environment and a human subjectivity. It is public knowledge that the fundamental reproach brought against us is that we stress the dark side of human life. Recently someone told me about a lady who, whenever she inadvertently utters some vulgar expression in a moment of anger, excuses herself by saying: "I think I'm becoming an existentialist." So it would appear that existentialism is associated with something ugly, which is why some people call us naturalists. If we are, it is strange that we should

---

* Published as a pamphlet in 1946, this is based on a public lecture by the same name Sartre gave at the Club Maintenant in Paris in October 1945. This translation is by Carol Macomber (Yale University Press, 2007).

† An attitude of passive withdrawal. Quietism is also a name given to a system of Christian mysticism recommending calm acceptance of things as they are.

‡ Characteristic of the middle class.

§ Jeanne Mercier, "Le ver dans le fruit. À propos de l'œuvre de M. J.-P. Sartre," *Le Devoir*, 16 February 1946, 8.

¶ Descartes's conclusion that "I think therefore I am," *cogito ergo sum* (Latin).

frighten or shock people far more than naturalism per se frightens or offends them. Those who easily stomach a Zola* novel like *The Earth* are sickened when they open an existentialist novel. Those who find solace in the wisdom of the people—which is a sad, depressing thing—find us even sadder. Yet, what could be more disillusioning than such sayings as "Charity begins at home," or even "Appoint a rogue and he'll do you damage, knock him down and he'll do you homage." We all know countless such popular sayings, all of which always point to the same thing: one should not try to fight against the establishment; one should not be more royalist than the king, or meddle in matters that exceed one's station in life; any action not in keeping with tradition is mere romanticism; any effort not based on proven experience is doomed; since experience shows that men are invariably inclined to do evil, there must be strict rules to restrain them, otherwise anarchy ensues. However, since it is the very same people who are forever spouting these dreary old proverbs—the ones who say "It is so human!" whenever some repugnant act is pointed out to them, the ones who are always harping on realistic litanies—who also accuse existentialism of being too gloomy, it makes me wonder if what they are really annoyed about is not its pessimism, but rather its optimism. For when all is said and done, could it be that what frightens them about the doctrine that I shall try to present to you here is that it offers man the possibility of individual choice? To verify this, we need to reconsider the whole issue on a strictly philosophical plane. What, then, is "existentialism"?

Most people who use this word would be at a loss to explain what it means. For now that it has become fashionable, people like to call this musician or that painter an "existentialist." A columnist in *Clartés*† goes by the pen name "The Existentialist." Indeed, the word is being so loosely applied to so many things that it has come to mean nothing at all. It would appear that, for lack of an avant-garde doctrine analogous to surrealism,‡ those who thrive on the latest scandal or fad have seized upon a philosophy that hardly suits their purpose. The truth is that of all doctrines, this is the least scandalous and the most austere: it is strictly intended for specialists and philosophers. Yet it can be easily defined. What complicates the matter is that there are two kinds of existentialists: on one hand, the Christians, among whom I would include Karl Jaspers and Gabriel Marcel, both professed Catholics; and, on the other, the atheistic existentialists, among whom we should place Heidegger,§ as well as the French existentialists and myself.[1] What they have in common is simply their belief that existence precedes essence; or, if you prefer, that subjectivity must be our point of departure. What exactly do we mean by that? If we consider a manufactured object, such as a book or a paper knife,¶ we note that this object was produced by a craftsman who drew his inspiration from a concept: he referred both to the concept of what a paper knife is, and to a known production technique that is a part of that concept and is, by and large, a formula. The paper knife is thus both an object produced in a certain way and one that, on the other hand, serves a definite purpose. We cannot suppose that a man would produce a paper knife without knowing what purpose it would serve. Let us say, therefore, that the essence of the paper knife—that is, the sum of formulae and

---

* Émile Zola (1840–1902) was a French writer and leading example of the new school of literary naturalism which emphasised a detached examination of the inexorable forces shaping human behavior, including emotion, heredity, and environment. His novel *La Terre* (*The Earth*) was published in 1887.

† *Clartés: l'hebdomadaire de combat pour la résistance et la démocratie* was a weekly newspaper published in Paris between 1945 and 1946.

‡ A cultural and artistic movement that began in the early 1920s and used unexpected juxtapositions and leaps to try to allow the unconscious to express itself.

§ Karl Jaspers (1883–1969) was a German-Swiss psychiatrist and philosopher and Gabriel Marcel (1889–1973) was a French philosopher and playwright. (Marcel was also probably the originator of the term "existentialism," which Sartre initially detested.) Martin Heidegger (1889–1976) was a seminal German philosopher of existentialism, phenomenology, and hermeneutics.

¶ A knife, similar to a letter opener, used for cutting open the pages of books produced using an older method where the folding of printed sheets creates closed edges that need to be cut before the book can be read. That is, it was a specialized tool with a very particular purpose.

properties that enable it to be produced and defined—precedes its existence. Thus the presence before my eyes of that paper knife or book is determined. Here, then, we are viewing the world from a technical standpoint, whereby we can say "production precedes essence."

When we think of God the Creator, we usually conceive of him as a superlative artisan. Whatever doctrine we may be considering, say Descartes's or Leibniz's,* we always agree that the will more or less follows understanding, or at the very least accompanies it, so that when God creates he knows exactly what he is creating. Thus the concept of man, in the mind of God, is comparable to the concept of the paper knife in the mind of the manufacturer: God produces man following certain techniques and a conception, just as the craftsman, following a definition and a technique, produces a paper knife. Thus each individual man is the realization of a certain concept within the divine intelligence. Eighteenth-century atheistic philosophers suppressed the idea of God, but not, for all that, the idea that essence precedes existence. We encounter this idea nearly everywhere: in the works of Diderot, Voltaire, and even Kant.† Man possesses a human nature; this "human nature," which is the concept of that which is human, is found in all men, which means that each man is a particular example of a universal concept—man. In Kant's works, this universality extends so far as to encompass forest dwellers—man in a state of nature—and the bourgeois, meaning that they all possess the same basic qualities. Here again, the essence of man precedes his historically primitive existence in nature.

Atheistic existentialism, which I represent, is more consistent. It states that if God does not exist, there is at least one being in whom existence precedes essence—a being whose existence comes before its essence, a being who exists before he can be defined by any concept of it. That being is man, or, as Heidegger put it, the human reality. What do we mean here by "existence precedes essence"? We mean that man first exists: he materializes in the world, encounters himself, and only afterward defines himself. If man as existentialists conceive of him cannot be defined, it is because to begin with

he is nothing. He will not be anything until later, and then he will be what he makes of himself. Thus, there is no human nature since there is no God to conceive of it. Man is not only that which he conceives himself to be, but that which he wills himself to be, and since he conceives of himself only after he exists, just as he wills himself to be after being thrown into existence, man is nothing other than what he makes of himself. This is the first principle of existentialism.

It is also what is referred to as "subjectivity," the very word used as a reproach against us. But what do we mean by that, if not that man has more dignity than a stone or a table? What we mean to say is that man first exists; that is, that man primarily exists—that man is, before all else, something that projects itself into a future, and is conscious of doing so. Man is indeed a project that has a subjective existence, rather unlike that of a patch of moss, a spreading fungus, or a cauliflower. Prior to that projection of the self, nothing exists, not even in divine intelligence, and man shall attain existence only when he is what he projects himself to be—not what he would like to be. What we usually understand by "will" is a conscious decision that most of us take after we have made ourselves what we are. I may want to join a party, write a book, or get married—but all of that is only a manifestation of an earlier and more spontaneous choice than what is known as "will." If, however, existence truly does precede essence, man is responsible for what he is. Thus, the first effect of existentialism is to make every man conscious of what he is, and to make him solely responsible for his own existence. And when we say that man is responsible for himself, we do not mean that he is responsible only for his own individuality, but that he is responsible for all men.

The word "subjectivism" has two possible interpretations, and our opponents play with both of them, at our expense. Subjectivism means, on the one hand, the freedom of the individual subject to choose what he will be, and, on the other, man's inability to transcend human subjectivity. The fundamental meaning of existentialism resides in the latter. When we say that man chooses himself, not only do we mean that each of us

---

*   René Descartes (1596–1650) and Gottfried Wilhelm Leibniz (1646–1716) were important early modern philosophers.
†   Denis Diderot (1713–84), Voltaire (1694–1778), and Immanuel Kant (1724–1804) were prominent thinkers of the Enlightenment.

must choose himself, but also that in choosing himself, he is choosing for all men. In fact, in creating the man each of us wills ourselves to be, there is not a single one of our actions that does not at the same time create an image of man as we think he ought to be. Choosing to be this or that is to affirm at the same time the value of what we choose, because we can never choose evil. We always choose the good, and nothing can be good for any of us unless it is good for all. If, moreover, existence precedes essence and we will to exist at the same time as we fashion our image, that image is valid for all and for our whole era. Our responsibility is thus much greater than we might have supposed, because it concerns all mankind. If I am a worker and I choose to join a Christian trade union rather than to become a Communist, and if, by that membership, I choose to signify that resignation is, after all, the most suitable solution for man, and that the kingdom of man is not on this earth, I am not committing myself alone—I am choosing to be resigned on behalf of all—consequently my action commits all mankind. Or, to use a more personal example, if I decide to marry and have children—granted such a marriage proceeds solely from my own circumstances, my passion, or my desire—I am nonetheless committing not only myself, but all of humanity, to the practice of monogamy. I am therefore responsible for myself and for everyone else, and I am fashioning a certain image of man as I choose him to be. In choosing myself, I choose man.

This allows us to understand the meaning behind some rather lofty-sounding words such as "anguish," "abandonment," and "despair." As you are about to see, it is all quite simple. First, what do we mean by anguish? Existentialists like to say that man is in anguish. This is what they mean: a man who commits himself, and who realizes that he is not only the individual that he chooses to be, but also a legislator choosing at the same time what humanity as a whole should be, cannot help but be aware of his own full and profound responsibility. True, many people do not appear especially anguished, but we maintain that they are merely hiding their anguish or trying not to face it. Certainly, many

believe that their actions involve no one but themselves, and were we to ask them, "But what if everyone acted that way?" they would shrug their shoulders and reply, "But everyone does *not* act that way." In truth, however, one should always ask oneself, "What would happen if everyone did what I am doing?" The only way to evade that disturbing thought is through some kind of bad faith. Someone who lies to himself and excuses himself by saying "Everyone does not act that way" is struggling with a bad conscience, for the act of lying implies attributing a universal value to lies.

Anguish can be seen even when concealed. This is the anguish Kierkegaard* called the anguish of Abraham. You know the story: an angel orders Abraham to sacrifice his son. This would be okay provided it is really an angel who appears to him and says, "Thou, Abraham, shalt sacrifice thy son." But any sane person may wonder first whether it is truly an angel, and second, whether I am really Abraham. What proof do I have? There was once a mad woman suffering from hallucinations who claimed that people were phoning her and giving her orders. The doctor asked her, "But who exactly speaks to you?" She replied, "He says it is God." How did she actually know for certain that it was God? If an angel appears to me, what proof do I have that it is an angel? Or if I hear voices, what proof is there that they come from heaven and not from hell, or from my own subconscious, or some pathological condition? What proof is there that they are intended for me? What proof is there that I am the proper person to impose my conception of man on humanity? I will never find any proof at all, nor any convincing sign of it. If a voice speaks to me, it is always I who must decide whether or not this is the voice of an angel; if I regard a certain course of action as good, it is I who will choose to say that it is good, rather than bad. There is nothing to show that I am Abraham, and yet I am constantly compelled to perform exemplary deeds. Everything happens to every man as if the entire human race were staring at him and measuring itself by what he does. So every man ought to be asking himself, "Am I really a man who is entitled to act in such a way that the entire human race should

---

*   Søren Kierkegaard (1813–55) was a Danish philosopher who, in his book *Fear and Trembling* (1843), described the biblical story of Abraham (Genesis 22) and presented it as a dilemma for the reader: either Abraham is no better than a murderer (or at least an attempted murderer), or moral duties are not the highest claim on human beings and Abraham is justified in his faith (which he has won through personal anguish).

be measuring itself by my actions?" And if he does not ask himself that, he masks his anguish.

The anguish we are concerned with is not the kind that could lead to quietism or inaction. It is anguish pure and simple, of the kind experienced by all who have borne responsibilities. For example, when a military leader takes it upon himself to launch an attack and sends a number of men to their deaths, he chooses to do so, and, ultimately, makes that choice alone. Some orders may come from his superiors, but their scope is so broad that he is obliged to interpret them, and it is on his interpretation that the lives of ten, fourteen, or twenty men depend. In making such a decision, he is bound to feel some anguish. All leaders have experienced that anguish, but it does not prevent them from acting. To the contrary, it is the very condition of their action, for they first contemplate several options, and, in choosing one of them, realize that its only value lies in the fact that it was chosen. It is this kind of anguish that existentialism describes, and as we shall see it can be made explicit through a sense of direct responsibility toward the other men who will be affected by it. It is not a screen that separates us from action, but a condition of action itself.

And when we speak of "abandonment"—one of Heidegger's favorite expressions—we merely mean to say that God does not exist, and that we must bear the full consequences of that assertion. Existentialists are strongly opposed to a certain type of secular morality that seeks to eliminate God as painlessly as possible. Around 1880, when some French professors attempted to formulate a secular morality, they expressed it more or less in these words: God is a useless and costly hypothesis, so we will do without it. However, if we are to have a morality, a civil society, and a law-abiding world, it is essential that certain values be taken seriously; they must have an *a priori* existence ascribed to them.* It must be considered mandatory *a priori* for people to be honest, not to lie, not to beat their wives, to raise children, and so forth. We therefore will need to do a little more thinking on this subject in order to show

that such values exist all the same, and that they are inscribed in an intelligible heaven, even though God does not exist. In other words—and I think this is the gist of everything that we in France call "radicalism"— nothing will have changed if God does not exist; we will encounter the same standards of honesty, progress, and humanism, and we will have turned God into an obsolete hypothesis that will die out quietly on its own.

Existentialists, on the other hand, find it extremely disturbing that God no longer exists, for along with his disappearance goes the possibility of finding values in an intelligible heaven. There could no longer be any *a priori* good, since there would be no infinite and perfect consciousness to conceive of it. Nowhere is it written that good exists, that we must be honest or must not lie, since we are on a plane shared only by men. Dostoyevsky once wrote: "If God does not exist, everything is permissible."† This is the starting point of existentialism. Indeed, everything is permissible if God does not exist, and man is consequently abandoned, for he cannot find anything to rely on—neither within nor without. First, he finds there are no excuses. For if it is true that existence precedes essence, we can never explain our actions by reference to a given and immutable human nature. In other words, there is no determinism—man is free, man is freedom. If, however, God does not exist, we will encounter no values or orders that can legitimize our conduct. Thus, we have neither behind us, nor before us, in the luminous realm of values, any means of justification or excuse. We are left alone and without excuse. That is what I mean when I say that man is condemned to be free: condemned, because he did not create himself, yet nonetheless free, because once cast into the world, he is responsible for everything he does. Existentialists do not believe in the power of passion. They will never regard a great passion as a devastating torrent that inevitably compels man to commit certain acts and which, therefore, is an excuse. They think that man is responsible for his own passion. Neither do existentialists believe that man can find refuge in some given sign that will guide him on earth; they think that

---

* In other words, they must be taken to exist necessarily, independently of any possible empirical evidence.

† This is a (rough) quote from Russian novelist Dostoevsky (1821–81), from Book XI, chapter 4 of *The Brothers Karamazov* (1880). "'But,' I asked, 'how will man be after that? Without God and the future life? It means everything is permitted now, one can do anything?' 'Didn't you know?' he said. And he laughed. 'Everything is permitted to the intelligent man,' he said."

man interprets the sign as he pleases and that man is therefore without any support or help, condemned at all times to invent man. In an excellent article, Francis Ponge once wrote: "Man is the future of man."[2*] This is absolutely true. However, if we were to interpret this to mean that such a future is inscribed in heaven, and that God knows what it is, that would be false, for then it would no longer even be a future. If, on the other hand, it means that whatever man may appear to be, there is a future waiting to be created—a virgin future—then the saying is true. But for now, we are abandoned.

To give you an example that will help you to better understand what we mean by abandonment, I will mention the case of one of my students, who sought me out under the following circumstances: his father had broken off with his mother and, moreover, was inclined to be a "collaborator."[†] His older brother had been killed in the German offensive of 1940, and this young man, with primitive but noble feelings, wanted to avenge him. His mother, living alone with him and deeply hurt by the partial betrayal of his father and the death of her oldest son, found her only comfort in him. At the time, the young man had the choice of going to England to join the Free French Forces—which would mean abandoning his mother—or remaining by her side to help her go on with her life. He realized that his mother lived only for him and that his absence—perhaps his death—would plunge her into utter despair. He also realized that, ultimately, any action he might take on her behalf would provide the concrete benefit of helping her to live, while any action he might take to leave and fight would be of uncertain outcome and could disappear pointlessly like water in sand. For instance, in trying to reach England, he might pass through Spain and be detained there indefinitely in a camp; or after arriving in England or Algiers, he might be assigned to an office to do paperwork. He was therefore confronted by two totally different modes of action: one concrete and immediate, but directed toward only one individual; the other involving an infinitely vaster group—a national corps—yet more ambiguous for that very reason and which could be interrupted before being carried out. And, at the same time, he was vacillating between two kinds of morality: a morality motivated by sympathy and individual devotion, and another morality with a broader scope, but less likely to be fruitful. He had to choose between the two.

What could help him make that choice? The Christian doctrine? No. The Christian doctrine tells us we must be charitable, love our neighbor, sacrifice ourselves for others, choose the "narrow way,"[‡] et cetera. But what is the narrow way? Whom should we love like a brother—the soldier or the mother? Which is the more useful aim—the vague one of fighting as part of a group, or the more concrete one of helping one particular person keep on living? Who can decide that *a priori*? No one. No code of ethics on record answers that question. Kantian morality instructs us to never treat another as a means, but always as an end.[§] Very well; therefore, if I stay with my mother, I will treat her as an end, not as a means. But by the same token, I will be treating those who are fighting on my behalf as a means. Conversely, if I join those who are fighting, I will treat them as an end, and, in so doing, risk treating my mother as a means.

If values are vague and if they are always too broad in scope to apply to the specific and concrete case under consideration, we have no choice but to rely on our instincts. That is what this young man tried to do, and when I last saw him, he was saying: "All things considered, it is feelings that matter; I should choose what truly compels me to follow a certain path. If I feel that I love my mother enough to sacrifice everything else for her—my desire for vengeance, my desire for action, my desire for adventure—then I should stay by her side. If, to the contrary, I feel that my love for my mother is not strong enough, I should go." But how can we measure

---

*   Francis Ponge (1899–1988) was a French essayist and poet. This quotation is from "Notes premières de 'L'Homme'" (1945).

†   Collaborating, that is, with the Nazi occupiers of France during World War II.

‡   A reference to Matthew 7:13–14, in which Jesus says, "Enter by the narrow gate; for wide is the gate and broad is the way that leads to destruction, and there are many who go in by it. Because *narrow is the gate* and difficult is the way which leads to life, and there are few who find it."

§   Sartre is referring to Immanuel Kant's view that it is immoral to treat another human being merely as a tool for achieving something else—human beings are things of intrinsic value, "ends in themselves." See the reading from Kant in the Ethical Theory section for more information.

the strength of a feeling? What gave any value to the young man's feelings for his mother? Precisely the fact that he chose to stay with her. I may say that I love a friend well enough to sacrifice a certain sum of money for his sake, but can claim that only if I have done so. I can say that I love my mother enough to stay by her side only if I actually stayed with her. The only way I can measure the strength of this affection is precisely by performing an action that confirms and defines it. However, since I am depending on this affection to justify my action, I find myself caught in a vicious circle.

Moreover, as Gide* once pointed out, it is almost impossible to distinguish between playacting and true feelings. To decide that I love my mother and will stay with her, or to stay with her by putting on a charade, amount to the same thing. In other words, feelings are developed through the actions we take; therefore I cannot use them as guidelines for action. This means that I shouldn't seek within myself some authentic state that will compel me to act, any more than I can expect any morality to provide the concepts that will enable me to act. You may say, "Well, he went to see a professor for advice." But if you consult a priest, for instance, it's you who has chosen to consult him, and you already know in your heart, more or less, what advice he is likely to give. In other words, to choose one's adviser is only another way to commit oneself. This is demonstrated by the fact that, if you are Christian, you will say "consult a priest." But there are collaborating priests, temporizing priests, and priests connected to the Resistance: which do you choose? Had this young man chosen to consult a priest connected to the Resistance, or a collaborating priest, he would have decided beforehand what kind of advice he was to receive. Therefore, in seeking me out, he knew what my answer would be, and there was only one answer I could give him: "You are free, so choose; in other words, invent. No general code of ethics can tell you what you ought to do; there are no signs in this world."

Catholics will reply: "But there *are* signs!" Be that as it may, it is I who chooses what those signs mean. When I was in a German prison camp, I met a rather remarkable man, who happened to be a Jesuit. This is how he came to join the order: he had experienced several frustrating setbacks in his life. His father died while he was still a child, leaving him in poverty, but he was awarded a scholarship to a religious institution where he was constantly reminded that he had been accepted only out of charity. He was subsequently denied a number of distinctions and honors that would have pleased any child. Then, when he was about eighteen years old, he had an unfortunate love affair that broke his heart. Finally, at the age of twenty-two, what should have been a trifle was actually the last straw: he flunked out of military training school. This young man had every right to believe he was a total failure. It was a sign—but a sign of what? He could have sought refuge in bitterness or despair. Instead—and it was very clever of him—he chose to take it as a sign that he was not destined for secular success, and that his achievements would be attained only in the realms of religion, sanctity, and faith. He saw in all of this a message from God, and so he joined the order. Who can doubt that the meaning of the sign was determined by him, and by him alone? We might have concluded something quite different from this set of reversals—for example, that he might have been better off training to be a carpenter or a revolutionary. He therefore bears the full responsibility for his interpretation of the sign. This is what "abandonment" implies: it is we, ourselves, who decide who we are to be. Such abandonment entails anguish.

As for "despair," it has a very simple meaning. It means that we must limit ourselves to reckoning only with those things that depend on our will, or on the set of probabilities that enable action. Whenever we desire something, there are always elements of probability. If I am counting on a visit from a friend who is traveling by train or trolley, then I assume that the train will arrive on time, or that the trolley will not derail. I operate within a realm of possibilities. But we credit such possibilities only to the strict extent that our action encompasses them. From the moment that the possibilities I am considering cease to be rigorously engaged by my action, I must no longer take interest in them, for no God or greater design can bend the world and its possibilities to my will. In the final analysis, when Descartes said "Conquer yourself rather than the world," he actually meant the same thing: we should act without

---

* André Gide (1869–1951), French author and winner of the Nobel Prize in Literature in 1947.

hope.* Marxists, with whom I have discussed this, reply: "Obviously, your action will be limited by your death; but you can rely on the help of others. You can count both on what others are doing elsewhere, in China, in Russia, to help you, and on what they will do later, that is, after your death, to carry on your work and bring it to fruition, which will be the revolution. What is more, you must rely on it; not to do so would be immoral."

My initial response to this is that I will always depend on my comrades-in-arms in the struggle, inasmuch as they are committed, as I am, to a definite common cause, in the solidarity of a party or a group that I can more or less control—that is to say, that I joined the group as a militant and so its every move is familiar to me. In that context, counting on the solidarity and will of this party is exactly like counting on the fact that the train will arrive on time, or that the trolley will not derail. But I cannot count on men whom I do not know based on faith in the goodness of humanity or in man's interest in society's welfare, given that man is free and there is no human nature in which I can place my trust. I do not know where the Russian Revolution might lead. I can admire it and hold it up as an example to the extent that it is clear, to date, that the proletariat† plays a part in Russia that it has attained in no other nation. But I cannot assert that this Revolution will necessarily lead to the triumph of the proletariat; I must confine myself to what I can see. Nor can I be certain that comrades-in-arms will carry on my work after my death and bring it to completion, seeing that those men are free and will freely choose, tomorrow, what man is to become. Tomorrow, after my death, men may choose to impose fascism, while others may be cowardly or distraught enough to let them get away with it. Fascism will then become humanity's truth, and so much the worse for us. In reality, things will be what men have chosen them to be. Does that mean that I must resort to quietism? No. First, I must commit myself, and then act according to the old adage: "No hope is necessary to undertake

anything." This does not mean that I cannot belong to a party, just that I should have no illusions and do whatever I can. For instance, if I were to ask myself: "Will collectivization ever be a reality?" I have no idea. All I know is that I will do everything in my power to make it happen. Beyond that, I cannot count on anything.

Quietism is the attitude of people who say: "Others can do what I cannot do." The doctrine that I am presenting to you is precisely the opposite of quietism, since it declares that reality exists only in action. It ventures even further than that, since it adds: "Man is nothing other than his own project. He exists only to the extent that he realizes himself, therefore he is nothing more than the sum of his actions, nothing more than his life." In view of this, we can clearly understand why our doctrine horrifies many people. For they often have no other way of putting up with their misery than to think: "Circumstances have been against me, I deserve a much better life than the one I have. Admittedly, I have never experienced a great love or extraordinary friendship, but that is because I never met a man or woman worthy of it; if I have written no great books, it is because I never had the leisure to do so; if I have had no children to whom I could devote myself, it is because I did not find a man with whom I could share my life. So I have within me a host of untried but perfectly viable abilities, inclinations, and possibilities that endow me with worthiness not evident from any examination of my past actions." In reality, however, for existentialists there is no love other than the deeds of love; no potential for love other than that which is manifested in loving. There is no genius other than that which is expressed in works of art; the genius of Proust‡ resides in the totality of his works; the genius of Racine is found in the series of his tragedies, outside of which there is nothing. Why should we attribute to Racine the ability to write yet another tragedy when that is precisely what he did not do? In life, a man commits himself and draws his own portrait, outside of which there is nothing. No doubt this thought may seem harsh

---

* "My third maxim was to try always to overcome myself rather than fortune and to change my desires rather than the order of the world, and generally to get in the habit of believing that there is nothing which is entirely within our power except our thoughts, so that after we have done our best concerning those things which lie outside of us, everything which our attempt fails to deal with is, so far as we are concerned, absolutely impossible. That alone seemed to me to be sufficient to prevent me from desiring anything in future which I might not achieve and thus to make me happy." *Discourse on Method*, Part 3 (1637), as translated by Ian Johnston.

† The working, non-property-owning class.

‡ Marcel Proust (1871–1922) was a French novelist, and Jean Racine (1639–99) one of France's most important playwrights.

to someone who has not made a success of his life. But on the other hand, it helps people to understand that reality alone counts, and that dreams, expectations, and hopes only serve to define a man as a broken dream, aborted hopes, and futile expectations; in other words, they define him negatively, not positively. Nonetheless, saying "You are nothing but your life" does not imply that the artist will be judged solely by his works of art, for a thousand other things also help to define him. What we mean to say is that a man is nothing but a series of enterprises, and that he is the sum, organization, and aggregate of the relations that constitute such enterprises.

In light of all this, what people reproach us for is not essentially our pessimism, but the sternness of our optimism. If people criticize our works of fiction, in which we describe characters who are spineless, weak, cowardly, and sometimes even frankly evil, it is not just because these characters are spineless, weak, cowardly, or evil. For if, like Zola, we were to blame their behavior on their heredity, or environmental influences, their society, or factors of an organic or psychological nature, people would be reassured and would say, "That is the way we are. No one can do anything about it." But when an existentialist describes a coward, he says that the coward is responsible for his own cowardice. He is not the way he is because he has a cowardly heart, lung, or brain. He is not like that as the result of his physiological makeup; he is like that because he has made himself a coward through his actions. There is no such thing as a cowardly temperament; there are nervous temperaments, or "poor blood," as ordinary folks call it, or "rich temperaments," but just because a man has poor blood does not make him a coward, for what produces cowardice is the act of giving up, or giving in. A temperament is not an action; a coward is defined by the action he has taken. What people are obscurely feeling, and what horrifies them, is that the coward, as we present him, is guilty of his cowardice. People would prefer to be born a coward or be born a hero. One of the most frequent criticisms of *Roads to Freedom** may be expressed as follows: "Frankly, how can you make heroes out of people as spineless as this?" This objection is really quite comical, for it implies that people are born heroes. Essentially, that is what people would like to think. If you are born a coward, you need not let it concern you, for you will be a coward your whole life, regardless of what you do, through no fault of your own. If you are born a hero, you need not let it concern you either, for you will be a hero your whole life, and eat and drink like one. What the existentialist says is that the coward makes himself cowardly and the hero makes himself heroic; there is always the possibility that one day the coward may no longer be cowardly and the hero may cease to be a hero. What matters is the total commitment, but there is no one particular situation or action that fully commits you, one way or the other.

We have now, I think, dispensed with a number of charges brought against existentialism. You have seen that it cannot be considered a philosophy of quietism, since it defines man by his actions, nor can it be called a pessimistic description of man, for no doctrine is more optimistic, since it declares that man's destiny lies within himself. Nor is existentialism an attempt to discourage man from taking action, since it tells him that the only hope resides in his actions and that the only thing that allows him to live is action. Consequently we are dealing with a morality of action and commitment. Nevertheless, on the basis of a few wrongheaded notions, we are also charged with imprisoning man within his individual subjectivity. In this regard, too, we are exceedingly misunderstood. For strictly philosophical reasons, our point of departure is, indeed, the subjectivity of the individual—not because we are bourgeois, but because we seek to base our doctrine on truth, not on comforting theories full of hope but without any real foundation. As our point of departure there can be no other truth than this: *I think therefore I am.* This is the absolute truth of consciousness confronting itself. Any theory that considers man outside of this moment of self-awareness is, at the outset, a theory that suppresses the truth, for outside of this Cartesian *cogito*, all objects are merely probable, and a doctrine of probabilities not rooted in any truth crumbles into nothing. In order to define the probable, one must possess what is true. Therefore, in order for any truth to exist, there must first be an absolute truth. The latter is simple, easy to attain, and within everyone's reach: one need only seize it directly. ∎

---

* *The Roads to Freedom* (*Les Chemins de la Liberté*) is a series of novels by Sartre revolving around a Socialist philosophy teacher and a group of his friends. Sartre intended it to be a sequence of four novels, but managed to publish only three: *L'âge de raison* (*The Age of Reason*, 1945), *Le sursis* (*The Reprieve*, 1945), and *La mort dans l'âme* (*Troubled Sleep*, 1949).

Suggestions for Critical Reflection

1. "[M]an is nothing other than what he makes of himself. This is the first principle of existentialism." What does Sartre mean by this? What are its implications?

2. One of Sartre's key claims in this essay is that "man is condemned to be free." How does he explain what he means by this? Why 'condemned'?

3. The contrast between human beings (for whom existence comes before essence) and artifacts such as paper-knives (for which essence precedes existence) is emphasized by Sartre, and is central to the philosophy of existentialism. How clear is this distinction? If it is clear for human beings and designed objects, how do you think it applies to non-designed objects (such as mountains) or to other living creatures (such as dogs)?

4. "When we say that man chooses himself, not only do we mean that each of us must choose for himself, but also that in choosing himself, he is choosing for all men." This is a striking and somewhat unexpected turn in Sartre's essay: why does he say this? How does he justify this claim?

5. "Choosing to be this or that is to affirm at the same time the value of what we choose, because we can never choose evil. We always choose the good, and nothing can be better for any of us unless it is good for all." What does Sartre mean by this? How important is it to his overall position? Is he right?

6. How does the story of Abraham illuminate or explain the kind of anguish Sartre discusses in his essay?

7. Sartre describes a pupil who comes to him for advice on a moral dilemma, and suggests that neither religion nor moral theory (in the shape of Kantianism) is able to provide him with any useful direction. How much more useful, if at all, is the advice the pupil eventually receives from Sartre, the existentialist? Is that—being useful in that way—the point of existentialism?

8. "In reality, however, for the existentialists there is no love other than the deeds of love; no potential for love other than that which is manifested in loving. There is no genius other than that which is expressed in works of art." What does Sartre mean by this? Is it an uncomfortable thought? Or is it a hopeful one?

9. Is existentialism a humanism? What exactly would it be to be "humanistic," and what do you think Sartre means by the term?

10. Sartre often stated his attraction to Marxist movements. If you have read the selection from Marx and Engels in this volume, consider in what ways (if any) Marxism is consistent with existentialism as Sartre defines it here.

11. Does existentialism lead to moral anarchy?

12. Sartre claims that his existentialist philosophy does without metaphysics, and treats essences as created and contingent rather than inherent and predetermined. But in a famous critique ("Letter on Humanism," 1947), Martin Heidegger writes, "Existentialism says existence precedes essence. In this statement he is taking *existentia* and *essentia* according to their metaphysical meaning, which, from Plato's time on, has said that *essentia* precedes *existentia*. Sartre reverses this statement. But the reversal of a metaphysical statement remains a metaphysical statement." What do you think about this criticism?

Notes

1 Heidegger refused to call himself an atheistic existentialist in his *Lettre sur l'humanisme* (1947).

2 "Notes premières de l'homme," *Les Temps modernes*, no. 1, October 1945.

ALBERT CAMUS

FROM *The Myth of Sisyphus*

Who Was Albert Camus?

Albert Camus was born in 1913 to a poor white family in Algeria, north Africa, at that time a French colony. He studied at the University of Algiers—studying part time and supporting himself through a succession of temporary jobs—and was also a serious soccer player, playing as goalkeeper for a high-profile university team until tuberculosis ended his career. After completing the equivalent of an MA degree (on the Greek philosopher Plotinus) he became a journalist. In 1935 he founded a theater company in Algeria called the Théâtre de l'Équipe, which aimed to bring excellent plays to working-class audiences. At the outbreak of World War II Camus was working in France for *Paris-Soir* magazine and was at first a pacifist. He became radicalized in his opposition to the German occupation after reading about executions of members of the French Resistance. He joined the Resistance cell *Combat*, which published an underground newspaper of the same name, and became editor of the newspaper in 1943. He was in Paris in 1944 when the Allies liberated the city, and reported on the fighting. After the war he founded the French Committee for the European Federation, one of several groups that joined together into the European Federalist Movement, a precursor of the European Union.

Camus was awarded the Nobel Prize for Literature in 1957, at 44 the second youngest person ever to receive that honor (after Rudyard Kipling, who received it at 42). Among his major works are the novels *The Stranger* (1942), *The Plague* (1947), and *The Fall* (1956), the plays *Caligula* (1938) and *The Misunderstanding* (1944), and the philosophical essays *The Myth of Sisyphus* (1942) and *The Rebel* (1951). The reading included here is the fourth and final part of *The Myth of Sisyphus*. Camus died in a car accident in France in 1960, at the age of only 46. In his coat pocket was an unused train ticket. He had planned to travel by train with his wife and children, but, fatefully, he accepted his publisher's last minute proposal to travel with him by car instead.

Camus was a political radical and a life-long anarchist (though he had conflicted views about the question of Algerian independence) who rejected any form of authoritarianism and campaigned against capital punishment. He also rejected belief in God. Although broadly left-wing in his views, Camus became a strong critic of Communism. This caused him to split from Jean-Paul Sartre, the well-known French existentialist philosopher, and although Camus's work is often grouped with Sartre's, Camus publicly denied that he was an existentialist.

Some Useful Background Information

1. For Camus, the human condition is that we live in a world that offers neither meaning nor clear understanding and yet—absurdly—we yearn for both. Our lives will end with an inevitable, final, and meaningless death, and nothing outside of ourselves determines or constrains what we should or should not do. Camus argued that the best response, that of the Absurd Hero, is to embrace this condition of absurdity. The alternative is to commit "philosophical suicide": to falsely endorse non-existent external standards—such as those from religion—in order to give life the fake appearance of meaning. In reality, though, according to Camus there is no escape from the Absurd. One of the main purposes of *The Myth of Sisyphus* is to examine what kinds of lives can be worth living despite their absolute meaninglessness. Futilely seeking to avoid death, Camus thought, prevents us from fully appreciating and experiencing life.

2. One of the consequences of this view of the human condition as being absurd is the importance of choice, and this is one of the main ways in which Camus's work is related to existentialism. If there are no external sources of meaning, there are no standards by which we can choose rightly or wrongly. We are absolutely free to make our lives any way we want. On the other hand, terrifyingly, we are

absolutely responsible for those choices—we cannot evade the responsibility to choose by appealing to some unavoidable external standard, as there are no such standards unless we choose them.

3. The well-known first line of the first section of *The Myth of Sisyphus* (not reprinted here) is "There is but one truly serious philosophical problem, and that is suicide." It is striking that Camus focuses his philosophical investigation not on a quest for understanding or analysis, but on the choice of an action. For him, philosophy is not the hopeless attempt to formulate a rational theory of a meaningless universe, but instead is the practical question of how (and whether) to live in that universe.

FROM *The Myth of Sisyphus**

The gods had condemned Sisyphus[†] to ceaselessly rolling a rock to the top of a mountain, whence the stone would fall back of its own weight. They had thought with some reason that there is no more dreadful punishment than futile and hopeless labor.

If one believes Homer, Sisyphus was the wisest and most prudent of mortals. According to another tradition, however, he was disposed to practice the profession of highwayman. I see no contradiction in this. Opinions differ as to the reasons why he became the futile laborer of the underworld. To begin with, he is accused of a certain levity in regard to the gods. He stole their secrets. Ægina, the daughter of Æsopus, was carried off by Jupiter.[‡] The father was shocked by that disappearance and complained to Sisyphus. He, who knew of the abduction, offered to tell about it on condition that Æsopus would give water to the citadel of Corinth. To the celestial thunderbolts he preferred the benediction of water. He was punished for this in the underworld. Homer tells us also that Sisyphus had put Death in chains. Pluto[§] could not endure the sight of his deserted, silent empire. He dispatched the god of war, who liberated Death from the hands of her conqueror.

It is said that Sisyphus, being near to death, rashly wanted to test his wife's love. He ordered her to cast his unburied body into the middle of the public square. Sisyphus woke up in the underworld. And there, annoyed by an obedience so contrary to human love, he obtained from Pluto permission to return to earth in order to chastise his wife. But when he had seen again the face of this world, enjoyed water and sun, warm stones and the sea, he no longer wanted to go back to the infernal darkness. Recalls, signs of anger, warnings were of no avail. Many years more he lived facing the curve of the gulf, the sparkling sea, and the smiles of earth. A decree of the gods was necessary. Mercury[¶] came and seized the impudent man by the collar and, snatching him from his joys, led him forcibly back to the underworld, where his rock was ready for him.

You have already grasped that Sisyphus is the absurd hero. He *is*, as much through his passions as through his torture. His scorn of the gods, his hatred of death, and his passion for life won him that unspeakable penalty in which the whole being is exerted toward accomplishing nothing. This is the price that must be paid for the passions of this earth. Nothing is told us about Sisyphus in the underworld. Myths are made for the imagination to breathe life into them. As for this myth, one sees merely the whole effort of a body straining to raise the huge stone, to roll it, and push it up a slope a hundred times over; one sees the face screwed up, the cheek tight against the stone, the shoulder bracing the claycovered mass, the foot wedging it, the fresh start with arms outstretched,

---

* Albert Camus, *The Myth of Sisyphus*, trans. Justin O'Brien (Alfred A. Knopf).

† In Greek mythology, Sisyphus was the founding king of the Greek city-state of Corinth, from a time long before written history.

‡ Æsopus is a river god (and the name of a river in Corinthia), and Jupiter is the Roman name for Zeus, the king of the Greek gods.

§ The ruler of the underworld in classical mythology, also known as Hades.

¶ The Roman name for the Greek messenger god Hermes, who among other roles conducted souls into the afterlife.

the wholly human security of two earth-clotted hands. At the very end of his long effort measured by skyless space and time without depth, the purpose is achieved. Then Sisyphus watches the stone rush down in a few moments toward that lower world whence he will have to push it up again toward the summit. He goes back down to the plain.

It is during that return, that pause, that Sisyphus interests me. A face that toils so close to stones is already stone itself! I see that man going back down with a heavy yet measured step toward the torment of which he will never know the end. That hour like a breathing-space which returns as surely as his suffering, that is the hour of consciousness. At each of those moments when he leaves the heights and gradually sinks toward the lairs of the gods, he is superior to his fate. He is stronger than his rock.

If this myth is tragic, that is because its hero is conscious. Where would his torture be, indeed, if at every step the hope of succeeding upheld him? The workman of today works every day in his life at the same tasks, and his fate is no less absurd. But it is tragic only at the rare moments when it becomes conscious. Sisyphus, proletarian of the gods,* powerless and rebellious, knows the whole extent of his wretched condition: it is what he thinks of during his descent. The lucidity that was to constitute his torture at the same time crowns his victory. There is no fate that cannot be surmounted by scorn.

If the descent is thus sometimes performed in sorrow, it can also take place in joy. This word is not too much. Again I fancy Sisyphus returning toward his rock, and the sorrow was in the beginning. When the images of earth cling too tightly to memory, when the call of happiness becomes too insistent, it happens that melancholy arises in man's heart: this is the rock's victory, this is the rock itself. The boundless grief is too heavy to bear. These are our nights of Gethsemane.† But crushing truths perish from being acknowledged. Thus, Œdipus‡ at the outset obeys fate without knowing it. But from the moment he knows, his tragedy begins. Yet at the same moment, blind and desperate, he realizes that the only bond linking him to the world is the cool hand of a girl.§ Then a tremendous remark rings out: "Despite so many ordeals, my advanced age and the nobility of my soul make me conclude that all is well." Sophocles' Œdipus, like Dostoevsky's Kirilov,¶ thus gives the recipe for the absurd victory. Ancient wisdom confirms modern heroism.

One does not discover the absurd without being tempted to write a manual of happiness. "What! by such narrow ways—?"** There is but one world, however. Happiness and the absurd are two sons of the same earth. They are inseparable. It would be a mistake to say that happiness necessarily springs from the absurd discovery. It happens as well that the feeling of the absurd springs from happiness. "I conclude that all is well," says Œdipus, and that remark is sacred. It echoes in the wild and limited universe of man. It teaches that all is not, has not been, exhausted. It drives out of this world a god who had come into it with dissatisfaction and a preference for futile suffering. It makes of fate a human matter, which must be settled among men.

---

* Forced to work for the (higher) gods.

† The garden of Gethsemane was the place where Jesus spent the night before his crucifixion and, knowing that he was about to be betrayed and executed, agonized about his fate before coming to terms with it.

‡ A tragic hero in Greek mythology, Oedipus was fated to fulfill a prophecy that he would accidentally kill his father and marry his mother, and thereby bring disaster down upon his family and his city. When he realizes what he has done he blinds himself. This story is the subject of three plays by Sophocles (c. 497–406 BCE): *Oedipus Rex*, *Oedipus at Colonus*, and *Antigone*.

§ This refers to his daughters Antigone and Ismene, whom Oedipus asked to hold one last time before his exile.

¶ A character in Russian author Fyodor Dostoevsky's novel *Demons* (1872, sometimes called *The Possessed*), who commits suicide because he is convinced that for life to be worth living God must exist, and yet he is also convinced that God cannot exist. To Camus this suicide is not an act of despair but of revolt, and an expression of the unbounded freedom that we have if God does not exist.

** A reference to the biblical passage, "Enter by the narrow gate; for wide is the gate and broad is the way that leads to destruction, and there are many who go in by it. How narrow is the gate and confined is the way which leads to life, and there are few who find it" (Matthew 7:13–14).

All Sisyphus' silent joy is contained therein. His fate belongs to him. His rock is his thing. Likewise, the absurd man, when he contemplates his torment, silences all the idols. In the universe suddenly restored to its silence, the myriad wondering little voices of the earth rise up. Unconscious, secret calls, invitations from all the faces, they are the necessary reverse and price of victory. There is no sun without shadow, and it is essential to know the night. The absurd man says yes and his efforts will henceforth be unceasing. If there is a personal fate, there is no higher destiny, or at least there is but one which he concludes is inevitable and despicable. For the rest, he knows himself to be the master of his days. At that subtle moment when man glances backward over his life, Sisyphus returning toward his rock, in that slight pivoting he contemplates that series of unrelated actions which becomes his fate, created by him, combined under his memory's eye and soon sealed by his death. Thus, convinced of the wholly human origin of all that is human, a blind man eager to see who knows that the night has no end, he is still on the go. The rock is still rolling.

I leave Sisyphus at the foot of the mountain! One always finds one's burden again. But Sisyphus teaches the higher fidelity that negates the gods and raises rocks. He too concludes that all is well. This universe henceforth without a master seems to him neither sterile nor futile. Each atom of that stone, each mineral flake of that night-filled mountain, in itself forms a world. The struggle itself toward the heights is enough to fill a man's heart. One must imagine Sisyphus happy. ■

Suggestions for Critical Reflection

1. According to Camus, hope is a mistake. Why does he believe this? Is he right? What do you think might be the benefits of abandoning hope?

2. If the absurd hero abandons objective values and does not seek explanation or justification, then why did Camus write an essay apparently trying to explain and justify the absurd worldview?

   Does Camus write philosophy or does he reject philosophy?

3. "One must imagine Sisyphus happy." Must one? Why? What happens to Camus's position if Sisyphus is not happy?

4. "There is no fate that cannot be surmounted by scorn." What do you think Camus means by this?

THOMAS NAGEL

The Absurd

Who Is Thomas Nagel?

Thomas Nagel, an important American philosopher, was Professor of Law and Philosophy at New York University until his retirement in 2016. He was born in 1937 in Belgrade, Serbia, to German Jewish refugees, and the family moved to the US in 1939. Nagel was educated at Cornell (BA), Corpus Christi College, Oxford (BPhil), and Harvard (PhD, completed in 1963). After working at Berkeley and Princeton, he moved to New York University in 1980. He is the author of a dozen books, including *The View from Nowhere* (1986) and *Mind and Cosmos: Why the Materialist Neo-Darwinian Conception of Nature Is Almost Certainly False* (2012), and many articles.

What Is Nagel's Overall Philosophical Project?

Throughout his career a main theme of Nagel's philosophical writing has been the difficulty of reconciling two fundamentally different points of view: our first-person, subjective, personal point of view, and the impartial, third-person, objective perspective.* The first-person perspective is typically thought of as being more partial than the third-person—partial both in the sense of being constrained by local horizons, and of being infected with personal concerns and biases. (For example, from *my* point of view it is right and natural to eat with a knife and fork, but this seems natural to me only because of the place and manner of my upbringing: speaking objectively, forks are no more nor less 'natural' than chopsticks or fingers.) As a result, subjective impressions are often thought of as being less reliable or 'true' than objective claims, and the first-person perspective tends to be treated as something to be avoided in serious

knowledge-gathering enterprises such as science or good journalism. Nagel's guiding philosophical question is this: *could* we completely understand the universe from the third-person point of view—that is, is the subjective completely reducible to (or eliminable in favor of) the objective? As he puts it in one of his books, he wants to know "how to combine the perspective of a particular person inside the world with an objective view of that same world, the person and his viewpoint included."†

The short version of Nagel's response to this problem is the following:

1. The subjective perspective is ineliminable in various highly important ways, and a refusal to notice this can lead to philosophical errors. "Appearance and perspective are essential parts of what there is." Our objectivity is limited by the fact that we cannot leave our own viewpoints entirely behind.

2. However, objectivity is also to be valued and fostered as a crucial method of coming to understand aspects of the world as it is in itself. It is important that we struggle to transcend our local horizons and try to get a better view of our place in the universe.

In the preface to his book *Mortal Questions*, Nagel describes his view of philosophy, and it is worth repeating here:

I believe one should trust problems over solutions, intuition over arguments, and pluralistic discord over systematic harmony. Simplicity and elegance are never reasons to think that a philosophical theory is true: on the contrary, they are usually grounds for thinking it false. Given a knockdown argument for an intuitively unacceptable conclusion, one should assume there is probably something

---

* "First-person" and "third-person" are terms taken from grammatical categories: "I am hungry" is a first-person sentence, as it's about the speaker; "She/he/it is hungry" is a third-person sentence, as it's about a third party. ("You are hungry" would be an example of a second-person sentence.)

† Thomas Nagel, *The View from Nowhere* (Oxford University Press, 1986), 3.

wrong with the argument that one cannot detect—though it is always possible that the source of the intuition has been misidentified.... Often the problem has to be reformulated because an adequate answer to the original formulation fails to make the *sense* of the problem disappear.... Superficiality is as hard to avoid in philosophy as it is anywhere else. It is too easy to reach solutions that fail to do justice to the difficulty of the problems. All one can do is try to maintain a desire for answers, a tolerance for long periods without any, an unwillingness to brush aside unexplained intuitions, and an adherence to reasonable standards of clear expression and cogent argument.*

What Is the Structure of This Reading?

Nagel begins by arguing that the reasons commonly given for thinking that life is absurd are bad ones. He then goes on to claim, however, that life really *is* absurd, and to give what he thinks is the correct diagnosis of this feeling. He considers whether this absurdity is something to be regretted, and compares his analysis of life's absurdity with that presented by Camus in "The Myth of Sisyphus" (see the previous reading), suggesting that, though similar, they differ in important ways and his own analysis is to be preferred.

The Absurd†

Most people feel on occasion that life is absurd, and some feel it vividly and continually. Yet the reasons usually offered in defense of this conviction are patently inadequate: they *could* not really explain why life is absurd. Why then do they provide a natural expression for the sense that it is?

I

Consider some examples. It is often remarked that nothing we do now will matter in a million years. But if that is true, then by the same token, nothing that will be the case in a million years matters now. In particular, it does not matter now that in a million years nothing we do now will matter. Moreover, even if what we did now *were* going to matter in a million years, how could that keep our present concerns from being absurd? If their mattering now is not enough to accomplish that, how would it help if they mattered a million years from now?

Whether what we do now will matter in a million years could make the crucial difference only if its mattering in a million years depended on its mattering, period. But then to deny that whatever happens now will matter in a million years is to beg the question‡ against its mattering, period; for in that sense one cannot know that it will not matter in a million years whether (for example) someone now is happy or miserable, without knowing that it does not matter, period.

What we say to convey the absurdity of our lives often has to do with space or time: we are tiny specks in the infinite vastness of the universe; our lives are mere instants even on a geological time scale, let alone a cosmic one; we will all be dead any minute. But of course none of these evident facts can be what *makes* life absurd, if it is absurd. For suppose we lived forever; would not a life that is absurd if it lasts seventy years be infinitely absurd if it lasted through eternity? And if our lives are absurd given our present size, why would they be any less absurd if we filled the universe (either because we were larger or because the universe was smaller)? Reflection on our minuteness and brevity appears to be intimately connected with the sense that life is meaningless; but it is not clear what the connection is.

*   Thomas Nagel, *Mortal Questions* (Cambridge University Press, 1979), x–xi.
†   Published in *The Journal of Philosophy* 68, 20 (1971): 716–27.
‡   To beg the question is to reason in a circle, where the truth of the premises presupposes the truth of the conclusion (and so can't independently support it).

Another inadequate argument is that because we are going to die, all chains of justification must leave off in mid-air: one studies and works to earn money to pay for clothing, housing, entertainment, food, to sustain oneself from year to year, perhaps to support a family and pursue a career—but to what final end? All of it is an elaborate journey leading nowhere. (One will also have some effect on other people's lives, but that simply reproduces the problem, for they will die too.)

There are several replies to this argument. First, life does not consist of a sequence of activities each of which has as its purpose some later member of the sequence. Chains of justification come repeatedly to an end within life, and whether the process as a whole can be justified has no bearing on the finality of these end-points. No further justification is needed to make it reasonable to take aspirin for a headache, attend an exhibit of the work of a painter one admires, or stop a child from putting his hand on a hot stove. No larger context or further purpose is needed to prevent these acts from being pointless.

Even if someone wished to supply a further justification for pursuing all the things in life that are commonly regarded as self-justifying, that justification would have to end somewhere too. If *nothing* can justify unless it is justified in terms of something outside itself, which is also justified, then an infinite regress results, and no chain of justification can be complete. Moreover, if a finite chain of reasons cannot justify anything, what could be accomplished by an infinite chain, each link of which must be justified by something outside itself?

Since justifications must come to an end somewhere, nothing is gained by denying that they end where they appear to, within life—or by trying to subsume the multiple, often trivial ordinary justifications of action under a single, controlling life scheme. We can be satisfied more easily than that. In fact, through its misrepresentation of the process of justification, the argument makes a vacuous demand. It insists that the reasons available within life are incomplete, but suggests thereby that all reasons that come to an end are incomplete. This makes it impossible to supply any reasons at all.

The standard arguments for absurdity appear therefore to fail as arguments. Yet I believe they attempt to express something that is difficult to state, but fundamentally correct.

II

In ordinary life a situation is absurd when it includes a conspicuous discrepancy between pretension or aspiration and reality: someone gives a complicated speech in support of a motion that has already been passed; a notorious criminal is made president of a major philanthropic foundation; you declare your love over the telephone to a recorded announcement; as you are being knighted, your pants fall down.

When a person finds himself in an absurd situation, he will usually attempt to change it, by modifying his aspirations, or by trying to bring reality into better accord with them, or by removing himself from the situation entirely. We are not always willing or able to extricate ourselves from a position whose absurdity has become clear to us. Nevertheless, it is usually possible to imagine some change that would remove the absurdity—whether or not we can or will implement it. The sense that life as a whole is absurd arises when we perceive, perhaps dimly, an inflated pretension or aspiration which is inseparable from the continuation of human life and which makes its absurdity inescapable, short of escape from life itself.

Many people's lives are absurd, temporarily or permanently, for conventional reasons having to do with their particular ambitions, circumstances, and personal relations. If there is a philosophical sense of absurdity, however, it must arise from the perception of something universal—some respect in which pretension and reality inevitably clash for us all. This condition is supplied, I shall argue, by the collision between the seriousness with which we take our lives and the perpetual possibility of regarding everything about which we are serious as arbitrary, or open to doubt.

We cannot live human lives without energy and attention, nor without making choices which show that we take some things more seriously than others. Yet we have always available a point of view outside the particular form of our lives, from which the seriousness appears gratuitous. These two inescapable viewpoints collide in us, and that is what makes life absurd. It is absurd because we ignore the doubts that we know cannot be settled, continuing to live with nearly undiminished seriousness in spite of them.

This analysis requires defense in two respects: first as regards the unavoidability of seriousness; second as regards the inescapability of doubt.

We take ourselves seriously whether we lead serious lives or not and whether we are concerned primarily with fame, pleasure, virtue, luxury, triumph, beauty, justice, knowledge, salvation, or mere survival. If we take other people seriously and devote ourselves to them, that only multiplies the problem. Human life is full of effort, plans, calculation, success and failure: we *pursue* our lives, with varying degrees of sloth and energy.

It would be different if we could not step back and reflect on the process, but were merely led from impulse to impulse without self-consciousness. But human beings do not act solely on impulse. They are prudent, they reflect, they weigh consequences, they ask whether what they are doing is worth while. Not only are their lives full of particular choices that hang together in larger activities with temporal structure: they also decide in the broadest terms what to pursue and what to avoid, what the priorities among their various aims should be, and what kind of people they want to be or become. Some men are faced with such choices by the large decisions they make from time to time; some merely by reflection on the course their lives are taking as the product of countless small decisions. They decide whom to marry, what profession to follow, whether to join the Country Club, or the Resistance; or they may just wonder why they go on being salesmen or academics or taxi drivers, and then stop thinking about it after a certain period of inconclusive reflection.

Although they may be motivated from act to act by those immediate needs with which life presents them, they allow the process to continue by adhering to the general system of habits and the form of life in which such motives have their place—or perhaps only by clinging to life itself. They spend enormous quantities of energy, risk, and calculation on the details. Think of how an ordinary individual sweats over his appearance, his health, his sex life, his emotional honesty, his social utility, his self-knowledge, the quality of his ties with family, colleagues, and friends, how well he does his job, whether he understands the world and what is going on in it. Leading a human life is a full-time occupation, to which everyone devotes decades of intense concern.

This fact is so obvious that it is hard to find it extraordinary and important. Each of us lives his own life—lives with himself twenty-four hours a day. What else is he supposed to do—live someone else's life? Yet humans have the special capacity to step back and survey themselves, and the lives to which they are committed, with that detached amazement which comes from watching an ant struggle up a heap of sand. Without developing the illusion that they are able to escape from their highly specific and idiosyncratic position, they can view it *sub specie aeternitatis*[*]—and the view is at once sobering and comical.

The crucial backward step is not taken by asking for still another justification in the chain, and failing to get it. The objections to that line of attack have already been stated; justifications come to an end. But this is precisely what provides universal doubt with its object. We step back to find that the whole system of justification and criticism, which controls our choices and supports our claims to rationality, rests on responses and habits that we never question, that we should not know how to defend without circularity, and to which we shall continue to adhere even after they are called into question.

The things we do or want without reasons, and without requiring reasons—the things that define what is a reason for us and what is not—are the starting points of our skepticism. We see ourselves from outside, and all the contingency and specificity of our aims and pursuits become clear. Yet when we take this view and recognize what we do as arbitrary, it does not disengage us from life, and there lies our absurdity: not in the fact that such an external view can be taken of us, but in the fact that we ourselves can take it, without ceasing to be the persons whose ultimate concerns are so coolly regarded.

III

One may try to escape the position by seeking broader ultimate concerns, from which it is impossible to step back—the idea being that absurdity results because what we take seriously is something small and insignificant and individual. Those seeking to supply their lives with meaning usually envision a role or function in something larger than themselves. They therefore seek fulfillment in service to society, the state, the revolution, the progress of history, the advance of science, or religion and the glory of God.

---

[*]   Latin: from the perspective of eternity.

But a role in some larger enterprise cannot confer significance unless that enterprise is itself significant. And its significance must come back to what we can understand, or it will not even appear to give us what we are seeking. If we learned that we were being raised to provide food for other creatures fond of human flesh, who planned to turn us into cutlets before we got too stringy—even if we learned that the human race had been developed by animal breeders precisely for this purpose—that would still not give our lives meaning, for two reasons. First, we would still be in the dark as to the significance of the lives of those other beings; second, although we might acknowledge that this culinary role would make our lives meaningful to them, it is not clear how it would make them meaningful to us.

Admittedly, the usual form of service to a higher being is different from this. One is supposed to behold and partake of the glory of God, for example, in a way in which chickens do not share in the glory of coq au vin.* The same is true of service to a state, a movement, or a revolution. People can come to feel, when they are part of something bigger, that it is part of them too. They worry less about what is peculiar to themselves, but identify enough with the larger enterprise to find their role in it fulfilling.

However, any such larger purpose can be put in doubt in the same way that the aims of an individual life can be, and for the same reasons. It is as legitimate to find ultimate justification there as to find it earlier, among the details of individual life. But this does not alter the fact that justifications come to an end when we are content to have them end—when we do not find it necessary to look any further. If we can step back from the purposes of individual life and doubt their point, we can step back also from the progress of human history, or of science, or the success of a society, or the kingdom, power, and glory of God,[1] and put all these things into question in the same way. What seems to us to confer meaning, justification, significance, does so in virtue of the fact that we need no more reasons after a certain point.

What makes doubt inescapable with regard to the limited aims of individual life also makes it inescapable with regard to any larger purpose that encourages the sense that life is meaningful. Once the fundamental doubt has begun, it cannot be laid to rest.

Camus maintains in *The Myth of Sisyphus*† that the absurd arises because the world fails to meet our demands for meaning. This suggests that the world might satisfy those demands if it were different. But now we can see that this is not the case. There does not appear to be any conceivable world (containing us) about which unsettlable doubts could not arise. Consequently the absurdity of our situation derives not from a collision between our expectations and the world, but from a collision within ourselves.

IV

It may be objected that the standpoint from which these doubts are supposed to be felt does not exist—that if we take the recommended backward step we will land on thin air, without any basis for judgment about the natural responses we are supposed to be surveying. If we retain our usual standards of what is important, then questions about the significance of what we are doing with our lives will be answerable in the usual way. But if we do not, then those questions can mean nothing to us, since there is no longer any content to the idea of what matters, and hence no content to the idea that nothing does.

But this objection misconceives the nature of the backward step. It is not supposed to give us an understanding of what is *really* important, so that we see by contrast that our lives are insignificant. We never, in the course of these reflections, abandon the ordinary standards that guide our lives. We merely observe them in operation, and recognize that if they are called into question we can justify them only by reference to themselves, uselessly. We adhere to them because of the way we are put together; what seems to us important or serious or valuable would not seem so if we were differently constituted.

In ordinary life, to be sure, we do not judge a situation absurd unless we have in mind some standards of seriousness, significance, or harmony with which the absurd can be contrasted. This contrast is not implied

---

* A French dish of chicken braised in wine.
† See the excerpt from Camus earlier in this chapter.

by the philosophical judgment of absurdity, and that might be thought to make the concept unsuitable for the expression of such judgments. This is not so, however, for the philosophical judgment depends on another contrast which makes it a natural extension from more ordinary cases. It departs from them only in contrasting the pretensions of life with a larger context in which *no* standards can be discovered, rather than with a context from which alternative, overriding standards may be applied.

V

In this respect, as in others, philosophical perception of the absurd resembles epistemological skepticism. In both cases the final, philosophical doubt is not contrasted with any unchallenged certainties, though it is arrived at by extrapolation from examples of doubt within the system of evidence or justification, where a contrast with other certainties *is* implied. In both cases our limitedness joins with a capacity to transcend those limitations in thought (thus seeing them as limitations, and as inescapable).

Skepticism begins when we include ourselves in the world about which we claim knowledge. We notice that certain types of evidence convince us, that we are content to allow justifications of belief to come to an end at certain points, that we feel we know many things even without knowing or having grounds for believing the denial of others which, if true, would make what we claim to know false.

For example, I know that I am looking at a piece of paper, although I have no adequate grounds to claim I know that I am not dreaming; and if I am dreaming then I am not looking at a piece of paper. Here an ordinary conception of how appearance may diverge from reality is employed to show that we take our world largely for granted; the certainty that we are not dreaming cannot be justified except circularly, in terms of those very appearances which are being put in doubt. It is somewhat far-fetched to suggest I may be dreaming; but the possibility is only illustrative. It reveals that our claims to knowledge depend on our not feeling it necessary to exclude certain incompatible alternatives, and the dreaming possibility or the total-hallucination possibility are just representatives for limitless possibilities most of which we cannot even conceive.[2]

Once we have taken the backward step to an abstract view of our whole system of beliefs, evidence, and justification, and seen that it works only, despite its pretensions, by taking the world largely for granted, we are *not* in a position to contrast all these appearances with an alternative reality. We cannot shed our ordinary responses, and if we could it would leave us with no means of conceiving a reality of any kind.

It is the same in the practical domain. We do not step outside our lives to a new vantage point from which we see what is really, objectively significant. We continue to take life largely for granted while seeing that all our decisions and certainties are possible only because there is a great deal we do not bother to rule out.

Both epistemological skepticism and a sense of the absurd can be reached via initial doubts posed within systems of evidence and justification that we accept, and can be stated without violence to our ordinary concepts. We can ask not only why we should believe there is a floor under us, but also why we should believe the evidence of our senses at all—and at some point the framable questions will have outlasted the answers. Similarly, we can ask not only why we should take aspirin, but why we should take trouble over our own comfort at all. The fact that we shall take the aspirin without waiting for an answer to this last question does not show that it is an unreal question. We shall also continue to believe there is a floor under us without waiting for an answer to the other question. In both cases it is this unsupported natural confidence that generates skeptical doubts; so it cannot be used to settle them.

Philosophical skepticism does not cause us to abandon our ordinary beliefs, but it lends them a peculiar flavor. After acknowledging that their truth is incompatible with possibilities that we have no grounds for believing do not obtain—apart from grounds in those very beliefs which we have called into question—we return to our familiar convictions with a certain irony and resignation. Unable to abandon the natural responses on which they depend, we take them back, like a spouse who has run off with someone else and then decided to return; but we regard them differently (not that the new attitude is necessarily inferior to the old, in either case).

The same situation obtains after we have put in question the seriousness with which we take our lives and human life in general and have looked at ourselves without presuppositions. We then return to our lives, as we must, but our seriousness is laced with irony. Not that irony enables us to escape the absurd. It is useless to mutter: "Life is meaningless; life is meaningless ..." as an accompaniment to everything we do. In continuing to live and work and strive, we take ourselves seriously in action no matter what we say.

What sustains us, in belief as in action, is not reason or justification, but something more basic than these—for we go on in the same way even after we are convinced that the reasons have given out.[3] If we tried to rely entirely on reason, and pressed it hard, our lives and beliefs would collapse—a form of madness that may actually occur if the inertial force of taking the world and life for granted is somehow lost. If we lose our grip on that, reason will not give it back to us.

VI

In viewing ourselves from a perspective broader than we can occupy in the flesh, we become spectators of our own lives. We cannot do very much as pure spectators of our own lives, so we continue to lead them, and devote ourselves to what we are able at the same time to view as no more than a curiosity, like the ritual of an alien religion.

This explains why the sense of absurdity finds its natural expression in those bad arguments with which the discussion began. Reference to our small size and short lifespan and to the fact that all of mankind will eventually vanish without a trace are metaphors for the backward step which permits us to regard ourselves from without and to find the particular form of our lives curious and slightly surprising. By feigning a nebula's-eye view, we illustrate the capacity to see ourselves without presuppositions, as arbitrary, idiosyncratic, highly specific occupants of the world, one of countless possible forms of life.

Before turning to the question whether the absurdity of our lives is something to be regretted and if possible escaped, let me consider what would have to be given up in order to avoid it.

Why is the life of a mouse not absurd? The orbit of the moon is not absurd either, but that involves no strivings or aims at all. A mouse, however, has to work to stay alive. Yet he is not absurd, because he lacks the capacities for self-consciousness and self-transcendence that would enable him to see that he is only a mouse. If that *did* happen, his life would become absurd, since self-awareness would not make him cease to be a mouse and would not enable him to rise above his mousely strivings. Bringing his newfound self-consciousness with him, he would have to return to his meagre yet frantic life, full of doubts that he was unable to answer, but also full of purposes that he was unable to abandon.

Given that the transcendental step is natural to us humans, can we avoid absurdity by refusing to take that step and remaining entirely within our sublunar* lives? Well, we cannot refuse consciously, for to do that we would have to be aware of the viewpoint we were refusing to adopt. The only way to avoid the relevant self-consciousness would be either never to attain it or to forget it—neither of which can be achieved by the will.

On the other hand, it is possible to expend effort on an attempt to destroy the other component of the absurd—abandoning one's earthly, individual, human life in order to identify as completely as possible with that universal viewpoint from which human life seems arbitrary and trivial. (This appears to be the ideal of certain Oriental religions.) If one succeeds, then one will not have to drag the superior awareness through a strenuous mundane life, and absurdity will be diminished.

However, insofar as this self-etiolation† is the result of effort, will-power, asceticism, and so forth, it requires that one take oneself seriously as an individual—that one be willing to take considerable trouble to avoid being creaturely and absurd. Thus one may undermine the aim of unworldliness by pursuing it too vigorously. Still, if someone simply allowed his individual, animal nature to drift and respond to impulse, without making the pursuit of its needs a central conscious aim, then he might, at considerable dissociative cost, achieve a life that was less absurd than most. It

---

*   Below the moon; Nagel is alluding to the classical and medieval contrast between the unchanging celestial sphere of the heavens and the region below the moon (i.e., the earth) where mortal things are created and destroyed according to physical laws.

†   Weakening—making paler—the sense of self.

would not be a meaningful life either, of course; but it would not involve the engagement of a transcendent awareness in the assiduous pursuit of mundane goals. And that is the main condition of absurdity—the dragooning of an unconvinced transcendent consciousness into the service of an immanent, limited enterprise like a human life.

The final escape is suicide; but before adopting any hasty solutions, it would be wise to consider carefully whether the absurdity of our existence truly presents us with a *problem*, to which some solution must be found—a way of dealing with prima facie* disaster. That is certainly the attitude with which Camus approaches the issue, and it gains support from the fact that we are all eager to escape from absurd situations on a smaller scale.

Camus—not on uniformly good grounds—rejects suicide and the other solutions he regards as escapist. What he recommends is defiance or scorn. We can salvage our dignity, he appears to believe, by shaking a fist at the world which is deaf to our pleas, and continuing to live in spite of it. This will not make our lives un-absurd, but it will lend them a certain nobility.[4]

This seems to me romantic and slightly self-pitying. Our absurdity warrants neither that much distress nor that much defiance. At the risk of falling into romanticism by a different route, I would argue that absurdity is one of the most human things about us: a manifestation of our most advanced and interesting characteristics. Like skepticism in epistemology, it is possible only because we possess a certain kind of insight—the capacity to transcend ourselves in thought.

If a sense of the absurd is a way of perceiving our true situation (even though the situation is not absurd until the perception arises), then what reason can we have to resent or escape it? Like the capacity for epistemological skepticism, it results from the ability to understand our human limitations. It need not be a matter for agony unless we make it so. Nor need it evoke a defiant contempt of fate that allows us to feel brave or proud. Such dramatics, even if carried on in private, betray a failure to appreciate the cosmic unimportance of the situation. If *sub specie aeternitatis* there is no reason to believe that anything matters, then that doesn't matter either, and we can approach our absurd lives with irony instead of heroism or despair. ■

Suggestions for Critical Reflection

1. "If *nothing* can justify unless it is justified in terms of something outside itself, which is also justified, then an infinite regress results, and no chain of justification can be complete." What argument is Nagel making here—what exactly is he trying to show? Is he right?

2. Nagel's diagnosis of the absurdity of life seems to depend upon our ability to occupy two different viewpoints—creatures that are not capable of taking these viewpoints (or any viewpoint) do not have absurd lives, according to Nagel. What are these viewpoints? Can it really make so much difference that we are capable of taking some viewpoint or other? If the absurdity is viewpoint-relative, does this show that life is really absurd or that it just appears so?

3. "We step back to find that the whole system of justification and criticism, which controls our choices and supports our claims to rationality, rests on responses and habits that we never question, that we should not know how to defend without circularity, and to which we shall continue to adhere even after they are called into question." What does Nagel mean by this? How does it contribute to his argument? How consistent is what Nagel says here with what he says in section I of the essay about some things being self-justifying?

4. Nagel suggests that "philosophical perception of the absurd resembles epistemological skepticism." Does it? How? What illumination does this comparison shed on Nagel's analysis of absurdity?

5. "We can approach our absurd lives with irony instead of heroism or despair." What do you think Nagel means by this? Is it an attractive stance?

---

* Latin: at first sight, before further investigation.

Notes

1   Cf. Robert Nozick, "Teleology," *Mosaic*, XII, 1 (Spring 1971): 27–28.

2   I am aware that skepticism about the external world is widely thought to have been refuted, but I have remained convinced of its irrefutability since being exposed at [the University of California,] Berkeley to Thompson Clarke's largely unpublished ideas on the subject.

3   As Hume says in a famous passage of the *Treatise:* "Most fortunately it happens, that since reason is incapable of dispelling these clouds, nature herself suffices to that purpose, and cures me of this philosophical melancholy and delirium, either by relaxing this bent of mind, or by some avocation, and lively impression of my senses, which obliterate all these chimeras. I dine, I play a game of backgammon, I converse, and am merry with my friends; and when after three or four hours' amusement, I would return to these speculations, they appear so cold, and strain'd, and ridiculous, that I cannot find in my heart to enter into them any farther" (Book 1, Part 4, Section 7; Selby-Bigge, p. 269).

4   "Sisyphus, proletarian of the gods, powerless and rebellious, knows the whole extent of his wretched condition: it is what he thinks of during his descent. The lucidity that was to constitute his torture at the same time crowns his victory. There is no fate that cannot be surmounted by scorn" (*The Myth of Sisyphus*, Vintage edition, p. 90).

KATHY BEHRENDT

Reasons to Live versus Reasons Not to Die

Who Is Kathy Behrendt?

Kathy Behrendt is a Canadian philosopher teaching at Wilfrid Laurier University in Waterloo, Ontario. She obtained a Doctorate in Philosophy at the University of Oxford in 2000, where she then taught for several years. Behrendt has published on issues of personal identity, memory, and the fear of death, among other topics. Her related published works include "Whole Lives and Good Deaths" (2014), which discusses narrative conceptions of the self in connection with the end of life, and "A Special Way of Being Afraid" (2010), which examines the fear of non-existence.

What Is the Structure of This Reading?

Behrendt frames this paper as a response to a line from philosopher Steven Luper-Foy: "any reason for living is an excellent reason for not dying." While this sentiment might seem at first sight to be obviously true, Behrendt shows that it is not only possible to disagree with it but that it might not even be an attractive position if it is true.

Her starting point is one well-known theory of the good life from ancient Greece: Epicureanism. For the Epicurean, a happy life is one which is peaceful, self-sufficient, filled with reliable pleasures (such as friendship), and free from anxiety or pain. Philosophy can help us to lead such a life, according to Epicurus, and one of the ways it does so is by freeing us from the fear of death—a natural but irrational fear which is the source of a great deal of unnecessary anxiety and (through the desire to cling to life) selfishness and immorality.

Behrendt points out that, according to Epicureanism, it is in fact not true that what makes life worth living is also a reason to prefer not dying. A modification of the Epicurean position produces a view, which Behrendt calls Acquisitionism, on which reasons to live are also reasons not to die—but this view is unattractive, she argues. A better view than either Epicureanism or Acquisitionism is another conception of the good life that Behrendt labels Completionism—but with Completionism we are again back to a view that accepts that death need not always be undesirable to those leading a good life. Indeed, for the Completionist, "death has a positive and necessary role to perform in helping to articulate and shape the primary reasons to live."

The final position that Behrendt considers is one formulated by Thomas Nagel. One can think of this account as a blending of Completionism with Acquisitionism and, if we accept it, it makes it once again true that reasons for living are always reasons for not dying. Behrendt does not issue a final verdict on whether the Nagelian conception of the good life is adequate, but concludes by noting that what might have seemed at first like an obvious connection between reasons to live and reasons not to die has turned out to be more complex than it appeared, and we are left not quite sure what we should want to say about it.

Some Common Misconceptions

1. Much of Behrendt's paper is presented as a response to the Epicurean understanding of life and death. Epicurus is often regarded as a "hedonist" philosopher, in that he advocates the pursuit of pleasure and avoidance of pain. The term "hedonism" is now often used to mean the unrestricted pursuit of physical appetites such as sexual gratification and the gluttonous consumption of food. To Epicurus, however, the best life is a moderate one in which pain is avoided and desires are limited to those things that can be easily acquired.
2. Neither Behrendt nor any of the philosophers she discusses are advocating *for* death. Epicurus's position is that death is simply nothing to the one who dies, because one no longer exists once death has come. Though this means that a person should not fear their own death because they can't be harmed by it, this doesn't entail that death is in any way positive (or that it doesn't seriously harm other people who are still alive—such as friends and family).

Reasons to Live versus Reasons Not to Die*

"Any reason for living is an excellent reason for not dying"—Luper-Foy, "Annihilation," 278

Some claims seem so clearly right that we don't think to question them. Steven Luper-Foy's remark is like that. It borders on the 'trivially true' (i.e. so obviously true as to be uninteresting). If I have a reason to live, surely I likewise have a reason not to die. It may then be surprising to learn that so many philosophers disagree with this claim—either directly or by implication. I will look at some of the things people say that stand in opposition to Luper-Foy's claim. I will also consider what is needed in order to agree with it. The views canvassed cover broad issues concerning life and death, and what matters to us with respect to both.

Epicurus† (341–271 B.C.) made claims about death that are still debated today. Perhaps his most notorious was that death is 'nothing to us' (*Leading Doctrines*, 2). There is a sense in which, for Epicurus, the claim that death is nothing to us is quite literally true. We have nothing to do with death because so long as we are alive, it is not present for us. And if it were present for us we would be absent (*Letter to Menoeceus*, 125). At no point do 'I' and 'death' coincide. So it cannot have an impact upon me.

Sometimes when reinforcing this point Epicurus emphasises that I will not sense or perceive anything when I am dead. Sometimes he merely emphasises that I will not exist when I am dead. There are unspoken assumptions in either case: either I need to sense something in order for something to be bad for me, or I need to exist in order for it to be bad for me. Both assumptions have come in for considerable criticism, especially the first one. But we can set this aside for the time being. Instead, I want to investigate how Epicurus deals with the issue of reasons for living. Understanding Epicurus'

views on life, it turns out, can help shed light on his view of death.

If death is nothing to us, do we have any reason to live? An uncharitable reading of Epicurus might say we do not. Certainly Epicurus and his followers were known for having challenging views about what in life is valuable. Life is good in so far as it yields pleasurable experience. But pleasurable experience is characterised by Epicurus in terms of the absence of pain. This being so, according to Epicurus, the benefits of pleasure do not increase with duration—more is not better. This can be difficult for people to understand and accept. But consider an analogy with health, which is sometimes used to explain the Epicurean view of pleasure: if you are healthy your health does not get better the longer it goes on. Likewise with pleasure in the Epicurean sense—the absence of pain, like the condition of being in good health, is a stable quality. It does not increase with time.

Epicurus would be the first to admit that this view of pleasure goes against the norm; his goal in part was to reform the common view. Thus it is not surprising that his understanding of pleasure is a far cry from the types of things many people often think of as pleasurable, e.g. sensual, often short-lived activities, such as the pursuit of physical pleasure beyond what is needed to survive and stave off appetites. Lucretius‡ (c.94–c.50 B.C.), a later follower of Epicurus, compared the relentless accumulation of pleasures to the pouring of water into a sieve or cracked vessel (*On the Nature of Things* 3.1005–1008)—a time-involving, never-ending and ultimately frustrating procedure. People who engage in such pursuits enjoy the act of drinking more than they appreciate the sensation of quenched thirst. Therefore they are constantly compelled to seek further pleasures. There are various names for such people but I am going to call them '*Acquisitionists*'; their key trait is that, for anything they deem good, the pleasure lies

---

* Kathy Behrendt, "Reasons to Live versus Reasons Not to Die," *Think* 10, 28 (Summer 2011): 67–76.

† Epicurus was an Ancient Greek philosopher who argued for a materialistic conception of the universe and defended a conception of the good life focused on tranquility and the avoidance of pain. He wrote numerous works, only a few of which have survived to the present day. See the introduction for more details regarding Epicurean philosophy.

‡ Titus Lucretius Carus (c. 99 BCE–c. 55 BCE) was a Roman poet and philosopher, known primarily for the six-book poem *On the Nature of Things*, in which he describes and defends Epicurean philosophy.

in the experience of obtaining it, and they will always crave more of it. By contrast to the Acquisitionist, Epicurus' view of non-time-bound pleasure invites us to rest content with the state of well-being that ensues when appetites and wants have been fulfilled.

What has this got to do with the relation between reasons for living and reasons for not dying? The Acquisitionist's compulsion to pursue and enlarge on fleeting pleasures is an ongoing endeavour that can be cut off by death at any time. Someone afflicted with this compulsion always wants more of what she wants, and so death stands in the way of her achieving this. Her reasons for living are reasons for not dying; she abhors and fears death because it interferes with a project that in theory has no end. That is part of why the thought of her own death produces fear and anxiety. However, once we rid ourselves of such wants, 'we no longer need unlimited time', according to Epicurus (*Leading Doctrines*, 20). We therefore stop being afraid that life is not eternal. We don't need to live forever in order to live well, since a good life can happen in a finite amount of time and isn't increased with duration. This is why, for the Epicureans, reasons for living are not reasons for not dying. Whatever it is that makes life good for an Epicurean, it cannot be anything we insist on pursuing ad infinitum.* The thinking person, who follows the 'mind' and not the 'body' does not 'avoid pleasure', but nor does he regret 'departure from life' (*Leading Doctrines*, 20); his pleasures are time-bound and death does not infringe on them. In short, and in contrast to the Acquisitionist, the Epicurean has reasons to live but they are not reasons not to die.

Some people think that Epicurus' difficult view of death is tied to his having rather spectacularly missed the point of life. He paints a picture in which our choices are between life as frustrated and fearful persons of the flesh trying to fill the cracked vessel of our endless, fleeting desires, and life as the person of the mind who basks in a state of simple well-being in the form of the absence of pain, with no great need to prolong this state. But perhaps these are not the only options. There are many valuable things in life that do take considerable time but don't demand endless renewal. Consider having a child, pursuing a career, undertaking a project of scientific discovery, or athletic

excellence, or artistic creation. These are all potential reasons for living. For many people, such things constitute *the* reasons for living. They propel us into the future and make us want to go on—as opposed to the day-to-day mundane things we do in order merely to pass the time we have been allotted.

These reasons for living take time to see through to the end. However, time is needed not because, like the Acquisitionist with the insatiable appetite, we just want to do these sorts of things again and again, but because in order to accomplish these tasks we need to follow a certain complex path. We need to do certain things in a certain order over a considerable stretch of time. If I want to become a successful lawyer I need to reach adulthood, and undergo a long period of education, apprenticeship, and work before achieving my goal. If I want to have and raise a child, biology determines that this too takes time. Successfully completing a marathon is unthinkable unless one follows a lengthy and structured regimen of training. But crucially, unlike the ongoing, endless pursuit of additional pleasures, *completion* of these goals and activities is also possible. The partnership in a firm can be obtained. The child can grow and thrive and be sent off into the world. The race can be run to the finish line. And so on.

The people who hold some form of this view are a diverse lot and differ amongst themselves on many of the details. For the purposes of this discussion, I am going to group them together and call them 'Completionists'. The key feature which they share is that they believe in and value time-extended but completable goals. The completion of valued life projects requires time, and the time required can be interrupted by death. Such an interruption, far from being nothing to them, would be a disaster, coming as it does before the goals are fully realised. As far as Completionists are concerned, Epicurus' composure about death was gained at the expense of ignoring these time-extended but completable goals.

Notice that the Completionists' disagreement with Epicurus here is not total. Like the Epicureans, Completionists also reject Steven Luper-Foy's claim. The reasons they give for living are not reasons for not dying. Or not ultimately—there is a qualification in this case. Prior to the completion of one's goals, these

---

* Latin: to infinity.

goals provide reasons to avoid death. But it is understood that the goals can be completed. So they cannot stand as permanent, unqualified reasons for wanting to avoid death. In fact, many Completionists emphasise that a limited life-span is necessary for us to form, pursue, and appreciate certain activities. I would not be motivated to become a top lawyer or star athlete if my time on earth were unlimited. I might not even be able to imagine goals for my self in the future if that future had no limit. I also may not value my accomplishments if they are amongst countless that I will be able to go on to pursue. Reasons for living here go hand-in-hand with reasons for dying. The time-extended but completable goals discussed have the fact of our mortality built into them, because mortality is part of what helps us formulate them and makes them valuable. So Completionists cannot embrace Luper-Foy's edict that any reason for living is an excellent reason for not dying. They have many reasons for living but these do not ultimately stand in the way of accepting death—indeed, death has a positive and necessary role to perform in helping to articulate and shape the primary reasons to live.

Does anyone other than the Acquisitionist agree with Luper-Foy? Maybe we should be satisfied with the Acquisitionist's endorsement. But even apart from Epicurus' criticisms, Acquisitionists are usually portrayed as shallow and unthinking. They are motivated by the spirit of acquisitiveness; emphasis is placed on the pursuit of more and further pleasures for their own sake, rather than on any satisfaction they bring about. The Completionist tends to view the Acquisitionist with despair—she is unwilling to undergo hardship for the sake of a long-term goal. And nothing will ever be finished for her, so she cannot achieve closure and contentment. That this is no way to live is another point the Completionists and the Epicureans can agree on. Furthermore, Lucretius' cracked vessel metaphor strikes a chord; there is something perhaps empty and unsatisfying in the constant accumulation of more short-lived pleasurable experiences. If we want to do justice to Luper-Foy's point, it would be nice to have a better representative of it than the Acquisitionist. Let's consider what we might need here, in light of where we have got to so far.

Epicurus and his followers cannot accept that any reason for living is an excellent reason for not dying, because the pleasures of life are not increased with time. While there are things we can enjoy in life, death does not detract from that enjoyment, which would not increase if we did not die. Completionists hold, against Epicurus, that death *can* undermine what is good in life. In particular, death is bad when it comes before we have completed certain time-extended goals. But once those goals are completed death is not a threat, and in order to form and appreciate those goals, it is necessary that we are beings who can and will die. Therefore in so far as those goals are our reasons to live, they are still not always reasons not to die. If we want reasons for living that are also reasons for not dying, it seems we need the following: reasons for living that are time-extended (*contra** the Epicurean), but are also open-ended, in the sense of not limited by time (*contra* the Completionist). And ideally, we would like those reasons not to consist entirely in obtaining the maximal experience of pleasure for its own sake (*contra* the Acquisitionist).

One person who may point us in the right direction here is Thomas Nagel.[†] He is amongst the many who do not accept Epicurean detachment about death. Death is bad, according to Nagel, and it is bad because it deprives us of the goods in life. These goods consist in not just momentary, experienced pleasures, but hopes and possibilities that death may undermine. A person, for Nagel, is 'identified by his history and his possibilities' more so than by his experiential state at any particular moment (5). So far this does not necessarily differ from the Completionist view that we need a decent stretch of time in order to complete meaningful goals. Both Nagel and the Completionist seem to agree that many of the goods of life are time-extended and death is bad in so far as it can curtail them. But Nagel adds a key point that pushes him into a separate camp, namely that the possibilities apparently open to a person may be unlimited. This changes matters considerably. As Nagel puts it, 'if there is no limit to the amount of life that it would be good to have, then it may be that a bad end is in store for us all' (10). What he is suggesting here is that death may always come at the wrong time, depriving us of possible goods of life.

---

* Latin: in opposition to, in contrast to.
† See the introduction to Thomas Nagel earlier in this volume.

Nagel is perfectly well aware that we cannot in fact live forever. Nature dictates this. So his talk of the limitless possible goods death deprives us of cannot mean 'possible' only within the current bounds of nature. There is clearly a limit to what possibilities are in fact available to us, given that we are mortal and our lives are short. But there may be no limit to the possibilities that we can imagine or conceive of for ourselves. It is when we dwell on these that we enter Nagel's realm of limitless possibilities for the self. Our sense of our own experience, says Nagel, 'does not embody this idea of a natural limit' (9–10); we can and often do plan as though there were no tomorrow. And even when we know it is not true, we are capable of imagining another career, another race, another goal worthy of pursuit, which could bring us further happiness. The Completionist's apparent acceptance of death under certain circumstances rings hollow when we let our imagination take flight and think of all the good experiences we have yet to have, or want to have again.

In Nagel we find the time-extended but open-ended reasons for living that we were looking for. These reasons to live propel us beyond the present experience and into the (theoretically open-ended) future. This is in contrast to the Epicurean view, where good is associated with an experiential state defined by the absence of pain, and does not increase with time. But it is also in contrast to the Completionist, who views the goods in life to be time-extended but completable; for here is a view that claims, in theory anyway, these goods may have no limit. In so far as death poses a threat to the realisation of the possible goods we can conceive of, the threat, like the possibilities themselves, is unlimited. Hence reasons for living, on Nagel's view, are always reasons for not dying.

Has this view avoided association with the shallow Acquisitionist position? That depends on what about Nagel's view we choose to emphasise. There are some apparent similarities with the Acquisitionist, in that the view Nagel considers implies that more of what is good is better, so to speak. Hence death's permanent potential to deprive us of the goods in life: 'death, no matter how inevitable, is an abrupt cancellation of indefinitely extensive possible goods' (10).

But Nagel also says that some things can be good or bad independently of how they feel for a person at the time. For instance, he disparages the 'man who wastes his life in the cheerful pursuit of a method of communicating with asparagus plants' (5). Similarly, but more seriously, he views the adult who suffers a brain injury and is reduced to the state of a contented child to be the subject of a great misfortune. The asparagus-man and the brain-injured person are in a contented state. The Acquisitionist would have trouble saying that anything is wrong for them or that they suffer any harm, so long as they can go on experiencing the pleasures of being fed and well cared for. Nagel's view that they do suffer harm connects with his belief that persons are defined not just in terms of their present state, but their history and possibilities. These possibilities must, for Nagel, be richer and more complex than the potential to live in a state of physical comfort indefinitely (otherwise he would not view these people as unfortunate). He speaks of the importance of success and failure and aspects of our life that are like processes rather than individual moments of well-being. 'Processes' here can plausibly include the longer-term goals of the Completionist—achievements which require time and, often, some pain and sacrifice. If we include such things amongst the possible goods of life, we arrive at something quite different from the Acquisitionist's understanding of the goods that death can deprive us of.

Despite such differences between himself and the Acquisitionist, Nagel will also have to contend with criticism of his claim that the goods of life may be 'indefinitely extensive'. The Epicurean objects to the notion of time-extended goods, and will criticise Nagel for suggesting that someone in a good state might still be deprived, and that this deprivation might be alleviated by additional time. The Completionist objects to the notion of *indefinitely* extended goods, and will criticise Nagel for suggesting that anything could retain its value indefinitely, or that we can imagine an open-ended future of limitless possibilities for ourselves.

It may be possible to maintain that any reason for living is a reason for not dying. But the claim is hard-won, if we are to give it the seriousness it deserves and ensure that the reasons in question are ones that we are prepared to live for, for all time. The Acquisitionist's reasons for never dying could wear thin after a finite amount of time; simply revelling in the experience of pleasure may lose its appeal given enough time, and thereby cease to be a reason for living. The Completionists arguably offer us better reasons for living (or at least what many of us would recognise as good and enduring reasons to go on). However, they added that those reasons gained their strength and possibly their coherence from being placed in the context of a finite, mortal lifespan. Nagel disagreed, and he is not alone in holding that the complex, rich and varied possibilities that give us, now, reasons to go on, can in some form provide grounds for continuing on indefinitely.

We cannot here resolve the disagreements that remain between the various parties. But we can at least note that Luper-Foy's claim that any reason for living is an excellent reason for not dying, regardless of its truth, is certainly not trivial. There are a number of ways of disagreeing with it. What is more, there are arguable advantages to disagreeing with it. The fact that the Epicurean and the Completionist have reasons for living that are not always reasons for not dying helps them accept their mortality. Their reasons for living won't necessarily place them in the unhappy position of having to dread or regret their inevitable demise. On the other hand, we may, like Nagel, think our reasons for living are always reasons for not dying—and excellent reasons at that, going far beyond the Acquisitionists' superficial, perhaps unsustainable, values. But if that is what we think then it is hard to avoid the view that, in so far as our reasons for living are sustainable and unlimited, a bad end is indeed in store for us all. ∎

Suggestions for Critical Reflection

1. The Epicurean position is meant to provide relief from the fear of death. But shouldn't one fear death, to at least some degree? Is indifference toward death helpful in relieving us of anxiety, or might it lead to a lack of sensible caution or a lack of appreciation for life?

2. According to the Completionist, "a limited life-span is necessary for us to form, pursue, and appreciate certain activities. I would not be motivated to become a top lawyer or star athlete if my time on earth were unlimited." Do you agree with this claim? Some have speculated that future technology may allow humans to live for an indefinite length of time. Would the prospect of immortality undermine the motivation to form and pursue life goals?

3. Are there good reasons to prefer the "richer and more complex" goals advocated by the Completionist and Nagel, such as long-term career and relationship success, artistic excellence, and the raising of children, over the simple and deliberately unambitious desires of the Epicurean? If so, what are those reasons? Are they moral reasons, or reasons of some other sort?

4. Behrendt suggests that Luper-Foy's statement strikes many people as an obvious (or "trivial") truth. His claim could, however, be interpreted in at least two different ways: (1) "*At any particular time*, any reason for living is an excellent reason for not dying *at that time*"; or (2) "Any reason for living is an excellent reason *to never die*." Which of these two interpretations seems more plausible? Are both interpretations contrary to the Epicurean and Completionist positions? Does Behrendt's argument hold equally with regard to both interpretations?

5. In the end, do you think that what makes life worth living is also a reason to prefer not dying? What kind of a harm, if any, is death to the one who dies?

6. Is "a bad end in store for us all"? (And what exactly is this supposed to mean?)

References

Epicurus, *Leading Doctrines*, in *The Philosophy of Epicurus*, ed. and trans. George K. Strodach (Chicago: Northwestern University Press, 1963).

Epicurus, *Letter to Menoeceus*, in *The Philosophy of Epicurus*.

Lucretius, *On the Nature of Things*, ed. and trans. Anthony M. Esolen (Baltimore: Johns Hopkins Univ. Press, 1995).

Luper-Foy, S. 'Annihilation', in *The Metaphysics of Death*, ed. J.M. Fischer (Stanford: Stanford University Press, 1993).

Nagel, T. 'Death', in *Mortal Questions* (Cambridge: Cambridge University Press, 1979).

PERMISSIONS ACKNOWLEDGMENTS

Appiah, Kwame Anthony. "How to Decide If Races Exist," *Proceedings of the Aristotelian Society* 106 (2006): 365–82. Reprinted with the permission of the Aristotelian Society.

Aristotle. Excerpts from *The Nicomachean Ethics*, Books I, II, V, and X, translated by Terence Irwin. Hackett Publishing Company, 1999. Copyright © 1999 by Terence Irwin. Reprinted with the permission of Hackett Publishing Company, Inc. All rights reserved.

Ayer, A.J. "The Claims of Philosophy," *Polemic* 7 (March 1947). Reprinted with the permission of Ted Honderich, Literary Executor to A.J. Ayer.

Beauvoir, Simone de. "Introduction," from *The Second Sex*, translated by Constance Borde and Sheila Malovany-Chevallier. Translation copyright © 2009 by Constance Borde and Sheila Malovany-Chevallier. Used by permission of Alfred A. Knopf, an imprint of the Knopf Doubleday Publishing Group, a division of Penguin Random House LLC. All rights reserved.

Behrendt, Kathy. "Reasons to Live versus Reasons Not to Die," *Think* 10.28 (Summer 2011): 67–76. Copyright © The Royal Institute of Philosophy. Published by Cambridge University Press. Reproduced with permission.

Bettcher, Talia Mae. "Trans Women and the Meaning of 'Woman,'" from *Philosophy of Sex: Contemporary Readings*, 6th ed., edited by A. Soble, N. Power, and R. Halwani. Rowman & Littlefield, 2013. Originally published as "Without a Net: Starting Points for Trans Stories," in the *American Philosophical Association Newsletter on Philosophy and LGBT Issues* 10.2 (Spring 2011): 2–5. Reprinted with the permission of the American Philosophical Association and Rowman & Littlefield.

Camus, Albert. Excerpt from *The Myth of Sisyphus*, translated by Justin O'Brien. Translation copyright © 1955; copyright renewed 1983 by Penguin Random House LLC. Used by permission of Alfred A. Knopf, an imprint of the Knopf Doubleday Publishing Group, a division of Penguin Random House LLC. All rights reserved.

Card, Claudia. Excerpts from "Recognizing Terrorism," *The Journal of Ethics* 11.1 (March 2007). Reprinted with permission from Springer Nature. Copyright © 2006.

Coates, Ta-Nehisi. Excerpt from *Between the World and Me*. Copyright © 2015 by Ta-Nehisi Coates. Used by permission of Spiegel & Grau, an imprint of Random House, a division of Penguin Random House LLC. All rights reserved.

Held, Virginia. "Feminist Transformations of Moral Theory," *Philosophy and Phenomenological Research* 50, Supplement (Autumn 1990): 321–44. Reprinted with the permission of the publisher, The International Phenomenological Society, via Copyright Clearance Center, Inc. "Terrorism and War," *The Journal of Ethics* 8.1 (2004): 59–75. Reprinted with the permission of Springer Nature. Copyright © 2004.

Marquis, Don. "Why Abortion Is Immoral," *The Journal of Philosophy* 86.4 (April 1989): 183–202. Reprinted with the permission of Don Marquis and The Journal of Philosophy.

Mendoza, Jose Jorge. Excerpts from "The Ethics of Immigration Enforcement," Chapter 5 of *The Moral and Political Philosophy of Immigration: Liberty, Security, and Equality*. Copyright © 2016. Used by permission of Rowman & Littlefield Publishing Group. All rights reserved.

Midgley, Mary. "Is a Dolphin a Person?" Chapter 9 of *Utopias, Dolphins and Computers: Problems of Philosophical Plumbing*. London: Routledge, 1996. Copyright © 1996 Mary Midgley. Reproduced by permission of Taylor & Francis Books UK.

Nagel, Thomas. "The Absurd," *The Journal of Philosophy* 68.20 (1971): 716–27. Reprinted with the permission of Thomas Nagel and The Journal of Philosophy.

Nozick, Robert. Excerpt from Chapter 7, "Distributive Justice," in *Anarchy, State and Utopia*. Copyright © 1974, 2008, 2013. Reprinted by permission of Basic Books, an imprint of Hachette Book Group, Inc.

Okin, Susan Moller. Excerpt from "Justice and Gender," *Philosophy and Public Affairs* 16.1 (1987): 42–72. Reprinted with the permission of the publisher, Blackwell Publishing, Inc., via Copyright Clearance Center, Inc.

Plato. Excerpts from Book II (357a–367e) of the *Republic*, translated by G.M.A. Grube; revised by C.D.C. Reeve. Copyright © 1992 by Hackett Publishing Company, Inc. Reprinted with the permission of Hackett Publishing Company, Inc. All rights reserved.

Rawls, John. Excerpts from *Justice as Fairness: A Restatement*. Cambridge, Mass.: The Belknap Press of Harvard University Press, Copyright © 2001 by the President and Fellows of Harvard College.

Sartre, Jean-Paul. Excerpt from *Existentialism Is a Humanism*, translated by Carol Macomber. Translation copyright © 2007 by Yale University

Press. *L'Existentialisme est un humanisme* © Éditions Gallimard, Paris, 1996. Reprinted with the permission of Yale University Press.

Singer, Peter. "Equality for Animals?" from *Practical Ethics*. Copyright © Peter Singer 1980, 1993, 2011. Published by Cambridge University Press. Reproduced with permission.

Thomson, Judith Jarvis. "The Trolley Problem," *The Yale Law Journal* 94.6 (May 1985): 1395–1415. Reprinted with the permission of The Yale Law Journal. "A Defense of Abortion," *Philosophy and Public Affairs* 1.1 (Autumn 1971): 47–66. Reprinted by permission of the publisher,

Blackwell Publishing, Inc., via Copyright Clearance Center, Inc.

Wellman, Christopher. Excerpts from "Immigration and Freedom of Association," *Ethics* 119.1 (Oct. 2008): 109–41. Copyright © 2008 by the University of Chicago. All rights reserved.

Young, Iris Marion. "Five Faces of Oppression," Chapter 2 of *Justice and the Politics of Difference*. Princeton University Press, 1990. Republished with the permission of Princeton University Press, via Copyright Clearance Center, Inc.

Images

Introduction
"Top Hat," by Eli W. Buel, ca. 1870. https://commons.wikimedia.org/wiki/File:Accession_Number-_1969-0183-0156_(2720792408).jpg

Ethical Theory
"Washington, D.C. Class in the Banneker Junior High School," by Marjory Collins, March 1942. Farm Security Administration–Office of War Information photograph collection (Library of Congress).

Ethical Issues
"2017.01.21 Women's March Washington, DC USA 00095," by Ted Eytan, 21 January 2017. Licensed under the Creative Commons Attribution-Share Alike 2.0 Generic License, https://creativecommons.org/licenses/by-sa/2.0/deed.en

Justice
"Shanty Homes near a Railway Station, Mumbai, India," by Anonymous (MM), December 2010. Licensed under the Creative Commons Attribution-Share Alike 2.0 Generic License, https://creativecommons.org/licenses/by-sa/2.0/deed.en

Equality and Fairness
"Upstate New York, 1963," copyright © Leonard Freed/Magnum Photos.

Life, Death, and Happiness
[No title], Anonymous, n.d. Licensed under the CC0 1.0 Universal Public Domain Dedication license, https://creativecommons.org/publicdomain/zero/1.0/